KU-773-649

ROBERT RHODES JAMES

THE
BRITISH
REVOLUTION

BRITISH POLITICS
1880–1939

METHUEN & CO LTD

LONDON

First published in two volumes
by Hamish Hamilton Ltd
90 Great Russell Street, London WC1B 3PT

First published as a one-volume University Paperback in 1978
by Methuen & Co Ltd
11 New Fetter Lane, London EC4P 4EE

© 1976, 1977 Robert Rhodes James

Printed in Great Britain at the
University Press, Cambridge

ISBN 0 416 71140 5

This paperback edition is sold subject to the condition that it
shall not, by way of trade or otherwise, be lent, resold, hired out
or otherwise circulated without the publisher's prior consent in
any form of binding or cover other than that in which it is
published and without a similar condition including this
condition being imposed on the subsequent purchaser.

To the memory

of my father

WILLIAM RHODES JAMES

born August 1886, died August 1972

Oh, why not sing anew the songs
We sang in Yesteryear?
And, why not laugh the laughter once again
That, in Yesteryear, we knew so well?
And, why not shed the tears again
That once we shed together,
And mourn again with bitter grief
The years and friends we lost?

What point in that? What point?
Why laugh, or sing, or weep again?
We, who travelled so hard, so long, so cruelly,
Are now tear-spent, songless, and with bruiséd hearts.
Let gentle silence fall across our puny hills.
Let others laugh, or weep, or mourn;
Let others praise, and raise, and lower their sad flags.
Because, God knows, we did enough of that, and more, in Yesteryear.

And, as God also knows, we shall conquer
Tomorrow, as you, my love, triumphed in Yesteryear.

CONTENTS

ILLUSTRATIONS

Between pages 144 *and* 145

ix

Nos. 1, 2, 3, 4, 6, 7, 14, 15, 16, 18, 19, 20, 23, 26 and 33 are reproduced by permission of the Mansell Collection, and no. 33 by permission also of *Punch*; nos. 5, 8, 9, 13 and 17 by permission of the Radio Times Hulton Picture Library; nos. 10 and 12 by permission of the National Portrait Gallery; no. 11 by permission of the Scottish National Portrait Gallery and of the Dowager Countess Rosebery; and no. 22 by permission of Glasgow Art Gallery. Cartoons by Sir David Low are reproduced by permission of the *Evening Standard*.

PREFACE

LORD ROSEBERY HAS written that the political ocean is never quiescent and that its most serene temper is the calm before the storm, 'often more awful than the storm itself'. To carry this apposite image further, the principal difficulty for the political historian is to determine between the surface waves and the deep tides and, most difficult of all, to deduce their true relationship and mutual significance. Politics are often depicted in terms of conflicts between individuals and factions whose results determine events in which, as Sorel has written, 'chance seems to be modifying the whole course'. Other historians, not enamoured of this interpretation, give priority to those deeper forces which they see as being far beyond the control and even influence of politicians and factions, which the latter do not comprehend or which they ignore until they are swept away by them to prosperity, oblivion, or ignominy. It is not often appreciated that these opposing views are, in fact, reconcilable.

The period of sixty years covered by this volume is one of the most tumultuous and complex in British history. The narrative itself opens with the General Election of 1880, when the profession of politics was severely limited, the privilege of the vote was confined to a minority of the adult male population, the secret ballot was still a suspected novelty—robustly denounced by Lord Palmerston in 1852 as 'a course unconstitutional and unworthy of the character of straightforward and honest Englishmen'—many hallowed corrupt practices still flourished, and the hustings, open voting, and practices immortalised by Charles Dickens in his account of the Eatanswill Election in *The Pickwick Papers* were very recent memories. Queen Victoria had nearly twenty years of her long reign and life before her. William Gladstone, who as a child had heard the guns triumphantly thundering in celebration of the victory at Waterloo, was beginning his second

Premiership, with two more to follow; Benjamin Disraeli—now adorned as the Earl of Beaconsfield—had just relinquished office for the last time, and memories of Lord Palmerston and Lord John Russell were very fresh.

By 1939 full universal suffrage had been achieved, which was in itself one evidence of the subtle political and social revolution which is the theme of this work. Winston Churchill—born in 1874, six years before this narrative opens—lamented in 1929 that 'the leadership of the privileged has passed away'. As a statement of absolute fact this was open to challenge, but no one could seriously question that there had been large and dramatic transformations in the character of national politics and, indeed, in the structure of the society of this remarkable nation.

There had been many other influences and changes not only in Britain itself but far from its shores, which had made their impact upon the development of its history. The Boer farmers, the Irish nationalists, the followers of Arabi in Egypt, of Gandhi in India, of Kemal in Turkey, of Lenin in Russia and of Hitler in Germany, had all played roles in what I have described as The British Revolution. British wealth and power, so substantial and so taken for granted in 1880 were, by 1939, so severely diminished that the nation was entering a desperate struggle for its very survival. This work is, in reality, the account of many revolutions, and indeed of some counter-revolutions as well, as the British nation moved from the relative calm and power of the nineteenth century into the unexpected storms, tumults, and perils of the twentieth.

My purpose has been to produce a narrative of tolerable length and balance which adequately describes and covers events and developments of considerable complexity and controversy, and to discern the 'waves' and 'tides' and their mutual significance. It might be argued that initially it gives undue prominence to the House of Commons and to its principal personalities, and to the varying fluctuations of what can be loosely called 'London politics'. It is true that to depict British politics in this first period simply as a gladiatorial contest between a few notables cheered on by an anonymous and ignored multitude would unquestionably omit certain significant elements. But in my judgement it is the case that until 1914 the real political decisions and struggles took place within a remarkably small segment of the population. This does not mean that the struggles were unreal or unimportant. If the principal cast was small and the electorate was a relatively limited participating audience, the active interest and involvement of that audience is not a nostalgic fiction. Politics was an eagerly followed drama, and the rise and fall of reputations at Westminister had a real public impact. This became less true after 1914, as the electorate widened greatly, the issues altered, the problems became more ominous, and new methods of public communication were created. It will be seen that the balance of emphasis and attention gradually changed, reflecting my interpretation of the subtle but very important differences in the character and structure of British politics and society during this period.

The range and detail of this period are so considerable that through necessity much has had to be omitted, and several important episodes have had to be handled somewhat swiftly. I would not expect the balance of my priorities to be accepted by all historians, but my dominant purpose has been to try to bring the individuals and the struggles of the past to life again, and to convey to the contemporary reader some element of the human dramas, achievements, failures, and perversities which, at different times and in different contexts, contributed to substantive changes not only to the course of British history but which are of a much wider modern significance.

As always, I have found the problem of references a very difficult one. I have tried to keep all footnotes to a minimum, and to present a bibliography that—although necessarily selective—may be of real value to the reader. The index contains brief biographies of the most significant individuals. This is, as I well know, a compromise, but I trust it may be recognised as a sincere endeavour to meet the requirements of the scholar and the concerns of the non-specialist reader.

*

This work has been in preparation for so long that the list of those individuals to whom I am indebted is so extensive that I hope they will accept a general statement of my profound gratitude. Furthermore, in my bibliography and footnotes I have been able to mention only some of the books and articles and manuscript collections which have been of such value to me. Thus, in saying, in Chaucer's valediction, 'Farwel my book and my devocion', I pay my grateful thanks to all who have helped me and who have shown me so many warm kindnesses throughout its extended journey.

But some have a very particular place in my gratitude. My beloved father, to whose memory this book is dedicated, was always gently impatient for the completion of this work, having been personally involved in some of the episodes I have described, and eager to read his youngest son's interpretation of them. Andrew Morgan unwittingly began the course of this book when he was a young history teacher and I his nervous pupil in 1948. To my wife, whose entire married life has had the shades of politics—ancient and modern, national and international—heavily in its background, my debt is beyond gratitude or expression.

It is given to few writers to say that they have lived and written in happiness and serenity, and have always been surrounded by kindness and understanding. For all who have provided me with these circumstances I can only say that this book truly belongs to them.

ROBERT RHODES JAMES

PART ONE

FROM GLADSTONE TO ASQUITH

CHAPTER ONE

PRELUDE, 1860–1880

IN THE year 1547 the House of Commons, which had previously assembled in various buildings in the fragmented history of its nascent but severely limited existence and influence, was given by the Protector Somerset the use of the exquisite, long-neglected, and deliberately impoverished Chapel of St. Stephen's in the Royal Palace of Westminster, hard by the swift-flowing Thames. It was appropriate to the mood of the time that a secular and subservient body should have been instructed to occupy, and thereby to humiliate further, one of the most beautiful of all buildings raised in England to the Glory of God, and which had brought to stone and mortar the soaring genius of the Perpendicular Style, of which King's College Chapel, Cambridge—almost certainly the work of the same hands— remains as evidence of what was lost by the desecration, and then destruction, of St. Stephen's.

The representatives of the *communes* took their places in the choir-stalls, which ran on either side of the Chapel, removed the altar and placed the Speaker's Chair in its place, with a bare table before it for the Clerk. St. Stephen's was sixty feet long and thirty feet wide. This tiny area was to be the meeting place of the House of Commons for nearly three hundred years, with constant complaints by generations of Members at the contrast between their miserable accommodation and the great houses in which the servants of the Sovereign and other grandees resided. As William Cobbett complained in 1833: 'Why are we squeezed into so small a space that it is absolutely impossible that there should be calm and regular discussion, even from that circumstance alone? Why do we live in this hubbub? Why are we exposed to these inconveniences?' One observer commented that 'When an important debate occurred . . . the Members were really to be pitied; they were literally crammed together, and the heat of the House

I

rendered it in some degree a second edition of the Black Hole of Calcutta.'

As the significance of the Commons rose, the asperity of these comments became more sharp, but the arrangements in St. Stephen's were little altered. The statues and carvings were callously mutilated, then the walls hidden by tapestries, and then, in the early years of the eighteenth century, covered with wooden panelling. Sir Christopher Wren added narrow galleries, and the great East Window was transformed into three tall, blank, windows. But the essentials remained, and endure to this day. The choir-stalls were converted into benches, but they still faced each other across the Floor, the Speaker's Chair still stood on the altar steps at the East End, with the Clerks' table before it.

It was an intimate place, oppressively stifling when filled, and compared by Macaulay with the hold of a slave ship, but convenient for the transaction of Parliamentary business, and for the purpose of Parliamentary revolution. It was to this rudely converted chapel that King Charles I came to attempt to seize the Five Members, and in it that Cromwell carried the Grand Remonstrance, and the Reform Bill of 1832 was passed. Here spoke Cromwell, Pym, Hampden, Walpole, the two Pitts and the two Foxes, Burke and Sheridan, Castlereagh and Canning, the young Robert Peel and the even younger William Gladstone. Here Samuel Johnson—resolved that the Whig dogs should not get the better of it—and the young Charles Dickens observed and reported. As the influence and power of the Commons increased and that of the monarchy and the Lords waned, the realities of political power increasingly moved towards this physically inadequate but politically enthralling room.

On the night of October 16th 1834, the Palace of Westminster was largely destroyed by a spectacular fire—long anticipated by experts—which drew admiring throngs in London and was watched with awe from the hill-tops of Surrey and Middlesex. Westminster Hall, which adjoined St. Stephen's, was saved, but St. Stephen's itself was gutted, only the lower chapel surviving. The two Houses of Parliament moved into temporary quarters while, in the usual atmosphere of bickering, jealousies, anguish and bitterness which invariably seem to mark the raising of significant edifices, the new Palace of Westminster arose on the site of the old. The combined genius of Charles Barry and Augustus Welby Pugin—at the outset 39 and 22 years of age respectively—

created a monument to the Gothic Revival yet which had, particularly in its proportions, a very English personality. From the clock-tower at the north end to the Victoria Tower at the south, they established one of the most remarkable silhouettes in nineteenth-century architecture. The unknown artisans, by their detailed workmanship, themselves created a monument to the standards of their age.

The new House of Commons was notably larger than St. Stephen's with larger galleries—that for the Ladies being hidden behind a steel grill—and more handsome artefacts, but the general arrangements were identical, and it could seat less than half of its full membership. The chief complaints of Members when they took possession in 1852 concerned acoustics and lighting. Over the protests of Barry, who felt so deeply about the matter that he never set foot in the Chamber again, the House ordered a glass ceiling to cover the ornately carved roof on which Barry and Pugin had devoted so much attention. Gas-flares, which burnt above this new ceiling, provided illumination. Members remained so dissatisfied with this cramped and poorly ventilated room that plans were prepared in 1868 for a much grander Chamber, almost double in size, in which every Member would have a seat, to be built in the adjoining Speaker's Court. But, thankfully, the plans were never executed, and the Members became increasingly reconciled.

This dank, tawny, room was to be, until it was destroyed by German bombs in May 1941, the home of the House of Commons. It inherited and incorporated not only the physical features of St. Stephen's but the customs which had grown up in the Chapel. The practice had been established from the earliest days that the Ministers and supporters of the King's Government sat on the benches to the right of the Speaker, with its critics and independents sitting opposite them. Although of a later growth, the concept of 'the Loyal Opposition' had also been established before St. Stephen's had been destroyed and the Commons had acquired their new abode.

*

The period between the formation of the Administration of Sir Robert Peel in 1842 and the death of Lord Palmerston in 1865 had been one of extreme political confusion, and by the mid-1860s the development of political parties as opposed to random groupings had not reached a level of much sophistication. But out of this complex struggle for mastery in which there had been few fixed points, there had mysteriously but definitely emerged the canalising of a number of interests into two general, if not as yet truly formalised, parties. Thus, by the middle of the 1860s the Liberal and Conservative Parties were uneasy coalitions, drawn together with relative degrees of discomfort and by thinly defined concepts of common interest, and liable to swift and easy fragmentation.

Leadership remained essentially dependent upon personal factors. Peel's Conservative coalition of the late 1830s and early 1840s had been shattered by the schism over the repeal of the Corn Laws in 1846 and the extraordinary but devastating combination of Benjamin Disraeli and Lord George Bentinck in vehement opposition to Peel's apostasy. From that trauma the Conservatives had taken more than twenty years to recover their bearings and develop any common philosophy. In this period of political fluidity Palmerston had exercised his formidable gifts of fusion, persuasion, personal style and great public popularity to establish a Liberal coalition which, as has been written, 'was primarily formed from an amalgam of old Whiggery and new radicalism, together with certain eccentric strains of Canningite toryism and Peelite conservatism.'[1] Lord Shaftesbury, one of the most significant of all nineteenth century social reformers, wrote after the election of 1857 that 'There seemed to be no measure, no principle, no cry, to influence men's minds and determine elections; it is simply "Were you or were you not? Are you, or are you not, for Palmerston?"'.

It was this coalition to which W. E. Gladstone, the erstwhile tormented Peelite, gave further cohesion and leadership after Palmerston's death in 1865. Meanwhile the Conservative coalition, whose Parliamentary strength lay primarily in the counties, had gradually fallen—not without considerable misgivings—under the control and guidance of Disraeli. These two exceptionally gifted men drew around them supporters and allies, and their duels gave to politics an excitement and drama which accentuated the divisions between their parties, and which remained primarily historical and personal rather than ideological. There were differences between these parties, but none could be described as fundamental. Both were cautiously committed to social reform, and both were irrevocably committed to the cause of Free Trade. But although the divisions might be subsequently regarded as minimal, at the time they loomed very

[1] Norman Gash: *Politics In The Age of Peel*, xii–xiii.

large and the political disputes were conducted with an intense vehemence and passion.

The passage of the Second Reform Act of 1867 by the first Disraeli government had been a substantial political gamble which had, at least temporarily, failed, and the Liberals had swept to a comfortable victory in the 1868 General Election. But, as they began to show clear signs of disintegration after 1871, the eloquence, philosophies, and personal magnetism of Disraeli held the Conservative coalition together and gave it hope for the future.

The structure of British politics had been changed in subtle but crucial ways in the 1860s and early 1870s. The electorate, although considerably enlarged after 1867, still represented only a small proportion of the adult male population, and there is good cause to regard the 1867 Reform Act as a spectacular exercise in calculated gerrymandering intended for the benefit of the Conservatives rather than as a mighty leap in the dark in the general direction of democracy. But the introduction of the secret ballot in 1872, urged by the Chartists forty years before, was a genuinely revolutionary change, whose implications were formidable. The hallowed and very expensive methods of bribery, intimidation, 'treating', imported electors, and other devices whereby the people's will had been signified were no longer guaranteed to deliver the desired results. Furthermore, the introduction of three-member constituencies and plural voting made it evident to at least some politicians—and notably a young and ambitious Birmingham businessman, Joseph Chamberlain—that entirely new organisational methods would have to be introduced. Disraeli also perceived this, and the Conservatives had taken the first serious steps towards a form of national organisation which was still very crude and inefficient, but which laid significant foundations for the future.

It was to be some time before these developments were to have clearly discernible consequences, but by 1880 several had already become apparent and were to become dominant. The Corrupt Practices Act of 1883 and the 1885 Reform Act were to be crucial in developing these processes, but it would be wrong to assume that the political structure and practices of generations changed overnight. Bribery in certain constituencies was still remarkably enduring: in Gloucester in 1880 it was estimated that out of 4,904 electors 2,756 were bribed. The Commissioners who examined a by-election at Sandwich in 1880 reported that 'it did not appear that the mode of taking votes by ballot had the slightest effect in checking bribery. On the contrary, while it enabled many voters to take bribes on both sides, it did not, as far as we could ascertain, render a single person unwilling to bribe for fear of bribery in vain.'[1]

Nonetheless, the General Election of 1880 was the last in which corrupt practices on the old brazen lines were widely attempted, and it was significant that great efforts were made to conceal them.[2] Gladstone rode to triumph in the constituency of Midlothian with the assistance of voters who had been hurriedly lured into the constituency, placed on the register, and not ill-rewarded for their civic virtue in a ferocious contest for votes between the Buccleuch and Rosebery interests and money. The agents of the Duke of Marlborough had to work hard to secure the re-election in Woodstock of the Duke's younger son, Lord Randolph Churchill. The practice of spreading the word, particularly in rural areas, that the ballot was not all that secret was still prevalent, and still not without impact.

But the old rules had changed, and were to change much more and very quickly. No single event or act had achieved this, rather a combination of events in which the seriousness and willingness to make changes in the quest for improvement, which was now so marked a feature of the mid-Victorian period, played a part which it is difficult to categorise or describe with precision, yet which was such a marked characteristic of the age. Joseph Arch wrote in his autobiography (published in 1898) that 'as a lad, every time I earned a penny by doing odd jobs or running an errand, I would buy some old papers. . . . I would read Gladstone's and Bright's speeches and from them formed my opinions'. Such opinions were in the direction of reform, usually vaguely defined, and based on the foundation of self-help.

Disraeli, in his later years, observed that England, being a land subject to fogs and possessed of a powerful middle class, required grave statesman. This had certainly not been his impression earlier in his career, but he adapted himself with great skill to the new mood and circumstances. Palmerston's timing in his death had been characteristically felicitous. Politics, and England, had become more serious. The political adventurer now had to be more careful. Politics had

---

[1] H. J. Hanham; *Elections and Party Management—Politics in the Time of Disraeli and Gladstone*, 267.

[2] It can also be genuinely described as a truly 'general' election. In 1859, 374 seats had not been contested; the number fell to 210 in 1868, 187 in 1874, and 110 in 1880.

gradually ceased to be the part-time occupation of only an aristocratic or nouveau-riche élite. The new prosperity had created new cities, new wealths, and new men, to whom London and the House of Commons were the goal of their new ambitions. Bagehot wrote in 1872 that 'The spirit of our present House of Commons is plutocratic . . . its most prominent statesmen are men mostly of substantial means, but they are mostly, too, connected more or less closely with the new trading wealth'. As a generalisation this was capable of refinement and was not the whole truth, but it contained a very strong element of the truth. As G. J. Holyoake commented in 1868, 'the House of Commons, like the London Tavern, is only open to those who can pay the tariff. . . . All that the sons of labour have gained, at present, is the advantage of being consulted.' The situation was still basically the same as it had been in the 1830s, when Macaulay had written to his sister that 'Every day shows me more and more strongly how necessary a competence is to a man who desires to be either great or useful'. Leslie Stephen wrote in 1867 that 'England is still an aristocratic country; not because the nobility have certain privileges, or possess influence in certain boroughs. A power resting upon such a basis would be very fragile and would go to pieces at the first strain upon the Constitution. The country is aristocratic, because the whole upper and middle, and a great part of the lower, classes have still an instinctive liking for the established order of things; because innumerable social ties bind us together spontaneously, so as to give to the aristocracy a position tolerably corresponding to their political privileges'.[1]

For a man who wished to enter politics and had the financial resources to undertake a political career, securing a seat in Parliament could be surprisingly easy, and no longer required the obligatory heavy expenditure which had in the past made contested elections of such financial benefit to the electors.[2] After 1883, although elements of corrupt practices continued in some areas, and the wealth of hopeful Members of Parliament was no disability to them, money by itself was no longer enough, and a young man no longer needed, as the young

[1] Quoted in H. J. Hanham op. cit.
[2] At St. Albans, between 1832 and 1852 some £24,000 was spent on corrupt practices, for a total electorate of less than 500. In Canterbury, between 1841 and 1852 £18,000 was spent on bribery. It was not to be wondered at that the electors of Barnstaple, appalled by the prospect of an uncontested election, tried to advertise for a candidate in *The Times*. For these and many other examples of corrupt practices see Charles Seymour: *Electoral Reform in England and Wales*.

Gladstone had done, a wealthy patron such as the Duke of Newcastle. For this, a certain price had to be paid. The development of local party associations gave them the power of selecting candidates; the fact that they were usually very susceptible to suggestions from the regional and national organisations did not remove this new influence. The balance of patronage had changed: now it was not the former grandees but the parties that were beginning to exercise it. The manner in which Chamberlain's 'caucus' ran Birmingham politics, and the fact that the pledge to Parnell was crucial to success in Ireland in 1885, were the first examples of tight control over candidates in a manner that was to develop rapidly in the early 1900s.

But in the 1870s and early 1880s, although the balance was changing, influence and wealth were often the decisive factors, and the position of the party associations and the central organisation often very weak. In 1874 Lord Randolph Churchill and Arthur Balfour virtually inherited family constituencies—Woodstock and Hertford—but although the practice continued for a suprisingly long time, the days of the virtual ownership of constituencies by the great families were passing. In Lancashire Conservatism the favour or frown of Lord Derby was critical to aspirants up to the Second World War, the Chamberlains dominated Birmingham for two generations, and no Rothschild ever met problems in the Vale of Evesham. But, as the electorate expanded, the importance of substantial personal wealth declined and the role of the central party organisations became more significant, and accordingly the possibilities for men of relatively modest means greatly improved. When Arthur Lee determined to enter Parliament as a Conservative in 1900 he went to the office of the formidable 'Captain' Middleton, of whom more will be heard, and was at once proffered the opportunity of a safe seat in Hampshire. Three days later he was the candidate, as he has related:

An emergency meeting of the constituency Association was called for the Thursday afternoon. This took place at the Town Hall, Fareham, and at 3 o'clock on a fine summer's day I found myself turned loose like a young bull into a ring of some 50 mature, if not crusted, local Conservative leaders, many of whom were resentful at being thus hustled, and highly suspicious of the whole proceeding. By an almost miraculous coincidence it had emerged that my grandfather Sir Theophilus Lee had for many years lived in the district, at

Bedhampton, and that my own father had been buried there. This had been quite unknown to me until the day before, but it at once made me a 'local man' and I did not fail to give so opportune a circumstance its full electoral value. Then I 'stated my views' on the political questions of the day at impressive length and with as much assurance as I could command . . . I found it comparatively easy to suggest easy familiarity with such problems as 'Home Rule', 'Local Veto', 'Church Dis-establishment' and 'Agricultural Reform'. Anyhow I succeeded in passing muster, and even in generating sufficient enthusiasm to enable my adoption to be carried by a unanimous vote.[1]

Lee had been lucky, but not exceptionally so. Good connections were all-important in that very close-knit political-social world. A blatant outsider like the Canadian self-made millionaire, Max Aitken, would have had considerable difficulties until he had worked his passage if he had not become the close friend of the Conservative leader, Bonar Law, who in 1910 drew the attention of the Unionist leaders of Ashton-under-Lyne to 'a young friend of mine . . . [who] now wants to stand for Parliament'. Aitken was swiftly accepted, and duly elected. In 1923 Victor Cazalet, not yet 26, was eagerly adopted as Conservative candidate for Chippenham on the basis of warm re-commendations from London. The situation was more complicated for the Liberals, but not much different in practice. In the 1880s H. H. Asquith, Augustine Birrell, Edward Grey and R. B. Haldane experienced relatively little difficulty in securing good seats at the first attempt and with little local influence.

Although the Member was expected to contribute to local party expenses, which varied very considerably and could be very formidable, his actual presence in the constituency between elections was not required save on special occasions. The great leaders would, from time to time, descend upon their constituencies as in a cloud of fire, deliver a major and lengthy address, and depart for London. Lesser breeds, particularly at the beginning of their careers, usually had to appear more often, but by modern standards the requirements of most constituencies in their demands on the attention of their Member were modest indeed. His biographer relates that Sir Henry Campbell-Bannerman, Liberal Member for the Stirling Burghs for forty years

[1] Alan Clark: 'A Good Innings'; The Private Papers of Lord Lee of Fareham, 78.

between 1868 and 1908, 'paid an annual visit to the five burghs to hold what he called a "colloquy" with his constituents, having a public meeting in each and meeting the leading citizens informally at the house of a prominent supporter. In those days the annual meetings between a Member and his constituents were serious affairs. His supporters described him as a model Member, taking trouble to understand their problems alive to their prejudices and always ready to support their interests. But he spent very little time in the constituency and sometimes he found it hard going . . . in a letter to Bryce he said: "I hardened my heart and thoroughly *did* my constituency which is a good thing over".' On one occasion there was a complaint by the secretary of the Liberal Association in Dunfermline, a Mr. Ireland, of Campbell-Bannerman's 'cavalier' treatment of his constituents, 'contenting yourself with one flying visit in the year of an hour or two's duration which is the only intercourse you have had with your constituents for some years', but Campbell-Bannerman took no notice and did not change his ways. His constituents regularly returned him, usually unopposed.[1]

This lofty approach was beginning to change in the 1920s, but only marginally. Unless the political winds were blowing very harshly against the party of one's choice, and barring total disasters, the process of actually getting into Parliament was not very difficult, and the burdens of Parliamentary life were not severe. The House of Commons did not often meet for more than six months in the year, and politicians of a later age are struck by the enormous volume of political correspondence conducted in Parliamentary Recesses, usually from large country-houses.

Until the activities of the Irish Nationalists made them necessary in the 1880s, the House of Commons had very few written rules and had had no need of them. It was governed by traditions which were instilled into the new Member with great severity and which he flaunted at his peril. The memory of Disraeli's disastrous maiden speech was still vivid. Presumptuousness was not tolerated. At the end of a major debate, after the final leading speakers had spoken, the House voted, and any Member who attempted to continue the debate would be silenced with bellows of 'Divide!'. 'The good sense and the good taste of the House of Commons', Disraeli had written, 'will be found on the whole to be the best regulators of the duration

[1] John Wilson: '*C-B*', 44–5 and 154.

of a debate.' The institution of Parliamentary Questions was in its
infancy, and had to be regulated after the Irish seized this opportunity
for further obstruction. But, as the 1880s continued, even the Irish
became more respectful of the hallowed traditions of the House and
swift to censure any infringement of them.

The late Victorian House of Commons had high standards. It had
gradually lost the raucous vulgarity which so shocked visitors earlier in
the century, but it remained a very masculine and irreverent assembly,
swift to mock pomposity, generous to sincerity and ability, but with a
certain cruelty and a suspicion of outside reputations that made it such
a formidable and incalculable body. 'It is a nerve-wracking place for
the ambitious man', Lee later wrote; 'he lives a jungle-life existence,
carrying his political life in his hand and knowing that if he slips the
denizens will tear him in pieces without any sort of compunction. I was
always conscious of this and although I sat in the Commons for 18
years I never faced the ordeal of speaking without anxiety and
apprehension.'[1] Disraeli described it as 'the most chilling and nerve-
destroying audience in the world.'

It was here, not in the country, that political reputations were made
or destroyed, because this was the national political stage. It had
drama, and the possibility of fame. It was here that Gladstone, Disraeli,
Palmerston, Lord John Russell, Lord Randolph Churchill, Chamberlain, Charles Stewart Parnell, and Arthur Balfour made their national
reputations. The development of the railways had not only revolution-
ised physical communications but also the availability of national
newspapers. These, during this period, paid considerable attention to
politics and particularly to Parliament, and this fact greatly and
significantly enhanced the national importance of a Parliamentary
reputation. F. E. Smith was to call Parliament 'the microcosm of the
talent of Great Britain' and urged that 'no man conscious of great
powers should ever, willingly, be excluded from it.' In the nineteenth
century this was indeed true, or at least was generally believed to be
the truth. The House of Commons was the goal that lured them from
all parts of the nation—David Lloyd George from Wales, Parnell from
Ireland, Andrew Bonar Law from Glasgow, Keir Hardie from West
Ham *via* Scotland, Asquith from Yorkshire, and Chamberlain from
the Midlands. Here, in this small Chamber, and in the ornate in-
timacies of the Palace of Westminster, the men of politics gathered to

[1] Clark, op. cit., 79–80.

further their reputations, to ply their trade, some to participate with eagerness, others considering themselves as privileged inside observers of the great game.

Often described as a club, it was in reality more like a theatre, in which the drama was always changing yet was always absorbing, and where new actors rose—and often fell—and in which chance and odd circumstance were expected and eagerly awaited. If, by the standards of later years, it was in many respects a leisurely life, for those who were privileged to belong to it, it was their real and their full life, and which they pursued with ardour and with style. When Sir William Harcourt said that his objective was 'to stand well with the House of Commons' he expressed a very widely held ambition.

But the real lure was the sheer excitement of politics, in which the rewards for the few were so considerable, when Office did indeed contain Power, and in which fortunes could fluctuate so dizzyingly. The civil service was in its infancy, a new creation, unsure of itself and of its relationship with its political masters. The philosophy that 'the Government governs best when it governs least' was widely believed, and the structure of Government was at best flimsy and insecure, in most aspects hardly advanced in expertise and experience than in the days of Pepys. And the world of the fledgling civil service was also the world of the politicians, that of family linkages, social ties, discussions at dinner-parties or at country week-ends. Official positions of significance were no longer at the disposal of Ministers as they had been in the past, but the relationship between political masters and public servants was close, intimate, and on the same level. Edward Hamilton, the close friend of Rosebery, served Conservative Governments. His week-end engagements covered Liberal and Conservative establishments and friends. He was, unconsciously, the bridge between the old partisan concept and the subsequent complete anonymity of the professional civil service. But in his time the official world was as small as, and as intimately linked with, the political and social world of London.

For the Victorian politician, the House of Commons was his place of business, his home of pleasure, his hope of fame. As Disraeli sardonically observed, the first requisite for success in the House of Commons was to be there. For those who were determined and had the financial resources, getting there did not provide major difficulties.

Succeeding there, and remaining there, were much more hazardous to achieve.

*

It is difficult, and invariably perilous, to endeavour to draw the portrait of a particular age. No period of British society until then is as copiously documented as nineteenth century England, but the historian, confronted by the extraordinary contrasts of accounts and approaches and the infinite variety of the contemporary experience of this turbulent period, emerges more with a quantity of contradictory conceptions than with a clear picture and understanding of the spirit, driving-power, doubts, uneasiness and momentum of Victorian Britain.

The physical results are themselves very contradictory, ranging from the superlative engineering feats of Brunel, the great new civic buildings in London and the major cities to the unplanned and squalid development of the towns, and the less happy manifestations of the Gothic Revival. Save in the Crimea, Britain was not involved at all in major conflicts since the Napoleonic Wars, and it had escaped—however narrowly—the violent internal social revolutions which characterised most European countries in the first part of the century.

But although the reality of Victorian society was not, on inspection, as serene as it later appeared, the contrast between the vast changes made on the face of Britain by the Industrial Revolution and the relatively small impact upon the basic structure of that society is very striking. There were agitations, difficulties, and change, but in reality the balance of power had not shifted dramatically. The historian, confronted with these and many other contrasts, gains piercing insights into sectors, and not least from the great contemporary fictional observers of society, but finds it difficult to see the whole. To describe mid- and late-Victorian England as a confused, exciting, and fascinating paradox is not to escape into banal generality but to advance in understanding.

But, clearly, there were ingredients in that paradox which were of central significance. The most important were the balm of wealth and power that Britain had acquired and continued to acquire from the beginning of the century. Either in commercial or in military power there was no real challenger close at hand. And while the most notable characteristics of the age were a seething dynamism, self-confidence and energy, yet these were also tempered by caution, apprehension, and by an instinctive self-protective belief in established institutions. For this society was much less confident and far less complacent than it was later depicted. It could see serious problems present or looming at home and abroad, and these concerns constituted the principal meaning, relevance, and content of contemporary politics.

But, after the turmoils and dangers of the first half of the century, by the 1860s it had appeared that Britain had entered into a period of almost indefinite prosperity and wealth. This mood of buoyant optimism had been reflected in the Report of the Census Commissioners in 1871 which had recalled and invoked the words of Milton:

> Lords and Commons of England, consider what nation it is whereof ye are, and whereof ye are the governors; a nation not slow and dull, but of a quick, ingenious and piercing spirit; acute to invent, subtile and sinewy to discourse, not beyond the reach of any point the highest that human capacity can soar to.

The period of British supremacy had been very brief indeed. Until the early 1870s, although Britain had developed rapidly into a major industrial nation, agriculture had remained the largest single industry. Now this major industry was suddenly and fatally stricken by the combination of a series of bad harvests and the availability of cheap American wheat. Although there was a temporary recovery in the 1880s, the blow was to be mortal. Between 1841 and 1901 some four million people left the land and moved into the towns and cities, increasing the proportion of urban dwellers from half the population in the 1850s to three-quarters by the beginning of the twentieth century; by 1914 nearly eighty per cent of the population of England and Wales lived in the towns and cities, and the bulk of the land fell into poverty and neglect. The extraordinary emptiness of the English countryside was to be, subsequently, one of the most vivid memories of those who remembered this period. Land under cultivation fell from some 17 million acres in the 1870s to less than 13½ millions by 1913, and Britain became a substantial food-importing nation for the first time in her history.

Up to the 1860s exports had provided a national bonus; from this time onwards, with a steadily mounting population, national economic survival depended upon the export of goods and services at a time when two new industrial giants—America and Germany—were

developing rapidly as formidable rivals. The *Annual Register* had
warned in 1867 that 'England . . . owes her great influence not to
military successes, but to her commanding position in the arena of
industry and commerce. If she forgets this, she is lost. . . . The signs,
for those who can read, are present, and can be plainly seen.' By 1880
they were to be even more clearly seen, but the response was insufficient. Britain was a very rich nation—in 1885 Sir Robert Giffen
estimated the value of British investments abroad at £1,302 millions—
and the value of its foreign possessions was beyond calculation. British
workmanship and technology were unequalled. But the brief hour of
supremacy had passed, as had the mood of buoyant optimism. The
'Great Depression' of the late 1870s may indeed, be, in retrospect, a
myth[1], but it was not regarded as such by contemporaries. Events such
as the collapse of the City of Glasgow Bank in 1878 were taken very
seriously indeed, and the agricultural depression was plain to see.

Macaulay had claimed in 1848 that 'the history of our country
during the last hundred and sixty years is entirely the history of
physical, of moral, and of intellectual improvement.' But by the end
of the 1870s there were some who were seriously questioning the
validity of these confident assumptions. The unexpected depression
created a revived awareness of the harsh squalor and misery that lay
so close to the surface of national prosperity, and which made the
contrast between the affluence of the few and the existence of the many
so glaring and painful. Laissez-faire and Free Trade were still
sacrosanct articles of national faith, virtually unchallenged and unchallengeable, but although there had been few signs of serious
industrial trouble there were indications of new stirrings in areas which
had been quiescent since the Hungry Forties. Joseph Chamberlain
had transformed Birmingham by a programme of energetic and
enlightened civic reform, and the new County Council was, in the
1890s, to do much for London. But social reform was sporadic, and
even major advances such as the 1870 Education Act in reality only
marked the beginnings of dealing with a much more profound problem,
which was that the great majority of the population of this powerful
nation lived in poverty, or near poverty, without education, and were
the first victims of any economic depression, while a small minority
enjoyed power and great affluence. The meek acceptance by the
deprived of this situation was still a dominant attitude, and the

[1] See S. B. Saul: *The Myth of the Great Depression 1873–1896.*

historian surveying the reality can only marvel at the passivity of the afflicted, and share Cobden's astonishment that 'the people at large' were so 'tacit in their submission to the perpetuation of the feudal system in this country.' But this was being challenged. The decline of Britain as a church-going nation, which had been taking place since the 1850s, was in itself a portent. In the 1880s these stirrings were to develop into something much more significant.

Of this teeming nation, whose population rose from 12 million in 1811 to over 40 million by the end of the century, and this in spite of massive emigration from Ireland, the vote in 1880 was the prerogative of two and a half million adult males. The electorate had more than doubled as a result of the 1867 Reform Act, but it was still a relatively small fragment of the nation. The programme of the Chartists in the 1840s had been only partly implemented, but not entirely forgotten, and the continuation of a situation in which the great majority of the population had not even this modest degree of influence over its destiny was bound to cause trouble.

Although much had changed since the 1840s, Britain still remained Disraeli's Two Nations, and the first regarded the latter with a deep apprehension. It was once remarked of the Liberal Lord Rosebery that he felt of democracy as though he were holding a wolf by the ears, and Rosebery was not alone. The sanctity of Property was the religion of the old and new moneyed classes. The London mob which had aroused such terrors in the past now only emerged very occasionally, and with little of the ferocity of the past, but its potentialities were vivid, as the Hyde Park riots of May 1866 had demonstrated. For all its surface glitter and apparent self-confidence, and which so impressed wealthy foreign visitors, the First Nation wielded its power with fear in its heart. It did not share that contempt for the docility of the British working class which so bewildered and angered Marx and Engels.

The dominant question for the First Nation was how to preserve its power without inviting its destruction. To what point could social reform be achieved without disturbing the basic structure of difference and division? Disraeli had persuaded the Conservatives to recognise the necessity of Reform in the 1860s by instilling into them the realisation that a policy of gradual and controlled reform, conducted by them on their own terms and at their own timing, contained the key. 'In a progressive country', he remarked, 'change is constant, and the question is not whether you should resist change which is inevitable, but whether that change should be carried out in deference to the manners, the customs, the laws and the traditions of the people, or whether it should be carried out in deference to abstract principles and arbitrary and general doctrines.'

But to have this opportunity required the necessity of Office. It was as this fact inexorably sank in that the far-flung Conservative coalition had begun to merge into something much more national and formidable. It could be said of Disraeli as Lord Beaverbrook wrote of Lloyd George many year later, that 'he did not seem to care which way he travelled provided he was in the driver's seat'. It was this message that he conveyed to his party, and it was in reality his most enduring memorial. The vital requisite for controlled reform was to be in the driver's seat. The doctrine of Imperialism abroad and social reform at home had seemed romantic and impractible when it was enunciated by Disraeli in the early 1870s, but by 1880 the Conservatives were beginning to see the point. Power was henceforth the ideology of their party—Power to preserve power, to control movements which, if ignored or alienated, could sweep them away. From this conclusion it was a very short step indeed to the conviction that for the Conservatives to be out of power would lead to national catastrophe. This belief gave to the Conservative Party a passion, a venom, a cohesion and an unscrupulousness which was to make it a dominant force, in office or out of it, for the next sixty years.

It would not be difficult to mock at these pretensions, but they provided the cement which bound the Conservative Coalition together and enabled it to expand its appeal so dramatically. Not only the Conservatives were apprehensive. Radicalism was a fine luxury for the established in good times but a dangerous plaything in bad. Gladstone in 1885 was alarmed by a tendency in Liberals to 'take into the hands of the State the business of the individual man'. When Chamberlain campaigned for this 'unauthorised programme' in the same year he was denounced as a revolutionary, yet he was very careful to emphasise that 'I am opposed to confiscation in every shape and form' and that 'nothing would be more undesirable than that we should remove the stimulus to industry and thrift and exertion which is afforded by the security given to every man in the enjoyment of the fruits of his own individual exertions.' As will be seen, other issues caused the great Liberal split of 1886, but a major element in the movement of the anti-Gladstone Liberals into the embrace of the

Conservatives was to be the fear of extra-Parliamentary forces which could cast down the accumulated wealth and influence of three generations. The horror of Joseph Chamberlain at land legislation in 1882, which he denounced as 'veiled confiscation', emphasised a belief in the rights of property which he was to demonstrate in his assaults on Gladstone's 'Newcastle Programme' of nearly a decade later, and were to make him and the Whig Lord Hartington natural recruits into the Conservative ranks.

In contrast to the Conservatives, the Liberal Coalition was in the 1870s a very curious amalgam indeed, and it was difficult to detect any cement at all in its haphazard structure. It had no lack of war-cries—indeed, a super-abundance of them—nor of talent, but it was riven in personalities and dogmas. It had no particular idea about what exactly it wanted to reform, or how. The old Whig element, which remained strong, had little interest in reform at all. Among those who termed themselves Radicals there was a very wide spectrum of objectives and philosophies, and it was this 'sectionalism' which most concerned Gladstone in the 1870s, and of which he wrote in 1877 that 'no more ingenious recipe could be found in a self-governing country for solving the problem, apparently so hopeless, how to devise a method under which, where the majority prevails by law, the minority shall be in fact supreme.' Gladstone himself, who described himself as 'an out-and-out inegalitarian' and 'a firm believer in the aristocratic principle—the rule of the best', responded to causes and problems, often with genius and deep perception, but he was at root a *responder*. In his old age he wrote that he perceived his most 'striking gift' as 'an insight into the facts of particular eras, and their relations one to another, which generates in the mind a conviction that the materials exist for forming a public opinion, and for directing it to a particular end.' The fact that his response usually emerged suddenly out of a process of deep thought and personal communion made him a highly uncomfortable colleague and leader. As he himself wrote:

> For years and years, well into advanced middle life, I seem to have considered actions simply as they were in themselves, and did not take into account the way in which they would be taken or understood by others. . . . The dominant tendencies of my mind were those of a recluse, and I might, in most respects with ease, have accommodated myself to the education of the cloister.

Gladstone was so complex a man that it is perilous to describe him in a brief compass, but this self-portrait held true throughout his life. As Lord Selborne wrote, 'He can hardly be brought to interest himself at all in matters (even when they are really great matters) in which he is not carried away by some too strong attraction; and, when he is carried away, he does not sympathise, or take counsel with, those whose point of view is at all different from his own.' After the Liberals fell to defeat in the General Election of 1874 he allegedly retired from public life, but his persistent eruptions—most dramatically over the Bulgarian Atrocities in 1876—had compromised the authority of the nominal leaders, Lord Hartington in the Commons and Lord Granville in the Lords, and had confirmed in the eyes of his admirers that he *was* the Liberal Party.

Gladstone had not only developed into the greatest public orator of his day, who could hold vast multitudes enthralled like the great preachers of old—and the comparison is a real one—but after Disraeli's departure to the Lords in 1876 he was also the most formidable and experienced Parliamentarian in public life. He had made his maiden speech in St. Stephen's Chapel, had passed through the agonies of the Corn Law schism and its aftermath, and in the swirling confusions of the 1850s had held his own through sheer ability and force of personality. His opponents, even Disraeli who affected to regard him with contempt, were afraid of him. His followers were awed by his powers and by his huge following, particularly in the North. Some of them considered him as the most valuable safeguard against the latent powers of the multitude, a kind of spectacular lightning-conductor for bitter feelings which, but for Gladstone, would have become highly and practically dangerous. Others were fearful of his unpredictability, and were baffled by the processes by which he suddenly and un-expectedly soared across ravines at whose edge he had trembled for years. Some regarded him as a true Radical, whose entire life had been a glorious progression from implacable Tory to root-and-branch reformer. But the political fact was that, however and for whatever reasons they had come to this conclusion, Gladstone was regarded by the bulk of Liberals as the holder of the true faith of Liberalism and of the Liberal cause. Thus, to a dangerous degree, it was *he* who provided the cement in the Liberal Coalition, and he alone. This fact was to dominate the policies and fortunes of the Liberals for the next fourteen years, and even beyond them.

*

Other movements had developed in the 1860s and early 1870s whose impact was not clearly apparent by 1880, but which were to have most profound consequences on the development of Britain over the next twenty years.

Viewed in calm retrospect, it is evident that the period 1870 to 1900 should be described as the Age of Imperialism. In these years the five major Imperial Powers—Britain, France, Germany, Belgium and Portugal—acquired by various methods some 12 million square miles of new territory. In 1900 it was estimated that the British Empire consisted of over 13 million square miles and 366,793,000 persons; the nearest challenger was France, with 3,740,756 square miles and over 56 million people; and Germany, with 1,027,120 square miles and over 14 million people. The bulk of the British, French and German acquisitions occurred in the years 1884–1900, in which the British acquired nearly three and three-quarter million square miles of territory and nearly fifty-seven and a half million people, and most of these new possessions came in the 'scramble for Africa' which was the principal phenomenon of these years.

This had been very difficult to foresee, so far as the British had been concerned, in the 1860s. India was recovering slowly from the after-effects of the Mutiny. Canada, given a new federated status, the six Australian colonies, and New Zealand, were far away. British possessions in Africa consisted of the Cape Colony, Sierra Leone, the Gambia, Lagos, and the Gold Coast settlement. The prevalent mood in high political circles in Britain was far from imperialistic, in the sense of expanding existing possessions. Even in radical circles the balance of argument had moved from the advocacy of separatism, and of abandonment of what Disraeli described as 'these Colonial dead-weights which we do not govern', to how best they should be administered. By the early 1860s no leading politician—with the possible exception of Lord Granville—could be described as a separatist, and Colonial Reform was one of the dominant themes in political discussion.

It was true that Cobden had spoken of 'the bloodstained fetish of Empire', and that John Stuart Mill had written that 'such a thing as the government of one people by another does not and cannot exist'. It was also the case that the very word Empire had a foreign, and, above all, a dictatorial connotation. As late as 1879 the Colonial Secretary, Lord Carnarvon, declared that 'I have heard of Imperial policy and Imperial interests, but Imperialism, as such, is a newly coined word to me', which he disliked 'for the obvious reasons that it suggests uncomfortable Continental associations'.[1] In 1876, when Queen Victoria assumed the title of Empress of India, *Punch* commented that:

> And, age by age, that name accurst
> Has still from first to latest
> Implied of Monarchies the worst,
> But ne'er with us the greatest.

But the subject of Empire was slowly becoming of revived interest to many Victorians. Huskisson's comment of 1828 that 'England cannot afford to be little. She must be what she is, or nothing' had perhaps an even greater significance in the 1860s, when the belief that a dynamic society must expand had many more adherents, and was well expressed by Adam Smith: 'It is a sort of instinctive feeling to us all, that the destiny of our name and nation is not here, in this narrow island which we occupy; that the spirit of England is volatile, not fixed.' Cobden had made it clear that he was not opposed to the *principle* of Colonies, but to the manner in which they were administered; in private correspondence he was more critical of the principle, but it was significant that latterly he kept such views to himself.

Matthew Arnold expressed a distaste for a narrow and insular mentality when he wrote in support of Heine's strictures on the British spirit in *Heine's Grave*:

> Yes, we arraign her! but she
> The weary Titan! with deaf
> Ears and labour-dimmed eyes,
> Regarding neither to right
> Nor left, goes passively by,
> Staggering on to her goal.[2]

At Eton, the schoolmaster William Johnson (who subsequently changed his name to Cory), dwelt heavily upon the grandeurs of the

---

[1] See Richard Koebner and Helmut Dan Schmidt: *Imperialism: the story and significance of a political word, 1840–1960*, for a detailed examination of this aspect of imperial thought and controversy.

[2] The metaphor became a popular one. As late as the Colonial Conference of 1902 Joseph Chamberlain spoke of 'the weary Titan' struggling under 'the too vast orb of its fate.'

past and the feebleness of the present. Among his pupils was a future Prime Minister, Lord Rosebery. As another pupil, Sir Henry Newbolt, wrote of Johnson:

> Beyond the book his teaching sped,
> He left on whom he taught the trace
> Of kinship with the deathless dead,
> And faith in all the Island Race.

The problem confronting the British in the 1860s was neatly expressed in the opening words of a pamphlet written by Joseph Howe in 1866 called 'The Organisation of Empire':

> Under the Providence of God, after centuries of laborious cultivation, the sacrifice of much heroic blood, the expenditures of a vast amount of treasure, the British Empire, as it stands, has been got together, and the question which is presented to us, in some form of Parliamentary or newspaper disputation almost every week is, *what is now to be done with it?*

If Howe's solution—responsible administration in the Colonies and representation at Westminster in a 'Parliament of the Empire'—was too extensive (and too vague) for contemporary appetite, the question that he posed was becoming a very real one.

The Radicals had found particular difficulty in determining their attitude to Empire, and the very existence of the colonies perplexed and divided them. By the 1860s few of the successors of Adam Smith and Jeremy Bentham could fully accept the philosophy of emancipation, and the argument that the desertion of the Colonies would be a worse crime than their seizure became more widespread. Many argued that they were an encumbrance—an opinion shared by Disraeli when he was Chancellor of the Exchequer in 1852—but what was to be done with them? Attention was accordingly given more to the task of improving the lot of the colonies than to abandoning them. Reform rather than Abandonment increasingly marked the Radical attitudes. The vision of Major John Cartwright—'the father of Reform'—a century before of 'a firm and brotherly league' of free and equal states with co-ordinated legislation and a common Crown became more attractive and comforting. It was extremely significant that when the severe repressive measures of Governor Edward Eyre of Jamaica aroused radical wrath in the 1860s, John Bright spoke at Rochdale of 'the legal putting to death of *subjects of the Queen and citizens of the Empire*'.[1]

In the middle and later 1860s this interest increased remarkably. A book by a young radical baronet, Sir Charles Wentworth Dilke, was published in 1869. Entitled *Greater Britain*, it attracted immediate attention and enjoyed a considerable success. 'The idea which in all the length of my travels has been at once my fellow and my guide—a key wherewith to unlock the hidden things of strange new lands—is a conception, however imperfect, of the grandeur of our race, already girdling the earth, which it is destined perhaps eventually to over-spread.' Dilke's book and his portrayal of the glowing future of the Anglo-Saxon race—for Dilke was thinking as much of America as of Britain—was warmly approved by the Radical Liberal W. E. Forster and by the historian J. A. Froude.

The year before, the Colonial Society was launched in London with the motto 'United Empire', and Gladstone and the Colonial Secretary, Granville, had attended its inaugural dinner. The aged but still influential ex-Premier Earl Russell wrote in a foreword to an edition of his speeches published later in the same year that his objective was 'the consolidation of the British Empire. In my eyes it would be a sad spectacle, it would be a spectacle for gods and men to weep at, to see this brilliant luminary cut up into spangles.' Froude, in his rectorial address at St. Andrew's University in March 1869, declared that 'Britain may yet have a future before it grander than its past; instead of a country standing alone, complete in itself, it may become the metropolis of an enormous and coherent Empire'. In a series of articles in *Fraser's Magazine* he had excoriated the old Manchester School and its narrow and insular outlook. Sir Charles Adderly, who had been under-secretary for the Colonies and who had played some part in the creation of the Dominion of Canada, delivered a robust assault on the old concept of the paternal role of the small Colonial Office, as personified to some by Sir James Stephen, Permanent Secretary from 1836–47, and derided as 'Mr. Mother-Country'. Adderly envisaged an Empire of self-governing dominion states, enjoying common citizenship, rights and duties; but it was significant that those colonies settled by aliens and military stations would be excluded from this process. Although little noticed at the time, the retirement of Frederick Rogers (later Lord Blachford) from the permanent-secretaryship of the

[1] Author's italics.

Colonial Office in 1871 marked the end of the direct influence of an individual who believed firmly in the inevitable disintegration of the Empire into autonomous states.[1]

It is important to emphasise the part played in the education of the men who were destined to be the chief apostles of the new expansionist conception of Empire in the 1880s and 1890s by influential leaders like William Johnson, Froude and Ruskin.

Froude's influence was considerable, and Ruskin's inaugural lecture as Professor of Fine Arts at Oxford, delivered in 1869, was one of the most significant and interesting of all contemporary utterances on the new expansionist vision of Empire. Among his audience on that occasion was Cecil John Rhodes, who had returned from farming cotton in Natal and working in the Kimberley diamond fields, to study at Oxford. An extract from Ruskin's lecture should be given:

> There is a destiny now possible to us, the highest ever set before a nation to be accepted or refused. We are still undegenerate in race; a race mingled of the best northern blood. We are not yet dissolute in temper, but still have the firmness to govern and the grace to obey. . . .
> This is what England must either do or perish; she must found colonies as fast and as far as she is able, formed of her most energetic and worthiest men; seizing every piece of fruitful waste ground she can set her foot on, and there teaching these her colonists that their chief virtue is to be fidelity to their country, and their first aim is to advance the power of England by land or sea; and that, though they live on a distant plot of land, they are no more to consider themselves therefore disfranchised from their native land than the sailors of her fleets do because they float on distant seas. If we can get men, for little pay, to cast themselves against cannon-mouths for love of England, we may find men also who will plough and sow for her, who will behave kindly and righteously for her, and who will bring up their children to love her.

The impact of this passionate declaration of faith on an audience of eager and impressionable young men was profound. When Rhodes declared at the age of twenty-four that 'I contend that we are the first race in the world, and that the more of the world we inhabit, the

[1] For a detailed study of the Colonial Office, see Chapter XIX (by R. B. Pugh) of *The Cambridge History of the British Empire*, Volume III.

better it is for the human race', he was already engaging upon that subtle but crucial extension of Ruskin's vision which was to bring it to the extreme racial faith of subsequent generations of imperialists, personified by Alfred Milner and Leo Amery. At its best, it was something larger and better, but when it fell below that level it degenerated swiftly into an arrogant racialism. But to men like David Livingstone, Charles Gordon, Evelyn Baring, Milner and Amery the concept of racial superiority had as its definite and absolute corollary responsibility and toil. It was *faith* in their race which acted as their driving force. Towards the end of his life Milner wrote what he called his 'Credo—key to my position', which may be inserted at this point to illustrate the development of the arguments with which Ruskin had amazed and inspired his undergraduate audience.

I am a Nationalist and not a cosmopolitan. . . . I am a British (indeed primarily an English) Nationalist. If I am also an Imperialist, it is because the destiny of the English race, owing to its insular position and long supremacy at sea, has been to strike roots in different parts of the world. I am an Imperialist and not a Little Englander because I am a British Race Patriot. . . . The British State must follow the race. . . . If the swarms constantly being thrown off by the parent hive are lost to the State, the State is irreparably weakened.

It was, characteristically, Disraeli who had first perceived the political importance of the new and marked change of intellectual attitudes towards Empire. When he rose to speak at the Crystal Palace on June 24th 1872, his audience had no foreknowledge of the message he was to deliver, for the cause and idea of the British Empire had never occupied Disraeli's attention or interest to any noticeable extent. Henceforward, it was to be the last great theme of his long and extraordinary career, that career which had seen the transformation of the cynical arriviste libertine to the solemn champion of the Conservative Party and the harbinger of Imperialism.

Reduced to its essentials, the Crystal Palace speech deliberately represented the Liberals as the destoyers of Empire and the Conservatives as its champion. 'The issue', Disraeli stated, 'is not a mean one. It is whether you will be content to be a comfortable England, modelled and moulded upon Continental principles and meeting in due course an inevitable fate, or whether you would be a great country, an Imperial country, a country where your sons, when they rise, rise to paramount positions, and obtain not merely the esteem of their countrymen, but command the respect of the world.' 'England', he declared, 'has outgrown the Continent of Europe. England is the metropolis of a great maritime Empire extending to the boundaries of the farthest Ocean.' The re-establishment of the Conservatives as the 'patriotic' and 'national' party was to pay important political dividends in the 1880s and 1890s.

But the immediate impact of Disraeli's speech was small, and the events of 1874–9 were to demonstrate that he had seen a possible political advantage in an Imperialistic doctrine before that doctrine had gained general acceptance or even recognition.

At the General Election of February 1874 the issues were primarily domestic. Gladstone's first (and incomparably greatest) Government had lost its reforming impetus. The animosity that it had aroused had out-weighed the approval. The party itself was divided on its future course. The Education Act of 1870 had aroused the fierce opposition of Midland Nonconformity, poised for the final blow against the influence of the Church in education, and angrily disillusioned by the compromise contained in the Act. The Nonconformist opposition to the Government first brought to national attention the name of Joseph Chamberlain, who had established himself in Birmingham as the forceful exponent of a new conception of civic administration and reform. The first Gladstone Government had disestablished the Irish Church, made the first venture into Irish land reform, opened the civil service to competitive examination, ended the purchase of commissions in the Army, introduced the secret ballot, established the principle of free elementary education, and by the Judicature Act of 1873 had reorganised the law courts and established the court of appeal. But it had also settled the *Alabama* dispute with the United States of America on terms which evoked criticism, and the virtual acceptance of the Russians' unilateral repudiation of the Black Sea clauses in the Treaty of Paris was also deemed unheroic. But the Liberal Government ran out of ideas and luck on domestic matters, and Gladstone himself became exhausted under the strain. Gladstone's election address in 1874 concentrated on the promise of the abolition of income tax, and was a bitter disappointment to the rising generation of Radicals, of whom Chamberlain and Dilke were the most conspicuous.

Chamberlain described Gladstone's manifesto as 'the meanest public document that had ever, in like circumstances, proceeded from the pen of a statesman of the first rank.' Disraeli's appeal was to a respite from 'incessant and harassing legislation', to a restoration of British influence in Europe, and 'to support by every means her imperial sway'. But it is extremely doubtful that the Imperial aspect had much influence. The electorate was bored with the hectic manner of Gladstonian government, and certain elements were responsive to Disraeli's accusation that Liberal reforms 'menaced every institution and every interest, every class and every calling, in the country'. At a time when the vote was substantially the privilege of the upper and propertied middle classes, such warnings had particular effect. And when Chamberlain declared that the Liberal leader was 'hardly in touch with the robust common sense of English liberalism' there were many who agreed with him.

Another element in the Liberal defeat was the unexpected emergence of an Irish Home Rule Party, the direct result of the 1872 Ballot Act and of the ferocious opposition of the Irish Catholic hierarchy led by Cardinal Cullen against the Irish University Bill of 1873, on which the Government had been defeated in the Commons on March 11th–12th 1873. Gladstone had resigned, with the invitation to Disraeli to form a minority government; Disraeli had refused, and the reputation of the Government had been further compromised. A series of minor scandals concerning the Post Office and the conduct of the Postmaster-General (W. Monsell) and Commissioner of Public Works (A. S. Ayrton), had followed. The removal of the Chancellor of the Exchequer, Robert Lowe, and other changes had not stemmed the rising tide of unpopularity that engulfed the Government. In 1874 the Conservatives secured an overall majority of fifty, but it could hardly be said that their victory was the consequence of the introduction of the Imperial issue.

Disraeli's first major Imperial coup came in 1875, when he in effect secured control of the Suez Canal by the purchase of the largest single holding—forty-four per cent—of the shares. Palmerston had strongly opposed the Canal, and Disraeli had described it as 'a most futile attempt and totally impossible to be carried out'. Ferdinand de Lesseps had proved Disraeli's claims incorrect, and the Canal had been completed in 1869. Egypt was part of the Ottoman Empire, but the Khedive Ismail was able to ignore the English protests to the

Sultan. He was less able to handle the financial aspects of the building of the Canal, and by 1869 was deeply in debt. In 1867 he had obtained from the Sultan the style and title of Khedive, and in 1873 he achieved permission to act as an independent ruler and to raise revenue and grant concessions without reference to the Sultan. But Ismail's capacity to spend money was awesome, and his many achievements for Egypt were overwhelmed by his chronic indebtedness. Thus it was that in 1875 he had to sell his 176,602 shares, out of a total of 400,000; with the assistance of the House of Rothschild, Disraeli secured them. Gladstone considered this 'an act of folly fraught with personal danger', but this was not the general reaction in England.

But although this action of Disraeli's was exceedingly popular, the bestowal on the Queen of the title of Empress of India in 1876 was less happily inspired. *The Times*, after initial approval, considered that it threatened the Crown 'with the degradation of a tawdry Imperialism'; Gladstone emerged from his retirement to denounce it as 'theatrical bombast and folly'; even the *Daily Telegraph*, a devout and docile admirer of the Government, expressed doubts, and the Liberals tabled hostile motions in both Houses of Parliament. The Queen was deeply angered by this hostility, and the episode confirmed her in her bias against the Liberal Party, on which Disraeli played with great skill. But the opposition did show that the glamour of Imperialism did not yet have a significant appeal to intelligent opinion. But it was significant that Disraeli had his champions. Edward Dicey—editor of *The Observer*—attacked Gladstone for upholding 'the anti-imperialist theory of British statecraft'. An official of the Madras Service, W. M. Thorburn, published in 1876 a book entitled *The Great Game*, advocating an expansive military Empire of a metropolitan character, which rapidly went through three editions. The first two contained an introductory chapter that deplored the absence of a forceful imperial policy; the third applauded Disraeli for providing one.[1]

A great moral issue arose in 1876. The Middle East crises of 1875–8 lie beyond this narrative, but no study of the movements of Imperialist sentiment in Britain can ignore the controversy over the Bulgarian Atrocities. First reports of the wholesale massacres of men, women and children by groups of armed Turkish irregulars called the Bashi-Bazouks were discounted by the British Government on the advice of the excessively pro-Turkish Ambassador at Constantinople, Sir H.

[1] See Koebner and Schmidt, op. cit.

Elliott. Disastrously, Disraeli tried to laugh off the reports. When Forster questioned him in the House on July 10th, Disraeli said that he doubted that torture had been employed by 'an oriental people' who 'generally terminate their connection with culprits in a more expeditious character'. The Tories leaped and roared at this sally. On July 31st Gladstone himself asked a question; the Prime Minister dismissed the allegations as 'coffee-house babble'. He subsequently blamed Elliott for his 'lamentable want of energy and deficiency of information', but it had been Disraeli himself who had made the most grievous blunder. He was justified in endeavouring to damp down hostility to Turkey at a time when his policy was based on supporting Turkey against Russian ambitions in the Middle East, but by adopting a flippant and contemptuous tone he had laid himself open to accusations of irresponsibility and even callousness.

The violent agitation that now arose owed nothing to Gladstone. In fact he behaved with almost excessive caution, and nearly missed the occasion. One of his biographers has written that 'never had Gladstone's instinct for right-timing been more perfectly exemplified',[1] which is a serious misunderstanding of the events of 1876.[2] It was not until September 6th that his famous pamphlet, 'The Bulgarian Horrors and the Question of the East', was published. It was—and remains— a startling document. One detects in its frenzy Gladstone the theological disputator rather than Gladstone the politician. It was a shrill, impassioned, and grotesquely vitriolic philippic. The Turks were depicted as 'the one great anti-human species of humanity', whose 'abominable and bestial lusts' were such that 'at which Hell itself might almost blush'. There was, however, one magnificent passage of inspired invective:

> Let the Turks now carry away their abuses in the only possible manner, namely by carrying off themselves. Their Zaptiehs and their Mudirs, their Bimbashis and their Yuzbachis, their Kaimakams and their Pashas, one and all, bag and baggage, shall, I hope, clear out from the province they have desolated and profaned. This thorough riddance, this most blessed deliverance, is the only reparation we can make to the memory of those heaps on heaps of dead; to the violated purity alike of matron, of maiden, and of child.

[1] P. Magnus, *Gladstone*, 242.
[2] See R. T. Shannon: *Gladstone and the Bulgarian Agitation.*

The last great duel between Gladstone and Disraeli—who in August, went to the Lords as the Earl of Beaconsfield—was in many respects their most significant. Disraeli's policy was, in Gladstone's eyes, not merely immoral in itself, but deliberately provocative. At the Guildhall on November 9th, he threatened Russia with war, and a famous music-hall refrain—'We don't want to fight, but by Jingo if we do,/We've got the ships, we've got the men, we've got the money too!'—had brought a new word into the language of political debate. Both parties were divided. Salisbury, Derby and Carnarvon were as alarmed by Disraeli's speeches as Granville, Hartington and Harcourt were by Gladstone's. The public utterances of both were marked by a personal animosity that was to affect Gladstone's career for the next twenty years. As Sir William Harcourt wrote to Dilke on October 10th, 1876, 'Gladstone and Dizzy seem to cap one another in folly and imprudence, and I don't know which has made the greater ass of himself.'

It seemed that it was Gladstone. His fury at the Turkish atrocities had led him into a series of wild panegyrics of the Russians. When, after a brave resistance, the Turkish armies were fought back almost to the walls of Constantinople itself, British opinion veered round sharply again. In London, Gladstone was vehemently unpopular, but elsewhere—particularly in the north of England and Scotland—his earnestness and fervour had made an immense impression. Froude, Ruskin, Carlyle and Tennyson gave him public support. But the events of 1878, culminating in the Congress of Berlin and 'Peace with Honour', seemed to give the victory to Beaconsfield.[1] In the speech from the Throne that ended the Session of 1877 there was a significant phrase:

> If, in the course of the contest, the rights of my Empire should be assailed or endangered, I should confidently rely on your help to vindicate and maintain them.

In the Lords (April 8th, 1878) Beaconsfield set out his new Imperial philosophy:

[1] But note should be taken of his letter to Salisbury, September 17th, 1878: 'So long as the country thought they had obtained "Peace with Honour" the conduct of Her Majesty's Government was popular, but if the country finds there is no peace they will be apt to conclude there is no honour.'

I have ever considered that Her Majesty's Government—of whatever party formed—are the trustees of that Empire. That Empire was formed by the enterprise and energy of your ancestors, my lords, and it is one of a very peculiar character. I know of no example of it, either in ancient or modern history. No Caesar or Charlemagne ever presided over a dominion so peculiar. Its flag floats on many waters; it has provinces in every zone, they are inhabited by persons of different races, different religions, different laws, manners, customs. Some of these are bound to us by the ties of liberty, fully conscious that without their connection with the metropolis they have no security for public freedom and self-government; others are bound to us by flesh and blood and by material as well as moral considerations. There are millions who are bound to us by our military sway, and they bow to that sway because they know that they are indebted to it for order and justice. All these communities agree in recognising the commanding spirit of these islands that has formed and fashioned in such a manner so great a portion of the globe.

This ideological basis for Imperialism aroused fierce controversy and hostility from the Liberals. Robert Lowe declared that 'when anything very foolish is to be done we are always told that it is an Imperial matter . . . Rome . . . was so imperial that its people were robbed to sustain the imperial policy'. The comparison with Rome was current. The banker and historian Frederick Seebohm urged that Britain should be the Athens, and not the Rome, of the English-speaking world.[1] Other comparisons lay at hand. Sir William Harcourt described the policy of the Government as 'an Imperial policy—a servile imitation of the imperialism of the Second Empire'; Gladstone declared that 'we do not want Bosnian submissions', and accused the nation of neglecting affairs at home 'to amuse herself everywhere else in stalking phantoms'. A. J. Mundella warned a Sheffield audience against being led captive by 'a sham imperialism'. 'What does imperialism mean?' Lowe enquired. 'It means the assertion of absolute force over others'.

Beaconsfield responded that there was only one responsibility from

---

[1] *Imperialism and Socialism* (1880) Seebohm's main contention—that imperialism was the banner of revolutionaries and radicals and thus threatened social order—was less characteristic.

which he shrank, 'that of handing to our successors a weakened or diminished Empire'. Lord Salisbury said that 'we are striving to pick up the thread—the broken thread—of England's old Imperial traditions'. He went on to produce another argument, which was just beginning to have a real attraction in certain circles: 'The commerce of a great commercial country like this will only flourish—history attests it again and again—under the shadow of Empire, and those who give up Empire to make commerce prosper will end by losing both.' This recalled Disraeli's own statement in 1863 that 'there may be grave questions as to the best mode of obtaining wealth . . . but there can be no question . . . that the best mode of preserving wealth is power'.

But the debate was not merely one that concerned theoreticians and politicians in Britain. In South Africa, the British High Commissioner, Sir Henry Barkly, and his Colonial Secretary, Richard Southey, urged upon the Colonial Office a policy of blatant acquisition. The Boers who had left Cape Colony on the Great Trek in the 1830s were now established in the Transvaal and the Orange Free State, a devout, independent, and sternly puritanical farming community. The discovery of diamonds at Kimberley in 1870 not only attracted some ten thousand prospectors to a hitherto deserted area but also made South Africa appear to be a kind of nineteenth-century El Dorado. Southey had been responsible for a very quick and sharp acquisition of the diamond fields by buying the disputed area of Griqualand West from the local chieftain. This gave the Boers a very real grievance, which was not diminished by the payment of £90,000 in compensation. Barkly and Southey now worked towards the annexation of the Transvaal itself, in the firm conviction that, as Barkly wrote to the Conservative Colonial Secretary, Lord Carnarvon, on May 25th 1874, Britain 'has only plainly and firmly to indicate her will, in order to seek submission to it'. Carnarvon, who at first favoured reconciliation with the Transvaal, was gradually propelled towards annexation. 'These South African questions', he wrote, 'are a terrible labyrinth of which it is very hard to find the clue'. Carnarvon had sponsored the Act of 1867 that had federated Canada; a similar federation of South Africa was a gleaming prospect.

The annexation of the Transvaal was in the event absurdly simple. The President, Burgers, was weak. The Republic was insolvent. There were unending, and increasingly menacing, disputes with native tribes. In 1875 the Boers suffered a severe defeat at the hands of the

Bantu, and turned to a force of desperadoes led by a Prussian ex-officer who received no pay but were permitted to take what plunder they could. They acted with great efficiency and brutality, and the prospect of a major war between white and black became grimly nearer as the Zulus, led by their monarch, Cetawayo, cried out for revenge.

Carnarvon's representative was Sir Theophilus Shepstone, the Minister for native affairs in Natal, an attractive, courageous and knowledgeable man with a deep affection for, and understanding of, the Zulus. Carnarvon sent him to Pretoria to discuss confederation with Burgers, and with the discretion to propose bringing the Republic under the British flag. He reached Pretoria early in 1877 to find the treasury bankrupt and the President desperate for assistance. Burgers and his colleagues were prepared to accept annexation on the conditions that they should receive pensions or positions and that they should be permitted to make a public protest against the annexation. Shepstone accepted both conditions, even approving the draft of Burger's statement of protest. At the time it seemed to be a matter of no significance, but Shepstone had ensured the re-establishment of a spirit of Boer nationalism at a time when the Republic was on the verge of collapse. The emergence of Paul Kruger—Burgers's putative opponent at the next Presidential election—as the champion of this nationalism was the first result of the annexation. The resentment against the Griqualand West coup and the incursion of exploiting outsiders into the Veld had already been seen in many ways. Perhaps of most significance had been the movement to restore the Afrikaans tongue, initiated by Arnoldus Panneris, a Hollander schoolmaster, and which had made surprising headway since 1873. The publication of the principles of the Afrikander Bond on July 4th 1879, showed that annexation had sharply quickened the pace of Boer nationalism. But these straws in the wind went utterly unperceived at the time in Government circles in Cape Town and in London.

Shepstone's annexation came as an unwelcome shock to the new High Commissioner, Sir Bartle Frere, on his arrival in South Africa at the end of April 1877. The fact that Carnarvon had empowered Shepstone to undertake a task of such importance undoubtedly undermined the authority of the High Commissioner. He proceeded to direct his attention exclusively to the Zulu problem, and came quickly to the conclusion that, as war was inevitable, it should be swiftly undertaken. He and the local Commander-In-Chief—General Thesiger (who succeeded to the title of Lord Chelmsford in December 1878)—appealed to the home Government for military reinforcements. The Cabinet urged Frere to handle the problem by negotiation, but eventually authorised the dispatch of troops. Frere delivered an ultimatum to Cetawayo on December 11th and deliberately launched the Zulu War.

This venture came at a moment when the glitter had begun to fall off what Wilfrid Blunt called 'Dizzy's suit of imperial spangles'. In reality, Beaconsfield had been extremely cautious in foreign policy; purchasing the Canal shares was one thing, direct intervention in Egypt's affairs, urged on him in 1878, was quite another. But in politics appearances are often as important as facts. Beaconsfield had rhetorically linked himself with a 'forward', 'patriotic', 'imperial' and 'national' foreign policy, and was now neatly caught on his own phrases. The combination of apparent flamboyant and unsuccessful adventures abroad and economic depression at home gave the Liberals—and particularly Gladstone—a magnificent target which they assailed with a rare unanimity. The issue of the Bulgarian Atrocities had aroused a very real passion which, as has been emphasised, owed nothing to Gladstone but which he exploited just before the outcry had faded. The despatch of the Mediterranean Fleet to Besika Bay and then through the Dardanelles left more enduring memories of recklessness than the alleged triumph of the Congress of Berlin. And then Beaconsfield's critics were given additional ammunition.

Contrary to Frere's expectations, the Zulu War was neither swift nor successful. On January 22nd 1879 Chelmsford suffered, at Isandhlwana, a shattering disaster. Misled by a Zulu feint, he took most of his force away from the main camp; when it returned it discovered that 52 British officers, 806 troops, nearly 500 natives and some non-combatants had been overwhelmed and killed. The news reached England on February 11th, and brought a storm of criticism down upon the Government. Even the reports of the epic defence of Rorke's Drift immediately afterwards, where a force of just over 100 men repulsed an immense Zulu attack, could not affect the political impact of the Isandhlwana disaster. Large reinforcements were dispatched, and the Government defended Chelmsford and Frere against severe Liberal criticisms. Sir Garnet Wolseley was sent out to replace

Chelmsford, and arrived just as Chelmsford was about to defeat the Zulus at Ulundi (July 1879). Cetawayo was deported and his territory divided up into eight principalities. The total cost to the British of this lamentable foray had been 76 white officers, over 1,000 men and over 600 native troops killed in action; this included the Prince Imperial of France (the only son of Napoleon III). Seventeen white officers and 330 men had died of disease, and a further 99 officers and 1,286 men invalided; 37 officers, 206 white troops, and 57 native troops had been wounded in action—an astonishingly small figure compared with the deaths suffered in action, and which illustrates the fierceness of the fighting and the valour of the Zulus. The cost in financial terms was over £5 million.[1]

Unhappily, Frere was not the only representative of the Government who had ambitions. Lord Lytton had been appointed Viceroy of India in 1876 with specific instructions to induce Sher Ali, the Amir of Afghanistan, to receive a friendly mission to his country. The negotiations at Peshawar early in 1877 foundered on the British condition that their agents should be admitted to the frontier positions. In July 1878 a Russian mission arrived in the capital of Kabul, and a British mission was turned back at the frontier. Lytton now urged military intervention on the Cabinet, which received the request badly. But Beaconsfield and Salisbury—the main advocates of a careful and restrained policy—eventually agreed, after an unexpectedly impassioned appeal by the Secretary for India, Lord Cranbrook, to leave matters to Lytton's judgement.

The dismal consequences were much the same as in South Africa. Lytton issued an imperious ultimatum and then invaded Afghanistan with three armies, one of which was commanded by Major-General Frederick Roberts V.C. Sher Ali was overwhelmed, and his son ceded the principal British demands in May 1879. The peace was brief. On September 3rd the British mission at Kabul was killed to a man, and the war had to begin all over again, in one of the most difficult regions for military operations in the world. Roberts' march to Kabul restored the military situation and made him a national hero, but the evil effects of Isandhlwana and Kabul combined to

---

[1] *Narrative of the Field Operations Connected with the Zulu War of 1879* (H.M.S.O., 1881). Gladstone's private comment may be noted: 'It is very sad, but so it is that in these guilty wars it is the business of *paying* which appears to be the most effective means of awakening the conscience.'

increase resentment at the apparent aggressive and costly nature of Beaconsfield's Imperialism.

If this was not entirely fair, neither was it wholly unjust. Beaconsfield had given encouragement to those tendencies which animated Frere and Lytton to act as they thought was now required and approved. When Beaconsfield developed his theme of 'Imperium et Libertas' in a speech at the Mansion House in November 1879, Gladstone categorised it as 'liberty for ourselves, Empire over the rest of mankind'. Imperialism had become a highly pejorative term in Liberal mouths. 'What is especially desirable to make clear', Joseph Chamberlain wrote to the editor of the influential *Fortnightly Review*, 'is that this infernal Afghan business is the natural consequence of Jingoism, Imperialism, "British interests" and all the other phrasing of this mountebank Government'. In one of those brilliant phrases that occasionally illuminate British domestic politics, Henry Dunckley (editor of *The Manchester Examiner and Times*) described Beaconsfield as an exponent of a system of government that was 'an absolute monarchy tempered by sacerdotalism'.

What was not perceived at the time was that the subject of Empire had become intellectually respectable, even in the most radical circles; that the public interest had been definitely aroused; and that forces out of the control of parties of governments were building up rapidly. Even at this stage, however, remarkably few were talking of the *expansion* of Empire. The first voice to argue that with real effect was J. R. Seeley, in 1881, following the path laid by Ruskin and Froude.

*

In 1876 Disraeli, confident that Gladstone's retirement was a definite fact, went to the House of Lords with the title of Lord Beaconsfield. Although he could still have his occasions, he had become a totem of past glories and was an old and lonely man, depicted by the young Max Beerbohm 'with his lustreless eyes and face like some Hebraic parchment'. 'Power!' he remarked. 'It has come to me too late. There were days when, on waking, I felt I could move dynasties and governments; but that has passed away.' It was difficult to discern in that pallid, sphinx-like and black-suited cynic sitting impassively for hours, arms enfolded, in that great gilded barn the House of Lords, the outrageous political and literary adventurer of the 1830s, the scourge of Peel in 1845–6 who, if he had leaned forward and had flicked his victim with a thong could not have devastated him more acutely or immediately, the self-styled educator of his Party, the great survivor, the brilliant, despised, and eventually revered opportunist of the '50s and '60s. Now, adulated by the Sovereign who had at first disliked him so greatly—and with such good cause!—and reverenced by his Party, Lord Beaconsfield was sinking into gloom-filled lethargy and seigneurial pessimism. The deplorable young Disraeli had moved, by careful and deliberate metamorphosis, into the respectable Disraeli, the saviour of the Conservative cause, and now into the immortal Lord Beaconsfield. As he faded, so did his Administration.

This was particularly evident in the House of Commons, where the Chancellor of the Exchequer, Sir Stafford Northcote, was worthy but not inspiriting, and the Home Secretary, R. A. Cross, despite considerable administrative talents, lacked authority. The real Conservative talents lay in the Lords, where Lord Salisbury, then aged 50 and who as the young Lord Cranborne in the 1860s had attacked Disraeli for his apostasy, and who had written of him that 'he is an adventurer; as I have too good reason to know, he is without principles and honesty . . . in an age of singularly reckless statesmen he is I think beyond question the one who is least restrained by fear or scruple', and had championed the cause of the old Conservatism with the passion of a Junius, had now found his destiny in the conduct of foreign affairs.

It was indeed fortunate for the Administration that Gladstone's appearances were only occasional, and that the Liberal leadership was flaccid. Lord Hartington, heir to the Duke of Devonshire, and who hardly represented the rising tide of Radicalism, was an angular man of middle age, who had entered Parliament in 1857, a Whig member of an historic Whig family, with a considerable capacity for silence. His position depended principally upon his great name, his not inconsiderable wealth, and the well-merited belief that he was not only shrewd but possessed that most rare of human qualities, common sense. But neither he nor his Party could rid themselves of the conviction that he was merely a *locum tenens*, awaiting an announcement of the return from Hawarden.[1]

---

[1] As the country estates of the leading politicians in this period were of some political interest, those of the most significant should be mentioned. Gladstone's home was Hawarden Castle, in Flint, just over the Welsh border from Chester. Beaconsfield's was Hughenden, close to High Wycombe, Buckinghamshire;

Beside him on the front bench sat Sir William Harcourt, an eager, opinionated, intensely warm and intensely insensitive politician-lawyer on the make. Harcourt's principal merit was gusto, plunging with zest and usually without too much thought into the most intricate and complex of problems. Harcourt loved politics with an all-consuming enthusiasm, blustering, shouting, red-faced, outraged, and yet also caressingly gentle and kind. Unhappily, he had a marked tendency to stamp upon his colleagues' toes with greater zeal and more manifest pleasure than on those of his political opponents. The Liberals, fearful of his temper and troubled about his judgement, yet impressed by his spirit, intellect, and capacity for hard work, eyed him with uneasy esteem.

More interest was shown in the rising Liberals, of whom Joseph Chamberlain, who entered the House in a by-election in 1876, was by far the most arresting.

Chamberlain had risen from a strict Unitarian family in London which had moved to Birmingham, where he had made his fortune and his name. The fortune came from the manufacture of screws and other larger enterprises; the name came from his progressive record as Mayor of Birmingham, his part in the National Education League's battles against the 1870 Education Act, his radical declarations, which included some faintly anti-royalist and Republican observations which aroused disproportionate dismay and opprobrium, and the creation of an organisation, the National Liberal Federation, which was compared to the American Caucus and was viewed with repugnance, alarm, or awed respect. The organisation was initially the response to the two-member constituency and the introduction of

Salisbury lived at Hatfield House, in Hertfordshire; Lord Rosebery moved between Dalmeny House, near Edinburgh, Mentmore, in Buckinghamshire, and The Durdans at Epsom, in Surrey; Joseph Chamberlain's home was at Highbury, near Birmingham; Hartington's was Holker Hall, Cartmel, in north Lancashire; Lord Spencer resided at Althorp, in Northamptonshire; Sir William Harcourt had a substantial residence in the New Forest (Hampshire) as did Arthur Balfour at Whittingehame, near Edinburgh, and Sir Stafford Northcote at Pynes, near Exeter in Devon. Many of these were inherited properties, and varied in size and luxury, the mansions of Rosebery and Salisbury being the most impressive and Chamberlain's probably the least. All of them had London houses as well, but it is striking how often these were regarded as regrettable necessities, and how eagerly the political world would quit London when Parliament adjourned and conducted political business through copious correspondence and visits to colleagues far away from the House of Commons.

plural voting, but it was developed into something more formidable than machinery for ensuring that party followers knew whom to vote for. The Federation, blessed at its birth by Gladstone personally, was clearly not only a vehicle for Chamberlain's ambitions but potentially a very formidable take-over bid for the entire Party organisation. Thus, although he sat on the back benches, a cold, carefully dressed, monocled newcomer to Parliament, he was at once recognised as a politician of the front rank. The House, and particularly the Liberals, had greeted him with bleak suspicion. There was, even at this stage, something chilling and implacable about him.

As John Morley was to write of him, 'his politics came to him, now and always, from a penetrating observation of things around him as they actually were.' It was evident that unlike most Members, his life was politics and politics was his life. 'The political creed is the whole man', as Beatrice Webb (then Beatrice Potter), who was briefly but deeply in love with him, wrote in 1884; 'the outcome of his peculiar physical and mental temperament, played upon by the experiences of his life.'[1] It was already known that he was of an independent spirit, the kind of man who spoke and acted as though he were on at least level terms of authority and influence with the major politicians of the day. He had not yet had the opportunity nor the facility to demonstrate to the House of Commons the debating style which flourished best when he was under fierce attack, which was slow to mature, and which made men increasingly chary of meeting him head-on in severe controversy. But already the House had seen enough of him to realise his considerable capacities and even more considerable potentialities.

For the Liberals, although they did not like the man, Chamberlain's youth, vigour, and power were in very welcome contrast to the lethargic occupants of the Opposition Front Bench, and indeed the remarkable feature of this Parliament lay in the number of men of future eminence who sat in relative obscurity on the back benches. Lord Randolph Churchill, the younger son of the Duke of Marlborough, had been elected for Woodstock in 1874, but his appearances in the House of Commons had been few. Arthur Balfour, elected for Hertford in the same year, was taking a relaxed approach to his Parliamentary responsibilities. But one back-bencher was neither obscure, nor unknown, nor relaxed, and had already established a

[1] Quoted in Peter Fraser: *Joseph Chamberlain*, p. 116.

unique reputation which even eclipsed the speculation about Chamberlain's future.

Charles Stewart Parnell had entered the House of Commons at a by-election as Member for Meath in 1875. His maiden speech ended with words of which greater notice should have been taken.

> Why should Ireland be treated as a geographical fragment of England, as I have heard an ex-Chancellor of the Exchequer call it some time ago? Ireland is not a geographical fragment, but a nation.

When Parnell entered the House, Parliamentary interest in the Irish Question was low. 'The Irish Question' had many definitions imposed upon it by the English. 'That dense population', Disraeli declared, 'in extreme distress inhabits an island where there is an Established Church which is not their Church, and a territorial aristocracy the richest of whom live in distant capitals. Thus, you have a starving population, an absentee aristocracy, and an alien Church, and in addition the weakest executive in the world. *That* is the Irish Question'. But it was The Question only in part. Disraeli—with much greater shrewdness and imagination than the majority of his English contemporaries—had touched upon certain of the more obvious and odious manifestations of English rule in Ireland, which he could well appreciate and comprehend. He knew that similar circumstances in England itself could only lead to bitter discontent and, possibly, revolution. But The Irish Question had a dimension that was unfathomable and incomprehensible to the English. It was true that agrarian poverty and exploitation lay at the root of much Irish hatred of the English; it was also true that religious factors were of major significance; and that long-hugged myths and jealousies played their part. But the abiding element, which the English could never understand, was the passionate desire of the Irish people to mismanage their own affairs in their own way. They also loathed being regarded as children and treated accordingly. This simple fact utterly escaped those Englishmen—many of them worthy and honourable—who endeavoured to resolve The Irish Question. A vast abyss lay between the two peoples, and it was one that no English politician understood, let alone endeavoured to bestride. Therein lay the roots of this vast, and as yet unfinished, tragedy.

The disestablishment of the Irish Church and the Land Act by the

1868–74 Liberal Government had made it a tenet of respectable Irish nationalism that the best hope for Ireland lay in alliance with the Liberals, and in the development of this conviction the roles of Cardinal Cullen and Isaac Butt, the leader of the Parliamentary Party, had been crucial. This enthusiasm had faded abruptly after 1870, and had helped to inspire the formation of the Home Rule Association, not a political party as such but designed, in the words of its founder, Isaac Butt, 'to bring the question before the public mind'. But there was another, and older, strand in the Irish cause, exemplified by the Irish Republican Brotherhood—the Fenians. It was accepted that Ireland had to take one course or the other, that of constitutional methods or that of violence; the possibility that they might be fused into one movement had not been seriously countenanced.

When Parnell made his maiden speech the Irish Parliamentary Party was a courteous and moderate group, anxious not to offend English opinion nor to interrupt the workings of the British Parliament. Butt was an able Dublin lawyer, in his early years a vehement Protestant Conservative and strongly opposed to any suggestion of the repeal of the Act of Union. But in 1852 he was elected for Youghal, and became increasingly the champion of the Irish tenants and Catholic education. It was not until the late 1860s, when he defended Fenians without fee, that he achieved a leading position. He had founded the Home Rule Association in 1870, and then, in 1873, the Home Rule League. But the General Election of 1874 had come too soon for the League, few of his fellow-members in the Irish party in the House were Home Rulers, and his position was precarious. His private life was open to criticism from the Catholic clergy; the Fenians supported him only out of gratitude for past services; the tenant farmers never gave him their full allegiance. Above all, he conspicuously failed to achieve anything tangible. His annual Home Rule Bill, a moderate proposal for limited self-government, was politely introduced, politely debated, and contemptuously voted into oblivion. But he was an eloquent speaker, and in other circumstances might have been highly effective. In introducing the Home Rule proposal for the first time he concluded a speech of one and a half hours with the words:

Give us a new participation in a new compact, carried not by fraud and coercion, but founded on the free sanction of the Irish people. Backed as I am now by sixty representatives of the Irish people, in

their name I offer you this compact, and I believe if it is accepted it
will be, humanly speaking, eternal.[1]

Although this appeal, and many others, were ignored, Butt per-
severed along the Parliamentary constitutional road, while impatience
grew in Ireland and turned to something considerably worse than
impatience when the full impact of the agricultural slump struck in the
late 1870s. The establishment of the militant Land League in County
Mayo by Michael Davitt in 1879 symbolised the change in mood and
temper.

Davitt had been born in 1846, and his childhood was dominated by
the harrowing experience of the Great Famine, the inhumanity of
landlordism, and the necessity for so many Irish people of the choice
of death or emigration. The Davitts had settled in England, where
Davitt's real education took place. Unlike most Irishmen of his generation he did not hate England; he hated the conditions under which so
many Englishmen lived as much as he hated those under which his
fellow-countrymen lived. He himself was a factory child, and at the
age of twelve lost his right arm in a factory accident; at the age of
nineteen he joined the Fenians. In 1870 he had been arrested and
imprisoned first in London, and then in Dartmoor, where he was most
evilly treated, and which destroyed his health. When he was released
seven years later his weight was 122 pounds, 'not, I think,' he wrote,
'the proper weight for a man six feet high and at the age of thirty-one.'
He paid the first of many visits to America where he had enunciated
the outlines of his developing new programme, and which matured
into the Land League. Davitt had turned aside from the extremism of
the Fenians, but he had taken up a weapon which was to prove much
more deadly—the cause of the impoverished and exploited Irish
tenant-farmer.

By this time Butt had been replaced by Parnell. On the day that the
new Member for Meath had taken his seat, the House of Commons had
been outraged by a performance of blatant and unprecedented
obstructionism committed by a coarse and ill-dressed Belfast provision
merchant, Joseph Biggar, who had himself lost patience with English
disdain for Irish grievances and the processes of correct Parliamentary
practice. Butt had been greatly distressed by Biggar's contempt for the
accepted usages of the House, but Parnell had been impressed. The

[1] David Thornely: *Isaac Butt and Home Rule* (1964), 231.

process which Biggar had started was now developed. To Butt's fury and humiliation, Biggar, Parnell, and a handful of Irish Members who shared their views took virtual command of the proceedings of the House of Commons. 'If we are to have Parliamentary action', Parnell had coldly remarked, 'it must not be the action of reconciliation but of retaliation', and proceeded to paralyse the British Parliament and to demonstrate the limitations of unwritten rules and accepted codes of behaviour.

The English stared with astonishment and then with anger at this outrageous spectacle, but were impotent. There was nothing to stop the iconoclasts, and they were wholly untroubled by ridicule or abuse. The Government, faced with a situation which was without precedent, attempted to respond. Two anti-obstructionist measures, passed after prolonged debate, proved to be easily circumvented; a Committee was set up to consider further and more effective measures; Butt un-availingly denounced Parnell's tactics to English cheers but to Irish hostility, and was doomed; in 1879 Northcote moved six resolutions to attempt to meet the problem, but five had to be abandoned and the sixth—after consuming three exhausting nights in debate—proved to be useless. Even the Irish who were most contemptuous of the 'con-stitutional' approach to Home Rule were impressed, and when Parnell publicly stated to the House of Commons that the Fenians who had been hanged for killing a policeman in Manchester in 1867 while attempting to rescue two of their comrades had not committed murder he won powerful new allies. In 1877 he displaced the forlorn Butt (who died in 1879) from the Presidency of the Home Rule Confederation; he was not yet thirty-one.

In appearance Parnell was tall, cold, and aloof, and—save when obstructing—of few words, yet those had an icy clarity that Bryce compared to a freezing wind on a winter's day. All leaders of revolutions are unusual individuals, but Parnell was one of the strangest of all. He was an aristocrat leading a predominantly middle class political party dependent upon the support of a peasant movement; a Protestant landowner at the head of an overwhelmingly Catholic movement bitterly opposed to landlordism; a man of action, he staked everything on constitutional methods sharpened by the threat of violence; super-ficially cold and aloof, not given to bandying civilities with his follow-ers and often openly contemptuous of their inadequacies, he evoked in them an awe and respect which made them suffer much without complaint and to accept his unpredictability, his hauteur, his chilling silences; and he was to destroy himself and—at least for a time—his cause, through a passionate love-affair.

In inheriting Butt's position, Parnell had inherited his problems, and these rapidly became much more acute. The bad harvests of 1877 and 1878 were followed by the failure of the potato crop in 1879, and created a desperate crisis in Ireland—a crisis of stark poverty. Most tenants were liable to eviction if they could not pay their rents, and in the circumstances of 1877–9 this possibility became a grim reality. It was under these circumstances that Davitt had founded the Land League in County Mayo, and whose appeal was immediate and widespread. Although the League's methods were constitutional— Davitt himself favouring 'a policy of parallel action between the revolutionary and constitutional movements'—the implications of its policies were revolutionary, and could well become so in reality if the already hapless condition of the agricultural tenants continued to worsen even-further. Parnell, while aware of the obvious dangers which were involved, accepted Davitt's invitation to become President of the Irish National Land League in October 1879. Thus, within four years of entering Parliament with little previous experience or even understanding of politics, Parnell had become a major political figure, and 'the New Departure'—the fusing into one national movement of all the elements of Irish protest and grievance—was created. The next stage was to secure candidates who would follow him personally, and by 1880 he had created a majority of Irish M.P.s sufficient to secure his election as Chairman of the Parliamentary Party.

But the scale and nature of Parnell's rapid rise were lost on the majority of British politicians, who took little interest in Irish affairs unless they were compelled to do so. Gladstone, the author of the disestablishment of the Irish Church and the Irish Land Act of 1870, who had written in 1845 'Ireland, Ireland! That cloud in the west, that coming storm, the minister of God's retribution upon cruel and inveterate and but half-atoned injustice', and who had declared in 1868 that his mission was 'to pacify Ireland', was particularly in-insensitive to the looming peril. When Beaconsfield in his 1880 Manifesto—which took the form of an open letter to the Duke of Marlborough, Viceroy of Ireland—described Home Rule as a menace 'scarcely less disastrous than pestilence and famine', it was denounced by the Liberals as a characteristic manoeuvre to cloud the main issues.[1] But Beaconsfield, who in 1836 had denounced 'this wild, reckless, indolent, uncertain and supersititious race, whose history describes an unbroken circle of bigotry and blood', had never visited Ireland,[2] and had wholly ignored the Irish Question during the six years of his Administration—had belatedly seen the signs. When the young Balfour lamented the defeat of the Government in April 1880, Beaconsfield simply replied, with great emphasis and solemnity, '*Ireland*'.

But the 1880 General Election was fought, outside Ireland, entirely on other issues. Gladstone's retirement had ended dramatically when he announced his candidacy for Midlothian in 1879 and conducted the first—and the greatest—of his campaigns that autumn. Superbly stage-managed by the Earl of Rosebery, the rising star of Scotland and already—at the age of thirty-two—widely spoken of as a future Prime Minister, Gladstone at Midlothian dwelt before vast audiences on the immorality of 'Beaconsfieldism' and on the iniquity of its foreign adventures. Characteristically, he did not offer specific remedies, nor a detailed programme but spoke as an inspired visionary on the attack. The impact in Midlothian in terms of votes was limited,[3] but elsewhere was evidently considerable.

The Conservatives offered feeble resistance. Deceived by two recent by-election victories in Liverpool and Southwark, Beaconsfield had sought the dissolution in March in full expectation of victory. Only too late was it recognised that the rudimentary organisation put together before the 1874 election by John Gorst—who had been ill-rewarded for his work—had been permitted to decline disastrously. The Liberals, in contrast, were far better organised and prepared, and not only in those constituencies where the National Liberal Federation claimed the dominant influence. The result was decisive. The Liberals won 349 seats, the Conservatives fell from 351 to 243, and the Irish Home Rulers numbered 60—of whom 37 could now be accounted Parnellites. The significance of this fact was overlooked in the hour of victory. Gladstone had swept aside Hartington's claims to the Premiership, as the Queen was most reluctantly forced to concede; Chamberlain exultantly claimed sixty Liberal victories for the Liberal

[1] It did little good in Ireland, either. The Home Rule Confederation urged its members to 'vote against Benjamin Disraeli as you would against the mortal enemy of your country and your race.'

[2] Gladstone had, once, for three weeks in 1877.

[3] The result of the election was: Gladstone 1,579; Lord Dalkeith 1,368.

Federation, and was hailed by *The Times* as 'the Carnot of the moment'. Chamberlain did not disagree. To Dilke he wrote that 'the victory which has just been won is the victory of the Radicals. Gladstone and the Caucus have triumphed all along the line.'

The Conservatives were shocked and disconsolate, and cast down by the most sombre forebodings. Salisbury wrote to Balfour that:

> The hurricane that has swept us away is so strange and new a phenomenon that we shall not for some time understand its real meaning. I doubt if so much enthusiasm and such a general unity of action proceeds from any sentimental opinion, or from a more academic judgement. It seems to me to be inspired by some definite desire for change; and means business. It may disappear as rapidly as it came, or it may be the beginning of a serious war of classes.

The Conservatives did not appreciate in that hour of depression how providential had been their defeat, and the Liberals, engaged in the exquisite task of Cabinet-making, had no premonition of the storms that were about to sweep down upon them.

CHAPTER TWO

THE LIBERAL INHERITANCE, 1880–1885

THE FORMATION of Mr. Gladstone's second Administration
was not a swift, smooth, or comfortable process.

The more radical elements in the party, convinced that the
great victory had been their achievement, sought a substantial
influence in the new Cabinet. But in the event they were reduced to the
ageing John Bright and the uncongenial W. E. Forster, while upon
Chamberlain was bestowed the Board of Trade, justly regarded as the
least significant place in the Cabinet; and although Sir Charles Dilke
received a senior post in the Government, he was not included in the
Cabinet. Gladstone himself took the Exchequer, Lord Granville
returned to the Foreign Office, Lord Kimberley went to the Colonial
Office, Lord Spencer became Lord President, the Duke of Argyll was
Lord Privy Seal, Hartington assumed responsibility for India,
Harcourt moved with ponderous relish to the Home Office, Lord
Northbrook went to the Admiralty and H. C. E. Childers—at the
Admiralty in the 1868–74 Administration—took over the War Office.
Rosebery had held himself aloof, although he could probably have
been persuaded easily enough to join if Gladstone had taken much
trouble over the matter—the first of a series of personal misunder-
standings that were to quickly dim the companionship and triumphs
of Midlothian.

It was not simply a matter of Gladstone's innate preference for
Whigs, as the disgruntled radicals averred, which caused this marked
imbalance. Gladstone was now in his seventy-first year; since 1874 he
had been very much out of touch with contemporary politics. His
appearances in the Commons had been few and brief, and he did not
know or understand the new men and the new moods. He accepted
Chamberlain with reluctance; the rest of his colleagues were familiar
faces from the past—comfortable and proven. The rising Conservatives

47

in 1951 were to experience very similar emotions when they beheld Winston Churchill's last Cabinet.

The radical discontent was at least partially responsible for the mood of the new House of Commons when it assembled at the end of April. As John Morley subsequently wrote:

> Mr. Gladstone found that the ministry of which he stood at the head was a coalition, and what was more, a coalition of that vexatious kind, where those who happened not to agree sometimes seemed to be almost as well pleased with contention as with harmony. . . .[1]

The principal problem was, however, much more profound. The 1868 Liberal Government had had a great deal of unfinished reforms awaiting its attention, and which it was eager to undertake in what Gladstone later nostalgically called 'the era of liberation'. In 1880 the situation was very different. The Liberals had fought the campaign in a purely negative manner, offering an end to 'Beaconsfieldism' but no real alternatives. The leadership had no defined policies or objectives, and no legislative programme at all. This was to haunt the Liberal Government throughout its existence.

Immediately after he had been re-elected Speaker, Mr. Brand noted in his diary that the Liberals were likely to be a difficult team to drive and that many members seemed determined to go their own ways. This was perceptive, but he might also have noted similar tensions in the disheartened and embittered Conservative Opposition.

The position of Sir Stafford Northcote, the Conservative leader in the House of Commons, was acutely unenviable, and cannot be described better than in words used by Disraeli himself in his biography of Bentinck:

> But he who in the Parliamentary field watches over the fortunes of routed troops must be prepared to sit often alone. . . . Adversity is necessarily not a sanguine season, and in this respect a politician is no exception to all other human combinations. In doors and out of doors a disheartened opposition will be querulous and captious. A discouraged multitude have no future. Too depressed to indulge in a large and often hopeful horizon of contemplation, they busy themselves in peevish detail, and by a natural train of sentiment associate their own conviction of ill-luck, incapacity, and failure, with the most responsible member of their confederation.

[1] Morley: *Gladstone*, III, 5.

It was hardly reasonable for the Conservatives to cast the odium for their misfortunes upon the able, genial, and patient Northcote, but Beaconsfield was beyond criticism on his pedestal—and would soon be translated to an even more exalted pedestal to which no criticism may be usefully directed—and the Conservatives were not in a very reasonable mood.

Northcote was competent and likeable, an experienced Minister and an adept Parliamentarian. But Rosebery subsequently put his finger upon his deficiencies as a party leader.

> Where he failed was in manner. His voice, his diction, his delivery, were all inadequate. With real ability, great knowledge, genial kindness, and a sympathetic nature—all the qualities, indeed, which evoke regard and esteem—he had not the spice of devil which is necessary to rouse an Opposition to zeal and elation. . . . When Northcote warmed there was, or seemed to be, a note of apology in his voice; there was also what is known as the academic twang, an inflection which cannot be defined, but which is not agreeable to the House of Commons.[1]

By this stage the bulk of the Conservative Party regarded Gladstone with emotions of fear and detestation which, had they but known it, were passionately shared by the Queen. He was, for one thing, a renegade, one of theirs, who had joined the enemy camp. Their assumption of his motives for this was not charitable, and they recalled with nostalgia the brilliant manner in which Dizzy had held him up to public derision as an unbalanced and unscrupulous fanatic. Disraeli may have actually believed this caricature, but his followers certainly did. They had thought he was finished in 1874, and had watched with anger and mounting horror his campaign against the Bulgarian Atrocities in 1876 and his triumphant renaissance in Midlothian, where he had seemed to them to have trumpeted the cause of class war in his desperate ambition for power. This was how they saw him, and why they hated him. The Conservatives may have been as bereft of policies as the Liberals, but at least they knew what they were *against*.

But they were also afraid of Gladstone. He had been in the House of Commons for nearly half a century and no one—not even Dizzy in his prime—had managed to crush him. He had had set-backs in debate, but they had been followed by devastating counter-attacks and

[1] Rosebery: *Lord Randolph Churchill*, 169.

he was, indeed, 'terrible on the rebound'. To an apprehension that was generally shared by his followers, Northcote added the fatal ingredient of respect. He had served as Gladstone's private secretary many years before and, like so many who had seen him at close quarters, had been impressed. It was Northcote who called Gladstone 'that Grand Old Man'; the phrase stuck, but it was not the kind of enconium that the Conservatives expected from their leader. Thus, when the Tories wanted Gladstone flayed, Northcote was courteously critical. When Gladstone slipped, and the Tories howled for the kill, Northcote issued critical admonitions to which Gladstone had no difficulty in responding with interest. Northcote was in poor health, but in any event he did not possess the qualities of fire and fury which the Opposition craved. The field was open for a challenger, and it was to come from a very unlikely quarter.

Ministers were quickly faced with an extraordinary and unforeseeable test. On May 3rd Charles Bradlaugh, newly elected as one of the two Liberal Members for Northampton, presented himself at the Table of the House and claimed to affirm rather than take the Oath of Allegiance. Bradlaugh was a well-known and courageous advocate of free-thinking, and his lusty denunciations of the Christian religion— 'the blasphemy against humanity, the mockery of humanity [which] has crushed our efforts, has ruined our lives, has poisoned our hearts, and has cursed our hopes'—had made his meetings the scenes of many violent confrontations. He also had advanced views on population control which were generally excoriated as outrageous, and when his reckless fire also fell upon the Monarchy he had succeeded in enraging a very formidable cross-section of public feeling.

The Speaker, confronted by the burly and intransigent figure of Mr. Bradlaugh demanding to affirm the Oath, decided to leave the issue to the House. Affirmation had been permitted in the Courts for a decade, and in Parliament for longer in the cases of 'Quakers, Moravians, and Separatists'. While Bradlaugh clearly did not fit into any of these categories, the principle of the right to affirm had been established, and Speaker Brand should have so ruled. But he did not, and much flowed from that failure.[1] The Government moved for a Select Committee which, by a majority of one, decided that Bradlaugh had to take the Oath. Bradlaugh defiantly announced that he would not, and would take his seat nonetheless.

[1] For an excellent account, see W. L. Arnstein: *The Bradlaugh Case.*

Meanwhile, the fires had begun to glow. Sir Henry Drummond Wolff, one of the Conservative Members for Portsmouth, had seen the opportunity of gravely embarrassing Ministers, and saw also that Bradlaugh's defiance of the Select Committee had aroused strong feelings in the House. On May 21st, when Bradlaugh reappeared, Wolff objected, and an extremely heated debate ensued. On May 24th, when it was resumed, Lord Randolph Churchill, the obscure, slight, and unprepossessing Member for Woodstock, denounced Bradlaugh's atheism and disloyalty, quoted from some of his more inflammatory writings, and—most interestingly of all—concluded with a direct appeal to Gladstone not to lead the Liberal Party through the lobbies 'for the purpose of placing on the benches opposite an avowed atheist and a professedly disloyal person'.

Although Gladstone doggedly maintained his position that the House could not deny a Member his right to take his seat, he was not carrying his supporters with him. Churchill had touched a very responsive chord in the Liberals. Another committee was established 'to search for precedents' and found none. The Government proposed that Bradlaugh be permitted to affirm and the matter be referred to the Courts, but the motion was defeated by 275 votes to 230. When Bradlaugh defiantly reappeared, he was committed to the Clock Tower, was unseated, was triumphantly re-elected, and the storms arose again. These scenes were to be repeated throughout this Parliament. There was something in the spectacle of Bradlaugh that aroused an atavistic reaction from the majority in the House of Commons, and the eloquence of Gladstone and the justice of his cause could not control these passions. It was a lamentable business in itself, but it was also a highly disturbing opening for a new Administration, and a swift check to the eager expectations of the great election victory.

But there were other consequences. Shortly after his speech, Lord Randolph joined Wolff and John Gorst on the front bench below the gangway, and the trio at once demonstrated a skill and independence which caught the attention of the House. Wolff and Gorst were experienced politicians, but Lord Randolph's quickness and self-confidence were a revelation. He was small in stature, slender in build, with a large moustache and rather popping eyes. He spoke with a lisp, and had difficulty in pronouncing the letter 's'. It was indeed difficult to see in this curious young aristocrat the man of whom Max Beerbohm was to write that he was, 'despite his halting speech, foppish mien, and rather coarse fibre of mind . . . the greatest Parliamentarian of his day'. Before 1880 he had made only one speech of any note in the previous Parliament—characteristically, it had been a memorable attack on his own Government—and although the details of his involvement in a somewhat discreditable episode involving his brother and the Prince of Wales in 1876 were known only to a few[1], the resulting ostracism of Lord Randolph and his young American wife from London society was common knowledge. He had gone with his father, the Duke of Marlborough—who had been persuaded by Beaconsfield to accept the Irish Viceroyalty in these highly embarrassing circumstances—to Dublin, and had been seen seldom at Westminster until the Bradlaugh affair.

But after that he was quickly noticed. 'He has certainly a pretty turn for sarcasm', the shrewd Parliamentary observer H. W. Lucy wrote in June, 'an honest contempt for bumptuous incapacity, and courage amounting to recklessness, which combine to make him equally dangerous, whether as friend or foe.' The three were joined by Arthur Balfour, whose approach to public affairs had been notably relaxed, and whose involvement in this iconoclastic group was as great a surprise as the discovery of Lord Randolph's unexpected skills as a Parliamentarian. Balfour was never, in reality, a total member of what was dubbed 'the Fourth Party' (the Irish being the Third), and which proudly proclaimed itself as such. But for the others there was considerable value in having the nephew of Lord Salisbury in the group, and Balfour himself certainly found it a useful and rewarding introduction to serious politics.

The Fourth Party, created out of the chaos of the Bradlaugh Case, was from the outset a much more serious phenomenon than many realised at the time. Those who regarded it as something on the lines of an undergraduate caper—despite the fact that both Wolff and Gorst were nearer fifty than forty—soon changed their opinion. The Opposition Front Bench became quickly embarrassed and humiliated, Gladstone took the Fourth Party seriously from the beginning, and Beaconsfield was so intrigued that he paid one of his rare visits to the Commons to see the 'Party' in action. They were often irresponsible, enjoyed their sudden fame and worked to maintain it, and had learned much about obstructive tactics from the Irish. But they had a serious core, and developed a serious purpose. Churchill's powers developed

[1] See Philip Magnus: *King Edward VII* for the most complete account.

so rapidly that within three months Northcote asked for a truce and the dissolution of the group, but Beaconsfield, while advising them to 'stick with Northcote, he represents the respectability of the party', went on to remark that 'I wholly sympathise with you, because I never was respectable myself'. Within a remarkably short time the Fourth Party had undermined the authority of Northcote, and Lord Randolph's high ambitions had been born.

*

The bitter consequences of the combination of the agricultural depression, bad harvests, and the neglect of the Conservative Government, now fell terribly upon Ireland. A pall hung over the country, reminiscent of that of the 1840s. 'I saw that for Irishmen to succeed', Davitt later wrote, 'they must be united and that they must have a practical issue to put before Englishmen and the world at large. . . . I made up my mind that the only issue upon which Home Rulers, Nationalists, Obstructionists and each and every shade of opinion existing in Ireland could be united, was the land question.' The vital element in the agrarian discontent which mounted during the summer of 1880 and exploded in the winter of 1880-1 lay in the agrarian poverty and subsequent evictions of defaulting tenants. The Liberals had no Irish policy at all and, indeed, little understanding of the ferocity of the storm which was descending upon them. There had been no reference to Ireland in the Queen's Speech, and it was rapidly evident that the Chief Secretary, Forster, was quite inadequate to the challenge. He took up a measure proposed by an Irish member to compensate those 'disturbed', but, after a stormy passage through the Commons in which the opposition was principally led by Lord Randolph, it was summarily rejected by the Lords. The action of the Lords was deplorable, but Ministers failed to discern its importance until too late. When Parnell asked Forster whether 'he proposes to employ the constabulary and military forces of the Queen for the purpose of assisting at the eviction of tenants who can be proved to be unable to pay their rents,' the Chief Secretary replied that 'we shall protect the officers of the courts of law in the execution of the law'.[1] The evictions mounted; so did the violence of the reaction in Ireland. Forster turned to buckshot; the Irish to more deadly methods.

The first tactic was one of non-co-operation with the landlords.

[1] Conor Cruise O'Brien: *Parnell And His Party*, 51.

Davitt declared in July that 'Today, from east to west, from north to south, not a man can be found who would dare to take the farm of an evicted tenant. If one should be found so recklessly indifferent, it would be simply impossible for him to live in that locality. The people would not buy from him; they would not sell to him; in chapel on Sunday he would have to sit apart by himself.' Parnell endorsed this tactic. Speaking at Ennis, in County Clare, on September 19th, he said:

> When a man takes a farm from which another has been evicted, you must show him on the roadside when you meet him [A Voice: 'Shun him'] in the streets of the town, at the shop counter, in the fair, in the market place, and even in the house of worship, by leaving him severely alone, by putting him into a moral Coventry, by isolating him from his kind as if he were a leper of old; you must show him your detestation of the crime he has committed.

The first, and most dramatic, victim was Captain Boycott. Boycott was an Englishman who leased a thousand acre farm from Lord Erne, and also acted as agent for Lord Erne's Mayo estates. His task was to collect the sum of £430 per annum from thirty-eight tenants, which, as has been written, 'brought Boycott much trouble and about £50 a year'.[1] In County Mayo, the birthplace of Davitt and the Land League, this difficulty was now greatly augmented. First, Boycott's own workers went on strike for higher wages, which Boycott had to concede. Then the tenants demanded a rent reduction of five shillings; Lord Erne offered a two shilling reduction, accompanied by a stern warning as to the consequences of defaulting. The tenants refused to pay, and the process-server had to be protected by the police. Boycott's workers were persuaded to leave him; Lord Erne's seat, Lough Mask House, had to be protected by armed policeman; and on September 25th, on the far side of Lough Mask, Lord Mountmorres was murdered. Boycott and his wife were beleagured, shunned by all. Eventually, after publicity to their plight had been given by the English press, they were rescued by a group of men from Ulster, protected by troops.

The Boycotts were unharmed, but the success of the 'boycotting' spread throughout the country while the asassination of Lord

[1] See T. H. Corfe: 'The Troubles of Captain Boycott', *History Today*, November and December 1964, and Joyce Marlow, *Capiain Boycott*.

Mountmorres had brought dread to all landowners. Boycott had indeed been put 'into a moral Coventry, by isolating him from his kind as if he were a leper of old'. While the League was making the strategy, Parnell was retaining his leadership of the general movement—a very difficult exercise in the ferment of the winter of 1879–80, but made immeasurably easier when he was specifically denounced by Ministers for the mounting chaos in Ireland. 'The landlords fear to evict', as Forster reported to Gladstone. 'Parnell is quite right . . . in saying that the League has stopped evictions, though he ought to have said "the League and its attendant outrages".'

But the evictions did continue, and the violence of the response continued. In the last three months of 1880 the situation reached crisis proportions. The desperate Forster appealed for more troops, more armed police, more buckshot, and the arraignment of the Irish leaders. Parnell and thirteen other members of the League were prosecuted— fruitlessly—for conspiracy, and the Viceroy (Lord Cowper) pressed urgently for the suspension of habeas corpus. With deep reluctance and dismay, the Government turned to coercion. The situation was grimly reminiscent of the 1840s, when Macaulay had asked of Ireland: 'How do you govern it? Not by love but by fear . . . not by the confidence of the people in the laws and their attachment to the Constitution but by the means of armed men and entrenched camps.' The thoughts of the Cabinet had indeed, in Morley's words, been 'violently drawn from Dulcigno and Thessaly, from Batoum and Erzeroum, from the wild squalor of Macedonia and Armenia to squalor not less wild in Connaught and Munster, in Mayo, Galway, Sligo and Kerry.'

At this point it was violently drawn to another inheritance from the Beaconsfield Government.

*

Gladstone, inveighing against the pursuit of 'false phantoms of glory' at Midlothian, and pleading the cause of 'the rights of the savage, as we call him', had also pledged himself to the restoration of the Transvaal to the Boers. The pledge had not been honoured.

The end of the Zulu war had changed the position of the Boers, but the movement for independence and the restoration of the Afrikaans language were signs that few outside heeded. Frere was not immediately recalled. He stood out for a federal solution, but it was only after negotiations with the Boers had failed in June 1880 that he belatedly returned to England. The event was not followed by the repeal of annexation nor even by an offer of self-government under the Crown, which Frere had unavailingly urged on Ministers.

The Government, acutely harassed by Bradlaugh, Ireland, and other unexpected distractions, received reassuring reports from the men on the spot. As late as mid-November the senior British official in Pretoria was confident, and the new Governor of Natal, Sir George Colley, recommended a reduction in the garrisons in the Transvaal. The patience of the Boers, however, had ended. On December 20th they rose, and the four small British detachments were quickly surrounded. Colley called upon the Boers to disperse, and to give urgency to his demand advanced at once to the border with 1,500 men. On January 29th he was, amazingly, beaten back at Laing's Nek. The Cabinet, now dimly aware that things seemed to have changed since 1877, welcomed an invitation from President Kruger to give facilities for a Royal Commission if the British forces withdrew. But Colley was determined to advance, and on February 26th marched to Majuba Hill with 359 men. By the 27th he and ninety of his men were dead, and sixty taken prisoner.

In Britain, national pride was deeply hurt. A British force destroyed by a collection of farmers! But although Gladstone had impetuously declared that an immediate grant of self-government to the Transvaal was out of the question on January 6th, he now chose to negotiate. Indeed, short of entering into a major war in South Africa, he had little choice. But the result was a compromise which dissatisfied all sides. The Pretoria Convention of August 1881 defined the boundaries of the State, gave it 'complete self-government, subject to the suzerainty of Her Majesty', prohibited slavery, and saddled the state with most of the debt accumulated since annexation. It was with great difficulty that Kruger was able to persuade the revived Volksraad to accept the settlement, and then only on the understanding that it was only 'for the time being and provisionally'.

In South Africa and in Britain Gladstone was violently attacked for the settlement, and cries of 'Majuba Hill!' joined the Conservatives' list of charges against him. The death of Beaconsfield early in 1881 had given them good opportunity of comparing his robust and patriotic policies with the pusillanimity of his successor. Majuba Hill gave added material. The 'Imperial' debate in domestic politics, which had swung so heavily against the Conservatives at the end of the 1870s, now began to show signs of moving in their favour.

The real lesson, however, had not been discerned in London by either party. It had been well put by a distinguished historian of South Africa:

> The prestige of the Imperial Government .. was far gone in the eyes of white and black alike. The long-enduring and sorely strained reputation of the handful of redcoats in which Governors had been wont to put their trust had been blown to the winds, Any future intervention in the affairs of Boers, who were satisfied that British soldiers could always be beaten, would have to be in force.[1]

Thus, a handful of Boers had played their part, at present unrecognised, in the overseas British Revolution. But, meanwhile, Ministers were oppressed by revolution, real and immediate, much closer to home.

*

It was characteristic of Gladstone to look beyond the limitations of coercion to the true causes of the Irish crisis, and of which the dominant one concerned the land. Meanwhile, however, the need to restore law and order was urged as paramount by Cowper and Forster, and the Protection of Person and Property (Ireland) Bill passed through the Commons amid scenes of wild disorder and suspensions of Irish Members which led to the introduction of the closure. On February 2nd Speaker Brand ended an historic continuous sitting of forty-one hours by dramatically taking the Chair and putting the Question on his own responsibility on the grounds that 'a crisis has arisen which demands the prompt intervention of the Chair'. On the following day the arrest of Davitt was announced, and in the resultant uproar thirty-six Irish Members were suspended. Many Irish believed that this would lead to the immediate withdrawal of the Home Rulers from Parliament, but Parnell, despite some past cryptic utterances on the possibility, continued the fight in London. Viewed in retrospect, this would have been the ideal moment for secession, but Parnell's developing conception of the most effective course of action involved fighting on several fronts, and Parliament was to remain the principal one.

[1] E. A. Walker: *A History of South Africa*, 393.

On April 7th Gladstone introduced his Land Bill, which provided for the provision of fair rents, fixity of tenure, and the right of the tenant to the free sale of his interest in his holding. It was a notable advance, but it was introduced in the context of coercion and appeared to be another concession to violence. In a sense it was, but it was in reality a response to the success of the Land League, and posed a considerable threat to it. In this difficult situation Parnell did not impede the passage of the Bill, but in Ireland deliberately attacked it. His new organ, *United Ireland*, was particularly virulent, and Gladstone, convinced that Parnell was out to wreck the Act, declared at Leeds on October 7th that 'the resources of civilisation are not yet exhausted'. Parnell retorted by a denunciation of the Prime Minister which categorised him as a man 'prepared to carry fire and sword into your homesteads unless you humbly abase yourselves before him and before the landlords of your country'. On October 12th the Cabinet agreed to Parnell's arrest, and he was seized the next day in Dublin and sent to Kilmainham Jail, Gladstone declaring (Liverpool, October 26th) that Parnell's resolve was to march 'through rapine to the dismemberment of the Empire'. Parnell, when asked what would happen if he were arrested, had replied that 'Captain Moonlight will take my place'. This turned out to be only partly true. The Land League was suppressed. A 'no rent' manifesto was issued by the League's leaders—of whom virtually all were in prison—but although agitation was renewed, it was not on the scale of the previous winter.

Parnell's imprisonment had several advantages for him. It gave him comfortable martyrdom, and removed him from politics at a very difficult moment, when the Land Act was beginning to be effective and the League was beginning to fade. But there were serious disadvantages for the New Departure in having its leaders in jail, and there was accordingly, a real possibility that the painful and difficult fusion of all the elements in the movement would collapse without the unifying personality of Parnell, whose personal prestige and influence were bound to diminish if he were incarcerated for too long. The 'no rent' manifesto, as Parnell had expected, was unsuccessful, and the violence in Ireland demonstrated that his movement was endangered by elements more extreme than the League. This point was not lost on Ministers. Complex negotiations were opened in December 1881 which led to the release of Parnell and his colleagues in May 1882. The Government pledged itself to deal with the question of rent arrears, while Parnell would use his influence against violence. Parnell also accepted that his proposed amendments to the Land Act— to which Ministers agreed—would be considered 'a practical settlement of the land question and would enable us to co-operate cordially for the future with the Liberal party in forwarding liberal principles and measures of general reform'. At the core of the so-called 'Kilmainham Treaty' was the understanding between the parties that while the struggle for Home Rule would be continued, all efforts would be made to curtail the land war and revolutionary activities by the Irish leader if the Government made significant concessions on land legislation.

The Kilmainham Treaty was negotiated principally by Chamberlain on Gladstone's behalf, and also involved Captain W. H. O'Shea, Member of Parliament for County Clare, and his wife.

O'Shea's previous career had been undistinguished. He had been born in Dublin in 1840, and had entered the Army. In 1868 he had married Katherine, the youngest child of Sir John Page Wood; one of her brothers was to become Field Marshal Sir Evelyn Wood, V.C. O'Shea left the Army, and attempted a number of unsuccessful business enterprises; the growing family was in fact maintained by Mrs. O'Shea's aunt, Mrs. Benjamin Wood, who bought for her a house near Eltham, in Kent. It would appear from all accounts that the marriage was not a happy one, although not noticeably strained. O'Shea had been elected for Clare in the 1880 election; in the summer of the same year Mrs. O'Shea had met Parnell, and what was to become one of the most famous and tragic of modern love-affairs had begun.

Although much has been written of the O'Shea–Mrs. O'Shea– Parnell triangle, there remains a great deal of acutely conflicting testimony and evidence, particularly about the extent to which O'Shea was or was not a *mari complaisant*, and, if so, from what time. The judgement of this commentator is that to accept that O'Shea was wholly ignorant of the fact that Parnell was his wife's lover for ten years, in the course of which she gave birth to three children, applies to him depths of stupidity—or to his wife a degree of ruthless and cynical cunning—which are both so improbable as to be unacceptable. To this commentator it is highly significant that at the time of the Kilmainham negotiations the liaison was known to members of the Government, including Gladstone, Chamberlain, Harcourt, Granville and Dilke, which made O'Shea an important channel for negotiation provided that the fact that he was an intermediary was kept secret.

There is no indication from the available material of the sources of the information given to the leading Ministers. When Gladstone received a letter from Mrs. O'Shea in May 1882 he consulted Granville, who noted in reply that 'She is said to be his mistress.' Perhaps of greater significance was the definite comment of Harcourt, the Home Secretary, to the same effect. Parnell's movements had been followed for some time, and it seems very improbable that his letters to Mrs. O'Shea from Kilmainham had not been opened and read.

But although the political world was a small one in 1880, and gossip was an engrossing part of it, it seems hardly credible that the Government would have entrusted so important a negotiation to an obscure and recently elected Irish Nationalist M.P. and determined to keep the fact secret unless they had had good reason to regard him as being in a very special position. Not all historical material is appended to paper. And this leads inevitably to the strong conjecture that it was O'Shea himself who had told them and persuaded them. This would certainly fit in with what we know about O'Shea's high political ambitions and character. His wife was about to give birth to a child (who died shortly afterwards) which he must have known was not his but Parnell's. He was accordingly in an admirable position not only to act as a go-between but to be of value to both sides, for which he fully expected to be rewarded in due course. This is deduction, but, in the judgement of this commentator, a reasonable one.

The announcement of the 'Kilmainham Treaty' provoked severe shocks both in Ireland and in England. Cowper and Forster resigned immediately, and Balfour gave the first indication of his powers with an attack on Gladstone in the Commons in which he described the arrangement as 'standing alone in its infamy'. But it was swiftly overtaken by a more dramatic event.

On May 4th Parnell was released. On May 6th the new Chief Secretary, Lord Frederick Cavendish—Hartington's brother—was assassinated by a group called The Invincibles in Phoenix Park, Dublin, while walking with the Permanent Under-Secretary, W. H. Burke, on the day of the arrival of the new Viceroy, Lord Spencer. The occasion and the manner of the murders—the men were stabbed with long surgical knives and then their throats cut—outraged British and moderate Irish opinion. This was Captain Moonlight in the broad day. Parnell was justifiably shaken, seeing the assassinations as a blow against his authority, and at once issued a strong condemnation.

In fact, the murders strengthened Parnell's position in Ireland. There is in the Irish character an element which has baffled the English down the centuries, and which is impossible to describe precisely. The English see it as a bewildering rapidity from gentleness to cruelty and back to gentleness again, almost in a twinkling. The English, slower to anger and much more cruel when angry, regard themselves—wrongly—as predictable, and the Irish as totally unpredictable. The fact is that both races are chronically unpredictable to each other. Thus, the violence of English reaction to the Phoenix Park Murders, and the fact that so much of it was directed at Parnell personally, caused a counter-reaction in Ireland which swept away the doubts and dismay which the Kilmainham Treaty had created. The murders convinced many Englishmen—not excluding many Liberals—that the Irish were brutal savages. *This* reaction confirmed Irishmen in their opinion of the English. The murders achieved nothing for the extremists—Parnell's condemnation was not challenged in Ireland—but the English reaction strengthened Parnell's position at a time when it could have been in great danger. As Conor Cruise O'Brien has rightly emphasised, 'What injured an Irish politician's reputation in England was likely to help it in Ireland and vice versa.'[1]

But in England this cast an even uglier light upon the Kilmainham Treaty. Forster compelled Gladstone to reveal parts of the arrangement with Parnell for co-operation with the Liberals in a memorable and highly charged exchange in the House of Commons. The Conservatives stormed and the Liberals, utterly baffled by the wildly varying fluctuations of their leaders' Irish policies, were angry and mutinous. To appease them, a new and stiffer Crimes Bill was hurriedly introduced and violently opposed by the Nationalists; the Arrears Bill turned out not to be generous enough, and the wave of crime in Ireland continued. In August an entire family at Maamtrasna—father, mother, three sons, and a daughter—were brutally murdered in their beds, only one little boy surviving. The evil effects of this terrible episode were long-enduring. The cause of those accused of the crime were championed not only by the Irish Nationalists but by Lord Randolph Churchill, to no avail.

But, although few could perceive it at the time, a crucial stage in the Irish crisis had passed. The combination of better harvests, the provisions of the Land Act, and sheer weariness in Ireland at the

1 O'Brien, op. cit., 82.

passion and cruelty of 1880–2, had made the successful suppression of the Land League possible. The extremists had harmed themselves with their excesses, but the crucial factor was that Parnell offered results through constitutional methods while having proved his independence and courage. This, clearly, was no Isaac Butt. The Irish National League, founded at the end of 1882, was a constitutional body dedicated to the establishment of Irish self-government through legal methods, and dominated by Parnell. The Catholic Church, whose position in the tumults had been definitely ambivalent, was sympathetic and interested. For an institution dedicated to the *status quo*, the Church in Ireland had been torn between that fundamental philosophy and the passionate nationalism of so many of its priests and the majority of its flock. It had executed as difficult and precarious a survival as Parnell had himself, and was thankful to support a movement whose implications were revolutionary but whose methods were not.

Although violence continued, in England as well as in Ireland, it faded sharply after 1882. Sheer exhaustion had played its part, but by no means the only part. Parnell had proved to the Irish that the constitutional approach, when fully backed in Ireland, could produce results. It had produced the Land Act, the Arrears Act—unsatisfactory though it may have been—and had utterly transformed the relationships between tenants and landlords, far beyond anything known in England, a fact which had occasioned the indignant resignation of the Duke of Argyll and the vehement attacks of Salisbury. 'Boycotting' had been more effective than murder, solidarity more effective than the houghing of cattle or burning of ricks. More had been achieved in two years by Parnell's methods than had been achieved in living memory. Bombs continued to go off in the Tower of London and in the House of Commons itself, and the Irish countryside remained dangerous. But these were increasingly regarded as the work of fanatics, and unworthy of a great cause. It was an astonishing transformation of mood, and was to survive longer than even Parnell could have envisaged.

Meanwhile, the Liberals were confronted by the angry Conservative drum-beat of Majuba, Kilmainham, and Maamtrasna. All they could offer in response to the mounting clamours of their opponents was a startling exercise in gun-boat imperialism.

*

British involvement in Egypt had inexorably increased since Disraeli's celebrated coup of 1875. From the purchase of the Canal shares Gladstone had said that this event—condemned as another of Beaconsfield's 'cruel and ruinous misdeeds'—could only result in political and even military involvement in the affairs of Egypt, and he had been right. European interest in Egypt now greatly increased, and the Khedive Ismail accelerated the process by his irresponsibility and profligate expenditure, which had so alarmed the French and the British that in 1878 the latter had sent two representatives to serve on an international commission initiated by the French. One was a Royal Artillery Major, aged 37—Evelyn Baring. A British and a French representative now served in the Khedive's Cabinet, but quickly concluded that the Khedive was incorrigible, and in 1879 the Sultan was induced by Anglo-French pressure to depose Ismail in favour of his son, Tewfik, who proved considerably more malleable. This was as far as the Beaconsfield Government was prepared to go, and Baring's appeals for a more active intervention were unheeded. The British policy followed the maxim of Palmerston that 'we want to trade with Egypt, and to travel through Egypt, but we do not want the burden of governing Egypt'. The British and French financial ministers were converted into permanent advisers, who could not be dismissed without the consent of the respective governments. But the Anglo-French collaboration was already becoming brittle. The Canal was assuming increasing importance to the British, who owned some eighty per cent of the shipping that passed through it, and their realisation of its strategic significance was becoming much stronger. Before the Gladstone Government took office, the 'Dual Control' was demonstrating signs of severe strain, which the French occupation of Tunis early in 1881 did nothing to reduce.

In 1881 a nationalist revolt broke out in Egypt, led by a Colonel Ahmad Arabi, and was successful and popular enough to impose terms upon the Khedive in September which included the dismissal of all ministers, the granting of a constitution, and an increase in the army. Both the British and French governments were nonplussed by this unexpected development, but the former was not anxious to intervene. The Gambetta-Ferry Government favoured intervention, but fell in January 1882. Gladstone turned to the Concert of Europe for guidance and assistance, to the exasperation of Hartington and Northbrook, and it was in its name that he subsequently professed to act.

By the late spring of 1882, in the judgement of the British and the French, the Arabi movement was getting out of control; there were serious riots in Alexandria early in June in which several Europeans were killed, and which Gladstone described as an 'international atrocity'. These were ascribed by the British—almost certainly incorrectly—to deliberate provocation by Arabi. The estimates vary greatly, from 300 killed to less than forty. At the time the higher figures were believed in England.

The Egyptians began to fortify the city against attack from the sea and to install batteries. A joint Anglo-French fleet, sent as a precaution against further outrages against Europeans, floated uneasily offshore. In January, before the fall of his Government, Gambetta had persuaded the British to concur in a Joint Note which pledged the two Governments to support the Khedive 'against the difficulties of various kinds which might interfere with the course of public affairs in Egypt' and to resolve 'to guard by their united efforts against all course of complications, internal or external, which might menace the order of things established in Egypt'. The French were now fading away, but the principle of the Joint Note still obtained strongly in London.

Ministers in London now became very belligerent. Granville was alarmed about the safety of the Canal, Hartington—who had not recovered from the shock of his brother's murder—was not enamoured of nationalist movements that employed methods of violence, and the reports from the British local officials were alarming. But the radicals were now equally aroused. Chamberlain was talking of 'the honour and interests of England' and was described by Granville as 'almost the greatest Jingo' in the Cabinet; Dilke strongly supported him, and Gladstone—who in 1877 had denounced the argument for intervention in Egypt[1]—was now convinced that Arabi was a despot and 'one of the greatest villains alive'. His first instincts had been sympathetic to Arabi—'Egypt for the Egyptians is the sentiment to which I would wish to give scope', he had written to Granville—but he had changed his views. The Khedive urged that the Anglo-French fleet should bombard Alexandria and send troops to destroy the Egyptian army. With the Prime Minister and the two most prominent radicals in this mood, the British Admiral commanding the fleet off Alexandria bombarded the

[1] *Nineteenth Century*, August 1877: 'Aggression on Egypt and Freedom In the East'.

city on July 11th. The French meanwhile, had withdrawn, leaving, as it transpired, Egypt to the British. On July 13th the Khedive sought British protection and denounced Arabi.

On July 22nd Gladstone informed the House of Commons that 'we should not fully discharge our duty if we did not endeavour to convert the present interior state of Egypt from anarchy and conflict to peace and order. We shall look . . . to the co-operation of the Powers of civilised Europe. . . . But if every chance of obtaining co-operation is exhausted, the work will be undertaken by the single power of England'. Arabi stated that 'irreconcilable war existed between the Egyptians and the English'. A British army under the command of Wolseley was despatched, a Vote of Credit for over £2 million was voted by the House of Commons, and only old John Bright—who wrote to Gladstone that 'I think on reviewing the doctrines connected with our foreign policy which I have preached and defended during forty years of my public life, you will not be surprised at the decision I am now compelled to take', and who told Rosebery that Gladstone's action was 'simply damnable, worse than anything ever perpetrated by Dizzy'—protested at this 'manifest violation of international and moral law' and resigned. Lord Randolph Churchill, who had sympathised from the outset with Arabi's purposes, joined Bright in his protests, but they were virtually alone. Gladstone informed the House of Commons that 'there is not the smallest rag nor shred of evidence to support [the] contention' that 'the military party was the popular party'. On August 19th Wolseley's army landed on Egyptian soil.

Wolseley's force consisted of some 30,000 men in all, and the fact that such a force had been assembled and transported at such short notice was in itself a remarkable feat. After occupying Port Said, Wolseley took the main part of his force down the Canal to Ismailia, with the purpose of advancing westwards along the Sweet Water Canal and its accompanying railway towards Cairo, so that he could place his army between Cairo and Arabi's force at Alexandria.

Arabi, who had raised a force of some 60,000 men, at once sent about 12,000 to Tel-el-Kebir, between Cairo and Ismailia, to confront the probable line of the British advance. A further 40,000 joined them at this position, which lay about thirty miles west of Ismailia, and began the construction of an ambitious trench-fortification (still visible today) running some twenty miles northward of the Sweet Water

Canal. It was built by hand in two weeks, a most remarkable and impressive feat. The trench consisted of a breastwork which was six feet high in places; although it was a relatively simple construction, with no communication trenches or traverses, it constituted a formidable military obstacle.

The British force was rather 'soft' after three weeks at sea, and the horses had been particularly affected by the voyage. The advance along the Sweet Water Canal and railway was accordingly slow and piecemeal, with a few desultory advance-guard actions. In seventeen days only twenty-five miles were covered. Three outpost positions were captured, and by September 12th Wolseley, with some 17,000 troops, sixty-one guns, and six cavalry regiments, was established around Kassassin, some eleven miles away from Arabi's trench, manned by over 20,000 men.

Wolseley conducted several personal dawn reconnaissances of the Egyptian positions. He noted that the Egyptians did not 'stand to' until 5.45 a.m., and concluded that a night flank march, with a surprise attack at first light was the most practicable method of assault. It was a courageous and almost foolhardy decision. It involved a march of over eleven miles in the dark across almost featureless terrain. In the event Wolseley's confidence in himself, his officers and his men, were fully justified. The Highland Brigade, which led the advance, was only 150 yards from its objective when it was seen by the Egyptians. The battle itself lasted for under an hour, although resistance was fierce in places. Artillery was brought up to enfilade the occupied sectors of the trench, the cavalry came in from the north to sweep the fleeing Egyptians before them, and the battle was over. The British losses were fifty-seven dead and twenty-two missing; the Egyptian casualties were terrible. It was, with the exception of Omdurman, the most devastating British military victory in the nineteenth century.

A company of the Scots Guards, with a divisional commander empowered to open negotiations, reached Cairo in the evening by train. There was no resistance of any kind. Arabi surrendered the Citadel and himself on 14th September; a few days later the Khedive was re-throned. After a great triumphal parade through the capital, Wolseley and his three divisional commanders embarked for England. The campaign had lasted for forty-seven days; it had cost under 450 British casualities. Gladstone ordered victory salutes of guns in Hyde Park and elsewhere to announce the victory of Tel-el-Kebir. The

British commanders returned to receive heroes' welcomes. The popularity of the Government soared. It was all very odd.

The aftermath was even odder. There was to be no question of annexation, a step which Gladstone described as 'at variance with all the principles and views of the British Government'. Ministers declared that the British occupation was temporary and that no commitments of a long-term nature had been incurred. These repeated assurances were quite genuine but quite unrealistic. Lord Dufferin was sent to examine the situation, and rapidly concluded that it would greatly benefit from major reforms under the supervision of British advisers. He emphasised that the country should not become a 'concealed protectorate', but the clear implication of his advice was that the condition of Egypt was still perilous, and that the same considerations that had inspired intervention still applied to remaining there. Ministers were extremely reluctant to face this fact. A reaction to the military invasion had set in afterwards in radical circles. Lord Randolph Churchill, ever unexpected, and influenced by Wilfred Scawen Blunt, denounced the campaign as 'a bondholders' war' and spoke disparagingly of 'tawdry military glories'. He fought vigorously for the captured Egyptian officers, contributed to the costs of Arabi's defence, and described his revolution as 'the movement of a nation'. The Tories were disconcerted, but, as Lord Randolph's son has remarked, 'They loved their country much; but they hated Gladstone more.'[1] But the Liberal Party was uneasy, and with good cause. When Churchill demanded an enquiry into the circumstances of the Alexandria riots, Ministers temporised. When one of Arabi's officers was sentenced to death after a farce of a trial the Government agreed to make enquiries; while thus engaged, the officer was hanged. The Opposition launched a fierce attack on Ministers; there was much troublement on the countenance of their supporters as they marched through the Lobbies to support them. Baring had returned to Egypt, and was to remain there, using as his mandate the declaration of Dufferin that 'it is absolutely necessary to prevent the fabric we have raised from tumbling to the ground the moment our sustaining hand is withdrawn'. That 'sustaining hand' was to prove of long duration. What Milner was to describe as 'the Veiled Protectorate' had been created.

*

[1] W. S. Churchill: *Lord Randolph Churchill* (one-volume edition, 1951), 214.

A very real dichotomy within the Liberal ranks was now becoming evident, of which Bright's resignation had been a portent, although it did not emerge into public gaze until the formation of the Imperial Federation League in 1884, of which Rosebery and Forster were active members. Whether one liked the fact or not, the British had acquired very substantial areas abroad and the question was exactly what Howe had posed twenty years before—'What is to be done about them?' The abandonment of India was, of course, unthinkable, but the new link to India, the Suez Canal, had led to a new involvement in Egypt which could easily lead to other commitments. The 'scramble for Africa' was just beginning. What should be the British reaction? The question was complicated by domestic political factors. The Conservative Primrose League, founded in 1883, had from the outset a markedly 'Imperial' tone, and its rapid success—it achieved over a million members by the end of the decade—could not be ignored. The popular excitement at Tel-el-Kebir and the fury at Majuba Hill were also significant. The 'imperial' debate, in terms of votes, was clearly changing. The creation of a new Empire in South Africa as a result of the energies of men like Rhodes, Goldie, MacKinnon and Johnston, owed nothing to Government encouragement. 'The Cabinet do not want more niggers', as Lord Kimberley remarked after a Cabinet meeting that had decided (March 22nd, 1884) against any increase in the Zululand Protectorate. Many Ministers viewed the gradual increase of British influence in Africa with regret. As Dilke wrote in 1890 in a sequel to *Greater Britain*, 'The only excuse that one can make is that, if we had not laid hands upon their territory, France or Germany would have done so.'

But there were other Ministers who took a very different line. Chamberlain, speaking about the German occupation of North-East New Guinea, declared that 'the English democracy will stand shoulder to shoulder throughout the world to maintain the honour and the integrity of the Empire'. And Dilke's views were broadly imperialistic. 'I am as great a jingo in Central Asia as I am a scuttler in South Africa', he wrote in 1885.[1] Gladstone told Lord Frederick Cavendish in November 1881 that he had to wage an almost daily battle 'on the side of liberty as opposed to Jingoism'. The niceties of Gladstone's distinctions between his actions in Egypt and elsewhere increasingly grated on his followers. He claimed that the invasion of Egypt had been undertaken 'from a love of peace, and, I may say, on the principle of

[1] Roy Jenkins: *Sir Charles Dilke*, 179.

peace'. Yet he defended himself in the Commons from taking action in the Sudan on the grounds that it would involve 'a war of conquest against a people struggling to be free . . . and rightly struggling to be free'. On that occasion (May 13th, 1883) Forster, by now an implacable foe, remarked that the Prime Minister 'can persuade most people of most things, and above all he can persuade himself of almost anything'. There was a certain truth in this cruel jibe.

The problem of the Sudan was a case in point. Mohammed Ahmed ibn Abdullah declared himself the new messiah—the Mahdi—and had raised the standard of revolt against the brutal and incompetent Egyptian rule. It was a good moment to do it, and his movement had spread rapidly. In 1883 the British Government sanctioned an attempt by the Egyptian Government to re-conquer the Sudan. The force, some 10,000 strong, was commanded by a British officer, General Hicks. On November 5th it was annihilated by the Mahdist army. The remnants of Egyptian authority in this vast area now consisted of a handful of beleaguered garrisons. Those on the Red Sea coast presented no difficulty, but those centred on Khartoum were a different matter. The Government was overwhelmingly in favour of evacuation south of Wadi Halfa. In an evil hour Gladstone acquiesced in the decision of an extra-Cabinet committee consisting of Hartington, Granville, Northbrook and Dilke (the new President of the Local Government Board and a member of the Cabinet) to dispatch General Charles Gordon to report back on the best methods of evacuation.

Gordon had resigned as Governor-General of the Sudan in 1881, and was temporarily without employment, but his glamorous exploits in China and the Sudan attracted the attention of Granville, and the campaign for his appointment included the Liberal *Pall Mall Gazette*. It was an extraordinary choice. Salisbury declared that the Government must have taken leave of its senses. In Cairo, Baring—now recalled from India where he had been sent in 1880 and appointed British agent and consul-general—gave his assent to Gordon's mission with great reluctance. Baring was in a difficult position, as it was he who had advised the Government to send 'an English officer of high authority to Khartoum with full power to withdraw the garrison and to make the best arrangements possible for the future government of that country', but he had not envisaged Gordon. Dilke, it appears, thought that Gordon was being sent to Suakim, on the Red Sea Coast. When he heard on January 21st that Gordon was going to Khartoum he wrote to Granville that 'if he goes up towards Khartoum, and is carried off and held to ransom—we shall have to send a terrible force after him even though he should go without instructions'.[1]

Gordon has been described by a cool and by no means friendly commentator as 'perhaps the finest specimen of the heroic Victorian type—a Bible-taught Evangelical, fearless, tireless, incorruptible; following the call of duty through fields of desperate adventure'.[2] Certainly his contemporaries viewed him in this light. He had served in the Crimean War, taken part in the British capture of Peking in 1860, and had served under the Chinese government from 1863–5 in the successful suppression of the Tai-Ping rebellion, acquiring the sobriquet of 'Chinese Gordon'. He had gone to the Sudan in 1873, and had made a mighty reputation. Recalled in 1881, he had viewed subsequent developments with consternation and wrath. About some matters Gordon had fanatical ideas, notably of the spread of Christianity and good government. His individuality and energy were notorious and his judgement erratic, but his following in Britain was enormous. Even Granville thought of him as 'a genius and a splendid character'. He was seen off from Victoria Station by a concourse of notables, including the Duke of Cambridge—the Commander-in-Chief of the Army—Wolseley, and Granville.

Gladstone quickly had serious doubts about the wisdom of Gordon's mission, but it was too late. Gordon demanded, and received, the title of Governor-General of the Sudan, and arrived in Khartoum on February 18th, 1884. He proceeded to bombard Baring and Ministers with grandiose proposals, and even attempted to propose terms to the Mahdi for ending his rebellion, which were curtly rejected. But in Britain the exasperation of Ministers and officials with this impossible man was overwhelmed by popular excitement at the spectacle of an heroic figure, and as the force of the Mahdi moved closer to Khartoum public apprehension for his safety became stridently expressed. At first Gordon would not withdraw and then he could not; the clamour for a relief expedition became so intense that the fate of the Government was in peril. Eventually, and with deep reluctance, Gladstone agreed in August after Hartington had threatened to resign, but it was not until October that a force of ten thousand left Cairo to undertake the fifteen hundred mile journey up the Nile.

It reached Khartoum at the end of January 1885 to find that it had

[1] Jenkins, op-cit., 180.   [2] R. C. K. Ensor: *England, 1870–1914*, 81.

been too late and that Gordon was dead. When the news reached Britain there was a storm of anger unprecedented since the news of the Buglarian Atrocities nearly a decade earlier, another clear indication that there was a real political and popular strength in the new imperialism. The Queen telegraphed her bitter displeasure *en clair* to Gladstone, the London mob howled for several weeks, and the Government narrowly avoided defeat in the House of Commons. The virulence against Gladstone personally was greater than at any time during his long and not uncontroversial career. The Cabinet, itself deeply divided, and after surviving by only fourteen votes on a Vote of Censure seriously considered resigning, and Gladstone was compelled to state that it was Government policy to crush the Mahdi—a commitment from which he thankfully and skilfully extricated himself in April when he took a startlingly belligerent line against Russian infiltration on the Afghan frontier at the obscure village of Penjdeh. The Russians drew back, the morale of the Liberals was raised, the Conservatives were astonished, and the Sudan was abandoned to the Mahdi. But the real issue had only been postponed. Gladstone was justified in writing immediately after this remarkable episode that the record of his Government 'has been a wild romance of politics with a continual succession of hairbreadth escapes and strange accidents pressing upon one another'.

The question now was how long this performance could endure.

*

The Conservatives, in the meanwhile, had not been without their own difficulties. The death of Beaconsfield had left Northcote and Salisbury as the party leaders, but the arrangement worked neither smoothly nor effectively. Who, in fact, was the leader? Who, in the event of the creation of a Conservative Government, would receive the Queen's Commission to form an Administration? Lord Randolph Churchill, although he had pursued a highly individualistic line on Irish questions and on Egypt—for which he had earned the respect and affection of the Irish—had emerged as a very definite contender for the leadership. His audaciously irreverent assaults on Gladstone ('the Moloch of Midlothian') and Chamberlain ('this Pinchbeck Robespierre') exhilarated large audiences in the country, drawn to his meetings by the rapidly spreading word of his Parliamentary stardom. In October 1882 an article signed 'Two Conservatives' appeared in the *Fortnightly Review* which was a detailed and unsparing attack upon the party leadership and the aloofness of its ruling circle and which was clearly the work of Gorst and Churchill. Shortly afterwards, in the House, Churchill was demanding: 'Is the attitude of the great Tory Democracy, which Lord Beaconsfield's party constructed, to be one of mere clogged opposition? And is it true, what our foes say of us, that Coercion in Ireland and foreign war is to be the "be-all and end-all" of Tory Ministers?'

Churchill's developing theme of 'Tory Democracy' was an early example of his particular genius for arresting and dramatic phrases. Although much derided at the time, it subsequently caught on, as did the even vaguer doctrine of 'Fair Trade', which provoked Chamberlain to a series of speeches in defence of Free Trade which sowed the first seeds of doubt in his mind about the sanctity of *laissez-faire*. Churchill did not push this particular heresy very far, and it faded from his speeches after January 1884, but it was characteristic of his originality that he was prepared to ask some highly uncomfortable questions about this particular shibboleth.

Churchill's great attraction to Conservatives was that he was always on the attack and afraid of no one, least of all Gladstone. 'I see no good object to be gained', he informed a deputation of Manchester Conservatives who were earnestly urging him to contest one of the constituencies in that city in December 1882, 'by concealing my opinion that the constitutional function of an Opposition is to oppose and not support the Government, and that this function during the three sessions of this Parliament has been either systematically neglected or defectively carried out'. T. P. O'Connor wrote shortly afterwards, with truth, that 'everybody now recognises that all the spirit and go which exist in the Conservative Party have been infused into it by this dashing, irrepressible, and, at first sight, frivolous youth. He has lived down the ridicule which used to be cast upon him by his friends as well as his foes, and at thirty-four he stands out as perhaps the one man of unblemished promise in his party.' Everybody, it may be added, except the Conservative hierarchy.

In his exuberance at the realisation of his developing powers, Churchill trampled recklessly on the sensitivities of older and less sparkling intellects. He mocked not only Northcote—labelled 'The Goat'—but his more earnest colleagues. He was not wise to describe W. H. Smith and Sir Richard Cross as 'Marshall and Snelgrove', nor to poke fun at 'the lords of suburban villas, of the owners of vineries and pineries'. He derided 'old men crooning over the fire at the Carlton Club', jeered at the 'old gang', and was imperious in his relations with those he did not respect. He held them up to ridicule in the House of Commons, at public meetings or cheerful dinner-parties, and he snubbed them in the Lobbies. As he advanced, an ever-increasing army of offended politicians viewed him with mounting uneasiness and personal resentments.

Although Churchill's rapid rise was viewed with dismay by the Opposition Front Bench and those 'respectable' elements in the Party about which Beaconsfield had warned him, Salisbury, from afar, had more mixed emotions. The relentless destruction of Northcote was certainly not opposed to his own ambitions, but the emergence of so formidable a challenger certainly was. Furthermore, Churchill's demagogery and the whole business of 'Tory Democracy' were un-congenial to him. Churchill, in two fiery letters to *The Times* and an article entitled 'Elijah's Mantle' in May 1883 clearly expressed his preference for Salisbury, but a reference to 'a statesman who fears not to meet and who knows how to sway immense masses of the working classes and who either by his genius or his eloquence, or by all the varied influences of an ancient name, can "move the hearts of house-holds" ' was regarded less as a tribute to Salisbury—who, despite an ancient name, was not known for his enthusiasm to meet immense masses of the working classes—than a blatant attempt to put Churchill's name in the list of contenders for Beaconsfield's mantle. The estab-lishment by Churchill and Wolff of the Primrose League later in the year, which had immediate success, and which Northcote and Salisbury joined with considerable reluctance, made the point clearer.

Salisbury was fifty-three years of age in 1883. Born in Hatfield House, he had endured a largely unhappy and unsuccessful childhood, dogged by poor health. After a visit to South Africa and Australia, he had become Conservative M.P. for the pocket borough of Stamford in 1853. Throughout his entire period of fifteen years in the House of Commons, he never fought a contested election, and after he succeeded as Marquess of Salisbury in 1868 he never visited the Commons again, and never gave evidence of any regrets for being removed from its atmosphere.

First as Lord Robert Cecil, and then, after the death of his elder brother in 1865, as Lord Cranborne, Salisbury had established himself as a serious Conservative journalist, writing principally in the *Quarterly Review* and *Saturday Review* for money as much as for recognition. He married, very happily, Miss Georgina Alderson in 1857 in the teeth of his father's objections, and gradually was less tormented by the periods of acute depression, accompanied by severe physical lassitude, which had been a marked characteristic. But he had been an obscure and solitary back-bencher, aloof, shy, and invariably shabbily dressed. He despised what he described as 'the world of conclaves and conspiracies, of pulse-feeling and thumb-screwing, of slippery intrigues and abortive stratagems', and wrote of Disraeli that 'he is bewitched by the demon of low dodging'.

Salisbury was a genuine intellectual, a Fellow of All Souls and of the Royal Society in his own right, deeply religious, suspicious of rhetoric and novelty, yet himself eloquent and pragmatic. Appointed Secretary of State for India in 1866, he resigned when it was evident that Disraeli's Reform proposals included household suffrage and redistribution. He refused to join Disraeli's government in January 1868 after denouncing the Reform Act with a vehemence that had personal as well as public motivations. Of Disraeli he wrote that 'he is an adventurer, and, as I have good cause to know, he is without principles or honesty'. His return to the India Office in 1874 had, accordingly, been very reluctant.

The key to Salisbury's increasing hold on the Conservative Party lay less in the fact that he was a grandee and a devout believer in the fundamentals of Toryism than in his blunt common sense and scepticism. Thus, in October 1871:

> We live in an age of blood and iron. If we mean to escape misery and dishonour, we must trust to no consciousness of a righteous cause, to no moral influence, to no fancied restraints of civilisation. These bulwarks may be of use when the millennium draws near; they are empty verbiage now. We must trust to our power of self-defence, and to no earthly aid.

Or, April 1881:

> To those who have found breakfast with difficulty, and do not know where to find dinner, intricate questions of politics are a matter of comparatively secondary interest.

And then, October 1884:

> If you will study history, you will find that freedom, when it has been destroyed, has always been destroyed by those who shelter themselves under the cover of its forms and who speak its language with eloquence and vigor.

Salisbury disliked public speaking—'This duty of making political speeches is an aggravation of the labours of your Majesty's servants which we owe entirely to Mr. Gladstone' he wrote on one occasion to the Queen—but from the beginning of 1881 he became one of the most active and conspicuous of the Conservative speakers, delivering more than seventy major speeches in the next four years. These were trenchant, well-prepared, and well received. The principal Conservative provincial leaders—Arthur Forwood in Liverpool, Sir William Houldsworth in Manchester, and Satchell Hopkins in Birmingham—were particularly grateful and impressed. To his reputation in foreign affairs Salisbury had now added a party following outside London which was greater than that of Northcote, and acted as a powerful, if less spectacular, counterweight to Randolph Churchill's meteoric campaign. Thus he was, in experience, intellect, and following increasingly seen as the natural successor to Beaconsfield, and was quietly consolidating this position. Its full strength was not to be demonstrated until December 1886.

*

At the end of 1883 the situation for the 'Dual Control' became much more serious when Churchill set out to capture the National Union of Conservative Associations. The National Union, founded in 1867, never occupied a very significant position and possessed virtually no funds. But it was in existence, its Council was elective, it did have an annual conference, and Churchill, with Chamberlain's example very much in his mind, saw in this moribund organisation considerable potentialities.

After the 1880 debacle Beaconsfield had established a Central Committee to reorganise the party organisation. It had not been notably successful, and Gorst—recalled to give it the benefit of his neglected experience—had soon resigned in disgust. The Central Committee, in its membership and approach, was the personification of 'the old gang', but it did have access to, and disbursed, the central party funds. It was Churchill's strategy at the end of 1883 to take the annual conference of the National Union by storm, to secure the election to the Council of his friends and allies, and to secure for it 'all power and finance'. 'This will be a bold step', he wrote to Wolff, 'the Austerlitz of the Fourth Party.' The combination of Churchill in his best demagogic form—'If you want to gain the confidence of the working classes, let them have a share and a large share—a real share and not a sham share—in your party councils and in your party government'—and careful polling of the delegates, nearly achieved the victory, but in the end Churchill's group only secured a fractional majority.

But it was enough for the moment. The new Council appointed an Organisation Committee with Churchill as its chairman, and promptly sought an interview with Salisbury. The implications were clear, and were made even clearer when Churchill embarked on a speaking tour in the Provinces which drew immense audiences and were reported at great length; to fervent applause Churchill then announced his intention of fighting John Bright in his citadel in Birmingham at the next election, a gesture of superb dramatic self-confidence and aggressiveness. Salisbury and Balfour—whose tenuous connection with the Fourth Party had now ended—viewed these developments with concern but decided on caution. In February 1884 Lord Randolph was elected chairman of the Council, and promptly demanded the surrender of the Central Committee, threatening public warfare unless the point was conceded. At this point Salisbury and Northcote decided to force the issue themselves, and Churchill resolved to fight. The tone of his letters to Salisbury now became sharp and at times personally offensive. The lines of battle were clearly drawn; on the one side, the voice of democratic involvement in party affairs, on the other an 'aristocratic and privileged' grouping consisting of 'certain irresponsible persons who find favour in your [Salisbury's] eyes'. This dispute was carried to the country, where Churchill declared that 'Governments will go wrong, Parliaments will go wrong, classes will go wrong, London Society and the Pall Mall clubs always go wrong, but the people do not go wrong' and stated that his political philosophy was 'Trust the people' and that 'I have no fear of democracy'. Salisbury, believing that he had a case for accusing Churchill of bad faith in the negotiations for a settlement, broke them off. Churchill promptly resigned from his chairmanship, and there was much excitement among the substantial elements in the Parliamentary Party which loathed and feared this impossible and disloyal young man with his brazen ambitions.

But the reaction outside London was quite different, and Churchill's wooing of the Provincial party leaders now paid great dividends. On May 16th he was unanimously re-elected Chairman, and Salisbury resolved to come to terms.

Gorst was not present at these negotiations (nor was Northcote), and was deeply embittered by what his son subsequently called 'the great surrender'. Churchill and Salisbury, recognising each other tacitly as equals, agreed that they would work in harmony, that the Central Committee would be abolished, that Sir Michael Hicks-Beach, in whom each had confidence, would become chairman of the Council, and that the Primrose League would be officially recognised. Gorst believed that Churchill had lost a great opportunity, and he rightly foresaw that the National Union would be put to sleep again. But Churchill's objectives had been more limited. It had become clear to him that the battle to win full control over the National Union was going to be a long and divisive one, and one that he might not have won in the long run. An election was close, and it was time to mend bridges. The Salisbury–Churchill pact doomed Northcote's ambition, and established a new duumvirate.

These acute divisions in the Opposition ranks had coincided with the relaxing of the immediate crisis in Ireland and the seizing of the initiative by the Government in the passage of a new Reform Bill which brought to the agricultural workers the extensions of the franchise given to the town artisans in 1867. This was Chamberlain's contribution, and it caught the Conservatives off-balance. The Conservatives refused to accept franchise reform without a simultaneous redistribution of seats, and for a time feelings ran high. The removal of the distinction between borough and county franchise in Ireland also alarmed the Conservatives, but they dared not press this matter too far. Although it appeared as though the issue would be 'the Peers against the People', as Chamberlain hoped, in the end party agreement was reached. Some two million new voters were enfranchised, there was a considerable redistribution, and the principle of 'one man one vote' was established, together with the abolition of the plural-member system. Of even greater immediate significance was the fact that the Act extended the franchise to Ireland on the same terms, increasing the Irish electorate by over half a million voters, and thus giving Parnell his opportunity for a clear Home Rule sweep outside Ulster. Given Parnell's ascendancy by this stage, it is doubtful whether this made much difference in terms of seats in Ireland, but it greatly improved his position in bargaining terms in England.

But this success for the Government was clouded by the disasters in the Sudan and severe internal differences over Ireland. The Crimes Act was due to expire in August, and Ministers were divided on its renewal. Chamberlain proposed a scheme of devolution introducing elective county boards with defined local responsibilities and a national council, a Central Board, which would assume many of the responsibilities borne by the Dublin administration. The Central Board Scheme split the Cabinet, was defeated by one vote on May 9th, 1885, and Chamberlain and Dilke resigned. Their resignations were not made public, and the search for a modus vivendi was continuing when, on June 9th, the Government was defeated in the House of Commons and thankfully resigned.

The Central Board Scheme was unacceptable to Parnell as an alternative to Home Rule, and, whether or not Chamberlain was deceived by the O'Shea who again acted as emissary[1] or not, it was a fatal misreading of Parnell's position to infer that such a watered-down version could be acceptable. In a dark moment for his cause, Parnell negotiated with Churchill—in itself a remarkable indication of how far and how high Lord Randolph had travelled over the previous five years. The discussion was confined to the issue of Coercion. Churchill said that if he were a member of the Government he would oppose the renewal of the Crimes Act. 'In that case', Parnell replied, 'you will have the Irish vote at the elections.'[2] The understanding was confirmed at least in one other meeting between the two. This episode demonstrated the Irish Nationalists' respect for Churchill's positions on the Irish Question, including his early denunciations of coercion and his fierce opposition to the introduction of the Closure in 1881. He was indeed, not only clearly the rising star of the Conservative Party but also the only one who had revealed any sensitivity to their cause. Northcote was not taken seriously by the Irish, and Salisbury's attitude towards Ireland was notoriously antipathetic. 'On Tory

[1] The claim is strongly denied by Henry Harrison in *Parnell, Joseph Chamberlain and Mr. Garvin.*
[2] W. S. Churchill; *Lord Randolph Churchill*, 395.

principles', he had written more than a decade earlier, 'the case presents much that is painful, but no perplexity whatever. Ireland must be kept, like India, at all hazards: by persuasion, if possible; if not, by force.' There were no indications that Salisbury had changed his mind on this matter, and he had been vehemently opposed to the principles of tenants' rights contained in the Land and Arrears Act. Churchill was accordingly the natural Conservative for Parnell to do business with. He subsequently claimed that 'there was no compact or bargain of any kind', but, as Rosebery has pointed out, when one man pledges action in a certain eventuality in return for certain favours it is difficult to describe it otherwise. The Conservatives did not renew the Crimes Act, and in November Parnell did advise Irish voters in Britain to vote Conservative.

On June 8th the Opposition moved an amendment to the Budget condemning the proposed increase in duties on beer and spirits. It was a torpid debate, until it became apparent that the Government was treating it as, in Dilke's words 'a question of life and death', a phrase repeated by Gladstone himself. At half past one in the morning of June 9th the division was taken, and amid scenes of tumult and cries of 'Buckshot!' and 'Coercion!' from the Irish it was announced that the Government had been defeated by twelve votes. Lord Randolph joyously leaped onto the bench to lead the Conservative exultations while Gladstone sat quietly writing to the Queen to inform her of the fall of his Government.

It was a curious incident which, as the Liberal Sir Wilfred Lawson remarked, reminded him of the verdict of a Dorset jury: 'Died on the visitation of God under suspicious circumstances.' Sixty-two Liberals had been absent, of whom only fourteen had been paired, while four had voted for the Opposition amendment. The Irish had combined with the Conservatives. As Conor Cruise O'Brien has commented, 'the unusually large muster of Parnellites on the decisive vote certainly suggests advance planning'.[1] On an issue of confidence the Liberal whips had either been exceptionally negligent or had been advised not to try too hard. The evidence strongly points to the latter conclusion.

Certainly, Ministers were delighted. Chamberlain confessed to a 'spirit of exultation' and wrote that 'the Tories have relieved us from a position of almost intolerable embarrassment'. Gladstone described it as 'a great personal relief'. The evidence of Gladstone's reaction is

[1] O'Brien, op. cit., 98.

ambiguous. His son wrote that 'Father I am sure knew nothing of the probability of defeat until the last moment. Tories taken aback, except Randolph who danced madly about like a Cherokee on the war path.' Mrs. Gladstone recorded that when her husband returned to Downing Street 'it had been a blow, he had gone in to win' but that 'before he fell asleep, came the lovely calm, the words coming from his lips, "All praise to God for his mercies".'[1]

Thus, under distinctly curious circumstances, ended the life of the Administration which had entered office with such high hopes little more than five years previously, which had endured so much, and which now gladly made way for the Conservatives while hopefully awaiting the election which, under the provisions of the Reform Act, could not come until November.

---

[1] Quoted in A. B. Cooke and John Vincent: *The Governing Passion*, 251.

CHAPTER THREE

THE HOME RULE CRISIS, 1885-1886

IN ATTEMPTING to dissect and describe a major political crisis the historian must be careful not to impose order and coherence, either in actions or individual motives, upon a human and confused business. This warning has particular application to the series of events which occurred between June 8th, 1885 and June 8th, 1886, and which together may be described as The Home Rule Crisis. No one at the time could forecast its course or outcome. Few, with the exception of Parnell—who nonetheless made at least one major miscalculation—took a consistent course. It can only be seen as a hectic struggle for political superiority in circumstances which no one had anticipated and which were unfamiliar to all participants. It brought old opponents into unexpected and uncomfortable alliance; it permanently ruptured former associations; and it transformed the nature of modern British politics. But few who were actually involved in the battle appreciated the scale of the stakes until it was over. The Conservatives won, and on balance narrowly deserved to, but were left with problems even greater than they had faced at the outset.

By June 1885, when the Gladstone Government was defeated, the political situation still greatly favoured the Liberals, and it was widely assumed that the increase in the franchise would increase this advantage when the General Election came in November. The Liberal organisation had decayed badly since 1880, but that of the Conservatives was in even worse condition; the appointment of 'Captain' Middleton[1] as National Agent in March 1885 was to produce considerable results, but these were not yet evident. In terms of policy, both major parties were divided and leaderless. No one knew how long Gladstone would continue in public life, nor how serious were his

[1] Richard William Evelyn Middleton, 1846–1905. Served in the Royal Navy 1860–77. Conservative Agent for West Kent 1883–4.

frequently expressed yearnings for retirement. The Conservatives had
no leader at all. Salisbury was unknown quantity in many respects,
and his particular brand of patrician High Church Conservatism
seemed highly inappropriate to the new conditions. Northcote was
clearly out of the running, although he himself did not realise it.
Churchill was too young and too new, and aroused at least as much
antipathy as enthusiasm. The remaining relics of the Beaconsfield era
evoked little interest, excitement, or respect. The Liberals at least had
considerable talent, while in these terms the condition of the Conservatives appeared absolutely forlorn. Through a series of startling
circumstances this balance was to be dramatically transformed.

Few of the Conservative leaders shared Lord Randolph's exaltation
at the fall of the Liberal Administration, and Churchill himself quickly
had second thoughts. Salisbury was particularly unenthusiastic. 'To
have to govern six months with a hostile but dying Parliament', he had
written on June 7th, 'is the very worst thing that can happen to us.'
When the Government was defeated and Gladstone announced his
intention to resign he wrote to Cranbrook that 'The prospect before us
is very serious. The vote on Monday night was anything but a subject
for congratulation.' The Conservative recollections of the events of
1873 were very sharp, when Gladstone had resigned but Disraeli had
declined to form an Administration and the Liberals had resumed
office, and had lurched towards ignominious defeat. The general
inclination of the Conservative leaders—with the exception of Northcote—was to follow Disraeli's example, but recognised that it would be
difficult to do so if the Queen asked them to form a Government and
Gladstone adamantly persisted in his resignation. Furthermore, there
was the factor of the rank and file, exhilarated by its achievement and
eager for office under almost any circumstances. And there was also
the unspoken but real query about what Lord Randolph would do
and say if the chance were not taken.

In spite of Salisbury's hesitations, it is clear that by June 11th he had
made up his mind to accept the Queen's Commission if it came to him,
as come it did. Northcote, who had believed until that moment that
he would be called to Balmoral, could not conceal his mortification.
Northcote had some reason for his chagrin. The Queen had written
to him on May 15th, 1881 to say that '*she* will look on Sir Stafford
Northcote as the Leader of the great Conservative Party, though it
may not be necessary to *announce* this *now*, and she wished that Sir

Stafford, who is so old and kind a friend, should *know* this'. But, as the Queen herself recognised, the situation had changed greatly by 1885. At Balmoral, Salisbury was very careful not to refuse to form a Government, while emphasising the difficulties under which a minority government would have to work. He returned to London to endeavour to form an administration.

The principal difficulty concerned Northcote and Churchill. The latter, who at this stage went into virtual seclusion, would accept no office if Northcote remained in the Commons, and Sir Michael Hicks-Beach—albeit with considerable unhappiness—supported him. Churchill cancelled all engagements and was virtually incommunicado. Faced with this impasse, some of the leading Conservatives argued that the 1873 option should be tried again, but Salisbury described such a course as 'abandoning the Queen'. At this point, on June 15th, Northcote suffered a major humiliation when Churchill, Gorst, and Wolff refused to accept his guidance on the Lords' amendments to the Redistribution Bill, arguing that they could not be considered until the ministerial crisis was resolved. Beach supported them—almost certainly without realising the full implications—and in the ensuing division the Opposition was hopelessly split. Northcote's bitterness and depression are fully understandable; 'the Queen's passing me over without a word of sympathy or regret is not pleasant'. In his diary he wrote: 'I have offered either to do this [First Lord and Leader of the House of Commons] or go to the Upper House, taking the India Office. I have offered to do whatever he [Salisbury] thinks best. I have not much heart in the matter. This has apparently been my last night in the House of Commons.'

It was obvious that things could not go on in this chaotic manner. On the following morning Churchill ended his period of withdrawal and saw Salisbury. Matters were settled to the satisfaction of both. Churchill would take the India Office, Salisbury would be Foreign Secretary as well as Prime Minister, Northcote would go to the Lords as First Lord of the Treasury, with the title of the Earl of Iddesleigh, Beach would lead the Commons, and Lord Carnarvon—whom Churchill had wanted excluded—would become Viceroy of Ireland. Northcote wrote of Churchill that 'he has practically got rid of me, and now he will prove a thorn in the side of Salisbury and Beach'. Salisbury had handled the crisis with considerable skill, but had not enjoyed the experience, which he described to G. E. Buckle as 'a revelation to me of the baser side of human nature'; to Cranbrook he was even more frank, and not least about the performance of Lord Randolph Churchill.

The final difficulty concerned arrangements with the Liberals for the passage of essential business, and the putative Conservative Government nearly never took office at all while these matters were being argued. But on June 23rd, two weeks after the fateful division on the Budget, the matter was settled, and what Chamberlain derided as 'the Ministry of Caretakers' formally took office.

From this point there was a very striking change in Irish attitudes. Churchill was an avowed opponent of the Crimes Bill, which was allowed to lapse. Carnarvon's ideas on resolving the Irish Question not only involved a policy of greater conciliation but were not dissimilar to Chamberlain's aborted 'Central Board' scheme and, indeed, went further. Salisbury was very uneasy, but permitted Carnarvon to continue his discussions.

In this atmosphere the Irish attitude towards the Liberals, and particularly Chamberlain, notably hardened. *United Ireland*, which had described Chamberlain as 'a sort of shop-keeping Danton' now strongly opposed a proposed visit to Ireland by Chamberlain and Dilke in insulting terms, and Cardinal Manning was cold to the idea. Archbishop Walsh, the new Archbishop of Dublin, refused to arrange any introductions as this 'would be interpreted as hostile to the excellent tenor and promise of Lord Carnarvon's conservative regime'. It was a very curt rebuff, and Chamberlain reacted sharply. He was preparing his own radical programme, the celebrated 'unauthorised programme', and as an immediate response to the way the Irish had treated him he dropped local self-government for Ireland from the list of his reforms. Chamberlain was a dangerous man to cross, as the Irish were to discover.

Meanwhile, Carnarvon was making some apparent progress. On August 1st he saw Parnell in an empty house in Mayfair (15 Hill Street), and found the Irish leader 'singularly moderate'. These discussions also impressed Parnell, and paved the way to his public advice on November 21st for the Irish voters 'to vote against the men who coerced Ireland'. Salisbury and Churchill, however, were becoming very uneasy. Salisbury—who had written, and firmly believed, that Home Rule threatened 'the highest interests of the Empire'— wrote to the Queen that 'he entirely agrees with Your Majesty in thinking that the nationalists cannot be trusted and that any bargain with them would be full of danger'.

Churchill was not aware of the extent of Carnarvon's discussions, and although he was a strong advocate of conciliation he baulked at anything approaching Home Rule. He was also acutely aware of the tactical political situation, and was convinced that the Nationalist movement contained so many mutually antagonistic elements that it could not hold together for long. Carnarvon was a highly intelligent and sensitive man, and as a result of his experience with the Canadian federation, and despite the failure of the federal proposal in South Africa, was a convinced believer in the concept of self-government within carefully prescribed limits. In other circumstances his venture might have had some chance of success; in the atmosphere of 1885, after all that had happened since 1880, and with a General Election imminent, there was very little. Nonetheless, the tone of his public statements and his conduct in Dublin led many people—and not excluding Gladstone—to believe that the Conservative Government was embarked upon a major change of British policy.

This impression was confirmed on July 17th, when Parnell moved for a new enquiry into the Maamtrasna murders of 1882. Beach was extremely cautious, but Gorst and Churchill made inflammatory speeches which were condemnatory of Spencer's administration and which particularly aroused the Ulster Conservatives, who were becoming very unhappy indeed about the trend of Government attitudes. Carnarvon was indignant, the Queen was dismayed, and Salisbury's diplomacy was exercised to calm them down. To the agitated Liberals, unaware of the divisions within the Government, this episode appeared to be clear evidence of a compact between the Conservatives and the Irish. On the same day Lord Ashbourne introduced a new Land Purchase Bill for Ireland which provided grants from the exchequer for tenants wishing to borrow money at relatively low interest for the purchase of their land. It was, as Ashbourne admitted, a modest proposal, but it was welcomed by Parnell and seemed to the increasingly alarmed Liberals to be another significant indication. The Irish Educational Endowments Bill and the Labourers' Bill, both of which became law before the end of the session, deeply confirmed this impression.

These overtures, far from being the Machiavellian intrigue that the Liberals believed them to be, were in fact unco-ordinated and formed no part of an agreed and coherent strategy. Ministers were, in fact, deeply divided, and confused. Churchill, for example, did not know of the Carnarvon-Parnell meeting until 1887, and Salisbury informed neither the Queen nor the Cabinet of this discussion. Parnell, reasonably, had assumed that Carnarvon was speaking with much greater authority than he had been. The revival of agrarian crime in Ireland alarmed Ministers, and particularly Ashbourne, but Carnarvon persistently minimised its significance. The 1885 harvest had been disastrous in parts of Ireland, and the old methods of refusal to pay rents, boycotting, and houghing of cattle had been revived.

The Conservatives began to feel trapped. Many believed that an unequivocal denunciation of Home Rule was essential if their supporters and the Ulster Conservatives were not to stampede. Salisbury personally agreed with the principle, but had his eye on the election. Carnarvon did not even agree with the principle. Churchill was obsessed by the tactical possibilities. Ashbourne and Cranbrook had become converts to coercion. On October 7th Salisbury delivered a major speech at Newport which was a classic of vagueness on Irish matters, and in which he spoke with calculated ambiguity of the creation of 'a large central authority' to prevent injustices from being perpetrated on the minorities by the Catholic majority. He had not endorsed Home Rule nor the principle of an Irish Parliament, but his studied imprecision persuaded the Liberals that he had and the Conservatives that he had not.

Gladstone had observed these movements with care, but ascribed to them a greater coherence of policy than in fact existed. Carnarvon had now become a devotee of a form of Home Rule, but there was no possibility of putting this past Salisbury, let alone the Cabinet. Carnarvon offered his resignation, but Salisbury was able to stall any decision. Gladstone resolved upon inaction, and to wait upon events. 'It is right I should say', he had written to Mrs. O'Shea on August 8th, 'that into any counter-bidding of any sort against Lord R. Churchill I for one cannot enter.' There was very little he could offer short of a full-blooded commitment to Home Rule, which had been already denounced by the improbable coalition of Chamberlain and Hartington.

*

Historians have often pondered on what Gladstone's preoccupations and concerns were in the six months which elapsed between the resignation of his second Government and his actions in December 1885. He spent virtually all of this period at Hawarden, was studiously occupied in research and correspondence which had little connection with contemporary politics, and what public observations he made were carefully Delphic. He made no public speech at all between the beginning of July and the beginning of November. Visitors came to Hawarden, but they were treated with great caution. His colleagues were baffled and offended, his opponents increasingly alarmed.

The truth was much less complicated. As has been emphasised before, Gladstone was not an innovator but a responder, and in 1885 he was temporarily lost—an affliction which strikes politicians of far less sensitivity than Gladstone at regular intervals. He entertained no dark schemes nor nourished any deep jealousies. Lost and puzzled, he waited upon events, and in the meanwhile employed his enormous energies in intellectual pursuits while awaiting political events. He was politically obsessed by Ireland, but this was not his only political preoccupation in these difficult months.

His relationship with Chamberlain had never been smooth. Although Chamberlain had proved himself an able and imaginative Minister, and had been one of the few real successes of the Liberal Government, the gulf of attitude and philosophy between the two man had markedly widened since 1880. It was not simply that Chamberlain was evidently hard, cold, ambitious, and coveted Gladstone's position. Gladstone was a political realist, and understood such matters. Nor was it only a matter of age, or of differing viewpoints on public affairs. It came down to a question of personal dislike. Gladstone did not like Chamberlain, nor did he trust him; at this time, furthermore, he underestimated him. Gladstone was sceptical of Chamberlain's integrity and capacity, and had already come to the conclusion that he was an opportunist without principle. This opinion was now fortified by Chamberlain's 'unauthorised programme', which was set forth in *The Radical Programme* and blazoned in a series of massively attended and widely reported speeches.

These were very good speeches indeed, delivered with a belligerence and style which Chamberlain had never achieved before. Much of the belligerence was delivered against his colleagues, notably Hartington, who was compared to Rip Van Winkle. 'If we cannot convince our allies of the justice and reasonableness of our views, then, with whatever reluctance, we must part company; we will fight alone; we will appeal unto Caesar; we will go to the people from whom we came and whose cause we plead.' In the midst of assaults upon his colleagues and 'the convenient cant of selfish wealth' there was a strong denunciation of Parnell (Warrington, September 8th) which was the first public sign of Chamberlain's anger at the rebuff that he had received.

The trouble was that the 'unauthorised programme', although cautious in its strategy—as Chamberlain explained, 'I am putting the rights of property on the only firm and defensible basis. I believe that the danger to property lies in its abuses'—was couched in vehement language, and some of its proposals were appalling to other Liberals. Items such as free primary education and local government for the counties were controversial—particularly the former—but the concept of much greater State intervention and the implicit abolition of *laissez-faire* were rather different. Iddesleigh, rather unexpectedly, denounced Chamberlain as 'Jack Cade', and Salisbury described him as 'a Sicilian bandit'. What was more ominous was the silence from Hawarden, broken by a manifesto which on the land issue demonstrated much more sympathy with the viewpoint of Hartington than of Chamberlain.

Chamberlain had launched his great effort without consultation with Gladstone, and by his language had achieved the alienation both of Parnell and Hartington. With the election looming, such conduct could only be interpreted by the Liberal leader in a hostile sense, and it was thus interpreted. Chamberlain, like many overtly ambitious self-made men on the make, was acutely sensitive. He was keenly resentful of any slight, real or imagined, and he hugged his grievances fiercely. He was vain and egotistical. But, as Beatrice Webb has rightly remarked, his 'intense sensitiveness to his own wrongs was not tempered by a corresponding sensitiveness to the feelings and the rights of others'. In Chamberlain's complex character the element of self-righteousness was very strong. His mind ranged neither wide nor deep. It was a precise instrument for dealing with defined problems and providing defined solutions. He was not a man given to doubts or qualifications. His private letters faithfully echo his public speeches. He simplified issues not because he was capable of making complex matters clear, but because his own understanding of them was simplistic. He was thus able to present them starkly and dramatically, because he saw them thus. The 'unauthorised programme' was a crude personal manifesto, but in the absence of any other one it achieved considerable attention. Chamberlain's vanity had been bitterly wounded by the Parnellite rejection; it was now inflamed by his large and enthusiastic audiences. These blinded him to the fact of his increasing isolation.

A visit to Hawarden early in October emphasised the gulf between Gladstone and Chamberlain. Nothing of real importance was discussed, both men were courteous but very careful. Gladstone had not liked the 'unauthorised programme', indeed he had a dislike for political programmes, preferring to discover some great central cause—as in the assault on 'Beaconsfieldism' in 1879–80—rather than a detailed programme which involved prior commitments. 'The unforeseen sometimes does much in politics', he wrote several years later, and in October 1885 it is clear that Gladstone was cautiously waiting upon events, increasingly convinced that 'a question of Irish government may come up with such force and magnitude as to assert its precedence over everything else'. But, although he told Chamberlain that 'he had an instinct that Irish questions might elbow out all others', he did not confide in him. Indeed, it is doubtful whether he had himself come to a definite conclusion at that stage. Gladstone wrote to the Queen that he 'recently thought it would be well to invite him [Chamberlain] to Hawarden, with a view to personal communication, which has now been effected, he thinks with advantage'.

It was a wary, uncomfortable, formality. Chamberlain's supporters subsequently blamed Gladstone harshly for not letting the younger man into his confidence, and not revealing the trend of his thinking. Throughout his life, Gladstone had been solitary when coming to momentous decisions; at this time he could have seen little value in exchanging confidences with a man who had launched his own campaign without discussion, let alone approval, on the eve of a major election. But Chamberlain's admirers, like Chamberlain himself, wanted it both ways. It was not the least of the factors that made Gladstone so suspicious and uneasy in Chamberlain's presence.

Meanwhile, the Unauthorised Programme blazed across the empty Liberal firmament, excoriated by Tory and Whig alike, and then, on November 21st, Parnell made his advice to the Irish electors plain. It was not to vote for the Conservatives, but to vote against the Liberals. With that declaration the plans both of Gladstone and Chamberlain had to be severely revised.

*

Chamberlain's political isolation was now augmented by a startling event.

Dilke's reputation had been considerably enhanced in office, and although he lacked the power-base of Chamberlain or the glamour of Rosebery, he was, like them, spoken of widely as a possible future Liberal leader. Dilke was in many respects an unattractive man, lacking intellectual or political originality, and was certainly a dull speaker, but he was very able, an assiduous worker and had a genuine following. Asquith wrote of him that 'his memory was over-stocked with detail, and there was a lack of the sense of proportion in his voluminous encyclopedia of political knowledge . . . this often gave an air of pedantry to really good stuff'.[1] He was not particularly liked by his colleagues, but he clearly was a force to be reckoned with among the rising Liberals.

In August 1885 Donald Crawford, Liberal M.P. for Lanark, instituted divorce proceedings against his young wife, citing Dilke as co-respondent on his wife's confession of adultery with him. Dilke described it as 'a false charge . . . made by conspiracy and careful preparation', and there were certainly some very suspicious elements involved. Mrs. Crawford's mother (Mrs. Eustace Smith) had once been Dilke's lover and her sister was the widow of Dilke's brother. Crawford's solicitor was the brother of a Mrs. Rogerson, who adjudged herself wronged by Dilke and who had written one of the anonymous letters that had caused Crawford's confrontation with his wife. There seems little doubt that Mrs. Crawford was a consummate liar in the witness box, and that she was also protecting another lover. But although this combination of women and one man who knew a great deal about Dilke and had good cause to wish to destroy him points to a conspiracy, Dilke's life was not unblemished. He was widely known as a man with 'a reputation'. Edward Hamilton wrote in his diary when the rumours of the divorce were circulating that 'it does not surprise anyone who knows Dilke. He is extraordinary free and easy with ladies'.

When the case came up in February 1886 the evidence against Dilke —the sole alleged co-respondent—was dismissed with costs, but Crawford was given his decree nisi, a decision which may have been justified in law but which baffled observers. Far more serious had been the decision of Dilke's counsel not to put him into the witness-box, on

[1] Earl of Oxford and Asquith: *Memories and Reflections*, pp. 154-5.

the grounds that 'in the life of any man there may be found to have
been some indiscretions'. The implications of this explanation were
clear, and Dilke found that although acquitted by the Court he had
been condemned outside it. In these circumstances there could be no
question of him being offered office in a Liberal Government, and he
was advised to invoke the intervention of the Queen's Proctor to re-
open the case. This second case, held in July, was disastrous. The
burden of proof was now on Dilke, and he and his counsel were
unable to shake Mrs. Crawford's detailed and sensational account of
their relationship. The jury took only fifteen minutes to decide that
they believed Mrs. Crawford's version, and Dilke was ruined. He had
just lost his Chelsea seat, and for a time there was even talk of him
being removed from the list of Privy Councillors and arraigned for
perjury. Although he returned to the House of Commons in 1892 for
the Forest of Dean and remained a Member until his death in 1911,
he never again held office nor exerted any political influence.

While it is difficult to disagree with the verdict of Dilke's most
recent biographer that 'he was the victim of a conspiracy, the main
lines of which (and, indeed, the identity of the other participants in
which) are shrouded in mystery and are likely always so to remain',[1]
the strong probability is that it was not a political but a personal
conspiracy. It is also possible that although the bulk of Mrs. Crawford's
story may have been false, the basic fact that Dilke had seduced her
may well have been true—which would help to explain why she
never withdrew her story after she had undergone a religious conversion to Catholicism and devoted herself to a life of good works.

To contemporaries, the matter was clear. Dilke had denied on oath
that he had been Mrs. Crawford's lover; a jury had decided otherwise.
He was branded as an adulterer and a perjurer and was, for practical
political purposes, finished. Chamberlain's one major ally in the
Liberal leadership had been removed.

*

The precise impact of the Irish vote outside Ireland on the 1885
General Election remains a matter of conjecture and controversy. To
a remarkable degree, in the light of later events, Ireland was hardly

[1] Roy Jenkins: *Sir Charles Dilke—A Victorian Tragedy*. The question of the alleged
involvement of the Roseberys in a conspiracy is discussed in the author's biography
of Rosebery, pp. 181-9.

mentioned at all in the English, Scottish, and Welsh campaigns and manifestos. Gladstone's Manifesto read:

> To maintain the supremacy of the Crown, the unity of the Empire, and all the authority of Parliament necessary for the conservation of that unity is the first duty of every representative of the people. Subject to this governing principle, every grant to portions of the county of enlarged powers for the management of their own affairs is, in my view, not a source of danger but a means of averting it, and is in the nature of a new guarantee for increased cohesion, happiness, and strength. History will consign to disgrace the name of every man who, having it in his power, does not aid but prevents or retards an equitable settlement between Ireland and Great Britain.

Three days before Parnell's pronouncement, the Bishop of Neath issued a denunciation of the Radicals as being 'fanatically anti-Christian', seizing upon the Chamberlainite advocacy of 'free schools' which had also aroused the condemnation of Cardinal Manning. There seems no reason to doubt the validity of the argument that these influences were very strong in the anti-Liberal vote in the cities in the election.[1] With Gladstone uncharacteristically quiescent—although calling in Midlothian for a majority independent of the Irish Nationalists—and with Chamberlain and Hartington in dispute, the Conservatives had an advantage which they seized in the cities.

Lord Randolph's campaign against Bright in Birmingham aroused the greatest excitement, and although Churchill was defeated (he was elected for South Paddington in the same election) and Birmingham remained solidly Liberal, elsewhere the Conservatives did very well, winning 116 out of the 226 borough constituencies, and there were high expectations of an overall Conservative victory. In the counties, however, the results of the new Reform Act strongly favoured the Liberals, and the pledge for free allotments—'Three acres and a cow', as it was derided by the Conservatives—played a part.[2] It was a considerable, and very significant reversal of the previous pattern. The final result was deadlock, with Parnell holding the balance. The

---

[1] See C. H. D. Howard, 'The Parnell Manifesto of 21 November 1885 and the Schools Question', *English Historical Review*, January 1947.

[2] Although probably not as great as was believed at the time (see H. Pelling: *Popular Politics and Society in Late Victorian Britain*, pp. 6–7.)

Conservatives were 249, the Liberals 335, and the Parnellite Irish 86. This time the latter were all Parnellites; by an overwhelming majority, Ireland had voted for Home Rule. Not a single Liberal was returned for an Irish constituency, sixteen Ulster Conservatives winning in the North.

A very confused period followed, while the politicians endeavoured to analyse the significance of the results and their immediate implications. Salisbury and Churchill, now increasingly concerned by Carnarvon's activities, were not enthusiastic for remaining in office unless they could attract some of the leading Liberals, notably Hartington and G. J. Goschen, but Salisbury—unlike Churchill—was firmly opposed to the idea of a coalition. Salisbury's opinion of Gladstone was that he was 'mad to take office, and that this will force him into some line of conduct which will be discreditable to him and disastrous, if we do not prematurely gratify his hunger'. Churchill also flirted seriously with Chamberlain—or, at least, made it seem serious —while in the Liberal ranks there was comparable confusion. Hartington, who had accused Parnell of exercising 'a grinding and widespread despotism' in Ireland, had now been the putative Liberal Prime Minister for ten years, and the strain was showing. Chamberlain's ambitions were very high. Goschen was intriguing actively for the creation of a new coalition party. The only event of major significance achieved by the Government—and it was almost ignored at the time—was the British annexation of Upper Burma in December after a swift military operation which had deposed King Theebaw and put his supporters to flight. This brought the whole of Burma under British rule, and was a significant extension of British power and influence in Asia and a check to French ambitions in Burma. For the Minister responsible it was another triumph, and Lord Randolph's reputation had risen further.

At this point Gladstone broke—or appeared to do so—his long and baffling silence on the Irish Question. On December 16th his son Herbert, sharing the suspicions of Chamberlain's motives and ambitions felt by Wemyss Reid, editor of the *Leeds Mercury*, gave the National Press Agency information concerning his father's altered views on Ireland and which implied that he had become converted to the principle of accepting Home Rule. It was stated that Gladstone would take office 'with a view to the creation of an Irish Parliament to be entrusted with the entire management of all legislative and administrative affairs, securities being taken for the representation of minorities and for an equitable partition of all imperial changes'.

Gladstone issued a denial that was so ambiguous, no doubt intentionally, that the confusion was augmented. Chamberlain and Hartington disassociated themselves publicly from this solution. Home Rule, in Salisbury's words, was converted at once from a chimera into a blazing issue. It completely eclipsed the Unauthorised Programme. The 'Hawarden Kite' did not greatly clarify the situation, but it gave the Conservatives their opportunity to depict Gladstone as a desperate man, intent on office at all costs. Chamberlain wrote to Dilke that 'my view is that Mr. G's Irish scheme is death and damnation; that we must try and stop it—that we must not openly commit ourselves against it yet—that we must let the situation shape itself before we finally decide'. Hartington complained to Granville in similar terms: 'Did any leader ever treat a Party in such a way as he has done?' Churchill and Salisbury, seeing the prospects before them suddenly becoming clearer, were resolved to pin Gladstone with Home Rule. From his close links with several Liberals—notably Labouchere—Churchill drew the conclusion, as he informed Salisbury, that 'the Radicals and the Irish want Home Rule, they know they cannot get it without Gladstone, Gladstone will give it and they go for him with all their strength and without risk of losing Joe and they calculate that their Whig falling off will be more than compensated for by the eighty-seven (sic) Irish votes'. This was a fair summation of a very confused situation. 'I fancy that a large number, perhaps the majority, of Liberals will support *any* scheme of Mr. G's', Chamberlain wrote to Dilke.

On December 15th Gladstone had gone to Eaton Hall, the grandiosely Gothic and gloomy seat of the Duke of Westminster, to see Balfour, who was a house-guest. His purpose was to urge a non-partisan approach to the Irish Question, with the co-operation on the Reform Act very much in mind. In this assumption he had been seriously misled by Canon Malcolm MacColl, the intermediary in the Reform Bill negotiations, that Salisbury was 'prepared to go as far probably as yourself on the question of Home Rule, but he seemed hopeless as to the prospect of carrying his party with him.' MacColl had himself not realised that Gladstone favoured an Irish Parliament—a key factor in the fundamental misunderstanding which led Gladstone to make his overture.

Gladstone argued to Balfour in his Eaton Hall discussion and in later correspondence that Home Rule had to be granted to prevent a resurgence of violence in Ireland, that the matter should not 'fall into the lines of party conflict', and that the Government should deal with the question.

There was no question of the Conservatives falling into what they regarded as a crude and obvious trap. Salisbury was intent on averting a break-up of his party, which he foresaw—rightly—as the obvious consequence of endorsing a policy of separation; Churchill had always made it clear that, although very prepared to conciliate Ireland, and to go a considerable distance in meeting legitimate Irish aspirations for self-government, Home Rule was an impossibility. The Conservative Party would not tolerate it, and he knew that the Protestants in Ulster would not.

Churchill was subsequently often blamed for discovering, if not actually creating, the Ulster hostility to Home Rule. The fact was that he was one of the very few English politicians who knew anything about Irish politics, and his brilliant exploitation of the simmering anger in the North was only that. He wrote to his old friend Justice FitzGibbon on February 16th that 'I decided some time ago that if the G.O.M. went for Home Rule, the Orange card would be the one to play. Please God it may turn out the ace of trumps and not the two'. This has been often seized upon to demonstrate Churchill's cynical irresponsibility in declaring that 'Ulster will fight, Ulster will be right'. What he did in fact was to give English Conservative leadership to a movement which would have found its leader in any event, and his action was to link the Ulster cause with that of his party for generations, as was Gladstone's espousal of Home Rule to link the Liberals with the Nationalists. In the context of 1886 it was only one element in the battle to defeat Home Rule; its full significance only emerged later.

If the Conservative leaders now saw their way clear, it was very largely because of their gleeful awareness of the deep fisures now opening in the Liberal coalition. Gladstone's aloofness and lack of leadership in the preceding months had demoralised much of the rank and file. Parnell said little, and bided his time. The Liberals who had lived through the awful vicissitudes of the Irish Question since 1880 and had seen the Irish vote turned against them in the 1885 election were not only confused but bitter. There was a wild mood in the

Liberal Party, and the Conservatives hastened to exploit it. Parnell, also, was having problems of his own. As T. P. O'Connor had been elected for two constituencies, there was a vacancy at Galway. O'Shea, who had been defeated in his bid for a Liverpool seat in the election despite the support of Chamberlain and Parnell, wanted Galway. Parnell decided to support his candidature, to the shock and anger of the local Nationalists. Eventually Parnell got his way, but not after a considerable amount of public unpleasantness which was eagerly picked up in London.

For a time the Conservatives were themselves acutely divided about how to act. 'I am feverishly anxious to be out', Salisbury wrote early in January. 'Internally as well as externally our position as a Government is intolerable.' Churchill was embittered and distressed by the rejection of a proposal for the projected Queen's Speech and had to be soothed, and then he and Beach, anxious to maintain Irish goodwill, threatened resignation unless a prepared coercion bill were dropped. Carnarvon's resignation was at length accepted, but acute disagreements arose over his successor, and the matter was still undetermined when the Government fell. In the end Churchill and Beach were placated, the Queen's Speech anticipated coercive measures in vague terms but was explicitly hostile 'to any disturbance of that fundamental law' (the legislative Union), and on January 26th Beach announced to the House of Commons—which had reassembled on the 21st[1]—the Government's intention.

The actual debate that evening was on an Opposition amendment to the Queen's Speech deploring the absence of any provision in it for the agricultural workers. It was a weird, carefully staged, occasion, Members speaking of allotments and peasant proprietors while behind them loomed the stark issue of Home Rule. The Government, accepting the Amendment as a vote of confidence, was duly defeated by seventy-nine votes, but Hartington, Goschen, and Sir Henry James were among the eighteen Liberals who supported it in the lobbies, and seventy-six Liberals abstained. The Conservatives—Salisbury carefully rejecting an appeal from the Queen for a dissolution—resigned the

---

[1] Bradlaugh had been re-elected for Northampton—for the fifth time—but when Beach raised the matter Mr. Speaker Peel emphatically ruled that he was entitled to take his seat and refused to accept the decisions of the previous Parliament. On January 27th 1891 the House expunged from its records the Bradlaugh Resolution of June 22nd 1880, three days before Bradlaugh's death.

next day, and left Gladstone, by now highly excited, to form an Administration as best he could.

The extent of the Liberal schism now became truly evident. Hartington, James, Goschen and Bright would not serve. Dilke was, as Gladstone curtly noted, 'unavailable'. Chamberlain was offered, and reluctantly accepted, the Presidency of the Local Government Board, having asked for and been denied the Colonial Office, and did so on the understanding that he would give 'an unprejudiced examination' to Gladstone's proposals. Harcourt went to the Treasury, John Morley, after only three years in the Commons, became Irish Secretary, and Rosebery became Foreign Secretary at the age of thirty-seven—an advancement which he quickly justified. But, compared with the previous Liberal Government, it was markedly undergunned, and lost more vital artillery when Chamberlain and George Trevelyan resigned on March 15th.

Chamberlain's links with Churchill had grown stronger since the Hawarden Kite, but it seems very probable that Gladstone could have retained him if he had tried. He did not try at all, and while it is going too far to conclude that he deliberately provoked Chamberlain's resignation he was not displeased when that event occurred. It was to prove a very costly misjudgement. On April 8th Gladstone introduced his 'Bill for the Better Government of Ireland' in an atmosphere of intense excitement and in a speech of over three and a half hours which was one of his most superb performances. This event in itself checked the confidence of the Conservatives and sent a ripple of political apprehension through the ranks of the hostile Liberals.

Gladstone's proposal was to establish an Irish Parliament and executive in Dublin which would have overall control but for certain specific reserved subjects, and Irish representation at Westminster would be ended. It was this proposal on which Chamberlain fastened, and caused the Government the greatest difficulty. When Gladstone offered to withdraw it, he laid himself open to the charge that the Irish M.P.s would have in effect two votes. Neither on this occasion, nor in 1893, was Gladstone able to devise a formula that satisfied his supporters or his wavering critics in his party. But the Bill as a whole was a remarkable tribute to Gladstone and his colleagues, particularly Morley. The 'reserved' subjects were very considerable, and would have made the reality of Home Rule considerably less than the independence for which the Irish had been agitating, and the attempts to protect the Protestant minority in the proposed Irish legislature resulted in so complicated an arrangement that it is difficult to see how it could have worked without intense difficulty and friction. The interests of Ulster were inadequately appreciated and met. But, given the situation and the shortage of time, the Bill was a very formidable achievement and received the qualified—but firm—endorsement of Parnell.

Everything now depended upon the dissident Liberals. Hartington and Salisbury had met early in April at the Turf Club at Churchill's suggestion, but there was little possibility of, or enthusiasm for, a Conservative-Liberal Unionist alliance at this stage. But the key factor was a Conservative pledge not to oppose any Liberal who voted against Home Rule—a pledge which was, with difficulty in many constituencies, scrupulously observed.

At this point a digression is necessary.

The formation of the Conservative Central Office in 1870 had been a response to the recognition of the problems created by the enlarged electorate, and also in tribute to the success of the Liberal Registration Association, established in 1861, and to which the National Union of Conservative Associations, founded in 1867, had not been an adequate answer. John Gorst had been the first Principal Agent, and his main task had been to ensure that every constituency had a candidate and that the development of local associations be actively encouraged. Gorst also maintained a list of approved candidates for submission to associations. They were not obliged to accept these recommended candidates, but the development of this practice gave the party leader —to whom the Principal Agent reported directly—an influence over the composition of the Parliamentary party which, although very limited, was much greater than ever before. A Conservative Prime Minister, with the power of patronage and honours, who particularly desired the selection of a candidate, or who indicated his preference for a particular *type* of candidate, did not have to dictate to the associations. A hint was enough.

In 1886, with Middleton in firm control, Salisbury's pledge that the Liberal Unionists should be given a clear run against the Liberals could be duly honoured in eighty-seven constituencies (out of ninety-three). Operating out of his cramped little rooms in St. Stephen's Chambers, Middleton's spider-web ran to every constituency and every association, and it was well-known that he spoke for Lord

Salisbury, and a courteous request that a certain candidate be favourably considered, or another be rejected, was in most instances decisive. Thus, by 1886, having started much later than the Liberals, and having neglected their organisation badly for ten years, the Conservatives were far ahead of their opponents, and had established the general principles which dominated the Conservative organisation until after the Second World War.

Thus, at this critical moment, the Conservatives possessed the essential machinery to ensure that their pledges could be honoured.

*

On May 5th the committee of the National Liberal Federation supported Gladstone—save in Birmingham, where a bloody contest was decided in Chamberlain's favour—as did most of the local associations. The extraordinary cohesive power that Gladstone still exercised in the party had never been more dramatically demonstrated, and the dissidents found themselves fighting for their political lives. The appearance of Hartington and Salisbury on the same platform in London on April 14th grievously damaged Hartington's authority among his followers, and made the outcome even more in doubt.

But on May 12th, fifty-two Liberals met at Chamberlain's house, and, not uninfluenced by a letter opposing Home Rule from John Bright, resolved to vote against the second reading. On May 15th Salisbury appeared to have wrecked the possibility of Conservative co-operation with the dissident Liberals when he delivered a vehement speech in London in which he compared the Irish with the Hottentots as incapable of self-government and put forward the Conservative alternative to Home Rule as 'Government . . . honestly, consistently, and resolutely applied for twenty years'. The motives for this speech remain unclear. He was certainly expressing emotions which he had held— and expressed—for some time; it may be that he blurted out these feelings, insensitive to the trouble they would cause to the dissident Liberals; it is also possible that he was deliberately sabotaging the movement towards a Liberal government under Hartington with Conservative support.[1] In any event, the speech did not—as the Gladstonians had hoped—bring Liberal unity. Too much had happened too quickly, and the internecine bitterness was too intense.

[1] See A. B. Cooke and John Vincent: *The Governing Passion*, 81, for this interpretation.

In particular, the debates between Chamberlain and Gladstone were marked by a clear and profound antipathy, and Hartington's revulsion from Home Rule was expressed in speeches of very high quality and obvious sincerity. It is, of course, possible to see in these events a variety of personal factors, of jealousies and ambitions; but the reality was that Home Rule was one of those issues which in itself and in its implications was genuinely divisive. When it came to the final choice, many Liberals could not and would not endorse it. The formation of the Liberal Unionist Committee—which held its first meeting on May 20th—demonstrated that the rift was too wide to be bridged.

Despite a last-minute attempt by Gladstone to conciliate his critics at a party meeting at the Foreign Office on May 27th—neatly sabotaged by Beach and Churchill in an exchange in the House which left the waverers with the firm impression that Gladstone had not been straight with them—the die was cast. Early in the morning of June 8th, the debate, in which Parnell made a magnificent contribution, was ended by Gladstone in one of his greatest speeches:

> Ireland stands at your bar, expectant, hopeful, almost suppliant. Her words are the words of truth and soberness. She asks a blessed oblivion of the past, and in that oblivion our interest is deeper than ever hers. . . . So I hail the demand of Ireland for what I call a blessed oblivion of the past. She asks also a boon for the future. . . . Think, I beseech you, think well, think wisely, think not for a moment but for the years that are to come, before you reject this Bill.

Matters had gone too far for rhetoric or appeals. The packed House immediately divided, and in the subsequent Division the Bill was defeated by 341 votes to 311 amid scenes of pandemonium. Ninety-three Liberals had voted against the Bill, and both the tellers against the Bill were Liberals. As Chamberlain strode exultantly out of the Chamber Parnell called out 'There goes the man who killed Home Rule.' Ministers agreed unanimously to advise dissolution rather than to resign, and the battle was taken to the constituencies.

Although Home Rule was the dominant single issue in the General Election, elections are never fought on single issues alone, and the result can hardly be interpreted only as a massive rejection of Home Rule—except, of course, in Ulster, when there were ugly riots, principally in Belfast—and an overwhelming Conservative victory. What the election did do was to demonstrate the price which the Liberals had to pay for disunity; in 114 constituencies in England, Scotland, and Wales there were Liberal candidates in contention, and many of these contests were fought with great bitterness. In the counties, not only as a result of disillusionment with the neglect of attention to land matters after the heady visions of the previous autumn, but also as a consequence of much greater Conservative effort after the shock of 1885, the Liberal cause faltered badly.

The outstanding contribution on the Conservative side was Lord Randolph Churchill's ferocious onslaught on Gladstone in his Address to the Electors of Paddington, in which the Liberal leader was depicted as 'an old man in a hurry', and which deserves to be read in full as an example of sustained invective.[1]

The Conservatives were now beginning to reap some advantages from 'Captain' Middleton's management of party affairs, and the considerable increase in the size and membership of the Primrose League—the direct result of the combination of the Home Rule and 'Imperial' issues, and upon which the Conservative leaders sedulously played. Middleton worked quietly, almost single-handedly, and with very limited resources. His great advantage over Gorst was that he was uninterested in a political career for himself, was self-effacing, and was on very close terms with the leader. His major contribution was to bring some order into the selection of candidates and to improve the quality of those who were recommended by the party to local constituencies. He also instituted *The Constitutional Year Book*, which was published annually from 1885 until 1939, and which was an invaluable, very professional, and usually very objective compilation of facts and statistics primarily intended for candidates and the party but also generally available to the public. In this venture one can see the beginnings of the Conservative Research Department, which was not to be formally instituted until 1930. Middleton had made himself—and the development was to become much more marked in following years —virtually a one-man Central Office and Research Department, working very closely with Salisbury and the Government Whips, and beginning to provide a cohesion and organisation which had never existed before. In 1886 the party began to receive the first benefits from this important development.

[1] See Winston S. Churchill: *Lord Randolph Churchill* (1951 edition) Appendix.

The crucial feature of the Corrupt and Illegal Practices Act, 1883, was that it had made effective national organisation dependent upon voluntary and unpaid workers. The 1880 General Election had been very expensive indeed for both parties—the exact cost is impossible to estimate, but it is known that the Conservatives spent some £100,000 on fifty-five seats in the Midlands; under the new Act they would be limited to £37,000. In one constituency (Leicestershire North) the Conservatives had spent £6,306 for 3,369 votes.[1] It was evident that under the new financial restrictions the entire nature of fighting elections—excluding direct bribes the most significant expenditure was in many cases paid canvassers—had to be transformed. Thus, the voluntary party devotee who was prepared to give his own time to the service of the party between elections as well as during them suddenly became a central figure. The Conservatives recognised this at once, and the dramatic improvement in their political position was the direct result of their realisation that the day of the mass party had arrived. The extraordinary success of the Primrose League drove the point home. Salisbury keenly disliked this development, and was profoundly concerned at the real possibility that a party machine might develop which dominated Parliament and made its members 'enslaved by the caucus', but he recognised the new realities and developed them after his own manner. Thus, as the Conservative machine developed to a high point of efficiency, and the party became a mass party for the first time, a subtle but vital balance between the old and the new was created, and has endured.

Although the National Liberal Federation had stood by Gladstone, the loss of the Birmingham machine was harmful in the Midlands, and the party as a whole was in disarray. In these dismal circumstances the Liberals were fighting to retain their position rather than to win the contest.

In the event, the result was not a complete disaster for the Liberals. The Conservatives won 316 seats, the Gladstonian Liberals 191, with seventy-eight Liberal Unionists and eighty-five Parnellites (O'Shea having lost in Galway, not altogether surprisingly in view of the fact that he had voted against the Home Rule Bill).

Although the Liberal Unionists now held the balance, and Salisbury

---

[1] These figures were given in a talk by Mr. G. C. T. Bartley—who fell foul of Lord Randolph Churchill—to a party gathering in 1883, and are quoted in Robert Mackenzie, *British Political Parties*, 164.

went through the motions of proposing that Hartington take the
Premiership in a coalition administration, he knew full well that this
was a political impossibility—particularly as he had taken care to
emphasise that he would not serve in a Cabinet with Chamberlain.
Thus, after these formalities had been concluded, an exclusively
Conservative Government was formed, with Lord Randolph—aged
thirty-seven—elevated to Chancellor of the Exchequer and Leader of
the House of Commons and Iddesleigh, rather unexpectedly, Foreign
Secretary. Hicks Beach became Chief Secretary for Ireland, and W. H.
Smith went to the War Office. The only real surprise was the elevation,
on Lord Randolph's urgings, of the politically unknown Henry
Matthews as Home Secretary, which proved a most unfortunate
appointment. Otherwise, it was very much the mixture as before, with
the veteran Lord John Manners creakingly bearing the banner of
Disraelian Young England at the Duchy of Lancaster. The intellectual
and political domination of Salisbury and Churchill was total.

On August 3rd the new Cabinet proceeded to Osborne to kiss hands.
'How long will your leadership last?' Rosebery asked Churchill. 'Six
months'. 'And after that?' 'Westminster Abbey!'

Gladstone wrote in his diary (December 29th) that 'It has been a
year of shock and strain. I think a year of some progress; but of greater
absorption in interests which, though profoundly human, are quite off
the line of an old man's preparation for passing the River of Death. I
have not had a chance given me of creeping from this Whirlpool, for
I cannot abandon a cause which is so evidently that of my fellow-men,
and in which a particular part seems to be assigned to me.'

On these contradictory but characteristic notes this narrative of the
Home Rule Crisis of 1886 may be conveniently ended.

CHAPTER FOUR

CROSS-CURRENTS, 1886–1892

AUGUST 1886 found the Liberal Party, on the morrow of defeat and division, in confusion and perplexity. The loss of the Hartingtonian Whigs was perhaps tolerable, the defection of Chamberlain less so; what was most serious of all had been the rasping and bitter nature of the reproaches which the erstwhile colleagues had hurled at each other over the past months. Gladstone had described Chamberlain as a trimmer, while Morley compared the latter to 'the envious Casca'. Hartington had only narrowly survived at Rossendale, and Henry James had only just scraped through at Bury, both against Gladstonian candidates, an important factor in Hartington's refusal of Salisbury's offer.[1] Dilke was gone. The party was wholly committed to Gladstone's Irish policy, and its fortunes dependent upon it.

Home Rule, as a cause, was one which many Gladstonian Liberals regarded with actual distaste; most were indifferent to it. Although Rosebery and Harcourt—to take the most conspicuous examples—had followed Gladstone, neither was deeply committed to Home Rule, and Harcourt's dislike of the Irish in general and Parnell in particular was ill-concealed. A new generation of talented Liberals, including Edward Grey, R. B. Haldane, and H. H. Asquith, was impatient that this measure should so dominate Liberal thoughts and ambitions.

But for Gladstone, Home Rule was the only issue that kept him in public life, and in those years he thought of little else. The decline in his powers now became even more marked, and was accompanied with an increase in excitability which often clouded his judgement. He remained an astounding phenomenon, and his public meetings in the 1886 election reminded observers of the passion and frenzy of the

[1] Until 1918, newly appointed Ministers had to seek re-election. Normally they were unopposed, but it was evident that this convention would not be followed in these cases.

glories of Midlothian. Both in Parliament and in the country he was an outstanding and dominating figure, and he enjoyed an immense personal following in the Liberal Party. But it cannot seriously be denied that this amazing longevity and energy were a source of deep misfortune for the party which he had in effect created, and whose character and policies had been so notably shaped by his towering personality, sincerity, political skill, and passion. He was thus at one and the same time the Liberals' greatest asset and their most grievous liability. Until Home Rule was passed, or Gladstone passed on, the Liberals were inextricably linked to that issue. When it prospered, their cause prospered; when it was in decline, they were in decline. And in the meanwhile other projects of social reform were delayed, neglected, and impeded. On all sides, 'Ireland blocked the way'. Gladstone was enthusiastic for Home Rule, so was John Morley. The bulk of the party, seeing the terrible damage already inflicted upon it, and fearful of worse to come, rallied around Gladstone because he was Gladstone, and not because of Home Rule.

Another consequence of Gladstone's longevity and new obsession was the postponement of the question of the future leadership of the party. Hartington and Chamberlain had not wholly lost hope of a reunified Liberal Party, but their chances for the leadership had vanished in the fire and fury of the Home Rule battle. The perennial Harcourt, 'his eye fixed firmly, but by no means unerringly, on the main chance' in Winston Churchill's phrase, aroused little enthusiasm. Morley, although Gladstone's *fidus achates*, was too new. Rosebery, picked out by Gladstone himself as 'the man of the future', would have been the choice of most had he not been so young and also in the House of Lords. But the fact was that, whether consciously or not, Gladstone had not given the party an obvious and generally accepted successor. This in itself was to cause serious strains and tensions at the top, and to give the party as a whole a sense of uneasiness and insecurity for the future.

By this stage it was evident that the Home Rule issue was emotionally closely linked with the new Imperialistic fervour which was to become so evident in the later 1880s, and which had a striking public demonstration in the Golden Jubilee celebrations and the first Colonial Conference in 1887. The Jubilee was a surprising popular triumph for Queen Victoria, who had become a remote and almost mythical figure since the death of her husband more than twenty years earlier, and whose active involvement in political affairs was not widely known. The establishment of the Imperial Institute in Kensington, the Conference of the Colonial leaders, the great naval review at Spithead, and the popular excitement, troubled many Liberals, and particularly those who sympathised with the new mood and resented the political advantages going to the Conservatives and the still-expanding Primrose League. The division within the Liberal leadership over its attitude to Imperialism now became marked, and was to destroy much of its effectiveness over the next twenty years. Liberals like Harcourt, Morley, and Campbell-Bannerman shared Gladstone's suspicions of the new movement, and were implacably opposed to any further colonial commitments; others, of whom Rosebery was the most prominent, were defiantly self-styled Liberal Imperialists. The Conservatives' blatant linking of the issues of Imperialism and Home Rule, arguing with increasing confidence that to be an Imperialist Home Ruler was a contradiction in terms, also had its effect. Even at this stage there were present the divisions within the Party that were to have such fatal results in the 1890s and early 1900s.

Thus, in the short run, the Liberals were irretrievably committed to the Irish Home Rule cause. In the long run there was a fundamental division in the Party about its future course and on the attitudes it ought to adopt in changing circumstances. And, while the Liberals battled with these perplexing issues, a new political power was developing which was eventually to replace the old Liberal Party as the party of the Left. Any understanding of the rise of the Labour Party must begin with a realisation of the decline of the Liberals from 1886–1906 and the factors that caused that decline. In 1886 there was no such thing as a Labour Party. Twenty years later fifty-three Members of the House of Commons described themselves as 'Labour', of whom twenty-nine were members of the new Party.

*

For the Conservatives, 1886 had been an *annus mirabilis*. They had converted the minority of 1885 into a handsome majority. Their opponents were divided and dispirited. Although the leading Liberal Unionists refused to join the Conservative Government, and were initially cautious about their relationship with it, the political and social affinities were close, and were to become steadily closer. By 1892 the Unionist coalition was a definite political reality. For nearly twenty years after 1886 this coalition was to enjoy almost uninterrupted political supremacy.

The Unionist Alliance, although the direct result of the events of April–June 1886, was some time in developing. The leaders found difficulty in adjusting themselves to the new situation, and for the rank and file the early strains on the alliance were severe. Although it was evident to the dissident Liberals that their survival depended upon the support—or at least non-intervention—of the Conservatives in the constituencies, this did not mean Coalition in the full sense of the word. As Chamberlain wrote to Hartington:

Of course, I would not join any coalition; it would be absurd in me, and I need not argue it. With you it is somewhat different. You might join and be perfectly consistent. But if you do you must make up your mind to cease to be, or call yourself, a Liberal. The force of circumstances will be irresistible, and you will be absorbed in the Great Constitutional Party.

Thus, at least for a period, there was no formal alliance beyond an electoral compact, and many of the dissident Liberals hoped that when the issue of Home Rule was removed or settled, unity might be restored.

The Conservatives played the game carefully so as not to offend their new allies. The Local Government Act of 1888, for example, put into effect reforms that Chamberlain had been campaigning for since the early 1870s. The 1892 Education Act, providing free education in the public elementary schools of England and Wales, the most important legislation enacted by this Government, similarly owed much to Chamberlain's influence and work. But the most significant feature of the first years of the Unionist alliance was the extent to which Chamberlain, Hartington and the Conservatives found that their views were very similar on both domestic and foreign issues. Chamberlain's imperialist attitude were gradually emerging, and he was as alarmed as any Conservative by what he considered to be the confiscatory and aggressive features of socialist and trade union attitudes. To Balfour he wrote on December 8th, 1894:

The intermediates—the men who hold the balance of elections—are disgusted and frightened . . . at the projects of confiscation which are in the air and [which] found expression at the Trade Union Congress the other day.

Gladstone's 'Newcastle Programme' of 1891 seemed to embody all Chamberlain's fears about the new Radicalism, and this was probably the final and decisive moment in his permanent estrangement from the Liberal Party. The 'programme' contained compulsory land acquisition, universal suffrage, and measures for employers' liability. Chamberlain attacked the Newcastle Programme root and branch, and this was really the end of 'Radical Joe'. By February 1894, when he spoke at Leeds, he was emphatically estranged. The objectives, he declared in this speech, of the 'new Radical' were 'to merge the individual into the State, to reduce all to one dead level of uniformity, in which the inefficient and the thriftless and the idle are to be confounded and treated alike . . . with the honest, and the industrious, and the capable.'

But personal factors played a very important part, as the Irish Question entered a particularly virulent and bitter period. As Winston Churchill has written of Chamberlain:

> The Irish were his most persistent foes.[1] They added to British politics a stream of hatred all their own and belonging to centuries from which England has happily escaped. They knew that more than any other man he had broken Mr. Gladstone and frustrated Home Rule. The malignity of their resentment was unsurpassed by anything I have ever seen in this confused world. He retorted with scorn and long, slow, patient antagonism. He made them feel they had been right to hate him.

The duels that now developed between Chamberlain and Gladstone, who sat beside each other in the House of Commons in icy proximity, were more intense and personal than even the Disraeli-Gladstone confrontations of the '60s and '70s. Chamberlain ascended to new heights of debating skill: 'He never spoke like this for us', Gladstone once remarked after a Chamberlain speech. The failure of the 1887 'Round Table' Conference and the continuation of the Irish debate

---

[1] And not only the Irish, i.e. Labouchere at Bradford, November 1888: 'Mr. Chamberlain had thrown over his old colleagues because the Radicals would not help him to supplant Mr. Gladstone; he had been activated by hatred and envy, declared Mr. Labouchere. Mr. Chamberlain had been called Judas. He did not approve of historical comparisons; they were seldom exact. Judas had some good about him. He betrayed his Master, but he did not afterwards stump Judaea, dine with Herod, sup with Caiaphas, sing the praises of Pilate, appear on platforms surrounded by Scribes and Pharisees, and then declare that he alone of the Apostles was a true Christian.' (*Maccoby: English Radicalism 1886–1914*, 112).

put aside the possibility of an early reconciliation. The movement away from the Gladstonian Liberals was steady. At Glasgow, on February 13th 1889, Chamberlain emphasised the nature of the division:

> In my opinion every Liberal who places the Union first of all is bound to make some sacrifices for what will be his paramount object. He is bound to make some sacrifices of extreme views. He is bound to put aside for a time some of his cherished ambitions. This is an elementary condition of all combinations whatsoever.

But the historian who omits the personal element in this dispute omits the dispute itself. Gladstone and Chamberlain saw in each other what each feared in himself, and thus assailed. Much has been made of the attraction of opposites, too little of the revulsion between similars. This, for all their differences of backgrounds and philosophies, was the essential Chamberlain–Gladstone dispute.

As a consequence of many elements, the Liberal Unionists were being propelled inexorably towards formal and complete coalition with the Conservatives. Although this did not occur until 1895, the movement towards Coalition was steady after the great Liberal split of 1886.

*

The Conservatives, after their triumph, were not in the mood for further excitements, and settled down contentedly to a period of power tempered by the practical realisation that their survival depended upon the perpetuation of the Liberal division. It was a time for cohesion and care. Salisbury's distaste for Chamberlain personally as well as politically was profound, although he appreciated the need to placate and satisfy him. Churchill, on the other hand, regarded Chamberlain as a natural ally, and saw him frequently. This was not the only factor that was placing an increasingly unbearable strain upon the relationship between Salisbury and Churchill. Churchill, although he proved an able Minister and a much better Leader of the House than many had expected, was proving an overbearing colleague, and behaved with an air of arrogance and impatience which exasperated the Cabinet and taxed Salisbury's soothing skills to their limit. When Churchill started interfering in foreign policy and making major public speeches without consultation, Salisbury had had enough. It was simply a question of when, and on what issue, Churchill would make his fatal mistake. It came in December, just before Christmas, on the matter of economies in the estimates of the War Office.

Churchill, from a position of weakness, and without calculation, made claim to virtual equality in the Cabinet with Salisbury. He grossly misjudged his man, his issue, and his occasion. He threatened to resign unless his demands over the War Office estimates were met. Salisbury in effect accepted his resignation, but carefully not in so many words. Churchill, trapped, was faced with the alternative of climbing down or actually resigning. When he, inevitably, chose the latter, and informed *The Times* of the fact, the Government tottered but did not fall. Churchill found himself in political desolation, his admirers appalled and baffled, his friends astounded and offended, and his many enemies exultantly merciless. Too late he realised the fact that his opponent had completely out-manoeuvred him, and that Salisbury was both a wily and a hard man. In retrospect, we can see that it was hardly a fair contest. 'His character', Salisbury wrote of Churchill, as if in dissection of a distant acquaintance who had aroused his dissatisfaction, 'moreover is quite untamed. Both in impulsiveness and variability, and in a tendency which can only be described by the scholastic word 'vulgaris', he presents the characteristics of extreme youth.' There was truth in this harsh estimate. Churchill had received many warnings but, in the continued exhilaration of his meteoric rise, had ignored them. Salisbury, eyeing him closely, had awaited the moment when Churchill's impetuosity and vanity would put him at his mercy, and then struck with cold efficiency.

Nonetheless, so high was Churchill's reputation and position that his crash made it appear that he must bring down Salisbury as well. But the calculations of the older man had been careful. Had he accepted battle on another issue, in other circumstances, and at another time, it might well have been different—but he had been careful not to do so.

Another offer to Hartington—this one even less serious than that of August—was made by Salisbury to step down in favour of him, but again had absolutely no chance of acceptance, a fact of which Salisbury was fully aware. But the progress towards achieving a Liberal Unionist participation in the Government succeeded when Goschen succeeded Churchill at the Treasury. Salisbury also used the occasion to resume control over foreign affairs by removing Iddesleigh; the distressed old man, who had read of his dismissal from the newspapers, collapsed and died at 10 Downing Street while making his formal farewell. Smith took Churchill's Leadership in the Commons and proved a considerable success, and Beach's failing eyesight—only temporary— gave Salisbury the opportunity of appointing Balfour to the post of Irish Secretary. Thus, the crisis passed, and Salisbury emerged from it infinitely stronger.

Churchill's extraordinary political career virtually ended at this point. Although he remained in politics, something in that febrile and tense personality was destroyed by this disaster and he was never the same man again. From 1891 until his death in 1895 he was in marked physical and mental decline. Rosebery's moving valediction on him should not be omitted:

> He will be pathetically memorable, too, for the dark cloud which gradually enveloped him, and in which he passed away. He was the chief mourner at his own protracted funeral, a public pageant of gloomy years. It is a black moment when the heralds proclaim the passing of the dead, and the great officers break their staves. But it is sadder still when it is the victim's own voice that announces his decadence, when it is the victim's own hands that break the staff in public.

> His career, although brief, had left its mark. 'Tory Democracy' may have been an imposture, as Rosebery argued and Salisbury certainly believed, but it had considerable and enduring effects. 'He made the people believe in us', one elderly Tory said of him, and it was not an ignoble nor an inaccurate epitaph. But Churchill had done more than coin phrases, superb though many of them were. He had restored Conservative morale at a critical moment. He had been the architect of what was to become the Unionist Alliance, another of his phrases destined to become reality. He had been the first to see the political implications of the Ulster issue, but his deep knowledge of, and genuine sympathy for, the Irish people gave him a very particular place in their affection and respect. He had been the leading spirit in the annexation of Upper Burma, and in his perception of British rule in India he had demonstrated a vision and understanding which made a profound impression upon his officials and advisers. In his brief period at the Treasury he had won new and unexpected admirers.

He leaves behind him an impression of youth, freshness, and vigour, of work unfulfilled, of promise uncompleted. For all his faults of judgement and character, Lord Randolph was a politician of the very front rank. But he was not vouchsafed time and experience, and we are left with a series of unanswered questions. To many of his contemporaries he always remained the most brilliantly equipped, fascinating, and perplexing individual in public life whom they had ever encountered. The more one examines his speeches and letters, the more one is struck by his fundamental seriousness and his acute perceptiveness. He possessed what the Welsh call 'the seeing eye'. His approach to questions was often intuitive, and often wrong, but his basic attitudes to democracy were far ahead of almost everyone in active politics in his time. He was Conservative only in name; he was in reality a rebel against his class and the structure of society, seeing the future and not fearful of it. It was this element above all others that Salisbury detected, and which was the root cause of their differences.

It is one of the persistent tragedies of life that nature endows certain individuals with outstanding intellectual qualities but denies them other essential necessities to success, while favouring others with lesser qualities but better fortune in health and personal circumstances. In the case of Lord Randolph Churchill it bestowed many qualities on a fragile frame. He was a solitary man, with a disappointing marriage, serious financial difficulties, and few personal friends. It could be argued by those who saw him, as did Lord Ripon, as 'a reckless and unprincipled mountebank', that he deserved his loneliness, and that his defects of character were bound to bring to nothing his abilities. But this is strikingly not the judgement of his most eminent contemporaries, and which included Gladstone, Rosebery, Beach, Parnell, Morley, and Asquith. They were touched by his courtesy, his moods of caressing gentleness, lack of jealousy—a quality that struck Rosebery particularly—and consideration and kindness. But to the world he showed a different face, and it is not to be wondered that so many found it repulsive and dangerous, and were joyous at his downfall.

It has been often argued that his deadly error in December 1886 was at least partly due to physical factors, and that he was already gripped by the disease that was to kill him so slowly. While this is possible, it seems much more probable that it was a political miscalculation by a young man hell-bent on power who was, not unjustifiably, intoxicated by his successes. It has happened before, and subsequently. In any event, it is not clear precisely what was the disease that destroyed him, or when he contracted it. The opinion of his medical advisers was General Paralysis of the Insane, a euphemism for syphilis, but there was no autopsy and, given the state of medical knowledge of brain conditions at the time, this verdict is not fully convincing to this commentator. Among other real possibilities of the source of his decline and death is a brain tumour, a diagnosis which the limited available evidence strongly indicates could have been the cause. But, whatever it was, the fact was that Lord Randolph Churchill, insane, died at the age of forty-five in London, in January 1895, and that it was left to his older son, whom he hardly knew and whom he somewhat despised, to revive his memory and to perpetuate his name.

Thankfully uncluttered by this turbulent and disturbing personality, the Salisbury Government braced itself to meet the burden of issues that now marched relentlessly upon it.

*

The resignation of Lord Randolph Churchill led directly, but unavailingly, to the last serious attempt to create a Liberal rapprochement. The much-heralded 'Round Table' Conference—in fact a series of meetings—held in London in January 1887 only served to demonstrate the differences and did nothing to bring the warring groups together. In Chamberlain's own words, 'All hope of reunion was at last abandoned.'

For the next six years, in Lucy's phrase, 'all Parliamentary roads led to Ireland'. We can now see that Parnell's '86' marked the peak of his power. But it did not seem so at the time, and indeed until the end of 1890 his position, and the fate of Home Rule, seemed assured. The Conservatives set out firmly to restore law and order on the one hand and, by judicious meeting of certain Irish grievances, to 'kill Home Rule by kindness' on the other.[1]

In Arthur Balfour the Unionists discovered an unexpectedly firm, sly, courageous and resourceful Chief Secretary. It became evident that behind a languid charm Balfour concealed many strong qualities, in which ambition and ruthlessness were not omitted. As Winston Churchill was to write of him many years later, with paternal and

[1] For the best account, see L. P. Curtis: *Coercion and Conciliation in Ireland 1880-1892*, Chapters XI–XV.

personal experience, 'had his life been cast amid the labyrinthine intrigues of the Italian Renaissance, he would not have required to study the works of Machiavelli'. A critical turning-point was his handling of the situation which arose in September 1887, when the police opened fire at a meeting at Mitchelstown and killed three people. The Irish and the Liberals were outraged, but Balfour emphatically supported the police and blamed the organisers of the assembly. Gladstone raised the cry of 'Remember Mitchelstown!', but the effect upon the Conservatives and the hard-pressed and demoralised Irish officials was very different. It may have been that Ireland between 1887 and 1892 required such a combination of strength and subtlety; what is without doubt was that the new Unionist Coalition did. Balfour swiftly became their hero, and the memory of Lord Randolph faded equally swiftly. As the Liberals and the Irish raged against 'Bloody Balfour' and the tumult rose, Balfour's imperturbable Parliamentary skill and Ministerial decisiveness gave new heart to the Government benches and established his position. In the Commons, with Churchill and Beach on the back benches, and W. H. Smith hardly in serious contention,[1] Balfour seized his opportunity to become the Conservative heir-apparent. The long rule of what was later derided as 'the Hotel Cecil' had begun.

The Irish Question now entered a period of extreme unpleasantness. To meet Irish obstructionism, a new Closure procedure was introduced, whereby the Speaker could accept a motion to end debate at any time from any Member and put it at once to the vote; if there were more than 200 votes in the majority voting for the proposal, the main Questions would be put immediately. This new procedure could have become—as many feared it would—a terrible weapon in the hands of any Government to curtail debate. But in Speaker Peel, one of the greatest of all Speakers, the minority's rights were firmly defended at all times, and the apprehensions of the opponents—by no means only Irish and Liberals—proved unfounded. Nonetheless, it marked a major change in the procedure and the character of the

---

[1] In the words of Herbert Paul: 'Mr. Smith's speeches were intelligible to careful listeners who understood the subject, and he knew how to arrange the business of the House. But as chief of a great party in a historic Assembly he left something to be desired.' (*A History of Modern England* (1906), Vol. V, 87). But, affectionately dubbed 'Old Morality' by Henry Lucy, Smith proved a popular and well-regarded leader during a period of exceptional virulence and difficulty, and the strain undoubtedly hastened his death in October 1891.

House of Commons. The 'Plan of Campaign', initiated in October 1886, incited tenants to withhold rents if the landlords refused what the tenants regarded as fair rents; the Criminal Law Amendment Act of 1887 was the Government's response, and gave it sweeping powers to 'proclaim' districts, to conduct trials of agrarian offences before courts of summary jurisdiction, and to declare specific organisations to be dangerous and liable to prosecution as such. Then, in May 1887 *The Times* initiated a series of articles on 'Parnellism and Crime', which deeply implicated the Irish leader in the Land League.

Parnell had prominently disassociated himself from the Plan of Campaign on the grounds that he would not support any actions which would alienate English opinion and harm the Liberals. *The Times* articles were designed to show that Parnell, behind a veneer of moderation, was in fact closely linked with the most violent aspects of the Irish agitation, that his movement was 'essentially a foreign conspiracy', and that the Liberals had allied themselves 'with the paid agents of an organisation whose ultimate aim is plunder and whose ultimate sanction is murder, to paralyse the House of Commons and to hand Ireland over to social and financial ruin'. The articles aroused only modest interest until, on April 18th, *The Times* published a facsimile of a letter allegedly written by Parnell, dated May 15th 1882, in which he expressed regret at his having been obliged, for political reasons, to condemn the Phoenix Park murders.

It was not know at the time, nor until a long time afterwards, that the Government was deeply involved in this calculated and well-planned attempt to destroy Parnell,[1] although many Irishmen and Liberals immediately suspected it at the time. The sensation was immense, and the charges against Parnell seemed to be confirmed by his own response. *The Times* challenged Parnell to bring an action if he dared, but Parnell merely denounced the letters as forgeries and seemed prepared to ignore the matter. In fact he was engaged in extensive and often heated discussion with the Liberal leaders about the best course to take, while *The Times* articles continued with more sensations.

F. H. O'Donnell, a popular Irish Nationalist of an eccentric manner and disposition, sued *The Times* for a reference to himself in their articles. The Attorney-General, Sir Richard Webster, appeared for

[1] See F. S. L. Lyons: 'Parnellism and Crime', *Transactions of the Royal Historical Society*, Fifth Series, Vol. 24 (1974).

the newspaper, and produced more facsimile letters allegedly written by Parnell. The Government, meanwhile, was considering how to maximise its advantage and, on the urgings of Chamberlain, initiated an investigation of the charges against Parnell; to the merited fury of the Liberals and Irish—who had wanted a Parliamentary investigation of *The Times*'s allegations—it appointed a special commission of three judges to look into the much wider and more fruitful questions of the complicity of the Land League and the Irish Parliamentary Party in agrarian and other outrages. This partisan manoeuvre was denounced in private by Churchill as 'a revolutionary tribunal for the trial of political offenders' and publicly by the Liberals and the Irish in exceedingly harsh debates. But Parnell, intent upon proving the letters published by *The Times* to be forgeries, reluctantly accepted the Commission which Morley justly categorised as 'one of the ugliest things done in the name and under the forms of law in this island during the century'.

The Government's discreditable strategem misfired. The proceedings of the Commission increasingly bored the public until on its fiftieth day, in February 1890, Richard Pigott appeared before it. After brutal cross-questioning by Sir Charles Russell it was established that this disreputable journalist had forged the letters so injudiciously accepted by *The Times*. J. L. Garvin's account of the scene should not be omitted:

> First the fatuity with which the forgeries had been accepted and paid for was disclosed. Then the lamentable Pigott with his bald head, red face, white whiskers, loose mouth, his disreputable but not unkindly lineaments, foolishly smiling—he looked like a church-warden or sidesman gone wrong—was racked and crushed in the witness-box. . . . Blackmailer, parasite, most mercenary of grubs in Grub Street, vendor of obscene books and photographs, he was hopelessly exposed.[1]

Pigott fled the country and committed suicide in Madrid; the reputation of *The Times* lay in ruins; the Government's strategy was shattered; and Parnell's prestige soared, even in England. The Liberals embraced him in ecstatic relief. The Eighty Club honoured him. Edinburgh gave him its freedom. He was warmly invited to Hawarden for discussions with Gladstone. Lord Randolph, who had so prophetic-

[1] Garvin: *Chamberlain*, III, 394–5.

ally attacked the Commission in private, now denounced it in the House of Commons with a ferocity that shocked even those who agreed with him, describing it as 'in every sense of the word an Elizabethan procedure. . . . What has been the result of this uprootal of Constitutional practices? What has been the result? Pigott! What has been the result of this mountainous parturition? A thing, a reptile, a monster. Pigott! What, with all your skill, all your cleverness, has been the result? A ghastly, bloody, rotten foetus—Pigott! Pigott!! Pigott!!! *This* is your Nemesis.'

The excitement and Liberal euphoria were deceptive and dangerous. The situation in Ireland itself continued to be bad, and the Irish Question remained highly volatile. A careful reading of Parnell's evidence to the Commission and of its Report emphasises that there was more substance to his critics' charges than the forgeries of Pigott. But the Pigott affair had other, much more fatal, consequences. It raised Parnell's position to such a height that, when the fall came, it was to be precipitous. It prompted many to disbelieve other charges which were in fact justified. And it linked the fortunes of the Liberals more than they had ever been before to the personal fortunes and strange personality of this complex man.

The period of Parnell's glory was brief indeed. In December 1889 Captain O'Shea instituted divorce proceedings against his wife, citing Parnell as co-respondent. Nearly a year elapsed between the filing of his petition and the hearing of the case, and Irish opinion, although disquieted, appeared to accept that this was another English attempt to discredit Parnell and on the same level as the allegations of *The Times*. Those who knew the facts were more apprehensive, but the general reaction was strongly supportive of Parnell. In the words of Conor Cruise O'Brien, 'the nationalist movement as a whole simply drifted towards the catastrophe, with a dumb confidence in its leader's ambiguous assurances, and a dumb expectation of another Pigott'.[1] 'One of the most marked traits in the psychology of Irish politicians', Davitt's biographer wrote, '—and perhaps the generalisation might be extended to politicians of other countries—is their capacity for imitating the ostrich whenever anything disagreeable appears on the horizon. They are inclined to make an excessive application to politics of the methods of Christian Science, and to imagine that to ignore an inconvenience is equivalent to annihilating

[1] O'Brien, op. cit., 282.

it. This was the principle on which Parnell's followers appear to have acted during the time when the O'Shea affair was in the air and had not yet been submitted to the tribunals'.[1]

But the Liberals were no better prepared. It was not until two days before the case was heard that Morley raised the matter with Parnell, received the firm assurance that he had no intention of retiring from the leadership, and assumed that Parnell would emerge from the matter unscathed. These reactions among the Irish and Liberal leaders, who were fully conversant with the facts, would be inconceivable except in the context of the Pigott affair, the extraordinary position of authority that Parnell had acquired, and their desperate wishful thinking.

It is still not clear why O'Shea intervened at this time. Considerable suspicion, then and later, fell on Chamberlain as the principal instigator. Much attention has been given to a statement by Sir Alfred Robbins, at the time the London correspondent of the *Birmingham Daily Post*, that in September 1889 he 'was asked by one on the inside of the liberal unionist "machine" whether Parnell would be politically ruined by a divorce, the then recent Dilke instance being given as a precedent, and Captain O'Shea, it was added, being willing to take proceedings'. This is very paltry stuff. Even if this was Chamberlain to whom Robbins was referring, one does not feel that Chamberlain required instruction from a journalist in the political implications of involvement in a sordid divorce case at that time. And no one could have foreseen how Parnell would handle the matter.

But there is much more compelling and serious evidence, although inconclusive, that Chamberlain was not uninvolved in O'Shea's action.[2] Chamberlain had been active in prompting the Government to set up the Special Commission, a fact which he denied in his personal account but which was subsequently revealed.[3] He had, as has been related, made use of O'Shea as an emissary in the past, had campaigned for him in Liverpool in 1885, and had supported his controversial candidature for the Galway seat in 1886. O'Shea had appeared before the Commission as a witness for *The Times* at Chamberlain's instigation, and had testified to the accuracy of Parnell's signature in the

[1] F. Sheehy-Skeffington: *Michael Davitt*.
[2] Although, interestingly, not from Parnell, who, although he believed that the proceedings were politically inspired, accused *The Times*.
[3] Chamberlain: *A Political Memoir*, 283, and Garvin, op. cit., III, 386–7.

Pigott letters; he had worked with Chamberlain in 1885–6 in seeking information detrimental to Parnell from the Home Office.[1] Thus, in spite of O'Shea's alleged duplicity in 1885, the evidence is overwhelming that Chamberlain worked with him closely thereafter. Why?

O'Shea took care to inform Balfour in December 1889 when he filed proceedings that Chamberlain was 'acquainted with the facts'. His counsel was the Solicitor-General, Sir Edward Clarke. Although it was quite proper for a Law Officer of the Crown at this time to accept private clients, the presence of Clarke in such a case, following Webster's appearance for *The Times*, necessarily arouses strong suspicions that the Unionists, having failed to destroy Parnell in *The Times* and the Special Commission, were making a third attempt. We now know that they were deeply involved in the first two ventures, and it is difficult to afford them the benefit of the doubt in the third. Clarke evidently relished his opportunity, and was devastatingly severe on Parnell, but he subsequently wrote that the two surviving children of Mrs. O'Shea were 'unquestionably' Parnell's,[2] a fact that demolished an important part of O'Shea's case as the deceived husband only recently aware of the true facts. It is not clear whether Clarke knew this at the time of the trial; it takes a considerable amount of credulousness to state that the thought had not crossed the mind of so experienced and politically dedicated a lawyer. There is nothing absolutely conclusive, but the number of coincidences is such that the allegations that O'Shea was driven on by factors wholly unconnected with contemporary politics become somewhat implausible.

But there were several factors that would have persuaded O'Shea to take action on his own account, of which the most compelling were financial. The belated death of Mrs. Wood in May 1889, at the age of ninety-eight, was an event of crucial significance. Mrs. Wood left all the considerable wealth to Mrs. O'Shea in such terms that it seemed not capable of claim by her husband nor within the scope of her marriage settlement. But O'Shea was not the only indignant claimant; several other relatives of Mrs. Wood were eager to contest her will, and were very ready to believe and to claim that its terms had been influenced by Mrs. O'Shea in her favour. O'Shea was by this time an embittered man politically, and was now embittered financially. We may discount the possibility that he was outraged by the realisation

---

[1] F. S. L. Lyons: *The Fall of Parnell*, 70.
[2] Clarke: *The Story of My Life*, 291–5.

of his wife's infidelity. But was he, in the eleven months between the filing of his petition and the hearing in court, engaged in blackmail? In short, was he seeking to be paid off for his silence? Mrs. O'Shea later told Henry Harrison that this was indeed the case, but that in view of the objections to Mrs. Woods's will it was not possible to meet his demands. The explanation may help to explain Parnell's confidence, and then his defiance. But it is unsatisfying by itself. One feels that other factors were involved, and that O'Shea did not act alone, nor for pecuniary reasons only. It was too convenient, too well-timed, and too well organised, to be dismissed as one of those historical events which, in the course of human affairs, occur at particular moments merely by chance. The arm of coincidence may indeed be long, but hardly as long as it was in this particular episode.

But the key factors in Parnell's downfall were his eagerness to marry Mrs. O'Shea, his aloof self-confidence, and his contempt for English courts and English opinion. Thus, when the case came to court on November 15th 1890 only one side of the case was given, O'Shea was awarded his decree nisi, and Parnell was depicted in the most severe and lamentable light. The revelations of what seemed to be a prolonged record of duplicity and tawdriness on Parnell's part provided excellent material for his enemies. More significantly, they put his colleagues and the Liberals in a difficult position which rapidly became untenable. It was this belief that they had been duped that imparted so much savagery to the political aftermath of the O'Shea divorce.

First reactions from Ireland, however, were very encouraging to Parnell, indeed so encouraging that the Irish Catholic leaders were unsure of their course and held silence. Of the leading Nationalists only Davitt urged Parnell to efface himself temporarily, at least until after he could marry Mrs. O'Shea, but with this exception there was initially no movement in Ireland to condemn Parnell nor to seek his resignation. Following the old pattern of Irish-English reaction, the abuse heaped upon Parnell in England was not likely to precipitate such a movement in Ireland, and for a brief period it seemed that Parnell might surmount even this episode as successfully as he had weathered previous storms.

But the Liberals, who had suffered so much for the Home Rule cause, were more keenly receptive to the uproar in England, and the rank-and-file, now convinced of a heavy victory in the next election, was dismayed at the prospect of fighting the rejuvenated Unionists with a discredited adulterer and deceiver at their side. This mood was very evident at the annual meeting of the National Liberal Federation on November 20th–21st at Sheffield, and the prospect of Parnell's voluntary retirement—even if only temporary—became very alluring.

Gladstone refused to condemn Parnell for his immorality, but he saw the political perils very clearly. Cardinal Manning urged him to repudiate Parnell, and, at the other extreme of the religious spectrum, the Nonconformists advised the same course. The Nonconformist influence may not have been what it once had been, but it was very raucous, and was still a very formidable political reality. Thus, it was eventually agreed on November 24th that Gladstone should write a letter to Morley which the latter would show to Parnell before the meeting of the Irish Parliamentary Party on the following day. The key passage, which stated that Gladstone's position would become 'almost a nullity' if Parnell remained was omitted from the first draft, but was in the final version. Gladstone also saw Justin McCarthy, Vice-Chairman of the Parliamentary Party on the 24th, and conveyed the same message. On the next day McCarthy found Parnell obdurate, and Parnell was re-elected Leader for the new session before he saw Morley and read Gladstone's letter. It is not clear whether this was wholly accidental, but from Parnell's attitude at this time it is difficult to believe that it would have had much influence. Parnell read it immediately after his election, and told Morley that he would not resign. Gladstone, shocked by the news, authorised the publication of his letter, which appeared on the next day. With that, the storm broke.

The Nationalists were in an agonising position. Many argued that Parnell should step down, but hated the idea of bowing to English clamour and the panic of the Liberals. Others, although alarmed by the situation, became more defiant in their support of Parnell for much the same reason. They all, as in the past, looked to Parnell for leadership and salvation. And at this point he made the rupture inevitable.

On November 26th there was an agitated and inconclusive special meeting of the Parliamentary Party at which Parnell refused a request to reconsider his position, and in which his haughty demeanour was such that Thomas Sexton commented to Tim Healy that an intelligent foreigner would have concluded that the entire Party was being tried for adultery, with Parnell as the judge. But Parnell appreciated the strength of the forces building up against him and realised he would

have to act, and act quickly. Characteristically, he resolved to go on
the attack. He prepared a Manifesto to the Irish people, published on
November 29th, which denounced Gladstone for attempting to
influence the Party's choice of leader, gave details of the Home Rule
settlement which the Liberals would introduce when elected, blamed
the Liberals—particularly Morley—for persuading him to attack the
Land Purchase Bill, and finally claimed that Morley had proposed that
Parnell or one of his colleagues should become Chief Secretary and
that the Nationalists should have one of the Irish law offices in a
Liberal administration.

This was a very tough counter-attack indeed. It was not an emotional
outburst, but a calculated stroke, characterised by language which was
obviously deliberately designed to outrage the Liberals and rally Irish
sympathy. The references to 'the integrity and independence of the
Irish parliamentary party having been apparently sapped and destroyed by the wirepullers of the English Liberal party' and 'the
English wolves now howling for my destruction' were bad enough, but
it was the final defiant claim that a postponement of Home Rule was
preferable 'to a compromise of our national rights' which the Liberal
connection would involve, that was bound to cause the deepest anger
in the Liberal ranks.

Parnell had clearly broken confidence in his revelations of the
Liberal proposals and had deliberately distorted what had actually
occurred in his discussions with the Liberal leaders. His outrage at the
proposals, furthermore, was in very marked contrast with his actual
public conduct when he had learned of them. Finally, he had never
indicated to his own colleagues this new sense of contempt for
Gladstone's proposed measures.

What Parnell was in reality doing was attempting to divert attention
—and particularly in Ireland—away from the divorce case and its
implications to the issue of who was to choose the leader of Ireland.
It was a bold stroke, but unsuccessful. After the first surge of instinctive
loyalty, second thoughts came very swiftly, and the intervention of the
Catholic hierarchy had already begun. The Manifesto in fact had
made the Liberals' point much stronger. Parnell was now attempting
to appeal to Ireland over the heads of the Parliamentary Party and the
Church, and although the anger of the Liberal leaders was naturally
intense, it was hardly less among the Nationalists themselves. A group
in the United States engaged in fund-raising, and which included

Dillon and T. P. O'Connor, had initially supported Parnell. When they read the Manifesto and had received a highly-charged cable from Sexton and Healy declaring that unless Parnell went 'general election lost, campaigners ruined, dissolution inevitable' and that on this there was 'practical unanimity', they denounced it in a counter-manifesto issued in Chicago on November 30th. On the same day Archbishops Croke and Walsh broke their silence, Walsh adding that Parnell's Manifesto was 'an act of political suicide'. And so it proved to be.

The battle for Parnell's leadership now moved to Committee Room Fifteen in the House of Commons. The debates were prolonged and bitter, and have been often described.[1] Parnell fought for his position with skill and passion. An attempt to negotiate new terms with the Liberals on substantive points was stillborn when the Liberal leaders refused to discuss them until the leadership issue was settled. The Irish retired back to Committee Room Fifteen and the temperature rose sharply, particularly when Healy called out 'Who is to be the mistress of the Party?' and was denounced by Parnell as 'that cowardly little scoundrel who dares in an assembly of Irishmen to insult a woman.' At 4.30 on the afternoon of December 7th Justin McCarthy rose and said with dignity that 'I see no further use carrying on a discussion which must be barren of all but reproach, ill-temper, controversy, and indignity, and I will therefore suggest that all who think with me at this grave crisis should withdraw with me from this room.' Forty-four left with him, leaving Parnell with his faithful but disconsolate remnant of twenty-seven.

Parnell resolved to fight on in Ireland, but his position was now hopeless. For a time he was misled by the fervour of Dublin itself and the enthusiasm of his most dedicated admirers, but from this point an ominous silence began to seep across Ireland—the bitter silence of the sense of betrayal. The first real test was a by-election at Kilkenny, where Davitt and Healy ran the anti-Parnellite campaign, and in which, on Healy's claim, some seventy of the eighty-two Irish Nationalist M.P.s were engaged. It was a terrible election, even by Irish standards. Parnell hurled himself into the battle, and was denounced by Davitt as 'an insolent dictator'. Healy was particularly savage, and Parnell responded in kind. Davitt accused him of insanity, and was injured in a scuffle, and Parnell was pelted with mud and lime. Davitt, the former Fenian, was now the champion of the

---

[1] For the best account see Conor Cruise O'Brien, op. cit., 313–46.

constitutional approach, while, as his situation became more desperate, Parnell appealed to older and darker forces. The Church, discreetly, became very active in the battle, and at the end of this cruel and often squalid contest Parnell's candidate was badly beaten.

But he fought on, with failing health and feverish passion, against relentlessly increasing odds. To many who had fought at his side for so long and who now fought against him, this was a period of agony, and they would have agreed with Dillon, who wrote on December 20th: 'I long with an unspeakable longing to get out of politics and have done with the sordid misery of that life, and get to read and think and live at least for a few years before I die, but I fear it is too late now.'[1] An attempt to reach a reasonable settlement was made at Boulogne at the end of December, in which Parnell proposed that he would retire from the chairmanship of the Parliamentary Party but would remain at the head of the National League. It was a skilful manoeuvre, coupled with the proposal that O'Brien should replace him and seek new assurances from Gladstone on Liberal policies. At a second conference at Boulogne, on January 6–7th, Parnell produced a memorandum of agreement, but Dillon was now to be his replacement. Dillon would have nothing to do with it, and it was evident that Parnell's attempt to relinquish the title of leader while retaining the reality of power was wholly unacceptable.

At this point the Unionists easily held, with an increased majority, a by-election at Bassetlaw, in spite of the personal involvement of Gladstone, the first serious disappointment the Liberals had received for nearly two years; shortly afterwards the Liberals won a by-election at West Hartlepool, but only after their candidate had been compelled to strongly endorse Gladstone's repudiation of Parnell. The Liberals could not change their conditions, and Parnell himself was by now intractable. The story of the Boulogne Negotiations—continued at Calais—is a complex one, but the important result was that they failed, and that it was Parnell who broke them off. The Liberals could have been more forthcoming, but by this time their feelings about Parnell were barely rational, and their eagerness to see him gone was greater than their willingness to reach an agreement on joint policies. If this was a disastrously short-sighted approach, it was entirely understandable. Parnell, also, was under severe physical and emotional strain. After this brief lull, the battle was continued with even greater

[1] Quoted in Lyons, op. cit., 192.

ferocity, and was only ended by Parnell's death at Brighton on October 6th 1891, by which time the Irish Nationalist Party and the cause of Home Rule itself had received further terrible blows.

This extraordinary and tragic episode was of profound political importance. As has been rightly written, 'Parnell directed a movement of revolutionary inspiration from within a relatively conservative and constitutional party. This is the peculiarity that made "Parnellism" such an equivocal term and so elusive and effective a force. . . . "We created Parnell", one of the ablest members of the party was to write, "and Parnell created us. We seized very early in the movement the idea of this man with his superb silences, his historic name, his determination, his self-control, his aloofness—we seized that as the canvas of a great national hero".'[1]

Now that was gone and all discredited. The Irish movement was cruelly split and in anguished disarray. It seemed that the patient work of decades had been utterly destroyed within sight of victory. With Parnell's death, the heart seemed to go out of Ireland, as though the tensions and hopes of his leadership and the ordeal of his final agony had produced a collective exhaustion from which it would take a generation or more to recover. Among even his most bitter enemies in Ireland there were now feelings of remorse and even of guilt at their part in his awful and abrupt downfall. For fifteen years Parnell had utterly dominated the Irish Nationalist Party, and if in Ireland itself his hold had been less total he had, more than any man since Grattan, won the claim to regard himself as the one leader of the Irish people. Had he been struck down by an assassin or died before 1891, his legacy would have been assured. But he had fallen under the blows of his own people in an atmosphere of rage and betrayal, himself fighting with violence and extremity of language, cursing and reviling as he went down. His harsh denunciations of his former followers and theirs of him could not be stifled by his death, and were to poison Irish politics until time brought calmer perspectives. But it was to be a very long time.

The Liberal Party could only watch the ghastly culmination of Parnell's career with helpless dismay. The crusade element in the Home Rule movement, which had been of significant importance since 1886, now vanished, having perished in 'the stench of the Divorce Court', and at Kilkenny. The approaching election now

[1] O'Brien, op. cit., 9–10.

loomed with a grim and forbidding aspect. The confidence of the Unionists was now surging. By the beginning of 1892 it was evident to all observers that it was going to be a very close-run thing.

*

The dramatically fluctuating fortunes of the Home Rule issue between 1886 and 1892 obscured other developments which, in their long-term effects, were to be of at least equal importance to the devastation of Gladstone's hopes for a large Home Rule majority.

During the early 1880s there had been little concept of 'labour' as a distinct class or problem, let alone a distinct political group. The enfranchisement of manual workers in the 1867 and 1885 Reform Acts and of agricultural workers in the 1885 Act had increased the political importance of these groups, but there had been no signs that this new voice might develop into an independent one. Disraeli had seen the potentialities of this new electorate, and Lord Randolph Churchill had calculatedly wooed it, and not without success. The Liberals, however, regarded it as their natural birthright vote, automatic to themselves, and did not work to bind it to their cause. The attitude, which was most notable at the local level, was that the duty of voting Liberal did not carry with it any privilege of involvement in the actual process of politics. From time to time a working class candidate was triumphantly flaunted, but in the main the associations preferred middle class candidates, spurning the eager Keir Hardie for the safe London barrister Sir William Wedderburn, to take but one example.

This attitude, which was very widespread, was serious enough for the future of the Liberal Party, but it was even more serious in the context of industrial and social unrest in which it was dominant.

The industrial discontent that flared up in 1886 and continued intermittently for the next three years provided indications that there was much bitterness under the surface of apparent prosperity. On 'Black Monday' (February 8th 1886) a mob smashed in windows in Pall Mall; two days later it was rumoured that a mob of 50,000 unemployed was marching from Deptford and Greenwich, looting and wrecking on the way. Although the apprehension was exaggerated, there was a new uneasiness. On November 9th there was further alarm when it was rumoured that a mob of unemployed proposed to join the Lord Mayor's Procession to call attention to their plight. In October 1887 there were further disturbances in London, including an invasion of Westminster Abbey by more than two hundred unemployed men. Between October 18th and 20th there were three days of rioting in Hyde Park, and on November 13th—'Bloody Sunday'—there was virtually a pitched battle in Trafalgar Square between an enormous crowd and some 4,000 policemen and 300 men of the Grenadier Guards with fixed bayonets; and the 1st Life Guards were called out before order was restored. And this in Jubilee Year!

The causes of this new unrest cannot be easily categorised. The slump of the seventies, the agricultural distress that drove farm-workers to the over-crowded cities, the growth of the scale of pro-duction and the consequent further weakening of the worker-master relationship, which encouraged both unskilled workers and dis-gruntled artisans to combine to protect themselves, were undoubtedly important contributing factors. But it is necessary to differentiate between blind inchoate striking-out of the under-privileged against exploitation and poverty, and organised labour movements. For it was in the latter that the destiny of 'labour' really lay.

The essential novelty of the 'New Unionism' that developed in the later 1880s was that men were organised in the industries that employed them rather than through their old crafts, although unions based on the latter still survived. But it is probable that the revival of collective action would not have been so speedy had there not been a remarkable demonstration of what could be achieved by these methods. This occurred in 1889.

The London Dock Strike, which lasted from August 13th to September 16th, has been seen, justifiably as one of the most im-portant single events in the history of the British Trade Union movement. It followed successful action earlier in the year by the Sailors' and Firemen's Unions, and John Burns has claimed that a gas workers' victory also had its effect; 'they [the dockers] caught the spirit that we were trying to inform them with and when the gas workers had won their victory . . . the dockers in their turn became restless.'

The London Strike was between casual dock workers, estimated at some 90,000, and the Directors of the four dock companies in the Port of London. The employers themselves were disunited; the members of the four Boards and the owners of many hundreds of wharves on the Thames were unable to work together in harmony.

The conditions of the dock workers were grim. Mayhew has

described the daily scene at 6 a.m. when the casual labourers gathered:

> As the foremen made their appearances, so began the scuffling and
> scrambling forth of countless hands, high in the air. All were
> shouting, appealing, coaxing. The scene is one to sadden the most
> callous, with thousands of men struggling for one day's hire, the
> struggle being the fiercer from the knowledge that hundreds must
> be left to idle the day out in want.

The men's pay was 5d an hour, out of which they had to 'treat'
the contractors who hired them (a tradition not extinguished until
1921). The only union was The Tea Operatives and General Labourers
Association, formed by a worker in the dock tea warehouses, Ben
Tillett.

The strike found the Dock Companies at a low ebb. On August 7th
Tillett requested the head of the South West India Dock to pay his
men 6d an hour and 8d an hour overtime in lieu of 5d and 7d, and to
guarantee a minimum engagement of four hours for each casual
worker taken on. This would have cost £100,000 a year. No reply
came, and 2,500 casual men at the East and West India group struck;
by the 16th those at the much larger Royal Victoria and Albert Docks
came out, as did the Irish workers building Tilbury Dock.

It is possible that the strike might have failed and certainly taken a
very different course, had it not been for John Burns, who took the
leadership in the struggle. It was not an occasion for half-hearted
measures. Picketing had to become 'unpeaceful', and was so. Organised intimidation and violence were certainly practised. But Burns was
also fully aware of the importance of public support, and had a
precocious sense of public relations. He organised a daily march
through the City to the West End, an orderly, impressive, demure
daily ritual that also raised funds from sympathetic bystanders.
Other unions helped to finance the strike, and when a strike account
was opened the Lord Mayor sponsored a fund that raised £1,400 and
Australian workers contributed £24,000. The Salvation Army provided soup kitchens and cheap food depots for the strikers. The Lord
Mayor—Sir James Whitehead—persuaded Sir John Lubbock,
Sydney Buxton and Cardinal Manning to form a committee to
find a solution. Eventually, 'the dockers' tanner' was conceded.[1] 'As a

---

[1] See Colonel R. B. Oram: 'The Great Strike of 1889' (*History Today*, August
1964) for further details.

An ironical, and rather melancholy footnote may be given to this victory. In

Trade Unionist', Burns wrote in the *New Review* (October 1889), 'my own notion of the practical outcome of the Strike is that all sections of labour must organise themselves into trades unions; that all trades must federate themselves, and that in the future, prompt and concerted action must take the place of the spasmodic and isolated action of the past.'

Although it was not until 1889 that Charles Booth published his electrifying statement—weightily supported by evidence—that some 30·7 per cent of the people of London were living at, or below, the poverty line, intelligent middle class interest in the condition of the poor had established, even before Booth made his researches public, massive evidence of the grim background to the unemployed marches and the revival of trade unionism. Britain's wealth had been built, and was being perpetuated, on cheap labour, and exploited cheap labour at that. One did not have to look far for evidence of poverty and malnutrition in London, and in the great industrial cities it was over-whelming. The subsequent idyllic concepts of English country life bore no relation to the actual realities in the last decades of the nineteenth century. The fact that Englishmen visiting Ireland were so shocked by conditions there is as illustrative an example as any of how awful those conditions were. But, since the 1840s, with the increase of national self-confidence and prosperity, a tacit acceptance of these conditions on the understanding that measures for amelioration would occur from time to time had been characteristic of what had once been so articulate and vehement an element in British post-Industrial Revolution society. Now, the calm was beginning to end.

It is important to emphasise that at this time, and indeed until much later, Socialism as such had very little impact upon the new Unionism. Furthermore, it was still assumed that the answer for working class discontent lay with the Liberals. Nevertheless, the middle class interest in the subject was to have important long-term consequences, and cannot be overlooked even at this early stage.

The Fabian Society came into existence at the beginning of 1884, as a by-product of a 'utopian' group called The Fellowship of the New

November 1923, Ben Tillett, in dire financial straits, approached the Conservative Prime Minister for financial support, in return for which he offered 'to fight Communism'. £2,000—or, failing that, £1,000—was the price he requested. (See R. R. James: *Memoirs of a Conservative*.)

Life founded by Dr. Thomas Davidson of New York in 1883. The Fellowship of the New Life was both too idealistic and insufficiently Socialist for those members who left to found the Fabian Society.

The quality of the Fabian Society has always lain in the intellectual questioning and disputes of its members. Among the original members were Frank Podmore, Edward Pease, and Hubert Bland,[1] and in May 1885 George Bernard Shaw and Sidney Webb (then a clerk in the Colonial Office) joined. Shaw also persuaded the formidable Mrs. Annie Besant—disenchanted by Secularism—to join at the same time; she was to become the celebrated organiser of the Bryant and May matchgirls' strike of 1888, but in 1890 she abandoned the Fabians for Theosophy and India, where she spent the rest of her life.

The Fabians, from the outset, were essentially middle class, intellectual, London-based and London-orientated. The 'Fabian outlook' was a curious blend of English Liberal tradition—notably J. S. Mill—Continental Positivism, and a certain vague Marxism. Although some of their early Tracts had a distinctly revolutionary flavour, the Fabians approved neither of revolutionary methods nor of the Marxist Social Democratic Federation (nor its leader, H. M. Hyndman), particularly after the fiasco in the 1885 General Election when two S.D.F. candidates stood for London seats and received twenty-seven and thirty-two votes respectively. The Fabians kept aloof from the unemployment troubles of 1886–7, and indeed actively disapproved of revolution by the proletariat. 'The unhappy people', Bland wrote, 'though not without their importance in a quasi-political movement, are *not* the people to make a political revolution, or even to carry out a great reform. The revolt of the empty stomach ends at the baker's shop.'[2] If this attitude may arouse resentment both for its tone and its content, it was not a wholly unfair deduction to draw from the recent history of British working class revolutionary movements. But, as other Fabians realised, this passivity was ending.

The contribution of the Fabian Society to the history of English

---

[1] Podmore retired from the Executive in 1888 to devote himself to literary and historical work. Pease was honorary secretary 1886–9, General Secretary 1890–14 and 1919–39. Bland was perhaps the most outspoken and vigorous of the early members, antagonistic to the Liberal Party and a keen advocate from the beginning of a new independent Socialist Party. He was married to Edith Nesbit, the distinguished writer of admirable children's stories.

[2] *The Practical Socialist*, October 1886.

Socialism remains controversial. Although it was primarily a London, middle class, self-conscious, intellectual group, its influence on younger people of the same class and background was profound, and it produced a series of proposals for social reform, many of which were put into practical effect. The foundation of the London School of Economics, and the Webbs' profound and enlightened involvement in educational reform were particularly important. Men of the calibre of R. H. Tawney, R. C. K. Ensor, G. D. H. Cole, Graham Wallas, Hugh Dalton, Clement Attlee, John Strachey and Hugh Gaitskell, came from the same background as the Webbs, and although the long-term influence of the Webbs may have been slight in proportion to their astonishing literary output, the manner in which they undertook their social investigations, and many of their conclusions, gave socialist reformers invaluable guidance and ideas.

If the Fabians had been meeting and talking in a vacuum their relevance would have been negligible, but they were not. Their own movement away from Liberalism to a new political and social philosophy was also taking place among more directly involved groups. Thus, as the Liberals preached the gradualist doctrine of Peace, Retrenchment, and Reform, and were alternately exalted and cast down by the gyrations of the Irish Question, the groups on which their future depended were beginning to ponder doubts about the merits of gradualism.

It was to be a long time—indeed, a surprisingly long time—before disillusionment with the Liberal Party became widespread in the trade union and intellectual sections of the new 'labour' movement. Respect for Gladstone personally, lethargy and apathy, the Liberal tradition, the conservatism and pragmatism of British trade unions, all formed a powerful negative coalition against converting irritation and disillusionment into actual revolt. The principal characteristic of British working class movements in the century, and particularly since the 1850s, had been to work within established institutions to bring reform, and of all these institutions the Liberal Party had become the most hallowed. But now, 'Ireland blocked the way'; furthermore, the radical assumption of a succession of progressive Liberal Governments with occasional brief Conservative interludes now had to be revised.

Gladstone's Newcastle Programme of 1891 offered a great deal to labour including 'one man, one vote' and land taxes, but even at that stage there were serious doubts about whether it would be implemented

—doubts which were to be amply confirmed. The 1886 Liberal Government had ignored—to its electoral cost—the allotment issue, and its only legislative achievement on social reform was the work of a private Member, Sir John Lubbock, a persistent and single-handed reformer who achieved a great deal. His Act prevented women and children from being employed for more than twelve hours a day, an item of legislation that throws a glaring light upon the indifference of Liberal leaders to the basic social questions of the day. Of equal significance was Gladstone's appeal to the miners of Nottingham in 1892 to give preference to Home Rule over the question of the eight-hour day, and thus sacrifice their 'own views and apparent interests' to a 'wider and weightier cause'. The fact that the Liberal Party was a middle class party with working class support was accepted so long as the party's priorities approximated to those of its mass support. But Irish Home Rule, Local Option—whereby a vote by three-quarters of the ratepayers could close all public houses in a district—disputes over Imperial policy, the role of the House of Lords, and Welsh and Scottish dis-establishment, were not the dominant concerns of labour in the 1890s.

At this moment there occurred an event that clearly demonstrated these schisms. In the General Election of 1892 Keir Hardie was elected to the House of Commons for West Ham South. His arrival at Westminster, bearded, wild-eyed, and wearing a cloth cap, aroused interest, derision, and trepidation. But his life and career were of great significance since, outside Irish politics, no one remotely like him had ever reached the House of Commons before.

Hardie had been born in Lanarkshire in 1856, an illegitimate child brought up in great poverty. As he later wrote, 'I am of the unfortunate class who never knew what it was to be a child—in spirit, I mean. Even the memories of boyhood and young manhood are gloomy.' He began work at the age of eight, and for years his family lived on the brink of destitution. From the age of ten until he was twenty-three he was a coal miner, but one who was determined to educate himself. He read widely and avidly, became a Christian, and developed his own personal and idiosyncratic version of radicalism which embraced strict temperance, a severe puritanism, a mystical attitude towards human progress, and a certain personal arrogance, vanity, and love of the dramatic which not everyone found endearing. Hardie's political philosophies changed, but were always intensely personal and

perplexing to those who tried to work with him. Originally he believed
in the inevitable alliance between Capital and Labour, whose interests
he regarded as identical, but harsh experience tempered this belief into
political atheism. He became secretary of the newly formed Scottish
Miners' National Federation in October 1886, and concerned himself
with the militant leaders of other miners' organisations. Hardie himself
became a militant, and his burgeoning doubts about the Liberal Party
as the true instrument for working class reform began to increase
greatly. In February 1887 the coalowners responded to a miners'
strike with police, and then troops, and the miners were routed. So,
also, were Hardie's dreams of a happy alliance between Capital and
Labour.

Moving to a larger stage, he interested himself in international
socialism, and visited London for the first time in 1887 and attended
the Trade Union Congress at Swansea, where he shocked the delegates
by a violent attack upon Henry Broadhurst, the very model of the safe
Liberal–Labour alliance leader, and by moving for larger working class
representation in Parliament with a new 'labour party'. This was
widely regarded as being in execrable taste, and was universally
denounced. But Hardie was still a Liberal, and probably would have
continued to be so if he had been shown any encouragement. Rejected
twice by Liberal associations—in both cases losing to prosperous
southern barristers—he was driven towards independence. He seemed
a transient phenomenon, interesting but laughable, and of little
account. But in reality he was a portent of doom to the Liberal Party.
He had been theirs for the asking, and they had ignored and humiliated
him. For this they were to pay a very heavy price.

In 1893 the Independent Labour Party was formally founded at
Bradford with the specific purpose of sending working class men to
Parliament who would be independent of the major parties. Although
the I.L.P. at this stage was never much more than a propaganda
society with little real support, and although 'Queer Hardie' lost his
seat in the 1895 General Election, the thought had been put forward
that it might be necessary to establish a new political confederation
which could combine the forces of the new unionism, the industrial
discontent, the intellectual radicalism which could find little satisfaction in a Liberal Party obsessed by other questions, and the growing
feeling that the traditional political parties could not and would not
meet the new imperatives of creating a more equitable society. It was

only a first and very tentative step, but, as the ancient proverb reminds us, in a long march the first step is the most important.

But despite these ominous developments, and the catastrophe which had befallen them over the fall of Parnell, there is little evidence that the Liberals felt much concern about their long-term future in 1892. As their correspondence and recorded discussions demonstrate, the Liberal leaders were troubled about tactics and their immediate prospects, and were deeply concerned by the traumatic events through which their confederation had passed since 1885. But hardly anywhere does one detect any apprehension that the structure of politics lay elsewhere than in the struggle for mastery between themselves and the Conservatives. What cries of alarm that arose were on the alienation of working class supporters by contemporary policies; that the alienation lay much deeper was hardly discerned at all. 'I am vexed to see portions of the labouring class beginning to be corrupted by the semblance of power as the other classes have been tainted and warped by its reality,' Gladstone wrote to Morley in 1892, 'and I am disgusted by finding a portion of them ready to thrust Ireland, which is so far ahead in claim, entirely into the background. Poor, poor, poor human nature'.[1] There were younger Liberals who clearly saw the perils of such attitudes, but in the vital 1890s their party held office only fleetingly, and in that interlude the opportunity was not seized.

[1] Gladstone Papers. Quoted in D. A. Hamer: *Liberal Politics in the Age of Gladstone and Rosebery*, 227.

CHAPTER FIVE

A LIBERAL INTERLUDE, 1892-1895

THE PROFESSION of politics is not a solitary exercise, and thus the observer is often baffled by those apparently inexplicable but very real moods of high exaltation or deep despair that sweep across political groupings, and for which there is no logical explanation beyond the obvious one that human associations are always very human, and consequently often very irrational. In 1892, the Conservatives, whose record since the beginning of 1887 had been disappointing in electoral and administrative terms, eagerly looked forward to the forthcoming elections and the prospect of defeat, while the Liberals were cast into the deepest gloom by that of victory. Individual Conservatives were dismayed at the prospect of losing office, individual Liberals were exultant at the prospect of gaining it, but the collective opinion was wholly contrary. The Conservatives wanted to get out, the Liberals did not want to go in. The former narrowly gained the advantage.

The overwhelming damage done to the Liberal Party by the downfall of Parnell and the lack of any real policies apart from Home Rule could not be repaired by the hasty adoption of every possible radical policy in the Newcastle Programme, nor by the lung-power of Liberal oratory. The rift between the Gladstonian Liberals and the Chamberlain–Devonshire[1] Liberal Unionists was now so substantial that the possibility of Liberal reunion could no longer be seriously discussed. There were indications that the magic of Gladstone's name was itself declining, even in the Liberal ranks, and particularly in those sections that were bored by the issue of Home Rule and were impatient for radical measures at home.

[1] In 1891 Hartington had succeeded his father as the eighth Duke of Devonshire, and had left the House of Commons after having been a Member for thirty-four years, and having been offered—each time under impossible circumstances—the Premiership on three occasions.

When the General Election came in the summer the Home Rule majority was only forty—315 to 355—and Gladstone himself was nearly defeated at Midlothian. The Liberal leadership had hoped for a majority independent of the Irish; now they were wholly dependent upon Irish votes and Irish co-operation in order to maintain themselves in office. The bitter divisions within the Irish Nationalists were demonstrated by the fact that only nine former Parnellites were returned. Gladstone was again—and for the last time—at Dalmeny with Rosebery when he learned of the final majority. One of the company ventured to suggest that it would be sufficient. 'Too small, too small', Gladstone sadly replied.

Salisbury did not resign at once, but decided to face the new Parliament, thus giving the Liberals over a month in which to regroup their forces for the new Government. They needed the time. On August 11th, a motion of no confidence moved by H. H. Asquith in a speech described by a Conservative as 'drastic, caustic, masterly,' was carried in the House of Commons by exactly forty, and the Liberals gloomily and apprehensively took office. The Queen, deeply chagrined by the prospect of Gladstone again, made the unprecedented announcement in the *Court Circular* that she had accepted Salisbury's resignation 'with great regret', and expressed in private her disgust at 'having all those great interests entrusted to the shaking hand of an old, wild and incomprehensible man of $82\frac{1}{2}$'; Gladstone for his part described the meeting between the Queen and himself as 'such as took place between Marie Antoinette and her executioner'.

The existence of the Queen's violent antipathy to Gladstone was not widely known in her lifetime, and his loyal silence on the matter was as noble as it was remarkable. But, for all her fulminations and the severe difficulties she caused him, Gladstone had a real respect for her, and to the end hoped that the relationship might be improved. The Queen, under the wise guidance of the Prince Consort, had come to recognise the perils of the blatant partisanship that had characterised the early period of her reign, and she had excellent advisers, of whom Sir Henry Ponsonby was the wisest. Her common sense, strong understanding of *realpolitik*, and devotion to her work invariably impressed those who had to deal with her. They were all, in truth, in awe of her, even Salisbury, and her influence remained strong. Now, in addition, she was more popular than at any time in her reign, and her rare public appearances produced immense crowds and enthusiasm. But although her antipathies were well concealed, in practical terms she was not unlike the House of Lords—politically quiescent when a Conservative Administration was in office, and a vigilant defender of the national interest when the Liberals were in power. Her impact on policy—particularly foreign policy—could be substantial, and her strong support of Rosebery and Cromer in the 1892–5 Government was to be of considerable significance. If she had little real power judged in normal terms, her influence was very great, and all in public affairs regarded her with respect and apprehension.

Rosebery, whose wife had died suddenly in 1890, and who had been in virtual seclusion since then, had refused to join the Government, and was only persuaded with very great difficulty to take the Foreign Office again. One of the most significant elements in persuading him was the pressure put upon him by the Royal Family. But he made it plain that he came in on his own terms. Gladstone's impatience with him for causing these difficulties was quickly fortified by alarm at Rosebery's policies. Reginald Brett recorded on September 7th of Rosebery that 'he is absolute at the F.O. He informs his colleagues of very little, and does as he pleases. If it offends them, he retires. We shall remain in Egypt, and the continuity of Lord S's policy will not be disturbed. All this is excellent.' There was some point to Harcourt's remark to Rosebery that 'without you the Government would have been simply ridiculous; now it is only impossible!'.

By now, Gladstone was a very old man. The solitary and melancholy Rosebery was aloof. John Morley and Harcourt were on bad terms. At some stage in the period of Opposition—it is not clear exactly when—Morley and Harcourt's son, Lewis (generally known by the unlovely soubriquet of 'Loulou') had come to agreement at Harcourt's New Forest home, Malwood, that Morley would support Harcourt for the leadership when Gladstone retired. The 'Malwood Compact' was showing severe signs of strain by the summer of 1892. Asquith has admirably portrayed this unlikely combination:

> They belonged not only to different generations, but in all essentials, except that of actual chronology, to different centuries. Both of them were men of high and rare cultivation; on the intellectual side, Morley was what Harcourt most loathed, an *ideologue*, and Harcourt was what jarred most upon Morley, a Philistine. Harcourt, with a supposed infusion (however diluted) of Plantagenet blood; the

grandson of a Georgian Archbishop; brought up with the tastes and habits of the castle in which he was born; but a natural mutineer, with a really powerful intelligence, a mordant wit, and a masculine and challenging personality, soon shook off his hereditary fetters, and seemed at one time to be in training for the post of the great Condottiers of the political world. Morley, sprung from the Lancashire middle-class, dipped but not dyed in the waters of Oxford, a youthful acolyte of Mill, had hovered for a time around the threshold of the Comtean conventicle. . . .

Political exigencies make strange stable companions, but rarely two, to all appearance, less well assorted than these. They had hardly even a prejudice in common. . . . Had they a common political faith? It is hard to say—except that, from different points of view, they were equally ardent disciples of what used then to be called the Anti-Imperialist and 'Little England' school.[1]

These clashes of personality and outlook at the top were serious enough, and were to have important and enduring consequences. But perhaps even more serious was the fact that, beyond Home Rule, the Liberals had no agreed programme and no strategy. In spite of his endorsement of the Newcastle Programme, Gladstone was not a believer in programmes but in great unifying single issues as in 1868, 1879–80, or 1885–6. A party, as he had declared in November 1885, should be 'an instrument for the attainment of great ends'. The trouble was that in the 1892 election many—if not most—Liberals had fought on those particular issues in the Newcastle Programme which had most attracted them or seemed most attractive to their constituencies. Home Rule—and Gladstone's own leadership—constituted the only unifying elements in this very heterogenous coalition, and the Liberals came to Westminster with firm but wildly differing priorities. For a time the excitement of Gladstone's last great campaign concealed this fatal deficiency, but when the Home Rule fight was lost nothing remained but a babel.

It was in justifiable low spirits and uneasiness that, on August 18th, the incoming Ministers travelled across the Solent to Osborne to receive their Seals of Office from their bleak and unsympathetic Sovereign. The ceremony took place in a cold and unbroken silence, and the party returned across the waters in a fierce storm amid

[1] Asquith: *Fifty Years of Parliament*, 1, 246–7.

flashes of lightning and crashes of menacing thunder. The Queen privately recorded her impression of the new Ministers as 'rather depressed and embarrassed'. The only surprise in the Cabinet was the elevation of Asquith, at the age of forty, to be Home Secretary, but the appointment of Sir Edward Grey to be Under-Secretary of State at the Foreign Office was almost as significant. Apart from these, and Rosebery, aged forty-five, it was an ageing, dispirited, and divided Government.

All Parliamentary roads led to Ireland. The Second Home Rule Bill differed from that of 1886 in many respects, but the key difference was that the Irish would have representation at Westminster but could only vote on Irish or Imperial concerns, a compromise which had to be abandoned under pressure after the Bill was introduced, and which made matters even worse. As in the 1886 Bill, questions of trade, foreign affairs, and military control were excluded from the scope of the proposed Irish Parliament. As in 1886, and despite the clear evidence of overwhelming Ulster feeling, the special problems and position of Ulster were ignored.

The Bill occupied virtually the entire time of the House of Commons from March until September 1893. It consumed eighty-five sittings, and was piloted throughout by Gladstone himself, a phenomenal performance for a man in his eighty-third year. Chamberlain, in his most relentless and trenchant temper, still sitting on the Liberal benches, and still referring to Gladstone invariably as 'My Right Honourable Friend' was by far his most formidable opponent. 'In the present controversy', Gladstone wrote of Chamberlain to the Queen, 'he has stood very decidedly first in ability among the opponents of the present Bill in the House of Commons.' Henry Lucy reported that: 'It is only when Mr. Chamberlain steps into the arena, and Mr. Gladstone swiftly turns to face him, that benches fill, drooping heads are raised, eyes brighten, the Chamber resounds with cheers and counter-cheers, and the dry bones of the debate rattle into strenuous life'.

Lord Randolph's elder son, Winston Churchill, then aged nineteen, was a witness of Gladstone's winding up of the Second Reading, and which he recalled nearly forty years later:

Well do I remember the scene and some of its incidents. The Grand Old Man looked like a great white eagle at once fierce and splendid.

His sentences rolled forth majestically and everyone hung upon his lips and gestures, eager to cheer or deride. He was at the climax of a tremendous passage about how the Liberal Party had always carried every cause it had espoused to victory. He made a slip. 'And there is no cause,' he exclaimed (Home Rule), 'for which the Liberal Party has suffered so much or *descended so low*'. How the Tories leapt and roared their delight! But Mr. Gladstone, shaking his right hand with fingers spread claw-like, quelled the tumult and resumed, ' But we have risen again'.[1]

Faced with the implacable Unionist opposition, the Government resorted first to the Closure and then to the Guillotine procedure, and, chunk by chunk, the Bill was rammed through. When Chamberlain depicted the Irish Members as 'nominated by priests, elected by illiterates, and subsidised by the enemies of our country', Gladstone accused him of using 'habitual, coarse, and enormous exaggeration'. On July 27th the accumulated passions of a long and a hot summer exploded when Chamberlain was replying to Gladstone. 'The Prime Minister calls "black" and they say "it is good". The Prime Minister calls "white", and they say "it is better". Never since the time of Herod has there been such slavish adulation.' There was a scream of 'Judas!' from the Irish, and the House fell quickly out of control. Members jostled each other, minor scuffles broke out, the galleries hissed in disapproval, and order was not restored until the majestic figure of Mr. Speaker Peel appeared. This was, however, the final point of passion in the long debate, and was not characteristic of its general temper. It was harsh in expression, bitterly fought at every point, but dominated by the restrained passion of Gladstone and Chamberlain. And at one point there was an incident that no one who witnessed it—including the young Winston Churchill in the galleries— ever forgot.

Chamberlain's elder son, Austen, had been elected for East Worcestershire in 1892. In appearance and dress, even to the monocle, he was startlingly like his father, and his maiden speech was an ordeal of very particular difficulty in which he acquitted himself well. On the first possible public occasion Gladstone—who had been genuinely impressed—turned to Joseph Chamberlain and remarked that 'it was a speech which must have been dear and refreshing to a father's

[1] Winston S. Churchill: *My Early Life*, 34.

heart'. Churchill relates that he saw Chamberlain's normally sallow countenance go pink, he started 'as if a bullet had struck him' and then he half rose and bowed, 'then hunched himself up with lowered head. . . . It was the way the thing was done that swept aside for a moment the irreparable enmities of years'.[1]

Gladstone's last and greatest effort was in vain. The House of Lords, the constitutional undertakers, contemptuously buried the Bill on September 8th after a debate of insulting perfunctoriness by 419 votes to forty-one. It was said that 'not a dog barked'. Gladstone wanted to dissolve Parliament and fight the Lords in the country, but was overruled by his colleagues. From this point the Liberal Government was lost.

*

On paper, this was a strong and talented Government, and more cohesive than the 1880–6 Governments. Gladstone, Harcourt, Morley and Rosebery provided the ballast and experience, supported by men of the calibre of Campbell-Bannerman (War), Henry Fowler (Local Government) and Lord Spencer (Admiralty), while Asquith and Edward Grey represented the very able group of young Liberals who had entered the Commons in the 1880s. But in practice it was sorely divided. Gladstone and Morley cared deeply about Home Rule, Harcourt and Rosebery hardly at all. On foreign and, above all, colonial policy, Rosebery found himself confronted by the hostile trio of Gladstone, Harcourt and Morley, yet this combination was beset by personal antipathies. Harcourt's well-known tendency to hectoring arrogance was now more raspingly apparent than ever. Gladstone was an old man obsessed by Home Rule, who viewed all other issues with impatience. Harcourt delighted in issuing fierce memoranda and commands to his colleagues from his Treasury desk. Morley sulked in Dublin, while Rosebery locked himself up in the Foreign Office and took command of foreign policy. As an indication of the manner in which this Cabinet operated, a letter from Asquith to Rosebery (February 10th, 1893) may be quoted:

I understand that on Monday a Bill (To 'amend the provision' for the Government of Ireland), which neither you nor I have seen, is to be introduced into the House of Commons. I send you word of

[1] Churchill, op. cit., 35.

this, as you may possibly like to be present, and hear what Her Majesty's Government have to propose.

Behind the personal differences they lay important issues, of which the most significant and divisive was over foreign—and specifically colonial—policy. Rosebery, having come in on his own terms, was determined to maintain a strong British presence in Egypt and to extend British influence in East Africa by taking over responsibility for Uganda from the ailing East Africa Company. On both points he was strongly opposed by Gladstone and Harcourt, yet on both, after sharp disputes, he gained the day. But the ill-feeling which had been generated was to prove enduring. The Queen was impressed by Rosebery's resolute handling of these matters; the anti-Imperialist section of the Liberal Party was not.

Gladstone did not have the authority to remove Rosebery, although he was sorely tempted. The titanic feat of piloting the Home Rule Bill through the Commons, only to see it arrogantly butchered by the Lords, was now followed by the refusal of his colleagues to follow his urgings for immediate dissolution. Those colleagues hoped—some none too secretly—that he would resign quietly and that there would be an agreed and orderly succession. Gladstone was indeed seeking a way out of his position, but it was to be on an issue of principle and conducted in a manner which was to make his successor's position as difficult—if not—impossible as could be contrived. It was not deliberately or calculatingly done, but no assessment of Gladstone can afford to omit that element of moral vanity in his personality, made more marked by age and disappointment.

The crisis that led to Gladstone's eventual resignation was over the issue of naval rebuilding. Concern at the relative strength of the Navy, particularly in the Mediterranean, was given dramatic emphasis by the loss of the battleship *Victoria* in June 1893. The Admiralty produced a desired and a minimum programme, and by the middle of December Spencer had agreed to the latter one. His arguments were accepted by the entire Cabinet, with the exception of the Prime Minister. Gladstone virtually cut off relations with his colleagues, and the Cabinet operated in limbo until Gladstone ended this embarrassing interlude with his resignation on March 2nd. If he had been asked to name his successor he would—the Naval Estimates notwithstanding—have recommended Spencer. He felt, with good cause, that his advice should have been sought by the Queen, but it was not. It was a heartless, brutal snub, which Gladstone felt keenly. It did not reflect well on the Queen, but for all her faults she was supremely honest. She loathed Gladstone, regarded him as unbalanced and irresponsible, and was glad to see him go at last. On March 3rd her Private Secretary called at the Foreign Office with a letter inviting Rosebery to form an Administration.

Why Rosebery? Subsequently, there were many Liberals who regretted the Queen's choice. But, at the time, there was virtually no questioning. He was the natural selection, 'the man of the future' as Gladstone had once described him. The Cabinet would not have Harcourt, and the intensive lobbying of the devoted Loulou had only served to demonstrate this fact. Most significant of all, Morley was deeply estranged and the Malwood Compact had been abrogated. All Loulou's attempts to stir up anti-Rosebery and pro-Harcourt feeling conspicuously failed. The Liberal Press came out strongly for Rosebery. It was an uncontested succession—or so it was thought.

*

Modern British politics present us with few careers and personalities of greater interest and complexity than that of Archibald Philip Primrose, fifth Earl of Rosebery. An early biographer, E. T. Raymond, has commented fairly that:

> By omitting certain sets of facts, and placing others in a strong light, he can be proved almost anything we like—a man before his age, a man behind it; a strong, far-seeing statesman, a sentimentalist bemused by his own incantations and watchwords; a patriot too pure for the vulgar commerce of politics, a politician too slippery to be trusted by men themselves not over-particular. . . . His admirers will have him all godhead. His detractors make him all clay feet.

The broad outlines of his career may be briefly summarised. He had been born in 1847, the elder son and third child of Archibald, Lord Dalmeny, and Lady Wilhelmina Stanhope, daughter of the fourth Earl Stanhope. He was educated at Eton, and then at Christ Church, Oxford, until, given the choice between relinquishing the ownership of a racehorse and remaining at Oxford, he chose the horse.

His father had died suddenly in 1851, and he succeeded his grand-father to the Rosebery title and estates in 1868. Ten years later he married Miss Hannah Rothschild, one of the greatest heiresses of the day. In his twenties he became increasingly interested in politics, and was identified with the Liberal Party from the beginning. In 1879, as has been recorded, he sprang into national prominence when he sponsored—and helped to finance—Gladstone's Midlothian campaigns. It would be difficult to overemphasise the importance of this episode on Rosebery's career. In Scotland, his reputation was, and always afterwards remained, immense. 'The first time I ever saw Lord Rosebery was in Edinburgh when I was a student', J. M. Barrie wrote, 'and I flung a clod of earth at him. He was a peer; those were my politics . . . [but] during the first Midlothian campaign Mr. Gladstone and Lord Rosebery were the father and son of the Scottish people. Lord Rosebery rode into fame on the top of that wave, and has kept his place in the hearts of the people, and in oleographs on their walls, ever since.' And Margot Asquith has related:

> Whenever there was a crowd in the streets or at the station, in either Glasgow or Edinburgh, and I enquired what it was all about I always received the same reply: 'Rozbury!'.

On the public platform he had a commanding presence and wonderful voice. As Augustine Birrell has written: 'His melodious voice . . . his underlying strain of humour, his choice of words, never either staled by vulgar usage or tainted with foreign idiom, and above all his "out of the way" personality, and a certain nervousness of manner that suggested at times the possibility of a breakdown, kept his audience in a flutter of enjoyment and excitement. He was certainly the most "interesting" speaker I have ever heard.'

In private he could be a fascinating companion. 'The marvel of his conversation', John Buchan has written, 'was its form. He spoke finished prose as compared with the slovenly patois of most of us, and his thoughts clothed themselves naturally with witty and memorable words'. And Winston Churchill has recorded:

> It is difficult to convey the pleasure I derived from his conversation, as it ranged easily and spontaneously upon all kinds of topics 'from grave to gay, from lively to severe'. Its peculiar quality was the unexpected depths or suggestive turns which revealed the size of the

1 Benjamin Disraeli 1869: by 'Ape', *Vanity Fair*

2 Lord Salisbury 1869: by 'Ape', *Vanity Fair*

3 Charles Stewart Parnell, 1880: by 'T', *Vanity Fair*

4 Lord Randolph Churchill and the Fourth Party, 1880
(John Gorst, Arthur Balfour, Sir Henry Drummond Wolff):
by 'Spy', *Vanity Fair*

5 'Vice Versa': the Old Chancellor of the Exchequer and the
New—Gladstone and Lord Randolph Churchill, 1886: *The Graphic*

6 The Lobby of the House of Commons, 1886: by 'Lib', *Vanity Fair*.

From left to right: Inspector Denning, Mr Milman (Clerk Assistant), Mr John Bright, Sir W. Harcourt, Mr Gosset (Deputy Serjeant), Mr Labouchere, Mr Bradlaugh, Mr Chamberlain, Mr Parnell, Mr Gladstone, Lord Randolph Churchill, Lord Hartington, Mr Chaplin, Mr G. Leveson Gower, The Hon R. Spencer,

7 H. H. Asquith: by 'Spy', *Vanity Fair*

8 Gladstone introducing the Second Home Rule Bill, 1893

9 Gladstone on the Treasury Bench, 1893: by Phil May

10 Sir William Harcourt: by F. Carruthers Gould

11 The Earl of Rosebery, 1885: by John Everett Millais

12 John Morley: by Harry Furniss

13 A. J. Balfour: by Phil May

14 Andrew Bonar Law: by
'Spy', *Vanity Fair*

15 Joseph Chamberlain in 1901: by
'Spy', *Vanity Fair*

16 Winston Churchill: by 'Spy', *Vanity Fair*

17 F. E. Smith: by 'Spy', *Vanity Fair*

subject and his own background of knowledge and reflection. At the same time he was full of fun. He made many things not only arresting, but merry. He seemed as much a master of trifles and gossip as of weighty matters. He was keenly conscious about every aspect of life. Sportsman, epicure, bookworm, literary critic, magpie collector of historical relics, appreciative owner of veritable museums of art treasures, he never needed to tear a theme to tatters. In lighter vein he flitted jauntily from flower to flower like a glittering insect, by no means unprovided with a sting. And then, in contrast, out would come his wise, matured judgements upon the great men and events of the past. But these treats were not always given.

To the public, Rosebery possessed political glamour. His wealth, particularly after his marriage to Hannah Rothschild, was considerable, and he lived in the grand style. 'There are many glass doors', Edward Grey wrote of Mentmore, the Rothschild-Rosebery palace in Buckinghamshire, 'but some are locked, and others open with difficulty—and egress and regress are more or less formal; you may *go* out or in but not *slip* out or in.' Rosebery's style, his ownership of racehorses, his intellectual interests and pursuits, combined to make him a refreshing and exciting political figure.

As has been indicated, his relationship with Gladstone had not been an easy one. It reflected both Gladstone's inadequacies in dealing with men and also Rosebery's acute sensitiveness. He refused office in 1880, in spite of much pressure: 'Lord Rosebery would accept nothing', Granville told the Queen, 'as he said it would look as if Mr. Gladstone had paid him for what he had done.' To Gladstone he wrote that if he took office 'I should feel that where I only meant personal devotion and public spirit, others would see and perhaps with reason personal ambition and public office seeking.' But a vacancy occurred at the Home Office in July 1881, and Rosebery had become a junior Minister with special, but undefined, responsibilities for Scottish affairs. This had not been a happy interlude. Rosebery's senior Minister had been Harcourt, and although the relationship between the two men had not been, at this stage, uncomfortable, Rosebery had quickly discovered that his actual responsibility for Scottish affairs was minimal. Gladstone, heavily occupied with other major problems, had insufficient time or inclination to respond sympathetically to the complaints of a junior Minister. Gladstone was also a firm believer in the values of seniority. It was unwise to have taken this attitude; Rosebery might have held only a junior position in the Government, but, although young, he was not a minor public figure. He very nearly resigned when Parnell was released from Kilmainham in April 1882, then stood beside his leader when Cavendish and Burke were assassinated.

In the autumn of 1882, when there was a Cabinet reconstruction, Rosebery was left out. Furthermore, his ambiguous position at the Home Office had preyed on his mind. With tactful handling all might have been well, but Gladstone did not handle the matter tactfully, and there was a somewhat sharp exchange of letters. In May 1883 Rosebery eagerly seized an opportunity to resign.

This episode was significant in many respects. It demonstrated the lack of real personal sympathy and understanding between Gladstone and Rosebery which was never to be fully created, and it also showed a defect in Rosebery's character which has been admirably summarised by Winston Churchill:

> In times of crisis and responsibility his active, fertile mind and imagination preyed upon him. He was bereft of sleep. He magnified trifles. He failed to separate the awkward incidents of the hour from the long swing of events, which he so clearly understood. Toughness when nothing particular was happening was not the form of fortitude in which he excelled. He was unduly attracted by the dramatic, and by the pleasure of making a fine gesture.

After telling Gladstone that he would never return to office except as a member of the Cabinet, Rosebery had ventured to Australia. This journey had had a decisive influence on his attitudes. The Empire was only just beginning to excite serious interest in Liberal political circles, but Rosebery had been, from his earliest days, a believer in the Empire. In 1874, in his first major public speech, he had drawn a picture of Britain as 'the affluent mother of giant Commonwealths and peaceful Empires that shall perpetuate the best qualities of the race', and in 1882, in his Rectorial Address at Edinburgh University he had compared the Empire to 'a sheet knit at the four corners, containing all manner of men, fitted for their separate climate and work and spheres of action, but honouring the common vessel which contains them.' Thus, in 1883 he went to Australia a supporter of Empire; he returned with a burning conviction in the future development of the colonies, and at Adelaide, on January 18th 1884, he made his famous declaration that: 'There is no need for any nation, however great, leaving the Empire, because the Empire is a Commonwealth of Nations.' On his return he described himself as a 'Liberal Imperialist', and said that 'Imperialism, sane Imperialism, as distinguished from what I might call "wild cat" Imperialism, is nothing but this—a larger patriotism.' He declared his support for the Imperial Federation League, and made a greatly applauded speech on the subject to the Trades Union Congress at Aberdeen.

Attempts to bring him back to the Government might have failed had not the death of Gordon, and the temper of public feeling against Gladstone, aroused him. He became Lord Privy Seal and First Commissioner of Works.

When he accepted Gladstone's offer of the Foreign Office in January 1886 at the age of thirty-seven, he was not particularly enthusiastic about Home Rule but was prepared to accept it as the only practical alternative to further coercion. This stand won him not only high office but enormous enthusiasm within the Gladstonian Liberal ranks, and his conduct of foreign affairs had been widely—and excessively—praised. He enunciated the doctrine of the continuity of British foreign policy, continued Salisbury's policies, and won golden opinions from all sides. When he became, in 1889, first Chairman of the new London County Council, this attracted the admiration of progressive Liberals everywhere, and particularly those at Westminster to whom Ireland obstinately barred the way to bold social reform.

And then, in November 1890, his wife died. This personal tragedy brought out a latent melancholia, and seemed to destroy what personal ambition he had ever possessed. Insomnia, which had always plagued him in moments of crisis, now became chronic. Until this disaster, Rosebery had everything. To Liberals, he was the young hero of Midlothian, the mature Minister, the radical social reformer, and one of the most arresting public speakers of the day. The Unionists respected him. He was known as a man of taste and style, civilised and alert, adept at all situations. His friends were awed by his wit and intelligence, and his brief biography of Pitt, published in 1890, had won new admirers.

But beneath this glittering surface there lay many doubts and indecisions, and a very taut and nervous personality. The death of Hannah Rosebery was a blow from which he never really recovered, and whose severity startled even those who thought they knew him best. Amateur psychologists may see in Hannah Rosebery the emotional replacement for the mother whom Rosebery had never liked and from whom he was distant, even as a child. Certainly she gave to him a strength and a confidence which he was never to recapture. Perhaps, with his fatalistic and gloomy view of life, he considered that a chapter had closed, and should not be reopened. Whatever the causes, the Rosebery after 1890 was a different man, in the sense that the latent weaknesses which were dimly evident to the more observant before then were now magnified.

But it is doubtful if any member of the Cabinet could have pulled together the Liberals in March 1894. The political circumstances of Rosebery's accession to the Premiership could not have been less inspiriting. It was, as Winston Churchill has written, 'a bleak, precarious, wasting inheritance'. The internal schisms were an added misery. Harcourt and his son did not accept their defeat; they attempted to secure conditions on foreign policy, and throughout the rest of the existence of the Government they made no attempt to conceal their contempt for the man who had destroyed their joint ambition. To say that they behaved badly is to place too charitable a judgement upon their activities during the following fifteen months.

Morley, too, was chagrined. It is difficult to explain his sudden movement away from Rosebery when the brief succession crisis was over without taking into account his intense sensitivity to small or imagined slights. Morley had come to value his position too highly. He was an intellectual who was fascinated by power, and his devotion to Gladstone had been total, almost filial. He was now emotionally overwrought, disconsolate, and affronted. He informed Rosebery that he would only be responsible for his department, and returned to Dublin, where he brooded bleakly for the rest of the life of the Government.

The Queen also oppressed Rosebery. She treated him in a different manner to that with which she had dealt with Gladstone, but with similar effect. Her letters to him were maternal but minatory. An early missive set the tone:

She does not object to Liberal measures which are not revolutionary and she does not think it possible that Lord Rosebery will destroy well tried, valued, and necessary institutions for the sole purpose of flattering useless Radicals or pandering to the pride of those whose only desire is their own self-gratification.

These were heavy burdens, and Rosebery was not the man to bear them. He began with a serious blunder when, in his first speech in the Lords as Prime Minister, he said in effect that Home Rule would have to be held in abeyance until there was an English majority that supported it. The Irish were appalled, the Unionists exultant. In the Commons that evening Labouchere seized his opportunity and carried an Amendment to the Address, by a majority of two, that practically abolished the powers of the House of Lords. It was, to say the least, an inauspicious beginning.

The first major crisis between Rosebery and Harcourt came over the latter's Budget of 1894. Harcourt's scheme—the creation of Alfred Milner, Chairman of the Board of Inland Revenue—included the introduction of a graduated death duty on property. It was a relatively modest step in itself, but its implications alarmed many, including Gladstone, who described it as 'by far the most Radical measure of my lifetime'. When Rosebery set out some of his own apprehensions in a memorandum, Harcourt retorted with a vehement onslaught, implying strongly that Rosebery was alarmed because of his own properties, and ending with the observation that 'the fate of the present Government and issue of the next Election are temporary incidents which I view with philosophic indifference.' Having delivered this highly personal philippic, Harcourt grandly agreed to the maximum being reduced from ten to eight per cent.

On Foreign Affairs, relations grew increasingly acrid as the year progressed. Again, on the main issue it was arguable that Harcourt was in the right, but, again, the manner in which he acted was intolerable. The defeat of Rosebery's proposed Anglo-Congolese Treaty in the summer of 1894 was more the result of French and German opposition than Harcourt's outbursts in the Cabinet, but the latter were not without their significance. Relations between the two men were now really bad; on one memorandum by Harcourt Rosebery minuted, 'Can *la betise humaine* further go?'.

The Cabinet did not pursue any fixed policy on any issue. Rosebery began an assault on the House of Lords that horrified the Queen—to the point that she seriously considered demanding a Dissolution—and was in effect disavowed by the Cabinet, which was indignant that it had not been consulted. Harcourt launched a personal campaign for Local Option. Morley publicly attempted to restore the Home Rule issue to its primacy. In January 1895, at Cardiff, Rosebery sounded forth on the issue of Welsh Disestablishment. The confusion was total. By-elections fell from bad to disastrous. From Gladstone, in nominal retirement, dank clouds of disapproval betokened a smouldering discontent. In the House of Commons Harcourt barely troubled to give the impression of supporting his leader, and Dilke and Labouchere seized every occasion for embarrassing the Government. This, in the circumstances, was not an especially arduous occupation. The loyal back-benchers gathered together in gloomy knots in the Lobby. Deputations to the equally bewildered Whips were fruitless. It was a hopeless, slithering, decline.

Gladstone's failure to consult his colleagues in the years of Opposition, the lack of agreed priorities, and the 'something-for-everyone' character of the Newcastle Programme, now had to be paid for. Rosebery was probably right in going for a large single issue, but not only did he not consult his colleagues but his proposals for the Lords were much too vague; the Conservatives could attack them for their imprecision, the Radicals for their moderation. Meanwhile the advocates of Welsh and Scottish disestablishment, Local Option, universal suffrage, and the rest, pressed the claims of their particular faiths upon Ministers with, in Rosebery's words, 'appeals, some of them menacing, some of them coaxing and cajoling, but all of them extremely earnest, and praying that the particular hobby of the writer shall be made the first Government Bill'.

Whatever chances Rosebery had of restoring the situation, were destroyed by the serious ill-health, aggravated by insomnia, which afflicted him from February to April 1895. On February 19th, goaded beyond endurance, he had virtually told his Cabinet to support him or let him resign, and his ultimatum had had a temporary success. But then, at a vital period in his party's fortunes he was prostrated, and whatever hope that lingered of his political recovery was lost. It was the coldest winter for more than fifty years; ice-flows were in the Thames, and there was considerable suffering, and a scourge of influenza of which Rosebery was the most conspicious victim. But influenza was hardly the only cause of Rosebery's collapse, and may be regarded as the final blow to an exhausted, lonely, and over-wrought personality.

In the January of that bitter winter, Lord Randolph Churchill was brought home to his mother's home in Grosvenor Square to die, from a tragic world tour which had had to be hurriedly curtailed. His last appearances in the House of Commons had been agonising for all, and the House had looked with sadness and pain at the spectacle of this trembling, rambling, inarticulate, and prematurely aged man. Most moving of all was the care and attention and courtesy with which Gladstone had listened to Lord Randolph's incomprehensible maunderings, and responded to them as though they had been serious contributions to debate. 'Lord Randolph stood at the Table, sad wreck of a man, attempting to read a carefully-prepared manuscript in a voice so strangely jangled that few could catch the meaning of consecutive sentences', Lucy recorded sadly. 'As soon as he rose Ministers began to move towards the door. When he had sat down he had talked the place half-empty—he at whose rising eight years ago the House filled to its utmost capacity.' Churchill's pitiable decline and death distressed Rosebery, his Eton contemporary and oldest and closest friend, very profoundly, and contributed substantially to his own melancholy.

The Conservatives in the Lords, exhilarated by the almost total popular indifference to the destruction of the Home Rule Bill, now proceeded to mutilate what progressive legislation the Government sent up to them. 'When the Conservative Party is in power', Rosebery wrote to the Queen, 'there is practically no House of Lords . . . but the moment a Liberal Government is formed, this harmless body assumes an active life, and its activity is entirely exercised in opposition to the Government. . . . It is, in fact, a permanent barrier against the Liberal party.' The Queen was not converted, describing any agitation against the Lords as 'a most revolutionary Proceeding'. The absence of public —or even party—reaction to Rosebery's attacks on the Lords encouraged the Conservatives to continue on their course. Their complete success on this occasion was to lure them into subsequent misfortune.

Thus, leaderless and disheartened, acutely divided among themselves, with the fate of their legislation at the whim of their opponents, the Rosebery Government drifted miserably towards disintegration. Campbell-Bannerman, whose rising stature was marked, eagerly sought the Speakership on the retirement of Speaker Peel—himself suddenly a shadow of his former greatness—and was distressed at

Rosebery's refusal to accept the proposal. The Parliamentary Party was becoming almost impossible to control. The Radicals were enraged by Asquith's bland attitude towards the deaths of two miners at Featherstone Colliery when troops opened fire during a bitter coal strike in 1893 which had eventually been resolved by Rosebery's mediation—his last triumph before the Premiership fell upon him. Campbell-Bannerman became locked in a prolonged, embarrassing, but eventually successful endeavour to remove the ancient and im- possible Duke of Cambridge from his post of Commander-in-Chief of the Army. The full story of how the aged, spirited, and reluctant Duke was prised from his cherished post may be described with some justification as one of the more comic interludes of the time. The high point was reached when the Prince of Wales, in what Campbell-Bannerman described to Rosebery as 'in quite a casual picktooth sort of manner', told the old Duke en route to Kempton Races that the Queen wanted him to resign. The Duke stiffened. The Queen pressed him. The Duke became obdurate. His friends rallied to his cause. 'The Kaleidoscopic changes in the old Duke's humour are rapidly driving C.B. and Bigge out of their minds', the Prime Minister's private secretary succinctly reported. It was decreed that he must retire on November 1st. He issued 'a piteous letter' begging reconsideration, and then raised the issue of his pension. Another agitated series of discussions ensued, centred on the Duke's demand for an additional £2,000 a year over his Civil List income of £12,000. The Cabinet would not put such a proposal to Parliament. The Duke was defeated. He tried to revive the matter with the Unionist Government, but without success. This episode not only engrossed the attention of the Queen and the Secretary of State for War and preoccupied the Prime Minister to an excessive extent at a difficult moment, but also gave Campbell-Bannerman's successor the opportunity to pass over Sir Redvers Buller—the Liberal choice—and to appoint Lord Wolseley, now in his dotage. The post was retained, and other more vital aspects of Army Reform seriously delayed. The consequences became apparent in 1899.

A proposal to raise a statue of Oliver Cromwell at Westminster aroused wild Irish fury, and had to be abandoned. It was eventually commissioned and undertaken at Rosebery's own expense, and placed outside Westminster Hall. When his horses won the Derby in 1894 and 1895 the condemnations of outraged Nonconformity fell upon him.[1] Relations between the Prime Minister and the Leader of the House of Commons were non-existent. The Queen was deeply disappointed by the tone and style of Rosebery's speeches, and wrote to him frequently and at great length on these and other topics. Questions were asked about the bestowal of honours on certain wealthy but obscure Liberals, the first public hint of scandals to come, and which, curiously enough, really originated with Gladstone.[2] It was not surprising that Ministers anticipated the demise of the Administration with eagerness.

Despite this dispiriting situation, new Liberal reputations were being made. Asquith had fully justified his early promotion, in spite of his somewhat detached attitude towards the Featherstone deaths. From relatively humble origins he had been a moderately successful barrister but a very successful political lawyer. In May 1894 he had married the ebullient and rich Margot Tennant—his first wife having died three years earlier—and had moved into a very different circle than his previous modest existence in Hampstead. He was clearly a coming man, with a certain gravitas which made him seem older than he was, eloquent, and incisive.

On the Liberal back benches, attention was being taken of a young Welsh lawyer, in his early thirties, who had first entered the Commons for Caernarvon Boroughs at a by-election in 1890. David Lloyd George was evidently a young man of burning ambition and rare eloquence whose eyes had been on a political career from an early age. He had not been brought up in the kind of poverty that he later affected to claim, but life in the small village of Llanystumdwy provided an education hardly commensurate with that of the majority of his colleagues in the House of Commons. Elected by a majority of eighteen votes in 1890, he had increased this to 196 in 1892, and

[1] Rosebery later commented that it was interesting to note that 'although without guilt or offence I might perpetually run seconds or thirds, or even last, it became a matter of torture to many consciences if I won'. When politicians run out of political luck, everything seems to go wrong.
[2] See H. J. Hanham, *Victorian Studies*, March 1960, 'The Sale of Honours in the Late Victorian England' and the author's *Rosebery*, pp. 379–81. Although it may not have been a 'sale', the most blatant case of the use of honours was the baronetcy conferred on Captain Naylor-Leyland in June 1895. Naylor-Leyland had been Conservative M.P. for Colchester until February 1895, when he resigned so suddenly and unexpectedly that the Liberals—obviously prepared—won the seat in the by-election. Naylor-Leyland, aged thirty-one, then announced he had joined the Liberals.

particularly in the debates on Welsh Disestablishment he had given clear evidence of formidable debating skills and independence, a scourge of Ministers and disdainful of Whips. He was to survive the 1895 General Election with a majority of 194, and to escape the disaster which was to overwhelm so many Liberals and to end several promising careers.

But it was evident that the Liberals could not long survive, and their leaders had little heart for continuing their wretched existence. A chance defeat in the House of Commons on June 21st on an Opposition motion condemning the Government's handling of cordite production gave them their opportunity to resign. The occasion had certain resemblances with the celebrated defeat of the Gladstone Government in June 1885. It had been a soporific debate, in an almost deserted Chamber. There was little merit in the Opposition's case, and Campbell-Bannerman—who earlier in the evening had received much praise for his handling of the affair of the Duke of Cambridge—had spoken convincingly. But the Ministerial ranks were thin, and after the Whips had exchanged the paper giving the figures, neither believing what they read, the result was a Government minority of seven votes (125 to 132). In the words of an observer, 'Mr. Campbell-Bannerman shut up his box with a snap, and moved to report progress, thus bringing Supply, and all contentious legislation, to a close'. It also brought the Rosebery Government to its conclusion.

The decision to resign was an emotional rather than a measured decision, and was strongly opposed by the party organisers, but the spectacle of Rosebery and Harcourt in full agreement, combined with Campbell-Bannerman's insistence on resigning, carried the exhausted Cabinet without difficulty. 'There are two supreme pleasures in life', Rosebery later wrote with feeling: 'One is ideal, the other real. The ideal is when a man receives the seals of office from his Sovereign. The real pleasure comes when he hands them back.' As the Queen noted: 'To him personally it would be an immense relief if the Government were to go out as the scenes in the Cabinet must have been quite dreadful.'

The record of this ill-starred Government was far from derisory. Rosebery's foreign policy, particularly in Africa, had been aggressive and, on the whole, successful. British influence in Egypt had been consolidated, and the British presence in East Africa firmly established. A clear warning had been given to France that the British regarded the

Upper Nile as being in their sphere of influence. Rhodes's advance northwards had been tacitly approved. Vital, and long overdue, reforms had been made in the armed services—albeit not sweeping enough. Fowler's Local Government Act had been a major advance, and Harcourt's Death Duties Budget had not only opened up new and dramatic possibilities for revenue collection for future Chancellors of the Exchequer but had established a precedent for the use of property for the State which was to have immense consequences. Given the hapless circumstances of its life, the Liberal Government achieved much more than was recognised at the time.

But it entered the 1895 General Election, called immediately after Rosebery had resigned and Salisbury had resumed his interrupted occupation of the Premiership, an army defeated before the battle. Edward Marjoribanks—now Lord Tweedmouth—and a former Chief Whip wrote to Rosebery from the National Liberal Federation offices that 'I've been here all this week with really little to do except interview a few callers and struggle with innumerable demands for speakers. "You must send us Harcourt, J. Morley, Asquith or Fowler" is the cry, and as three out of the four seem determined to crow only on their own dunghills there's small chance of gratifying the criers.'

Significantly, 124 Unionists were returned unopposed, whereas only ten Liberals had uncontested elections. 'Captain' Middleton's organisation was now operating with great efficiency. Gladstone did not stand, Harcourt and Morley were among the ranks of the defeated Liberals (both returned to the Commons shortly afterwards), and the Unionist majority was 152. Rosebery wrote to Ripon that 'I expected this overthrow, and think it a great blessing to the Liberal Party'. To Gladstone he wrote that 'the firm of Rosebery and Harcourt was a fraud upon the public', and let it be publicly known that he would have no relations with Harcourt.

Thus it remained for another year, in spite of occasional, not altogether full-hearted, efforts to bring the deeply estranged leaders together. In that year the gulf between the two widened, and Rosebery thankfully seized an opportunity, provided by a speech by Gladstone on the Turkish massacres of Armenians, to resign on October 8th 1896. In his farewell speech in Edinburgh on the following evening he picked out Asquith—who was present—for particular praise, but for the next two years the Liberals were led by the uneasy partnership of Harcourt and Morley. But Rosebery, depicted as 'the veiled prophet' by the *Daily Chronicle*, retained—and perhaps even enhanced—his unique fascination for the Liberals. It was only slowly that they realised that his ambitions had been destroyed and his spirit broken by private and public misfortunes from which he was destined never to recover. He was still young, and had an immense popular following. But that inner core of resolution and self-confidence, so vital to success in politics, and so difficult to describe, had died.

One of the best portraits of Rosebery's mood is supplied by Edward Hamilton, who stayed with him at The Durdans on June 11th 1899 and recorded in his diary that he found his friend absorbed in Napoleon and Chatham and 'all the less inclined to join in the political throng and all the more minded to hold aloof. In fact he declines point blank to take up any other attitude than that which he has taken up since he retired. He will not admit that he owes anything to his colleagues, after their outrageous behaviour towards him when he was trying to lead them. No one was ever subject to greater ignominy than he was during his short reign. Moreover, public life or rather active participation in public life is, he declares, very distasteful to him; and I am sure that this is a much more genuine feeling than most people would imagine. What he likes—at least this is my belief— is to figure largely in the mind of the public and at the same time to be independent and thus not over-weighted with responsibility. And this is just what he has got though he declines to admit it. . . . He refuses to budge one inch in the direction of emerging from his shell. He declares he is a fatalist, and it is only by fate that he could possibly find himself so situated as to be forced into taking the helm again. He sincerely hoped that such a fate did not await him. . . . I am sure he is not intentionally deceiving me and others: though he may be deceiving himself, as I believe he is doing.'

Hamilton's account and conclusions are confirmed by all other sources, save the last. Rosebery was not deceiving himself; he meant every word. Unhappily, others could not or would not accept that this brilliant man, fifty years of age, had renounced politics. But he had.

Salisbury invited Chamberlain, Devonshire, Sir Henry James, Goschen, and the Marquis of Lansdowne to join his new Cabinet. All accepted, and, six months after his death, Lord Randolph Churchill's proposed Unionist Alliance of 1886 was thus formally signified, and the Liberal Interlude was concluded.

*

At this point it is necessary to take stock of the general situation as it existed in June 1895, and to turn aside from political fluctuations and fortunes.

The relative decline in British trade and industry from the 1870s onwards was significant, but should not be exaggerated. For example, British seaborne trade in the period 1880–1900 averaged £710 million a year, three times that of France and ten times that of Russia; seventy per cent of the foreign trade of China was, in effect, in British hands. Nevertheless, Britain was now third in the production of steel, her consumption of raw cotton was virtually stagnant, and save in ship-building and mercantile business, there were few exceptions to the general picture of both a real and relative slowing-up of the British economy. Agriculture, beginning to recover from the disasters of the 1870s, now suffered further blows. The Parsons turbine and the Dunlop pneumatic tyre were the only significant technological con-tributions made by Britain in this period, in sharp and painful contrast with the ingenuity and inventiveness of the rapidly ascendant Germany and the United States. Wages were increasing—by about seventy-seven per cent in real wages since 1860, a quarter of this achieved in the decade 1890–1900—but although it would be absurd to portray Britain as a poor nation, or even a nation becoming poorer, the full effects of the loss of momentum in the 1870s were being seen in the 1890s.

One effect concerned British attitudes to the outside world. The actual increase in British overseas trade from the territories acquired after 1880 was, by 1901, only 2½ per cent of the total.[1] But the economic interest in these, and prospective, acquisitions was now increasing. The new attitude has been well summarised by Dr. C. J. Lowe:

> Essentially the problem by 1900 was that with the decline in comparative industrial efficiency, the British share of world markets, though still enormous, was shrinking: hence both a determination to hold on to those still possessed and the imperialist idea of develop-ing new, closed, markets for the future.[2]

This new attitude was best expressed by Rosebery in a speech on March 1st, 1893 at the Royal Colonial Institute:

[1] J. Hobson: *Imperialism*, 35.
[2] C. J. Lowe: *The Reluctant Imperialists*, 4–5.

There is another ground on which the extension of our Empire is greatly attacked, and the attack comes from a quarter nearer home. It is said that our Empire is already large enough, and does not need extension. That would be true enough if the world were elastic, but unfortunately it is not elastic, and we are engaged at the present moment, in the language of the mining camps, in 'pegging out claims for the future'. We have to consider, not what we want, but what we shall want in the future. . . . We should, in my opinion, grossly fail in the task that has been laid upon us if we shrink from responsibilities and decline to take our share in a partition of the world which we have not forced on, but which has been forced upon us.

It was this speech in particular that Gladstone had in mind when he subsequently wrote that Rosebery had shown himself 'to be rather seriously imbued with the spirit of territorial grab, which constitutes for us one of the graver dangers of the time'. But Gladstone, in this as in so many other matters, spoke the language of an earlier era. By the 1890s the dominant tones in British Imperial discussion were those of expansion and consolidation; the controversies arose over the methods whereby British interests could be best served.

In retrospect, it may appear remarkable that the British clung doggedly to Free Trade in a world that was steadily becoming more Protectionist. But Free Trade was one of the established dogmas of Victorian Britain. The fact that the United States—as a result of the McKinley Tariff of 1890 and the Dingley Tariff of 1897—had become among the most highly protected countries in the world and that even the Dominions, notably Canada in 1879 and Australia in 1900, were moving in the same direction seemed to make the British more implacably resolved than ever to cling to a system that had, in their eyes, given them their world position and would do so in future. The Labour Party was to prove itself the most dogmatic Free Trade group of all, and was to provide in Philip Snowden in 1929–31 the last convinced Free Trade Chancellor of the Exchequer. In the 1900s onwards, the issue of Tariffs was to be one of the dominating ones in British politics. But, as the century neared its end, Free Trade still stood hallowed and revered in England alone. Germany was in effect protectionist since 1879, Russia since 1882, and France and Austria-Hungary in the same year. As the years passed, the tariff walls grew remorselessly higher against British products.

There had been a quiet revolution in British Government in the 1870s and 1880s. The creation of elective County Councils in 1887 was the most significant single development, for, as completed by the creation of district and parish councils in 1893, it based the whole of English local government upon direct popular election.

This really was a revolution. Democracy did not exist on a national scale, but it was being established in the towns and in the counties. The fact that women could vote for, and serve on, these new Councils was in itself a startling development that was to have its effect on the movement for Women's Suffrage which now began to develop seriously.

In education, the really important decisions were taken between 1870 and 1902. Few measures of Victorian Parliaments aroused fiercer opposition than W. E. Forster's Education Act of 1870, which provided elementary schools at public expense for the first time. The denominational schools had been virtually the only former institutions of this kind, and, as has been noted, the reactions in Nonconformist circles had been particularly bitter, and had brought the National Education League and Joseph Chamberlain into national prominence. But the public elementary schools were established, and in 1892 all fees for such education were abolished. The Technical Instruction Act of 1889 recognised what other countries had realised a quarter of a century before, that an industrial society depended for its very existence upon such instruction. In 1899 a single Department of Education was set up, presided over by a senior Minister. These advances paved the way for the Education Act of 1902.

The expansion of Universities and the establishment of the system of national free libraries emphasised the fact that the quality of British education was rising sharply in the latter quarter of the century. Unhappily they only served to repair the ravages of neglect and complacency. Illiteracy was destroyed, but only for future generations. It would be a very long time before the quality of the eduction in State schools approximated to the standards of the private fee-paying schools. A really full education remained the prerogative of the upper and wealthy middle classes, and the most that can be said is that the existence of the gulf was recognised, and belated steps were being taken to bridge it.

One of the most interesting developments in the 1890s was that of the 'popular' Press. The key feature of the 'new journalism' was commercialism, and its pioneer was Alfred Harmsworth, subsequently Lord Northcliffe, who made the discovery that news, or a version of it, could be sold at as great profit as any other form of merchandise. He started his first newspaper at the age of twenty-five, and it was well on the way to foundering when he offered a prize—a pound a day for life—for anyone who guessed the value of the amount of gold in the Bank of England on a given day. Circulation soared to a quarter of a million and Harmsworth moved on with his brother (later Lord Rothermere) to buy the *Evening News*, which sold at a halfpenny and showed strong signs of American newspaper influence; its editor, Kennedy Jones, had in fact studied the American Press with care. In 1896 the Harmsworths founded the *Daily Mail*, which was an immediate success, with a circulation of 543,000 within three years, a figure unapproached by any competitor.

Harmsworth was undeniably a genius, and was himself a natural journalist. Under his control the new journalism provided its readers not with news but stories. The sub-editor now became the crucial figure, re-writing reports and lacing them with his own headlines and interpretations. If Providence did not provide news, it could be manufactured, as in the notorious case in 1900 when the *Daily Mail* published the story of the massacre of the white residents of Peking; it was a pure invention, but neither the repute nor the sales of the *Daily Mail* suffered thereby, thus providing Harmsworth with another interesting lesson.

Harmsworth was the first to discover the enormous potentialities of a large and just-literate readership; he also saw that advertising was the key to really large financial success. Salisbury described the *Daily Mail* as 'written by office boys for office boys'. He was right, but office boys were developing into voters. Where Harmsworth had sowed, others reaped with him. A new figure, the newspaper magnate, entered British social life and politics. In time many of them made vast fortunes and developed megalomania in lesser or greater forms. They assumed an apparent omnipotence and inspired aversion and fear until Baldwin showed that their political influence was in fact negligible. But this was not to come until 1931.

The Harmsworth, and subsequently the Beaverbrook, Press was in business to make money. The popular press accordingly pandered to what it deemed were popular tastes, and the strident nationalism and Imperialism of the 'new journalism' in the later 1890s was not the least of the factors that drove intelligent and sensitive men into opposition of their cause, believing, probably wholly mistakenly, that the popular press was responsible for creating emotions that were in reality there, and merely being commercially exploited.

The revival of Trade Unionism in the late 1880s had been given a substantial impetus by the London Dock Strike of 1889. Concern about the legal position of the Unions increased in the 1890s; employers, alarmed by the impact of foreign competition, were beginning to combine effectively, and the Courts were upholding them. The right to picket was successfully challenged in the courts, and resulted in the Trades Union Congress resolving—by a small majority—to summon a special conference of trade unions, co-operative societies and Socialist bodies to make plans for Labour representation in Parliament in 1899. Significantly this was strongly opposed by the miners, who already had a firm grip on Liberal representation for mining areas.

In 1892 total membership of trade unions was 1,576,000; by 1900 it was 2,022,000. The most notable industrial dispute of the 1890s were the miners' strike and lock-out of 1893 and the engineers' strike of 1897. The former lasted for fifteen weeks, and included the riot at Featherstone, but in many respects the engineers' strike was more significant. After seven months the men were totally defeated. There were two lessons to be drawn from this episode. The Unions must, by fusion or federation, become larger units if they were to achieve results; and that political action was likely to be more rewarding than crude, isolated industrial protest. This had been preached for years by the Fabians; now it was realised that their answer was the correct one. Closely linked to this realisation was the new interest being shown by the Unions in the condition of life of the working classes.

These new movements coincided—and the coincidence is important —with the decline of the Liberals. From 1886 to 1895 Ireland had dominated all other issues. In 1895–6 Harcourt and Rosebery were not on speaking terms. After Rosebery retired as leader in the autumn of 1896 Harcourt took his place, only to find his position compromised and his authority fatally undermined. For all his talk and bluster, Harcourt was essentially a radical middle class London attorney, and his sympathies and comprehension of public affairs were not closely linked with nascent working class groups. The Fabians had long since been disillusioned by the Liberals; working class disillusionment was much more slow in developing, but it was in the late 1890s that those who urged separate Labour representation in Parliament began to make serious progress.

The Socialist-union conference called in 1899 met in London on February 17th–18th, 1900, and agreed to set up the Labour Representation Committee (the L.R.C.) to promote and co-ordinate plans for Labour representation in Parliament. It is perhaps possible to exaggerate the importance of this conference, but some of its decisions were crucial. In the first place, the Unions agreed to a levy—'10 shillings per annum for every 1,000 members or fraction thereof'—to finance the new party; of equal importance was an amendment proposed by Keir Hardie that the Committee's function was to establish 'a distinct Labour Group in Parliament, who shall have their own Whips and agree upon their policy, which must embrace a readiness to co-operate with any party which for the time being may be engaged in promoting legislation in the direct interest of Labour, and be equally ready to associate themselves with any party in opposing measures having an opposite tendency'; a third important decision—proposed by G. N. Barnes—was to the effect that candidates need not be working men themselves.

These decisions meant in effect that the new party was to be based very much on the pattern of the Irish Nationalist Party under Parnell. It was to have a regular source of income from the Unions; it was to act in Parliament as a separate Party, but was to co-operate with any other party which was acting in the best interests of the working classes. Dogma, in short, was to be emphatically subordinated to the requirements of practical politics.

There was at this stage no question of establishing a new party with a specific programme of reform, and there was considerable vagueness as to the exact role to be played in Parliament when, and if, it had any elected representatives. The first secretary of the L.R.C. was a young Scottish journalist, Ramsay MacDonald, who was, like Keir Hardie, an illegitimate child brought up in poverty.

The early history of Labour politics was somewhat confused, even to contemporaries. There was the Independent Labour Party, based in Scotland; the Marxist Social Democratic Federation (S.D.F.); and the Fabians. Each was represented on the L.R.C., with five members out of twelve, but were seriously at odds with each other. The S.D.F. found the Committee too tame for their brand of social reform, and quickly retired in 1900. In the 1900 General Election the L.R.C.

endorsed fifteen candidates, but could do little for them except supply leaflets and give them their blessing. Total expenditure in the election by the L.R.C. was £33. Only two of the sponsored candidates— Hardie and Richard Bell—were elected. Bell turned out to be a Liberal on every issue except when the interests of his Union—the Railway Servants—were involved. Hardie was difficult, erratic, passionate, humane and independent, whose very confusion of purpose gave him much attractiveness but with few merits as a leader, or even a guide. It was not, either in quantity or in quality, a very impressive start. Nevertheless, it was a start, and a further development in the slowly unfolding British Revolution.

*

It is desirable to examine other, more familiar, institutions in the 1890s.

The Navy was showing clear and, for those who cared to look closely, alarming signs of decrepitude. It is perhaps too harsh to say, as Professor Marder has remarked, that 'although numerically a very imposing force, it was in certain respects a drowsy, inefficient, moth-eaten organisation'.[1] The Spencer Programme of 1894–6 retained the Navy's numerical superiority, but its qualitative superiority was more questionable. The Navy had no Staff College. Excessive emphasis was placed on appearances and precise seamanship. There was ignorance of and indifference to new scientific developments. There were virtu-ally no war plans, a fact that first became evident in the Fashoda Crisis of 1898. Gunnery was regarded with dislike and distaste. Practice firing was limited to 2,000 yards—little more than in Nelson's day—and the percentage of hits in practice, even at this range, was less than one in three. Target practices at sea were limited to one every three months. The Navy urgently required reorganisation from the top to the bottom, and it was to receive this revival under the hands of the amazing Admiral 'Jackie' Fisher. Fisher became Commander-in-Chief of the Mediterranean Fleet in 1899, was Second Sea Lord 1902–3, and First Sea Lord 1904–8. He arrived just in time. Between 1899 and 1904 the Navy Estimates had trebled, and by 1904 they stood at £37 millions. Fisher not only produced a revivified Navy but did so at less cost, which earned him the gratitude and awe of politicians no less than that of the more far-seeing officers of the Navy.

A. J. Marder: *From the Dreadnought to Scapa Flow*, Volume 1.

Fisher's reforms fall in a later period. It suffices at this stage to comment on the fact that the basis of British world policy in the nineteenth century, whether admitted or not, lay in her supremacy at sea, and that this was, for all who cared to see, a very much less impressive foundation than appeared at first glance.

The British Army was hardly in more impressive condition, but serious and partially successful attempts had been made to reform it. Edward Cardwell's tenure of the War Office in 1868–74 had removed some of the more spectacular anomalies. Small units were withdrawn from the Colonies, the War Office was centralised in London, short-service commissions were introduced, the Army equipped with the breech-loading rifle, the regimental system reorganised on a territorial basis, flogging in peacetime was abolished, and the system of 'Purchase' ended. Cardwell was less successful in other respects. The 'linked battalion' system had serious weaknesses, and the cavalry retained its privileged position; the artillery, far from being modernised, went back to muzzle-loading cannons. Until 1886 no mobilisation scheme existed at all, and no mobilisation regulations were issued until 1892. The machine-gun was not properly developed, and had not been fully introduced by the Boer War. The condition of the Ordnance Factories was described in February 1899 by the Director-General of the Ordnance as 'full of peril to the Empire'. Campbell-Bannerman's removal of the Duke of Cambridge as Commander-in-Chief in 1895 was a step forward in that it removed a considerable impediment to energetic reforms, but his replacement, Wolseley, by now a shadow of his former self, was a somewhat marginal improvement.

The British Army, like the Royal Navy, was awesome at a distance. Its competence and courage in the field were well known, and were to be seen again in the Sudan Campaign of 1897–8. In theory, 600,000 men were available for mobilisation, but in fact the practical limit for a quick mobilisation was 85,000. It was not until the Boer War that the urgent necessity for its major overhaul was fully demonstrated. But it must be emphasised that hardly anyone—if anyone—thought of the Army ever becoming involved in a major war against a comparable military power. As a young subaltern, Winston Churchill later wrote:

Nobody expected to get killed. Here and there in every regiment or battalion, half a dozen, a score, at the worst thirty or forty, would pay the forfeit. But to the great mass of those who took part in the little wars of Britain in those vanished light-hearted days, this was only a sporting element in a splendid game.

The Navy, then and always, had strong political allies; the Army, virtually none at all. The link between the politicians and the soldiers was at best tenuous; normally they operated separately, with a certain mutual contempt. For all the Cardwell and other reforms, the British Army in its essentials had advanced very little since the Crimean War. The worst abuses and weaknesses had gone, but many still remained. Compared with the vast and well-equipped European armies, the British Army was a negligible factor in power calculations. And, as the events of 1899 were to prove, it was not even prepared for the kind of minor colonial war which was its raison d'etre. 'The Government', as Wolseley complained in 1899, 'are acting without complete knowledge of what the military can do, while the military authorities on their side are equally without full knowledge of what the Government expects them to do.' From this complacency there was to be a sharp awakening.

*

The last decade of the nineteenth century saw the deaths of Parnell and Randolph Churchill, and, in May 1898, Gladstone's long life at last ended.

For more than fifty years Gladstone had astounded, angered, awed, and inspirited his countrymen. Now, a harsh fate determined that he should be stricken with one of the most acutely painful of all forms of cancer and that his extraordinary physique should resist its advance so relentlessly. At the end, as the shadows darkened over him, the fierce controversies faded. The wealthy young Conservative, the early defender of slavery and privilege, the stern but tormented Churchman and 'out and out inegalitarian' had developed slowly and painfully into the earnest and at times inspired champion of the deprived, the assailed, the weak, and the defenceless. His life had a nobility which transcended all defects, and which expunged all errors and failings. And no episode in that complex journey was more noble than the last one, so tragically drawn out, so exquisitely painful, and whose outcome was so inevitable. Let Morley describe the end:

On the early morning of the 19th [of May], his family all kneeling around the bed on which he lay in the stupor of coming death, without a struggle he ceased to breathe. Nature outside—wood and wide lawn and cloudless far-off sky—shone at her fairest.

*

The 1890s have been varyingly assessed by different commentators. Inevitably, each sees in this period particular facets of significance. It was undoubtedly a more exciting decade than its predecessors. It was a period of a greater relaxation in morals and in a wider and more enjoyable life[1]—demonstrated in the enormous new popularity of spectator-sports, particularly Association Football and cricket—for more people. There was a distinct relaxation of social and religious taboos and, in this respect, the increased use of contraceptives was significant. It will be recalled that in 1878 Charles Bradlaugh had been imprisoned for advocating birth control; by the 1890s the use of reasonably efficient contraceptive devices had become much more widespread in the educated and upper classes, and the marked decline in the birth rate of this minority element was one of the most interesting social phenomena of the decade. Divorce—as the Dilke and Parnell cases demonstrated—was still socially unacceptable, but opinions were changing even on this. The continuing decline in church-going, particularly in the Church of England, was very striking; although the Nonconformists lost less ground, even their records showed a noticeable reduction.

There was, in the England of the 1890s, an evident sense of change, of greater intellectual activity, and the emergence of new approaches and attitudes towards the accepted tenets of mid-Victorian England. But there were few clear indications of the directions into which these new energies and attitudes would move.

---

[1] It was in the 1890s that some manual workers began to have the long-sought advantage of the Eight-Hour day.

CHAPTER SIX

THE SOUTH AFRICAN LABYRINTH, 1895–1899

LTHOUGH Salisbury's offer to the Liberal Unionists occasioned little remark, there was very considerable and widespread surprise at the decision of Chamberlain to go to the Colonial Office, a Department that had held a low status in the political and official hierarchy. But Chamberlain's ambitions had been centred on that backwater for several years. To his American fiancée he had written in 1888 of the South African situation that 'I mean some day to be Colonial Secretary and to deal with it', and to the same correspondent he had written that 'I am inclined to advocate a bold policy [in South Africa], fully recognizing Imperial responsibilities and duty, but then I intend that it should be the policy of the Imperial and not of the Cape Government, and should be carried out by officials taking their instructions from the former.' For the first time, therefore, London would call the tune in Imperial, and particularly South African, affairs.

The Conservatives viewed their formidable colleague without enthusiasm, and Salisbury's attitude was even more bleak than that of his colleagues. He had once described Chamberlain as 'a Sicilian bandit', and had not in reality changed his view. Lady Frances Balfour noted in November 1895 that 'I never heard him talk of any colleague as he does of him, says Chamberlain wants to go to war with every Power in the world, and has no thought but Imperialism.'

Amongst other emotions, there was a strong element of jealousy in the Conservatives' attitude to their former foe. He was, as Winston Churchill later wrote, 'incomparably the most live, sparkling, insurgent, compulsive figure in British affairs. . . . He was the man the masses knew. He it was who had solutions for social problems; who was ready to advance, sword in hand if need be, upon the foes of

167

Britain; and whose accents rang in the ears of all the young peoples of the Empire and lots of young people at its heart.' If this was hyperbole, it was as Chamberlain saw himself at this time. Throughout his career Chamberlain had been the principal actor upon small stages. His ambition went far beyond Birmingham sewers, radical programmes, or Home Rule. His intelligence, his vanity, and his ambition required a much more significant theatre and audience. He had now discerned where these were to be found, and he applied himself relentlessly to their conquest. He was now at the height of his powers, possessing, as Beatrice Webb wrote, 'energy and personal magnetism, in a word masculine force, to an almost superlative degree'. It was to prove to be a catastrophic combination once again.

Salisbury, whose instinct for serious politicians was usually very sound, saw this clearly. There were other things the Conservative leader knew, and feared, about Chamberlain, after long experience of him as an opponent and as an uneasy ally. He was a hard man, and had grown harder in the Home Rule disputes. His eye was always on the reality of power, and not on position. His approach had always been combative and relentless, but had become more cold and ruthless since 1885. His mind was remarkably clear. It was limited in scope, the range was not long, and the breadth was not great, but the clarity was impressive. He was a man who believed that a politician must always have a policy. It could be amended, modified, or even reversed, but at all times the politician must present himself to his following with decisive leadership. His approach had become markedly more logical and precise, and lacking in that confusion of objective and intent that characterises most politicians. He dealt with situations as they arose, and always had a policy to deal with them. He had survived the break with Gladstone, and had fought his former colleagues with fire and logic. They hated him for it, and the Conservatives did not love him for what he had done. But they had need of him, much though they feared his independent power base, his dedication to the task in hand, his implacable resolve, his popular support, and his unquenched ambition.

If many Conservatives were awed by Chamberlain, Salisbury was not. He had never trusted him nor liked him, nor even greatly respected him. Now, he trusted him less than ever. But Salisbury was ageing prematurely, tired and vague, increasingly detached from the burdens of office. His eye remained clear, and he saw more sharply than his colleagues the perils of Chamberlain's energy, ardour and inexperience in foreign affairs. He endeavoured to warn others of these dangers, but his word no longer carried the old authoritative urgency, and he had lost the mental and physical energy to press his arguments quietly yet with overwhelming effect. He was in a tragical decline, seeing all, yet helpless. Balfour, for all his cleverness and guile, did not possess Salisbury's long-term vision, his acute understanding of human nature, his experience, nor his Christian cynicism. Thus, swiftly Chamberlain became dominant, while Salisbury lamented in vain. The destiny of the Unionist Government, and much else besides, was now in the hands of this impatient, hard, and limited man.

The gulf between Salisbury and Chamberlain had always been, and would remain to the end, vast and incapable of being bridged. Salisbury was a deeply religious man, devoted to his family, and a warm encourager of lively and uninhibited disputation between his children and himself. He was an intellectual, who read much and pondered greatly. Hatfield in his lifetime was a place of accepted custom and tradition, yet of intense spirit and happiness, where he presided benignly but acutely over a family of outstanding intellect and charm, which argued incessantly at the highest level. At Highbury, Chamberlain dominated a pretentious, gloomy, and although devoted, subservient *ménage*. As Beatrice Webb noted, there was 'very *much taste*, and all very bad', and her description of the principal room as 'forlornly grand' may serve as an accurate portrait of the household. He relished good champagne, and cultivated orchids with skill, application, and success. But the food was, although grand and expensive, in quality poor. Chamberlain's family, and particularly the women, were there to comfort and applaud him, and not to contradict or dispute. Salisbury, ill-dressed and vague, was an authentic grandee; Chamberlain, immaculate and sharp, remained an authentic *arriviste*. Chamberlain was not an intellectual, nor did he have the experience, imagination or dedication to close the gulf between himself and Salisbury. Nor, did he discern any reason why he should. And so he rushed along, while the much older man viewed his progress with mounting concern and anguish, incapable of restoring the political balance.

*

Chamberlain came to the Colonial Office in July 1895 with emphatic opinions, and in his first major speech, on August 22nd, he further developed a theme much in evidence in his recent declarations that the colonies were 'undeveloped estates' that merited development. Once Chamberlain had seized on an issue, he carried it through to what he regarded as its ultimate conclusion. He had come to agree fully with Rosebery's dictum that the Empire was 'the greatest secular agency for good the world has ever seen', and that it should not simply be maintained but actually expanded. 'I and those who agree with me believe in the expansion of the Empire', he said in the Commons on March 20th, 1893, 'and we are not ashamed to confess that we have that feeling, and we are not at all troubled by accusations of Jingoism.' The Boers did not know that it was he who had been the principal impelling force that had persuaded the Gladstone Government in 1884 to send 4,000 troops into Bechuanaland to end Boer encroachments there, but there were many other indications that Chamberlain was not likely to be a friend of the Republics. A man who said that it was Britain's duty to extend her control over 'those friendly chiefs and peoples who are stretching out their hands towards us' and that 'the British race is the greatest governing race the world has ever seen' aroused justifiable concern in the Transvaal and Orange Free State.

The Colonial Office itself was fully aware of the issues now at stake in South Africa. Until the early 1890s it had been tacitly assumed in London and at Cape Town that the Cape Colony would inevitably acquire an economic domination, and that the problem of the Boer Republics would solve itself by their becoming a negligible economic, political and military factor in South Africa. The spectacular advances of Rhodes's British South Africa Company had seemed to support this assumption. Since 1889 Rhodes had acquired vast new areas of territory, and in October 1893 the Company had routed the Matabele in an ugly little war in which a small mounted force under Dr. Jameson and equipped with the revolutionary quick-firing Maxim gun had achieved an overwhelming victory. The Colonial Office stood aside, although it approved of further Cape advances, and Liberal indignation quickly faded away. 'Local Imperialism', it appeared, had all the advantages and involved no commitments or expenditure.

But by 1895 it was evident that these assumptions had proved to have been disastrously wrong. The discovery of the Witwatersrand

Gold Field in 1886 in effect trumped Rhodes's ace. His belief that the true Rand was in southern Zambesia had been falsified; it was at Johannesburg. The total revenue of the Transvaal in 1886 was £196,000; within ten years it was nearly £4 million. Thus, far from the expanding Cape Colony eventually absorbing a poor and backward farming community it now began to look as if it would be the Transvaal that would be the centre and leader of a new confederation inimicable to British and Cape Colony interests. When it seemed in October 1892 that the Transvaal might actually invade Zambesia, a Colonial Office memorandum starkly pointed out that

> . . . unless we are prepared to resist this by force, we shall have to abandon Mr. Rhodes and the British South Africa Company and the whole idea of British supremacy in the interior to a 'New Republic' which will be hostile to British capital and enterprise.[1]

If there was apprehension in London and in Cape Colony at the dramatic change in the South African situation, there was fear also in the Transvaal.

Since the discovery of the Rand, settlers had poured into the Republic, mainly from Britain and Cape Colony. There was no proper census undertaken, and it is not possible to estimate their total numbers with any precision. A census of Johannesburg in July 1896, however, revealed that of a white population of 50,907 only 6,205 were Transvaalers. The main groups of the 'Uitlanders' were the British (over 16,000) and over 15,000 from Cape Colony. It is probable that, by the mid-1890s, the number of adult Uitlander males in the Transvaal actually exceeded that of adult Boer males.

The massive infiltration represented a number of grievous political, social and economic problems for the Republic. The development of the Rand had not brought proportionate wealth for the Boers themselves; indeed, in several respects they were worse off than before. Much of the produce of the new inhabitants was brought in by the new railways; by 1890 the supply of free land—on which the Boer agrarian economy was based—had virtually stopped, and large areas were being purchased by foreigners. Outbreaks of rinderpest, plagues of locusts and a severe drought further impoverished the farming community.

The Transvaal Government was ill-equipped to handle the situation.

[1] Colonial Office Memorandum on 'The Swazi Question', October 19th, 1892. Quoted in Robinson and Gallagher: *Africa and the Victorians*, 413.

It was xenophobic, incompetent, grasping, and riddled with corruption. The formidable President Kruger was himself ageing, was surrounded with inefficient or actively dangerous colleagues, and was notably more dictatorial than ever before.

Paul Kruger had grown up with the Republic. As a child of ten he had gone with his parents on the Great Trek out of Cape Colony in 1835. In the troubled years of the Republic he had risen quickly as a conciliator and a moderator of fierce rivalries. It was he who, on the morrow of Majuba, had urged moderation on the angry Volksraad. He was a devout, and almost childlike, believer in the literal truth of the Bible. He was uncouth in speech and manner, and subject to almost uncontrollable rages when thwarted. He cared passionately for his country, and personified the Republic's motto, Unity Gives Strength, and which included the corollary that opposition and party strife were undesirable. Yet, in spite of his authority and reputation, the Presidential election of 1892 had been a very close thing. Wily and skilful himself, yet he was a poor judge of character, a defect that became more obvious with old age.

It was not surprising that foreigners, of whom he was deeply suspicious, found him politically slippery and personally repulsive. One English visitor found him sitting in a leather armchair 'in dirty-looking clothes, his hair and beard long, a big Dutch pipe in his mouth, and a huge red bandana handkerchief hanging out of the side pocket of his loose jacket'; a huge spitoon was at hand, to which he had frequent recourse, although with indifferent aim. Yet everyone of stature who had dealings with him was impressed. Rhodes, who knew a strong man when he met one, always regarded Kruger as a formidable opponent. Although unlettered and uneducated, his energy was considerable, his intelligence was keen, and his obstinacy well-established.

His contempt for, and fear of, the mercenary outsiders who had entered his country and coarsened its life was understandable. An English journalist—Flora Shaw—described Johannesburg in 1892 as 'hideous and detestable; luxury without order, sensual enjoyment without art, riches without refinement, display without dignity,' and her appraisal was echoed by many other observers.

Until it was too late, Kruger had thought that he could use these interlopers and then dispose of them; it was not until the early 1890s that he fully realised that they had come to stay and represented a real threat to the Republic.

It is necessary to look at the system under which the Transvaal was governed, for it lay at the heart of the subsequent crisis, and which was to have such profound consequences for Britain and the course of British politics.

The Volksraad consisted of between twenty-four and twenty-eight representatives, who were virtually all landed Boers. Originally a Uitlander could obtain citizenship and the full franchise for £25 after five years' residence. In 1890 the period of residence was extended to fourteen, and no Uitlander under the age of forty could vote for the Volksraad, the President, or the Commandant-General. A second Volksraad for the Uitlanders was introduced, but its powers were so circumscribed that they were vitually non-existent. There was little attempt by the Uitlanders to become full citizens of the Republic; between 1890 and 1896 only 2,087 were naturalised. This fact did not, however, inhibit them from seeking full voting rights. As early as 1887 they had begun to organise themselves into groups for this purpose, but until 1892 these efforts had been relatively feeble. But they did obtain control of the Johannesburg Sanitary Board, and it was the curt rejection of 1892 of its request for wider powers that resulted in the creation of the Transvaal National Union, which resolved to 'obtain by all constitutional means equal rights for all citizens of the Republic, and . . . the redress of all grievances'.

This was an ominous development. There is no firm evidence that the formation of the Union was encouraged or inspired from the outside, and it seems to have been an entirely local organisation. In the 1892 Presidential election it supported Joubert against Kruger— to Joubert's considerable embarrassment. But the fact was that the Union was led and dominated by British settlers from Cape Colony, and it was not long before its political potentialities were being studied eagerly and attentively in Cape Colony.

Whether regarded from the north or the south, the Transvaal was a formidable barrier to British expansion in Africa. Furthermore, there were strong indications that her nuisance value was even greater than this. The activities of W. J. Leyds—a hard, ambitious, dour Hollander almost as much disliked by the Boers as by the British—were a case in point. Leyds had become State Secretary in 1888, and had developed the lucrative system of selling 'concessions'—which were in effect monopolies—which also had a political aspect. Leyds wanted powerful capitalist influences in Europe to have a stake in the Transvaal which they would be prepared to defend. In brief, he wanted British money to be countered by French, Dutch and German money. When, in 1894, Kruger called the controversial dynamite concession 'the cornerstone of the independence of the Republic' he meant what he said. He was, in a blundering fashion, playing off the great powers. Leyds was passionately anti-British, and although his attempts to enlist strong European support for the Republic failed, these activities were an additional factor in the increasing unease and resentment with which the British viewed the situation. The Liberal Colonial Secretary, Lord Ripon, wrote to Kimberley in November 1894 that:

> . . . The German inclination to take the Transvaal under their protection is a very serious thing. To have them meddling at Pretoria and Johannesburg would be fatal to our position and our influence in South Africa. . . .

Neither Kimberley nor Rosebery had to be told of this danger by the Colonial Secretary, and Kimberley—with Rosebery's full support—warned the Austrian Ambassador at the end of October 1894 that 'the maintenance of the Cape Colony was perhaps the most vital interest of Great Britain'. The British were looking at Europe as closely as they were South Africa.

The influence of Cecil Rhodes was the decisive factor in bringing a potentially critical confrontation to a head. In 1894 Rhodes began to greatly interest himself in the Uitlander cause. His motives were, as usual, very mixed. To ignore the visionary and idealistic side of his strange character is as foolish as to overlook the hard ruthlessness of the capitalistic entrepeneur. Dogged by ill-health, obsessed by visions, and haunted by the prospect that his dream of a federated South Africa under British domination would not be accomplished in his lifetime, Rhodes was a sick, eager, and impatient man.

He was in a postion of rare power and influence. His reputation extended far beyond the confines of Cape Colony, whose Premier he had been since 1890. In Britain he had powerful allies, and not least in the Liberal Party. In Cape Colony he was admired by all parties, and even in the Transvaal he was viewed with respect—and in some cases with more than respect. The young Jan Smuts was to write of him in July 1896 that, 'the Dutch set aside all considerations of blood and nationality and loved him and trusted him and served him because they believed that *he* was the man to carry out that great idea of an internally sovereign and united South Africa in which the white man would be supreme—which has been the cry of our forefathers even as it is our cry today. Here at last our Moses had appeared—and it made no difference that he was an Egyptian in blood.'

This great position, and very much more, was now to be put to ridiculous and terrible hazard.

*

In May 1894 the Transvaal Government ordered some British subjects to serve on a commando. In the subsequent spate of Uitlander protests, the leader of the Johannesburg Uitlanders, Lionel Phillips, asked the British High Commissioner at Cape Town—Sir Henry Loch—if the Uitlanders could count on his support in the event of an uprising. It was Phillips' understanding that Loch had said that he could count upon support from Cape Colony in such an eventuality. Loch then proposed to the Colonial Office that he should be authorised to use the Bechuanaland Police to support an Uitlander rising in Johannesberg, prior to the intervention of the British garrison in South Africa, which he wanted increased by 5,000 men.

Loch was not actually suggesting that a rising should be provoked; he was making contingency plans for what seemed a real possibility. But his plans were emphatically rejected by the Colonial Office, and the most severe criticism of the suggestion was written by the Permanent Under-Secretary, Sir Robert Meade. What he described as Loch's 'extremely dangerous proposal' would encourage the Uitlanders 'to make excessive demands'; it was imperative that 'every nerve should be strained to prevent such a disgrace as another S. African war'. Lord Ripon expressed his approval of Meade's attitude.

Loch was succeeded by Sir Hercules Robinson, High Commissioner 1881–9, now aged and in bad health; he was Rhodes's nominee, and had served on the board of one of Rhodes's companies. His appointment was widely criticised, not least by Chamberlain. The High Commissioner's Colonial Secretary, Sir Graham Bower, has described the difference between Loch and Robinson:

Sir Hercules was cold and calculating, very cautious and without any personal ties or personal friendships or hatreds. His first interest was to secure his safety. Sir Henry Loch was hot-headed, vain, impulsive, and with strong likes and dislikes. In the case of Sir

Hercules my difficulty generally was to get him to move at all. I spent my time with Sir Henry Loch in figuratively holding on to his coat-tails.

Before the Rosebery Government fell in June 1895 plans for a rising in Johannesberg and subsequent planned assistance from Cape Colony were well advanced. Rhodes was putting pressure on London to hand over the Bechuanaland Protectorate to the British South Africa Company, and it was essential to the plan that the township of Gaberones—on the Transvaal border—should be in Rhodes's hands. No decision had been reached by the Liberals, and Rhodes's agent in London—Dr. Rutherford Harris—put the matter before Chamberlain on August 1st. Also present at this meeting were Chamberlain's Under-Secretary, Lord Selborne, and Earl Grey. Reports of the meeting vary, although it does seem to be the case that when Harris was about to deal with the matter of why the British South Africa Company wanted Gaberones so urgently, Chamberlain swiftly changed the subject. Grey said that he subsequently saw Chamberlain alone and told him that a Uitlander rising was imminent, and that it was essential to place an armed force on the border. Grey's honesty— although not his intelligence—has never been impugned, and there is no reason to question his account, as it is confirmed by subsequent events.

Harris reported to Rhodes on August 13th:

Chamberlain will do anything to assist except hand over the administration protectorate provided he officially does not know anything of your plan. He does consider Rhodes' ingenuity resource can overcome any difficulty caused by refusal protectorate now.

Harris telegraphed further on August 20th that Chamberlain had been informed of the reason for the Company's interest in the Protectorate. On the same day Chamberlain ordered Robinson to obtain the land on which Gaberones stood from the local chief for the Company. On October 18th this acquisition was publicly announced. It is, of course, not certain that the Liberals would have proved implacable to Rhodes's persistence, but it was of real significance that Chamberlain easily and swiftly accepted the request which Rosebery and Ripon had refused. Chamberlain knew full well why Rhodes wanted Gaberones, and was from the outset a conscious but careful accomplice in the projected invasion of an independent and sovereign state. He covered his tracks well enough for contemporaries, but his active involvement in the scheme is now clear. The acquisition of Gaberones for the British South Africa Company was the key decision.

In August there had been another crisis. In order to encourage his new railway from Dalagoa Bay, Kruger raised the rates on the Cape line to Johannesburg. When Rhodes retaliated by organising supplies by ox-wagon, Kruger closed the drifts (the fording-places). Chamberlain delivered what was in effect an ultimatum to Kruger, and ordered troops to South Africa. Kruger had to climb down, and in the excitement no notice was taken of the formation of a new volunteer corps by Dr. Jameson.

Meanwhile, the organisation of the Johannesburg rising was proceeding. 'Never before', James Bryce has commented, 'was there except on the stage so open a conspiracy.' Some 3,000 rifles were smuggled in, but only half were unpacked. A ridiculous code was devised. The return of prosperity on the Rand had cooled the ardour of many of the Uitlanders. At Johannesburg, the preparations continued in an *opera bouffe* atmosphere.

There were several fatal misunderstandings. Five Uitlander leaders wrote an undated letter appealing for assistance. They were under the impression that they would summon Jameson at the proper time; Jameson considered that he was the best judge of that, and assembled less than 500 men on the border; Rhodes himself thought that he was in charge of the timing of the operation.

In London, Chamberlain continued to encourage the operation while taking care to have no personal involvement. Robinson was fully aware of what was to happen. To Bower he remarked that 'the whole thing is, I believe, sheer piracy, but I know nothing about it and have nothing to do with it'.

He was instructed by Chamberlain to proceed to Pretoria as soon as the provisional government had been declared in Johannesburg and order the immediate election of a Constituent Assembly to be elected by every adult male in the country. Chamberlain would announce his support for his action, and would also talk of a large military force being held in readiness to proceed to South Africa. Jameson would carry the British flag with him, for raising in Johannesburg. The British Cabinet was wholly unaware of the Colonial Secretary's deep involvement in this adventure; it was not until December 26th that

Chamberlain mentioned to Salisbury that a rising would occur 'in the course of the next few days'. As has been written, 'Chamberlain and Rhodes worked together to solve the Transvaal problem by a *fait accompli* with no objection from Salisbury'.[1] But there is no evidence that Salisbury realised the full implications of what his Colonial Secretary was doing.

On December 17th, when everything was—or seemed to be—ready, an utterly unexpected hitch occurred. President Cleveland sent to the United States Congress a belligerent anti-British message concerning the Venezuela boundary dispute,[2] and for the moment it appeared that there was a major international crisis. In these circumstances Meade urgently proposed postponement of the Transvaal business 'for a year or so', a letter which confirms beyond any reasonable doubt the extent of the knowledge of the Colonial Office of what was afoot. Chamberlain replied rather ambiguously, but it seems certain that his letter was interpreted by his officials to mean—and was meant to mean—that the balance of advantage lay in immediate action. One of Rhodes's agents, Rochfort Maguire, was summoned to the Colonial Office, and afterwards telegraphed to Rhodes in this sense. Although the actual telegram has not yet been discovered, there is little doubt as to what it said.

Meanwhile, the position of Dr. Jameson was not enviable. Disputes had now broken out at Johannesburg among the Uitlander leaders over the issue of raising the British flag, and this procrastination and timorousness daily reduced the chances of his success. On December 25th Jameson received telegrams counselling further delay—but nothing from Rhodes himself. Jameson thus decided to go in, and on December 29th, with 356 men, he rode into the Transvaal, having cut the telegraph lines to the Cape but, through characteristic ineptitude, *not* those to the Transvaal. He sent a telegram to Harris that 'unless I

---

[1] Lowe: *The Reluctant Imperialists*, 217.

[2] The Venezuela Dispute subsided swiftly because, although a belligerent mood certainly existed in the United States Congress, it was not echoed on Wall Street nor in the business and trading communities. But another factor was the conciliatory reaction of the British, and the impression made by Balfour's statement that 'The time will come, the time must come, when some statesman of authority will lay down the doctrine that between English-speaking people war is impossible.' It is not too fanciful to date the beginning of what Churchill was to call 'the special relationship' from the Venezuela Dispute. The concept of Britain and the United States as natural allies was slow to develop on both sides of the Atlantic, but the events of December 1895 gave it a powerful impetus.

hear definitely to the contrary shall leave tomorrow evening'. This arrived at Cape Town on Saturday 28th; Harris did not read it until the Monday, when he came into his office. By then the lines had been cut and Jameson had started his mad adventure. Much too late, Rhodes tried to stop him.

On January 2nd, after a brief fight with the Boers, within ten miles of Johannesburg, Jameson and his force were forced to surrender. By then, Robinson had repudiated him and Chamberlain had backed this repudiation. More honourably, Rhodes would not do so, thus destroying the unique position which he had created in Cape Colony with the Dutch. The Johannesburg 'rising' was a fiasco. The Jameson Raid itself marked a crucial step on the road to war between the Transvaal and Britain. Its immediate aftermath was to confirm the deep rift that had now opened in South Africa.

The Jameson Raid has many interesting points in common with the Bay of Pigs fiasco of 1961.[1] With overt encouragement from London, a highly dangerous gamble had been taken on the basis of ignorance of the strength of Uitlander feeling and power and of Boer military competence. The Colonial Office followed the policy of making the adventure possible, standing prepared to make full use of it if successful, yet without any control over how the operation was to be conducted. But the assumption that disassociation from it if it failed would be easily accomplished was swiftly proved false. International opinion was shocked by the Raid; the prestige and position of Rhodes suffered a fatal blow; the British were internationally humiliated, while the reputation of the Transvaal soared. On January 3rd the Kaiser sent Kruger a telegram of warm congratulation, and sought support from France and Russia in what would have been in effect a Three-Power guarantee of the independence of the Transvaal. Troops were ordered to proceed to Delagoa Bay for transit to Pretoria. The French and the Russians rejected the Kaiser's overtures, and the Portuguese refused to permit the troops to land. The British sent a squadron to sea that was capable of overwhelming any other Navy in the world. British dismay at the failure of Jameson was followed by indignation at the Kaiser's actions. The scene was now set for the great crisis of 1896-9.

Chamberlain's objectives in South Africa were not altered by the

---

[1] As Salisbury commented to Chamberlain, 'If filibustering fails it is always disreputable.' (Salisbury to Chamberlain, 30th December 1895.)

fiasco of the Jameson Raid. Indeed, they now became more implacable. On January 4th 1896, only two days after Jameson's surrender,
he instructed Robinson to press vigorously for redress of Uitlander
grievances 'as the Representative of the Paramount Power' and to use
'firm language'. The War Office, at Chamberlain's request, ordered
troops to Mafeking on the pretext of preventing further incursions of
the Jameson type. But Robinson obstinately refused to play Chamberlain's game, and countermanded the troop movements. When
Chamberlain hinted that 'large forces including cavalry and artillery'
could be dispatched to the Cape, Robinson ignored the implied offer.[1]
The High Commissioner knew that the Johannesburg Rising must
end in complete surrender and that the Colonial Secretary's hopes of
extracting something from the ruins of the Jameson venture were
illusory. 'Months afterwards', Bower has related, 'Mr. Chamberlain
reproached me with not taking a hint, and with spoiling his policy at
Pretoria'; when Bower referred to the military and international
complications of that policy, Chamberlain replied curtly, 'that was my
business, not yours'.[2] Chamberlain's only achievement was to get the
death sentences on the four leaders of the Reformers—including
Frank Rhodes—commuted and other penalties reduced.

　　Chamberlain's next move was to try 'to make a great coup and get
Kruger over here . . . if he will walk into my parlour it will be very
nice of him'.[3] But Kruger was only interested in the abolition of the
London Convention of 1884 and particularly the obnoxious Article
Four, which forbade the Republic to conclude treaties without
British consent. If he came to London, it would be as an aggrieved
party claiming and receiving monetary compensation and political
redress, not to discuss Uitlander reforms. A somewhat sour exchange
of letters between Leyds and Chamberlain brought this episode to an
end. It was simply a manoeuvre by Chamberlain to bring the discussion and public interest back to the alleged misfortunes of the
Uitlanders, and had no serious purpose as a discussion on the outstanding issues between London and Pretoria.[4] His final letter to
Leyds warned that the British Government 'as representing the
paramount Power in South Africa . . . cannot be blind to the danger

---

[1] Garvin, op. cit., 111, 99.
[2] Bower's *Reminiscences*, 264 (Quoted in Marais; *The Fall of Kruger's Republic*, 106).
[3] Garvin, op. cit., 127.
[4] C.O. 537/130 (Minute of January 26th, 1896) makes this evident.

which threatens its future if legitimate causes of discontent continue to be ignored by the Government of the South African Republic'.

Against all Chamberlain's attempts to keep up heavy pressure on Kruger, the High Commissioner stood obstinately in the way. He told the Colonial Secretary bluntly that Kruger would rather face war than discuss his internal affairs and that in such an eventuality the Orange Free State and a large section of the Dutch in Cape Colony and Natal would support him.[1] A proposal by Chamberlain 'in view of possible eventualities' to strengthen the Cape Colony and Natal garrisons was also firmly resisted. Fairfield and Bower spoke the same language. Chamberlain temporarily abandoned his belligerent stance. When Bower told him that if he adopted a warlike attitude he would have to get another High Commissioner, Chamberlain replied, 'I know that.'[2]

Early in 1897 Robinson was recalled as High Commissioner. 'I would like to infuse a little more spirit into Sir H. Robinson', Chamberlain had complained, 'and I wish he would show his teeth occasionally.' A more vigorous and aggressive High Commissioner lay at hand, and with the appointment of Sir Alfred Milner the South African crisis entered a new stage.

Robinson was not the only opponent of Chamberlain's policy who was removed. Fairfield and Meade retired towards the end of 1896, and the British Agent at Pretoria was replaced by Conyngham Greene, who favoured a more aggressive policy. Graham and Wingfield, who replaced Fairfield and Meade, were also less in favour of allowing a period of calm to occur in which British relations with the Boers could be improved.

Chamberlain himself was under heavy pressure. The widespread allegations abroad that the British Government had been deeply implicated in the Raid were indignantly and vigorously denied, but now they were current in London. Some members of Rhodes's entourage—and probably encouraged by Rhodes himself—deliberately fostered them. The British South Africa Company's solicitor, Bouchier Hawksley, let it be known that he possessed incriminating documents concerning Chamberlain's personal complicity. The rumours spread swiftly, and raised, as Chamberlain's biographer has written, 'fungoid growths in the shade'.

No examination of what followed can ignore two central features of Chamberlain's character. He was a fighter, and he deeply resented

[1] Marais, 117-18.   [2] Bower, *Reminiscences*, 291.

humiliation. He now fought back at his critics at home while keeping Rhodes amenable, and adopted a determined policy to crush the Transvaal at the earliest opportunity.

The Kaiser's telegram of congratulation to Kruger had a profound effect upon British reactions to the Raid. Thus, when Jameson and his fellow officers faced the judges at Bow Street they were hailed as heroes rather than prisoners, and the Poet Laureate, the lamentable Alfred Austin, published an immensely long panegyric on the raiders in *The Times* which contained the stanza:

There are girls in the gold-reef city,
    There are mothers and children too!
And they cry 'Hurry up! for pity!'
    So what can a brave man do?
If even we win, they'll blame us:
    If we fail, they will howl and hiss.
For there's many a man lives famous
    For daring a wrong like this!

The manner in which the origins of the Raid were investigated by a Select Committee of the House of Commons was blundering but, from Chamberlain's point of view, highly successful. Its Report blamed Rhodes but acquitted Chamberlain—who was himself a member of the Committee. One of the Liberal members, Sydney Buxton, had declared that the Opposition 'would give the Government their most earnest support in endeavouring to clear the name of England of any moral stain that might attach to it', and this was indeed the principal objective of the Committee. It was significant that whereas Rosebery described the Raid as 'an Elizabethan venture', and he was only willing to 'lay a meagre and a tardy chaplet on the opulent shrine of the Colonial Secretary', Harcourt had warmly praised Chamberlain. The Committee tiptoed with elaborate caution around such potentially dangerous subjects as the 'missing telegrams', which Rhodes refused to produce, and the mysterious activities of Flora Shaw, the colonial correspondent of *The Times*, who had been closely concerned with the conspiracy and was in Chamberlain's confidence. Miss Shaw—the future Lady Lugard—handled the Committee with skill and aplomb, but it was not a particularly difficult body to handle. Bower became Robinson's scapegoat; Fairfield was cast to play the role for Chamberlain, but died before the Committee met.

The proceedings of what became cynically known as 'the Lying-In-State at Westminster' have been exhaustively examined by historians.[1] The gullibility of the Liberal members—notably Harcourt and Campbell-Bannerman—was remarkable; Labouchere proved unequal to the task of probing the truth of what had happened. It was a classic cover-up. All independent observers were outraged by the Committee's performance, and Harcourt's position never recovered in the Liberal party. In the debate on the Report on July 27th, 1897, Chamberlain vehemently defended Rhodes—with, it is alleged, copies of the 'missing telegrams' in the pocket of a pro-Rhodes M.P. in case he did not fulfil his part of the bargain. The story has never been substantiated. But this defence was, for many people, the last straw.

The effects of the Raid and its aftermath were legion. Rhodes's position in South Africa was fatally compromised; Boer self-confidence and suspicion of British ambitions were alike intensified, and preparations went forward for a more major confrontation; the Germans, sobered by the response to their challenge, began to build a Navy; in 1897 the Orange Free State joined in an offensive and defensive alliance with the Transvaal; Chamberlain nurtured revenge; South Africa was now divided into two camps. The shadows of this absurd and contemptible foray were to prove long and dark.

*

Although severely checked in South Africa, British progress elsewhere in the Continent was dramatic, and made the reverse even less endurable. Early in 1897 Sir George Goldie, on behalf of the Royal Niger Company, established British influence firmly on the Upper Niger. Lugard now began his remarkable second career in West Africa, and Nigeria was in effect established as a British possession. And then, in 1897–8, the British reconquered the Sudan. This operation had been carefully prepared by Cromer and his staff, most notably Colonel Reginald Wingate, to ensure political and public support in Britain. Milner's *England in Egypt* and the memoirs of Slatin Pasha, for ten years the prisoner of the Mahdi and his successor Abdullahi, the Khalifa, made an immense impression. The decision to act was, however, dominated by factors of European *realpolitik*

[1] See Jean van der Poel: *The Jameson Raid*; Marais, op. cit.; P. Stansky: *Ambitions and Strategies*; Woodhouse and Lockhart: *Rhodes*; Elizabeth Longford: *Jameson's Raid*.

rather than moral outrage, and particularly to check French ambitions while gratifying the Germans and the Italians, who had recently suffered a terrible defeat at Adowa at the hands of the Abyssinians. For the Anglo-Egyptian army, now transformed, the expedition was to be an act of revenge.

The task was given to General Sir Herbert Kitchener, whose irascibility in the Army was equalled by political astuteness in London, where he had the support and friendship of the Salisburys. He aroused fierce, and very contradictory, opinion, but he was ruthless, hard-working, and professional. The Sudan Campaign was essentially a matter of logistics, in which Kitchener excelled. The final stand of the Khalifa's army was at Omdurman, outside Khartoum, on September 2nd 1898, and was the most dramatic and devastating massacre in modern military annals. In a few hours, at trifling loss to the British, the Dervish army of 50,000 was slaughtered or dispersed. Although the Khalifa escaped—to be hunted down and killed a year later—his rule was destroyed in five hours. The British were not gentle victors, and their conduct—and that of Kitchener—came under strong criticism from the elder son of Lord Randolph Churchill, who had fought in the battle with the 21st Lancers, and who published a year later an account of the campaign—*The River War*—which was at once recognised as a classic of military history and was an extraordinary achievement for a young man not yet 25. But nothing could dim Kitchener's sudden fame and eminence.

The strategic importance of the reconquest of the Sudan was swiftly and dramatically emphasised. Immediately after Omdurman Kitchener received intelligence that a French officer, Captain Marchand, had reached Fashoda—some 350 miles to the south—and had raised the French flag. Grey had made it plain on March 28th 1895, that any French advance into the Nile Valley 'would be an unfriendly act and would be so viewed by England'. Salisbury was prepared to be conciliatory, but Chamberlain was emphatic.[1] The confrontation between Kitchener and Marchand brought Britain and France to the verge of war, but, once again, *force majeure* was triumphant, and the Anglo-French Convention of 1899 merely confirmed the fact. Thus, only the continued intransigence of the Boer Republics marred the general picture of British advance and

---

[1] All the leading Liberals supported the Government's handling of the Fashoda crisis. The protests of Lloyd George were not regarded as significant.

success in Africa, and this obstruction became increasingly intolerable.

Chamberlain had now found the instrument for his policy. Alfred Milner had been born in 1854, the only son of an English mother and a German father (whose own father had been English). On the death of his mother he came to England at the age of fifteen, and was educated at King's College, London, and Balliol College, Oxford, where he was a contemporary of Asquith and Arnold Toynbee. The latter made, at the time, the greater impression, and Milner's first public work was done in the East End of London. Milner was also subsequently impressed by Parkin's lectures on Imperial Federation, and had developed serious and intransigent views upon the destiny of Britain.

From 1884–9 he was private secretary to Goschen, and stood for Parliament as a Liberal candidate in 1885. Significantly, he never once mentioned Gladstone's name in his campaign, and was defeated after a raucous campaign; his early distaste for popular politics grew rapidly. In 1889 he went to Egypt to serve under Cromer as under-secretary for finance; in 1892 his *England in Egypt* made his name in Britain. Between 1892–7 he was Chairman of the Board of Inland Revenue, and was responsible—as has been noted—for Harcourt's Death Duties proposals of 1894. In 1897 he became, at the age of forty-three, British High Commissioner in South Africa.

Milner subsequently bore the brunt of the criticism for the sharp change in the course of British policy towards the Boer Republics that occurred after 1897. Certainly, he was from an early stage convinced that a show-down was inevitable, and he was contemptuous of what he derided as 'the no-war policy' in the British Government, and particularly the pacific attitudes of the Commander-in-Chief in South Africa, General Sir William Butler. He came to these conclusions with disturbing rapidity, and Smuts was justified in describing him as 'a proud, high-strung, impatient, ironclad man'. By the middle of 1898 the Boers were in no doubt that a formidable new figure had appeared on the scene.

John Buchan, a sincere admirer and follower, characterised what was probably Milner's principal defect—and also gives us the clue to Chamberlain's choice—when he wrote of him:

His spiritual integrity made it difficult for him, when he had studied a problem, to temporise about the solution which he thought inevitable. . . . When he had satisfied himself about a particular course—and he took long to satisfy—his mind seemed to lock down on it, and after that there was no going back.

As early as February 1898 Milner was writing with a certain exultant grimness of 'the great day of reckoning'.

But Milner was not alone in this view, and it was by no means a wholly unreasonable one. The Boers were now arming themselves rapidly; no concessions were made towards the Uitlanders or the British; Leyds was still engaged in his European activities; the Transvaal Government remained corrupt and incompetent. As one South African historian has written:

> It is only the narrowest interpretation of South African history that can seek to explain the eventful years leading to the Boer War by dwelling exclusively upon the sins of Downing Street and British Secretaries of State.[1]

Milner, like Rhodes and Chamberlain, not only saw the Uitlanders as the Achilles Heel of the Transvaal Republic, but appears to have been genuinely convinced of the justice of their cause. He had no doubt that the Kruger regime was despicable and incompetent, nor that the fundamental superiority and civilising mission of the British race in Africa must triumph. He saw the situation in clear terms. Simply to depict him as cold-bloodedly preparing for war is to over-simplify and under-estimate both the situation and Milner's character. Milner's tragedy was that he had so few doubts, and that, having locked his mind into a general situation based on his Egyptian experience, he could not appreciate the vastness of the gulf which separated that experience and those general principles with the actual situation that existed in South Africa. He went out looking for trouble, if not a *causus belli*, and he swiftly found the former.

One of the first significant episodes occurred in December 1898, when a Uitlander—Edgar—was shot dead by a constable in Johannesburg. The Boer authorities said that Edgar was resisting arrest after a street brawl; the Uitlanders said that he had been shot down in his own house. It was the kind of incident which, when it

---

[1] C. W. de Kiewet: *The Imperial Factor in South Africa*, 15.

occurs in an atmosphere of tension and suspicion, arouses a disproportionate amount of heat and fury.

The constable—Jones—was charged by the young State Attorney, J. C. Smuts, with culpable homicide. He was also permitted bail. The Uitlander leaders demanded a charge of murder and opposed bail. Jones was acquitted and the judge, in discharging him, uttered some appropriate words of encouragement to the police in their difficult task of keeping law and order. Smuts very properly ordered another trial—when it took place, in February, Jones was again acquitted—but tempers were now running high. An Edgar Committee was formed, and the South Africa League planned a monster meeting of protest and petitioned the British Vice-Consul. Smuts declared the meeting illegal—which it was—and after it took place on December 24th ordered the arrest of two leading officials of the League. Another meeting, which was technically legal because it was held in an enclosed space—in fact a circus building—was deliberately broken up by the police.[1]

This was exactly the situation Milner had been waiting for, to give him the opportunity of laying the Uitlanders' grievances before the British Cabinet and British public opinion. But at this point he was in England, for consultations with Chamberlain, and to his dismay, the Acting High Commissioner—General Butler—took a very different view. Butler refused to transmit the Uitlanders' petition to London and gave his opinion that the real culprits were the League and the Johannesburg rabble.

Milner took steps to ensure that future petitions would be received in a notably more sympathetic manner and began a campaign to oust Butler, whom he described in a letter to Selborne as 'out-Krugering Kruger', from his command. 'Henceforward', Smuts's biographer has written, 'he and Conyngham Greene maintained the closest possible relations with the South African League and used it as an instrument of Imperial policy'.[2] Butler's independence of attitude was to destroy his career, and his prolonged opposition to Milner was not forgotten. When his name was proposed in 1902 to command a Corps, Balfour—by then Prime Minister—wrote to the King with characteristic tartness that:

[1] For a markedly biased and high-flown account of the Edgar Crisis, see Garvin, III, 381–3.
[2] W. K. Hancock: *Smuts: The Sanguine Years*, 83.

General Butler is a candidate of great ability and military knowledge. Unfortunately he has never in the exercise of his military duties been able to forget that he is a politician: while his politics are of a kind which seriously interfere with the discharge of his military duties. He made (as Mr. Balfour is informed) most embarrassing speeches in the course of the Egyptian Campaign: and had practically to be recalled from S. Africa because, in spite of warnings, he ran deliberately counter to Lord Milner's policy. A soldier who invariably believes that the enemies of his country is right, is seriously handicapped in the discharge of his proper duties.[1]

1899 thus opened with a decided check for the Uitlanders and for Milner. At a conference at Highbury he made it plain that he wanted to 'work up to a crisis'. Chamberlain, while emphasising the importance of not precipitating matters, supported the principle. But the Cabinet was very uneasy at the prospect of further South African complications, and British public opinion was far from belligerent. On board ship, returning to Cape Town, Milner wrote to Selborne, who was becoming his closest confidant:

My views are absolutely unaltered, but I have come to the conclusion that having stated them, it is no use trying to force them upon others at this stage. If I can advance matters by my own actions, as I still hope I may be able to do, I believe that I shall have support when the time comes.[2]

This was indeed true; Chamberlain had assured Milner that 'if the situation came to danger, he would be supported through thick and thin. He would never be let down'.[3]

On Milner's return the pace quickened. In February 1899 a protest to the Transvaal Government by Chamberlain concerning the dynamite concessions was curtly rejected. In March a well-organised Uitlander petition, with over 21,000 signatures, reached Milner. This time it was ceremoniously received, and was at once transmitted to London. 'The condition of Your Majesty's subjects in this State', the petition declared, 'has become well-nigh intolerable. . . . They are still deprived of all political rights, they are denied any voice in the

---

[1] P.R.O, Cab 40, 27/28 (July 23rd, 1902).   [2] *The Milner Papers*, I, 301-2.
[3] Garvin, III, 379.

Government of the country and they are taxed far above the requirements of the country.' On April 28th Selborne cabled to Milner at
Chamberlain's 'express wish' to 'send fully your views expressed as
frankly as you consider it to be possible or advisable consistently with
your position in South Africa'. As Chamberlain's biographer has
written, 'Milner was invited virtually to address Parliament and the
country through the written word. After fourteen months of constraint
he let himself go.'[1]

The resultant explosion reached Chamberlain on May 5th—a fact
which demonstrates that it had been composed some time before—
and contained this devastating phrase:

> The spectacle of thousands of British subjects kept permanently in
> the position of helots . . . does steadily undermine the influence and
> reputation of Great Britain and the respect for the British Govern-
> ment within the Queen's Dominions. . . . I can see nothing which
> will put a stop to this mischievous propaganda but some striking
> proof of the intention of Her Majesty's Government not to be
> ousted from its position in South Africa.

The Cabinet considered this startling document on May 9th, and it
was at this meeting that Balfour began to move in the general direction
of the Chamberlain–Milner line. But other Ministers, notably Salisbury,
were becoming very uneasy. 'This country, as well as the Cabinet',
Salisbury wrote on July 18th, 'excepting perhaps Mr. Chamberlain,
were against a war.' He was to write subsequently on Milner:

> What he has done cannot be effaced. We have to act on a moral
> field prepared for us by him and his jingo supporters. And therefore
> I see before us the necessity for considerable military effort—and
> all for people whom we despise, and for territory which will bring
> no profit and no power to England.[2]

At the end of May an attempt was made, in a conference at
Bloemfontein, to solve the franchise issue. 'Milner is as sweet as
honey', Smuts noted, 'but there is something in his very intelligent
eyes that tells me that he is a very dangerous man.' Milner proposed
a five years' retrospective franchise; Kruger responded with an offer

---

[1] Garvin, op. cit., 395.
[2] Salisbury to Lansdowne, August 30th, 1899 (Newton: *Lansdowne*, 157).

of a seven years' franchise with conditions which would in no way affect the Boer supremacy. When, at one stage, Kruger cried out that 'It is my country that you want' he struck one of the few notes of realism in the conference. Nevertheless, it was unwise of Milner to break it off after only six days with the declaration that 'this Conference is absolutely at an end, and there is no obligation on either side arising out of it'. Chamberlain, who had had real hopes of a Boer climb-down, was dismayed; Milner wrote to him (June 14th) that he had probably erred, but his letter ended:

> Though I think the beginning of a war would be *very unpleasant*, owing to our scattered outposts and the fact that the thinly populated *centre* of the country is quite Dutch, I do not think the result doubtful, or the ultimate difficulty, when once we had cleared the Augean Stable, at all serious.

At this point (June 14th) the 'Helots' Dispatch was published. War began to loom ominously closer.

Neither Chamberlain nor Milner thought that it was inevitable, nor did they think it would even be necessary. Their policy was essentially one of steady pressure, with force held confidently in the background. 'The Boers', Milner wrote to Chamberlain on July 26th, 'are still bluffing and will yield further if pressure is kept up.' Neither feared war if the Boers were intransigent, but at this stage they were not working towards a war, a fact that made their policy even more perilous. If they had ever considered the military situation seriously—and neither did, save in general terms—their policies might well have been changed. For the British were in no condition to back up their threats with force.

The general condition of the British Army was not good. It consisted of 124,000 men serving abroad—of whom 73,000 were in India—and 125,000 in the home battalions. The Reserve, which had been much neglected, totalled some 90,000 men. Counting all regulars, reservists, and volunteers, there was a theoretical total of 600,000; in fact, the practical limit for a quick mobilisation was 85,000 and the standard was not high. Poor terms of service and series of easy contests against natives were an inadequate background for a war against skilled marksmen and riders in a foreign country.

In May 1899 there were in South Africa 10,300 British troops and twenty-four field guns, split between the Cape and Natal. No plan of campaign existed, and the British had virtually no maps. They had one map of Natal, 'on a scale of five miles to an inch prepared locally for educational purposes', and another to a scale of 12½ miles to the inch covering Cape Colony, Natal, the Orange Free State, but only part of the Transvaal. Even by October, when war broke out, the British forces in South Africa totalled 27,054, dispersed, which was opposed by over 35,000 mounted Boers, which were—although perhaps of not as high a quality as the victors of Majuba—still the best marksmen in the world. General Butler, for one, had no illusions about the disparity in quality as well as quantity, but his days as Commander-in-Chief were numbered, and he was recalled at the beginning of August. Nevertheless, his lack of enthusiasm for a confrontation did not help. As he subsequently wrote, 'I held the balance. There would be no war while I was there',[1] a fact that was perfectly evident to Milner. When Milner said that the Boers would not fight, Butler retorted that 'they would fight for their independence'. He considered that 40,000 troops would be insufficient for the task, and, as Milner subsequently wrote of him: 'His great merit was that he knew the size of the job.' He was one of the few who did. But his attitudes contributed to subsequent reverses. On June 22nd he was instructed by the War Office to purchase wagons and transport mules; he retorted that such action would merely increase 'the ferment which [I] am endeavouring to reduce by every means. . . . I believe war would be the greatest calamity that ever occurred in South Africa'. Butler's resignation was accepted on August 8th after a blunt meeting with Milner.

The policies of Chamberlain and Milner now began to become even closer. The publication of the 'Helots' dispatch had had a deep impact in Britain. But the new Liberal leader, Campbell-Bannerman, declared on June 17th that nothing in the South African situation justified war; more seriously, the Cabinet was now very alarmed, and Salisbury's reports to the Queen reflected this concern. On July 11th he reported:

Lord Salisbury was much impressed with the more pacific tone of the Cabinet. Some members were averse to any abatement of their indignation towards the Transvaal. But the majority of the Cabinet were impressed with the want of support such a war would seem likely to command with public opinion in the country.

[1] Butler: *Autobiography*, 414.

Even more significant was a report from Selborne to Milner on June 25th:

> The warnings Mr. Chamberlain and I gave you about the state of public opinion here have been abundantly justified. . . . The idea of war with the South African Republic is very distasteful to most people . . . we simply cannot force the pace . . . the worst service we could do the Empire would be to outrun public opinion.

Nevertheless, some deliberate pace-making in Britain was begun, and Chamberlain's speeches began to strike a more menacing note. The Cabinet increasingly came to accept his diagnosis that a policy of steady pressure with an implicit military threat would succeed in gaining the necessary concessions from Kruger. Salisbury instinctively disagreed, but his influence was waning rapidly. Indeed, in Mid-July it did seem that the Boers were backing down on the matter of the franchise, and Chamberlain authorised a statement—to Milner's dismay—that 'the crisis between Great Britain and the Transvaal may be regarded as ended'. When Milner protested that the real issue was not the franchise but 'the practical assertion of British supremacy', he was assured by Selborne that British policy was back 'on the old right track'. On August 24th Chamberlain wrote:

> It is clear that we cannot go on negotiating forever; we must try to bring matters to a head. The next step in military preparations is so important and so costly that I hesitate to incur the expense . . . so long as there seems a fair chance of a satisfactory settlement. But I dread above all the continuing whittling away of differences until we have no *causus belli* left.

Two days later, at Birmingham, he said of Kruger that 'he dribbles out reforms like water from a squeezed sponge', and went on to declare that 'the issues of peace and war are in the hands of the President. . . . Will he speak the necessary words? The sands are running down in the glass.'

They were indeed. It takes two to make a war, and by this time there was an ugly mood in Pretoria. Deneys Reitz, the son of a former President of the Orange Free State, wrote of the atmosphere in Pretoria:

> Looking back, I think that war was inevitable. I have no doubt that the British Government had made up its mind to force the issue, and

was the chief culprit, but the Transvaalers were also spoiling for a fight, and from what I saw in Pretoria during the few weeks that preceded the ultimatum, I feel sure that the Boers would in any case have insisted on a rupture.[1]

Smuts now prepared a military appraisal on the assumption that war was imminent, and which envisaged a whirlwind attack on the British in Natal and then in Cape Colony. (Fortunately for the British, the plan was not adopted.) Kruger refused to consider a suitable response on the franchise issue. On September 27th the Orange Free State publicly declared its support for the Transvaal, which meant that the Boers could put into the field at once over 50,000 mounted infantry; they had rifles and ammunition for 80,000, the total they hoped to reach by enrolling Cape Dutch volunteers. The rains had renewed the veldt grass—a vital prerequisite for campaigning. Milner advised the government not to issue an ultimatum until the expected 10,000 troops from India were on the Transvaal border. 'Personally I am still of opinion not to hurry in settling ultimatum', he wrote, 'as events of next few days may supply us with a better one than anybody can compose. Ultimatum has always been great difficulty, as unless we widen issue there is not sufficient cause for war, and if we do, we are abused for shifting our ground and extending our demands.' When Milner's papers were published, the last sentence was prudently omitted. The British belatedly ordered substantial reinforcements to South Africa under the command of General Sir Redvers Buller. But they had not arrived when the Boer Republics issued an ultimatum at the beginning of October and began hostilities almost at once.

It was, in any event, a matter of who got in his ultimatum first. As Chamberlain wrote on September 29th, if the Boers took the offensive 'the Lord will have delivered them into our hands—at least as far as diplomacy is concerned.' But the Boer ultimatum of October 9th settled the matter for most Englishmen. G. K. Chesterton has written:

> The nation seemed solid for war. . . . I saw all the public men and all the public bodies, the people in the street, my own middle class and most of my family and friends, solid in favour of something that seemed inevitable and scientific and secure. And I suddenly realised that I hated it. . . . What I hated about it was what a good many people liked about it. It was such a very cheerful war. I hated

[1] Deneys Reitz: *Commando*, 19.

its confidence, its congratulatory anticipations, its optimism of the Stock Exchange. I hated its vile assurance of victory.[1]

There were no forebodings of disaster. Chamberlain wrote to Hicks-Beach on October 7th that:

My own opinion is, as it always has been, that both Milner and the military authorities greatly exaggerate the risks and dangers of this campaign. I have never believed that the Boers would take the offensive at this stage—nor do I fear a British reverse if they do. There must be risks in all wars, but I think the risk of a successful attack on a fortified position chosen by us is a very small one. When all the reinforcements are landed my own feeling is that we shall be quite a match for the Boers even without the army corps.

In the general excitement only a few dissenting voices were heard.

In the Parliament elected in 1895 the star of Lloyd George had risen very considerably, but he had demonstrated little interest in South African affairs, and was an ill-concealed admirer of Chamberlain, despite political differences. This respect was reciprocated. But Lloyd George reacted immediately to the outbreak of the war with a denunciation of the Government and of Chamberlain personally which was certainly not calculated, and which demonstrated the best part of his complex and not wholly attractive personality. In the fervent mood of the day, it took courage to point out that the British were fighting 'a little country, the total of whose population was less than Carmarthonshire—the British Empire against Carmarthonshire!'. Thus began a campaign that almost cost Lloyd George his seat in Parliament and his life, but which made him a national figure. On September 15th John Morley protested at Manchester at the possibility of war with 'this weak little Republic'.

It will bring you no glory. It will bring you no profit, but mischief, and it will be wrong. You may make thousands of women widows and thousands of children fatherless. It will be wrong. You may add a new province to your Empire. It will still be wrong.

Gladstone had been dead for a year, but his voice still lived in the land. For the moment it was a faint one, but was shortly to be heard

[1] The full extent of public enthusiasm for the war is difficult to gauge. Richard Price's *An Imperial War and the British Working Class*, emphasises the prevalence of middle class volunteers, particularly in 1900–01.

with more insistence as the British marched confidently towards a series of military and political disasters.

But, if to many contemporaries the origins of the Boer War were complex, the issue itself seemed quite clear. 'What is now at stake', Chamberlain wrote to Salisbury, 'is the position of Great Britain in South Africa and with it the estimate formed of our power and influence in our Colonies and throughout the world.' Salisbury himself, although deeply unhappy about the situation, expressed the dilemma well when he wrote to the Queen on September 23rd:

> On the one hand we cannot abandon them [the Uitlanders] without great injustice—nor without endangering Your Majesty's authority in the whole of South Africa. On the other hand we are most earnestly anxious to avoid any rupture with the Boers, if it is possible. But they do not assist us to do so. . . .
>
> It is impossible to avoid believing that the Boers really aim at setting up a South African Republic, consisting of the Transvaal, the Orange Free State, and Your Majesty's Colony. It is impossible to account in any other manner for their rejection of our most moderate proposals. . . .

In this estimate Salisbury probably represented the majority opinion in Britain. If the Government as a whole entered the war without enthusiasm, yet it had no premonition of defeat. Elsewhere, the war was greeted with undisguised eagerness and excitement, and particularly in the Unionist Party. In one of his less happy hours Kipling denounced Kruger as 'Cruel in the shadow, crafty in the sun . . . sloven, sullen, savage, secret, uncontrolled.' Serious questioning of the justice and necessity of the war was confined to a small and derided section of the Liberal Party.

CHAPTER SEVEN

THE BOER WAR AND TARIFF REFORM, 1899–1905

THE INTELLIGENCE DIVISION of the War Office was maintained at a cost of £11,000 per annum, and two officers were responsible for the entire colonial Empire. The expenditure on Intelligence at the time by the German General Staff was some £250,000, and that of the Transvaal Republic was some £90,000. Section B of the Intelligence Division revised and issued in June 1899 a document entitled 'Military Notes on the Dutch Republics of South Africa'. It is an instructive document. After describing the Boer custom of military councils deciding daily military business in the field, it comments that:

> It is obvious, this system of leaving not only administrative details, but even strategical and tactical questions, to the decision of a large body of officers, elected by the votes of the burghers they command, must inevitably involve inefficiency and renders it improbable that a burgher force, under such conditions, will ever carry through any great enterprise requiring steadfastness of purpose, or, that in case of defeat, it would be in a position to contrive any prolonged resistance . . . although the Transvaal has spent large sums during the last three years on their military forces, they have made but little progress towards the improvement of their primitive organisation.

The document pointed out that Boer mobilisation—as the Jameson Raid had demonstrated—would be rapid; the Corps of Staats Artillery had greatly improved, although 'the standard at present reached is inferior to that of the Royal Artillery'; Joubert, the Commandant-General, was described as 'a man of vacillating purpose, and is easily influenced by those near him'. The assessment continued:

The Boers indeed today frankly own, to use their quaint expression, that 'God Almighty gave them their lives for some better purpose than to be shot at like bucks in the open', and that they consider as sheer folly that willingness to face death which English soldiers display. The real genius of the Boer is in fact to fight under cover, and this dislike to risk death seriously diminishes his military value in offensive operations or in any position the flanks of which can be turned. . . .

The Dutchman is, in fact, by race and instincts of a stolid stubborn nature, but it would be absurd to expect from untrained farmers that readiness to face death at the bidding of a superior which history emphatically teaches can only be created and fostered by discipline. . . .

It may therefore be anticipated that while the Boers will show some of their old skill in guerrilla warfare on ground favourable to such tactics, yet they will have but little chance of success if compelled to meet in the open plains of the Free State or Transvaal an adquate force of disciplined troops complete in all three arms, and it appears certain that, after serious defeat, they would be too deficient in discipline and organisation to make any further real stand. . . .

These somewhat condescending judgements were now to be put to the test.

Details of the proposed expeditionary force were sent by the War Office to the Admiralty on September 20th; ten days later the Admiralty was told to take up the required shipping. On October 7th the mobilisation order was issued and the Royal Proclamation calling out the Reserves was published. The mobilisation was efficient; ninety-nine per cent of the Reservists reported for duty, and over ninety per cent of them were fit for active service. The first Regular units embarked on October 8th, and embarkation was completed— with the exception of one cavalry regiment, delayed by horse-sickness —on November 7th.

Superficially, this was admirable. Closer inspection was less impressive. To make the force complete, staffs were taken from units which it was thought (wrongly) would not be required. It was also discovered that 'staffs of many formations, such as those of mounted infantry, ammunition columns and medical field units, did not exist'.[1]

[1] Maurice: *The War in South Africa*, 8–10.

One small, but not untypical, example may be given. By the end of November one battery of field artillery had lost its captain, the senior subaltern (the only one with four months' experience in field artillery), five sergeants, a corporal bombardier, 'four shoeing smiths, two trumpeters, the wheeler, six gunners and five drivers'. In December the battery commander was sent to South Africa. Ten days later the battery was mobilised; when it was brought up to strength, no member of it had ever seen the guns, which they were to operate, fired.[1]

Then, there was the case of the Royal Army Medical Corps, found to be in deplorable condition; an eminent surgeon who brought a hospital to South Africa said of the doctors in the Corps that 'you would get a few good ones, but the majority of them were shocking'.

Perhaps the same harsh judgement could be applied to the British senior officer. One British correspondent, L. S. Amery, subsequently wrote:

> All I saw during those [first] weeks left on my mind an ineffaceable impression of the incapacity of many of our senior officers, of the uselessness of most of our then army training for the purposes of modern war, especially in South African conditions, and of the urgent need of complete, revolutionary reform of the Army from top to bottom.[2]

The British Commander-in-Chief, when offered the two volumes of information on the Boer Republics prepared by the Intelligence Branch, returned them immediately with the curt statement that he 'knew everything about South Africa'. Winston Churchill, who went to South Africa as a journalist, and was to win national fame by his escape from a Boer prisoner of war camp, sailed with Buller to South Africa on the liner *Dunottar Castle*—which did not raise her speed above the normal commercial rate—and has penned this portrait:

> Buller was a characteristic British personality. He looked stolid. He said little, and what he said was obscure. He was not the kind of man who could explain things, and he never tried to do so. He usually grunted or nodded, or shook his head, in serious discussions; and shop of all kinds was sedulously excluded from his ordinary

[1] Ibid., footnote to pp. 11–12.
[2] L. S. Amery: *My Political Life*, I, 118.

conversation. He had shown himself a brave and skilful officer in his youth, and for nearly twenty years he had filled important administrative posts of a sedentary character in Whitehall.[1]

Churchill might have added that Buller, in addition to his taciturnity, had a notorious addiction to the bottle; as Balfour was to write on December 18th, 'for ten years he has allowed himself to go downhill'.

While the Commander-in-Chief and is staff proceeded on their leisurely and agreeable way to South Africa, matters were proceeding in an unexpected and untoward manner on the veldt.

On one point at least, the British Intelligence had been correct. Joubert was a feeble and unimaginative commander. With every advantage on his side, he engaged in desultory seiges of British garrisons in the Transvaal. Ladysmith, Mafeking and Kimberley were invested somewhat lethargically, and large Boer forces were needlessly tied to these irrelevancies. While the younger Boer commanders chafed impatiently, the British slowly gathered their forces together in Cape Colony.

Buller at once broke up his Army Corps into three divisions, and they proceeded northwards into a series of disasters. In one week in December—'Black Week'—Methuen was repulsed at Magersfontein trying to do 'a Tel-el-Kebir'; Gatacre was thrown back at Stormberg; and Buller, advancing ponderously on Ladysmith, was forced to retire at Colenso. The British forces were at every stage out-witted and out-manoeuvred by the Boer soldiers, who fought with precision and skill. Buller's nerve was broken. He recommended the abandonment of Ladysmith; the Government promptly relieved him of his command and sent out Lord Roberts, whose son had won the V.C. at Colenso but had died of his wounds.

1899 thus closed in humiliation and reverse. One bright gleam of hope was that the Empire had rallied to the Imperial cause. Canada sent 8,400 men, Australia over 16,000, and New Zealand, 6,000. Far from the Cape Colony being divided, 30,000 volunteers enlisted in the Colony on the British side. To Chamberlain in particular, these were encouraging indications of the rightness of his actions and the solidarity of Imperial unity at an hour of crisis.

But in England opinions were most sharply divided, particularly in

[1] Churchill: *My Early Life*, 228.

the Liberal Party where the dilemma of the late 1880s and 1890s was sharply revealed.

Rosebery, although he distrusted and disliked Milner—unlike Asquith—regarded the Boer ultimatum as decisive, and came out strongly in favour of the war, quoting Chatham's phrase: 'Be of one people; forget everything for the public.' In this attitude he was warmly supported by Asquith and Edward Grey and by some fifty Liberal M.P.s. At the other extreme were Harcourt, Morley, Labouchere and the young Lloyd George, quickly dubbed the 'pro-Boers', and vehemently opposed to the war. In the middle were Campbell-Bannerman, Herbert Gladstone, and some twenty Liberals who disliked the war intensely but who considered that the Boer ultimatum had given the Government no choice. The Annual Register for 1900 estimated the Liberal supporters of the Government in the House of Commons at sixty-two; the 'pro-Boers' at sixty-eight; twenty-seven who were uncertain, and the Campbell-Bannerman middle-of-the-roaders. This internecine controversy was a deep and bitter one, and whenever the war issue arose in the Commons the Parliamentary Liberal Party shivered into angry fragments. The war itself might be going badly, but the domestic political battle was proceeding very satisfactorily for the Unionists.

Then, the war itself took a dramatic change for the better in 1900. Roberts concentrated his forces and marched on Bloemfontein. At the end of February a large Boer force of 4,000 men was surrounded and forced to surrender. One by one, the beseiged towns were relieved. From this point it was a story of unbroken British success, culminating in Kruger leaving the Transvaal on September 11th and the Transvaal being formally annexed on October 25th. The war was over. Roberts returned home in triumph, Milner received a peerage, and Kitchener was left to clear up the few guerrilla commandos who had refused to surrender. It had been a war fought with very little bitterness, and marked on both sides by chivalry and respect. Prisoners were well treated; the wounded were cared for; neither side had any compunction in surrendering when surrounded and outnumbered. Each side developed a considerable respect for the other. It was, in a very real way, the last of the old-fashioned wars. The early British reverses had shocked the nation, but had been swiftly succeeded by a string of emphatic victories. In spite of much verbal abuse of Britain no other power had come to the aid of the Boers, and the other Colonies had vigorously supported the British. It seemed that the Boer problem, which had exercised British attention for two decades, had been solved in a matter of months.

It was in these highly encouraging circumstances that, in September 1900, the Cabinet decided on a new election. The Liberal position was hapless. On July 27th, for example, on a motion proposed by a prominent 'pro-Boer', Sir Wilfred Lawson, to reduce the Colonial Office Vote, Campbell-Bannerman had advised a general abstention. Grey led thirty-seven Liberals to support the Government, while over thirty Liberals supported Lawson.

The Unionists accordingly entered what the Liberals angrily called 'the Khaki Election' with every possible advantage. In terms of domestic legislation, the only real achievement had been the Workmen's Compensation Act of 1897, which gave automatic compensations by employers for industrial accidents, and the election was dominated by the war and the Liberal divisions. Chamberlain was now the truly dominating figure in British politics; the Unionist party was absolutely united; the Liberal leadership was weak and not inspiriting, and the party was riven. It was not an election which the political purist could contemplate with much satisfaction. Morley declared that 'a ring of financiers . . . mostly Jewish, are really responsible for the war', and the anti-semitic campaign instigated by Lloyd George was eagerly echoed by John Burns and Keir Hardie. Burns declared that the British Army had become 'the janissary of the Jews', and he, Hardie, and eighty-one executive officers of the trade union movement signed a resolution that blamed the war not only on the capitalists and the press, but on the fact that they were 'largely Jews and foreigners'. One Unionist pamphlet exhorted:

Electors, be up and doing. Your Children Call Upon You. They will ask you hereafter how you voted in the crisis of the Empire. Don't let your reply be 'For a Small England, a Shrunken England, a degraded England, a Submissive England'.

No!

To the Poll, then, to the Poll to

Vote for the Unionist Candidate

and for

GREATER BRITAIN

In the circumstances, the Liberals did remarkably well. Particularly difficult was the position of those Liberals who had supported the war, but were still attacked as pro-Boers and anti-British. The pre-election Unionist majority of 130 was increased to 134, but very significantly, this was eighteen smaller than the majority of 1895. A new Unionist M.P., Winston Churchill, who had been elected for Oldham, wrote to Rosebery—who had not taken an active part in the election—that 'I think this election, fought by the Liberals as a soldier's battle, without plan or leaders or enthusiasm, has shown so far the strength, not the weakness, of Liberalism in the country'.[1] But the Liberal dissensions increased after the election, until it seemed that the party was hell-bent on self-destruction. The gulf between men of the stamp of Rosebery, Grey, Asquith and Haldane on the one hand and Morley, Harcourt and the rising young Lloyd George on the other, was so wide that it seemed impossible ever to bridge.

In 1902 Salisbury at last retired, and was succeeded as Prime Minister by Arthur Balfour. It was a wholly unchallenged succession, dutifully endorsed by a special Party meeting. But no one doubted who was the strongest man, with the greatest personal following, in the Unionist ranks. It was Chamberlain's hour.

But the Boer War now entered a long and dismal period for the British. The Boer commandos, led by men of the calibre of Smuts, Botha, and De Wet, harried the British lines. The only answer was to increase the British forces and denude the countryside of succour for the Boers. The deliberate burning of farms as an act of war seems to have begun in April 1900, and *The Times* reported (April 27th) that a column left Bloemfontein 'with definite instructions to render untenable the farms of men, who, having surrendered, were found to be still in league with the enemy, or were making use of British magnanimity as a means to save their property'. As early as March 11th Roberts had complained about the continued Boer abuse of the white flag. In May Botha protested about the burning of farmhouses. In June Roberts issued a proclamation that farmhouses in the vicinity of damaged railway lines would be destroyed in reprisal. In August it was announced that any building that had harboured the enemy would be razed to the ground. Meanwhile, Botha was also destroying farmhouses with the object of intimidating Boers who were contemplating surrender or had done so. These punitive measures had the

---

[1] But the Liberals did not contest 143 seats, another indication of their disunity and low morale.

same result. The smoke rose into the air and the victims had to search desperately for succour. 'The Devil is walking up and down this land and people have gone mad', Lionel Curtis, a strong admirer of Milner, wrote in October 1900. 'We are doing things that 100 years ago Wellington would have none of and which a year ago we should have said was impossible.'[1]

The British and the majority of the Boers were now in a very real quandary. In March, when the war seemed virtually over, Roberts had issued a proclamation permitting Boers who laid down their arms and took an oath of neutrality to return to their farms. Many thousands availed themselves of these terms. Now, it appeared, the war was not over at all.

The first indication of serious trouble occurred on September 3rd, when Roberts reported that a British officer had to look after a party of Boers, with women and children, who had come to him for help. On September 22nd an order was issued to establish refugee camps in Pretoria and Bloemfontein 'for burghers who voluntarily surrender'. Botha, considerably alarmed by the attraction of this offer, intensified his measures of intimidation, while at the same time issuing a number of allegations against the British which, although thinly based on fact, had a considerable impact abroad.

By November, farm-burning by the British had become virtually indiscriminate. In effect, it was impossible to draw any distinction between farms; every one was potential—if not an actual—source of supply for a Boer commando living off the land. Behind the protests of the Boers there lay a genuine military apprehension. The trickle of refugees became a torrent. On December 21st Kitchener drew the attention of officers to the fact that an experiment of moving all women and children to camps had reduced the morale of the men on commando.

Early in 1901, there was a brave but abortive attempt by the Boers to invade Cape Colony; the Dutch in the Colony would not support them. On March 8th-15th there was a meeting between Kitchener and Botha at Middelburg which achieved nothing. Kitchener proposed that farmhouses and their occupants should be put outside the scope of military operations, but Botha refused in terms so callous that repelled even so favourable an observer of the Boer conditions as Miss Emily Hobhouse, who subsequently wrote:

[1] *With Milner in South Africa.*

From the date of the Middelburg Conference the Boers washed their hands, as it were, more completely of the families of surrendered burghers, and, regarding them as English subjects, sent them into the English lines.

From the one side or the other it was clear that the Boer women with their little ones must suffer. They were between the devil and the deep sea.[1]

The Boers themselves were in no position to look after their own refugees, and conditions in their camps were unspeakable. The flood of Boer refugees now descended on the British, in a pitiable condition. They brought with them diphtheria, typhoid and a virulent strain of measles which was particularly lethal to children. They were also badly under-nourished, and their open life on the veldt left them easy victims to infection. The British were already badly short of medical supplies for their own troops, who were ravaged by enteric and dysentery; up to the end of May 1902 the British lost 13,750 dead and 66,500 invalided from disease. The medical facilities—bad at the outset—had completely broken down. This background shows why it was that the death-rate in the 'concentration' camps was so appalling. The number of deaths in the camps totalled some 4,000 women and 16,000 children. It was not surprising that world, and British, opinion was outraged.

On June 14th, 1901, Campbell-Bannerman, shocked by Miss Hobhouse's reports, declared that:

> A phrase often used is that 'war is war', but when one comes to ask about it one is told that no war is going on, that it is not war. When is a war not a war? When it is carried on by methods of barbarism in South Africa.

This brought the Liberal schisms to a head, and led to the formation by the Liberal Imperialists of the Liberal League, led by Rosebery, Asquith, Haldane and Grey. On December 15th, at Chesterfield, Rosebery advised the party to abandon 'the fly-blown phylacteries of obsolete policies' and 'clean the slate'. Campbell-Bannerman reacted sharply, and began to demonstrate real signs of political leadership. The controversy in Britain now reached new heights of bitterness and passion. If the Jameson Raid had been her Bay of Pigs, the Boer War

[1] Emily Hobhouse: *The Brunt of the War and Where It Fell*, 102.

was her Vietnam. The circumstances under which Lloyd George narrowly escaped with his life from the Birmingham Riot of December 18th, 1901 have been often described, but they deserve repetition. No one was in any doubt, from the tone of the Unionist press in Birmingham, that Lloyd George's increasingly personal assaults on Chamberlain's competence and integrity—and particularly upon his brother's association with a company which had prospered greatly from Government contracts—represented an outrage to which the citizens of the city should respond. A well-armed mob of over thirty thousand persons surrounded the Town Hall, many of them surged into the meeting, the windows were smashed, the platform received a blizzard of missiles, and Lloyd George only escaped disguised as a policeman. The episode—strongly reminiscent of the Aston Park Riot of 1885 directed against Lord Randolph Churchill and Sir Stafford Northcote—was significant in that Chamberlain could easily have prevented it, but did not; that it established Lloyd George's reputation for physical courage, which his detractors have subsequently sought to deride; and that it made his national reputation. Mob brutality in Britain, particularly when it is obviously carefully planned, has a devastatingly counter-productive effect. The incident also demonstrated that Chamberlain had learned nothing about the true nature of British politics. In one night of brutality, in which two people were killed and over forty seriously injured, he had made Lloyd George's name a household word.

'Joe's war' ended in May 1902 on a sour and disagreeable note. It had cost the British 5,774 killed, 22,829 wounded, and over 16,000 dead from disease. The Boer losses are not known, although it is estimated that they lost some 4,000 killed in action. It had cost Britain £222 million.

Although the Boers had lost, the terms of surrender were generous. They included a money grant of £3 million to rebuild and restock farms, an act that did much to reduce the bitter feelings left by the last two years of the war. Abroad, the war had brought Britain nothing but obloquy outside the Empire, and her isolation in Europe had been painfully evident. It was this realisation that created the climate of opinion in which the new Foreign Secretary, Lord Lansdowne, started to reshape British foreign policy with the settlement of outstanding differences, particularly with France. The drastic overhaul of the British Army, so long overdue, was put in hand.

The loss of the glitter of victory was one factor that affected the Unionist fortunes. The end of the war, furthermore, although it did not result in Liberal reunion, at least removed the most crucial abrasive element in the party's internal affairs.

The first turning-point came in 1902, with the Education Act. The Act of 1870 had created a dual system with two sets of schools, one wholly provided and maintained by religious authorities, and the other by elected school boards. The 1902 Act, the work of Balfour and a rising civil servant, Robert Morant, swept away the boards, and made the new local authorities wholly responsible; it also required the religious-supported schools to provide their facilities free of charge to the authorities. These proposals aroused intense opposition. As they also strengthened the position of the Church of England Schools and restored them to equality with Nonconformist ones, the fury of the latter was intense, and was concentrated particularly upon Chamberlain. Many Nonconformists refused to pay the new Education Rate, and in Wales there was a successful capture of county councils; these then refused to levy any education rates until they had complete control of the money, and forced the Government to pass legislation giving it powers to by-pass the local authorities. This was a very significant increase in the powers of the central government, and confirmed the purpose of the 1902 Act to give the new Board of Education control over the policy of national education.

The 1902 Education Act can now be seen as a logical development of previous Acts, a legislative action of far-reaching effects, and a substantial step forward in the provision of national State education. At the time, it aroused intense passions, and the Liberals found themselves united for the first time in six years. This was a considerable check for the Unionists, but far worse was to come.

*

It is never difficult—in retrospect, particularly—to trace the processes of Chamberlain's thought. In the 1880s he had followed Lord Randolph about the country lauding Free Trade when Churchill was temporarily toying with 'Fair Trade', and the experience had made him question the essential validity of the case for Free Trade. There was now additional evidence. British exports to the Empire actually declined between 1883 and 1892, and the value of imported goods into Britain had risen sharply, by nearly £100 million, while foreign imports into the Empire countries rose. For a nation that depended upon trade for its existence, these figures were ominous. But economic factors were not the only ones. By 1902 Chamberlain's political position had slipped, and he was frustrated by his failure in South Africa and by his inability to persuade Hicks-Beach to introduce a modest Old Age Pension scheme. He was, accordingly, looking for a new national issue.

In 1897 Queen Victoria had her second—the Diamond—Jubilee. It marked the high point of national enthusiasm for the Empire, and was both in popular and political terms a spectacular occasion. Rudyard Kipling, the most sensitive, prolific, and influential writer in England since Dickens, had become, as H. G. Wells later wrote, 'almost a national symbol. He got hold of us wonderfully, he filled us with tinkling and haunting quotations. . . . He helped to broaden my geographical sense immensely, and he provided phrases for just that desire for discipline and devotion and organised effort the Socialism of our times failed to express.' Kipling was much more than the Jingo poetaster that many—including Max Beerbohm—have portrayed him. If he exalted the cause of Empire he also warned against its perils and, having been brought up in India, saw clearly the moral pitfalls of Imperialism. He also understood, as no other contemporary writer did, the difficulties and strains under which the servants of the Empire lived, and he was their spokesman and their champion. His contempt for flag-waving politicians was best expressed in a famous passage in *Stalky and Co.*, but is to be seen often elsewhere in his writings. Immensely popular, almost a national institution, derided by the anti-imperialists, his influence on popular attitudes in the 1890s was immense.

During the Jubilee the experiment of 1887 of the Colonial Conference of Colonial Prime Ministers had been repeated. Chamberlain presided, and it was attended by the Prime Ministers of Canada, Newfoundland, New South Wales, Victoria, South Australia, West Australia, Queensland, Tasmania, New Zealand, Cape Colony and Natal. Chamberlain proposed closer federation and a 'Council of the Empire' which he hoped might develop into 'that Federal Council to which we must always look forward as our ultimate ideal'. He also proposed 'an Imperial Zollverrein'. Both proposals were in effect, turned down flat. But Chamberlain was not disposed to abandon his plan so easily. In 1902, making use of the presence of Colonial Prime

Ministers at the Coronation of King Edward VII, another Colonial Conference had been held. It was notable for two reasons. The idea of 'Imperial Defence' was unenthusiastically received and, in effect, rejected in spite of cogent arguments by Chamberlain. But the Prime Ministers did agree to accepting the principle of Imperial Preference in general terms. This move forward was to have decisive importance on Chamberlain's outlook.

In the 1902 Budget Hicks-Beach introduced a registration duty on imported grain, corn, flour, and meal, emphasising that this was not to be regarded as a Protectionist measure. Chamberlain persuaded the Cabinet to respond favourably to a request by the Canadian Government for preference. In November 1902 the matter was discussed in the Cabinet. Chamberlain concluded that it had agreed that the tax would be maintained, and that the preferential remission for countries of the Empire would be increased. This was not the interpretation of the new Chancellor of the Exchequer, Ritchie, who proceeded to repeal the duties in his 1903 Budget. Until December 1916 no Cabinet Minutes were taken or distributed to Ministers, and the only record of Cabinet proceedings was a confidential letter to the Sovereign by the Prime Minister. This inefficient arrangement was bound to lead to misunderstandings, and this was to prove one of the most celebrated.

On May 15th 1903, at Birmingham, Chamberlain delivered one of the most sensational speeches in modern British politics. He called it 'A Demand for Enquiry', but it was in fact a trenchant and provocative exposition of the case for Imperial Preference and Tariff Reform, arguing that the key to Empire was commerce, coupled with a critical analysis of the deficiencies of Free Trade. He also spoke warily of 'sacrifices', referring to the inevitability of higher prices for imported food. To make the sensation even more complete, Balfour on the same day explicitly relegated Imperial Preference to 'a hypothetical future'.

Politics leaped into intense life. The Liberals sprang together, and Asquith started a tour of speeches in which he hammered away at Chamberlain's proposals. 'To dispute Free Trade, after fifty years' experience of it, is like disputing the law of gravitation', Campbell-Bannerman declared, thus characteristically putting his finger on the fatal defect in Chamberlain's approach. He was disputing not a policy, but a religion—and without advance notice. Ironically, in this matter he was right, but in the manner of his heresy he doomed it to failure. The Protectionist issue was to divide and haunt the Unionists for nearly thirty years, and was to be to them what Home Rule had been for the Liberals. The Unionists reacted in dismay, and split into Tariff Reformers and Free Traders; one of the most vigorous of the latter was the young Winston Churchill, ambitious, impatient, and already highly discontented at his lack of advancement, and whose progression to the Liberal party was now accelerated.

Balfour attempted to hold the Cabinet together. Compromise solutions were created, but could not bridge the deep fissure opened in the Cabinet. Balfour proposed retaliatory measures against high tariff countries, with no food taxes. In September he issued a pamphlet of considerable skill but which satisfied neither side. It had already become virtually a theological dispute.

On September 9th Chamberlain offered Balfour his resignation on the understanding that his son, Austen, would enter the Cabinet, so that he could propagate his cause. On September 14th Balfour in effect dismissed Ritchie and Lord Balfour of Burleigh, two prominent and intransigent Free Traders. On the following day the Free Trade Duke of Devonshire and Lord George Hamilton resigned, but under Balfour's urgings the former withdrew his resignation when he was privately told of Chamberlain's resignation. It seemed that Balfour had achieved a remarkable coup by shedding the extremists of both sides and retaining the Duke. Hartington—as his contemporaries still called him—was now an old man, and no longer particularly active in politics, but he aroused respect and confidence to a quite remarkable extent. For two weeks the political world breathlessly awaited his decision. Loud and angry accusations were made by both sides against Balfour's tactics, and the Free Traders put intense pressure upon the Duke. Persuaded that his honour was at stake, and somewhat confused, he resigned on October 6th and Balfour's elaborate scheme collapsed in ruins.

Many historians have been baffled by Balfour's tactics during this crisis, and have pondered upon his strategy. To this commentator, the strategy seems clear enough—it was to preserve the unity of the Unionist party, and to avoid a catastrophic split on the scale of 1846. If he had declared himself for one side or the other he would, as he saw the situation, become 'another Peel'. Furthermore, it was a vital part of his policy to keep the Unionists in office. He had a genuine, if very exaggerated, fear of the domestic social policies of the Liberals and their new Labour allies. He was fearful about the possibility of

the return of Home Rule as a major issue. He also was determined to
make permanent his reforms in Defence matters, to the point when a
Liberal Government would find it very difficult, if not impossible, to
reverse them. For this he needed time.

This was the strategy. From it the tactics flowed, but here he came
up against problems of personality which he could not surmount, and
he grievously underestimated the passions which lay behind the issues
of Free Trade and Protection. Balfour was not a passionate man, and
he failed to make allowances for the burning convictions, which in
some instances amounted to frenzy, that these issues aroused. At the
time, and by many historians subsequently, he has been depicted as
fatally weak and indecisive. Now, with a clearer perspective, we can
see this his strategy had its merits, and that his tactics were coherent
and intelligent. And, if nothing else, he bought his Government two
more years of office, in which many of his most cherished reforms were
established permanently.

Chamberlain now embarked upon the last great campaign of his
career. A Tariff Reform League was founded to raise subscriptions and
finance the campaign; a Tariff Commission supplied facts and
figures; although seventy, Chamberlain himself was in his most
vigorous form. But as his campaign developed it became less concentrated on Imperial Preference and more insistent on the advantages
of Protection. Chamberlain captured the Liberal Unionist organisation, and had large and enthusiastic support in the Unionist Party.
The debate raged throughout 1904 and 1905, to the agonised embarrassment of the Government and the increasing advantage of the
Liberals.

Misfortunes now descended upon the Government in a cataract.
An attempt to deal with labour problems in South Africa by bringing
in some 50,000 Chinese coolies to work in the mines for three years
resulted in outraged protests from the Liberal and Labour parties. The
conditions under which the Chinese lived and worked were unspeakable, and the Government's lack of interest in the subject
appalled middle class philanthropists and trade unionists alike. The
attitude of regarding human labour as a commodity seemed to expose
a particularly odious aspect of the Tory mentality, and 'Chinese
slavery' was a potent factor in the further decline of the Unionists in
1904–5. George Wyndham, the talented Irish Secretary, was virtually
forced out of office by the Ulster Conservatives as a result of the

activities of his Permanent Under-Secretary, Sir Anthony McDonnell, a Catholic Home Ruler. A Licensing Bill in 1904 further demonstrated the Government's ill-fortune. It was an honest attempt to deal with drunkenness by improving the licensing system; with considerable skill this was portrayed as another attempt by the Tories to assist the brewers. 'The Licensing Bill', Lloyd George declared 'is a party bribe for gross political corruption—an act which Tammany Hall could not exceed.'

The fundamental problem of Balfour's leadership was not his alleged timorousness and irresolution, but that it revealed just how profoundly Conservative a man he was. In certain areas—education was the most notable example—he was far ahead of most of his contemporaries in understanding and enlightened courage, but in others he was wholly insensitive. His refusal to accept Keir Hardie's proposals for the use of public money in creating jobs for the unemployed was a case in point, and the Unemployed Workmen Act of 1905 was a feeble palliative. His brother, Gerald, was once described by Maud du Puy as 'really the most conservative man that I have ever met. Believes the higher set of people, the House of Lords, etc., set a good example to the lower classes of people—and ever so much more stuff that I had read of but never met anyone that believed it'.[1] Balfour, for all his charm and real ability, also had certain ineradicable prejudices and fears. It was said of him by Ramsay MacDonald that 'he saw life from afar', and certainly he had little understanding of, and no sympathy with, proposals for substantial social reform. He was, like Salisbury, a vehement believer in the *status quo*, while fully admitting the need for certain changes which were necessary for the national good and for the maintenance of that *status quo*. But no further. New ideas and radical proposals were alien to him and to his concept of what the Conservative Party was, and was not. The division between the Cecils and Lord Randolph had had a strong ideological as well as personal content. Now, as the 'Imperial' issue was becoming actually harmful to the Unionists, Balfour's hostility to social reform became a major liability.

This attitude was now put to the test.

Until 1901 it had been assumed that the Trade Union Act of 1871 afforded absolute protection to union funds, and that a union could not be sued for damages as a result of industrial action. In 1901 the

[1] Gwen Raverat: *Period Piece*, 22.

Taff Vale Railway Company sued the Amalgamated Society of Railway Servants. The High Court found for the Company; the judgement was reversed in the Court of Appeal, but was upheld in the House of Lords.

This was a thunderbolt to the Unions. In a fatal moment for his Government and party, Balfour refused to entertain the unionists' proposal for remedial legislation, and they turned elsewhere. Their previous relative lack of interest in the Labour Representation Committee was now transformed, and L.R.C. membership rose dramatically from 376,000 in 1901 to 861,000 in 1903. Furthermore, in 1903 the unions increased its contribution from 10 shillings per thousand members to almost £5; a fund for the payment of future Labour M.P.s was established; and it was resolved that its candidates must 'strictly abstain from identifying themselves with or promoting the interests of any section of the Liberal or Conservative parties'. In fact, MacDonald and Herbert Gladstone—the Liberal Chief Whip— came together to make an electoral compact, whereby the majority of L.R.C. candidates would not have to face Liberal opposition. This was a secret compact, but one of great importance both for the Liberals and for the new party, and represented a form of united front against the Unionists. By 1905 the L.R.C. had fifty candidates in the field, of whom only eighteen would face Liberal opposition. In ten double-member seats one Liberal and one L.R.C. candidate fought side by side. The L.R.C. candidates, furthermore, fought on the Liberal policies.

This development made the electoral position of the Unionists more precarious than ever. Their internal difficulties became steadily worse. On November 3rd 1905, Chamberlain described Balfour's Parliamentary tactics of evading debates on Free Trade as 'humiliating' and demanded a dissolution. On November 14th he in effect captured the National Union. With the Central Office in decline since Middleton's retirement, this was a significant pointer.

But the fundamental point about party organisations in both parties was that they had no say or involvement in the formulation of policy. Thus, the capture of the National Union by the Tariff Reformers in 1905 reflected the new balance in the party, and made the position of the dwindling band of Free Fooders even more precarious, but the impetus and organisation had come from above. The Union, in short, was *used*—the rank and file did not spontaneously reach the conclusion that Tariff Reform should be the dominant policy of the party. A. L. Lowell described the situation in *The Government of England*, which was published at this time:

> The Whips may be said to constitute the only regular party organisation in the House of Commons, unless we include under that description the two front benches. The very fact, indeed, that the ministry and the leaders of the Opposition furnish in themselves the real party machinery of the House, avoids the need of any other. The ministers prepared and carry out the programme of the party in power, while a small coterie of leaders on the other side devise the plans for opposing them . . . in neither of the great parties is there anything resembling a general caucus for the discussion and determination of party policy. Sometimes a great meeting of the adherents of the party in Parliament is called at one of the political clubs or elsewhere, when the leaders address their followers. But it is held to exhort not to consult.[1]

If this was true of the situation in Parliament, it was even more evident in the country. The developing central, regional and local organisations were essentially to provide the voluntary support necessary in the post-Corrupt Practices Act situation—to raise money, to develop enthusiasm for the Cause, and to give a flattering sense of participation in great affairs. But their place was certainly not to concern themselves with issues of strategy or policy, which were reserved to the awesome and sapient leaders in Parliament, who would tell the armies what to do. Until the Labour Party came along, with very different attitudes and practices, which gave some people new ideas, this relationship was accepted and hardly challenged. There were occasional grumblings, but little more.

*

Subsequently, the Balfour Government was viewed in a more generous light than it was at the time. The Education Act of 1902, the Irish Land Purchase Act of 1903, the Licensing Act of 1904, the Anglo-Japanese Treaty of 1902, the Entente with France in 1904, and the creation of the Committee of Imperial Defence in the same year, were major achievements. Much of the credit for the *entente cordiale* with France went to the King, and certainly a triumphantly successful

---

[1] Quoted in Robert Mackenzie: *British Political Parties*, 71.

State Visit to Paris and the King's known fondness for France were no disadvantages in securing popular support for the new departure, but the driving force was that of Balfour, and he was entitled to remark later to Lansdowne of the King that 'So far as I can remember, during the years which you and I were his Ministers, he never made an important suggestion of any sort as to large questions of policy.' King Edward passed into legend as The Peacemaker, Arthur Balfour went down to political eclipse.

The reform of the Army had been put in hand, and the tremendous Selborne-Fisher naval programme, beginning in 1902, covered the entire field of naval activity—personnel training, redeployment of reserves, gunnery training, battle tactics, naval training and the development of the 'all big-gun ship', the *Dreadnought*, launched in February 1906. These latter advances were to be imperilled by the Liberal Government in the first two years of its existence, but the effect of the Selborne-Fisher programme was to transform the Navy.

But it was the establishment of the Committee of Imperial Defence, presided over by the Prime Minister, that was the most important development of all. 'But for Balfour's far-seeing initiative in 1904', Lord Hankey has written, 'our defensive preparations could not conceivably have been brought to the pitch that was attained in 1914.'[1] It was somewhat ironical that Salisbury had been virtually forced out of the Foreign Office in 1900, to be replaced by Lansdowne, because of Salisbury's entrenched hostility to an Anglo-German rapprochment. The attempts of Lansdowne and Chamberlain to achieve this had been curtly rebuffed, and the realisation that the Germans were now serious about naval equality and regarded themselves as a putative world power led to new assessments about future dangers. The *entente* with France was not an anti-German move, but it fitted very closely with the strategy now being urged on Ministers by a new generation of Froeign Office officials alarmed by the increasing power of Germany and its belligerence. The brutal tone of German warnings to France in the 1905 Morocco Crisis gave their arguments additional force.

Balfour's problems when he assumed the Premiership were many. His party had been in office for seven years and had gone through the perils and anxieties of a major war, whose cost, coinciding with a temporary slump, caused poor economic conditions. His attempt to

[1] Hankey: *The Supreme Command*, I, 45.

keep the party together over Tariff Reform were perhaps too ingenious, but it is difficult to see how the split could have been averted, and Balfour ensured that it did not—as seemed probable at one stage—bring the Government down in 1903. Balfour himself was deficient neither in courage nor dexterity. Abused by his opponents and constantly criticised by both extreme elements in his own party, he maintained an imperturbable calm. He did not kindle warm emotions, and he was himself somewhat cold-blooded and aloof. He did not excel at the demagogic arts. He was, by background and inclination, far removed from the problems that beset the vast majority of the people. He was a 'politician's politician', who aroused admiration and respect, yet who could not stem the tides sweeping against his party and his government. Perhaps no single man could have. The marvel was that he withstood them for so long and achieved so much. As Austen Chamberlain has commented:

> Balfour's courage never failed; he maintained consistently the line he had marked out for himself and he accomplished . . . by his own force of will . . . great reforms which, however criticised at the moment, have stood the test of time and still dominate the scene. . . . It is not easy to find a parallel to such an achievement in so short a time and amidst such difficulties.[1]

At this point Ministers were further embarrassed by the public eruption of a classic dispute between the Viceroy of India, Lord Curzon, and the Commander-in-Chief, Lord Kitchener. Curzon was a man of so many mixed aspects that, despite several biographies and analyses, it is difficult to give a clear portrait of him. It is to Winston Churchill that we owe the best portrait:

> The contradictory qualities which dwell in the characters of so many individuals can rarely have found more vivid contrasts than in George Curzon. The world thought him pompous in manner and in mind. But this widespread and deep impression, arising from the experience and report of so many good judges, was immediately destroyed by the Curzon one met in a small circle of intimate friends and equals—or those whom he treated as equals. . . . Helpful with comfort and sympathy on every occasion of sickness or sorrow in his wide circle, unpopular with most of those who served him, the

---

[1] Austen Chamberlain: *Down The Years*, 206–7.

master of scathing rebukes for subordinates, he seemed to sow gratitude and resentment along his path with evenly lavish hands. Bespangled with every quality that could dazzle and attract, he never found himself with a following. Majestic in speech, appearance, and demeanour, he never led. He often domineered; but at the centre he never dominated.[1]

His Viceroyalty attracted very varying estimates, both then and subsequently. It was his conviction that the real leader must be a master of detail, and he despised the view that 'it is supposed to be a mark of efficiency and even greatness to get your work done for you by other people. I frankly disagree. I say that if you want a thing done in a certain way, the only manner in which to be sure that it is done is to do it yourself.'[2] No Viceroy ever worked harder, and his achievements were considerable. But he made enemies, and the most formidable was Kitchener, who had close political contacts in London, notably with Lady Salisbury. It was a brutal clash of opposing personalities, and Kitchener won. Curzon returned to England an embittered man, and the Liberals made much capital over the defeat of a civilian administrator by a military clique. There was more to it than that, but the charge had a certain validity.

*

It is always perilous to fix dividing-lines in the study of history. Nevertheless, the nineteenth century did end with a satisfying neatness in many respects. Gladstone died in 1898, Queen Victoria in 1901, and Salisbury in 1903; Harcourt died in 1904; Chamberlain was totally incapacitated by a stroke in 1906, and although he lived until 1914 his career ended completely with his stroke; the Duke of Devonshire died in 1908. Most modern historians of the period have regarded Chamberlain with coolness, while conceding his enormous influence and importance. Although it would be unfair to blame him wholly for the great Liberal break-up of 1886, Chamberlain's political mind was such that it is difficult to believe that his influence in the Liberal Party would have been benignant, or that he would have been a comfortable colleague. As Rosebery once wrote in another context, 'independence in a great orator on the Treasury Bench is a rocket of

[1] Churchill: *Great Contemporaries.*
[2] Kenneth Rose: *Lord Curzon and His Circle*, 26–7.

which one cannot predict the course'. Chamberlain's defection from the Liberals had delivered that party a temporarily crippling blow and he was, in the 1890s and early 1900s, their most implacable foe. But it is doubtful if he damaged the Liberals to the same extent that he did the Conservatives. The Jameson Raid and the Boer War did much harm to the cause of Imperialism; the Tariff Reform pronouncement of 1903, and the subsequent campaign, smashed the Conservatives for more than a decade. The sudden removal of this powerful, determined, single-minded man from politics in 1906 was accordingly an event of great importance.

Salisbury's last years had been clouded by private grief, ill-health and sombre forebodings. He lamented the South African War, and his failure to avert it. The death of his wife in 1899 had been a blow from which he never recovered, but even before this disaster it had been evident that he was worn out and in melancholy physical decline. He had been seventy-two when he had thankfully retired in 1902, and his death followed not long after, on August 22nd 1903, in his beloved Hatfield, surrounded by his family, and with one of his sons reading the prayers. Complex in so many things, doubtful of so much, his Faith had always been serene and assured. It would be wrong to depict him as the last relic of a fading age. He possessed certain aspects of political character which are timeless. He is one of those rare public figures of whom one can say with real confidence that he could have succeeded at any time and in any circumstances.

It is of Salisbury, more than any other modern politician, that the historian invokes Boswell's celebrated tribute to Samuel Johnson:

> His superiority over other learned men consisted chiefly in what might be called the art of thinking, the art of using his mind; a certain continual power of seizing the useful substance of all that he knew, and exhibiting it in a clear and forcible manner; so that knowledge, which we often see to be no better than lumber in men of dull understanding, was, in him, true evident, and actual wisdom.

Yet, for all that we know of him, he remains mysterious and elusive —a wise and percipient man, yet wedded emphatically and without apology to an older order. A conciliator in foreign affairs, highly cautious, yet with a streak of recklessness. An intellectual, yet with a sharp understanding of the value of exploitation in immediate human relationships. Gentle, yet remorseless when occasion demanded. Tolerant, and yet with certain immovable prejudices. Forgiving, and yet often unpitying. Idealistic, yet cynical. Kind, yet also cruel. All in all, the most formidably equipped politician for all seasons that England had produced since Robert Cecil, first Earl of Salisbury, had made his family's eminence and fame.

Other giants of late-Victorian politics, notably Parnell and Lord Randolph Churchill, who might have been expected to be active in politics in the 1900s, had died in their middle forties, and others, like Rosebery and Dilke, although still in public life, were out of the front line for ever. The future lay with a new generation. Some, like Asquith, Grey, Curzon, the Irish leader John Redmond, Lloyd George, Austen Chamberlain, and Edward Carson, had begun their political careers before 1900. Others, such as Bonar Law, Winston Churchill, Ramsay MacDonald, Arthur Henderson and F. E. Smith, entered Parliament in the years 1900–6. There were some exceptions. Arthur Balfour's remarkable career had only reached its half-way stage when he became Prime Minister in 1902; John Morley was in active politics until 1914; Campbell-Bannerman lived until 1908. But Morley was no longer the force he had once been; Campbell-Bannerman's hour came too late; and Balfour's position never really recovered from the holocaust of 1906.

The outstanding feature of British politics from 1903 to 1914 was to be the absolute superiority of the Liberal Party. From the opening of the Free Trade battle in 1903 the Liberals were no longer in decline, and no longer wearily resigned to decades of futile and debilitating Opposition. The vaunted Conservative organisation had crumbled. Middleton had lost interest in his work after the death of Salisbury, and his successors—a Captain Wells, who lasted briefly, and a Colonel Haig—were failures. Admittedly, they could hardly have operated in a worse period, and the blame cast upon them for the 1906 débâcle is obviously harshly unfair. But the fact that Middleton's once superb machine had declined so quickly and so catastrophically added another ingredient in the Unionist misfortunes. And for this, also, Balfour must bear a large part of the censure, as the Central Office was under his personal and direct control.

The Liberals now possessed a marked superiority of talent. Asquith was clearly the coming man. Born in 1852 in relatively humble circumstances, he had had the benefit of a Balliol education during the early part of that College's golden period. He had gone into law, but was not notably successful. In 1886 he entered Parliament for East Fife at the age of thirty-three, and swiftly made a good impression. Asquith had about him, from the beginning, a massive intellectual quality and steadiness of purpose that was impressive and even daunting. At the Home Office in the hapless Gladstone–Rosebery Government he had made an excellent impression, although, viewed from this distance, he appears to have been somewhat unimaginative and conventional. But his brisk no-nonsense competence and skill in debate stood out conspicuously in that Government, and when Rosebery resigned from the Liberal leadership in October 1896, he picked out Asquith as the future leader of Liberalism. His marriage to Margot Tennant had brought him into more glittering circles, and by the end of the 1890s references to the fact that Margot was 'ruining' him were not infrequent; certainly this was the opinion of Haldane, formerly one of Asquith's closest friends and himself a politician of much promise. 'London Society', Haldane wrote tartly many years later, 'came, however, to have a great attraction for him, and he grew by degrees diverted from the sterner outlook on life which he and I for long shared. . . . From the beginning he meant to be Prime Minister, sooner or later.'[1] But too much should not be made of these charges; it is possible that, by 1915, his will had been sapped by years of good living and intellectual complacency. But Asquith's physical strength and resilience were considerable, even in 1915, and there were no indications of decline in the first ten years after his marriage.

When Harcourt had retired at the end of 1898, taking Morley with him, there was a real possibility that Asquith might succeed him, and if Campbell-Bannerman had not been interested in the leadership it seems probable that he would have done so. But Asquith was extremely reluctant to oppose Campbell-Bannerman, and 'C-B' took the leadership. But it had been a significant indication of Asquith's position in the party that his name had been canvassed so seriously.

It was unquestionably a lucky escape. Within a few months the South African cauldron began to bubble ominously. Asquith, a close friend and admirer of Milner and Rosebery, supported the Government. In 1901 he was one of the vice-presidents of the Liberal League, which was in effect if not in title opposed to Campbell-Bannerman's interpretation of the Liberal future. But it was noticeable that in this

[1] Haldane: *Autobiography*, 103.

unhappy period of the history of the Liberal Party, Asquith was cautious. While maintaining his position, he did not give the hierarchy much cause for antagonism, and when the Free Trade storm broke in 1903 he was first in the field to give sound proof of his Liberal bona fides. His biographers ascribe much of this to good fortune; but it is noticeable that Asquith had a habit of being in the right place at the right time. He was a formidable politician.

Asquith did not possess an original mind, and he had moreover a certain degree of intellectual priggishness, with a capacity for supercilious dismissal of men who did not come up to the Balliol standard; politics being what it is, there were not many who could aspire to such a level of excellence. With the great majority of his colleagues— particularly Lloyd George and Winston Churchill—he was contemptuous of 'socialism'. His attitudes were conservative, he had no interest in working class attitudes and aspirations, he believed in the rule of the elite. He was not a man who was sensitive to new movements which might imperil his fundamental philosophies. His admiration for Rosebery and Balfour was significant, and was based not only on intellectual respect. Yet he was always ready to respond to arguments whose implications were radical and even modestly revolutionary. The secret of his quality lay in his availability to a good case. Once persuaded, he would put the full strength of his intellectual and political power behind it. His intellect was powerful and fair, and was seen at its best in the reconciliation of differences and in pin-pointing the crucial features in a complicated dispute. He was a professional politician in a very exceptional way. As Gilbert Murray has written:

> Asquith made a sharp difference between business and the rest of life, and, during the times when I knew him best, he treated politics strictly as business. He worked at them, made his decisions, dismissed them and did not want to talk about them afterwards. Nearly all politicians like talking politics; Asquith preferred literature or history or simple amusement or at least something that was not 'shop'.

Behind Campbell-Bannerman, Asquith, Grey, Morley, and Haldane there were younger men of outstanding promise. Lloyd George was already a major figure as a result of the vehemence of his opposition to the Boer War and his unremitting pursuit of Chamberlain; Reginald McKenna, Lewis Harcourt, Winston Churchill—who finally left the

Unionists in 1904—and Charles Masterman were evidence of the talent available for the future. In contrast, the Conservatives looked out of date and lack-lustre. It was a remarkable reversal of fortunes.

*

What was the condition of England in the early 1900s?

Her industrial stagnation was now recognised, and was giving cause for concern. The rate of increase of the population was slackening considerably. The population was 41·15 million in 1900 and rose to 45·65 in 1913, but this net increase was more the result of a lower death-rate. In 1900 the male expectation of life was forty-six and for a woman fifty; only 14·8 per cent of the population was over fifty. By 1910 the life expectation had risen to fifty-two for a man and fifty-five for a woman, the proportion of the population over fifty had risen to 16·1 per cent.

The causes of the industrial stagnation were many, but the central one was that a nation depending upon its exporting capacity must inevitably suffer from a situation whereby every major purchasing country was raising protective tariff barriers. The figures themselves told the story. The British proportion of world trade in manufactured goods fell from 22·8 per cent in the early 1880s to 10·2 per cent by the early 1890s. There was then a recovery, but never to the previous level. The increase in the volume and cost of imports was maintained without a corresponding increase in exports. The first Census of Production in 1907 revealed that roughly a quarter of the goods consumed were imported. Comparing 1890 with 1901, the value of exports in these years rose by some £19·6 million, whereas that of imports rose by £107·699 million.[1]

One very significant factor was that, in the 1880s and 1890s, the British had done particularly well with the export of machinery; but, as these were principally to her main competitors, the British were in effect creating the industrial competition which was now challenging them.

It was becoming one of the cardinal tenets of industrialists and Unionist politicians that the increased activity of the Trade Unions

[1] W. Page: *Commerce and Industry: Tables of Statistics for the British From 1815*, 71–2, The actual figures were:
Exports: £328,252,000 in 1890; £347,864,000 in 1901.
Imports: £420,692,000 in 1890; £528,391,000 in 1901.

was in itself impairing industrial development. There was something in this, but the root causes of the trouble lay far deeper. Although the average unemployment figure in the years 1901–10 was 6 per cent— which was actually higher than the average in the previous decade (5·2 per cent)—the slumps were far less drastic, and in the years 1911–13 unemployment fell to figures of 3·1, 2·3, and 2·6 respectively. Of considerably greater importance were the figures of man-hours lost by strike. In 1901 they totalled 4·13 million; in 1911 they were 10·16 million; in 1912 they reached 40·89 million. Although the figure fell to a 'norm' figure of 9·8 million in 1913, this was still more than twice the 1901 figure.

But we should go deeper than statistics. The condition of the people should have been a cause for great concern. One of the shocks of the Boer War had been the revelation of the lamentable physical condition of the working class, seen in the young men who had volunteered for service. The great majority were rejected on physical grounds, particularly in the big cities. In Manchester, for example, 12,000 men volunteered and 8,000 were rejected immediately; eventually 1,200 (ten per cent) were accepted, and this at a time when the Army standards had been reduced to the lowest level since the Napoleonic Wars. In 1901 Seebohm Rowntree published a study of the city of York under the stark title of *Poverty*. It will be remembered that Charles Booth in 1889 had produced for London a figure of 30·7 per cent living at or below the poverty line; Rowntree's studies in York produced a figure of 27·84 per cent. It was significant of the changed temper in British life, and the effects of mass-circulation newspapers, that these statistics created a far greater sensation than Booth's study had done. Overcrowding in the cities, bad housing, totally inadequate sanitation, employers' exploitation and low wages presented a series of problems, none of which had been adequately understood, let alone solved by 1914, or even by 1939.

The wealth of the nation still lay in very few hands. That wealth was increasingly being used for grandeur and pleasure, and in this marked tendency the influence of the hedonistic King Edward VII was not beneficial. The ostentatiousness of the New Wealth was its most lamentable feature, and the social historian becomes bemused and impatient by the records of vast slaughters of pheasant, grouse, and deer, the gargantuan meals, the lengthy country-house weekends, and the lavish competition between the great hostesses in London. The

New Wealth was flaunted, and the contrast between the circumstances of the favoured few and the miserable many became more glaringly obvious than at any time since the Regency. This was not the least of the factors that made Salisbury, himself rich but frugal, despair of the new age. To the favoured, it was a glittering, enthralling, period. Others viewed it differently. This was the social background to the decline in productivity, the unrest of the working classes, and the increasing inclination to resort to industrial action and even violence. The revolution of the have-nots against the haves had not yet fully developed, but there was clear evidence of new forces in British society. Apprehension at these developments explains much of the reactions of the Conservatives in these years, and was to give to party politics a degree of bitterness unparalleled even at the height of the Home Rule struggle. In fact, the Liberals were equally baffled and alarmed. After the Conservative defeat of 1906, Balfour wrote that:

> What has occurred has nothing whatever to do with any of the things we have been squabbling over the last few years. Campbell-Bannerman is a mere cork, dancing on a torrent which he cannot control, and what is going on here is a faint echo of the same movement which has produced massacres in St. Petersburg, riots in Vienna and socialist processions in Berlin.

But the have-nots, in addition to their other deprivations, did not have the vote—or at least, not many of them. In 1900 the adult population of Britain totalled 22·675 million; the electorate was under 6·75 million. Only 58 per cent of the adult male population had the vote, and this was to be the situation until the General Election of 1918.

But interest in politics was still very great. In the 1900 election 74·6 per cent of the electorate voted; in 1906 the figure was 82·6 per cent, and in the first of the two elections of 1910 it rose to the figure of 86·6 per cent. The opinion of many commentators that popular interest in politics was less than in the 1870s and 1880s seems to be decisively belied by these figures. The passions that party politics evoked in the years 1900–14 also casts serious doubt on this generalisation. Furthermore, at no stage, even in 1911, did the politics of discontent take really serious extra-Parliamentary forms; indeed, had Balfour had a more acute realisation of his country he would have realised that the advent of Labour M.P.s in 1906 was a reassuring sign, and not one of incipient revolution. If there was to be a revolution, it was going to be a constitutional and Parliamentary one.

The Boer War did not mark the end of Imperialism, but it certainly marked the end of a period in which it had been the political prerogative of the Conservatives. The debates, often harsh and strident, and always divisive, within the Liberal Party had given it a much better claim to represent a public opinion that believed in the Empire but had become disenchanted with foreign adventures while grievous social problems remained unresolved at home. The Liberal Imperialists —who now had a dominant position in the party—had contributed a great deal, and had learned a great deal. The party, except on its extreme fringes, was no longer hostile or unsympathetic to Imperial responsibilities nor to the concept of Empire itself. To a remarkable extent, the Liberals had now accepted the Rosebery formula of the 1880s of 'a sane Imperialism' which would have been unthinkable in 1895. But the Liberal Imperialists had learned that blind devotion to the cause of Empire no longer existed. The Boer War had indeed been, in Kipling's words, 'No end of a lesson'. If it had been swift, sure, and triumphant, the political consequences in Britain might have been transitory. As it was, the revelations of arrogance and incompetence left a lasting impression upon Englishmen who had been victims of those same attitudes in their domestic affairs. The Boer War led to drastic and long overdue reforms in the British Army—although not drastic enough. But it also struck at certain casual assumptions in domestic politics, which now had to be revised. In the new attitude towards Empire, the Liberals—unwittingly, perhaps—were the principal beneficiaries.

In 1900 J. A. Hobson had published his celebrated diatribe on Imperialism which, in the long run, had an impact upon intellectuals comparable to that of Seeley in the opposite direction in 1883. Politicians, however, survive or disappear in the short run. The appeal of the Liberals in 1905 lay in the fact that they were emphatically for the Empire, but opposed to its more dangerous—and expensive— excesses. Thus, they had blundered upon the key for popular support in this confused and complex period.

In South Africa, Milner had endeavoured to make annexation work, with the assistance of a new generation of young men—derided as 'the Milner kindergarten'—from Oxford, who included Leo Amery, Philip Kerr (later Lord Lothian), John Buchan, and Lionel Curtis. But

Milnerism was fatally discredited and Milner himself left South Africa in 1905, having refused an offer to succeed Curzon as Viceroy of India. For the last three years as High Commissioner his methods had aroused increasingly virulent criticism in the Liberal and Labour ranks, particularly over 'Chinese slavery', and he had incurred the formidable and unremitting hostility of Campbell-Bannerman.

One major consequence of the war had been to expose Britain's isolation in Europe. The Anglo-Japanese alliance of 1902 had done nothing to change this situation, but it was to have substantial results. It was the first formal recognition of equality in modern history between a European great power and a non-European one. Without this alliance, it is highly improbable that the Japanese would have embarked upon their successful war with Russia—described by Balfour as 'not an unmixed curse'—and thus helped to precipitate the abortive Russian revolution of 1905. From the British point of view, the object of the alliance was to restrain Russian ambitions in the Far East, and as such was highly successful. But it also committed them to support for Japanese ambitions, particularly in Korea, and thus marked a very significant move away from the policy of avoiding formal international commitments that had been dominant since 1878.

The Anglo-French Entente of 1904 was, in essentials, a successful attempt to settle a number of matters which had caused friction between the two countries abroad, particularly in Africa. At the time there was no intention that this should draw Britain into closer involvement with France on a *European* basis, but it was a shift in policy which was to have vast consequences. Europe was slowly dividing itself into two camps; the British had taken the first step towards taking sides, in involving herself in European entanglements against which Rosebery in particular had constantly urged. It was significant that Rosebery was the only leading British politician to attack the Entente; in public, he said that it was more likely to lead to war than to peace; in private he said that it would lead 'straight to war'.

*

Balfour's last flickering hope of evading disaster had been the continuance of Liberal dissensions. For a brief moment in November 1905 it seemed as if he had calculated correctly. Rosebery had demanded, and had not received, specific assurances about the abandonment of Home Rule from Campbell-Bannerman. But here there had been a serious misunderstanding; Asquith had been privy to, and had approved, the Liberal leader's guarded declaration, and was amazed and incensed when Rosebery denounced Campbell-Bannerman at Bodmin on November 25th. This had been the last of several misunderstandings in the Liberal League. But this was by no means the only factor in Balfour's calculations. On November 25th he had circulated to the Cabinet a memorandum arguing for resignation—rather than dissolution—early in December. His eyes were more on Chamberlain, who on November 3rd had derided his Parliamentary tactics as 'humiliating' and had declared that he would 'rather be part of a powerful minority than a member of an impotent majority', than on Rosebery. But the Bodmin speech, and the subsequent turmoil, provided an apparent flicker of hope to the stricken Ministry. It was to prove illusory.

On December 4th Balfour resigned, and Campbell-Bannerman was requested by the King to form an Administration. Grey, Asquith and Haldane had agreed in September, while staying at Grey's hunting-lodge at Relugas, not to take office unless Campbell-Bannerman went to the Lords. C-B, fortified by his wife, refused, and the 'Relugas Compact' quickly disintegrated. Significantly, it was Asquith who first urged its dissolution. He became Chancellor of the Exchequer, Haldane Secretary of State for War, and Grey Foreign Secretary. Lloyd George became President of the Board of Trade. Winston Churchill, whose rising reputation was further enhanced by the publication during the election campaign of his superb biography of his father, became Under-Secretary for the Colonies, and thus—as the Colonial Secretary was Lord Elgin—chief spokesman for the Department in the House of Commons. Morley went to the India Office. By December 11th the main offices had been filled and the new Ministers found their way to Buckingham Palace, with considerable difficulty, in a thick and impenetrable fog; after over an hour groping in the Mall and around the uncompleted Victoria Memorial they reached their destination. The first Liberal Government for over a decade was in office.

Of all the leading Liberals, only Rosebery was excluded, and he had, in effect, excluded himself. He was offered the post of Ambassador in Washington, but refused, and he forbade his elder son to accept Campbell-Bannerman's invitation to second the motion for the Address in the new Parliament. It was not long before he found other reasons for disassociating himself from the Liberal Party whose leader he had been. He was fifty-six, and still a magnetic political figure, but his period in the wilderness had baffled friends and alienated moderates; by now he was politically déconsideré and knew it. The personal magnetism which he exercised had not dimmed in his ten years of political solitariness. 'I sometimes think,' Edward Grey wrote, 'that the reason why Rosebery attracts so much attention is that the genius in him lifts him up so that he is conspicuous in the crowd, a head taller than it. . . . It's as if God dangled him amongst us by an invisible thread.' In 1902, at Glasgow, 32,000 people applied for tickets to hear him deliver a Rectorial Address; over 5,000 were present in the hall to hear him. As Churchill has written of Rosebery's numerous adherents and admirers: 'At first they said "He will come". Then for years "If only he would come". And finally, long after he had renounced politics for ever, "If only he would come back".' Now, even that hope had disappeared.

The new Government was immensely strong, and was generally welcomed. *The Times*, deeply irritated by the unfortunate turn of events, merely announced that 'Sir Henry Campbell-Bannerman has succeeded in forming his Ministry'. Parliament was promptly dissolved.

The Prime Minister's performance in the election was somewhat cursory. He made only two major speeches, at the Albert Hall on December 21st, and in Liverpool on January 9th, and spent the whole of the campaign in Scotland, contenting himself with one printed address to his constituents, by whom he was returned unopposed. In neither did he produce any specific proposals, and concentrated upon criticising his predecessors. These were, however, effectively delivered. A vague reference to making the land 'less of a pleasure-ground for the rich and more of a treasure-house for the nation' sounded good, and there was one passage in the Albert Hall speech—otherwise unexciting and almost inaudible—which was extensively quoted:

The Government has executed what one might call a moonlight flitting. It has run away, not in the broad day of summer, not even in the twilight of October, but in the midnight of December.

We were told—told emphatically and abundantly—that the method of their going would be a masterpiece of tactical skill.

Tactics! Tactics! Ladies and gentlemen, the country is tired of their tactics. It would have been better for them if they had had less of tactics and more of reality.

But they have lived for some years on nothing but tactics. And now they have died of tactics.

It was left to other Liberals—notably Asquith—to spell out the detailed programme dealing with education, drink, trade union reforms, and old age pensions. The Unionist reaction was purely defensive. Balfour spoke scathingly of 'the long catalogue of revolutionary change' proposed by the Liberals, and Chamberlain, after castigating the 'essentially Home Rule and Little Englander Government' devoted his energies to Tariff Reform and Birmingham. 'Captain' Middleton, the awesome 'Skipper' of the Unionist machine, had retired, and had proved to be irreplaceable. Operating quietly, and with considerable acumen, he had been the hidden force in the Salisbury supremacy, and after Salisbury's retirement and death his zest for politics had faded. His rival, Schnadhorst, had never approached Middleton's power, nor his grasp of national and local politics, and Schnadhorst, too, proved to be irreplaceable by the Liberals. Archibald Salridge was still dominant in Liverpool, but only there. Operating out of tiny rooms in St. Stephen's Chambers, with few facilities in staff or finance, Middleton had done more than any other single individual to bring coherence and cohesion into the Unionist coalition, and had shown the way for future central party organisation. But it was to be many years before the lessons that he had quietly imparted were to be fully appreciated.

Looking back, and recalling the schisms in the Unionist ranks and the long list of their by-election disasters since 1903, a Liberal victory seems inevitable. It did not seem so at the time. There were surprisingly few in the Unionist ranks who fully appreciated the magnitude of the disenchantment of the electorate with the Balfour Government.[1] On the other side, many years of Opposition, of false dawns, of hopes shattered, and imminent victories torn away, had left the Liberals hardly daring to hope that their hour of opportunity had come. When Winston Churchill went to see Morley after the latter's appointment as Secretary of State for India, he found him despondent:

'Here I am,' he said, 'in a gilded pagoda.' He was gloomy about the

[1] See, for example, Winterton: *Orders of the Day*.

forthcoming election. He had too long experience of defeat to
nourish a sanguine hope. He spoke of the innate strength of the
Conservative hold upon England.

Even among those who were confident of victory, there were few who
had any premonition of the enormous scale and sweep of the Liberal
triumph. On the second day of the results Balfour himself lost his seat
in Manchester, and after that it was an avalanche. Brodrick, Lyttelton,
Gerald Balfour, Walter Long and Bonar Law were among the
Ministerial casualties. Except in Birmingham, where Chamberlain's
hold was complete, the Unionists crumbled. 377 Liberals were elected,
with a further 24 'Lib-Labs'; the Irish totalled 83, and the new
Labour Party had 29 M.P.s; the Conservatives were scythed down to
132, with 25 Liberal Unionists. In total Irish and Labour M.P.s, the
Government could count on a majority of 356, a figure unequalled
since 1832. Even if all other parties combined against them—a highly
unlikely event—the Liberals and Lib-Labs had a majority of 132.

In the astonishment at this landslide, some highly significant facts
were overlooked at the time. The vagaries of the British electoral
system have rarely been demonstrated with greater emphasis than in
1905. The Unionists received 43·6 per cent of the popular vote, and
returned 157 M.P.s: the Liberals received 49 per cent, and had 401
M.P.s. In terms of seats won, the Liberals and their allies had won a
total, unimaginable victory; but the proportion of votes showed the
extent to which Morley had been right—in spite of everything that
had happened since 1900, Britain was still a very Conservative country.
Another very significant aspect of the result was that, in the Unionist
ranks, the 'Free Fooders' did badly; of the 157 elected, 109 were
Chamberlain supporters, 32 can be classified as 'Balfourians', and only
11 were self-styled Free Fooders. Chamberlain, in purely party terms,
had won the battle. His immediate supporters were exultant, and,
with Balfour out of Parliament, believed that his hour had come. But
the strain had been too great. Chamberlain was now over seventy. In
1902 he had been seriously injured in a cab accident in London. He
had lived a full life in defiance of the advice of his doctors, one of his
more admirable aphorisms being that more people died from taking
exercise than from any other cause. Within months of the election he
suffered a stroke (July 17th 1906) which incapacitated him totally.
There was to be no recovery, no return. He lingered on until the eve

of the Great War, in 1914, but his extraordinary career effectively ended in 1906.

But in the Liberal and Labour exhilaration, there was no premonition that this was to be the last General Election in which the Liberals had more Members of Parliament than the Unionists, nor that in less than five years the triumphant majority of 1906 was to be cut down to exact parity. No notice was taken of a significant remark by Balfour on January 15th at Nottingham, to the effect that it was the duty of all to ensure that 'the great Unionist Party should still control, whether in power or whether in Opposition, the destinies of this great Empire'.

Even a swift glance at the political situation should have provided the cause of Balfour's statement. In the Commons the Government had a majority of 356; in the House of Lords the Unionists had a majority of 391. The exultant Liberals were shortly to learn the bitter truth of Rosebery's warnings of 1894.

CHAPTER EIGHT

THE TRIBULATIONS OF THE LIBERALS, 1906–1910

THE EXULTANT Liberal Ministry opened the first Session of the new Parliament with a fanfare of projected legislation, of which the most important were an Education Bill to remedy the Nonconformist grievances of the 1902 Act, a Trade Disputes Bill to reverse the Taff Vale Judgement, and a Plural Voting Bill to prevent the owners of several property qualifications from voting more than once.

This was a very talented Government—perhaps the most talented of any modern Administration—and it entered office confidently. The first and real surprise was Campbell-Bannerman himself. Indolent, affable, and easy-going, he had always commanded a certain respect, but had never been regarded as a probable Prime Minister. He had emerged from the party disputes over the Boer War with heightened authority, but he never could be described as a widely popular figure in the country nor as a dominant Parliamentarian. Balfour dismissed him as 'a mere cork', but it was quickly evident that it was Balfour, and not Campbell-Bannerman, who was out of touch with realities. When Balfour returned to the House of Commons as Member for the City of London on March 12th, he delivered one of those clever debating speeches which in previous Parliaments had delighted his supporters and humiliated his foes. This time, and before this new Parliament, it was ill-received, and was contemptuously dismissed by a speech by Campbell-Bannerman which lasted barely four minutes, and which opened with the devastating words: 'The right hon. gentleman is like the Bourbons. He has learned nothing. He comes back to this new House of Commons with the same airy graces, the same subtle dialectics, and the same light and frivolous way of dealing with great questions. He little knows the temper of the new House of Commons

231

if he thinks those methods will prevail here'; and he ended: 'I say, enough of this foolery. . . . Move your amendments and let us get to business.' The speech did not destroy Balfour, but it made Campbell-Bannerman. As a result of the lingering death of his wife, followed by his own decline which resulted in his death two years later, his appearances in the House became very few, but his authority was unchallenged.

Balfour was far from finished, and it was on the Education Bill that he showed his hand. He and Lansdowne, the Unionist leader in the Lords, had agreed, as Balfour had written to him on April 13th, that 'the two Houses shall not work as two separate armies, but shall co-operate in a common plan of campaign'. He now made it plain in public that the Lords were going to deal with the Bill in detail. 'The real discussion of this question', he declared, 'is not now in this House . . . the real discussion must be elsewhere.' The bluntness and nakedness of this statement startled even some of the Unionists. It was the first shot in a struggle that was to bring the Unionists substantial short-term advantages, and which was eventually to rebound disastrously against them and their chosen instrument of obstruction, the House of Lords.

The mood of the Unionist minority was aggressive. Its excited reactions to a most untypical maiden speech by F. E. Smith, a brilliant, arrogant, and tragically flawed man, was evidence of their violent temper.

Smith's speech contained one particular thrust that established his position, when he provoked Lloyd George into an angry denial that he had claimed that the Unionists would introduce slavery on the hills of Wales. Smith continued:

> The Rt. Hon. gentleman would no doubt be extremely anxious to forget it but, anticipating a temporary loss of memory, I have in my hand the *Manchester Guardian* of January 11, 1906, which contains a report of his speech. The Rt. Hon. gentleman said: 'What would they say to introducing Chinamen at one shilling a day in the Welsh quarries? Slavery on the hills of Wales! Heaven forgive me for the suggestion!'
>
> I have no means of judging how Heaven will deal with persons who think it decent to make such suggestions.

When he rose to speak, F. E. Smith was unknown. When he sat

down his reputation was made. The reports of his triumph spread rapidly through the demoralized Unionists throughout the country. There was rarely a debut like it before; certainly never one since.

The Conservative Party does not show up to advantage in Opposition. Regarding itself as the natural governing party, it views years in Opposition as unnatural interludes in the real purpose of this confederation. In Opposition, the Conservatives are not choosy about their weapons or their tactics. By deliberately fostering these attitudes, Balfour was also creating the passions that were to cost him the Unionist leadership.

Balfour, having thrown down the gauntlet on the Education Bill, then prepared the amendments which the House of Lords was to make to it. It was this kind of tactic that made Lloyd George retort to the claim that the Lords were 'the watchdog of the Constitution', by claiming that they were 'Mr. Balfour's Poodle'. The Lords duly mutilated the Bill, and the Government passed, by a majority of 416 to 107, a motion disagreeing with the amendments *en bloc*. The Lords promptly passed a motion insisting on the amendments. Private attempts at compromise were unsuccessful, and the Government had to abandon the Bill. Campbell-Bannerman wanted to dissolve on the cry of 'the Peers against the People', but the perils of such a course were many and considerable. The Lords, advised by Balfour, were very careful to accept the Trade Disputes Bill, but they threw out the Plural Voting Bill on Second Reading after a cursory debate of barely one and a half hours.

In the 1907 session the effects on Liberal morale of these unexpected setbacks were evident. A feeble Education Bill was introduced, was cursed by both sides, and was ignominiously withdrawn. An Irish Devolution Bill was hailed with contempt by the Irish and derision from the Unionists; it, too, was hastily withdrawn. A Licensing Bill was announced, but Ministers became increasingly apprehensive about taking on a fight with the Lords on the subject of temperance reform, an issue dear to Liberal hearts but never very close to the hearts of the British electorate. Faced with this impasse, the Government decided, not without dissensions, to pass a resolution declaring that the will of the Commons must prevail. It was a heated debate which lasted three days, in which Lloyd George and Churchill thundered at the Tories, Churchill describing the Lords as 'a one-sided, hereditary, unprized, unrepresentative, irresponsible absentee'.

But resolutions, however fierce, had no legal or constitutional effect, and the Unionist leaders were untroubled.

Ensor was representative of Liberal opinion when he wrote of this performance:

> In the light of post-war democracy no student can avoid asking, how practical men like Balfour and Lansdowne—the former of high and latter of flexible intelligence—could be so short-sighted . . . scarcely distinguishing in their minds between the Constitution and the dominance of their own order, they felt justified in using any resource of the former, however unfairly one-sided it might otherwise have appeared, in order to crush the challenge to the latter.[1]

Thus Ensor, and others, have regarded Balfour's tactics in a *class* sense. But this was only partially true. Politics is about power; deprived of it, one uses what weapons are available to harass and embarrass one's opponents. All the Unionists had after 1906, apart from obstruction in the Commons, was the House of Lords, until the nation could be brought back to Conservatism. These tactics had worked admirably in 1893–5, and, for the two years of Campbell-Bannerman's Premiership it worked well again. Ideology was important, but in fact Balfour and Lansdowne were playing party politics. Until too late, they did not realise how dangerous the new game was.

Old, tired, but defiant, Campbell-Bannerman would have dissolved Parliament at once and fought the Lords, but neither his Party nor his colleagues wanted another election so soon, having savoured office after a decade of impotence. Subsequently, the predicament of the Government was greatly complicated by the rapid decline of the Prime Minister. The death of his beloved wife had been a devastating blow, and may have contributed to his first heart attack in October 1906. In June 1907 he suffered another, and in November a third. Most of his colleagues viewed his probable departure with apprehension, convinced, as Haldane wrote, that 'C.B. is the only person who can hold this motley crew together'. But on February 12th 1908 he presided over his last Cabinet and made his final appearance in the House of Commons; on the following day he had another heart attack, and it was obvious to those close to him that the end was approaching.

Not all Liberals viewed the prospect of Asquith, the natural successor, with much enthusiasm, but Campbell-Bannerman dictated a

[1] R. C. K Ensor, op. cit., 387-8.

letter which was read to the Cabinet and which put the succession beyond doubt. But the Prime Minister did not resign, and the Cabinet —and particularly Asquith—became uneasy and restive. In fact, the cause lay less with C-B than with the King, who did not wish to cut short his holiday at Biarritz. Thus, it was not until April 3rd that the dying Prime Minister was permitted to resign, and Asquith was summoned to Biarritz to kiss hands upon his appointment. Campbell-Bannerman died, still in 10 Downing Street, on April 22nd. He fully deserved Lloyd George's tribute that 'he was a big figure, and got bigger as he advanced'. But it was also the case that for nearly a year— a vital year for the Government—he was a lonely, sad, and ailing man.

But Campbell-Bannerman's brief Premiership was not devoid of achievement. The most considerable was the granting of self-government to the Transvaal, in which Churchill and Smuts were deeply involved. It was bitterly opposed by the Unionists, and described by Balfour as 'the most reckless experiment ever tried in the development of a great colonial policy', warning that the Boers would make 'every preparation, constitutionally, quietly, without external interference, for a new war'. Churchill, in one of a series of remarkable speeches as junior Minister at the Colonial Office that marked him out for rapid promotion, appealed in vain for the Opposition to make self-government 'the gift of England' rather than that of a Party. The Unionists, inflamed by Liberal attempts to censure Milner, and by what Chamberlain described as Churchill's 'insulting protection' of him, were irreconcilable. Fortunately, their virulent opposition had little effect on the Boer leaders—notably Botha and Smuts—who were highly impressed by British magnanimity and understanding. The intervention of South Africa in both world wars on the British side— and particularly in 1939—stemmed directly from this reaction. Campbell-Bannerman's denunciation of 'methods of barbarism' paid handsome dividends for British long-term interests.

This was very much a personal triumph for Campbell-Bannerman, and it was followed by the grant of self-government to the Orange Free State. These generous acts led directly to the creation, in 1908, of the Union of South Africa, made by the elected representatives of Cape Colony, the Transvaal, Natal and the Orange Free State, and ratified by the British Parliament. No one contributed more to this result than the Prime Minister of Cape Colony—Dr. Jameson. In politics, time often brings strange reverses; this may be regarded as one of the strangest of all.

Subsequently, with the advantages of hindsight, we can look on this settlement with something less than the enthusiasm with which liberals everywhere hailed it at the time and for a long time afterwards. It was very much self-government for the whites in South Africa; it was impossible to foresee the evil long-term consequences of such an arrangement. But one must be fair. Politicians can only legislate for the present and for the foreseeable future; it is only long afterwards that the full effects of their actions can be adequately gauged. Judged by the standards, and the conditions, of the time it was a notable achievement.

But at home, the Lords were now in full cry. Land Reform was the main object of the 1907 Session, and four Bills were introduced, one for England, one for Ireland, and two for Scotland. The English and Irish Bills were brutally mutilated by the Lords and the Scottish pair were contemptuously thrown out.

It was perhaps surprising that any legislation got through at all. Lloyd George, at the Board of Trade, was showing just how able a Minister he was. The Merchant Shipping Act of 1906 confined pilots' licences to British subjects, restricted the employment of foreign seamen, provided better food, accommodation and terms of service in British ships, and compelled foreign ships to conform to British standards if they used British ports. The Patents Act of 1907 was another excellent and practical measure, although, by compelling patentees to work their patents in Britain within three years, it, too, was somewhat protectionist in tone. Other measures that escaped the Lords' veto provided free medical inspections and meals for elementary school children, another modest, but in its implication very progressive, advance in social reform.

Lloyd George was also responsible for taking (for the first time) a Census of Production, and for settling a major railway dispute in 1907 that imperilled the nation with a General Strike. He also created the Port of London Authority, that gave London a single central authority to administer the vast tangle of small companies and docks.

Haldane, meanwhile, was being highly—although less obviously—active at the War Office. His most important acts were the creation of a General Staff on the German pattern, and the establishment of an Expeditionary Force of six infantry divisions and one cavalry division, with artillery, transport, medical and all other logistic elements ready for rapid mobilisation and movement overseas, with suitable reserves ready. A Territorial Force—merging the Old Yeomanry and Volunteers—was also created, consisting of fourteen Divisions and fourteen mounted brigades, with their own transport, medical and other services.

In this work Haldane of course did not act alone. The Royal Commission that had investigated the lessons of the Boer War provided much valuable material; the Committee of Imperial Defence rather lost its strategic value under the Liberals, but was of considerable use in making contingency plans and undertaking specific studies, and the compilation of the War Book was one particularly significant aspect of its work. Haldane has perhaps been overpraised but it can be said of him that he provided exactly the right personal encouragement for reforms, and had clear enough ideas of what was necessary. In August 1914, twenty infantry divisions and one cavalry division, with full equipment, were mobilised swiftly and efficiently and dispatched to France. Its quality was outstanding. And this was accomplished at the same time as economies were achieved in the cost of the Army.

One controversy that gradually became more acrimonious during these years concerned conscription. The voices advocating it included that of Lord Roberts, and Haldane's opposition to it contributed to the subsequent charges that he had not properly prepared the nation for war. There was no question of a Liberal Government introducing conscription, and the Unionists had been highly embarrassed by Roberts's campaign. But in denouncing it, Haldane was able to divert Liberal attention away from the implications of his own policies. Few of Haldane's colleagues were greatly interested in military affairs, and he was given a remarkably free hand, as was Grey in the Foreign Office. In both cases there was actual deception by these Ministers of the Cabinet and the Liberal Party.

The first, and most significant, deception occurred following the Franco-German Morocco Crisis, when Grey had authorised Anglo-French military conversations in January 1906. Campbell-Bannerman, Asquith and Haldane were also consulted; the rest of the Cabinet was not, and there was to be a memorable explosion in 1911 when the Cabinet first heard of the action. Although these conversations did not bind either side, they were a truly momentous step away from isolationism. The failure to consult the Cabinet has had many ingenious explanations; the real reason was that pacifism was still strong both in it and in the Liberal Party, as the events of August 1st-3rd 1914 were to prove, and as the virulent opposition of Lloyd George and Churchill to the expanded Naval Estimates in 1908 emphasised.

Haldane was not anti-German, a fact that was to end his political career. Grey, however, had become increasingly persuaded by his Foreign Office advisers of the reality of German ambitions and by the threat posed to France. Sir Eyre Crowe's famous 'Memorandum on the present State of British Relations with France and Germany' (January 1st 1907) spelt this out very clearly. German actions—and particularly the expansion of the German Navy—did much to convince other sceptical Ministers, notably Churchill and Lloyd George, that a real threat existed. Little was attempted to resolve the increasing tension between the two nations, and British policy—unknown to the majority of the Cabinet—increasingly assumed a hostile Germany. On August 31st 1907, Britain moved even further away from isolationism by signing the Anglo-Russian Convention, the decisive step towards the Triple Entente. This was deeply repugnant to the left wing of the Liberal Party and the Labour Party, to whom association with the Tsarist autocracy had a profound symbolic meaning. The Liberal Party swallowed it, but with evident unhappiness. Had it known of the Anglo-French military commitment the alarm and disillusionment would have been formidable indeed. It is still difficult to gauge whether Grey's secretiveness—learned from Rosebery—was in the long-term national interest.

*

Meanwhile, the Government was enduring harassing fire from another, and quite unexpected, source. In 1903, chagrined by years of futile polite agitation, a group of feminist extremists founded the Women's Social and Political Union at Manchester. Its founder, head, and driving spirit was Mrs. Emmeline Pankhurst. In 1907 the extremists formed the Women's Freedom League.

Their first victim was the mild Grey, who supported women's suffrage, but who had one of his meetings rudely interrupted in the 1905 Election Campaign. Churchill, more understandably, suffered similar harassment. This was just the beginning. Everywhere, it was the Liberals who suffered, on the grounds that they were the Government Party. At times the lives of Ministers were even in danger, and public attitudes veered sharply between admiration and sympathy for women imprisoned for their political ideals and made to endure forcible feeding when they went on hunger strike, to outrage when houses were burned down and physical violence was attempted on leading politicians.

Perhaps the violence and hysteria of the Suffragette movement were symptomatic of the fever that ran through the country during this time, and which made 'the Edwardian Age' so much less placid to contemporaries than to subsequent observers. It was particularly hard that Liberals, like Grey and Lloyd George, who favoured women's suffrage were also objects of abuse and attack. Every Liberal candidate was exposed to the danger of his meetings being broken up by screaming women, and it was understandable that in these violent circumstances Liberal sympathy for the cause of female suffrage dimmed sharply. Some Liberals—notably Asquith and Churchill—were actively opposed to the idea, and ensured that every attempt to pass a Suffrage Bill went down to defeat.[1] Throughout these years, the Suffragettes provided an additional, and fierce, distraction for Ministers, which aided neither their cause nor the process of Government. Of greater significance politically was the fact that the Liberals abandoned franchise reform as a possible initiative, partly because of the issue of women's suffrage and also because it would inevitably bring up the fact that the Irish Nationalists were grossly over-represented.

*

When Asquith succeeded the dying Campbell-Bannerman in April 1908—kissing hands in the incongruous surroundings of the Hotel du Palais at Biarritz, and tactfully averting a characteristic proposal by the King that the members of the new Cabinet should accept their Seals of Office in the Hotel Crillon in Paris—he made only a few changes in his Government, of which the most important were the elevation of Winston Churchill to the Cabinet as President of the Board of Trade and the promotion of Lloyd George to the Exchequer.

---

[1] The debates on the issue were characterised by observations which read oddly today, but which were widely applauded (or at least accepted) at the time. Among the most vehement opponents of women's suffrage was F. E. Smith, who put forward to the House of Commons the asinine proposition that 'I venture to say that the total sum of human happiness, knowledge and achievement, would remain unaltered if . . . Sappho had never sung, Joan of Arc had never fought, Siddons had never played, and if George Eliot had never written'.

Most unfortunately, he did not remove John Burns from the Local Government Board. Burns, who had started in the early Labour movement, had rapidly proved himself an entrenched conservative. He was responsible for poor-law, municipal government, housing, town-planning, and public health. For the following nine years this Department was an oasis of reaction in a generally progressive Government.[1]

By this stage the Liberal situation had become very serious indeed. Few measures of real significance had been passed without the personal blessing of Balfour and Lansdowne. As Roy Jenkins has commented:

> For three years the smallest Opposition within living memory had effectively decided what could, and what could not, be passed through Parliament. In the language of the day, the cup was full, and the sands were exhaustively ploughed.[2]

If Asquith's inheritance was a bleak one, he was admirably qualified to lead a brilliantly talented but somewhat confused Government. He was to prove, in the best sense of the word, an opportunist, giving his Ministers remarkable latitude and his full support when he agreed with their case. 'When the need required it,' Churchill later wrote, 'his mind opened and shut smoothly and exactly, like the breech of a gun.'

His cool deliberation was at once put to severe test. His situation was far from encouraging. The record of the Government in by-elections was confirming the success of Balfour's tactics. Exasperated by the lack of progress, the Independent Labour Party put up its own candidate—a strange young man called Victor Grayson—at a by-election in the Colne Valley; Grayson, describing himself as a 'clean Socialist', won in a three-sided contest in a seat held by the Liberals. This was an unpleasant jolt both to the Liberals and the leaders of the Labour Party in the Commons. Fortunately, perhaps, Grayson was not a very influential or able man, was addicted to alcohol and exciting society, and disappeared in very mysterious and unexplained circumstances after he lost his seat in the 1910 election.

But Grayson did represent a growing impatience in the Labour

---

[1] It would be sad to omit the famous story that when Burns was invited by Campbell-Bannerman to join the Government he cried out, 'Well done, Sir 'enry! That's the most popular thing you've done yet'. (See, *inter alia*, Hugh Dalton: *Call Back Yesterday*, 147.)

[2] Roy Jenkins: *Mr. Balfour's Poodle* (1954).

Movement with the slowness of the arrival of the Promised Land; it aroused all the feelings against the MacDonald–Gladstone Pact—the feeling that, as four members of the Independent Labour Party Council declared in a pamphlet published in 1910 under the title *Let Us Reform the Labour Party*, 'Labour must fight for Socialism and its own Land against BOTH the Capitalist parties IMPARTIALLY'. In 1908 the Liberals lost no less than eight by-elections, and Winston Churchill was defeated at North-West Manchester, when seeking re-election on his appointment to the Board of Trade.[1] If this went on, the great Liberal Dawn of 1906 would turn out to be bleak indeed.

But deliverance was to come from the Opposition. Up to this point, the Lords had not dared to mangle Money Bills, and it was evident to Ministers that the Government's only serious hope of passing major social legislation was to incorporate it in Finance Bills. Lloyd George, in framing his first Budget, had to raise substantial new revenue for Old Age Pensions and the increased naval expenditure which he and Churchill had opposed so vehemently that Asquith had written in his diary at one stage that 'there are moments when I am disposed summarily to cashier them both'. It is extremely doubtful if Lloyd George framed the Budget deliberately to confront the Lords. Few thought that the Lords would be mad enough to reject a Money Bill, and those Ministers who thought it possible welcomed the prospect.

The Budget required the raising of £16 million. To do this, Lloyd George increased Death Duties on estates over £5,000, and income tax—from 1s. to 1s. 2d. in the £—and introduced a super-tax of 6d. in the £ on the amount by which all incomes of £5,000 or more exceeded £3,000. There were heavier taxes on tobacco and spirits, and the liquor licence duties were increased. The only concession was the introduction of children's allowances. The really dramatic innovation, however, were the Land Taxes—a duty of twenty per cent on the unearned increment of land values, to be paid whenever land changed hands, and also a duty of ½d. in the £ on the capital value of undeveloped land and minerals. This meant, of course, a complete valuation of the land of Britain. It is not surprising that many Ministers regarded this as very strong meat to swallow. In the picturesque phrase of John Burns, his Cabinet colleagues deliberated upon this alarming document 'like nineteen rag-pickers round a 'eap of muck'. But it went through the Cabinet after a series of tussles.

[1] He was almost immediately returned for Dundee.

The reactions of the Unionists were immediate and intense. Rosebery called it 'inquisitorial, tyrannical and Socialistic'; Sir Edward Carson described it as 'the beginning of the end of all rights of property'; Balfour condemned it as 'vindictive, inequitable, based on no principle, and injurious to the productive capacity of the country'. From Highbury, the stricken Joseph Chamberlain echoed these assaults.

A Budget Protest League was formed, and it was at once evident that the Government was in for a fight. Its supporters, restive and dispirited for so long, gleefully took up the battle for 'the People's Budget', described by Lloyd George as 'a war Budget—for raising money to wage implacable warfare against poverty and squalidness'. In the Commons, the Unionists waged a marathon battle against the Bill, forcing the Government to employ the 'kangaroo' closure, and occupying virtually the entire time of the House. In the country, the Liberals took up the Unionists' challenge with gusto, and Churchill became President of the Budget League, and he and Lloyd George went on the stump to great effect—to such effect indeed that the King joined in the protests at the violence of their language. The Budget Protest League began to wither in the face of this counter-assault, and Unionists themselves were becoming uneasy about the effect on public opinion of the squealings of the landed and moneyed classes.

This was exactly the kind of situation in which Lloyd George thrived, and in a speech in Limehouse, in July, he raised the issue of the class war in language not heard from a leading politician since Chamberlain had assailed Salisbury in 1883 as the representative of a class 'that toils not, neither does it spin'. The fire and eloquence of Churchill, however, were a considerable surprise, and incensed the Unionists far more, and not least because they strongly questioned his sincerity. In fact, Churchill had become enraptured by the issue of social reform,[1] and was proving a remarkably successful Minister. His speeches on the Budget further enhanced his reputation with the

[1] It was of Churchill that Charles Masterman wrote to his wife in February 1908 that 'He is full of the poor whom he has just discovered. He thinks he is called by Providence—to do something for them. . . I challenged him once on his exposition of his desire to do something for the people. "You can't deny you enjoy it all immensely—the speeches and crowds, and the sense of increasing power." "Of course I do," he said. "Though shalt not muzzle the ox when he treadth out the corn. That shall be my plea at the day of judgement".'

Liberals, and led to a corresponding further decline in his relationship with the Opposition.

There remained the House of Lords. Joseph Chamberlain, from his sick-bed, urged the Lords to reject the Bill—a curious final intervention, and one that added to his unenviable record for destroying parties. The Liberal leaders—at least Churchill and Lloyd George—viewed the prospect of the Lords mangling or rejecting the Bill with enthusiasm. Lloyd George rose to the occasion with a speech at Newcastle-upon-Tyne on October 10th in which he accused the Lords being about to initiate a revolution 'which the people will direct', and describing the Lords as '500 men, ordinary men chosen accidentally from among the unemployed'; the people, he prophesied, would ask also who made 10,000 people owners of the soil 'and the rest of us trespassers in the land of our birth'. Other ugly questions would be asked as well, he said, and added:

> The answers are charged with peril for the order of things the Peers represent; but they are fraught with rare and refreshing fruit for the parched lips of the multitude who have been treading the dusty road along which the people have marched through the dark ages which are now emerging into the light.

On November 10th 1909, the Unionists decided to kill the Budget. It was as much an emotional as a political decision. Lloyd George may not have framed the Budget to precipitate a head-on clash with the Lords, but his subsequent speeches had succeeded in provoking them mightily. At the end of November the Lords threw out the Finance Bill by 350 to 75. 'Liberty', Lloyd George thundered, and with good cause, 'owes as much to the foolhardiness of its foes as it does to the sapience and wisdom of its friends. . . . At last the cause between the Peers and the People has been set down for trial in the grand assize of the people, and the verdict will come soon.'

Parliament was promptly dissolved after the Liberals had passed a resolution condemning the action of the Lords. The great Constitutional Struggle of 1910–11 had begun.

*

In spite of many achievements in most difficult circumstances, it would be to understate the case to say that the first three years of the Liberal Government had been a considerable disappointment to its

supporters. Its two major popular successes had been the Trade
Disputes Act of 1906 and the Old Age Pensions Act of 1909. The latter
gave a non-contributory pension of five shillings a week to persons over
seventy and seven shillings and sixpence to married couples, provided
that income from other sources did not exceed ten shillings a week.
This very modest grant[1] aroused at the time intense enthusiasm, and it
was indeed a very significant step, described by Rosebery—now firmly
in spirit if not in fact in the Conservative camp—as 'so prodigal of
expenditure that it was likely to undermine the whole fabric of the
Empire'.

One other notable advance had occurred. The Morley-Minto
Reforms in India made the legislative councils, hitherto nominated, at
least partially elective, and increased their scope. Indians were also to
be allowed to become members of executive councils. These changes
did not alter the reality of the situation in India, but they marked the
first tentative steps in the direction of the Chelmsford Reforms of
1919–20 to the granting of Dominion Status in 1935. This new phase
was agreed at the fifth Colonial Conference in 1907, which also
marked the failure of plans for Imperial Preference when Canada and
the Transvaal insisted that each member must have the right to
determine its own fiscal system.

There had been other achievements. Churchill, at the Board of
Trade, had become an ardent believer in social reform—albeit with an
important qualification. 'He desired in Britain', as Charles Masterman
commented rather sharply, 'a state of things where a benign upper
class dispensed benefits to an industrious, *bien-pensant* and grateful
working class.' Churchill's social reform phase was not to last very
long, but while it lasted it had excellent practical results. The establishment of Labour Exchanges and the protection of certain 'sweated'
trades in the Trade Boards Act of 1909 were notable acts of social
improvement, and the Coal Mines Act of 1908 had established a
statutory eight-hour day in the mines; this was the first occasion on
which the working hours of adult males was limited by statute, and it
was a significant portent.

Churchill had demonstrated considerable ability at the Colonial
Office, and enhanced that reputation at the Board of Trade. His
freshness, youth and exhilaration, combined with an insatiable hunger
for work, genuinely impressed all who worked with him. 'More than

[1] Its cost in the first financial year was £6 million.

any man of his time', the Liberal journalist and commentator, A. G. Gardiner, wrote of him in 1908, 'he approaches an issue without mental reserves and obscure motives and restraints. You see all the processes of his mind. He does not "hum and ha". He is not paralysed by the fear of consequences, nor afraid to contemplate great changes. He is out for adventure. He follows politics as he would follow the hounds.' But, already, he had acquired formidable opponents. The Unionists regarded him as a turncoat; not all Liberals were wholly convinced of his full dedication to radical policies. As Asquith's daughter later wrote: 'It was not in principle or theory that he differed from the rank and file of his party. It was the soil from which he had sprung, his personal background, context and experience which made him seem a foreign body among them, and as such, at times (unjustly) suspect.' His handling of the 1911 railway strike was to heighten many of these suspicions.

The claim of the Liberals that they were 'the fathers of the Welfare State'—a claim ceaselessly and wearyingly reiterated in later years by Liberal orators—has some basis in fact. But it was a cautious reforming Government of the nineteenth century Liberal pattern, in which individual Ministers dealt with problems as they arose or which particularly interested them. There was no driving force towards reform, and no central planning or direction. If Burns, at the Local Government Board, had been more energetic, competent and imaginative— or had been replaced by someone who was—the social record of the Government would have been considerably more impressive; but the mere fact that Burns remained in this office until his resignation over the intervention in the war in August 1914 emphasises the character of the Asquith Government. It tinkered—often very effectively—with social problems on the classic nineteenth century pattern; at no point did it deal with fundamental social problems; at root, it was emphatically a Free Trade and Laissez-Faire Government. It moved slowly and carefully, under a leader whose conservatism was deeply ingrained, who distrusted enthusiasm, who dealt with matters as they arose, and who was a master of political judo. By these tactics he held his government together and, on the whole, dominated it; but domination is not always the same as leadership. The vital feature of the Welfare State— massive State intervention in the life of the individual—was conspicuously absent in the pre-1914 Liberal Government, and no assaults on Socialism were more trenchant and swingeing than those delivered by Lloyd George and Churchill. In its approach, if not in some of its measures, this was a Government of which Mr. Gladstone would have been proud.

*

The enormity of what the Lords had done in rejecting the Finance Bill can hardly be over-emphasised. They had left the Government with no choice other than that between resignation and dissolution. The Legislature had refused Supply to the Government, and it simply could not go on. The Unionists' retort was that Lloyd George had himself broken the conventions of the constitution by 'tacking' legislation—such as the Land Valuation Bill—onto the Finance Bill. This, it was riposted, was necessary as a result of the performance of the Lords since 1906. 'We all know', Balfour had said on June 24th 1907, 'that the power of the House of Lords . . . is still further limited by the fact that it cannot touch Money Bills, which if it could deal with, no doubt it could bring the whole executive government of the country to a standstill'. This was precisely what had occurred, and Balfour had been to a large extent responsible for the situation.

In spite of the emotive cry of 'the Peers against the People', the Liberals fought the General Election of January 1910 under several disadvantages. Asquith described the issues as being 'the absolute control of the Commons over finance, the maintenance of Free Trade, and the effective limitation and curtailment of the legislative powers of the House of Lords'. In effect, the election was to be over the Budget of 1909; compared with 1905, it was a somewhat slender and un-exciting platform, and Asquith's performance was noticeably lacking in vigour; Lloyd George characteristically added some much-needed colour.

Asquith fought the campaign under one disability which was not known at the time. He opened with a speech at the Albert Hall with the declaration that 'We shall not assume office and we shall not hold office unless we can secure the safeguards which experience shows us to be necessary for the legislative utility and honour of the party of progress.' This was interpreted widely to mean that Asquith had secured the agreement of the King to redress the Liberal disadvantage in the Lords by the creation of a mass of new Peers.

In fact, the matter had been raised with the King, who had made it absolutely plain that he would not agree to such a creation without another General Election. This was made clear again to Asquith by Lord Knollys on December 15th—five days after the Albert Hall speech—in a letter to Asquith's secretary. This was of course a very real personal and political intervention by the Sovereign, but was accepted by the Prime Minister. Unfortunately, the matter was not made completely clear, and from the outset there was an imprecision and vagueness in the relationship between the Sovereign and the Prime Minister which was to bedevil the whole of the constitutional crisis of 1909–11.

Although the Unionists did not maintain their momentum of 1907–9 in by-elections—indeed, they lost all the seats they had won in the previous three years—they won 116 seats and became the majority party in England. Scotland and Wales redressed the balance, but the Liberals' overall advantage had gone. With 275 seats to the Unionists' 273, they now needed the 40 Labour and 82 Irish Nationalist votes to have a working majority. This, in the long run, was the real significance of the election result.

Ministers were now in a profound quandary about which course to follow. Asquith was pestered with unsolicited suggestions. Some Ministers wished to deal with the Lords' power of legislative veto once and for all. Others urged resignation. Others—notably Grey—were for reforming the Lords. Another problem was that the Irish had disliked the liquor taxation in the Budget and had even voted against the second reading. It was to the credit of Ministers that they opposed making any concessions to the Irish on this issue, desperately though they needed their votes. But each side was fully aware of the fact that a new relationship had opened between the Government and the Irish.

The major problem, however, was the matter of the King's 'guarantee' to create Peers. The clear implication given by Asquith in the Albert Hall speech had been that such a guarantee had been given. On February 21st he had to tell the Commons the facts. 'I tell the House quite frankly', he said, 'that I have received no such guarantee and that I have asked for no such guarantee.' The shock to the Liberal rank and file was palpable, and morale slumped. So bad was the situation that some Ministers considered the possibility of immediate resignation, but Asquith stood firm. It was as well that he did. At this point it seemed that, in spite of the election result, Balfour's tactics had played off with brilliant success, and that the Liberals were in a condition of paralysis and despair.

After much discussion and dissension, the Cabinet resolved to proceed by passing resolutions in the Commons which declared (a) that the Lords could not in future amend or reject a Money Bill (the Speaker to determine whether a Bill was, or was not, a Money Bill); (b) that if a Bill were rejected by the Lords it would become law provided that not less than two years elapsed between the introduction in the Commons and its third reading there; and (c) that the maximum duration of Parliaments should be reduced from seven years to five. After the passage of the Resolutions, a Parliament Bill containing their provisions was formally introduced on April 14th. On April 28th the Lords, accepting the decision of the electorate, passed the Finance Bill without a division.

Ministers had resolved that if the Lords rejected the Parliament Bill, steps would be taken—by the exercise of the Royal Prerogative if necessary—to ensure that it was given statutory effect. If that failed, the Government would resign or advise a Dissolution, with the clear implication that the King, in granting the Dissolution, would give assurances that in the event of a Liberal victory he could create sufficient Peers to pass the Bill through the Lords. This was the situation at the end of April when Parliament adjourned for the Easter Recess and the Prime Minister went off on a cruise on the Admiralty Yacht *Enchantress* with Churchill and his young wife as companions.

At this point a major distraction occurred. King Edward VII died suddenly and unexpectedly on the evening of May 6th after a brief illness. No one was prepared for this development. The new King, behind an impressive facade, was ill-equipped for the responsibilities now suddenly cast upon him. 'His planned education', as one of his official biographers has emphasised, 'ended just where and when it should seriously have begun. He was (until he had painfully taken his own education in hand late in life) below the educational and perhaps intellectual standard of the ordinary public school-educated country squire'.[1] King George's interest in intellectual matters was not only non-existent, but was actively hostile. Unlike his father, his tastes were modest and frugal, and although possessed of a formidable temper his preference was for a simple, ordered life. His wife, a lady of great beauty and presence, was austere and shy, and fully shared the King's attitudes. But if King George V was a man of limited intellect,

[1] John Gore: *King George V, A Personal Memoir*, 247–8.

he possessed great application and dedication, which were to give him a shrewdness and wisdom which earned him great and merited respect from his Ministers.

But in 1910 it was evident that he was hopelessly ill-prepared to deal with a complex, bitter, and perilous constitutional crisis. As Asquith subsequently wrote of the King he was 'with all his fine and engaging qualities, without political experience. We were nearing the verge of a crisis almost without example in our constitutional history. What was the right thing to do? This was the question which absorbed my thoughts as we made our way, with two fast escorting cruisers, through the Bay of Biscay, until we landed at Plymouth on the evening of Monday, May 9th.'

What, indeed, was to be done? There were very real humane considerations about confronting the inexperienced King, grieved by the loss of his father, with a major crisis of this complexity. Garvin, in *The Observer*, urged 'The Truce of God', a phrase that caught the popular feeling. This was the background—emotional and political—to the attempt to settle the crisis by negotiation which occupied nearly five months, and which postponed consideration of the most difficult problem of all—whether a guarantee by one Monarch, however reluctantly and cautiously given, was binding upon his successor.

The Constitutional Conference eventually broke down on one point, but it was politically crucial. The Unionists insisted that all constitutional legislation, if rejected twice by the Lords, should be submitted to a national referendum. Lansdowne, the most vigorous advocate of this point, had Home Rule firmly in mind; so had the Liberals, now dependent upon the Irish vote. On almost every other point agreement was reached; the Lords could not reject Money Bills, and if other measures could not gain the support of both Houses two years running the matter would be settled by a Joint Sitting, with the Lords' representation scaled down so that a Liberal Government with a majority of fifty could get its legislation through—after a time. But Lansdowne's intransigence on the constitutional legislation was complete, and it caused the conference to fail.

It is instructive to note how far the party leaders—with the exception of Lansdowne—had got away from their supporters. The rank and file were not consulted at all, and a proposal by Lloyd George—warmly supported by Churchill—for a Coalition made surprising progress before Balfour was told by Akers-Douglas, a former Chief Whip, that the Unionist Party would not tolerate it. This was a curious return to the theme of 'Efficiency' which had been argued by Rosebery seven years earlier, and it was significant that it now attracted Lloyd George and Churchill. The chimera of the great Centre Party was certainly not new, and had been eagerly canvassed by Chamberlain and Lord Randolph in the late 1880s. But that at a time of intense political warfare the most belligerent members of the Cabinet should be advocates of a new alliance was curious indeed.

But all this was unreal. Even if the Constitutional Conference had been successful, it is difficult to see how the Unionist or the Liberal rank and file could have accepted it. The Liberals had just risked all on the issue of the Peers against the People, and the Unionists were adamant on Home Rule. Both Balfour and Asquith made real efforts to reach a solution, but it was perhaps just as well for Asquith that, by the end of the first week in November, both the formal Constitutional Conference and the Coalition proposal had completely dissolved. After 'a rather intimate talk' with Balfour, Asquith reported to his wife that the Unionist leader was 'very pessimistic about the future, and evidently sees nothing for himself but chagrin and a possible private life'. Balfour, at least, was now grimly aware of the position into which he had led the Unionists.

The Cabinet met on November 10th and resolved to go to the country again. It was now essential for Asquith to extract a positive statement from the King, concerning the creation of Peers after the election, that he understood King Edward VII to have conceded. It was a delicate business, and it is difficult to avoid the conclusion that Asquith bungled it when he saw the King on November 11th. The King thought that he would not be asked to commit himself until *after* the election, and he agreed to this with much relief. Clearly, something had been missing in Asquith's presentation of his request, and it is probable that his manner was not well suited to handling the King, who favoured clarity and directness. 'Unaccustomed as he was to ambiguous phraseology', Sir Harold Nicolson has written, 'he was totally unable to interpret Mr. Asquith's enigmas.'[1]

Four days later, on November 15th, the King was accordingly dismayed to learn from Knollys—who saw Asquith on the 14th—that Asquith wanted the guarantee *before* the election. 'What he *now* advocates', Knollys reported, 'is that you should give guarantees *at*

[1] Nicolson: *King George V*, 130.

once for the next Parliament.' The King's other private secretary, Bigge, accordingly telegraphed to Asquith:

> His Majesty regrets that it would be impossible for him to give contingent guarantees and he reminds Mr. Asquith of his promise not to seek for any during the present Parliament.

This created another crisis—one between the Sovereign and the Cabinet. It was resolved by the compromise proposal put forward by the Cabinet that although the King should give the undertaking, it should not be made public until the Cabinet thought it necessary.[1]

And there was now another crisis—between the King's two private secretaries, Knollys and Bigge. Of the two, Bigge was the closer to the King, having served him for several years; but Knollys, as King Edward's confidant and adviser, had the far greater political experience. Knollys was in spirit a Liberal, and he thought the Lords 'mad' to reject the Budget. He now advised the King to accept the Cabinet's compromise proposal; Bigge, on the other hand, strongly urged him to reject it in a series of vigorous memoranda. 'Is this straight?' he demanded. 'Is it English? Is it not moreover childish?' On November 16th the King travelled up to London with the determination to refuse the Cabinet's proposal and to send for Balfour. At this point Knollys told him a straight lie; Balfour would not, he said, take office and form an administration if invited to do so by the King. As Knollys told him a straight lie; Balfour would not, he said, take office Government, and had told Knollys positively in this sense. The King was unaware of this until 1913, after Knollys had retired. By his action, Knollys saved the King from an act which would have imperilled the political position of the Monarchy, but it says something for the King's common sense that he considered Knolly's information decisive. It is not surprising that when Balfour discovered Knollys's role he was incensed, a fact which in itself reveals the passions now aroused. Balfour was not normally a man who permitted public controversy to cloud private life; Knollys, henceforth, was an exception.

Thus, on the afternoon of November 16th, the King, with deep repugnance, gave his assent. But it remained, as the King wrote, 'a secret understanding that in the event of the Government being returned with a majority at the General Election, I should use my Prerogative to make Peers if asked for. I disliked having to do this very

[1] See Nicolson, op. cit., 136, for the text of the Minute.

much, but agreed that this was the only alternative to the Cabinet resigning, which at this moment would be disastrous'.[1] Thus, the way was cleared for the second general election in a year—and the second, moreover, in which the electorate and the majority of men in public life were unaware of the secret understanding between Sovereign and Prime Minister.

It was not surprising that public interest in the second election of 1910 was considerably lower than it had been in the first. Nevertheless a remarkable 81·1 per cent of the electorate voted—as opposed to 86·6 per cent in the first election—which demonstrated the fact that politics still occupied a commanding interest in the life of the country. The campaign itself was not devoid of interest and even excitement. Lloyd George in particular was in fine fettle; he declared that 'an aristocracy is like cheese; the older it is the higher it becomes'. When the Unionists alleged that the Liberals and Irish were being supported by American funds after Redmond had toured North America (it was, in the circumstances, somewhat tactless of the Canadian Prime Minister, Laurier, to make a handsome personal contribution) Lloyd George maliciously enquired 'since when has the British aristocracy despised American dollars? They have underpinned many a tottering noble house'. Churchill's cousin, the Duke of Marlborough, who had married Consuelo Vanderbilt and was spending part of the Vanderbilt fortune in restoring Blenheim to its former grandeur, was among those who considered this thrust to be uncomfortably close to the mark. Churchill may have thought so, too.

The campaign also further weakened Balfour's position as leader. With considerable tactical neatness the Liberals argued that if the Unionists believed in a Referendum for Home Rule they should accept one for Tariff Reform. Balfour was caught by this tactical stratagem, and appeared to give his blessing to the idea. The fury of the Tariff Reformers—by now a substantial majority of the Parliamentary party—was considerable, although not public. Balfour was now regarded as a renegade by both extremes and ineffectual by the moderates. His languid leadership grated increasingly on a party avid for office, which wanted action and not philosophical discourses. The fact that he was admired by the Prime Minister in particular was regarded as a positive disadvantage; the Unionists wanted a fighting leader, who would more accurately reflect their detestation of the

[1] Nicolson, op. cit., 129.

Liberals. Already, the opposition to his leadership was gathering momentum, and Leo Maxse—the Tariff Reform editor of the *National Review*—coined the phrase 'Balfour Must Go', swiftly adapted to 'B.M.G.'. There were renewed jibes at 'the Hotel Cecil', and it was evident that what Garvin described as 'the Byzantine theory of Unionist leadership—the theory of speechless loyalty to a hereditary succession' was in jeopardy.

The results of the election were a deep disappointment to all parties. Over fifty seats changed hands, but in net terms the Liberals lost three seats and the Unionists one, while the Irish Nationalists and Labour each gained two. The second election of 1910 had been a virtual replica of the first.

*

At the beginning of the new Parliament, Joseph Chamberlain made his last visit to the House of Commons to be formally sworn in. Arthur Lee helped Austen Chamberlain to carry him into the Chamber, having waited until the last Member had left. 'For a few moments he sat, piteously but proudly motionless, whilst his eye slowly surveyed the empty benches and galleries, and then he indistinctly repeated the Oath after the Clerk. To sign the Roll was for him a physical impossibility, but Austen guided his hand sufficiently to make a shaky cross, and then after another poignant pause we carried him out again. As he passed the Chair the Speaker leaned over to touch his helpless hand, and the tragic ceremony was over'.[1]

*

Asquith went into the post-election situation hoping and believing that it would not be necessary to ask the King to implement his secret guarantee. There were some Ministers—notably Churchill, now at the Home Office—who actively wanted the creation. He wanted the Parliament Bill pushed through swiftly and, if progress were delayed, 'we should clink the coronets in their scabbards'. Asquith favoured less heroic stances. Birrell spoke of 'the sudden emergence of a certainty' after the second 1910 election, and so it appeared to all except a substantial portion of the Unionist Party.

The difference between the attitudes of Balfour and Lansdowne again became important. Balfour accepted the verdict of the electorate,

[1] Clark, op. cit., 113.

and assured Knollys (January 10th 1911) that the Opposition would not publicly question the Government on the King's participation. But, on January 29th, Lansdowne saw the King—with Asquith's very reluctant approval—and gained the distinct impression that the King loathed the prospect of the mass creation, and that at least some Ministers were equally unhappy. This gave Lansdowne fresh hope that the 'guarantee' was in fact nothing but a gigantic bluff.

The idea of throwing out the Parliament Bill—an issue on which two General Elections had been held within a year—now began to be seriously canvassed among the Unionist Peers, supported by some Unionist M.P.s, including Austen Chamberlain and F. E. Smith. This was not a rational, nor a deeply-considered step. It was symptomatic of the degree to which many Unionists had lost their sense of political balance. It was not long before a distinct and eventually bitter cleavage developed in the Unionist party between those who knew that the game was up and those who did not.

As an initial tactic, the Unionists took an uncharacteristic interest in House of Lords Reform—on their own terms. As Asquith caustically commented:

> The motive for this feverish exhibition of destructive and constructive ardour is not far to seek. The Tory Party were determined at all hazards not to face another General Election with the incubus of the House of Lords on their back. There must be something to put in its place, something—it did not matter for the moment very much what—but something which could be called a Second Chamber, with a coat, however thin, of democratic varnish.

These endeavours came to an abrupt conclusion when Morley pointed out that the Parliament Bill would apply equally to any new constitution of the Lords as to the old. Lansdowne's reforms were not greatly mourned by either side. Haldane described the debate as 'sombre acquiescence punctuated every now and then by cries of pain'. Meanwhile, at the beginning of March, the Parliament Bill had passed the Commons by a majority of 368 to 273 on second reading. Throughout the early summer it progressed through the Commons. It reached the Lords late in June.

Even the Coronation of King George V and a summer of quite exceptional heat did not push the political battle into the background, and Lloyd George was booed, when entering Westminster Abbey, from the stand reserved for Members of Parliament and their families. The national rejoicings were also marred by a major seamen's strike, and other indications of serious industrial unrest. The sweltering heat of London—the temperature remained in the 90's for weeks, and 100 degrees was recorded on one occasion at Greenwich—no doubt also played its part in what followed.

A kind of madness now gripped the Unionist extremists. The Parliament Bill was massacred in Committee by the Lords, and the Government now determined—very belatedly—to play its trump card, the threat to make a mass creation of Peers. But passions were now at such a pitch that many Unionists simply would not believe the validity of the threat, even when told of it by Balfour on July 7th. The division between those who would 'die in the last ditch' against the Government and the 'hedgers' now became public and acute.

The King, in mid-July, accepted the advice of the Cabinet that the anticipated eventuality had arisen. He did, however, stipulate that the Lords should be given one last chance, and be at least given an opportunity of reconsidering their position. Asquith agreed. Balfour and Lansdowne were told of the position by Lloyd George on July 18th, and, more formally, by letter by Asquith on the 20th. Even Lansdowne realised that the situation was not recoverable. On July 21st he summoned a meeting of 200 Unionist Peers at Lansdowne House, and argued that, in view of the King's guarantee, it was no longer possible 'to offer effectual resistance'. But, like many political generals before and since, he was unable to call the troops back. Some, like Curzon, changed their position, but most of the 'ditchers' were irreconcilable. Under the titular leadership of the eighty-seven-year-old but still lively Earl of Halsbury, they resolved to fight.

In this crisis, Balfour offered no effective leadership. His private contempt for the ditchers was profound; he was, furthermore, heartily sick of the whole business. He published a letter of support for Curzon which further enraged the ditchers. When, on July 24th, they howled Asquith down in the House of Commons when he rose to explain the Government's action of the Lords' Amendments, the demonstration was as much against Balfour as against the Prime Minister. From that moment his leadership was doomed. It was a disagreeable episode, described by Churchill as 'a squalid, frigid, organised attempt to insult the Prime Minister', but characteristic of that torrid summer.

The Constitutional Crisis, amidst stifling heat and in circumstances of high drama, moved towards its close. Relations between the hedgers and ditchers deteriorated further. One 'die-hard' newspaper wrote of the Peers who had voted for the Bill or who had abstained that 'no honest man will take any of them by the hand again, their friends will disown them, their clubs will expel them, and alike in politics and social life they will be made to feel the bitter shame they have brought upon us all'. On July 25th the supporters of Lord Halsbury gave a dinner at the Hotel Cecil, at which Austen Chamberlain referred to 'this revolution, nurtured in lies, promoted by fraud, and only to be achieved by violence', in which the Prime Minister had 'tricked the Opposition, entrapped the Crown and deceived the people'. The Government unenthusiastically prepared its list of five hundred Peers, and, when the Parliament Bill returned to the Lords on August 9th, Morley stated bluntly that if the Lords did not accept it, rejection would be followed by 'a large and prompt creation of peers'.

Although, even at this point, there were those Unionists who could not grasp the reality of the threat, Curzon's efforts, supported by the King, began to make a distinct impression. After a debate in the Lords, on August 9th–10th, of great passion and tension, and in suffocating heat, the Lords passed the Parliament Bill by 131 votes to 114. The King thanked God for deliverance from 'a humiliation which I should never have survived'. His estimate of politicians, never high, had not been raised by his experiences. As his official biographer has written, 'King George remained convinced thereafter that in this, the first political crisis of his reign, he had not been accorded either the confidence or the consideration to which he was entitled.'[1] The list of Liberal Peers was put aside.

*

The Constitutional Crisis of 1909–11 was, of course, the culmination of the battle opened by Balfour in the Education Bill of 1906. The unscrupulous tactic of using the Unionist majority in the Lords to humiliate and negate the Liberal majority had worked with brilliant success up to the rejection of the Budget. Even that action had its credit side for the Unionists, as it forced an election on the Government considerably earlier than it had wanted. It also made the Government look weak and pusillanimous, and to some extent undermined its position as the great reforming party. It now seems clear that Campbell-

[1] Nicolson, op. cit., 139.

Bannerman's desire to dissolve early in 1907 was soundly based, as was Gladstone's in 1893. If the challenge had been taken up earlier, the Liberals might have been spared much. The policy of 'filling the cup', of forcing the Lords to extremes, eventually succeeded, but not before the Liberals had suffered severely themselves. In 1906 they had had the greatest majority of modern politics; by early in 1910 this superiority had been swept away, never, as it happened, to be restored, Most seriously of all, the Constitutional Crisis had absorbed the attention of Ministers for two years, and held up other legislation. It was, all in all, a tragic irrelevancy.

Asquith's own leadership is open to criticism. Until forced by events, and by the extremism of his opponents, he was anxious to negotiate a settlement which would have left the situation basically unchanged. This was characteristic. Asquith was constitutionalist, a gradualist, a believer in established institutions, responsive to enlightened proposals for social reform, but essentially cautious and moderate. He tended to assume in his opponents the same basic philosophy, but Balfour's reasonableness when he fully grasped the enormity of the implications of his strategy was unrepresentative of the fierce mood of the Unionist Party, determined as it was to claw down the Liberals by virtually any means. At no point does Asquith appear to have grasped the extremes to which most Unionists were prepared to go, nor the intensity of their feelings against the Government. His relations with both Kings had been unfortunate, and in his dealings with the Unionists in 1910 he had shown an alarming lack of sensitivity towards the feelings of his own followers.

Thus, the Liberals had won the Constitutional battle that had raged since 1906, and whose first rounds had been fought in 1892–5. But if ever there was a Pyrrhic victory in politics, this was it.

CHAPTER NINE

THE DARKENING SCENE, 1911–1914

SINCE THE defeat of the Second Home Rule Bill in 1893—and, indeed, since the death of Parnell in 1891—the Irish Question had been quiescant in British domestic politics. This calm was deceptive. As Professor Mansergh has written:

> The fall of Parnell marked the beginning of a period of profound disillusion in Ireland, a period in which is to be noted little of obvious interest or activity in the political field and which was yet a period of significant development in national consciousness.[1]

The ending of Parnell's domination—and the circumstances of his downfall—had heralded a return to the harsh faction-battles of Irish domestic politics. For a decade, in spite of the passage in the Commons of the second Home Rule Bill in 1893, the Nationalist movement remained in a state of shock, tormented by internecine feuds. It was not until 1900 that the Parliamentary Party was nominally reunited under the leadership of John Redmond.

Redmond was a gentle, civilised, attractive man. He had been an ardent admirer of Parnell, and he had stood by him resolutely to the end. Like Parnell, he believed that Home Rule must come from Westminster, and must be sought in the constitutional processes. But he did not have a comparable burning passion against England, nor did he ever manage to combine so effectively the militant and constitutional aspects of the Parnellite movement. Although he was capable of fierce statements, his kind personality removed any sting from them. In character and approach he was considerably closer to Isaac Butt than to Parnell.

The Unionist policy of 'killing Home Rule by kindness', combined with a firm application of the law seemed to have had a very considerable measure of success by 1905. The land question, which had lain at

---

[1] N. Mansergh: *The Irish Question.*

the heart of the Irish Question for the whole of the nineteenth century, had apparently been finally resolved in Wyndham's Land Purchase Act of 1903. It was believed that, with the solution of this hitherto intractable problem, the wider problem itself would be solved. This was not the case. Indeed, the cause of Irish Nationalism entered a new and more complex phase.

The formation in 1893 of the Gaelic League, and the remarkable Irish literary revival at the turn of the century, were manifestations of a new form of Irish Nationalism. Although it was less easy to quantify or identify than the previous forms, in many respects it was a far more serious threat to English domination. Gladstone had rightly said that Irish nationalism was not a passing mood but an inextinguishable passion. The Unionists, in the years 1886–1905, had treated it as a series of specific problems, of which the Land Question had been the most serious and the most important. In fact, the very solution of the Land Question had removed a problem which had obsessed Irishmen for generations, and left them more free to occupy themselves with the wider cause of Irish independence.

Sinn Fein ('Ourselves Alone') was founded by Arthur Griffith in 1905, who wrote in 1910 that:

> Ireland has maintained a representation of 103 men in the English Parliament for 108 years. The 103 Irishmen are faced with 567 foreigners. . . .
>
> Ten years from now the majority of Irishmen will marvel they once believed that the proper battleground for Ireland was one chosen and filled by Ireland's enemies. . . .

Sinn Fein achieved little of practical political importance before 1914, but its very creation, at a time when most Englishmen believed that the Irish Question was solved, was in itself significant. So were the strikes organised by the Irish Transport Workers' Union during 1912 and 1913, run by James Larkin and James Connolly. The differences between Irish Labour and Sinn Fein were those of priorities. Irish Labour believed that social reform must precede independence; Sinn Fein argued that independence must come first. In fact, as subsequent events were to demonstrate, the differences between Sinn Fein and Irish Labour were neither serious nor profound. After 1913 Irish Labour became more nationalistic in outlook, a fact signified by Connolly's increasing participation in the national movement.

Unionist satisfaction at the economic position in Ireland reads oddly when compared with the actual facts. The improvement was only relative. Rural poverty may have been reduced; urban poverty was still appalling. Housing conditions in Belfast and Dublin were among the worst in Europe. Wages were very low. The death rate in Dublin was 27·6 per 1,000 in 1911, the highest of any capital in Europe and higher than that of Calcutta. These were fertile breeding-grounds for sectarian bitterness. The old division between 'Constitutional' and 'violent' approaches to Home Rule in Ireland had become more sophisticated and complex. Sinn Fein had little connection with the Fenians, and scorned the efficacy of sheer physical force to defeat the British. Nevertheless, a far wider gulf separated the Sinn Feiners from the Irish Nationalists at Westminster. It was indeed ironical that these nationalist movements were in revival at a moment when it appeared that the 'Constitutional' approach was at last on the verge of success.

Any examination of the Irish Question from 1912–14 must be made in the context of the political temperature of Britain at the close of 1911. The relationship between the two major parties had deteriorated further, and there was a profound rancour and bitterness in the political battle. The political struggle in Britain rests, in the last analysis, upon mutual acceptance of certain conventions. In their use of the Lords between 1906 and 1911, the Unionists had broken at least one of those conventions. As it approached its culmination, the dialogue between the two parties was harsh, and often hysterical. In the Unionist ranks, the more extreme elements were now in the ascendant, but, in spite of the violence of the Constitutional struggle, it would have been difficult to anticipate the lengths to which the Unionists were prepared to go in their passionate vendetta against the Liberal Government.

This was a period of fever, of violence, and of extreme tensions. 1911 saw the most serious industrial unrest in modern British history; at Liverpool there was savage rioting, and two strikers were shot dead. Unrest flared violently in the South Wales coal fields. There was a railway strike, in the course of which Churchill called out troops without waiting for the local authorities to ask for them; Lloyd George saved what was developing into an ugly situation. Reaction in the Labour Party to Churchill's methods was extremely hostile, and prompted a memorable attack on the Home Secretary by Ramsay MacDonald. In reality, Churchill's conduct in the South Wales miners' dispute had been exemplary, and it was ironical that his name should be excoriated for 'Tonypandy' whereas his impetuous actions in the railway dispute were forgotten. But in Labour memories the two incidents became intermingled, and these episodes marked a significant change in the attitude of the Labour Party towards this colourful, dramatic figure. In the Liberal Party as well, Churchill was being regarded with increasing suspicion and apprehension; to the Unionists he was anathema. These shadows gathering over the most brilliant early career since that of Lord Randolph Churchill were to assume important proportions by 1914.

Tension was also growing abroad. As the Lords were debating the Parliament Bill, the Agadir Crisis was assuming very serious proportions. In September 1911 Italy declared war on Turkey and invaded Tripoli, and the long-delayed dismemberment of the Ottoman Empire began in earnest. The naval race between Britain and Germany maintained its menacing momentum. The Suffragettes developed new methods of violence.[1] It was a time of *sturm und drang*.

*

The recrudescence of the Irish Question in British politics coincided almost exactly with the accession of Bonar Law as Balfour's successor to the Unionist leadership. Balfour's resignation was announced on November 8th. The National Union was due to meet at Leeds the following week, and there was a remarkable concurrence of feeling in the Parliamentary Party that the issue must be resolved before then. A meeting of Unionist M.P.s was arranged for November 13th.

The principal contestants were Austen Chamberlain and Walter Long, the latter justly described by the former as 'a long-time Conservative, a typical country gentleman, and senior to me both in length of service in the House and in Cabinet rank, and he aroused none of the jealousies or doubts which were inseparable from my position'. The problem was not simply that Austen Chamberlain was a Chamberlain, nor that he was still a Liberal Unionist, while Long was a determined Tory squire with impeccable credentials and moderate intellect. The shadows of the Tariff Reform and the constitutional crisis hung over both of them, the Party was in a hectic and

---

[1] The Prime Minister was particularly unimpressed with their extreme methods. As Mr. Fulford has commented, 'The more the women marched, the less his reason marched with them.' (*Votes for Women*, 184).

vehement mood, and the two were personally on very bad terms. After a short period of fierce lobbying by their partisans, they agreed to step aside if a compromise candidate could be found.

As Amery has written of Chamberlain:

> The trouble with Austen was not undue humility or diffidence. He had quite a good opinion of himself. But he had an exaggerated fear of being regarded as pushful. . . . There was in him none of Churchill's ready assertion of a conscious fitness to lead. So he made no attempt to fight for his own hand.[1]

To the surprise of Law and Chamberlain, Bonar Law also came forward—in the view of many contemporaries, pushed forward by his Canadian adventurer friend and recently elected M.P. for Ashton-under-Lyne, Max Aitken, an interpretation not now accepted by historians. The matter was handled by a very small section of the party hierarchy, and Law was submitted to the party meeting as the only candidate for the new Leader in the Commons. Chamberlain, in seconding Law's nomination, admitted that 'there has been a little feeling that the matter has been taken out of the hands of the Party, and too much settled for you before you came to this gathering'. There were many who agreed wholeheartedly, yet in the circumstances they had little choice. Law was unanimously elected Leader.[2]

Law was a cautious and reserved man, 'meekly ambitious' in Asquith's phrase, and one who has been regarded without undue enthusiasm by most historians. He was in many respects an attractive man. He was modest, calm, and unassuming. He was utterly devoid of pomposity. He had no interest in political or social gossip. He was a total abstainer, and wholly unenamoured of the pleasures of the table.[3] The sudden death of his wife in 1909 had accentuated a habitually gloomy and pessimistic outlook on life. His habits were simple, although he was relatively wealthy, and his private character was absolutely beyond reproach. He was a kindly man, to whom his few close associates were utterly devoted. There was a gentleness, compassion and simplicity in his character which was rare and refreshing. As

[1] Amery: *My Political Life*, Vol. I, 386.

[2] For the best account of this curious episode see Robert Blake: *The Unknown Prime Minister*, pp. 71–86.

[3] 'The food on Bonar Law's table', as Beaverbrook has commented with feeling, 'was always quite execrable. Its sameness was a penance and its quality a horror to me.' This should not be taken too seriously. Beaverbrook's standards were not low.

J. M. Keynes—who subsequently served him at the Treasury—has written of him:

> Many politicians are too much enthralled by the crash and glitter of the struggle, their hearts obviously warmed by the swell and pomp of authority, enjoying their positions and their careers, clinging to these sweet delights and primarily pleasing themselves. These are the natural target of envy and detraction and a certain contempt. They have their reward already and need no gratitude. But the public have liked to see a Prime Minister not enjoying his lot unduly. We have preferred to be governed by the sad smile of one who adopts towards the greatest office in the State the attitude that whilst, of course, it is nice to be Prime Minister, it is no great thing to covet, and who feels in office, and not merely afterwards, the vanity of things.

It is necessary to probe further. Andrew Bonar Law had been born in New Brunswick in 1858, a child of the Manse, and something of his Scottish Presbyterian background seems to have remained with him all his days. He had made a considerable fortune as an iron merchant in Glasgow before entering Parliament in the 1900 Unionist victory, and had the misfortune to make his maiden speech on the same evening as the dashing son of Lord Randolph Churchill, for whom he developed an enduring antipathy. In an age when it was regarded as imperative that a political career should start very early, the observations of an unknown Scottish businessman in his forties were not regarded as of much moment. Such men are familiar to the House of Commons. They enter obscurely, make some speeches of practical common sense, earn a certain respect, are asked to undertake the most boring of Parliamentary chores, and then either die, lose their seats, or drift into the House of Lords. Cromwell approved of such men, and so has the House of Commons down the ages. But their station is lowly and is destined to remain so; they are the foot-soldiers of politics—and particularly Tory politics.

But Bonar Law was of a different calibre. He had not come to Westminster to drift into placid backwaters. The very frugality of his life and his quiet glumness soon earned him many, and exceptionally devoted, friends. He had trained himself in local mock Parliaments—a great feature of those times, and long gone—to speak at length without notes, his mastery of complicated statistics was notable, and his bluntness and direction of expression were only to be emulated sub-sequently by Clement Attlee, with whom he had much in common. Like Attlee, Bonar Law had his points of principle on which he would not be moved. Like Attlee, he was distrustful of more glittering politicians, while at the same time being fascinated by them. In appearance, the sombre Law appeared incongruous on a public platform with F. E. Smith and Sir Edward Carson—until he began to speak. A later generation witnessed a similar phenomenon when Attlee appeared with Stafford Cripps or Aneurin Bevan.

Law was an expert upon, and passionately concerned with, two subjects above all others—Tariff Reform and Ulster. Although he had served as a junior Minister in the Balfour Government, Joseph Chamberlain was his lode-star, and, after Chamberlain's disintegration in 1906, his most ardent advocate. On Ulster, he was not open to dis-cussion or argument, and believed implicity in the creed of Lord Randolph Churchill.

Law was a ruminative, somewhat introspective, lonely man. He had no vices—unless teetotallism, continuous pipe-smoking, lack of interest in food, and a mania for chess can be so described (and a case could be made out)—and he could certainly not be described as an intellectual. But he was thoughtful, serious, dedicated, and softly determined. He was also highly ambitious, but reticently so. The Unionist Party, after a surfeit of catastrophic brilliance, was in the mood for blameless reliability in 1911. In Lloyd George's words, 'the fools chose the right man by mistake'. But perhaps the reasoning was not as faulty as Lloyd George—who never comprehended Tories—appreciated until October 1922 when the modest iron-merchant from Glasgow struck him down as completely as he had Churchill and Asquith. Bonar Law has often been depicted as a dull man, a plodder. But a man who dully plods his way to the leadership of his party within ten years of entering politics, holds a position of commanding influence for six years, and ends up as Prime Minister is not to be casually treated. Bonar Law was shrewd, quick, professional, and with an inner hardness and craftiness which some crudely describe with the adjective 'tough'. The judgement of A. G. Gardiner was to the point:

He is as unimaginative as the ledger in his country-house. His speech is dry and colourless, his voice thin and unmusical. . . . He is as innocent of humour as a dirge and had never made an epigram.

But he can sting. His qualities are an unhesitating fluency, an orderly argumentative progression, a certain business-like exactness, and an unaffected sincerity.[1]

Asquith and his colleagues made the great mistake of regarding Law with considerable contempt and condescension. He was to the Liberal leader and many of his colleagues (particularly Churchill) 'the gilded tradesman'. Of the Liberals only Lloyd George seems to have appreciated the calibre of Bonar Law, his adroitness in debate, and the moral and political toughness that lay beneath the unprepossessing façade.

On the subject of Home Rule, Law was a deeply committed man, far more committed than Balfour. The prospect of handing over Protestant Ulstermen to the rule of the Catholic South genuinely repelled him. As his biographer has commented:

We may then safely take with a grain of salt Bonar Law's strictures upon such topics as Welsh Disestablishment or the Franchise Bill, but upon Irish Home Rule . . . he meant every word he said.[2]

One may perhaps be reminded of Disraeli's aphorism that 'a little sincerity is a dangerous thing, and a great deal of it is absolutely fatal.'

Meanwhile, Ulster had found a leader. Sir Edward Carson, who led the Ulster Unionists from February 1910, was as strange a man to find in that position as Parnell had been to lead the Catholic Southern Nationalists in the 1870s. Carson was a Southern Irishman who sat as Member for Dublin University until he accepted the Ulster leadership. Until he became the leader of Ulster he had had no connection with Northern Ireland that would have led men to anticipate his emergence. He was a hypochondriac, a serious and responsible constitutional lawyer, and in reality a moderate man. It was particularly difficult for a fellow lawyer like Asquith, who knew Carson so well, to take Carson's violent language too seriously.

This was another mistake. As George Bernard Shaw once remarked: 'We must also bear in mind that political opinion in Ulster is not a matter of talk and bluff, as it is in England . . . there is a strength in [the Ulsterman's] rancour which lifts it above rancour.' Carson knew this. His appearance was magnificent, his mien decisive and intimidating, and he had something of Parnell's quality of icy delivery. His

[1] A. G. Gardiner: *Pillars of Society.*
[2] Robert Blake: *The Unknown Prime Minister.*

merciless destruction of Oscar Wilde had demonstrated his forensic persistence and quickness. His assault on the Admiralty in the famous Archer–Shee case was a celebrated episode. But, up to February 1910, he had not made a deep impression upon the House. From that moment he was a changed man. Like Law, he meant every word that he said on the matter of Home Rule. Ulster was determined not to be coerced by the South. In Carson they had found what they had hitherto lacked, a real leader. Thus, Carson, the outsider, understood better, and was closer to, his followers than Redmond. And, whereas Redmond was deeply committed to constitutional methods, Carson was fully prepared to countenance extremist actions if need be. There were those who thought that this was all a gigantic bluff, and that he was at heart a moderate and a man of peace; but Carson's manner, methods and language made even the most sceptical begin to doubt. Carson was the leader, but his most effective lieutenant was Captain Craig, who demonstrated a flair for stage-management of Ulster demonstrations.

The Liberals embarked on Home Rule once again with little enthusiasm. Politicians on both sides steeled themselves for the wearying repetition of the old, long familiar arguments. Once again, and with greater justification than in 1892–3, the Unionists alleged the existence of a political deal between the Government and the Irish Nationalists. The facts spoke for themselves. From 1906 to 1910, with a comfortable independent majority, Home Rule had been ignored. Now, dependent upon the Irish vote for their existence, Ministers had no choice. 'Unless an official declaration on the question of Home Rule be made', Redmond wrote to Morley, 'not only will it be impossible for us to support Liberal candidates in England, but we will most unquestionably have to ask our friends to vote against them . . . as you know very well, the Opposition of Irish voters in Lancashire, Yorkshire and other places, including Scotland, would certainly mean the loss of many seats.' No formal compact was required; the situation was stark and clear to each party. On this basis, the Liberal Government was propelled unhappily forward.

The Third Home Rule Bill was introduced in April 1912. Its novelty was to embrace the federal conception of Home Rule, on which Asquith laid emphasis in the speech he made introducing it. But in essentials, it was not very different from the Bill of 1892, inasmuch as the Irish Parliament was to have powers severely circumscribed to the point when, as Sir Harold Nicolson has commented, it was nothing more than 'a glorified County Council'. But although it did not go far enough for Sinn Fein, it went far further than the Ulster Unionists were prepared to tolerate. The Session that opened in February 1912 was to be one of the most arduous in modern political history. With a break of eight weeks in the summer of 1912, and another early in 1913, Parliament sat virtually continuously until August 1913. Once again, 'all Parliamentary roads led to Ireland'.

The issues involved were at once simple and also complex. With the majority in the Commons, and with the Lords' powers cut, the passage of the Bill was virtually inevitable. This was the major difference between 1886 and 1893. Everything hinged on the position of Ulster. Historically, politically and economically the north-eastern corner of Ireland had little affinity with the rest of the country. Since the seventeenth century four of the Nine Ulster Counties—Antrim, Armagh, Down and Londonderry—had had populations which were overwhelmingly Scottish in origin and Protestant in religion. In two other counties—Fermanagh and Tyrone—the Catholics and Protestants were more or less equally divided. In the remaining three—Donegal, Monaghan, and Cavan—there was a Catholic majority numerically, but with a powerful and wealthy Protestant minority.

On the face of it, the case of the Ulster Unionists in claiming the Nine Counties was not a strong one. Indeed, in 1912 the Nine Counties were represented at Westminster by seventeen Unionists and sixteen Irish Nationalists, and a by-election at the beginning of 1913 actually gave the Nationalists a majority in the Nine Counties.

It was always the claim of the Irish Nationalists that Ireland was one, and that partition was unthinkable. In part, this was an emotional feeling. But it was also a practical one. The four north-eastern counties provided the only modern industrial plant in Ireland, and the wealth of Belfast was regarded as crucial to the economic existence of a future Irish State. Belfast was the centre of resistance to Home Rule. In 1886 it had welcomed Lord Randolph Churchill rapturously, and in 1893 it had been the scene of the great Ulster Convention at which one speaker had declared that 'as a last resort we will be prepared to defend ourselves'. By 1911, when the ill-fated *Titanic* was built there, Belfast had the largest shipyard in the world. The city also harboured, as Morley once wrote, 'a spirit of bigotry and violence for which a parallel can hardly be found in any town in Western Europe'. In September 1912, 417,444 Belfast citizens signed a 'Solemn Covenant' prepared by Craig 'never to recognise a Dublin Parliament'. It requires emphasis that the temper of Belfast, and of Ulster Nationalism, was militant long before Carson, Craig, Law and F. E. Smith—a very recent and opportunistic convert to the cause of Ulster—appeared on the scene. But their intervention gave the issue a new, and more ominous, dimension.

Law quickly made it plain that his attitudes towards the Government were different to those of Balfour. In his first speech as Leader, at the Albert Hall, he described Ministers as 'humbugs' and as 'artful dodgers', a manner derided by Asquith as the 'new style'. If it was somewhat rough and unsophisticated, it was greatly to the taste of the Unionists. And on the Irish Question, Law was in deadly earnest. 'It may seem strange to you and me', he remarked to Lord Riddell, 'but it is a religious question. These people are . . . prepared to die for their convictions'.

As the Home Rule Bill proceeded slowly through the House of Commons, the Ulstermen began to prepare. On January 5th 1912 they started drilling a Volunteer Force; on April 9th Carson, Lord Londonderry, Law and Walter Long took the salute of 80,000 Orange Volunteers. A counter-attack was launched. On October 3rd of the previous year Churchill had told his Dundee constituents that 'we must not attach too much importance to these frothings of Sir Edward Carson. I daresay when the worst comes to the worst we shall find that civil war evaporates in uncivil words'. To prove his point, with real courage, Churchill—now First Lord of the Admiralty—accepted an invitation to speak at a Home Rule meeting in Belfast in March, and in the Ulster Hall, the very place in which Lord Randolph Churchill had made his famous speech in January 1886. Eventually the venue was changed to the Celtic football ground—in the Nationalist part of the city. Feeling at this act of sacrilege was very intense. Troops— seven battalions of infantry and a squadron of cavalry—were brought in, but the meeting itself passed off without any serious incidents, in spite of the inevitable interruption by a suffragette. The visitor was then hastily dispatched to Larne and back to England by a circuitous route. Courage was required for this expedition, and it was a quality which Churchill possessed to the full. But the incident did nothing to soothe the passions of the situation.

The Ulster retort was a spectacular Easter Demonstration in Belfast, which included the breaking-out of a gigantic Union Jack— said to be the largest ever woven, forty-eight feet by twenty-five feet— an interminable march-past of Volunteers, and much violent speech- ifying, in which Law described Belfast as 'a besieged city'. This was, however, mild compared to what he said at a Unionist rally on July 12th, at Blenheim Palace:

I can imagine no length of resistance to which Ulster can go in which I should not be prepared to support them, and in which, in my belief, they would not be supported by the overwhelming majority of the British people.

This was coming very close indeed to encouraging defiance of the constitutional conventions. Just in case this point had not been taken, Law made it emphatically clear:

In our opposition to them we shall not be guided by the considera- tions or bound by the restraints which would influence us in an ordinary Constitutional struggle. We shall take the means, whatever means seem to us most effective, to deprive them of the despotic power which they have usurped and compel them to appeal to the people whom they have deceived. They may, perhaps they will, carry their Home Rule Bill through the House of Commons—but what then? *I said the other day in the House of Commons, and I repeat here, that there are things stronger than Parliamentary majorities.*

Law did not confine his threats to the Commons or to the public platform. He astounded King George by calmly informing him on May 12th that he would be fully justified in using the Royal Veto on the Home Rule Bill—constitutional usage since the death of Queen Anne notwithstanding—and implied that he would be liable to strong criticism if he did not exercise his duty.

Meanwhile, the Home Rule Bill debates were characteristically prolonged and rancorous, and included one suspension of the House and an occasion on which an Ulster M.P. accurately hurled a copy of the Standing Orders at Churchill. On January 16th 1913, the Bill was given its Third Reading in the Commons by 367 votes to 257. On January 30th it was thrown out by the Lords by 326 to 69. On March 10th a new Session began, and the Bill started all over again. On July 7th it received its Third Reading in the Commons; on July 15th the Lords rejected it once again. The exhausted Parliament adjourned on August 15th, and was in recess for the rest of 1913.

*

Home Rule, although the major political preoccupation at this time, was not the only one. Throughout 1912 and the early part of 1913 it was closely rivalled by the strange affair of the Marconi Scandal.

The broad outlines of what actually occurred are as follows. In March 1912 the Postmaster-General, Herbert Samuel, provisionally accepted a tender from the English Marconi Company for the construction of a chain of wireless stations in the Empire; this caused a sharp rise in Marconi shares, accentuated by the extensive publicity given to the importance of wireless communications after the disaster of the sinking of the liner *Titanic* after striking an iceberg on April 10th.

The managing director of the English Marconi Company was Godfrey Isaacs, a brother of the Attorney-General, Sir Rufus Isaacs, who was also managing director of the legally independent American Marconi Company. Godfrey Isaacs decided to expand the American company—in which the English company had a majority shareholding—by floating a new issue of shares on the British market on April 18th. On April 9th he invited two of his brothers—Harry and Rufus—to buy a large block of the new shares at a price considerably below the probable market price. Harry Isaacs bought 56,000; Rufus Isaacs at first did not like the idea, but a few days later bought 10,000 from Harry Isaacs at £2 a share. He then sold 1,000 to Lloyd George and another 1,000 to the Liberal Chief Whip, the Master of Elibank, at no profit to himself.

On the next day—April 18th—the new issue was floated and the shares jumped to £4 each. All three Ministers promptly disposed of their shares at a handsome profit. Subsequently they bought more shares, and, as the value of the shares dropped, they made a net loss. For some strange reason, this fact has been often cited in defence of the Ministers, as though the purpose of making a profit had been far from their thoughts, and their losses in some way made their offence innocuous. The fact remained that three senior Cabinet Ministers had bought shares on a privileged basis from a major Government contractor and had made a considerable initial profit on the transaction. The fact that, encouraged, they subsequently tried again and got their fingers burnt is hardly to be regarded as a convincing defence of their activities. Viewed in the most charitable possible light, they acted with great imprudence. A more realistic assessment would be harsher.

Well-informed rumours began to circulate in the City, and at length emerged in a violently anti-Semitic journal called *Eye Witness*, edited by Hilaire Belloc and Cecil Chesterton (brother of 'G.K.'). (A somewhat ironical development, when Lloyd George's anti-Semitism in his Boer War period is recalled.) Samuel, who was wholly uninvolved, was also mentioned in these attacks; he wanted to bring an action for libel, but was dissuaded by Asquith. In August Isaacs was also persuaded by Asquith not to take legal action.[1] Asquith, indeed, wrote to him:

> I expect [it] . . . has a very meagre circulation. I notice only one page of advertisements and that occupied by books of Belloc's publishers. Prosecution would secure it notoriety, which might yield subscribers. We have broken weather [*he went on somewhat irrelevantly*], and but for Winston there would be nothing in the newspapers.

In private, Asquith was very angry. But either he was very much implicated in a serious attempt to mislead the House of Commons later in the year or he did not fully ascertain the facts at this early stage. Neither conclusion reflects to his advantage.

On October 11th Samuel moved to appoint a Select Committee to investigate the whole story of the Marconi contract. In the debate, both Isaacs and Lloyd George specifically, and with much heat, disclaimed any dealing in the shares of 'the Marconi Company'. They were careful to word these denials so as to cover only the English Marconi Company, but the impression given was that they had not had dealings in any Marconi shares at all. In spite of the torrid atmosphere of politics at the time, these denials were accepted by the House of Commons and by the Opposition, and the matter appeared to be concluded.

This conclusion was abruptly amended when it was learned early in 1913 that Samuel and Isaacs proposed to sue the French newspaper

---

[1] It is, however, open to doubt whether Asquith—as Samuel has stated in his *Memoirs*—knew of the full details before January 1913. The latter is the date given by Asquith in his account to the King, but the matter remains in doubt. It is, however, an important point, as it concerns the extent of Asquith's involvement in the Lloyd George–Isaacs disclaimers in the Commons in October 1912.

Le Matin and that Isaacs would admit that he and Lloyd George had bought shares in the American Marconi Company. Hardly less startling was the news that F. E. Smith and Carson would defend the Ministers at a time when they were the foremost advocates of extreme measures in Ulster and were making violent inflammatory speeches against the Government. Smith defended his decision in characteristic-ally majestic terms, invoking the hallowed traditions of the English Bar at a time when he was defying and deriding certain fundamental tenets of English Law, thereby giving rise to the justified conclusion that although he was very clever he was not very intelligent (or, alterna-tively, that he was morally and professionally schizophrenic). Perhaps the truth lies in Arthur Lee's reminiscence: 'He once said to me jestingly: "At least I can say this, that never in my life have I attempted to resist temptation", and he pressed his reckless course without illusions and certainly without fear.' Bonar Law was not the only Unionist who found this performance stupid and totally incompre-hensible, and the episode marked a decisive turning-point in Smith's fortunes with his party.

But matters now became much more serious for the Government. It transpired that the Master of Elibank had not only invested some £9,000 of Liberal Party funds in the Marconi shares but had left the country to go to the remote township of Bogota and accordingly would not be available to give evidence before the Select Committee. Colombia was far distant from Westminster, and caustic references to this fact became frequent at Unionist meetings. Matters were hardly improved by the blatant partisanship of both sides on the Select Committee. After much fury and other disagreeableness, the Com-mittee eventually reported on purely party lines, and a very fierce debate in the Commons ensued. The Ministers not only survived, but Asquith appointed Isaacs to the highest judicial post in the land, Lord Chief Justice, an act which provoked Kipling to pen one of the most vitriolic political verses in modern politics. Isaacs' career prospered thereafter. He became, as Lord Reading, British Ambassador in Washington and subsequently Viceroy of India. If he never quite succeeded in escaping from the shadows cast by the Marconi affair, his sufferings were minimal. Lloyd George's career received only a very temporary setback. Within a very short time he was even posing as the victim of a conspiracy to malign his character. Nerve was one of Lloyd George's most remarkable political attributes. Lloyd George and

Isaacs were lucky in their Prime Minister, but their gratitude took a strange form.

Not altogether surprisingly, this episode did little to elevate the stature of the Government nor to reduce the political temperature. Moral strictures by Lloyd George became even less supportable for the Unionists, aware as they were of other aspects of his private life. The antagonism between the parties, which had been accelerating since 1906, was now greater than anyone in English public life could recall.

*

Marconi was a symptom of a much deeper bitterness. By the end of the Session in August 1913 the Home Rule Bill had been twice passed by the Commons and twice rejected by the Lords. Under the terms of the Parliament Act, its final passage could not be long delayed. The Ulster Volunteers were drilling and preparing for armed resistance; plans for an alternative government were far advanced; weapons were being purchased, and by various methods being brought into Ulster. On Roberts' personal recommendation, a retired officer, Lt.-Gen. Sir George Richardson, K.C.B., a veteran of Afghanistan and the Boxer Campaign, was in command in Belfast. The Government was not well served by the Chief Secretary, Augustine Birrell, a man of great charm but consistently out of touch with reality in Ireland, and who declined to regard the situation with adequate seriousness.

Up to this point, it must be emphasised, there had been no serious discussion about treating Ulster separately. The Unionist case was that Home Rule was impossible because of the special position of Ulster. Carson's line, however, was somewhat different. He recognised that Ulster could not prevent Home Rule; but he was determined that Home Rule should not include Ulster; he was fully prepared to come to an arrangement on these lines with the Government.

The King was, by this stage, becoming justifiably alarmed, particularly when Law had advised him that he ought to dissolve Parliament on his own responsibility. While the King was fully aware of the fact that no Monarch had dismissed a Prime Minister since 1834, that the precedent was not promising, and that much had happened since then,[1] he was justifiably agitated. But Law had also raised another very disconcerting possibility: If Home Rule had to be imposed on

---

[1] Rosebery was among those who, when their advice was sought, pointed out the dangers involved in the Monarchy in taking such an action.

Ulster by military force, would the Army obey such an order? The King laid these dilemmas before Asquith on August 11th in the form of a handwritten memorandum, in which he described his personal position and raising the possibility of 'a settlement by consent'. Asquith dismissed the King's arguments somewhat briskly, and on September 22nd the King wrote to Asquith again:

> Will it be wise, will it be fair to the Sovereign as head of the Army, to subject the discipline, and indeed the loyalty of his troops, to such a strain?

Asquith replied that there were 'no sufficient grounds for the fears—or hopes—expressed in some quarters, that the troops would fail to do their duty'.

Nevertheless, as the King urged, it was necessary at least to attempt a negotiated settlement of the crisis. In the late autumn of 1913 it was begun in an atmosphere of distinct coolness between Bonar Law and Asquith. Although it came to nothing, the ingenious mind of Lloyd George produced a scheme whereby the Home Rule Bill would not come into effect in Ulster for five or six years. This eventually emerged in the following March in an offer by Asquith that any County in Ireland could vote itself out of Home Rule for six years. This merely succeeded in enraging both sides. 'We do not want sentence of death with a stay of execution for six years', as Carson retorted; the Nationalist dismay and resentment was equally strong. The latter was increased by the decision of the Government in December to forbid the embargo on importing arms into Ireland that had been relaxed since 1906, and which had enabled the Ulstermen to arm themselves.

Passions on both sides were now rising to a very dangerous level. Lord Roberts drafted a letter for publication (in fact never published), approved by Carson and Bonar Law, to the effect that in the event of Civil War the normal rules of military discipline did not apply. Excitement was also growing in the Empire. The Orange Association of Manitoba prepared to send a regiment of volunteers to Ulster, and other Canadian states—notably Winnipeg, Saskatchewan, Alberta and Vancouver—pledged support to the same cause. Nationalist movements sprang up in New Zealand, South Africa, and the United States. At Dublin, in November 1913, Law made a clear appeal to the Army to disobey orders. Matters were further complicated by the attitude of Ministers. Many—particularly Asquith—did not take the

Ulster threats seriously; few were enthusiastic about Home Rule. By
the beginning of 1914 they had succeeded in disillusioning and
infuriating both sides. Their subsequent actions made the situation, if
anything, even worse.

In March 1914 Churchill—whose prestige with his own party was
in marked decline—made another hapless intervention in the Irish
Question with the purpose, as he subsequently frankly admitted, 'to
ingratiate myself with my Party'. On March 14th he made a highly
belligerent speech at Bradford in which he declared that there were
'worse things than bloodshed even on an extended scale', that Britain
must not be reduced to the condition of Mexico, and that if her civil
and Parliamentary institutions were to be brought to the crude
challenge of force he could only say 'Let us go forward together and
put these grave matters to the proof.' The Cabinet had set up a small
Committee to handle the Ulster problem on March 11th, which consisted of Crewe (who, through illness, took no part), Churchill,
Birrell, J.E.B. Seely (Secretary for War) and Simon. On March 17th it
reported with recommendations for increased guards on depots and
movement of troops. Churchill reported that 'the forthcoming practice'
of the Third Battle Squadron would take place off the Isle of Arran.
In fact, the naval movements to Lamlash had already been ordered.
To the Unionists this seemed clear evidence of attempts to coerce the
Ulstermen, and even to countenance the use of force.

Meanwhile, Seely ordered Major-General Sir Arthur Paget,
Commander-in-Chief Ireland, to concentrate and reinforce his troops
at a number of important points. Asquith cancelled the warship
movement to Lamlash—although not before much political damage
had been done—but Seely's order to Paget was the vital spark.

Seely—later Lord Mottistone—was a lively, dashing, cheerful man
of action, whose career had many points in common with that of
Churchill. Like him, he had distinguished himself in the Boer War,
had entered the Commons as a Conservative and had joined the
Liberals over the Free Trade issue. But if Churchill was impetuous,
Seely's impetuousness was in a different class. It is difficult to consider
that he was very intelligent, and he was a strange successor to Haldane
at the War Office.

Paget came to London and obtained several undertakings from
Seely, of which the most important was that any officer whose domicile
was in Ulster could 'disappear' if ordered north. Paget informed his

senior officers of this concession and also told them that any not
domiciled in Ireland but who refused to undertake active operations
against Ulster should send in their resignations. This was a subtle, but
crucial, extension of Seely's orders. General Sir Hubert Gough and
sixty of the seventy officers of the Third Cavalry Brigade said that they
would prefer dismissal if ordered north. The War Office ordered
Gough and his three colonels to London. They proceeded to negotiate
with Seely, demanding a written assurance that they would not be
called upon to enforce Home Rule upon Ulster. Asquith, on March
23rd, wrote out a cautious letter to Gough exonerating him from the
charge of disobeying orders. Disastrously, Seely—with Morley's
assistance—added two paragraphs of which the second one stated
that the Government 'have no intention whatever of taking advantage
of the right to crush political opposition to the policy or principles of
the Home Rule Bill'.

Gough returned to the Curragh, the hero of the hour. The Liberals
and the Nationalists were enraged, and Asquith's removal of Seely
could not materially change the situation. The Unionists were convinced that Seely and Churchill had planned a massive use of force
against the Ulstermen which they had been compelled to abandon.
Unionist feeling against Churchill ran very high, and Asquith's
position was seriously affected. As Ensor subsequently wrote: 'His
followers supposed that this betokened a drastic policy, such as only a
prime minister could put through; in fact, it heralded a policy of
surrender, such as only a prime minister could put over.' The long-term
effects of the so-called 'Curragh Mutiny' were to be substantial. But
the immediate were also significant. In May the Ulster Volunteers
smuggled in at Larne some 30,000 rifles and three million rounds of
ammunition without military or police interference. The feeling in the
South that the Government was in effect condoning the Ulster cause
and bowing to Ulster pressure was greatly augmented. There was a
rush to join the Irish Volunteers. Ireland advanced rapidly closer to
Civil War.

The inter-party discussions continued throughout the summer. On
July 18th, advised by Asquith, the King summoned a formal conference under the chairmanship of the Speaker at BuckinghamPalace;
it opened on July 21st. The differences were irreconcilable, and no
progress was made after four days in which, as Churchill has related,
the conference 'toiled round the muddy byways of Fermanagh and

Tyrone'. A proposal by Asquith to exclude six of the Nine Counties from Home Rule was rejected by both Redmond and Carson. On July 26th the National Volunteers carried out a gun-running at Howth. Soldiers were called out, and, in Dublin, were stoned by an angry crowd. They fired, killing three civilians and wounding thirty-eight. Civil War seemed imminent. All plans were ready. Lord Milner was urging the immediate setting up of an Ulster Provisional Government.

But on July 24th, at the end of a Cabinet meeting concerned with the breakdown of the Buckingham Palace Conference, just as Ministers were rising to depart, Grey informed them of the text of an ultimatum sent to Serbia by Austria-Hungary. To quote Churchill's account:

> The parishes of Fermanagh and Tyrone faded back into the mists and squalls of Ireland, and a strange light began immediately, but by perceptible gradations, to fall and glow upon the map of Europe.

PART TWO

FROM ASQUITH TO CHAMBERLAIN

CHAPTER TEN

WAR AND COALITION, 1914–1915

FROM 1870 UNTIL July 1914 the principal preoccupations of British politicians had been domestic, with Imperial interludes. After a visit to Britain in 1899, von Bülow wrote that:

> British politicians know little of the Continent. They do not know much more of Continental conditions than we do of those of Peru or Siam. To our ideas they are rather naïve. They are naïve in their candid self-seeking and again in the way in which they give their confidence. They believe with difficulty that others have bad motives. They are very calm, very easy-going, very optimistic.

This domestic preoccupation was not surprising, and was particularly evident in the years 1906–14. The Tariff Reform–Free Trade battles of 1903–5 had been followed by the long drawn-out struggle between the Conservative-dominated House of Lords and the Liberal Government that had not been resolved until August 1911; this, in turn, was followed immediately by the Home Rule crisis, which opened at the beginning of 1912 and was not resolved by August 1914. Other matters of concern, such as the serious industrial unrest of 1911 and 1912, the suffragette movement, and the controversies over the implementation of the social programme of the Liberal Government, ensured that the domestic political scene was heated, time-consuming, and absorbing—and irrelevant to the new challenges from abroad.

In retrospect, it is evident that by at least 1909 a definite change had occurred in Britain's relationship with Europe. It was not so evident to contemporaries. The established principle of British foreign policy since the 1870s had been non-commitment to foreign alliances, and particularly European alliances, while at the same time preserving British interests and keeping a wary eye on the ambitions of the major European powers. But by 1909 this principle had been slowly and irreversibly eroded. The Three times between 1898 and 1901 there were serious attempts to build an Anglo-German Alliance, to which the unmistakable response was the Second Navy Law of 1900 and the threat of a German battle fleet of thirty-four battleships and fifty-two cruisers within sixteen years. The German assumption that the British could not find allies elsewhere in Europe seemed well-founded in 1900; all over the world there seemed unlimited possibilities for serious clashes between the British on the one hand and the French and the Russians on the other. Thus, Joseph Chamberlain's threat that the British, if spurned, would turn elsewhere was not taken seriously in Berlin.

Von Bülow would have been well advised to have read the wise remark of the French historian Sorel, written in 1893, upon the British:

> Their history is full of alternations between indifference which makes people think them decadent, and a rage which baffles their foes. They are seen, in turn, abandoning or dominating Europe, neglecting the greatest continental matters and claiming to control even the smallest, turning from peace at any price to war to the death.

The British emergence from European isolation had not been a planned operation. It was a slow dawning of recognition that a new peril lay close. The Anglo-Japanese Treaty of 1902, the entente with France in 1904, and the convention with Russia in 1907, were not connected parts of a coherent strategy, but were separate, individual, *ad hoc* defensive arrangements. But, when assembled together, they represented a very important change from the situation that had existed when Salisbury had ceased to be Prime Minister. The very fact that the major differences between Britain and Russia and France had been resolved was in itself of very considerable importance, and signified that the British, after a long absence, were now concerned with European power politics.

The Algeciras Crisis at the beginning of 1906—which occurred almost immediately after Sir Edward Grey came to the Foreign Office—had been an important demonstration that the new entente with France was not to be easily fractured. It also gave impetus to the secret Anglo-French military, and subsequently naval, conversations. Furthermore, Russia had supported the French, and the international recognition of the mandates of France and Spain in Morocco was manifestly the result of British and Russian support for the French. The Anglo-Russian Convention of 1907 may not have been popular in Britain—particularly in the Liberal Party—but it, too, marked another important development of what was to become called the Triple Entente. Europe was moving slowly and uneasily into two armed camps and Britain was clearly showing her preferences.

The character and capacity of Edward Grey remain subjects of deep controversy. He enjoyed to a very exceptional extent the trust of his colleagues and the respect of his political opponents. The warmth and kindliness of his character glow down the years; he was not regarded as partisan; his social radicalism—which was genuine—won him admiration among the Liberals, and his record of sympathy towards Imperialism and British interests evoked strong support among the Conservatives.[1] But it is difficult to believe that Grey fully appreciated the direction in which British foreign policy was now moving. He believed in the Concert of Europe. He believed in the preservation of peace. He had little understanding of the brutal realities of European power-politics. He lacked Rosebery's or Salisbury's intuitive knowledge of how nations saw their futures or sought their aspirations. He viewed Europe from afar. Furthermore, he was under pressure from all sides. The Liberals loathed expenditure on armaments, the overwhelming mood of the Liberal Party was pacific, and French and Russian ambitions were viewed by many with no less suspicion than those of Germany. He followed Rosebery's tactic of secrecy in his conduct of foreign affairs, and his colleagues were in general very inadequately informed of his actions, and of their implications. Thus, when the crisis came at the end of July 1914 few Ministers had any realisation of the trap in which they had been caught. But in the Services, and in the Foreign Office itself, where the powerful personality of Sir Eyre Crowe was dominant, there was strong pressure to convert loose entente agreements into precise and binding alliances. Grey, while aware of the strength of these arguments, did not or would not carry them out. He achieved the worst of all possible situations, in which there was no clear understanding by the European powers of what the

[1] The title of 'the Unionist Party', first suggested by Lord Randolph Churchill in 1886 to cover the Conservatives and those Liberals who opposed Irish Home Rule, lasted until 1921, and the party still calls itself 'the Conservative and Unionist Party'. But in this volume it will be described as the Conservative Party throughout.

British would or would not do in the event of a serious crisis, and yet had permitted commitments which severely reduced the freedom of manoeuvre which had been the key element of British European policy. Of these facts the majority of the British Cabinet were wholly unaware. Thus, Britain drifted along, while war-fever began to mount.

On this latter point, a digression may be permitted. One of the most interesting aspects of popular literature in Europe from 1900 onwards was the considerable preoccupation with future wars. In 1900 a German writer, Karl Eisenhart, described a war against Britain; an English author, Colonel Maude, published in the same year *The New Battle of Dorking* which envisaged a French invasion of Britain. In *The Invaders* (1900), Louis Tracy related the fortunes of a secret Franco-German invasion. In Max Pemberton's *Pro Patria* (1901) a secret Channel Tunnel from which Britain was to be invaded by the French was opportunely discovered by a British officer. In March 1900—at the height of the Boer War—*Le Monde Illustré* devoted an entire issue to an illustrated account of a Franco-British war; a 'Capitaine Danrit' (whose real name was Driant, and who was killed at Verdun) described a swift invasion and total defeat of Britain, proving that 'Britain is really a colossus with feet of clay'.

Such publications had been intermittent since the 1870s, and the first authentic example was probably Sir George Chesney's *The Battle of Dorking*, first published in the May issue of *Blackwood's Magazine* in 1871. The interesting features of the publications at the beginning of the century were their quantity and their choice of enemies. Until the early 1900s, British authors usually chose France as the enemy, and the French were divided between Germany and Britain; after 1904 Germany held the field. In Germany itself there was little interest in this *genre* until about 1904, but subsequently it was as popular in that country as elsewhere; on the whole, England had the edge over France as the likely foe.

Perhaps the most sensational single work—and unquestionably the only example of real and lasting literature—was Erskine Childers' classic *The Riddle of the Sands* (1903), which described how a young and rather pompous amateur yachtsman cruising with a friend in the Friesland Islands blundered across a German rehearsal for a full-scale invasion of England. No less a person than the Kaiser himself appeared, and it was not surprising that in Germany copies were confiscated. In England it had a spectacular success, and several hundred thousand copies of the cheap edition were sold. More was to be heard later of the author, at that time a clerk in the House of Commons.

Few could rise to this standard, but William Le Queux and Guy du Maurier—whose play, *An Englishman's Home*, opened in 1908 and ran for eighteen months—approached it. In 1906 Le Queux serialised in the *Daily Mail* an account of a German invasion of England that sold a million copies when published in book form, and was translated into twenty-seven languages; in the German edition the ending—a total German defeat—was tactfully omitted. The work was specially commissioned by Harmsworth, and Le Queux not only spent four months in the probable invasion area but had worked out with Lord Roberts the most likely German tactics. For sales reasons, the final account involved battles up and down the country, and *Daily Mail* sandwich men, dressed in Prussian uniforms and helmets, stalked the streets. The success was phenomenal. Lord Roberts wrote an introduction to the book version:

> The catastrophe that may happen if we still remain in our present state of unpreparedness is vividly and forcibly illustrated in Mr. Le Queux's new book which I recommend to the perusal of every one who has the welfare of the British Empire at heart.

Humour was, alas, rarely seen, although the opening chapter in *The Riddle of the Sands* is a very notable exception. Another was the young P. G. Wodehouse's *The Swoop! Or How Clarence Saved England*, a sadly neglected work of this brilliant writer, which relates how nine invasion armies stormed wildly across the country, wholly ignored by the inhabitants. Russians, Germans, Swiss, Chinese, Young Turks, Moroccan brigands, the Mad Mullah and the Prince of Monaco were actively involved. In these irritating excitements cricket, golf, and normal life continued unperturbed; Londoners complained of the noise; the news of the invasion was given in the Stop Press between the racing results and the cricket scores. Eventually the locals became annoyed, the invaders fell into severe disputes with each other, and went home. The book was not a commercial success.

Another interesting point about this literature—which had become very voluminous by 1914—was the fact that very few of the authors foretold the future with any accuracy. There were, however, some notable exceptions. A Captain Guggisberg in 1903 described a German invasion of Belgium and a consequent British involvement in a European war. H. G. Wells anticipated the tank in his short story 'The Land Ironclads', and, astonishingly, the atomic bomb—by name—in *The World Set Free*, giving the year 1959 when every Power 'went to war in a delirium of panic, in order to use their bombs first', and describing the consequent 'unquenchable crimson conflagration of the atomic bombs'. This, also, was a commercial failure. When Conan Doyle, in the July issue of the *Strand Magazine* in 1914, anticipated the defeat of Britain as a result of a naval blockade by enemy submarines he was formally, officially, and majestically censured for alarmism by responsible naval opinion.[1]

These works have much more than a mere antiquarian interest. Their volume and popularity give at least some measure of the alarm and interest in war matters that existed in Europe from 1900 onwards. Henry Newbolt has written of his generation that 'we spent all our lives among warring nations, and in grave anticipation of the supreme danger which broke upon us at last'. The popular reaction to the Dreadnought crisis in 1908 and the vehemence of the popular Press undoubtedly played its part. Writing in the *Nineteenth Century* in August 1911, General Sir Reginald Hart declared that 'War represents motion and life, whereas a too prolonged peace heralds in stagnation, decay, and death'. Certainly in the Services, there was little doubt of who the future enemy was to be.

Their view was given strong support by the actions of the German Government. The British made many mistakes in this period, but their recognition of the essential belligerence and expansionism of Germany was well-founded. France, although with an immense army, was weak at sea. The large and rambling Austrian-Hungarian Empire was in clear decomposition, and the deposition of the Sultanate in Turkey and the accession of a group of arrogant, brutal, and ambitious officers under the evil genius of Enver Pasha had done nothing to reverse the relentless disintegration of the Ottoman Empire. Here, too, the Germans were eager and active. Wherever one looked in Europe during these years, the presence of German interest and ambition was evident, and it was not at all fanciful to see the very real possibility of a Europe—and even a Middle East—dominated by Germany. It was

[1] See I. F. Clark: *The Tale of the Future* (1961). Quoted in A. J. Marder: *From the Dreadnought to Scapa Flow* (vol. I, 1961), p. 3.

this prospect that so concerned the Foreign Office, and it was based upon the new stern realities of the situation.

But—and this was particularly true of the public awakening to the softly developing crisis—it was the building of a modern North Sea Fleet which provided a direct challenge that could not be ignored. All attempts to end the naval race by negotiation failed; the last ones were in 1912, when Haldane proposed to the Kaiser a lowering of the British superiority rate, and in March 1913, when Churchill proposed a 'naval holiday' in battleship construction. The German Government proceeded relentlessly on its course. The Cabinet decided to retain a sixty per cent superiority of Dreadnought strength and build two keels to one; it was also decided to increase the association with the Dominions for Imperial defence and to withdraw from the Mediterranean, leaving that area to the French, and concentrating on the North Sea and the Channel. It was this decision which, perhaps almost more than the military conversations, put the British in really close association with the French. Formal letters between Grey and the French Ambassador on November 22nd 1912 stated that these arrangements did not bind either Government; but each also agreed that, if danger threatened either, the two Governments would consult. Remorselessly, the freedom to manoeuvre independently, which was at the heart of late-Victorian foreign policy, was disappearing.

This became grimly evident in the Agadir crisis of 1911. The Germans had a real grievance that the French were not honouring the Algeciras agreements of 1906, but the German methods—the dispatch of a warship to Agadir, a closed port, and demands for French concessions in the Congo—compromised their case. As Asquith pointed out to the King on July 4th:

> The sudden discovery of German 'subjects' and 'threatened interests' in the immediate neighbourhood of the only harbour on the western coast of Morocco which can be developed into a naval and commercial base, facing the Atlantic, is an interesting illustration of 'Real-Politik'.

The crisis was important for another reason. It drew Lloyd George out of his marked pacifist stage. 'I think *au fond* he has a strong element of Jingoism in his nature', Winston Churchill had written to Rosebery in 1905. 'I should not be surprised to see that develop with the exercise of power.'[1] His Mansion House speech of July 21st was a personal and national turning-point:

> I would make great sacrifices to preserve peace. I conceive that nothing would justify a disturbance of international goodwill except questions of the gravest national moment. But if a situation were to be forced upon us, in which peace could only be preserved by the surrender of the great and beneficent position Britain has won by centuries of heroism and achievement, by allowing Britain to be treated, where her interests were vitally affected, as if she were of no account in the Cabinet of Nations, then I say emphatically that peace at that price would be a humiliation intolerable for a great country like ours to endure.

This was a very serious crisis, at which, at one point, war seemed more probable than peace. But although it was resolved, it had momentous consequences. The revelation to the Cabinet of naval unpreparedness, furthermore, resulted in Winston Churchill replacing Reginald McKenna at the Admiralty. Churchill's period as First Lord was to be tumultuous and controversial, but the advantages far outweighed the errors that he committed. Churchill's sense of the melodramatic, his overwhelming egotism and lack of tact in dealing with men older and more experienced than himself, made him many enemies in the Navy, and not all his actions proved to be wise. But he injected into naval affairs an energy and a decisiveness which had been lacking under McKenna, and which were to ensure that the Royal Navy remained, by 1914, the greatest sea power in the world. Since they had first met in 1906, Churchill had held a high regard for the opinions of the former First Sea Lord, Lord Fisher, now in retirement but still intensely active and vehement. Between 1911 and 1914 they were in constant communication and in substantial agreement about what must be done. The conversion of Churchill and Lloyd George, the two most vigorous opponents of the Dreadnought programme of 1907–8, was a most significant event. Although they were at loggerheads over the issue of the Naval Estimates early in 1914, this was a formidable combination.

The general deterioration in Anglo-German relations, and in particular the potentially perilous situation in the Balkans, combined to edge Britain towards total European involvement. From this Grey

[1] Rosebery Papers (Churchill to Rosebery, May 9th, 1905).

and the Cabinet shrank, yet the actions of the British Government between 1907 and 1914, taken collectively, presented it with less and less opportunity for disengagement. All plans for the part to be played by a British Expeditionary Force were based on the assumption of joining with the French Army against Germany, and British naval dispositions were also based on the same premise.

The inflexibility of the plans of all the Great Powers has been constantly emphasised by historians of the pre-war period, and this emphasis is fully merited. The concept of 'contingency plans' did not exist. The German military plan was for a bold sweep through Belgium to envelop the French defences; this presupposed British neutrality. The German *naval* plans, however, assumed hostile British participation. The French plan was for an immediate assault upon the lost provinces of Alsace-Lorraine, with the British Army protecting their left flank and the Navy guarding the Channel and the North Sea. Russian support, to divert and hold down substantial German forces, was also assumed. The British position did not mean automatic participation in a Franco-German war, but the distinction was somewhat unrealistic. The plans themselves were dangerous enough— the assumptions were even more perilous. Until something happened, no one really knew what would happen.

The pacific element in the Cabinet, the Liberal Party, and particularly in the Labour Party, was powerful. To this group, prospect of involvement in a European war was anathema, and was rarely considered probable. Two leading Liberal dailies, the *Daily News* (edited by A. G. Gardiner) and the *Manchester Guardian* (edited by C. P. Scott), and the weekly *Nation* (edited by H. W. Massingham), were strongly opposed to any British intervention in any European war. It had been with considerable difficulty, and at the cost of a Cabinet crisis, that Churchill had been able to get his Estimates for 1914-15 agreed, and then only on the understanding that those for 1915-16 would show substantial reductions. At the height of the debates in the Cabinet at the end of July 1914, Asquith noted of the strongly anti-interventionist views of Lord Morley (Lord President of the Council) and Sir John Simon (Attorney-General) that 'This no doubt is the view for the moment of the bulk of the party', and all the available evidence strongly supports this conclusion. Up to August 3rd Ministers were being vigorously urged by Liberal and Labour associations throughout the country to keep Britain out of the European crisis.

This crisis, when it came on July 24th, was wholly unexpected. Between January 29th and July 24th the Cabinet discussed foreign affairs only twice—on May 14th (when the suggestion that military conversations with Russia should be opened was turned down, although naval co-operation should be extended) and on May 21st when the deportation of a Turkish officer at Durazzo by Austria and Italy without consultation was raised by Grey; in addition, on June 26th it was agreed to grant £100,000 to Persia 'to keep the gendarmeries going', and on July 2nd a possible British base in the Persian Gulf was discussed. There was no general discussion on foreign affairs before July 24th. The British and German Governments had come to an agreement concerning the Baghdad–Berlin Railway in June; relations with Russia over Persia had reached a low point.

All politicians were obsessed by the Irish Question, and the real possibility of civil war. The European situation seemed calm. There was, accordingly, no immediate appreciation of the seriousness of the situation when the assassination of the Archduke Prince Ferdinand of Austria in Sarajevo set in motion immense forces. The successfully resolved crises in the Balkans in 1912 and 1913 had lulled apprehensions. Thus, it was only very slowly that the magnitude of the new crisis impressed itself vigorously upon Ministers. On July 24th, after hearing of the brutal Austrian ultimatum to Serbia, Asquith noted that 'Happily there seems to be no reason why we should be anything more than spectators.' Morley's account records that after Grey's statement about the developing situation on the Continent and the need for a fundamental decision about Britain's role, 'the Cabinet seemed to heave a sort of sigh, and a moment or two of breathless silence fell upon us'.

When it became apparent that this was a real war-crisis, the Cabinet broke apart. By July 28th it was evident that, out of twenty Ministers, there was a potential 'peace party' of ten, of whom Lloyd George, Morley, Burns, and Harcourt were the most significant. It is very doubtful that a positive declaration by the British Government at this stage would have stopped the ponderous war-machines that were now heaving laboriously into action all over Europe; but the British Government was in no condition to deliver such a declaration. On July 29th it proceeded cautiously towards the heart of the matter, the threatened neutrality of Belgium. Morley described the discussion as 'thin and perfunctory', and Asquith reported to the King that:

After much discussion it was agreed that Sir E. Grey should be authorised to inform the German and French Ambassadors that at this stage we were unable to pledge ourselves in advance either under all conditions to stand aside, or in any conditions to join in.

Asquith, Grey, Churchill—'with his best daemonic energy', in Morley's words—and Haldane were the most vigorous advocates of intervention, and certainly Churchill was the most vehement, **demanding** immediate mobilisation. Asquith, although in basic agreement with Grey, was cool. His main preoccupation was to keep the Cabinet united during what Churchill called 'this flaming week'. Although Asquith supported Grey, his attitude on the main question strengthened only gradually. As late as August 1st he was writing that 'I am still *not quite* hopeless about peace, tho' far from hopeful'.

'The Cabinet', as Churchill has written, 'was overwhelmingly pacific.' On the 28th it approved his decision—actually taken in the first place by Prince Louis of Battenberg, the First Sea Lord—to postpone the dispersal of the First and Second Fleets after manoeuvres. But the dissensions were acute. 'Had it not been for Asquith', Grey has written, 'the outbreak of war might have found us with a Cabinet in disorder or dissolution, impotent to take any decision.' But resolution of the crisis needed time. The French expostulated, the European war-machines were in motion. On July 31st Grey informed the French that he was still unable to 'give any pledge at the present time'. He also asked the French and German Ambassadors whether their Governments would respect Belgian neutrality, and asked the Belgian Government whether it would fight if invaded. The French and Belgians replied affirmatively; the Germans refused to make any statement one way or the other. On July 30th Austria declared war on Serbia, and Grey's proposal for another London conference to settle the Balkans dispute was abortive.

On August 1st the British Cabinet was on the point of disintegration, and the City of London was strongly pacific. That evening Germany and Russia were at war. Anti-war demonstrations were hurriedly planned in London. On August 2nd Burns resigned when it was agreed that the German Fleet would not be permitted to enter the Channel. Other resignations loomed. On the same day the Unionist leaders sent a letter urging support of France and Russia but making no reference to Belgium. Burns was adamant against involvement,

Morley and Beauchamp were close behind him, and it was evident that Lewis Harcourt (Colonial Secretary) and Sir John Simon were on the verge of resignation. 'We came, every now and again, near to the parting of the ways', Asquith recorded. But Lloyd George was beginning to move in the direction of the interventionists. When the Cabinet met on August 3rd Burns, Morley, Simon and Lord Beauchamp had resigned. Churchill had made overtures to the Conservative leader Bonar Law for a possible Coalition Government, but he was acting alone and Law did not respond. With this exception, there was no consultation at all between the principal party leaders on a matter of such momentous importance for the nation. But the news of the German ultimatum to Belgium and its rejection earlier that morning had transformed the situation, and it was Lloyd George who successfully appealed to the four Ministers to postpone their resignations and to sit on the Treasury Bench.

Grey's statement in the Commons that afternoon is often cited as one of those rare occasions when a speech swings the House of Commons. It can now be seen that its principal legal point—British commitment to Belgium—was dubious, and that Grey's claim that 'if we are engaged in war we shall suffer but little more than we shall suffer if we stand aside' should have been more thoroughly questioned. But that extraordinary phenomenon, which we can only call war-fever, had gripped the House of Commons as avidly as it had Europe. When the Cabinet met on August 4th, only Burns and Morley had resigned, Redmond had declared the support of Ireland, and only a fragment of the Labour Party had expressed its opposition to war. The only business was to approve the issue of an ultimatum to Germany to withdraw from Belgium, to expire at 11 p.m.

Outside Parliament, the movements to oppose the war had been overtaken by events. The attitude of the Labour Party was somewhat confused, and it, also, had serious divisions. On Sunday, August 2nd, there had been a demonstration against the war in Trafalgar Square, addressed by Keir Hardie, H. M. Hyndman, George Lansbury and Arthur Henderson. But at a meeting on the following morning of Labour MPs it was clear that they were seriously divided. In the event, only Ramsay MacDonald and the Independent Labour Party members opposed the war. After Grey's triumph, only MacDonald had asked the fundamental question, Was Britain in danger? On August 5th he resigned as leader, and was replaced by Arthur

Henderson. He was at the time, and for many years, most cruelly excoriated. But this courageous action was to begin the process whereby he was to rise to be the first Labour Prime Minister of Britain.

But he and his tiny band were a minority indeed. Other bodies, such as the hastily formed Neutrality Committee and the Neutrality League, had hardly begun activity before war was declared. A full-page appeal by the League against the war was published in the *Daily News* on August 5th, a pathetic memento of a movement that never had time to plead its cause. The violation of Belgium had united the Cabinet, the Liberals, and the country. The carefully prepared plans of the War Office and the Admiralty were now put into operation. Europe marched joyously, and with ardent expectations, into catastrophe.

*

Britain went to war in a glow of national unity. The German invasion of Belgium seemed to sweep away the disputes and controversies that had occupied the nation for the previous decade. Home Rule was to be postponed until the end of the war, and Irishmen from north and south enlisted in the British Army. The struggle between the Conservative Opposition and the Liberal Government was covered by a display of all-party concord. The Liberal Party and the trade unions pledged their support. In the Commons on August 3rd Ramsay MacDonald had courageously declared that 'whatever may be said about us, we will take the action . . . of saying that this country ought to have remained neutral, because in the deepest parts of our hearts we believe that that was right and that that alone was consistent with the honour of our country and the traditions of the Party that are now in office.' But MacDonald's was almost a lone voice raised in protest, and after his replacement as chairman of the Parliamentary Labour Party by Arthur Henderson opposition to the war, to all practical purposes, did not exist. It was this unity which, although sorely tried, was to bring Britain through a war whose magnitude was undreamed of in August 1914.

But the events that had preceded the war in British domestic politics could not be swept aside. No Act of Oblivion could be passed. The circumstances of the political struggle had been drastically changed, and were to be even more drastically changed before the end of the war, but the struggle itself could not for long be suppressed.

As Mr. A. J. P. Taylor has emphasised,[1] the Englishman in 1914 was a very free agent. Since 1905, State expenditure on the social services had roughly doubled, but the impact was small. The State now protected the very needy to a modest extent, and rather less than eight per cent of the national income went on taxes. There was no compulsory military service, no limitations on the freedom of the law-abiding citizen to go where he liked, do what he liked, and buy what he liked. The apparatus of the State, familiar in France and Germany, and to an even greater extent in Russia, barely existed at all in the England of 1914. Unemployment stood at just over three per cent. On the debit side, however, was the fact that although income tax did not start until a man's income exceeded £160 per annum there were less than one and a quarter million taxpayers —or less than seven per cent of the occupied population. Some two and a half per cent of the population owned two-thirds of the nation's wealth. The average annual wage of the industrial worker was £75 per annum; that of the salaried middle class was £340. As Charles Masterman has written, 'the rich despise the Working Class; the Middle Class fear them'. But although this situation was potentially dangerous, there seemed to be no problems that could not, eventually, be solved without any untoward disturbances. Britain was still a very rich nation. Her navy had an immense reputation, and, numerically, an overwhelming preponderance over any possible rival. The Empire was united. It was perhaps in this self-assurance and confidence that Britain presented to superficial observers her most formidable and impressive characteristics.

*

The opening six weeks of the war constituted in many respects the most dramatic and exciting period of all. Europe surged to the colours. There was never a more popular war. The generals and the admirals were at last able to put in motion, and test in action, their long-prepared plans. The Russian steamroller started to move purposefully westwards. The Schlieffen Plan progressed smoothly. The French marched ardently into Alsace-Lorraine. The British Expeditionary Force was conveyed swiftly and efficiently across the Channel in conditions of deep secrecy to take up its allotted position on the

[1] *English History, 1914–45,* 1.

French left flank. The Navy at once initiated the blockade of Germany, and one of its first actions was to cut the Germans' Transatlantic cable.

In a sense, everything was going to plan and nothing was going to plan. The most striking feature of these opening manoeuvres was their remarkable lack of mutual relevance. Europe was marching and counter-marching, immense armies were deploying into well-rehearsed positions, but the relationship between these formidable movements was, initially, difficult to determine. Indeed, were it not for the very hugeness of these forces, one has the feeling that they might have marched indefinitely without making serious collision.

The first month of the war saw the plans of every belligerent go bitterly agley. The Germans had not expected a Russian invasion of East Prussia, and were temporarily thrown off balance. Then, the Russians were brought to a shattering halt at Tannenberg. The French were bundled ignominiously out of Alsace-Lorraine. The Belgian resistance was more severe than the Germans had anticipated; the massive German bombardments of the Belgian fortresses were infinitely more severe than anyone had expected. The Schlieffen Plan then went forward after this temporary setback with an ease which the Germans had never expected. The German armies marched through militarily deserted countryside while their lines of communication became dangerously extended. On August 22nd two British divisions of the B.E.F. blundered into six divisions of the German 1st Army at Mons. It is difficult to say which side was the more surprised; probably the Germans. If the dramatic appearance of the British in Belgium was a shock to the Germans, the vigour and efficiency of their fighting was even greater. Since the Boer War the British Army had laid great emphasis upon musketry, and the devastating effect of the British rifle-fire at Mons passed into legend. But it was impossible to hold the position when the French 5th Army on the British right fell back, and the retreat from Mons began. On August 26th the IInd Corps, under Smith-Dorrien, fought a brilliant but costly rearguard action at Le Cateau. After this the British retreat could continue undisturbed. They marched 200 miles in thirteen days, almost due south. The bewilderment and exhaustion of the troops were alike considerable. Unmolested, the German 1st Army continued its sweeping movement to the south-west.

Britain had gone to war in a somewhat magisterial manner. At 10.30 p.m. on the evening of August 4th the King held a Privy Council which was attended by only one Minister—ironically, Beauchamp, the First Commissioner of Works, who succeeded Morley as Lord President of the Council on the following day—which sanctioned the proclamation of the declaration of war with Germany. The Cabinet was not involved. The Empire was not consulted. Each Governor-General, as the King's representative, issued the royal proclamation. No objection was necessary. The Empire was solidly for the war.

Asquith did not consider that the emergency justified any major changes in the Government. No consideration was given to the possibility of a Coalition. Relations between the two parties were so bad that it would have been difficult for either side to work harmoniously with the other, and there was, in addition, the antipathy between Asquith and Bonar Law. Had Arthur Balfour still been the Conservative leader, it might possibly have been different. Asquith always showed Balfour particular favour, and he had retained his position on the Committee of Imperial Defence.

There was, however, one notable change in the Cabinet. Lord Kitchener, the conqueror of the Sudan, the (eventual) victor in South Africa, and also the victor over Curzon in India, and, since 1911, 'British representative' in Egypt, was regarded as a great capture as Secretary of State for War. Kitchener's prestige was enormous, and this widespread confidence was not wholly misplaced. Kitchener was not as great a man as his contemporaries generally believed, but he was a far greater one than his many subsequent detractors have alleged. On all the big issues he was right. When everyone said that the war would be brief, Kitchener startled the Cabinet when he sombrely retorted that it would be long. Enormous new armies had to be created and equipped. He took on his shoulders all the burdens of the Army. The officers of the General Staff, so laboriously created by Haldane, were bundled off to the war and their places filled by nonentities. Kitchener's achievements were astounding, and, for a time, the Cabinet was awed. 'All-powerful, imperturbable, reserved, he dominated absolutely our counsels at this time', as Churchill has recorded. But Kitchener did too much; the burden was too great. Edward Grey's estimate of Kitchener is perhaps the most fair:

> His conception of work was that it must be a one man job. He shouldered the responsibility, and did the work of a Titan; but he did not realize that general responsibility must be shared with the

Cabinet, and strategic responsibility with the most independent and expert military brains, organized in a General Staff; he abided loyally by this decision, which he accepted; but he seemed to regard it rather as a supersession of himself than as an addition of strength. Nor did he realize that for an Army such as he was raising, the whole industries of the country must be organized for war, and that this could not be done inside the War Office.

Yet no one but Kitchener measured the dimensions of the war with such prescience; no one but he foresaw how great would be the need for men, and from the first moment he prepared accordingly. He inspired the country with the magnitude of the military need, and gave it confidence. It may be that before his end came all that was in his power to contribute to winning the war had been given. But without that contribution the war might have been lost, or victory rendered impossible.[1]

There was a considerable gulf between Kitchener and the rest of the Cabinet. Kitchener, like most soldiers, was a Conservative. He regarded his political colleagues with, at best, distaste. To Rosebery he remarked that the Cabinet merited the Victoria Cross for declaring war with such inadequate resources. He was dismayed by the paucity of the British military capacity. 'Did they (the Government) consider when they went headlong into a war like this, that they were without an army, and without any preparations to equip one?' he enquired with justification. He also remarked that 'my colleagues tell military secrets to their wives, except X who tells them to other people's wives'. Kitchener's taciturnity and lack of confidence in his colleagues was both distressing and disconcerting to them. Lloyd George subsequently compared him to 'one of those revolving lighthouses which radiate momentary gleams of revealing light far out into the surrounding gloom and then suddenly relapse into complete darkness'. Matters were complicated further by the bad relations that existed between Kitchener and Sir John French, commanding the B.E.F. French, at least for the first six months of the war, had the full confidence of Asquith, and was also close to Churchill. Again, Kitchener was right.

Asquith's decision to invite Kitchener to join the Cabinet does not appear to have been thought out in advance. Kitchener had been about to return to Egypt on August 3rd, and had reached Dover when

[1] Grey: *Twenty-Five Years*, 246.

he was recalled to London and asked to hold himself ready for consultation. When, on August 5th, Asquith invited him to become Secretary for War, the Prime Minister did so apparently on the grounds that no member of the Cabinet was suitable, and he himself described it as a 'hazardous experiment'. It was an enormously popular decision, and henceforth, whether they liked it or not, Ministers were tied to Kitchener. If his reputation with the Cabinet steadily declined, that with the public steadily rose, to the point that removing him became a political impossibility.

The structure of government was unaltered by the outbreak of war. Parliament dispersed for the summer recess on August 10th. There were some important measures—including the closing of military areas to aliens, the forbidding of trade with the enemy, and the requisitioning of merchant ships—taken by proclamation. But the theme was, as Churchill declared, 'business as usual'. It was to be a long time before the fatal inadequacy of this approach was appreciated. The first War Budget, in November, raised the 9d income tax paid by those with an income between £160 and £500 a year to 1s 6d. The duty on tea was raised from 3d to 8d per pound, and that on beer raised by a penny. That was all. *The Economist* described the measures as constituting 'an unprecedented sacrifice'. 'No government action', the President of the Board of Trade informed the Commons, 'could overcome economic laws, and any interference with those laws must end in disaster.'

When the war broke out, Britain had less than 250,000 men in the Regular Army, scattered around the world. Expenditure on the Army before the war was running at less than £30 millions, whereas that on the Navy was over £50 millions. The effect of this order of priorities was quickly apparent. The British Army was admirably trained and proficient with the rifle. But it was too small. Each Division had only twenty-four machine-guns, or two per battalion. It had virtually no hand grenades, entrenching tools or howitzers. There was almost no mechanisation; the British Army had a total stock of eighty motor vehicles, whereas each Division had 5,600 horses. There were no field telephones or wireless equipment. Haldane had done a great deal, but his widely praised economies now began to reveal their serious impact on the efficiency of the Army.

But the main problem was simply one of size. On August 6th Parliament authorised an increase of half a million men; on September 15th it authorised another half-million. In November another million was added, and then, in December, a third and fourth million. Over two and a half million men had enlisted before voluntary recruitment came to an end in March 1916. Such an enormously increased Army had to be based upon the existing cadres, and to rely heavily upon the officers and non-commissioned officers of the Regular Army. But, by the end of 1914, this vital experienced material had been decimated in France. Unlike any other army in Europe, therefore, the British had to start from the beginning in creating their new armies. The combination of old or failed officers and raw troops was not an efficient one. This citizens' army did wonders, but it was, from the very outset operating under grievous limitations.

This was, furthermore, to be a volunteer army. Of all the major belligerents Britain was the only one that put its faith in voluntary recruitment. The pre-war Liberal hostility to the idea of conscription was firmly retained and, as the volunteers poured in at a rate that overwhelmed the arrangements for coping with them, they seemed to be justified. The long-term social perils of this policy were not perceived in 1914, nor even in 1915.

The doctrine of 'Business as Usual' also applied to the central government. The Cabinet, which met irregularly, remained the private gathering of His Majesty's Ministers under the chairmanship of the Prime Minister. No records were kept, except for the formal letter written by the Prime Minister to the Sovereign, which remained a private communication. This method was not often very illuminating, even to the King, and Asquith's reports—which compare very unfavourably in content with those of Salisbury and Balfour during the Boer War—frequently contained such statements as this in 1916:

> Considerable discussion took place, without any definite conclusion being reached, on a number of miscellaneous topics.

The imperfections of this arrangement had been evident long before 1914, and had been at least partly responsible for the confusion in the Balfour Government in 1903 over the corn duties.[1] Nothing, however, had been done. No knowledge of Cabinet decisions was disseminated, and no positive instructions given to Departments. As Curzon subsequently wrote:

[1] See Volume I, p. 208.

The Cabinet often had the haziest notion as to what its decisions were. . . . Cases frequently arose when the matter was left so much in doubt that a Minister went away and acted upon what he thought was a decision, which subsequently turned out to be no decision at all, or was repudiated by his colleagues.

A good example of the remoteness of the Cabinet from the really important decisions concerned the deployment of the B.E.F. On August 6th a Council of War, consisting of sixteen men—'most entirely ignorant of their subject' as General Sir Henry Wilson tartly commented—debated the matter; only four Ministers—Asquith, Churchill, Grey and Haldane—attended. The meeting had to accept Wilson's brusque statement that the B.E.F. had no choice, and must go to Maubeuge, on the French left. On the following day the Cabinet insisted that, of these seven divisions, two must stay at home. Kitchener persuaded them to change the destination from Maubeuge to Amiens. Under pressures from Wilson and the French, Kitchener changed his mind on August 12th. On September 1st he sent French one of the remaining divisions. Thus, without the Cabinet having any real say in the matter at all, the B.E.F. was committed as part of the French Army, tied irrevocably to the decisions and actions of the French commanders.

Attempts to improve this slipshod organisation were unimpressive. In November a War Council was set up, in which all the deficiencies of the Cabinet system were repeated and a few new ones added for good measure. The War Council consisted of Asquith, Grey, Lloyd George, Churchill, Kitchener, Sir Archibald Wolfe Murray (Chief of the Imperial General Staff), Fisher[1] and Balfour. McKenna, Lewis Harcourt and Admiral Sir Arthur Wilson were subsequently added. The War Council met irregularly, and only when the Prime Minister deemed it necessary. It did not work to an agenda. It did not forward its conclusions to the Cabinet. Its proceedings were kept by the secretary of the Committee of Imperial Defence, Maurice Hankey, in manuscript. It received very few departmental memoranda. In no sense did it superintend the day-to-day operation of the war. There was, furthermore, a fatal misunderstanding about the role of the Service members. The atmosphere of Council meetings was that of a

[1] Fisher had replaced Battenberg as First Sea Lord after a scurrilous Press campaign against the latter's alleged German connections.

Cabinet meeting to which Service advisers had been invited, to speak when spoken to. 'It is a mistake to call us members of the War Council', Fisher subsequently stated: 'it was no such thing. We were the experts there who were to open our mouths when told to.' The awesome presence of the taciturn and glowering Kitchener effected the total silence of Wolfe Murray. This new organisation was not a success; indeed, it did little more than to add a committee to the government structure and take up the time of busy men.

But the problem went far deeper than one of organisation. Men and attitudes are always more important than organisation.

With the exception of Kitchener and Churchill, there was not a single member of the Government or the War Council with any practical military experience of any kind. Virtually none had hitherto shown any interest in the subject. The majority, indeed, regarded it with repugnance. Some—notably Lloyd George—picked up the essentials in due course; the majority did not. Virtually from the beginning of the war there was a mutual antipathy between the military and the politicians, which was to develop into a wide and bitter gulf. There was no individual comparable to General Ismay in the Second World War, who had the confidence of all. Kitchener could have played such a role, but chose not to, and in any event was unsuited to it. The soldiers played politics—notably French and Sir Douglas Haig—and the politicians played at war. Churchill initially, and then closely challenged by Lloyd George, hungered for active and personal control over military matters. Each side cultivated the Press and was not reticent in its complaints about the other. What began as an uneasy entente gradually degenerated into a ferocious, squalid, and implacable enmity.

Furthermore, the Government lacked leadership. In a revealing self-portrait, Asquith once wrote that:

> Some people, sadly wanting in perspective, went so far as to call you 'chivalrous'; it would be nearer the truth to say that you had, or acquired, a rather specialised faculty of insight and manipulation in dealing with diversities of character and temperament.[1]

This was no longer enough. Asquith's techniques of managing a Cabinet had worked well in peacetime, although in both the Constitutional Crisis of 1909–11 and the Home Rule Crisis of 1912–14 its

[1] Roy Jenkins: *Asquith*, 336.

limitations had been apparent. They were grievously inadequate for wartime leadership. The preservation of Cabinet unity was important, but not as important as the reaching of quick decisions and following a policy. As Churchill commented in a 1915 Cabinet memorandum:

> Nothing leads more surely to disaster than that a military plan should be pursued with crippled steps and in a lukewarm spirit in the face of continued nagging within the executive circle. Unity ought not to mean that a number of gentlemen are willing to sit together on condition either that the evil day of decision is postponed, or that not more than a half-decision should be provisionally adopted. . . . The soldiers who are ordered to their deaths have a right to a plan, as well as a cause.

Asquith had been Prime Minister for six and a half years by August 1914. He was in his sixty-third year. It has been frequently emphasised that he had never, since his second marriage, been averse to the pleasures of the table, and he was the first Prime Minister in modern times to appear in public evidently the worse for drink. But although his mind remained clear, cool, and logical, and he dominated his colleagues, close observers were concerned at his lassitude, his casualness save when aroused, and intellectual arrogance. He was at this time conducting an extraordinarily voluminous, and rather pathetic, correspondence with a young lady of twenty-one, Miss Venetia Stanley. Perhaps too much has been made of this. Asquith was not the first, nor assuredly the last, Prime Minister who needed an emotional outlet which he could not obtain from his marriage, family, or colleagues. But although he had always firmly drawn the line between 'shop' and relaxation, it seemed to some of his colleagues that the latter was becoming too prominent in his life. This may have been unfair, but it can hardly be contested that Asquith's bland and often dilatory methods of conducting political business were totally unsuited to the conduct of a major war.

He still enjoyed very considerable prestige, and his air of calm and magisterial wisdom continued to dominate men who had worked with him for so long, and who had developed not only respect but personal affection for him. But, if at this early stage doubts began to arise about the suitability of his talents for this situation, they were only doubts. At the time, only Churchill and Lloyd George were seriously critical of the manner in which the war was being conducted, and both were careful not to criticise Asquith personally. Later, it was different. As Lloyd George was subsequently to write: 'There was no co-ordination of effort. There was no connected plan of action. There was no sense of the importance of time.' Churchill, characteristically, favoured leadership of a decisive, semi-authoritarian, nature: 'No man', he wrote afterwards, 'had the power to give clear, brutal orders which would command unquestioning respect. Power was widely disseminated among the many important personages who in this period formed the governing instrument.'

By September the war plans of every belligerent were in even greater disarray. The Germans, with Paris seemingly at their mercy, swung eastwards. A vital gap opened between the German armies. Joffre stood and fought on the Marne, and the Germans began to fall back. The pursuit was not—indeed could not—be swift enough. On September 14th the Germans stopped on the River Aisne and dug in. The British and French forces were checked, some 200 miles from the sea. There then followed the celebrated 'race to the sea', which was in fact a series of attempts by each side to outflank the other before the Channel was reached. By October the opposing trench-lines writhed savagely from the Channel to the borders of Switzerland, and the first real lessons in trench warfare were being painfully learned. A melodramatic, if militarily justifiable, attempt by Churchill—in person—to hold Antwerp had ended in disaster, although it is probable that the few days gained were vital to the saving of the Channel ports. At the time, the sacrifice of the untrained marines of the Royal Naval Division—Churchill's own creation—brought him much obloquy. Subsequently, he was credited —not least by himself—with having won for the Allies 'the race to the sea'. Both censure and praise were exaggerated; the latter, certainly, ignores the fact that the brunt of the resistance was borne by the Belgians.

To this point, the B.E.F. had not been fully engaged, and its role —although important—had been peripheral to the main battles; it took virtually no part in the Battle of the Marne. Its first major battle, the so-called First Battle of Ypres (October 12th–November 11th), was a victory of sorts, but at appalling cost. More than half the original B.E.F. had now become casualties; one-tenth had been killed.

All this had been a considerable shock to the British public. In all, over a million men had been killed in the first fury of the war, and the

British losses, although small in comparison with those of the Russians, French, Austrians and Germans, were, in relation to the numbers engaged, very heavy. But it was the series of reverses at sea that caused the greater dismay.

In this respect it can be argued that the British public had expected too much. Certainly they had never expected what actually happened. The *Goeben* and *Breslau* evaded British and French warships in the Mediterranean and reached Constantinople, the first decisive step in the series of events that was to bring Turkey into the war, at the beginning of November, on the German side. On September 22nd three British cruisers were sunk by a single German submarine in the North Sea with the loss of nearly 1,500 officers and men. In the South Atlantic and Pacific a German squadron under Admiral von Spee roamed almost at will, completely destroying a small British force under Admiral Cradock at Coronel. In the Indian Ocean the cruiser *Emden* almost completely paralysed the movement of British vessels. In December a German cruiser force shelled the Hartlepools, Whitby and Scarborough, killing 137 people and injuring 592.

Of much greater seriousness, although it was not yet perceived, was the German superiority in submarines, a matter on which Churchill's judgement had proved to be seriously at fault. The British attitude to submarine warfare was a mixture of the moralistic and pragmatic. Merchant ships were armed, *ordered* to paint over their names and port of registry, and to fly the flags of neutral nations when in British waters. Some were converted into 'mystery' or 'Q' ships, heavily armed and manned by naval crews, and initially had considerable success.

At this stage, the so-called Cruiser Rules were accepted by all maritime nations. Under these, an unarmed merchant ship could be stopped, searched, and if a neutral unharmed and if a belligerent sunk, after the crew had been permitted to take to the boats. This practice was in general scrupulously observed by the Germans in the early stages of the war, and it placed their boats frequently in peril.

Churchill's approach was aggressive. Merchant captains were forbidden to obey a U-boat's command to stop, and ordered to counter-attack. The purpose was deliberate—to compel the Germans to abandon the Cruiser Rules and to take the risk of sinking a neutral ship, 'and thus', in Churchill's own words, 'embroiling Germany with *other* Great Powers'. Much, meanwhile, was made of the bestiality of this new form of warfare, and there was still little recognition in the Admiralty of the threat which the U-boats constituted to British naval superiority.

The early British reverses at sea were embarrassments rather than a dire threat to British naval supremacy, but they had a disconcerting effect. Battenberg was hounded from office by a vicious Press campaign, but was sacrificed readily enough by Churchill; his replacement by the aged Fisher had, initially, excellent results. A gigantic ship-building programme was put urgently in hand. The *Emden* was hunted down and sunk. Von Spee's squadron was destroyed at the Falkland Islands. The blockade proceeded efficiently. The German High Seas Fleet did not emerge in force, and the two fleets sparred uneasily with each other at a distance in the grey expanses of the North Sea, the monotony only varied by isolated actions such as that at the Dogger Bank, hailed as a great British victory but in reality only a relatively minor German reverse. In retrospect, it is clear that the British were winning the sea war; at the time it did not appear thus. When, at the end of October, the new battleship *Audacious* was sunk, the Cabinet decided that the news should be rigidly suppressed. In September it passed what was in effect a formal vote of censure on the officers of the Royal Navy. From general criticism of the Navy it was only a very short step to personal criticism of the ebullient Churchill.

Thus, everything had gone differently to what everyone had expected. The Western Front was established, and the machine-gun, the spade, and barbed wire were the masters. As French subsequently lamented:

> No previous experience, no conclusions I had been able to draw from campaigns in which I had taken part, or from a close study of the new conditions in which the war of today is waged, had led me to anticipate a war of positions. All my thoughts, all my prospective plans, all my possible alternative of action, were concentrated upon a war of movement and manoeuvre.

It was evident that some serious re-thinking would have to be done. The Germans, advancing in massed close formation, had been shot down by the British and French in rows with contemptuous ease. The Russians had been out-generalled and out-fought. The French doctrine—more a religion than a tactic of war—of attack *à l'outrance* had resulted in dreadful casualties and the first blunting of the ardour with which the French army and nation had gone to war. Both the French and the Germans had used their young officer cadets, the St. Cyr cadets at the Marne and the German officer-cadets on the Aisne; in each case it had been a massacre of the innocents. The ponderous German artillery had proved unsuitable for open warfare; the French seventy-five, the finest field gun in the world, was of little use against trenches. The British had virtually no artillery at all, and very few shells. The British had lost their army, and now had to fight a type of warfare for which they had no training and for which they had no equipment. But the predicament of the Russians was perhaps the worst of all. By the end of 1914 they had lost over a million men, more than a million precious rifles, had barely a week's reserve of shells, and, since the Turks closed the Dardanelles in November, had lost their warm-water outlet to the West.

It was also becoming evident that this was to be a different war in other respects. The rigour of the German repression of civilians in Belgium was equalled by the Russian ferocity in East Prussia. This was going to be a brutal war, and it was already apparent that it was one in which few distinctions were going to be made between civilian and military in culpability and suffering. The peoples of Europe began to understand the full implications of 'Total War'. These implications had not yet, however, been appreciated in Britain.

*

From August 1914 until the end of 1915 the two dominant problems for the British were *how* the war was to be fought and *where* it was to be fought.

The question of 'how' was not merely technical, although that aspect was of great importance. The conflict between laissez-faire methods and the concept of 'the nation in arms' was fundamental, and it should not be seen in party political terms. There were those in the Liberal Government—notably Lloyd George and Churchill—who gradually leaned towards the 'nation in arms' concept; there were Unionists who shrank instinctively from the prospect of military and industrial conscription. But the movement against the Asquith Government was based on the growing conviction that pre-war methods were fatally inappropriate. Unhappily, the conviction took a long time to develop.

The dilemma of 'how' and 'where' came together when the strategy of the war was being considered. The British had entered the war with very little in the way of strategical concepts, and they, like every other belligerent, had been trapped by events and chance. The fact that the British Army in France was in effect part of the French Army had at once eliminated any freedom of manoeuvre or disposition that it might have possessed; the losses sustained in the B.E.F. had finally confirmed that situation.[1] As the events of 1915 were to emphasise, the British Army was barely capable of acting in an effective subsidiary capacity in France.

The fact that the Army was in France, however, was of crucial importance. Beyond strategical and tactical arguments there were other ones. As Eyre Crowe had written to Grey on July 31st:

> The Entente has been made, strengthened, put to the test and celebrated in a manner justifying the belief that a moral bond was being forged. The whole policy of the Entente can have no meaning if it does not signify that in a just quarrel England would stand by her friends. This honourable expectation has been raised. We cannot repudiate it without exposing our good name to grave criticism.

The subsequent debate between 'Westerners' and 'Easterners' cannot be interpreted in purely rational terms. The British had incurred a strong moral and military burden in France, which many were determined to honour. But of greater importance was that defeat in France would mean, militarily, the end of the war. The guns could be heard in Kent. The enemy, it seemed indeed, was hammering at the door. In the face of such indisputable facts, the argument that the war could best be won elsewhere seemed lunatic.

Furthermore, how was the German Army—the principal enemy— to be defeated if troops and equipment were to be taken away from this decisive theatre and employed elsewhere? From these arguments —many of which were incontrovertible—there stemmed a passionate commitment by many soldiers and politicians that everything must be subordinated to the war in Flanders. No one, at the beginning of 1915, had any real concept of the magnitude of what that war was to

---

[1] British casualties up to the end of November 1914 were 842 officers and 8,631 other ranks killed; 2,097 officers and 37,264 other ranks had been wounded; 688 officers and 40,432 other ranks were listed as missing, making a total of 3,627 officers and 86,327 men who had been killed, wounded, or missing in the first four months of the war, of whom the majority had fallen in the First Battle of Ypres.

involve. In January 1915 the War Office submitted to the Cabinet a memorandum that declared that 'Germany can do no more in the way of increasing her armies, and will, a very few months hence, begin to feel the want of resources in men to keep her existing armies up to strength.'

The argument of the 'Westerners' was, however, made suspect by certain discomfiting facts. The first of these was that although the trench systems of the opposing armies were nothing to what they were to become, they already presented a very severe obstacle to any attacking force. The losses already suffered by troops, even with supporting artillery, assaulting well-trained soldiers in good positions had been unimaginably horrific. The survivors of Pickett's Charge at the Battle of Gettysburg could have borne testimony to these perils. The commanders blamed their lack of success on various factors, of which, for Sir John French, the lack of adequate shells was already becoming the most important. But, even with the trench system as it was early in 1915, the only way in which the deadlock could be broken was by the frontal assault and breakthrough. There was no alternative, no way round. It was already becoming apparent that this could only be achieved after the introduction of entirely new methods, of which the first was the use of gas by the Germans at Ypres in April 1915. Gas was, however, a perilous weapon, subject to the vagaries of the wind, and as likely to inflict equal injuries on the assailant. Its initial shock value was very great, but it was not the answer to the impasse. The commanders on both sides became obsessed by the havoc that could be rendered by artillery, if only the guns were more accurate and the shells more lethal. After which, the infantry would advance. It is easy to deride these commanders, but they were confronted by an unparalleled situation in which the only gift that modern technology appeared to offer was the skill of the artilleryman. And at this point that skill was notoriously deficient. The politicians, and Kitchener, viewed with dismay the prospect of incurring losses on the scale of First Ypres and of sending troops to 'chew barbed wire in Flanders', in Churchill's words, but they were to a considerable extent dependent upon the opinions of the officers on the spot and of French policies.

The other point that reduced the impact of the 'Westerner' argument was the simple fact that this was a war that did not merely concern France. The Russians were in dire straits. The Balkan States and Italy were hovering on the verge of intervention—but on which side? Turkey posed a continuing threat to the British position in Egypt—a fact dramatically emphasised by a daring attack on the Suez Canal in January 1915—and in Persia, and, most of all, to the Russians' south-eastern flank. Meanwhile, in Africa, an entirely separate war was being fought.

Thus, the dilemma of 'how' and 'where' was a very real one, and it was one, furthermore, to which there was no real answer. The truth of Kitchener's sombre dictum that 'we must fight war not as we would but as we must' was being fully justified within five months of the outbreak of hostilities.

The result of the debate between the 'Westerners' and the 'Easterners' throughout 1915 was a series of disastrous compromises. The British fought everywhere, and achieved nothing save further appalling casualties. No real order of priorities was agreed. With resources that were barely sufficient for one military campaign, the British were eventually running four—in France, Gallipoli, Salonika and Mesopotamia. The deficiencies of the pre-war system of Ministerial responsibility were well shown up by this situation. As General Sir William Robertson subsequently wrote:

> The Secretary of State for War was aiming at decisive results on the Western Front; the First Lord of the Admiralty was advocating a military expedition to the Dardanelles; the Secretary of State for India was devoting his attention to a campaign in Mesopotamia; the Secretary of State for the Colonies was occupying himself with several small wars in Africa; and the Chancellor of the Exchequer was attempting to secure the removal of a large part of the British Army from France to some Eastern Mediterranean theatre.

The debates on the conduct of the war were not confined to Ministerial circles. The Opposition had agreed to the suspension of normal party warfare, but the announcement that the Government proposed to put certain Home Rule measures through created a violent Parliamentary storm. Bonar Law compared the action of the Government with the German invasion of Belgium, and led a mass walk-out of his party from the Commons, which Asquith derided as 'a lot of prosaic and for the most part middle-aged gentlemen, trying to look like early French revolutionaries in the tennis court'. Asquith viewed alliance with the Conservatives with profound repugnance. When, in May 1915, it was inevitable, he did so with barely concealed distaste. 'To seem to welcome into the intimacy of the political house-hold, strange alien, hitherto hostile figures', he wrote, was a 'most intolerable task.' Until then, with the exception of Balfour's member-ship of the War Council, no Conservative had any part in the conduct of the war. Bonar Law was invited to one meeting of the War Council in March 1915; it was not a successful experiment, and was not repeated. The less seen of Mr. Bonar Law and his associates, it was felt in Liberal circles, the better. This was politically and nationally unwise. For the first nine months of the war, the Liberals bore com-plete responsibility for its conduct.

It was ironical, but very understandable, that it should be against Churchill, who favoured Coalition, that the bulk of the Conservative hostility was directed. His pre-war record had not endeared this brilliant, arrogant, impulsive, egocentric and flamboyant personality to the Opposition. Bonar Law openly detested him. Now there were the apparent fiascos of the 'Dunkirk circus'—where Churchill had directed a demonstration in September—and Antwerp. Fisher's honeymoon with Churchill had been short-lived, and he was reopening his contacts with the Opposition. Admiral Beatty put his finger on the basic problem: 'The situation is curious, two very strong and clever men, one old, wily and of vast experience, one young, self-assertive, with a great self-satisfaction, but unstable. They cannot work together, they cannot both run the show.' Churchill's own Director of Opera-tions regarded him as 'a shouting amateur', and there was mounting criticism within the Admiralty of the First Lord's personality and methods, and not least his frequent absences and involvement in matters beyond his official position. These criticisms were echoed in the Navy, in the newspapers, and in the Opposition ranks. Churchill's friend, Lord Beaverbrook, has described his position:

> His attitude from August 1914 was a noble one, too noble to be wise. He cared for the success of the British arms, especially in so far as they could be achieved by the Admiralty, and for nothing else. His passion for this aim was pure, self-devoted, and all-devouring. He failed to remember that he was a politician and as such treading a slippery path; he forgot his political tactics. . . . As he worked devotedly at his own job, the currents of political opinion slipped by him unnoticed.[1]

[1] Beaverbrook: *Politicians and the War*, 125.

This was a kindly judgement. Churchill was obsessed by the war
and by his position in its conduct. To his colleagues he seemed to be
everywhere, eager, intrusive, voluble and often hectoring, and always
seeking the limelight. He began to bore and irritate them, and confidence in his judgement and capacity was being eroded. He was
being, like his father, a young man in a hurry, and Ministers and
important elements in the Navy increasingly put down to vaulting
personal ambition what he genuinely regarded as his intense patriotism
and passion to win the war. And so he crashed along, arousing mistrust
and active dislike, but heedless of the resentment he caused.

The peril of Churchill's position was greatly increased by the fact
that he had never struck deep roots in the Liberal Party. His strength
had lain in the confidence and respect—sometimes amused and often
exasperated—with which the Liberal leaders, and particularly
Asquith, regarded him. By the beginning of 1915, however, much of
this confidence had begun to falter. In particular, Asquith's opinion
of his judgement and reliability had been undermined. 'To speak
with the tongue of men and angels', he noted at this time of Churchill,
'and to spend laborious days and nights in administration, is no good
if a man does not inspire trust.' Ths hostility of the Conservative Press
was unrelenting, led by *The Times* and the *Morning Post*.

Churchill's dismay at the events of the war at sea had been manifest
since the autumn of 1914. From the outset his attitudes had been
belligerent. He had wanted to chase the *Goeben* and *Breslau* to Constantinople. He had armed the British merchant marine and ordered
it to adopt aggressive manoeuvres against U-boats. He had authorised
the bombardment of the Dardanelles' outer defences on November
3rd before war with Turkey had been declared. At the first meeting
of the War Council early in November he had urged an attack on the
Dardanelles. He was playing with a scheme to send old battleships
up the Elbe. His eager, questing, original mind chafed at opportunities
forsaken and others ignored. Churchill's mind, Lord Halifax subsequently commented with truth, was 'a most curious mixture of a
child's emotion and a man's reason'. The historian, reading his
letters, memoranda, and comments, can easily understand why he in
turn baffled, impressed, bewildered, and enraged those with whom he
had public business. Hankey later wrote that Churchill 'had a real
zest for war. If war there must needs be, he at least could enjoy it.'
'He is a wonderful creature', Asquith wrote of him in October, 'with

a curious dash of schoolboy simplicity (quite unlike Edward Grey's) and what someone said of genius—"a zigzag streak of lightning in the brain".' It was his extraordinary fluctuation between real wisdom and superficial folly which made him so uncomfortable and so dangerous a colleague and Minister. His judgement rested almost entirely upon intuition. Often it was right, but, in F. E. Smith's words, 'when he is wrong—My God!'

But by the end of 1914 two other important individuals had come to much the same conclusion as Churchill, that it was urgently necessary to look elsewhere than France for immediate results. Lloyd George and Hankey, acting entirely independently, produced memoranda at the end of December that urged investigation of other alternatives to the Western Front. These papers coincided with an appeal for assistance, if only a diversion, from Russia to reduce the Turkish pressure in the Caucasus. In fact, the threat to the Caucasus had disappeared by the time the Russian appeal was received in London, but this was not known until some time later.

It was this conjunction of events that gave Churchill his opportunity early in January to put a plan for a naval forcing of the Dardanelles to the War Council. Having obtained provisional assent, he used the replies of the Admiral at the Straits—Carden—to persuade the War Council of the soundness of a plan which had been regarded as impossible by responsible naval and military opinion as late as 1907 and by Churchill himself in a memorandum in 1911.[1] Churchill marshalled his arguments with great care and thoroughness; his colleagues were swept along by his infectious enthusiasm. Only Kitchener and Fisher were doubtful; Kitchener because he did not want another military commitment, and Fisher because he saw in the operation a possible diminution of the strength of the Grand Fleet. More fundamentally, they regarded the operation as irrelevant to the main purpose of the war—to defeat the Germans on land and sea. But neither, after the events of the past few months, had any clear policy by which this might be achieved, and the prospect of a swift, easy, and spectacular victory over one of Germany's principal allies enraptured the War Council. 'The idea caught on at once', Hankey has recorded of the vital Council meeting of January 13th. 'The War Council turned eagerly from the dreary vista of a "slogging match" on

[1] 'It should be remembered that it is no longer possible to force the Dardanelles, and nobody would expose a modern fleet to such peril.'

the Western Front to brighter prospects, as they seemed, in the Mediterranean. . . . Churchill unfolded his plans with the skill that might be expected of him, lucidly but quietly and without exaggerated optimism'. Fisher's recollection supported Hankey's: 'He was beautiful! He has got the brain of Moses and the voice of Aaron. He would talk a bird out of a tree, and they were all carried away with him. I was not, myself.' The Council resolved that 'the Admiralty should also prepare for a naval expedition in February to bombard and take the Gallipoli Peninsula, with Constantinople as its objective'.

Churchill had managed to persuade Fisher, but it was not long before the old man's doubts returned. The senior officers of the Admiralty, hardly involved at all in the strategical discussions, were even more doubtful, but Asquith—at Churchill's prompting—suppressed a memorandum to the War Council that spelt out these doubts. Of the Ministers, only Lloyd George expressed reservations, and Hankey, in a series of prescient memoranda, vainly appealed for a more thorough appraisal of the various factors involved. All doubts were swept aside, and it was with full War Council approval that the naval assault was launched on February 19th.

But it was not long before serious shadows began to darken the gleaming expectations held out by Churchill to his colleagues. Disputes arose with Kitchener about the availability of troops to follow up the successful forcing of the Straits. An attempt to make use of an offer of Greek troops was peremptorily vetoed by the Russians—a fact that has been over-emphasised in almost all accounts of the campaign, for it is very doubtful if Venizelos was in any position to provide the troops, and even more doubtful if they would have been of any decisive value.

The approval given by French to the expedition had been reluctant, and based entirely on the understanding that it was to be a solely naval attack, and that the War Council consented to further offensives in France. In fact, the military demands of the Dardanelles expedition became quickly apparent. After observing the situation, Lt. General Birdwood reported privately to Kitchener that there was no chance of the Navy getting through by itself, and an army that consisted mainly of an Australian and New Zealand (ANZAC) Army Corps and a French division was made available in Egypt. Units of the Royal Naval Division were ordered to the Middle East and, on March 10th after three weeks of haggling, the last Regular Division in Kitchener's possession, the 29th, was sent. The War Council records make clear that Churchill's argument was that the troops would not be used in the forcing of the Dardanelles, but were required 'to occupy Constantinople and to compel a surrender of all Turkish forces remaining in Europe after the fleet had obtained command of the Sea of Marmara. . . . The actual and definite object of the army would be to reap the fruits of the naval success'. The island of Lemnos was loaned by Greece—commandeered by the British would probably be a more apt description—and Admiral Wemyss was dispatched there to establish an advanced base. As he had no facilities whatever, Wemyss found his task difficult.

French was not the only commander who viewed these developments with concern. General Sir John Maxwell, the British commander in Egypt, considered that his position was difficult enough already, and he could obtain no clear account from London of the use to which troops were liable to be used in the Dardanelles offensive.

At the Dardanelles Admiral Carden was encountering serious difficulties. The weather, always bad in the Aegean at that time of the year (a point which might have been taken into account) was hindering him badly. His ships were old, and the crews mainly the residue from the Grand Fleet. His only minesweepers were East Coast fishing smacks crewed by civilians and commanded by a naval officer with no experience whatever of minesweeping. The Outer Defences were easily subdued, but when the warships entered the Straits their difficulties became serious. The minesweepers could make little headway against the fierce Dardanelles current, and were subjected to constant harassing fire. The mobile Turkish batteries were only a nuisance to the warships but unnerved the minesweeper crews. Turkish resistance to landing parties of marines became more resolute. By mid-March an impasse had been reached. Carden was subjected to a flow of admonitory telegrams from Churchill, but the fact remained that he could not advance until the minefields were cleared. He accordingly was forced to reverse his tactics; the suppression of the batteries would precede the clearing of the mines. On the eve of the attack on March 18th he collapsed, and was replaced by Rear-Admiral de Robeck.

Meanwhile, it had been decided to send out a senior officer to command the 70,000-odd British, French and Dominion troops made available for the operation. The choice—Kitchener's, with Churchill's warm support—had fallen upon General Sir Ian Hamilton, commanding the Central Force in England. Hamilton was sixty-two. He was a man of great physical courage, recommended thrice for the Victoria Cross. He also possessed much charm and political adroitness, and had been one of the most trenchant critics of Roberts' conscription campaign. Events were to prove him sadly inadequate to his responsibilities, but he hardly had a fair chance. He was appointed at twelve hours' notice, had to gather an improvised staff together, and hastily quit London on Friday, March 13th. As one of his staff subsequently wrote:

I shall never forget the dismay and foreboding with which I learnt that apart from Lord Kitchener's very brief instructions, a pre-war Admiralty report on the Dardanelles defences and an out-of-date map, Sir Ian had been given practically no information whatever.

He arrived, with his hotchpotch and bewildered staff, just in time to witness the celebrated débâcle of March 18th.

This famous attack has been the subject of many accounts. It opened propitiously, in perfect weather, but shortly before 2 p.m. the French battleship *Bouvet* was rocked by a giant explosion, spun over, and disappeared. The British battleships *Invincible* and *Ocean* were sunk, and *Inflexible* crippled. The French battleship *Gaulois* was also badly damaged. The minesweepers had not even reached the edge of the minefields. The Turks had shot away virtually all their heavy ammunition, but they still had sufficient ammunition to dominate the sweepers. The Turks had had forty men killed and seventy wounded. Out of 176 guns only eight had been hit, and four put out of action. The Allied losses were over seven hundred officers and men. The real lesson of March 18th was that the Dardanelles was impassable unless the sweeper force was drastically reorganised. This was realised by Roger Keyes, de Robeck's Chief of Staff, but even he admitted that to compose such a force would take three weeks.

A fact to which sufficient emphasis can hardly be given was that the soldiers were very keen to intervene. Birdwood had never believed that the Navy, by itself, could get through the Dardanelles; Hamilton had seen for himself what had happened on March 18th; Kitchener, by the dispatch of Hamilton, had gone a long way towards accepting Birdwood's arguments. On March 22nd, on board the battleship

Queen Elizabeth at Mudros, Hamilton and de Robeck agreed on a joint operation. Hamilton returned to Alexandria to reorganise his army, now scattered around the Eastern Mediterranean in spectacular confusion. Thus, without the knowledge or approval of the War Council or the Cabinet, the decision to open a major military campaign was taken in a matter of minutes by the senior naval and military officers on the spot. Churchill was eager to renew the naval attack, but was not able to convince his Service advisers. The action of Hamilton and de Robeck was decisive. 'The silent plunge into this vast military venture', Churchill later recorded, 'must be regarded as an extraordinary episode.' The War Council did not meet for ten weeks after its meeting of March 10th.

Meanwhile, French had launched his assault in France. The Battle of Neuve Chapelle (March 10th–13th) merely confirmed all previous lessons of trench warfare against entrenched positions. British casualties were 583 officers and 12,309 other ranks. In April the Germans hit back in the Second Battle of Ypres (April 22nd–May 31st) and nearly broke through. In May the British attacked at Aubers Ridge and Festubert. Vast casualties were suffered;[1] no gains were made. French claimed that the cause was a deficiency of shells. On April 21st, in the House of Commons, Lloyd George strongly defended Kitchener against these charges, reporting that there had been a nineteen-fold increase in shell production since September 1914. This temporarily only checked the allegations, which broke out with redoubled vigour after French's further setbacks in May.

By itself, what developed into the 'shells scandal' was not sufficient to topple the Government, although it shook it. For one thing, the issue involved personal criticism of Kitchener, the one Minister in whom the Opposition had confidence. Bonar Law had his followers under control over the issue of shells, but it represented another opportunity for criticisms of the general conduct of the war in the Conservative Party.

There was a strong tendency among some Ministers to regard this unrest in the Opposition and in the Press as factious and unpatriotic. Churchill's project to commandeer *The Times* was a case in point. There was certainly no comprehension of, nor sympathy with, the

---

[1] Losses at Aubers Ridge were 458 officers and 11,161 other ranks; at Festubert 710 officers and nearly 16,000 other ranks. In addition to these losses, the cost of the Second Battle of Ypres had been 2,150 officers and 57,125 other ranks.

problems of the Opposition, which were put succinctly by Curzon in a memorandum to Lansdowne in January 1915:

> We are expected to give a mute and almost unquestioning support to everything done by the Government; to maintain patriotic silence about the various blunders that have been committed in connexion with the War. . . . The Government are to have all the advantages, while we have all the drawbacks of a Coalition. They tell us nothing or next to nothing of their plans, and yet they pretend our leaders share their knowledge and their responsibility. . . . I do not think this state of affairs can continue indefinitely, both because the temper of our party will not long stand it, and because, in the interests of the nation, the position is both highly inexpedient and unfair.

*

Hamilton, after reorganising his forces in Egypt, launched his attack on the Gallipoli Peninsula on Sunday, April 25th. By the end of a tumultuous day the British and Dominion troops, at heavy loss, were hanging on to precarious positions. In the following two weeks they suffered further heavy casualties, had only succeeded in establishing their foothold on the Peninsula, and Hamilton was calling for reinforcements. In a period of less than two weeks, on two small fronts, the British, Dominion, and French forces suffered over 20,000 casualties out of a total strength of 70,000 men, and of whom 6,000 had been killed. At the tip of the peninsular they were definitely halted on the slopes of Achi Baba and, to the north, on the harsh cliffs of Sari Bair. The British had acquired another major campaign, but were not yet fully aware of the terrible sacrifices which that insatiable fragment of ground was to demand over the next months.

On May 7th there occurred a dramatic incident which was to play its part in the eventual entry of the United States into the war, and over which considerable mystery remains. The Cunard liner *Lusitania*, with a number of Americans aboard, was torpedoed and sunk by a German submarine off Kinsale, on the southern Irish coast. The great ship sank within minutes, and 1,201 persons lost their lives. There was intense outrage in Britain and America at this further example of German 'frightfulness', an emotion which was sedulously encouraged by British Intelligence and its agents abroad.

But there were certain aspects of this tragedy which were perplexing, if not downright suspicious, and recent research has raised certain questions which have not been adequately answered.[1] Above all is the suspicion that the sinking was deliberately calculated—or, at the least, was fervently hoped for—by the Admiralty. Even though this has not been proved, it is now clear that the *Lusitania* was carrying considerable quantities of war material, and it would appear almost certain that her sudden destruction—virtually a nose-dive into the sea—was the result of a massive internal explosion and could not have been wholly caused by a single torpedo, at a time when they were so notoriously ineffective that most German submarine commanders preferred to use their guns on the surface. The episode did not bring America into the war, and President Woodrow Wilson was to ride to an unexpected re-election a year later on the cry that 'he kept us out of the war'. But official American–German relations, already cool, had suffered a major deterioration. And in Britain this event, coming at the moment it did, was not helpful to the rapidly declining position of the British Government.

The check at Gallipoli coincided with both the loss of the *Lusitania* and French's disastrous assault at Aubers Ridge. French then informed the military correspondent of *The Times* that the attack had failed as a result of a shortage of shells, and on May 14th *The Times* published his telegram that 'the want of an unlimited supply of high explosive shells was a fatal bar to our success', and commented in a leading article that 'British soldiers died in vain on Aubers Ridge . . . because more shells were needed. The Government, who have so seriously failed to organise adequately our national resources, must bear their share of the grave responsibility.'

The fact that *The Times*' attack was launched against Kitchener personally, however, reduced much of its impact, particularly on the Opposition. It was Fisher's dramatic resignation early on the following day that was the final factor that made the position of the Government impossible. Fisher's discontent with Churchill had preceded the Dardanelles operation, but had been mightily augmented by it. The almost universal judgement in the Admiralty was hostile to the campaign, and was burdened by recurring criticism of Churchill personally. These criticisms were conveyed to the Opposition, and by the end of April—two weeks before Fisher resigned—Law and his col-

---

[1] Colin Simpson: *The Lusitania* (1972) makes a very effective case for the argument that the ship was deliberately sacrificed, but it is not fully proven.

leagues were fully informed of the hostility of the bulk of the Board of Admiralty to the mercurial First Lord. Fisher's resignation, therefore, was not unexpected to them, and their profound antipathy to Churchill ensued that they would not look charitably upon his explanation. In the event, he was not given an opportunity to explain.

Asquith, having at first refused Churchill's offer to resign, now quickly realised that his own position was in serious danger. Law had seen Lloyd George, and had made it plain that the Conservatives could not support Churchill in a quarrel of such magnitude with Fisher. Lloyd George, whose sense of political possibilities was acute, eagerly accepted Law's statement and threatened resignation unless a Coalition was formed. Asquith had no wish to have a Coalition, but he acted with decision and celerity to preserve his own position. The Conservatives made it clear that Churchill would have to be sacrificed, and Haldane as well. Churchill fought desperately to survive, but to no avail. His bitterness at his downfall was intense, and he subsequently commented:

> Asquith did not hesitate to break his Cabinet up, demand the resignations of all Ministers, end the political lives of half his colleagues, throw Haldane to the wolves, leave me to bear the burden of the Dardanelles, and sail on victoriously at the head of a Coalition Government. Not 'all done by kindness'! Not all by rosewater! These were the convulsive struggles of a man of action and of ambition at death-grips with events.[1]

The Ministerial Crisis of May 1915 remains a somewhat mysterious episode, but its root cause was the pervasive feeling in the House of Commons—and not confined to the Opposition—that the Government was inadequate to meet the burdens of the war. The 'shells scandal' and the Fisher resignation brought to a head a judgement which had become very widespread, and which was not unjustified, that the Government was simply not equipped in procedures, personnel, or attitudes to wage the war competently. Unhappily, the cure was to prove at least as bad as the disease.

---

[1] Churchill: *Great Contemporaries*. See also Martin Gilbert: *Winston Churchill*, Volume III, Chapters 13 and 14.

CHAPTER ELEVEN

THE FALL OF ASQUITH, 1915–1916

APOLITICAL COALITION is a loveless relationship, created only out of dire necessity and resented for that in itself, and in which the partners eye each other warily and not without hostility. Coalition is, of its very nature, contrary to the basic tenets of politics, and it is not surprising that most politicians abhor both the concept and the reality. Coalition means the abandonment of the deliciously enjoyable dramas of partisan politics. Coalition means co-operation with men against whom a politician has been in dispute for years. Coalition means the subordination of political dogmas and creeds to new and uncomfortable necessities. Coalition means that there are fewer positions available to the party faithful. Coalition, in short, means the sacrifice of almost everything that renders political life so stimulating and rewarding.

A successful Coalition requires a decent minimum of mutual confidence and respect between its leading members. It would be quite unreasonable to expect complete mutual confidence; human nature —and, above all, political nature—could hardly stand such a severe test. But the Asquith Coalition was remarkable in that even the minimum requirements were not met. A few months earlier Asquith had come across a statement of Bolingbroke's: 'Sir, I never wrestle with a chimney-sweep', and noted 'A good saying, which I sometimes call to mind when I am confronting Bonar Law'. In November 1915 Law wrote to Asquith:

> The criticism which is directed against the government and against yourself is chiefly based on this—that as Prime Minister you have not devoted yourself absolutely to co-ordinating all the moves of the war because so much of your time and energy has been devoted to control of the political machine.

At no point during the Asquith Coalition were relations between Asquith and Law anything but distant. For this situation both men were to blame, but the greater responsibility was Asquith's. He regarded Law's timidity and caution as signs of weakness, and, if anything, his contempt for the Conservative leader was increased by the experience of working with him. This was to be a fatal error, as Law had a genuine regard for Asquith and a profound mistrust of Lloyd George. If Asquith had made an ally of Law—as he could easily have done—his position would have been greatly strengthened by the Coalition. But he made no move. Asquith wrote to Law, 'My dear Bonar Law'; Law replied, 'Dear Mr. Asquith'. This mode of address adequately symbolised the gulf between the two men.

In the Coalition as a whole, feelings were even stronger. Many Liberals bitterly—and not unjustifiably—resented the imperative Conservative veto, based wholly upon personal prejudice, against Haldane. 'You cannot imagine', Augustine Birrell wrote to Redmond, 'how I loathe the idea of sitting cheek by jowl with these fellows.' The Conservatives regarded the Liberals with no greater enthusiasm. Walter Long wrote to Carson on May 25th that he did not expect the Coalition to work 'when it comes to daily administration. I loathe the very idea of our good fellows sitting with these double-dyed traitors.' The repugnance with which Asquith viewed his new colleagues was thinly disguised, and in many instances warmly returned.

The Coalition had been forced upon Asquith, but he was able to maintain the Liberal dominance in the new Cabinet. The Conservatives were emphatic about the exclusion of Haldane and Churchill's removal from the Admiralty, but were surprisingly docile on other appointments. Remarkably, even Churchill was retained, with the post of Chancellor of the Duchy of Lancaster, and with a seat on the new version of the War Council, called the Dardanelles Committee. And, almost immediately after the formation of the Coalition, Churchill was able to persuade the Committee and the Cabinet to send substantial reinforcements to Gallipoli.

Churchill had gone down fighting, but it had been impossible to keep him at the Admiralty. He had tried everything—even including a proposed rapprochement with Fisher, which had been indignantly rejected—but his position was hopeless. In later years Churchill convinced himself that he had been destroyed by Tory hostility and Asquith's weakness. Churchill had formidable powers of self-deception.

His loyalty to Asquith was now fatally undermined; his dislike of Bonar Law substantially augmented.

But in the difficult circumstances Asquith had done very well for Churchill and the Liberals. All the key posts remained in Liberal hands. Lloyd George went to the new Ministry of Munitions; Grey stayed at the Foreign Office; McKenna took the Treasury, and Simon the Home Office. Kitchener stayed at the War Office. Law went to the relative backwater of the Colonial Office; Curzon became Lord Privy Seal; Sir Edward Carson became Attorney-General, with a seat in the Cabinet; Walter Long became President of the Local Government Board. Of the Conservatives only Balfour (Admiralty) occupied a major Cabinet post. The Liberals held the twelve key positions, the Conservatives had eight minor posts, and Labour received one Cabinet office, Arthur Henderson taking the Board of Education. Asquith's only failure concerned Redmond, who declined an invitation to join.

This was a remarkable exercise in political legerdemain. It was, however, just a bit too clever. Asquith did not realise that his best chance of remaining Prime Minister was to be head of a genuine and strong Coalition. But the failure was deeper. Despite all the experience of the war, there were no changes in the manner in which the Government itself operated. The Dardanelles Committee did not differ in substance from the old War Council. It was replaced in November 1915 by a War Committee which faithfully reproduced all the weaknesses of the previous arrangements. The old failures of leadership and coherence remained; the internal discord and mistrust between Ministers added an additional element of weakness.

Although the Coalition brought into the Cabinet the dilemmas of how the war was to be fought and where it was to be fought, the Conservative impatience with the old attitudes was an instinctive rather than a logical one. They knew that something was wrong, but they had few practicable alternatives to offer. The idea of nationalising key industries or of the Government stifling private enterprise was as loathsome to them as it was to the Liberals. In military matters their resources were so slender that their response was to rely upon the military authorities to an even greater extent. In any serious dispute between the Services and the Government the Conservatives were almost certain to support the former.

Nevertheless, a fundamental change of outlook existed, and was to become even more marked in 1916. The Conservatives, in short, were moving, however irrationally, blunderingly and nervously, towards the 'nation in arms' concept from which the Liberals still shrank. Thus, a highly improbable alliance between the Conservatives and Lloyd George began slowly to develop. This process was gradual, and shadowed by old antipathies; indeed, up to the Ministerial Crisis of December 1916 Law distrusted Lloyd George to a far greater extent than he had lack of confidence in Asquith. But, as the war marched on its terrible course, the Conservative leaders found themselves in increasing, if reluctant, sympathy with Lloyd George's attitudes and objectives. They mistrusted and disliked him still, and knew him too well to be overwhelmed by the charm which he could use so effectively on others. They had good cause to hate him, and yet the exigencies of the situation created a slow but perceptible change in their attitudes.

A strange light still flickers around Lloyd George's personality and career. That he was an adventurer and an opportunist is evident enough, but he has succeeded well in obscuring the motives that drove him onwards, and has eluded his several biographers. Mere ambition cannot adequately explain it, although he was a profoundly ambitious man. Principle did not figure conspicuously at any stage in his long career, yet on several occasions—notably in the Boer War—he had courted political disaster for the sake of principle. He rose as the champion of the under-privileged; he was to become obsessed by the menace of organised labour and international communism. An ardent pacifist in the Boer War, initially a very reluctant supporter of intervention in 1914, he was to be the only Minister who served in high office throughout the war; was to attain international stature as a great war leader; and, in October 1918, was to advocate the continuance of the war until Germany had been totally overrun. The leading Radical of the early 1900s, he did more than anyone else to destroy the Liberal Party and to place his own fate in the hands of the Conservatives. The self-appointed spokesman for Welsh non-conformity, his own private life—in matters financial and sexual—left much to be desired. He followed no star save his own, dwelt on no philosophy save his own, and yet was, at his peak, one of the most powerful and persuasive speakers that British Radicalism has produced. His early speeches can still be read with excitement. Thus, on Joseph Chamberlain in 1903, at Oldham:

Mr. Chamberlain has appealed to the workmen, and there were very fine specimens of the British workmen on his platform. There were three Dukes, two Marquesses, three or four Earls. They had gone to help the workman to tax his own bread. The Corn Laws meant high rent for them, and when a statesman of Mr. Chamberlain's position comes forward and proposes a return to the old Corn Law days, Lords and Dukes and Earls and Squires all come clucking towards him like a flock of fowls when they hear the corn shaken in the bin.

But Lloyd George was at his best when he dwelt on deeper matters. Thus, at Swansea, in October 1908:

What is poverty? Have you felt it yourselves? If not, you ought to thank God for having been spared its sufferings and temptations. Have you ever seen others enduring it? Then pray God to forgive you, if you have not done your best to alleviate it. By poverty, I mean real poverty, not the cutting down of your establishment, not the limitation of your luxuries. I mean the poverty of the man who does not know how long he can keep a roof over his head, and where he will turn to find a meal for the pinched and hungry little children who look to him for sustenance and protection. That is what unemployment means.

Lloyd George was an instinctive politician. His reading was not extensive, and he always preferred an oral to a written argument. It was said of him with justice that when he was alone the room was empty. He was, unlike most politicians, an eager and excellent listener. He did not impose his views on his audiences, he reacted instinctively to what the audience wanted to hear. He drew into his mind and memory the views and experience of others; he was prone to make snap decisions on the basis of his impression of a man's capacity; he had an unfortunate tendency to making swift estimates, and he always preferred the colourful and articulate in mankind. The fact that he was not over-encumbered with principle or prejudice often gave him an air of cynicism and blatant opportunism; yet it was, particularly in war, a source of strength. Unlike Churchill, he did not attempt to impose things on people; he drew from people.

He could be a bully, and he personalised politics to an excessive extent. He was a good hater, and was relentless in his persecutions. His character was not devoid of cruelty, and he was not the kind of person to whom one would wish to be beholden on any matter affecting one's well-being or fortune. His energy was prodigious, and at this time in particular people felt in his presence a vitality which they could see in no other politician—all the more impressive because it lay in the man. Churchill had run around in a fever of activity that seemed juvenile and melodramatic, as if rushing around on the spur of the moment was synonymous with real action. Lloyd George gave the impression of tremendous mental and physical energy held on a leash, and with a much more impressive evidence of shrewdness and timing. And some, at least, detected in the small, vibrant, eager personality an element of cold ruthlessness which the sentimental, romantic, and warm-hearted Churchill did not possess, and which Asquith reserved for domestic political matters which closely affected himself.

His oratorical styles in Parliament and on a public platform were entirely different. In the House of Commons he adopted a deliberately low key, characterised by studied moderation and courtesy. On the platform a new man stood forth, brilliant, exciting, witty, provocative, and emotional. His Parliamentary speeches were devoid of remarkable and memorable phrases; his speeches outside Parliament were replete with them. For the platform the purple passage and the piercing personalities; for Parliament, calmness and sweet reason; for private conclave, a ready ear, a keen intelligence, and no claptrap. A most formidable combination!

Churchill has written of Lloyd George that 'he had the greatest capacity in the art of *getting things done* of any man in public life that I have known'. Lloyd George's record at the Board of Trade and at the Treasury certainly demonstrated the validity of this tribute. Lloyd George had perhaps the most acute and perceptive intelligence of any individual in public life. His charm has been commented on by all who knew him. It could be—or appear to be—a genuine, unforced charm, and few did not succumb to it, even those who knew him for what he was and were unimpressed by the Celtic extravaganzas. His private secretary once confessed that, after listening to Lloyd George singing Welsh hymns, he was almost persuaded of his religious convictions. He was, if nothing else, the most brilliant actor in British politics since Disraeli—and, like Disraeli, perhaps the actor was the real man.

From an early stage in the war, Lloyd George had prised the control of munitions away from the War Office and Kitchener. Kitchener, under pressure, set up an Armaments Output Committee on March 31st, 1915; it became independent of the War Office on April 28th. By May it was in virtual control of the material side of armaments. When the Coalition came in May 1915 Lloyd George took over the new Ministry of Munitions and hurled himself energetically into its development. His subsequent claims must be approached with caution; Kitchener had laid the foundations, and the proportion of 'duds' in British shells in the Battle of the Somme in 1916 revealed that complaints that quality had been sacrificed to quantity were not unjustified. Nevertheless, Lloyd George had been right. The production of war matériel required a separate Ministry and full-time devotion to the task. The Ministry of Munitions was to become one of the great success-stories of the wartime administration. Shell production in December 1914 was 871,700; in December 1915 it was 23,663,186; in December 1916 it was 128,460,113. Production of guns increased six-fold between June 1915 and June 1916.

This new creation, and the manner in which it was run, represented a very sharp departure from 'business as usual'. Lloyd George was now thrusting forward as the most vigorous and articulate exponent of 'the nation in arms'. Above all, he gave an impression of direction and confidence which was in marked contrast with the Government as a whole.

His position was not yet strong in the Government. The Conservative suspicions and resentments remained. Neither the King nor the Army viewed him with enthusiasm, and he was already trying the patience of the Liberal and Labour parties, who were beginning to detect in him a tendency to authoritarianism from which they instinctively rebelled. But Lloyd George bided his time, watched events carefully, and lost no opportunity for advertising his own achievements, to the point that some of his speeches in support of his colleagues sounded uncommonly like Motions of Censure upon them.

*

Throughout 1915 Ministers grappled earnestly but futilely with the deteriorating military situation. It was a year of virtually unrelieved disaster. In the battles of Neuve Chapelle (March), Second Ypres (April), Festubert (May) and Loos (September) the British suffered more than 150,000 casualties. The total Allied casualties in Gallipoli amounted to some 250,000, of whom nearly 200,000 were British and Dominion. In August, Ian Hamilton had made his supreme effort, and had bungled it. The decision to abandon this tragic venture was not an easy one, and Churchill fought bitterly for its continuation. But Churchill was now in eclipse. At the beginning of November the Dardanelles Committee was ended, and replaced by a War Committee consisting of Asquith, Balfour, Grey and Lloyd George; the Conservatives were incensed at the omission of Law, who joined it shortly afterwards with McKenna—four Liberals and two Conservatives. Churchill, for the first and last time in his career, resigned, and made a defiant speech in defence of the Dardanelles operation before placing himself 'unreservedly at the disposal of the military authorities'. Asquith—and, much more surprisingly, Law—expressed formal regrets at his departure; others were more critical of his description of the Dardanelles operation as 'a legitimate war gamble'. *The Times* commented that 'Nobody imagines that his disappearance from the political arena will be more than temporary'. To the regret of many, this forecast proved to be true. Churchill entered into his responsibilities on the Western Front with ardour and deep seriousness, but with his attention still concentrated upon political developments in London. In the maelstrom of events, Churchill's dramatic donning of khaki aroused little public or political interest. Churchill and his circle regarded his fortunes as central to the fate of the nation; but the nation had more immediate preoccupations than the fate of one egotistical and apparently failed middle-aged politician.

In Mesopotamia, a bold and foolish march into the desert towards Baghdad had ended in disaster. By the end of 1915 virtually no progress had been made on the Western Front; Gallipoli had had to be abandoned, the evacuation of the Allied troops being the only thoroughly successful and professional feature of the enterprise; Bulgaria had entered the war on the side of the Central Powers; Serbia had been totally defeated; a vast and absurd new commitment in Salonika had been undertaken. The only gleams of solace were the continued superiority of the British at sea; the accession of Italy on the Allied side; and the ever-increasing volume of fresh troops from the Dominions. But these were only flashes in the darkness. London was being bombed, which was not serious physically but unnerving psychologically; the condition of the Russians was grievous; the Turks were more firmly in control of the Straits than ever; the Western Front had now acquired its own hideous character.

In most wars it is possible to trace the success or failure of the combatants in territory gained, towns captured, casualties suffered. In the Great War the historian reads constantly of epic struggles to seize a shell-crater in what was once a farm, of major engagements to wrest a shattered patch of woodland, or of how Captain X or Sergeant Y died heroically in a raid on trench HK3. It was an unglamorous, beastly, vicious, and debilitating conflict, with much physical discomfort, boredom, and peril, but which was endured not merely with stoicism but often with enthusiasm. In spite of everything, the competing armies had faith and confidence. The real comradeship of the trenches bound them together, and the will to win was overpoweringly infectious. This is difficult to recapture, and for some impossible to comprehend, but it was the dominant element on both sides in that ghastly, unending, duel.

Amidst these misfortunes for the British, there was no financial or economic crisis. The British economy—assisted by the blockade of Germany—proved itself fully capable of meeting the financial demands of the war. McKenna's first Budget, in November 1915, imposed an excess-profits duty of fifty per cent—in 1917 raised to eighty per cent —on any increase in pre-war profits. It did nothing to reduce war-profiteering, but it provided the Treasury with a handsome income. But McKenna also imposed duties of thirty-three and one-third per cent on a number of 'luxury' items such as motor cars, clocks, and watches. One of the reasons Asquith had privately advanced for not sending Law to the Treasury had been because of his Protectionist views; in the eyes of many Liberals, McKenna had delivered a serious blow against Free Trade. Income tax rose to 3s 6d in the pound, and more War Loans were floated. Had it not been for heavy loans to her allies—£1,825 millions in all, met largely by American borrowings— the British could have handled their war with no serious losses, and, indeed, made a profit as well.

The dominating problem was not, in 1915–16, economic. It was one of manpower. By the end of 1915 the British had suffered casualties of 21,747 officers and 490,673 men, of whom about 200,000 were dead or missing. By the middle of 1915 the recruiting figures were already dipping drastically. The first enthusiasm was gone, and the ever-lengthening casualty lists cast a pall over the nation. The French,

Russian and German losses had been far greater than those of the British—by the end of 1915 the French had endured casualties amounting to over 50,000 officers and nearly two million other ranks of whom dead or missing totalled over one million—but conscription had to some extent spread the losses better.

Behind the issue of conscription there lay the broader issue of the attitude of the Government to the war, and, even more important, that of the nation itself towards the war.

Edward Grey has written that:

Conscription in the early days of the war was impossible; public opinion was not ready for it; it would have been resisted. Voluntary enlistment gave the country a good start in good-will and enthusiasm; conscription would have given it a bad start. There would have been division of opinion, much resentment; the country might even have foundered in political difficulties.[1]

It is probable that this was an incorrect assessment, and it is arguable that in fact the beginning of the war had been the one moment when conscription would have been freely accepted. But the Liberal Government had never considered it, and the moment had passed.

The roots of the hostility to military conscription lay deep in British history, attitudes, and society. The case for conscription had been made before the war, but had made virtually no impact. Liberals in particular were instinctively opposed to the proposal; the Labour movement, fearing that it would be the first step towards industrial conscription, was adamantly hostile. But the hostility lay much deeper. The State, it was argued, was entitled to ask for the citizen's services; it was not entitled to demand it.

The attitude of Labour reflected this general attitude. Under the Defence of the Realm Act (D.O.R.A.) the Government had taken strong powers. The Munitions of War Act gave the Government authority to deal with industrial stoppages and to assume direct control of certain factories in which no normal trade union activities would be permitted. This was a blow to Labour's high opinion of Lloyd George—the first of many. A voluntary War Munitions Volunteer Scheme was put into operation; under the Act, the Government had the power to direct those workers who joined this scheme.

[1] Grey, op. cit., 72.

Joining, in short, was the only voluntary aspect of it. Munitions Tribunals were set up to deal with infringements of the Act. Most significant of all, a National Register of everyone between the ages of fifteen and sixty-five was initiated. These actions were viewed with considerable hostility by the Labour movement. When Lloyd George visited Glasgow on Christmas Day, 1915, he had a rough reception. The Socialist journal *Forward* was suppressed for a report that began:

> The best paid munitions worker in Britain, Mr. Lloyd George (almost £100 a week) visited the Clyde last week in search of adventure. He got it.

Greeted with cries of 'Get your hair cut' and other unfriendly observations, Lloyd George was virtually howled down. An official version of what occurred was issued, in which no mention was made of the disturbances, nor of the fact that Lloyd George's speech had never been delivered. No reference was made to David Kirkwood's statement that 'I can assure him that every word he says will be carefully weighed. We regard him with suspicion, because every action with which he is associated has the taint of slavery about it.' These were, of course, extreme attitudes, and Glasgow Socialism had a vivid character of its own. Labour now had a stake in the Coalition Government, and it recognised, however uneasily, the duty of the Government to harness the nation's industrial capacity. But military conscription, with the possibility of industrial conscription, was another matter.

Thus, even if the Government had been united on the need for conscription—which it certainly was not—it had to move circumspectly. In October 1915 the Earl of Derby was appointed Director-General of Recruiting, with instructions to find a way out of the dilemma. Derby's difficulties were not lessened by the fact that he had become convinced that conscription was essential. What emerged as 'the Derby Scheme' was a classic but ingenious compromise proposal. Adult males were to be persuaded to 'attest'—i.e. to give an undertaking to serve if and when called upon to do so. No married men would be called up so long as unmarried men were available—a qualification that had the result that might have been expected. Those men who had important skilled occupations or exceptional personal reasons would be exempted. Tribunals were to decide on the latter cases.

This was a very clever scheme, combining an adroit link between voluntary recruiting and compulsion. As has been remarked, it was 'a gigantic engine of fraud and moral blackmail, but, given that the Government had to find soldiers somehow, it was a very astute piece of political tactics. If it succeeded, well and good—the sanctity of voluntaryism had been maintained; if it failed, the case for conscription would be well-nigh irresistible.'[1]

The answer came soon. Within six weeks Derby reported that only half—just over a million—of the total number of single men of military age had attested; the same ratio existed for married men. The demands of the trenches could not be met in this way if the magical— and somewhat arbitrarily determined figure—of seventy divisions, with full support, laid down by Kitchener was to be met.

The next stage was the Military Service Act, hurriedly drafted and introduced in January 1916, which declared that all single men between eighteen and forty-one—including widowers without children —would be deemed to have enlisted and to have been transferred to the Reserve, whence they would be called up as required. One Liberal Minister—Simon—resigned in protest, and the Liberal and Labour parties and Press were deeply unhappy about the Bill. Henderson resigned on January 10th, and the two junior Labour Ministers followed his lead; on the next day Asquith addressed the Parliamentary Labour Party and persuaded the Labour Ministers to remain. The T.U.C. voted overwhelmingly against the Bill, but the Labour members of the Government stayed on the grounds that industrial conscription was not involved, but the Act was passed, although some fifty Liberals voted against it in the Commons. Two vigorous opponents in the Cabinet—Runciman and McKenna—did not carry their disagreement to resignation.

Whether it liked it or not, the Government was now fully embarked on the road to conscription, and the pressures on it to go further mounted, actively encouraged by Lloyd George. At one stage Asquith seriously considered resignation, and the Government seemed on the brink of collapse. A feeble compromise Bill was introduced on April 27th, which so disappointed both sides that it had to be ignominiously withdrawn. In May a second Military Service Bill was brought forward, that introduced at long last the principle of universal conscription. The Easter Rising in Dublin and the surrender of General

---

[1] A. J. Marwick: *The Deluge*, 77.

Townshend at Kut were the final factors that made the House of Commons act.

The conscription issue was of great political importance. It exposed the divergence of outlook between Liberals and Unionists in the Government and in the House of Commons; it became a symbol of two attitudes to the war—the vigorous and determined, the half-hearted and timorous. The actual effects of conscription on the armies were not great. Claims for exemption were nearly three-quarters of a million, and the Ministry of Munitions had already 'starred' a million and a half men in crucial war-work. In the first six months of conscription the average monthly enlistment was not much over 40,000—less than half under the voluntary system. Furthermore, the Act did not apply to Ireland. The manner in which conscription had come did Asquith no good politically,[1] although it is difficult to see what other course he could have followed.

But attitudes to the war were now definitely changing. Impatience with lack of success was becoming increasingly demonstrated. The war had become something less than a glittering adventure. One significant example of the degree to which the war now extended in the normally easy-going British society was shown in the changing attitude towards conscientious objectors. In December 1914 a No Conscription Fellowship had been set up for young men of military age; it had not received much custom hitherto, but by the end of 1915 it was active. It was as a result of their activities that the Derby Scheme considered appeals for exemption on grounds of conscientious objection—a new phrase in the English language.

The local tribunals did not always view such applications with sympathy. One classic exchange took place in Bradford.

Member: What would you do if a German came to you with a bayonet fixed?

Applicant: I shouldn't know what to do . . .

Member: If the only way to save your mother were to kill a German, would you still let him kill her?

Applicant: Yes.

Member: You ought to be shot.[2]

---

[1] As Hankey commented: 'The fact was that the people who wanted compulsory service did not want Asquith, and those who wanted Asquith did not want compulsory service.'

[2] John Rae: *Conscience and Politics*, 106

The Military Service Bill had been pushed through with such speed that there were bound to be difficulties and anomalies, and there was certainly hostility to conscientious objectors by the Boards and the Army, but, considering the passions of the time, they did not fare too badly. 2,919 men served in the Non-Combatant Corps, and 1,969 who refused to do so were court-martialled. Several were sentenced to death, but it is now clear that there was no real possibility of the sentences being carried out, and all were quickly commuted. Commanding officers who treated objectors badly were rigorously dealt with. Nonetheless, the legend of a military plot to send objectors to France, try them summarily for capital offences, and execute them has proved very enduring.[1] But although the objectors were turned over to the civilian authorities, their lot was not always easy.

The issue was subsequently evaded by various methods. Some 7,000 objectors agreed to perform non-combatant services, and another 3,000 went to labour camps. Tribunals often deemed an objector's occupation to be of national importance and exempted him on other grounds. There were, in all, less than two thousand who absolutely refused all compulsory service. Lloyd George, once the champion of the oppressed and the pacifist pro-Boer, was among the loudest in demanding severe treatment for such people. This attitude further improved Lloyd George's standing among all patriotic men and women who 'wanted to get on with the war', and, in particular, among the Conservatives. It was another step towards 10 Downing Street— and another away from the Radical support that had given Lloyd George his political opportunity.

At this point, the virtually forgotten Irish Question returned.

*

'This has taken everyone by surprise.' With these words James Stephens—a Registrar at the National Gallery of Ireland—opened his personal daily narrative of the Easter Rising in Dublin.[2] It was an exact statement of fact. 'The general state of Ireland, apart from recruiting, and apart from the activities of the pro-German Sinn Fein minority, is thoroughly satisfactory', the Director of Military Intelligence had reported to London two weeks before the Rising. 'The mass of the people are sound and loyal as regards the war, and the country

[1] Ibid.   [2] James Stephens: *The Insurrection in Dublin* (1916).

is in a very prosperous state and very free from ordinary crime.' There were a quarter of a million Irishmen—Northern and Southern— serving in the British Army or in associated forces such as the Royal Irish Constabulary. Even Patrick Pearse—who proclaimed the Republic in April 1916—wrote in 1915 that 'the last sixteen months have been the most glorious in the history of Europe. . . . The old heart of the earth needed to be warmed with the red wine of the battle-fields', which merited James Connolly's withering retort: 'No, we do not think that the old heart of the earth needs to be warmed with the red wine of millions of lives. We think anyone who does is a blithering idiot.'

Later, it was clear that the Rising did not come out of a clear blue sky. As Stephens wrote immediately afterwards: 'If freedom is to come to Ireland—as I believe it is—then the Easter Insurrection was the only thing that could have happened.' But, at the time, the sur-prise was total, and nowhere more than in Dublin, whose amazed citizens found themselves in the middle of street-fighting, and stood bemusedly watching Volunteers in Phoenix Park and British troops clattering down the streets. As Stephens wrote:

> None of these people were prepared for Insurrection. The thing had been sprung on them so suddenly that they were unable to take sides, and their feeling of detachment was still so complete that they would have betted on the business as if it had been a horse race or a dog fight.

The Easter Rising and its concomitant activities were, even by Irish standards, a spectacular shambles. After the outbreak of war the Irish Volunteers had not disbanded, and continued to drill. Birrell, the Irish Secretary, took the view that it would be unreasonable to disarm them without disarming the Ulster Volunteers; in this attitude expedience also played at least some part. The British had quite enough on their hands without taking on the Irish Volunteers—few in number and poorly armed—and Birrell was the last man to seek trouble.

Furthermore, Ireland was to all appearances patriotic and quies-cent. Redmond had given eloquent expression to his own patriotism in the House of Commons, and his son had been killed on the Western Front. As an issue, Home Rule was in the past. Ireland would receive her independence when the war ended and the Bill became law. Thus, it was widely believed, every attempt made by Irishmen to defeat Germany was a step towards the long-awaited independence.

But the Volunteers were planning for a rising with German assistance on Easter Sunday 1916. Their plans were elaborate, and involved a rising in Dublin itself, assaults on British garrisons, and a march on the capital. It was a bold attempt to effect a *coup d'état*. The British had ample warnings, but ignored them.

There were many fatal defects in the plan, of which the most conspicuous was the half-hearted attitude of the Germans. Sir Roger Casement, who had earned international recognition for his exposure of the methods employed by the Belgians in the Congo, had gone to Germany after a fund-raising visit to the United States in December 1914, but had found little practical support. An attempt by Casement to recruit an Irish Legion from among Irish prisoners of war had been a dismal failure. All that the Germans would do was to ship Casement and two associates to Ireland in a submarine and to send a shipload of arms and ammunition captured by them at Tannenberg in the steamship *Aud*.

The ensuing events had a high element of comedy in them. The *Aud* eluded the British Navy by adopting a number of obvious subterfuges which were for some time successful, but failed to keep a rendezvous. Casement and his companions were picked up, drenched and exhausted, within a few hours of staggering ashore. The captain of the *Aud* scuttled his ship when the suspicious British ordered it to berth under naval escort.

There was a crucial difference of outlook among the Volunteers' leaders. John MacNeill was the President and Chief of Staff of the Volunteers, and Patrick Pearse was Director of Organisation. The total force of the Volunteers was never more than 16,000. MacNeill had no knowledge of the *Aud* or of Casement's imminent arrival, and had always insisted that the Volunteers should not rise save in self-defence. Pearse was a member of the Irish Republican Brotherhood and it was the I.R.B. leaders who were determined to have their revolution. They accordingly published, on April 19th, a forged letter —the 'Castle Document'—purporting to show that the authorities proposed to arrest the Volunteers' leaders and dissolve the movement. This forced a decision from MacNeill, which he now rescinded on the evening of April 21st, in spite of Pearse's bitter protests. But the Military Council of the I.R.B.—Pearse, Connolly, MacDonagh,

Plunkett, Clarke, MacDermott, Ceannt—was determined to proclaim the Republic.

Easter Sunday passed peacefully. On Easter Monday, 1,200 Volunteers in Dublin, led by Pearse and acting quite independently, seized the General Post Office and other strategic points and declared the establishment of the Irish Republic. Dubliners returning from their Easter holiday in the country discovered their city in a state of insurrection. Throughout the events that followed they were either apathetic onlookers or vehement against the Volunteers; as Stephens noted, it was the women in particular who were the most angry and resentful.

The British, after their initial amazement—on the afternoon of Easter Monday an English officer walked into the General Post Office and tried to buy a book of stamps from the astounded Volunteers—reacted vigorously. Four days of severe fighting ensued, in which some 100 British soldiers and 450 Volunteers were killed. The total casualties on both sides were 1,351, and very substantial damage was done. Over 100,000 people had to be given public relief, and the centre of Dublin was in ruins. It seemed that it had been a gallant, futile venture, in the Irish tradition. As Stephens wrote:

> For being beaten does not greatly matter in Ireland, but not fighting does matter. 'They went forth always to the battle; and they always fell.' Indeed, the history of the Irish race is in that phrase.

The Rising was widely condemned in Ireland. The *Irish Catholic* denounced it 'as criminal as it was insane,' and 'traitorous and treacherous to our native land'. The Bishop of Ross described it as 'a senseless, meaningless debauch of blood'. Stephens noted that the Dubliners, and particularly the women, were 'actively and viciously hostile to the rising'. In essentials, Birrell and the Viceroy had been right. The I.R.B. was an impotent minority party; the Volunteers had no basis of popular support. The reactions of the British were entirely understandable. Ireland had been promised her freedom when the war ended, and had joined with the British in the war against Germany. Irishmen, no less than Englishmen, Scotsmen or Welshmen, owed allegiance to King and Country. Together they were falling in battle in terms of thousands. Here was a reckless minority which had traded with the enemy and raised arms against the ordered Government.

The Government handed the matter over to the military, and dispatched General Sir John Maxwell—former General Officer Commanding in Egypt and a persistent difficulty to Ian Hamilton—to Ireland to declare martial law and bring matters under control. This was swiftly done. Military justice then followed. Only the ring-leaders would suffer. Sixteen were court-martialled and shot—not all at once, but over a period of days. Immediately, Irish opinion was transformed. The blundering incompetents became martyrs. Yeats, who a few years earlier had written contemptuously of Ireland as 'a little greasy huxtering nation groping for halfpence in a greasy till', now wrote that 'A terrible beauty is born'.

Out of many tragedies, one in particular should be recorded.

Francis Sheehy-Skeffington, the youthful biographer of Michael Davitt, was, like his admired subject, an individualist. A contemporary of James Joyce at University College, Dublin, he had taken up the causes of nationalism, pacifism, socialism and the emancipation of women with ardour and independence. His convictions about Irish Independence did not embrace the use of violence, and he was a vehement opponent not only of war but of the actions by his country-men in the Rising. He tried to organise a citizens' force to prevent looting in Dublin, and was arrested by the British. Tragically, he fell into the hands of one Captain Bowen-Colthurst, himself an Irishman, who had him and two equally innocent men—Thomas Dickson and Patrick MacIntyre—shot without any form of trial. After repeated efforts by Dillon, Bowen-Colthurst was court-martialled and his conduct investigated by a Royal Commission of Inquiry. He was found guilty but insane. After a period in Broadmoor he emigrated to Canada, where he lived until 1965. To read Sheehy-Skeffington's study of Davitt—written before he was thirty—is to appreciate what was lost by the action of a mad officer.[1] Particular poignancy is pro-vided in the cold record of Sergeant Aldridge, given to the official enquiry:

You told us that Captain Colthurst said he wanted the three men out to speak to them?—Yes.

[1] Sheehy-Skeffington's biography of Davitt was published in 1908, and reprinted, with an introduction by Professor F. S. L. Lyons, in 1967. Its concluding section, with its warnings against 'the Irish tendency to hero-worship', deserves to be remembered, including this phrase: 'It is only the commonplace man who grows cold and conservative with age; the rare spirits who have made the world worth living in widen their outlook and strengthen their faith in progress year by year.'

Did he speak to them?—Only to tell them to go to the wall.
Did he accuse them of anything?—No.
Did he ever explain to them that he was going to shoot them?—No.
Did he ever ask them if they had anything to say?—No.
Did you feel that you had no alternative but to obey his orders?—
No. I did not understand that he was going to have them shot. It
was a surprise to me, and the men themselves did not realise what
was going to happen. When he asked for the seven men (for the
firing party) I thought he wanted them as an escort.
Did anybody make any sort of protest at all?—No; there was no
one there to do it.

It is easy to blame both the Government and Maxwell. Yet, by the
lights of the times, they had been lenient. This was to be one of the
last of a long, long series of examples of how little the British, after
four hundred years, understood the Irish.

Yet, there was still hope. Asquith seriously considered the immediate granting of Home Rule. Lloyd George negotiated on his own
with Carson and Redmond, and secured agreement whereby twenty-
six counties would receive Home Rule at once, with the six Ulster
Counties to remain British until after the war, when their position
would be reviewed by an Imperial Conference. This was a solution
that offered real chance of success. But, once again, Lansdowne was
implacable. Compromises had to be made to meet Unionist demands,
until Redmond refused to go further. The attempt to negotiate a
settlement broke down. Ireland was ruled by Dublin Castle, as before.
The Irish Nationalist Party at Westminster was virtually destroyed by
this final failure. The dead Volunteers became martyrs. The extremists
made spectacular gains. Sinn Fein, which had in fact played no part
in the Rising, became a force and no longer a minority voice. Its
amended Constitution in 1917 declared that 'Sinn Fein aims at
securing the international recognition of Ireland as an independent
Irish Republic', and drew into it all the principal elements of the
revivified Irish nationalism. The relative political importance of
Redmond's party and Sinn Fein were exactly reversed. The subsequent proposal to impose conscription upon Ireland was the final
stroke. The Irish Question now entered a new, and decisively terrible,
period, 'Death answering to Death like the clerks answering one
another at the Mass', in the tragic words of Lady Gregory. Stephens

concluded his account of the Easter Rising with the words: 'The Volunteers are dead, and the call is now for Volunteers.' And still the English did not understand. They had crushed a small rebellion. They had created an immense revolution.

There remained the embarrassing question of what to do with Casement. On June 29th he was convicted of high treason and sentenced to death. His appeal was rejected, and the Attorney-General, F. E. Smith (now Sir Frederick Smith), refused to give leave for a further appeal to the House of Lords. The only hope for Casement lay with the Home Secretary's prerogative of mercy.

Exceptionally, but justifiably, Herbert Samuel referred the matter to the Cabinet. On July 19th it decided unanimously that Casement should be hanged, and on August 2nd stood by this decision in spite of urgent appeals from abroad, notably from the United States. Casement was duly executed on August 3rd. Another incompetent revolutionary had become a martyr, and the manner in which his homosexual diaries were shown to individuals who had been disposed in his favour added a peculiarly nauseating touch to the macabre business. Asquith, Grey, and Lansdowne had originally wanted him declared insane, but after a professional report that he was 'abnormal but not certifiably insane' they bowed to the majority feeling in the Cabinet. After the Maxwell executions they perhaps had no alternative, but the effects were disastrous. As the British Ambassador in Washington reported of the Irish-Americans, 'there is blood in their eyes whenever they look at us'.

Mr. Taylor has written that 'This was the only national rebellion in any European country during the first world war—an ironical comment on the British claim to be fighting for freedom'.[1] The Easter Rising was not, in the first instance, a 'national rebellion'. The actions of the British Government and General Maxwell turned it into one. Some six months before his death Pearse had written:

The lawyers have sat in council, the men with the keen, long faces
And said, 'This man is a fool', and others have said, 'He blasphemeth';
And the wise have pitied the fool that hath striven to give a life
In the world of time and space among the bulk of actual things
To a dream that was dreamed in the heart, and that only the heart
  could hold.

[1] Taylor, *English History 1914-1945*, 56.

O wise men, riddle me this: what if the dream come true?
What if the dream come true? and if millions unborn shall dwell
In the house that I shaped in my heart?

The Easter Rising and its sequel cast long and dark shadows. Birrell
clearly had to go, although Asquith accepted his resignation with
reluctance. The Under-Secretary, Sir Matthew Nathan, was also
removed, although he had had a better understanding of Irish affairs
than most of his predecessors. But he had made several very fundamental errors. He over-valued the role of Casement, and assumed
that, when Casement was captured, the moment of peril was past.
On April 10th he had told Birrell that he did not believe that the
Volunteers meant insurrection, nor that they had the means. On
Easter Sunday, April 22nd, he had written to Birrell that 'I see no
indication of a rising'. Most damning of all was the evidence that the
Viceroy, Lord Wimborne, had wanted the known leaders of the
Volunteers arrested on the Sunday, and that Nathan had hesitated.
Nathan had been exceptionally unlucky, another in the long and
uncompleted list of those destroyed by the Irish Question.

Birrell's loss was not a serious one. Sixteen years after the Rising,
when its full effects were plain for all to see, he wrote blandly in
reminiscence:

> It was a supreme act of criminal folly on the part of those who were
> responsible for it, for it never had a chance, and was really nothing
> more than a Dublin row.

Of much greater significance was the fact that Redmond's political
fate was sealed by 'the Dublin row'. He had condemned the Rising,
and had said that 'the overwhelming mass of the Irish people' regarded
it, as he did, 'with a feeling of horror and detestation'. On May 3rd,
when the executions were in full swing, he issued a statement condemning the Rising as a blow against Home Rule and declaring that
'Germany plotted it, Germany organised it, Germany paid for it'.
That statement ended his career as an Irish leader. As John Dillon
wrote to T. P. O'Connor in the autumn of 1916, 'enthusiasm and trust
in Redmond *is dead*, so far as the mass of the people is concerned'.

Dillon had been in Dublin throughout the Rising. On April 30th
he wrote to Redmond to impress upon the Government 'the *extreme*
unwisdom of any wholesale shootings of prisoners. The wisest course

is to execute *no one* for the present. This is *the most urgent* matter for the moment . . . *So far* the feeling of the population in Dublin is *against* the Sinn Feiners. But a reaction might very easily be created. . . .' Redmond did see Asquith about the executions, but with no success: 'He said some few were necessary, but they would be very few. I protested.' Redmond then issued his statement condemning the Rising and blaming it upon German influence.

Dillon might have saved the Nationalist Party. On May 11th and 12th in the House of Commons he spoke of the Volunteers in warm terms, and cried to the Government:

> We have risked our lives a hundred times to bring about this result [Anglo-Irish union]. We are held up to odium as traitors by the men who made this rebellion . . . and you are washing out our whole life-work in a sea of blood.

The breakdown of the Lloyd George negotiations, and, above all, the disclosure that the Nationalist leaders were prepared to omit the six Ulster counties from Home Rule, finished the Nationalist cause in Ireland. The Irish leaders themselves considered that Lloyd George had double-crossed them, and it was several months before Redmond would have any dealings whatever with Lloyd George. Already, he could dimly see the truth of the words spoken by Pearse at the court-martial which was described as a trial: 'We seem to have lost: we have not lost.'

*

The end of 1915 had seen the formal abandonment of 'side-shows' and the concentration on the Western Front. General Sir Douglas Haig had replaced Sir John French as Commander-in-Chief in France; Sir William Robertson had become Chief of the Imperial General Staff, and had re-created the General Staff. When Kitchener returned from his visit to the Middle East in November he found these two men in their positions, and his powers drastically curtailed. These two determined, obstinate men henceforth dominated British strategy. Kitchener's star was in the descendant. He contemplated resignation, but was persuaded to stay. The politicians regarded him as a useless but crucial ornament, a kind of national talisman, but little more. Their over-estimation of Kitchener in 1914 was hardly less reasonable than their under-estimation of him in 1916.

The first effects of the Haig-Robertson combination were seen in the Battle of the Somme, which opened on July 1st. Haig had originally wanted to attack further in the north, but the agreement to have an Anglo-French offensive dictated that it should be in the Somme. Already, the French were heavily engaged at Verdun, first attacked in February, with the result that the Somme battle became more irrelevant than ever. But it had acquired its own momentum, and Haig was no longer troubled by its locale. It was a catastrophic British defeat. On the first day the British suffered 57,000 casualties, of whom 19,000 were killed.[1] On one day! But, undeterred, Haig hung on, and the battle raged until November, by which time the British had suffered 420,000 casualties and the French 194,000; the German losses were also heavy, 465,000. The secret to success in trench warfare—the tank—had arrived, but the few available were used in small groups. Two days after their first use—on September 15th—Haig asked for a thousand. Although they were as yet unaware of the fact, the British had at last a weapon that could win the war. The Somme was a bitter battle, and something more than a bitter disappointment.

It was not the only one. On May 31st the Battle of Jutland had been fought. The British lost three battle-cruisers, three cruisers, and eight destroyers; the Germans lost one battleship, one battle-cruiser, four light cruisers and five destroyers. The Germans issued a statement on June 1st which was in effect a claim of a great victory; the Kaiser declared a national holiday and bestowed the Ordre Pour Le Mérite on Admirals Scheer and Hipper. The Admiralty asked Jellicoe for his comments on the German communiqué; these had not been received by the 2nd, by which time the news was beginning to reach the country through the foreign press. The Admiralty accordingly issued the German statement without any comment. The effect of this upon British morale was severe, and in New York British stocks fell sharply. To make matters worse, Balfour put out a factual statement on June 3rd that concentrated on the British losses and seemed to confirm the German claims. It was as if Nelson had been defeated at Trafalgar. The true facts came out later; at the time public confidence was grievously, and unnecessarily, shaken. An optimistic article by Churchill— sponsored by the Admiralty—could not correct the first impressions.

[1] Over 1,000 officers and 20,000 men killed, fatally wounded, or missing; over 1,300 officers and 34,000 other ranks wounded.

The Times, indeed, commented tartly that 'this use of Mr. Churchill—who has no association whatever with the Government, who apparently aspires at this moment to lead an Opposition, and whose strategical utterances during the war have hardly been models of accuracy—was the most amazing confession of weakness on the part of the Admiralty'. It was certainly an odd tactic.

The Germans, realising that they had only just escaped complete defeat, turned to the submarine offensive. Scheer's official despatch of July 4th, indeed, stated bluntly that 'a victorious termination of the war within measurable time can only be attained by destroying the economic existence of Great Britain, namely, by the employment of submarines against British commerce'. The results were soon apparent. In November the President of the Board of Trade, Runciman, circulated a memorandum which stated that, if present shipping losses continued, Britain would collapse by the summer of 1917. He had no suggestions to offer, and his contribution has been described, not unjustly, by Christopher Addison as 'the most invertebrate and hopeless of any memoranda presented to the Government during the war by a responsible head of a department on a great issue'.

But Runciman's dilemma was acute. The obvious answers—control and regulation—were anathema. The alternative to a controlled economy was a negotiated peace. In November Lansdowne circulated a memorandum to the Cabinet seeking specification of British war aims and, by implication, a settlement on the pre-war status quo. It received short shrift.

Asquith's troubles were now piling heavily upon him and his Government. Everywhere the war was going badly. The Kitchener Armies were being destroyed on the Somme, and on June 5th Kitchener himself had perished as well, in the cruiser *Hampshire* en route for Russia. It is difficult to say whether the British were more shaken by this event than by the failures at Jutland and the Somme. But the political consequences were profound.

A month elapsed between Kitchener's death and the assumption of office by his successor. Asquith proposed to take his time over the matter. What actually occurred has become the object of considerable controversy. One account has it that Asquith, faced by the alternative of Bonar Law or Lloyd George, procrastinated and hoped to put in Derby, but that Law and Lloyd George delivered a joint ultimatum which he had to accept. Mr. Jenkins has, however, raised some pertinent questions about this version.[1] The King, and the generals, did not view the prospect of Lloyd George with much satisfaction, but Asquith seems to have recognised that he was clearly the best man for the job. In the event, Lloyd George succeeded Kitchener at the end of June. Margot Asquith later considered that this was the beginning of the end of Asquith's Premiership. Certainly, Lloyd George began to act more boldly. He publicly advocated the doctrine of the 'knock-out blow' and spoke belligerently of fighting to 'a decisive finish'. The Northcliffe Press, unsparing in its criticism of Asquith, began to call for new leadership and to use Lloyd George's name frequently in this connection. *The Observer*—an Astor paper—joined the opposition to Asquith. The decision of the Government to permit Royal Commissions to enquire into the Dardanelles and Mesopotamia campaigns was a serious blunder, and particularly affected relations within the Cabinet, never good at the best of times. And these were not the best of times.

But Asquith's position was still a strong one. The Unionists may have been increasingly admiring of Lloyd George's energy and capacities and increasingly impatient of Asquith, but their mistrust of Lloyd George remained. Law considered that Lloyd George was 'a self-seeker and a man who considered no interest except his own', and who wanted merely 'to put Asquith out and to put himself in'. It was neither an uncommon nor a wholly unfair judgement. There was still a Liberal majority in the House of Commons and in the Government, and remarkably many Conservatives still regarded Asquith as indispensable. Even those who did not feared the effects on national unity of division and discord in the Government. Bonar Law's attitude has been described by his friend Max Aitken, shortly to become Lord Beaverbrook:

Since the formation of the Coalition Government, no one had been a more loyal member of the Cabinet in the face of much provocation, and the appeal to loyalty was to the Prime Minister's hand. At the same time, a kind of scepticism about strong emotions and distrust of ardent passions or sharp measures, mixed with a contempt for personal ambition, made him by instinct, if not by reason, regard the rise of Lloyd George to supreme power as a dangerous portent in politics.[2]

[1] Jenkins, op. cit., 406–9.   [2] Beaverbrook: *Politicians and the War*, 353.

Asquith was, however, fighting a mood rather than an effective political combination at this stage. The pent-up frustrations of two years of war, in which no gains could be counted and only hideous losses incurred, required a scapegoat. This was a natural feeling, even if it was unfair. Similar emotions were evident in France, Russia, and even in Germany. Beaverbrook's words admirably sum up the mood against Asquith in the early winter of 1916:

His complete detachment from the spirit of the struggle; his instability of purpose; his refusal to make up his mind on grave and urgent issues of policy; his balancing of one adviser against another till the net result was nil; his fundamental desire to have a peaceful tenure of office in the midst of war, could in the long run have only one result. The men who were in tune with the atmosphere of the war—the bold, the eager, the decisive spirits—first fell away from him and then combined against him. And while all this was going on, he was immersed in his own social circle and engaged in responding to the devotion of his friends.'[1]

By the end of November a Ministerial crisis was imminent.

*

The position of a Prime Minister is always a strong one. He has in his hands the political careers of his colleagues. He has the weapon of Dissolution. He controls patronage and preferment. If he resigns, he can take his Government with him. He can divide his opponents by raising some and lowering others. He has the power—implicit and explicit—of the Party Machine. Asquith, in November 1916, did not possess all these advantages; it would be difficult, in wartime, to justify a general election, and such a course could only have been taken either in concert with his Conservative and Labour allies or as a result of breaking up the Coalition. Nevertheless, the inherent advantages possessed by a Prime Minister were with him.

Asquith had been Prime Minister since 1908. In that period he had presided in peacetime over a Cabinet of exceptional ability and also exceptional divisive potentiality. He had survived the Ministerial Crisis of May 1915, since then had kept the Coalition together, and had brought it through the crises of the Dardanelles evacuation, the

[1] Beaverbrook, op. cit., 226.

divisions over Conscription, and even that in Ireland. It cannot be pretended that it was a harmonious Cabinet, but it had held together.

The question was how long Asquith could maintain this delicate balance. Hankey's comments are of particular interest:

> The machinery of the War Committee was at this time working smoothly. An Agenda paper was issued before each meeting. Full records were as before kept in manuscript. The conclusions after being approved and initialled by the Prime Minister—in this matter Asquith was prompt and punctilious—were circulated to the Cabinet whose members were thus kept fully abreast of what was going on.

It was Hankey's opinion that 'with a loyal and united team' this system might have been adapted to meet the problems of the latter part of the war.

> But, with a Government composed of members of opposite political parties who had never been able entirely to forget their differences and in an atmosphere poisoned by the Dardanelles and Mesopotamia Commissions, this proved impossible even under so patient and experienced a leader as Asquith.[1]

The autumn meetings of the War Committee had been long, exhausting, and usually inconclusive. On November 8th, in a debate on the disposal of assets in Nigeria, Bonar Law had had a very rough passage in the House of Commons, and the Government had been nearly defeated. As in the celebrated 'Three Acres and a Cow' debate of January 1886,[2] the issue of Nigeria itself was irrelevant. It provided an issue on which the greatest number of Conservatives could be gathered to vote against the Government, and which would provide Carson with a suitable opportunity to attack Law personally.

The old alliance between Carson and Law had been broken since the former had resigned from the Government in November 1915. Carson invariably injected into his political and forensic life a strain of personal bitterness and animosity that made him a very formidable opponent but which also often poisoned his personal relationships. It is difficult to categorise or explain the causes of his resentment against

---

[1] Hankey, op. cit., II, 543–4.
[2] See Volume I, 96. The Norway Debate of May 1940 was another comparable occasion.

Law—a resentment that was not returned. Those Conservatives who wanted to topple Asquith knew that the weak point in the edifice was Law's position. Law was indispensable to Asquith; he had also made it plain when he took office that he did so on the condition that he retained the support and confidence of his party. At that time he had said:

> I say quite plainly that if I found that in this new position I had lost the confidence of our party I should feel I was of no further use to the Government. Certainly, so long as I myself believe that, whatever its defects, I can see no better way of carrying on this war, I should not oppose it, but if the party to which I belong had lost confidence in me I should not for a moment dream of continuing to be a member of the Government.

Thus, in striking at Law, the Conservative opponents of the Government were striking at Asquith. Added force was given to their attack by Carson's personal hostility towards Law.

In the event, the Government just survived; most important, Law had a small majority—seventy-three to sixty-five—of the Unionists who voted; but 148 did not. Among those who voted against the Government was Churchill, now definitely returned to the political front, clearly out to make trouble, and deeply discontented with his lot. One significant absentee was at once noted: Lloyd George had not voted. Indeed, he had that evening been dining at the home of Lord Lee of Fareham—the former Arthur Lee—with Carson and Milner. It is not quite clear whether Lloyd George, as he claimed to Bonar Law on the following morning, had been paired; it is very probable that he was not, and that his absence was deliberate. It was certainly interpreted as such at the time, and awoke politicians and political commentators to the interesting fact that the Government was now being attacked from front and rear.

It had survived, but only barely. Law rejected Aitken's proposal that he resign and force the issue. His loyalty to Asquith was strong. So was his mistrust of Lloyd George. As a party leader himself, he had an instinctive distaste for rebels, and at least part of his support for Asquith was based on the 'dog don't eat dog' principle. These feelings were considerably strengthened by a discussion with Churchill at Cherkley on November 12th, vividly described by Beaverbrook.[1] Law

[1] Beaverbrook, op. cit., 105–6.

disliked Churchill very strongly, and after he had endured a characteristic Churchillian harangue he threatened him with a general
election. With Law in this mood, and with Asquith showing no
inclination whatever to resign, the possibilities of a successful coup
against the Prime Minister seemed to suffer a serious setback. The
malcontents—Liberal and Unionist—were once again confronted by
the realities of the political situation and the strength of the position
enjoyed by a Prime Minister determined not to be pushed out.

The Lansdowne Memorandum[1] gave them another opportunity for
attacking the Government. Asquith did not support Lansdowne's
pessimistic view of the situation, but the Memorandum was immediately leaked to the Press, and the impression was quickly gained that
Asquith himself was not opposed to the views it contained. It was
ironical that Lansdowne, who had so often deliberately harmed
Asquith in the past, should now unwittingly deliver this severe blow.

Before he left with Asquith to attend an Allied conference in Paris
on November 14th, Lloyd George used Aitken to sound out Bonar
Law on the possibility of their urging the creation of a small War
Committee, to be independent of the Cabinet, and without the Prime
Minister at its head. Lloyd George's principal preoccupation at this
point was not Asquith, but Sir William Robertson. When Aitken put
the idea to Law, the Unionist leader was 'desperately "sticky"'.
Law's dislike and distrust of Lloyd George were as great as ever, and
he was, moreover, oppressed by his own problems as Conservative
leader. When he heard that Carson agreed with Lloyd George on the
matter he felt that he would have at least to give consideration to the
proposal, although he was clearly unenthusiastic. When Lloyd George
got back from Paris,[2] he invited Law to dine with him alone, but Law
refused. On the following day Law told Asquith of what was in the
wind.

Asquith did not express surprise, and commented that he could not
believe that Lloyd George's ambitions would be content with chairmanship of such a body. In this he struck a receptive chord in Law.

[1] See p. 63.
[2] This conference had exposed the differences in attitudes towards the military
shown by Asquith and Lloyd George. Lloyd George wanted Ministers to meet before
the military conference was held; in the event he did not get his way, and the
Ministers accepted the decisions of the generals. Lloyd George returned from Paris
even more convinced than ever that the generals, if left to themselves, would lose
the war.

He also expressed doubts about including Carson on the basis of his previous performance as a member of the Government.

On November 20th Lloyd George, Carson and Bonar Law met at the Hyde Park Hotel. Law's attitude remained one of scepticism and suspicion of Lloyd George's motives. Nevertheless, he did see the advantages of getting Carson on to the Committee. This was the first meeting of the 'Triumvirate', and its results were to be momentous.

There were further meetings on the following three days, in which Law became increasingly attracted by the War Committee idea. By Saturday, November 25th, he was ready to accept a written agreement, prepared by Aitken, which was in the form of a public announcement by Asquith, and to submit it to the Prime Minister. It would announce the creation of 'a civilian General Staff' of which Asquith would be president, and Lloyd George the actual chairman. The members would be Lloyd George, Carson and Bonar Law himself. It was a skilfully worded document, designed to placate Law's suspicions of Lloyd George's motives and to give Carson and Lloyd George what they wanted.

On the next day (Sunday, November 26th), Law presented this paper to Asquith. The Prime Minister had, on Thursday 23rd, been alerted by the curious fact that the *Morning Post*, an old ally of Carson's but never enthusiastic about Lloyd George, came out for a Lloyd George premiership and styled him the 'saviour of society'.

In his reply to Law's missive, Asquith wrote that, after due reflection, he was not taken by the idea of the small War Committee, and put forward some very reasonable and acute criticisms of the proposal. It was a measured, calm, precise response. Again, one has the impression of a great judge giving mature consideration to a project, analysing it, and returning a fully considered and unanswerable opinion. And there was a sting in the tail, when the judge came to deal with the plaintiff Lloyd George:

He has many qualities that would fit him for the first place, but he lacks the one thing needful—he does not inspire trust. . . . Here, again, there is one construction, and one only, that could be put on the new arrangement, that it has been engineered by him with the purpose, not perhaps at the moment, but as soon as a fitting pretext could be found, of his displacing me. In short, the plan could not, in my opinion, be carried out without impairing the confidence of loyal and valued colleagues, and undermining my own authority.

This flung the 'Triumvirate' into some confusion. Carson was all for fighting Asquith, but Law had not yet reached this point, and Lloyd George, although quite untroubled by the severe comments on himself, began to back-pedal.

Carson and Aitken had no doubts or hesitations, and began to use their formidable newspaper contacts to good purpose. A Ministerial Crisis is difficult to create by Press agitation, but a Little Ministerial Crisis can be built up into a Big Ministerial Crisis with judicious fire and brimstone applied at the right moment. Aitken, who was convinced that Asquith must go, was particularly active. On November 29th the *Daily Chronicle*, an influential Liberal newspaper, came out with strong criticism of the manner in which the war was being conducted. The *Daily Express, Daily Mail, Morning Post* and *Times* echoed these charges, and they constituted a formidable coverage of the national Press. All week the barrage against the Government was maintained.

On the Thursday (November 30th), Bonar Law told his Conservative colleagues in the Government what had transpired. Not unnaturally, they were affronted by the fact that they had not been consulted; none of them liked the proposals themselves, and particularly the elevation of Lloyd George. Lord Robert Cecil, in fact, openly accused Law of 'dragging the Conservative Party at the coattails of Lloyd George'. The Ministers favoured a reorganisation of the present War Committee but would not support the 'Triumvirate's' proposals. Law stood by them, and the meeting broke up in disagreement.

On the next day (Friday, December 1st) Lloyd George in effect told Asquith that unless he accepted the terms of the Triumvirate, he would resign. In reply Asquith admitted that the system needed revision, but insisted that the Prime Minister must remain head of any reorganised War Committee. Lloyd George considered this 'entirely unsatisfactory'.

The key to the situation was Bonar Law. If he backed Lloyd George, Asquith's position would be extremely serious. If he did not, Lloyd George would have either to suffer a serious humiliation or resign alone. There are moments in politics when a man needs friends. Lloyd George had none in the Coalition Cabinet. He was fighting alone, and had reached a crisis-point.

If Bonar Law was to be moved, his close friend Aitken was the only person who could achieve this. On the evening of December 1st he dined alone with Law at the Hyde Park Hotel, and pressed Lloyd George's case upon him. At length Law decided to see Lloyd George at once, and they went in a taxi to the Berkeley Hotel, where Lloyd George was dining with the Governor of the Bank of England, Lord Cunliffe.[1] Lloyd George joined Aitken and Law—patiently waiting in the taxi—and returned to the Hyde Park. Lloyd George handled Bonar Law dexterously and sympathetically. On the following morning he sent Law a copy of Asquith's letter to him and a brief note that read: 'The life of the country depends on resolute action by you now.'

Bonar Law called a meeting of his Conservative ministerial colleagues for the Sunday (December 3rd) morning. Balfour and Lansdowne were not present. The Ministers came in a passion, having read or been told about an article in *Reynolds' News* that morning which gave the full story from Lloyd George's angle. It was, as Beaverbrook subsequently commented, 'like an interview with Lloyd George written in the third person'. The Ministers were deeply chagrined, and instructed Law to transmit to Asquith a resolution recommending the resignation of the Government; if this were not done, they authorised Law to tender their resignations.

Some historians have accepted Beaverbrook's opinion that this was a purely anti-Lloyd George move, designed to expose Lloyd George's isolation, and bring Asquith back on the Conservatives' terms. This interpretation seems both too naïve and too subtle; it imposes clarity of thought and action upon an angry and confused meeting; it does not credit the Conservative Ministers with much intelligence or competence. This was an ultimatum to Asquith that a major reconstruction from the top was necessary, and on the Conservatives' terms. Curzon, who wrote an account for Lansdowne, took a strong anti-Asquith line, and said that the object of the resolution was to bring Lloyd George face to face with the fact of political responsibility: 'His Government will be dictated to him by others, not shaped exclusively by himself.'

Law saw Asquith—who had been urgently summoned back from

[1] 'I had the means of finding Lloyd George at that time at any hour of the day or night', Beaverbrook has recorded.

his weekend in Kent—after lunch with Aitken. Aitken had tried to persuade Law not to show Asquith a passage from the Conservative resolution which rebuked Lloyd George for his disclosures to the *Daily Chronicle*, *Daily Express*—Aitken's own work—and *Reynolds*. At the meeting with Asquith, Law did not give him the resolution. Law's account is that he forgot to show him the actual paper, although he described its contents. In any event, Asquith took Law's message to be that all the Conservative Ministers were in complete hostility to him.

Much heat has been engendered about this meeting, and of Law's failure to give a copy of the resolution to Asquith.[1] Law's explanation is so simple and human that it sounds very authentic, but, given Aitken's urgings to him at luncheon, this commentator is sceptical. It is difficult to determine whether it had any real consequence on the eventual result, but it certainly complicated matters. And it must have determined Asquith on his next move, which was to see Lloyd George and virtually give him everything he had asked for. Law joined this meeting at the end, and they decided that all Ministers other than Asquith should resign and the Government be reconstructed on the basis of the new arrangement. It seemed an admirable compromise. Lloyd George would get his War Committee; Asquith would remain Prime Minister, and with 'supreme and effective control of War Policy'. Asquith was not unjustified when he wrote that evening:

> The 'Crisis' shows every sign of following its many predecessors to an early and unhonoured grave. But there were many wigs very nearly on the green.

On the following morning (Monday, December 4th) the wigs were back on the green.

The cause was a leading article in *The Times*, which attacked Asquith personally. Furthermore, it showed clear signs of having been written by someone with very good inside information indeed, and implied that Asquith had made a complete surrender of his powers to Lloyd George. Asquith assumed at once that Lloyd George was the informant. He did not know that Lloyd George had been seeing Northcliffe regularly during the previous weeks, and that there had been three meetings in the previous three days, but his assumption

---

[1] See Robert Blake, *The Unknown Prime Minister*, 317–25; Beaverbrook, op. cit., 419–36; Jenkins, op. cit., 438–40.

that Lloyd George had been up to his old tricks was not surprising. Some confusion exists about Lloyd George's part in the *Times* article, which was written by the editor, Geoffrey Dawson. It has also been alleged that the sole purpose of Northcliffe's discussions with Lloyd George was to offer him a post on his newspapers. It requires considerable credulity to accept this version implicitly; in any event, it is doubtful whether these conversations about Lloyd George's future career did not include some chance observations on the current political situation. The last of these conversations took place on the Sunday evening. Dawson's claim—supported by Mr. Taylor[1] and Dawson's biographer—that his sole informants were Waldorf Astor and Carson does not wholly exonerate Lloyd George. From whom else would Carson get his information? Asquith's conclusions may not have been correct, but they certainly were not unjustified.

Asquith at once wrote a curt letter to Lloyd George, reminding him of their arrangement. Lloyd George replied that he had not read *The Times*, and advised Asquith to take no notice of what Northcliffe said. Asquith, at 12.30 told the King that the Cabinet had resigned, and that the Government would be reconstructed. That afternoon there were two inconclusive but significant meetings with Law, at which Asquith made it clear that he was reconsidering the War Committee arrangement, and that other ex-Ministers—Liberal and Conservative—were hostile to it. Law emphasised that it was vital to keep to the arrangement. Later Asquith wrote to Lloyd George in effect throwing over the arrangement, and making it quite clear that this was to be a reconstruction on his, and not on Lloyd George's, terms.

Thus, Asquith had determined to fight. Lloyd George was determined to fight as well. On the following morning, as soon as he had read Asquith's letter, he withdrew from the arrangement. This was expected. What was not expected was a letter from Balfour, who had been unwell for several days, which in effect supported Lloyd George. But Asquith, heavily pressed, does not seem to have grasped the implications. Balfour, with characteristic feline subtlety, was on the move.

At one o'clock on that fateful Tuesday, December 5th, the Liberal ex-Ministers met to consider the situation created by Lloyd George's

[1] Taylor: *Beaverbrook*, 118.

withdrawal, and concluded that Asquith could best meet the challenge by resigning himself.

Asquith hoped that the Conservative ex-Ministers would support him, even if the new Government did not include Law or Lloyd George. Their answer was that they could not, and that the arrangement over the War Committee must stand. Balfour had meanwhile sent another letter from his sick-bed at Carlton Gardens, which made his movement even clearer. Later in the afternoon Asquith told his Liberal colleagues that he would resign, and at 7 p.m. he did so, still believing that he would win his struggle. The King summoned Bonar Law and, at the end of a somewhat chaotic interview, invited him to form a Government.

Thus matters stood on the evening of December 5th. Through a series of events, not all of which his critics controlled, Asquith had resigned after eight years and 241 days as Prime Minister, and Bonar Law had been invited to form an Administration.

It has been often alleged that Asquith's resignation was a manoeuvre to expose and crush his critics. It is difficult to accept this sweeping conclusion. Asquith had chosen to reconstruct his Government on his own terms, and not those of Bonar Law and Lloyd George. He thought he could do it. He could not. Continuance in the premiership in these conditions had become impossible. There was no alternative to resignation once the Liberal and Conservative ex-Ministers—for different reasons—had advised such a course.

All that remained was aftermath. There was a conference of the leading politicians at Buckingham Palace on the afternoon of December 6th, attended by Asquith, the recovered Balfour, Lloyd George, Bonar Law and Arthur Henderson, and with the King in the chair. Lloyd George later alleged that everyone was ready to serve under Balfour, and that Asquith dramatically declared that 'What is the proposal? That I who have held first place for eight years should be asked to take a secondary position.' There is no reference to this in the accounts of Balfour or Stamfordham, and it would seem to be another example of Lloyd George's dramatic inventiveness that make his *War Memoirs* occasionally interesting. What is uncontested is that Balfour urged Asquith to serve under Law, and that Asquith refused.

The conference only emphasised the political realities of the situation, which were well summed up by Balfour. Asquith could not form a Government. Lloyd George was indispensable. If Asquith would not serve under Bonar Law, then a Government would have to be formed either by Law or Lloyd George. After again consulting his colleagues, Asquith wrote to Law to reiterate that he would not serve under him. At seven o'clock Law went to Buckingham Palace to decline the King's Commission; at 7.30 Lloyd George was invited to form a Government, and accepted.

Thus, almost soundlessly, Asquith fell. Churchill subsequently expressed the opinion that if Asquith had taken the battle to the House of Commons he would have won a vote of confidence, instead of fighting what Churchill called 'secret, obscure, internal processes'. This seems highly improbable. Certainly, it would have been a bitter debate, and matters had gone too far already to be thus retrieved.

Tactically, Asquith made many errors. He fought hard to keep the premiership, but although he was consistently out-manoeuvred by Lloyd George and was over-influenced by the *Times* article of December 4th, it was not really tactics that ended his premiership. The fact was that he no longer possessed the confidence in the House of Commons or in the Cabinet that was required to beat off such a major challenge to his leadership. That authority had gone; it was a matter of how and when the attack was mounted. When it came, Asquith was utterly defeated. But he still had many friends in the Liberal Party who were incensed by Lloyd George's activities, and who remained loyal. Although Lloyd George had won, he had done so with Conservative support. It was in fact a major Conservative victory, and the wounds inflicted on the Liberal Party by the events of December 1st–7th were never to be healed.

Asquith had been brought down by his own inadequacies. The feeling against him was well expressed at the time by Haldane:

Asquith is a first-class head of a deliberative council. He is versed in precedents, acts on principle, and knows how and when to compromise. Lloyd George cares nothing for precedents and knows no principles, but he has fire in his belly and that is what we want.

CHAPTER TWELVE

A NATION AT WAR, 1916–1918

THE GREAT WAR illuminated the strengths, and also the deficiencies, of the British society that had been developing for the previous half-century. It is a baffling feature of the British character that it responds to major challenges and crises with exhilaration, and demonstrates depth of courage and initiative that lie dormant in quiet times. It is the element that has brought the British to remarkable heights and has brought them also to the edge of disaster. It is also the factor that makes them such an enigma to their foes and so infuriating an ally to their friends.

The effects of the war on British society were highly complex, and were not to be seen clearly for several years. At the time, it was a period of confusion, excitement, tragedy and disillusionment.

The most remarkable immediate revolutions were technological. The disparity in quality between British and German steel emphasised the fact that Britain had been overtaken in what had been her principal product both in quantity and quality. In 1914 Britain did not possess a chemical industry. The National Physical Laboratory— founded in 1902—limped along on a government grant (in 1914) of £7,000 a year. The Imperial College of Science and Technology had not been established until 1907. The war exposed these, and many other, painful deficiencies in a modern industrial nation. These were seen in many areas. Wireless telegraphy had hardly been exploited; in the manufacture and use of the internal combustion engine Britain lagged behind her Continental rivals; the demand for new munitions of war revealed that the country was seriously deficient in such matters as the production of optical glass, dye-stuffs, magnets, drugs, tungsten and zinc that were vital for the war effort. They emphasised what had been only dimly apparent to contemporaries before the war, that Britain from being a great industrial nation had become a great trading nation.

356

Some of these weaknesses could be cured—in time. In August 1915 the Government announced the establishment of an Advisory Council to a Committee of the Privy Council devoted to scientific and industrial research. It received a grant of £25,000 for the first year, and £40,000 for the second. As from December 1st, 1916, it was reorganised as a separate Government Department of Scientific and Industrial Research (D.S.I.R.) with, at last, substantial funds behind it. But its contribution could only be fragmentary and limited in the immediate crisis.

The technological contributions that were made by the British owed more to individual enthusiasms and private enterprise than to Government sponsorship or encouragement. The tank was a case in point. The idea itself had been mooted before—notably by Ian Hamilton in somewhat vague terms in his evidence to the Royal Commission on the Boer War—and it began to make progress shortly after the outbreak of war, principally as a result of the keen interest shown by Churchill. In August 1915 the project was transferred to the Ministry of Munitions, and the firm of William Foster and Co. produced the first prototype, called 'Little Willie'. It was succeeded in turn by 'Big Willie', eventually rechristened 'Mother', which was ready for tests in January 1916. By the autumn of 1916 a number were available for action at the Somme. Very little interest had been shown in the project by the War Office, and the Western Front generals were at best unenthusiastic. There was no attempt to examine the tactical and strategical implications of the new weapons, which were frittered away at the Somme in 'penny packets'. Nevertheless, Haig was impressed enough to order a thousand of the cumbersome, fearful new invention, but no further study was made of how it was to be employed, with the result that at Cambrai (November 20th, 1917) the tanks tore a gaping hole in the German lines which could not be exploited. The British had in fact found the answer to the perennial problem of the Western Front.

It is easy to criticise the reaction of the soldiers. They had not yet realised—nor, indeed, had anyone—the one gleaming lesson of twentieth-century warfare; that strategy follows, and does not precede, the scientist and the technician.

Much more success had been achieved in the air. At the outbreak of war the Army and the Navy had their own flying services, the Royal Flying Corps and the Royal Naval Air Service, with a Joint Air

Committee of the Committee of Imperial Defence to secure co-operation. Service aviation thus got off to a bad start, and the mutual jealousies and animosities between the army and naval aviators was to plague British aviation up to the eve of the Second World War. The attempts to concentrate the services under one Air Council were poisoned by personal antipathies and the interventions of Northcliffe, Rothermere, and others who flung themselves into the political and personal problems with greater enthusiasm than they demonstrated for the technical and operational ones.

But the technical performance was remarkable. In 1914 the British possessed 272 machines, and were heavily dependent on other countries for aero-engines. By the end of the war the new Royal Air Force had over 22,000 effective machines; most impressive of all, the British aero-engines were the best in the world. The reconnaissance aircraft possessed by the B.E.F. in 1914 had a maximum speed of 80 m.p.h., a rate of climb from ground level of between 300 and 400 feet a minute, and were equipped with engines of between 60 and 100 horse-power. In 1918 the fastest fighter-aircraft could reach 140 m.p.h. and had a rate of climb from ground level of 2,000 feet per minute. By 1918 the British had developed the first heavy bomber, the Handley Page V/1500, which had a maximum flying height of 25,000 feet and was capable of bombing Berlin from French airfields. Other new bombers—notably the Vickers Vimy, which achieved the first transatlantic flight in 1919—were also available by the end of the war. Many of the technical innovations were German, but in many cases the British developed them more efficiently; the synchronised machine-gun firing through the propellor was a case in point.

In wireless, also, the British had had a bad start. Supplies of radio valves from the pioneer companies—Marconi, Edison, Swan and Cossor—were inadequate, and contracts were given to the principal producers of electric light bulbs, thus bringing firms of the experience of General Electric, British Thompson-Houston, and British Westinghouse into this new field. These companies were to bring strong pressure to bear after the war for the official encouragement of national broadcasting, and to create in effect a new industry of enormous potentiality. For these advances the war was entirely responsible.

The war had no responsibility for the one spectacular scientific contribution—the artificial disintegration of the atom by Rutherford at Manchester in 1918. The revolution this gave to British physics needs no emphasis. The Cavendish at Cambridge and the Clarendon at Oxford became the best physics laboratories in the world. The man who developed the latter was Professor F. A. Lindemann, whose main contribution in the war had been in the highly dangerous techniques of obviating the effects of aircraft spins, which until then were almost invariably fatal. We shall hear more of this curious man.

In a sense, Britain was so backward technically and scientifically in 1914 when compared with Germany and even France, that any advance would have been notable. But the outstanding feature of the period 1914–18 was that the strange pause in industrial and technical inventiveness in Britain that had existed since the 1870s came to an end. Until 1916 there were few official organisations that could harness and exploit these developments, and the pressures to create such organisations grew, and were the vital background to the burst of government sponsorship of the war effort in the last two years. But, typically, the gains were to be thrown away. The central organisations were to be swiftly dismantled; the supply of Government funds was to be cut off, few of the great advances made were to be properly exploited. The old traditions of laissez-faire and Free Trade were to prove more durable than the new technology created by the war. In 1919 the British lapsed into the pre-1914 system with an audible sigh of relief, and all the advantages of the war were needlessly thrown away. Most tragic of all was the virtual abandonment of the new aircraft industry, which by 1919 was producing the best aircraft in the world and was eager for new advances. Not until 1935 was it to be given another opportunity to demonstrate its quality.

*

Thus, before the fall of the Asquith Coalition in December 1915, British industry and society had already changed to meet the new challenges of wartime conditions. One remarkable feature was the changed status and responsibilities of women. The statistics tell only part of the story. It was subsequently estimated that, in July 1914, there were 23,721,000 women in Britain, of whom 4,809,000 were under ten years of age. The total in occupations or professions was 5,966,000, of whom 2,178,000 were in industry. By July 1918 the total in occupations or professions was 7,311,000 (an increase of 1,345,000). The number of women in commerce increased from 505,000 to

934,000; in transport from 18,000 to 117,000, and in national and local government (including education) from 262,000 to 460,000. The number of women over the age of ten not in occupations fell by 450,000; the only profession in which numbers fell was domestic service. In July 1914 these totalled 1,658,000; in July 1918, 1,258,000 —a fall of exactly 400,000.

The importance of women's work was recognised at the outset of the war. A 'Central Committee for the Prevention and Relief of Distress', headed by the President of the Board of Trade, was set up on August 4th, and asked local authorities to set up similar bodies at the local level. The Board of Education asked local education authorities at least to consider providing instruction in new industries or under-developed ones, in areas where unemployment would be caused by the war. The Board of Agriculture was made responsible for instruction for women over school-leaving age. On August 20th the Central Committee for Women's Employment, headed by Queen Mary, was set up, 'to consider, and from time to time report upon, schemes for the provision of work for women and girls unemployed on account of the war'.

These organisations were basically relief projects; this relief was certainly needed, as a substantial proportion of the women employed by the outbreak of war were in luxury trades. By September 1914, forty-four per cent of the total number of women in industry were either unemployed or on short time, as opposed to twenty-seven per cent of men.[1]

The Central Committee for Women's Employment attempted to increase the number of firms and workers participating in government work, and in some cases through its Contracts Department actually intervened to spread the work on large orders as widely as possible among small firms. It also interested itself in the development of new trades for women and even on occasion provided loans on wages which were to be repaid out of profits. Emergency workshops, in which women could be trained either from scratch or to move into other work, were set up; experimental schemes in training in domestic economy and home help were also initiated.

Most useful of all was the work done by the local committees for the Prevention and Relief of Distress. By January 1915 there were

[1] I. O. Andrews and M. A. Hobbs: *Economic Effects of the War Upon Women and Children in Great Britain*, 23.

approximately seventy workrooms and training centres administered by these local bodies, and they had enrolled 8,963 women.

By the end of 1914 the 'relief' side of this work had become of lesser importance. The problem had changed from there being a surplus of labour to an acute shortage. Early in 1915 the Government began to campaign for women workers, and urged them to register for war service in industry at the Labour Exchanges. By April 1915, 47,000 women had registered, but only 440 had been placed.[1]

The Munitions of War Act, 1915, created a Labour Regulation Department and Labour Supply Department in the new Ministry of Munitions. The country was divided into forty-three districts, with three Commissioners in each district. A Central Labour Supply Committee was also set up to advise the Minister on the most productive use of available labour. Women also had to register under the National Registration Act. This was a long stride in the direction of government direction of labour, although the main weapons of the government ramained, to the end, those of persuasion rather than of compulsion. The Ministry embarked upon a substantial programme urging employers to bring schemes of 'dilution' of women into industry, issuing pamphlets and bulletins to industrialists, while at the same time fostering the local authorities' interest and organisation in persuading women to work in industry.

All this aroused strong opposition in the trade unions. Women were reluctant to attempt agricultural work, and the National Federation of Women Workers was severe in its criticism of the recruiting of women for rough, dirty and sometimes dangerous work without proper safeguards; they were also concerned—and rightly—by the considerable possibility of exploitation of cheap labour by certain industrialists. The invasion of industry by women, however, caused a minor revolution in attitudes to working conditions, the provision of canteens and washing facilities. At the end of 1915 the staff of the Director of Welfare for Controlled Factories had inspected the 1,396 controlled factories employing 198,661 women, and reported that 31 per cent of the factories merited an A rating; 49 per cent B; and 20 per cent C. This new interest by the Government in factory conditions constituted, in itself, a considerable development.

Politically, the war had abruptly ended the Suffragette Movement's

[1] *Hansard*, April 27th, 1915, 563.

activities. There was a split between the majority, which was prepared to drop the matter of female suffrage for the duration, and the determined activists. The movement fragmented, but the war gave it the victory so long denied to it. Not that it was a total victory, and its origins were curious. The 1918 Representation of the People Act started its life in 1916 as a measure to provide for the registration of voters who had moved as a result of war work. This led to the proposal to enfranchise soldiers over twenty-one, which, in turn, led to a demand that women should not be excluded. A conference, presided over by the Speaker, recommended a six months' residence qualification for males, instead of occupancy. It also recommended (by a majority) that women over thirty should have the vote if they themselves, or their husbands, could meet the *former* property qualifications. Thus, the division between the sexes was carefully maintained.

The Representation of the People Act, 1918, was the most dramatic single advance towards a full democracy. With one stroke it added two million women and six million men to the electorate. It established the principle of 'one man, one vote', the only exceptions being the University seats and a vote for business premises; the second exception seems, in retrospect, even more astonishing than the first. The women had won a victory, but perhaps it was, in relation to their contribution to the war effort, a somewhat meagre one.

*

The full extent of the new political situation on the accession of Lloyd George was swiftly seen. Not a single Liberal member of the 1915–16 Cabinet was retained, and only a few lesser Liberals took office under the new Prime Minister. Edwin Montagu (India) and Churchill (Munitions) were brought in some six months later—the latter to the dismay and fierce opposition of the Unionists. Bonar Law did not exaggerate when he told a Conservative gathering in November 1918:

> By our own action we have made Mr. Lloyd George the flag-bearer of the very principles upon which we should appeal to the country. It is not his Liberal friends, it is the Unionist Party which has made him Prime Minister, and made it possible for him to do the great work that has been done by this government.

Lloyd George's personal influence was, however, initially overwhelming. The old Cabinet system was swept away, and replaced by a small War Cabinet of five—subsequently increased to seven—Ministers, of whom only one (Bonar Law) had any departmental responsibilities. The Ministers were Lloyd George, Curzon, Law, Lord Milner and Henderson. Smuts joined in June 1917, and Carson in July. This reorganisation of function and personnel was accompanied with a transformation of the machinery of the Cabinet. In this, Hankey's views and Lloyd George's coincided almost exactly. Cabinet meetings were to an agenda; minutes were taken, printed, and circulated; departments were informed of decisions concerning their operations, and the Cabinet Secretariat followed up to ensure that the decisions were in fact being carried out. These changes resulted in much more efficient control at the top and a far more practical and businesslike approach. From December 1916 to October 1919 the War Cabinet met more than 650 times, and much of the work previously done in full Cabinet—or not done at all—was delegated to committees. Other Ministers were only summoned to Cabinet meetings when their departments were involved.

All this was certainly to the good, and the effects were permanent. Other innovations did not survive Lloyd George. The creation of a personal Secretariat in St. James' Park—the 'Garden Suburb'—was viewed with suspicion in some quarters. In part, this new organisation pandered to a particular aspect of Lloyd George's character—'of secretaries', Thomas Jones (one of them) has related, 'Lloyd George never could have enough'—but it also represented his reaction to the fact that the Prime Minister has no department. The Garden Suburb became in effect Lloyd George's private army, and was accordingly increasingly regarded with the mixed feelings that accompany private armies in politics as elsewhere. Subsequently there tended to be a confusion between the official Secretariat and the Garden Suburb in the popular comprehension. 'Hankey and his Secretariat was essential', Sir Henry Wilson has written, 'whereas Philip Kerr, Ned Grigg,[1] etc., are poisonous.'[2] By 1922 the Civil Estimates, under the item 'Cabinet Office', recorded a staff of 129 persons and a cost of over £38,000.

Another important innovation that did not survive the war was the creation of 'functional' Ministries on the same lines as the Ministry of Munitions. Labour, Shipping, Food, National Service and Food

[1] Later Lord Lothian and Sir Edward Grigg, respectively.
[2] C. E. Callwell: *Wilson*, II, 343–4.

Production now became matters that merited separate departments, and new men. They had substantial powers, but these were seldom used; the new system, like the old, relied upon co-operation of industry and labour for success.

It would be dangerous and inaccurate to see in these changes any detailed plan of action brought by the new Prime Minister. As Professor Marwick has rightly commented, 'Lloyd George was nothing of a theorist, very little of a planner; his concern was to get things done, his strength that he would give a hearing and a trial to all suggested means towards this end'.[1] Indeed, Lloyd George's genius as a war leader lay in his immediate reactions to problems with immediate—virtually instinctive—solutions. The results were not always successful, but there was, from the outset, a sense of pace and urgency in the Lloyd George regime that was in marked contrast with his predecessor. The crisis had brought the politicians and the industrialists reluctantly—and in some cases without fully realising it—to the situation of accepting the 'nation in arms' concept to an extent that had been unthinkable in 1914 or even 1915. There were still pockets of resistance, and many of the changes were accepted on the explicit understanding that there was to be no permanence in them. Circumstances impelled changes which might have been far-reaching upon British industry and society, but which in fact were not.

In one vital respect there was little change. Lloyd George was never in a position to control the conduct of the war in a Napoleonic, or even in a Churchillian, sense. 'Of all the civilians I have known', John Buchan wrote, 'Lloyd George seems to have possessed in the highest degree the capacity for becoming a great soldier. But he might have lost several armies while he was learning his trade.' Lloyd George certainly possessed drive, imagination, and single-minded pursuit of the enemy, and his scepticism of the capacities of the senior British commanders—notably Haig and Robertson—was not ill-founded. But his lack of knowledge of military matters meant that his contribution tended to be a negative one; whenever driven to suggest alternatives they were usually even more disastrous than the disease they were meant to cure.

Ironically, the change in Government had actually increased the independence of the Service Departments. Carson, now at the

---

[1] Marwick, op. cit., 252.

Admiralty, accepted everything from his advisers and became an implacable opponent of anything that did not appeal to them. Derby, who had become Secretary of State for War, was completely under the influence of Robertson and Haig. Haig was a match for Lloyd George in intrigue, and cultivated powerful allies with the King and in the Conservative Party. This created a very serious situation, whose military implications were not fully seen until early in 1918. The relationship between Asquith and the senior commanders had been bad in that the latter were in complete control, and civilian control was virtually non-existent. Now, the control was retained, but a strong reciprocal mistrust and suspicion developed between the Prime Minister and the senior military advisers, to the point that Robertson described the Cabinet as 'the enemy' and the Prime Minister as 'the wrong 'un'. Thus, from the beginning, Lloyd George had to handle the military with caution.

The situation at the outset of 1917 has been described with characteristic sharpness by Beaverbrook:

> The politicians gave little credit to the generals.
> The generals denounced the politicians.
> The soldiers and sailors serving in the forces had little confidence in either.
> The public had no heroes.[1]

Lloyd George's position was complicated further by the fact that Northcliffe—who controlled not only *The Times* but half the daily papers sold in London—was a strong supporter of the military, and was described by Lloyd George (later) as 'the mere kettledrum of Sir Douglas Haig and the mouth-organ of Sir William Robertson'. This particular obstruction was neatly—but only temporarily—removed in May 1917 when Lloyd George appointed Northcliffe to head a British mission to the United States over the strong objections of the Foreign Secretary (Balfour), the British Ambassador in Washington, the President of the United States, and the American Secretary of State. But Northcliffe remained an implacable critic of Lloyd George, and his newspapers consistently supported the soldiers against the politicians.[2] It is to Churchill that we owe the best account of the picture that was conveyed:

[1] Beaverbrook: Introduction, *Men and Power*, 1917–18.
[2] Nonetheless, Northcliffe's star was fading. On his return in November he publicly refused to take the Air Ministry and abused the Government. In Beaverbrook's

The feeble or presumptuous politician is portrayed cowering in his office, intent in the crash of the world on Party intrigues or personal glorification, fearful of responsibility, incapable of aught save shallow phrase-making. To him enters the calm, noble, resolute figure of the great Commander by land or sea, resplendent in uniform, glittering with decorations, irradiated with the lustre of the hero, shod with the science and armed with the panoply of war. This stately figure, devoid of the slightest thought of self, offers his clear far-sighted guidance and counsel for vehement action or wise delay. But his advice is rejected; his sound plans put aside; his courageous initiative baffled by political chatterboxes and incompetents. As well, it was suggested, might a great surgeon, about to operate with science and the study of a lifetime upon a desperate case, have his arm jogged or his hand impeded, or even his lancet snatched away from him, by some agitated relation of the patient. Such was the picture presented to the public, and such was the mood which ruled.[1]

Nonetheless, although the Service commanders were still firmly in control, now, for the first time, their actions were under scrutiny and had to be justified. And Lloyd George could get results by untraditional methods. His action in going behind the backs of the Board of Admiralty to discover the views of junior officers on the convoy system would have been unthinkable to Asquith; but the results were admirable.

The fairest summary comes in a letter from Balfour to Lord Robert Cecil on September 12th, 1917. Balfour had few illusions about Lloyd George; indeed, he had few illusions about any politician. He considered that Lloyd George was 'impulsive', and went on:

> ... he had never given a thought before the war to military matters; he does not perhaps adequately gauge the depths of his own ignorance; and he has certain peculiarities which no doubt make him, now and then, difficult to work with. But I am clearly of the opinion that military matters are much better managed now than

---

words: 'Night of gloom closed in upon Northcliffe. His gaiety and high spirits were memories of the past. Although he gave much attention to his newspapers, his shadow was no longer lengthening across the land' (op. cit., 89–90). He died insane, in 1922.

[1] Churchill: *The World Crisis 1916–18*, Part I, 244.

they were in the time of his predecessor . . . [Asquith] never seriously attempted to co-ordinate in one homogeneous whole the efforts of soldiers, sailors, and diplomatists, and the result was disaster. . . . Is there any one of his colleagues in the present War Cabinet you would like to see in his place? Is there any member of the late government you would like to see in his place?

By the middle of 1917 all the major steps had been taken at last to put Britain on a war footing. If the results—particularly in industry— had been a series of compromises between laissez-faire and government control, the Government now possessed the powers at least to direct industry. It had the power to conscript young men and to influence the deployment of labour; it could, to a substantial degree, control prices. Towards the end of 1917, for example, flour and potato subsidies were introduced, and food prices controlled by what Beveridge called a mixture of 'costings, conference, and compromise'. Farmers had a minimum guaranteed price, and agricultural workmen a guaranteed minimum wage. Bulk purchasing of raw commodities from abroad became the rule rather than the exception. Compared with the situation in 1914 and 1915, this cumulatively represented a real economic revolution. The machinery of State interference, virtually non-existent in 1914, had been created, and was working with— on the whole—remarkable absence of serious friction. The emphasis upon co-operation rather than compulsion was probably the right one; it was certainly the only one that had a chance of substantial success. 'As the war continued', wrote Evelyn Wrench, 'we became increasingly accustomed to restrictions of every sort. When the fourth anniversary came, government control was so much part of our lives that we found it difficult to jump back in our minds to the pre-war world in which we lived in July 1914.'[1]
One of the most impressive features of the war had been the manner in which the Dominions had rallied to the British cause. The performances of the Canadian, Australian, New Zealand and Indian armies had been such as to arouse the admiration and enthusiasm of all observers. This revived high hopes among the Imperialists of the Milner school—particularly now that Milner had made a remarkable renaissance and was in the War Cabinet. In short, might not the old dream of Imperial Federation be turned into actuality as a result of

[1] E. Wrench: *Struggle 1914–20*, 333.

the experiences of the war? Certainly, enthusiasm for the Empire had never been greater. Unfortunately, as the meeting of the Dominion Premiers in 1917 demonstrated, these national achievements actually worked *against* federation. Lloyd George's plan of creating a real Imperial War Cabinet was largely based on the hope that it would increase civilian control over the military. Both his hopes and those of the Imperialists were dashed. The self-governing Dominions were to remain emphatically self-governing, and they gave no support to Lloyd George's schemes.

It was ironical that the unity of the Empire in the war was, in the long run, a step towards further independence of the self-governing Dominions. Furthermore, in the greatest British possession of all—India—there were indications of stirrings against the British supremacy. British policy towards India from 1905 onwards was one of 'gradualness', but at so slow a pace that the final grantings of genuine self-government on the Australia-Canada-New Zealand-South Africa pattern was scarcely envisaged at all. All reforms were based on increasing Indian consultation and participation without sacrificing the reality of British rule. The Morley–Minto Reforms of 1909 were based on this premise; so were the Montagu–Chelmsford proposals of 1917, eventually embodied in the Government of India Act of 1919. Under the Act, Indian membership of the Viceroy's Executive Council was increased; an elective majority in the legislative assembly would be Indian; and in the Provinces the system of 'Dyarchy' was created, whereby the Governor-in-Council had special reserved powers and Indian ministers were responsible for the administration of certain areas of responsibility—education, health, and local government. The 'reserved' powers were, of course, the real powers.

Seen through British eyes, these were substantial concessions to Indian nationalist feeling; indeed, they were opposed by F. E. Smith as going much too far. In the pre-1914 context, they represented a considerable step forward. But in the post-1914 context they were inadequate. Thus, the war that seemed to demonstrate the vast strength and unity of the British Empire struck a mortal blow at the edifice.

*

1917 proved nearly disastrous for the Allies. It opened with the renewal of unrestricted submarine warfare by the Germans, which had immediate success, and very nearly ended the war. By April one out of four ships leaving British ports was sunk. In February the total shipping losses—British, Allied, and neutral—were 540,000 tons; in March, 593,841 tons; in April the total was 881,027 tons, of which 542,282 tons were British. Between February and June some 3·3 million tons of shipping were lost to the submarine campaign, of which almost two million were British. This came on top of the very real success of the 'restricted' submarine campaign; in the last month— January 1917—of restricted submarine activity the Germans sank nearly 370,000 tons of British and foreign shipping. Jellicoe was not being alarmist when he wrote late in October 1916 that this rate of loss might compel the Allies to make peace in the summer of 1917.

The Admiralty had no answer to this menacing situation except to search and destroy the submarines by various methods. By February 1917 there were some three thousand vessels engaged in this work, and operating with an alarming lack of success. In February the British sank three submarines and a fourth was blown up by a mine; in March another four were sunk; in April only two. The Germans had one hundred and eleven submarines available for active service in February, of which about a third were on operations at a given time. Thus, in spite of massive anti-submarine activity by the British, the rate of destruction was less than the rate of new building. Meanwhile, the total of merchant losses rose to crisis level.

The obvious answer was to revert to the older system of convoy, but the Admiralty produced formidable arguments against adopting this policy. The total of arrivals and departures from British ports was 2,500 a week, and it would be impossible to organise this vast number into protected convoys. Furthermore, it was argued, the convoy system required a high standard of sea discipline of which most merchant captains were incapable. The faster ships would have to go at the pace of the slowest, and would present a much easier target.

Lloyd George doubted these arguments on the first occasion that he heard them in October 1916. As the months passed his doubts had increased. He sought advice from junior officers, who were wholeheartedly in favour of the convoy system. Coal convoys to the French ports were operating efficiently and safely, the Grand Fleet, of course, moved in convoy, and the figure of 2,500 included *all* sailings, including ships of all nationalities, and coastal trade.

On April 25th Lloyd George received the approval of the War

Cabinet to visit the Admiralty in person on the 30th to discover the situation. But by this stage the balance of Admiralty opinion had already changed. An experimental convoy left Gibraltar early in May and arrived without mishap. At the end of May the first convoy from America—curiously enough, the American naval authorities also opposed the convoy system—sailed across the Atlantic in safety. By the end of September the convoy system was in full operation with complete success. British shipping losses fell from over 365,000 tons in July to about 200,000 tons in September. This was the turning-point.

The battle of the seas was not won by the convoy system; but it was saved by it. It was not until July 1918 that the tonnage of new shipping was greater than the amount lost, but the tide had been turned in the autumn of 1917 when the convoys began in earnest. The early Admiralty calculations had proved wrong, and the amateur civilian politicians and junior naval officers had been proved right. Lloyd George's personal intervention—although it has been over-dramatised —had been decisive.

The German adoption of unrestricted submarine warfare had nearly ended the war, but its consequences were disastrous. The attitude of the Germans to the United States is difficult to comprehend. The sinking of ships such as the *Lusitania* and the *Arabic* in May 1915 had outraged American opinion, but calmer reflections could only lead to the conclusion that neutrals who travelled in wartime on British, French or German ships could not expect immunity from enemy attack. But the new methods were different. Even in the period of restricted submarine warfare, a German submarine went across the Atlantic; after calling at Newport, Rhode Island, it proceeded to sink five ships off Nantucket Island. When an American destroyer attempted to pick up survivors it was ordered to move out of the way so that the submarine could torpedo another ship. An American ship was sunk off Cape St. Vincent in the same month. The resumption of unrestricted submarine warfare included permission for *one* American ship a week to cross the North Atlantic, which was in itself a declaration that other American ships would be sunk on sight. Wilson broke off diplomatic relations on February 3rd. On March 1st the Zimmerman Telegram,[1] offering Mexico an offensive alliance against the

---

[1] For the best account of this episode see Barbara Tuchman: *The Zimmerman Telegram.*

United States, and which had been intercepted by the British, was published. This was in itself 'an unfriendly act' in the full sense of the phrase. Three American ships were sunk with great loss of life on March 18th. On April 2nd Wilson made his historic speech to Congress; by the afternoon of April 6th the United States was at war.

This massive new ally could not be of much direct help in 1917. As Wilson's confidant Colonel House noted on December 16th after an alarming talk with the Secretary of the Navy: 'We have no large guns; if we had them we have no trained men who would understand how to handle them. We have no air service, nor men to exploit it; and so it is down the list.' The situation was not quite so disastrous as this, but it would be some time before the presence of the United States in the war could be fully felt.

Joffre had at last been relieved of his command of the French forces at the end of 1916, and had been replaced by a dashing and heroic new personality. General Nivelle was sixty in 1916, and he seemed to have the secret to the impasse on the Western Front. The terrible Battle of Verdun, in which more than a million casualties were suffered by the opposing armies, had ended in a French victory of sorts. The German strategy of 'bleeding France white' at Verdun had boomeranged badly, and, together with their losses at the Somme, 1916 had been as bitter a year for the Germans in the West as it had been for the Allies. Verdun had become for the French a symbol of their resistance to the enemy, and the battle had been fought with barbaric fury by both sides. On October 24th General Nivelle had electrified France with the recapture of Forts Douaumont and Vaux and advanced over nearly two miles of ground which had taken the Germans almost eight months of furious fighting to capture. On December 15th Nivelle launched another attack, which was even more successful.

Nivelle's 'answer' to the Western Front situation was simply a more sophisticated use of artillery. The enemy lines would be overwhelmed with a tremendous surprise bombardment, while the advancing troops would proceed behind a 'creeping' barrage which was far deeper than those previously attempted. Exhilarated by his successes on a small front against an exhausted enemy in poor positions, Nivelle now expounded his faith in these methods on any front in any circumstances.

Nivelle's plan was to concentrate a 'mass of manoeuvre' of twenty-seven divisions. This would mean that the British should keep the Germans fully stretched on their part of the front and should also take over part of the French line to allow the concentration of the mass of manoeuvre. Haig was impressed, but was also anxious to drive forward to the north to secure the Belgian ports and drive the Germans out of western Belgium. He eventually settled on a major offensive at Ypres. Nivelle was not interested, but agreed that if his own offensive failed Haig could have his troops back and could deliver his Ypres attack. Nivelle did not expect to fail.

Lloyd George, who was keenly interested in British support to the Italians at this point, and who was more sceptical than ever of Haig, was suddenly and dramatically converted to Nivelle's plans. It was a curious reversal of the usual situation. Haig was cautious in his estimates of Nivelle's chances, whereas Lloyd George was now Nivelle's most enthusiastic champion. So enthusiastic was he that he proposed to the French that Haig should be subordinated to Nivelle. The French, not surprisingly, were quick to accept this proposal. Briand proposed to Lloyd George that, in effect, the French Commander-in-Chief should have total authority over the British forces, so that Haig would be reduced, for all practical purposes, to 'an Adjutant-General in charge only of discipline and personnel'.[1] On February 24th the War Cabinet agreed that Lloyd George should take measures to ensure the unity of command on the Western Front, but it is doubtful whether they had a full realisation of what Lloyd George was up to; they did know, however, that all this was being done without the knowledge of Haig or Robertson.

Haig and Robertson reacted violently. Haig and Nivelle agreed that Haig would be under Nivelle's orders in the coming battle but would be free to determine his own actions in his own sector. Haig also alerted the King to the situation, which was timely, for Lloyd George had characteristically kept the King wholly uninformed of what was going on. Derby and Curzon backed Haig strongly, and the War Cabinet hastily passed a vote of confidence in him. The result was to make Haig's position stronger than ever, but relations between himself and Robertson, on the one hand, and Lloyd George, on the other, were lastingly damaged.

[1] Woodward, *Short Journey*, 263.

It was an odd, but illuminating, episode. Lloyd George's total lack of confidence in Haig had occasioned this attempt to strip him of his powers, but the methods he used to achieve this were admirably qualified to bring Haig strong support in the Government and in the Press. Lloyd George never seems to have considered the public outcry that must surely have followed the publication of the news. Haig and Robertson had won this round, but Lloyd George was ever a determined man.

The much-heralded Nivelle Offensive virtually eliminated France from the war. Ludendorff had already begun the construction of a new line of defences in September 1916 which was built with immense skill and ingenuity, with much of the work done by prisoners of war and pressed civilians. It was originally intended as a precautionary measure, but Ludendorff became increasingly attracted by the opportunity of shortening his line, moving his men back to a greatly improved position, and thereby to save some thirteen divisions. The area evacuated would be utterly devastated, and it is an interesting commentary on the humanitarian feelings that still remained that the Crown Prince of Bavaria protested strongly against this devastation and that the French and British troops were shocked and embittered by the cutting down of fruit trees and the pollution of wells. Across the former main street of a flattened village an unknown German left the message: 'Do not be angered; only wonder.'

This withdrawal, which began on March 16th, destroyed the whole point of Nivelle's offensive. Furthermore, the Germans knew all about it, having captured the complete plans in a trench raid. The results were what might have been expected. The Canadians and British seized Vimy Ridge, but the British did not exploit this fine victory.[1] This battle cost 158,000 casualties, of whom nearly 30,000 were killed, but the British could point to a significant success, which was more than the hapless French Army could. The Nivelle attack opened on April 16th; after five days virtually no progress had been made and terrible losses had been suffered. In spite of increasing doubts by the French Government—shared by Haig—that there was no point in continuing the offensive, Nivelle persisted until sections of his army were in mutiny and the Government removed him. His successor was Pétain, who described his policy as 'Aggressive-Defensive'. Haig noted

[1] The best account of this battle is Edward Spears: *Prelude to Victory*.

in his diary that 'doubtless in his mind he figures the British Army doing the aggressive work, while the French Army "squats" on the defensive'. This was indeed what happened, but Haig was not an unwilling ally. He still assumed that victory could be achieved in 1917.

This was the background to the Flanders offensive that opened on July 31st. Lloyd George fought a stubborn action to hinder Haig in going forward. In the Cabinet, only Milner supported him. As Haig knew full well, the French were in no condition to support him with adequate attacks as they had originally promised. He withheld this information from the War Cabinet, which unhappily approved his offensive. Its unhappiness continued as Haig's attacks secured no notable gain in August, by which time the British casualties amounted to 3,424 officers and 64,586 men. The second stage opened on September 20th after the special Committee on War Policy appointed by the Cabinet had approved it by a majority. The subsequent fighting around Passchendaele acquired a terrible quality of its own. The British gained their principal objective, but at a cost of 244,987 casualties; all these gains were to be lost in the following March.

*

Most understandably, morale at home now began to cause serious concern. The new machinery of controls did not begin to make its real impact until towards the end of the year, by which time the British were beginning to see the consequences on their daily lives of the submarine campaign and the drain of the war to an extent that they had not before. The Russian Revolution of March 1917 was eagerly welcomed in the Labour Party, and it gave a new impetus to those who advocated peace by negotiation. The Independent Labour Party and the British Socialist Council, which was a Marxist body, set up a United Socialist Council, which in June summoned a convention at Leeds which endorsed the Russian peace programme for a peace with 'no annexations and no indemnities' and called for the setting up of workers' and soldiers' councils. Eleven hundred delegates assembled and MacDonald and Snowden attended.

It was at this point that Lloyd George made a political error that was to have far-reaching consequences.

Arthur Henderson had been a loyal and important member of the Government since May 1915. The division in the Labour Party between himself and the minority of opponents of the war had never been serious, and party co-operation had been retained to a certain extent. In May 1917 a conference on war aims was called by the Petrograd Soviet with the formal approval of the Provisional Government (which itself was replaced by a new coalition on May 20th). The Petrograd Soviet then issued invitations to an International Socialist Congress on War Aims at Stockholm in order that 'the work for peace started by the Russian Revolution [might] be brought to a conclusion by the efforts of the international proletariat'. The Executive of the Labour Party voted to send three representatives to visit Petrograd to determine Soviet intentions, and chose George Roberts, a right-wing personality, William Carter of the miners, and Ramsay MacDonald. The new Russian Foreign Minister asked that MacDonald be given permission to go to Petrograd. The Government were in a difficult position, and decided to send Henderson to report on the situation. Henderson was not in favour of the Stockholm Conference nor of the re-institution of the International, and his mission was attacked by Snowden and others on the grounds that he did not represent Labour opinion.

Six weeks in Petrograd convinced Henderson that if Russia were to be kept in the war the British Labour Party should accept the Russian peace programme and send delegates to the Stockholm Conference. The War Cabinet was hostile to these arguments when Henderson presented them—Lloyd George was absent—on July 26th. On the next day Henderson, MacDonald and G. H. Wardle (acting Chairman of the Parliamentary Party) went to Paris to attend a meeting called by the French United Socialists to discuss the method of proceeding at the Stockholm Conference.

It was this visit that started the storm. *The Times* on August 1st launched a sharp attack on Henderson:

> It is plain that no man harbouring such ideas and endeavouring to realise them by furtive co-operation with persons like Mr. MacDonald is fit to keep in a War Cabinet. His action is indefensible, and, if his colleagues are wise, they will renounce all further attempts to defend it.

The kernel of the difficulty was that Henderson considered it essential that German delegates should attend Stockholm; Lloyd George initially agreed and then, at French insistence, changed his mind.

On the afternoon of August 1st the Cabinet discussed Henderson's position, with Henderson himself waiting outside for an hour 'on the doormat', at the end of which he was, in Lloyd George's words, 'in a highly resentful frame of mind'. Henderson in effect challenged the Cabinet to demand his resignation. Lloyd George persuaded him to explain his position in the Commons that evening, which he did. Lloyd George's own speech was a dexterous affair, in which he spoke principally of the value of Labour participation in the Government. By the evening of August 1st Henderson was an angry man. The events of the next two weeks made him angrier still.

A Party Conference had been called for August 10th to consider the Stockholm invitation. Lloyd George claims that at a meeting of the Cabinet on August 8th Henderson gave his colleagues the impression that the motion would be defeated 'by a fair majority', a statement denied by Henderson and his biographer. In any event, on the 10th Henderson spoke vigorously for British representation at Stockholm, and the motion was carried by 1,846,000 votes to 550,000. A long wrangle on representation then followed, and it was with some difficulty that Henderson persuaded the conference to defer a decision until August 21st.

This caused consternation in the Cabinet; *The Times* declared that 'the hand of Germany is discernible throughout', and Henderson resigned in a dignified letter on the following day. Lloyd George's reply was anything but dignified, and was released to the Press before Henderson had had any chance to respond. In no uncertain terms Lloyd George accused Henderson of not informing the Conference of a telegram he had received on the 9th to the effect that the new Kerensky Coalition, formed on the 6th, had changed its attitude to Stockholm. The implication that Henderson had misled both his Cabinet colleagues and the Conference was plain enough, and was made even more plain by a violent attack on Henderson that Lloyd George delivered in the Commons on August 13th. It was now that Henderson revealed the 'doormat incident' on August 1st. The effect on the Labour Party was considerable. As Snowden wrote in the *Labour Leader* on the 16th:

This incident shows plainly that while Mr. Henderson was in the Cabinet he was never of it, and that the Prime Minister regarded him as useful only for the purpose of deluding democracy into the belief that it was exercising an influence upon the policy of the Government.

Labour was by no means united on the wisdom of the Stockholm Conference. Indeed, when the Party Conference resumed on August 21st, a motion to reaffirm its previous decision was carried by only 3,000 votes after the miners reversed their vote. The miners also carried a motion on representation that in effect barred the Socialists. Nevertheless, the consequences of the doormat incident and its sequel were very considerable. Henderson was bitterly personally estranged from Lloyd George, and resolved that he would never join a government in which Labour did not predominate. Lloyd George assumed that Henderson's successor in the Cabinet, G. N. Barnes, would also be his successor in the party leadership. This assumption was incorrect. Henderson, without really meaning to, had at last created some unity of outlook in the Parliamentary Party towards the war.

His energies were now devoted exclusively to the party's problems and its future. The Labour Memorandum on War Aims, drawn up at the end of 1917, was a significant step that caught the attention of President Wilson among others. The American Ambassador, Walter Hines Page, wrote to Wilson in January 1918 that 'the Labour Party is already playing for supremacy'. It would have been more accurate to have said 'working for political independence'.

In September Henderson submitted a memorandum to the National Executive that proposed 'the reorganisation of the Party with a view to a wider extension of membership, the strengthening and development of local parties in the constituencies, together with the promotion of a larger number of candidates, and the suggestion that a Party programme be adopted'. This was referred to a sub-committee, of which MacDonald and Sidney Webb were members, and which produced a draft constitution. It contained few novelties, except in the section relating to the party's objectives, and particularly the celebrated Clause IV, originally drafted by Henderson in standard cautious trade union language, but subsequently amended—almost certainly principally by Sidney Webb—to read:

To secure for the producers by hand and brain the full fruits of their industry, and the most equitable distribution thereof that may be possible upon the basis of the common ownership of the means of production and the best obtainable system of popular administration and control of each industry or service.

In June 1918 the Party conference adopted a policy statement also compiled by Webb called *Labour and the New Social Order* that incorporated the concept of the national minimum wage and standard working conditions with a maximum working week of forty-eight hours; it urged the democratic control of industry; the subsidisation of social services by heavy taxation of large incomes; and The Surplus for the Common Good, whereby the balance of the national wealth would be devoted to increasing the opportunities in education and culture for the people. This distillation of previous resolutions was certainly not an extreme manifesto. The debates within the Party on the draft constitution emphasised the dislike of the trade union leaders for socialist theory, and their clear intention to make the Party, in the words of one unionist leader, 'our political arm'.

But this programme—coupled with the decision in November 1918 to withdraw from the Coalition and fight alone—gave Labour the opportunity to project itself for the first time as a separate party and as a positive alternative to Liberalism and Conservatism. In the second 1910 election Labour had fielded 78 candidates, fighting upon the Liberal programme; in the 1918 election it was to sponsor over 360 candidates, fighting on its own programme. All this might have happened in any event; but the alienation of Henderson gave immense impetus to the movement towards separation. The consequences of the doormat incident remain with us to this day.

Labour was not the only element that was questioning the value of the war. On November 29th Lansdowne published in the *Daily Telegraph* a letter on war aims which aroused even more excitement and controversy than his leaked memorandum of a year before. It was condemned in violent terms from the usual quarters, Northcliffe describing it publicly as 'the stupid, senile manifestation of an old man who has lost control of himself', and both the *Daily Mail* and the *Morning Post* described it as an offer of surrender. The Liberal papers, however, and particularly the *Daily News* and the *Manchester Guardian*, warmly welcomed Lansdowne's initiative, and Gardiner described it as 'a torch in the darkness' which 'has made it respectable and even patriotic to think'; from Labour, George Lansbury welcomed the letter and wrote that 'we are not going, because of old quarrels, to belittle the great word he has spoken now'. The Conservatives would have no part of his action, which was strongly condemned by his former close colleague Bonar Law at a meeting of the National Unionist Association on November 30th. As Lloyd George commented: 'The direction in which [his sword] was waveringly pointed was no longer heeded by the exclusive regiment he once led.' It did, however, force Lloyd George to make a belated and generalised declaration on British War Aims to the Trades Union Conference on January 5th, 1918.

But these protests against the war had little substantial political impact. War-weariness had not yet reached the point when alternatives were seriously considered. Clemenceau's dictum that 'the war aims for which we are fighting are victory' echoed the dominant feeling in Britain and also in Germany. But, for all the major belligerents, 1917 had been the worst year of the war. Russia had crumbled and was out of the conflict. The Italians had been swept back at Caporetto. The French armies had survived mutiny, but were on the defensive. On the other side, although Austria-Hungary and the Ottoman Empire were virtually *in extremis*, the Germans were massively formidable. For the Allies the best hope lay in the Americans; for the Germans, a decisive blow on the Western Front before the Americans arrived. When 1918 dawned, the surviving belligerents were still fighting for victory.

*

Lloyd George was a Prime Minister without a Party. He had now moved too far from Labour to have any substantial hope of future support from that quarter. The Liberals who had remained faithful to Asquith—estimated at over 100—regarded Lloyd George with even greater animosity than did Asquith himself. Thus, Lloyd George was wholly dependent upon the Conservatives and those Liberals who had followed him for his retention of power. In these circumstances his room for manoeuvre was limited, and everything depended upon the skill with which he managed the forces on which he relied. For a man who had always lived by his wits, and whose political antennae were exceptionally sensitive, this situation was admirably suited to his character. As he once wrote: 'I never believed in costly frontal attacks either in war or politics, if there were a way round.' Furthermore, his fundamental opportunism gave priority in his calculations to the retention of power; as Beaverbrook[1] has observed, his object was to remain in the driver's seat, and the direction in which he was travelling was of less concern to him. Anything served his purpose. All was grist to his mill. He had colleagues, supporters and admirers, but no friends. The maxim that there are no friendships at the top in political life was certainly true when Lloyd George was Prime Minister.

But it was this ruthlessness, guile and pragmatism that made him a great War Minister. He himself has described the ideal:

> But a War Minister must also have vision, imagination, and initiative—he must show untiring assiduity, must exercise constant over-sight and supervision of every sphere of war activity, must possess driving force to energise this activity, must be in constant consultation with experts, official and unofficial, as to the best means of utilising the resources of the country in conjunction with Allies for the achievement of victory. If to this can be added a flair for conducting a great fight, then you have an ideal War Minister.[2]

Judged by these dazzling standards, Lloyd George was deficient in certain respects, but no qualification can be entered against his energy, imagination and enterprise. The reorganisation of the Cabinet had resulted in vastly more efficient control at the top, the dissemination of decisions among departments, and an infinitely greater practical and businesslike approach. The creation of 'functional' Ministries and the introduction of professional businessmen to run them marked the end of the former laissez-faire attitude to the running of the war. As has been emphasised, all this did not form part of a grand overall plan of government control and direction, and the changes were made on a pragmatic basis; but the cumulative effect was that, by the beginning of 1918, Britain was at long last geared for the tests of total war. But it was Lloyd George's continued attempts to seize control of the direction of the war from Robertson and Haig that brought the last major crisis faced by the Lloyd George Coalition.

By the end of 1917, after the dreadful cost of the Passchendaele offensive, relations between Lloyd George, on the one hand, and Haig and Robertson on the other were at their nadir. It may have been true that

---

[1] Max Aitken had become Lord Beaverbrook on the formation of the Lloyd George Government.
[2] Lloyd George: *War Memoirs*, I, 602.

Lloyd George knew little about military matters, but he had learned a great deal about the military mind the hard way since August 1914. He had been sceptical about Gallipoli, but ignored. He had been bewitched by Nivelle, and deceived. He had been reluctantly persuaded to go along with the disastrous British summer and autumn campaign of 1917. He had rightly over-ruled naval advice on the convoy system. If he viewed the military experts of the nation, from Kitchener and French to Haig and Robertson, without awe it was not altogether surprising. But he was serving as head of a government which had not reached his conclusions, was dependent upon a party whose instinctive reaction was to support soldiers against politicians, a Press that was overwhelmingly pro-military, and in an uneasy relationship with a monarch who was in close touch with Haig and had views of his own. The principle of civilian control over the military continued to exist in theory rather than fact. Lloyd George had to move warily. He could not act frontally, and his attempts to undermine Haig's position had failed, at the cost of creating a profound mutual mistrust.

The faults were by no means all on one side. Lloyd George had a marked tendency—not uncommon in men who had risen by methods he had employed—of seeing conspiracies against him on all sides. He came to believe that there were intrigues afoot in the army against the government and—more importantly—against him personally, and he told Lord Esher—who passed on the information to Haig—that 'his means of information are varied and go deep into the camp of his opponents. Of this there was ample proof from what he said to me. Conversations with pressmen, communications with critics and wreckers of the Government, all brought to him by agents who have a footing in what he calls "both camps".' In his War Memoirs he was subsequently to write that there had been a cabal to 'enthrone a Government which would be practically the nominee and menial of the military party'. No evidence that such a cabal existed, or that there was ever a 'military party' as such, has emerged. In his later account Lloyd George no doubt deliberately dressed up the grumbling of the military commanders into the garb of a deep-rooted campaign against him; it is very possible that he believed this lurid portrait.

By the end of 1917, Lloyd George had no confidence in Haig and Robertson, and Haig and Robertson had none in Lloyd George. Robertson wrote to Haig on December 8th, 1917, of 'the impossibility of honestly working with such a man'. Haig warmly agreed: 'How

unfortunate the country seems to be to have such an unreliable man
at the head of affairs in this crisis', he noted in his diary on September
24th. Haig, like Kitchener in his duel with Curzon, had powerful
allies whom he carefully cultivated. He could count upon Conservative and Royal support in the event of a crisis, and the military
reverses of 1917 had not seriously affected his national position. Haig
could adopt as devious and pragmatic methods as Lloyd George
himself, and had some understanding of the dark arts of propaganda
and influence-peddling. Robertson, however, did not possess Haig's
connections or guile. He emerges from all accounts—including his
own, which is unusual in soldiers' memoirs—as an attractive and
bloody-minded professional of limited but clear perspectives. His
celebrated retort, 'I've 'eard different', to eloquent analyses was
unlikely to attract politicians—and particularly Lloyd George—but
gave confidence to others. Nonetheless, his taciturn contempt for
politicians and other amateurs was not conducive to the successful
prosecution of the war; his judgements were not often justified by
events; and, as he was about to discover to his cost, he had no powerful
allies, not even Haig.

In spite of the American declaration of war, whose effects were
only slowly beginning to be felt, the military situation at the end of
1917 was not good, and was obviously not going to get any better
after the collapse of Russia. In December Haig issued instructions on
defensive measures on the Western Front. This was indeed necessary.
For two years all British plans had been for the attack, and the
British defensive positions were at no point remotely comparable to
those of the Germans. The British calculated that by the end of
February 1918 the Germans would have 185 divisions on the Western
Front, giving them a superiority over the British and French of some
200,000 men. This disparity was not, in itself, of critical importance;
in the great assaults of 1916–17 the Allied superiority over the Germans had been considerably greater. What was serious was the condition of the Allied lines and the enormous amount of work necessary
to put them into reasonable shape. The new lines gained in the
Passchendaele offensive were the worst of all, providing little effective
defence and unspeakable living conditions, and there was a chronic
shortage of men and equipment to make them capable of withstanding
the major German attack that was now expected.

The question of manpower was clearly crucial. In December the

War Cabinet set up a special committee to consider the problem, consisting of Lloyd George, Curzon, Barnes, Carson and Smuts. It had to consider the whole question of manpower—industrial as well as military—and its conclusions were sobering. In short, the barrel had nearly been scooped dry. Haig and Robertson asked for 615,000 new men, and pointed to the two million troops in the Middle and Near East. The Cabinet came to the conclusion that only 100,000 new men in the 'A' class could be available for the Army, and Lloyd George was adamantly opposed to withdrawing men from the Middle East.

Indeed, it was in this area that the British had made their most substantial advances. The army of Mesopotamia was in Baghdad, and General Allenby—atoning for a somewhat undistinguished per-formance as an Army Commander on the Western Front—had entered Jerusalem on Christmas Day. Militarily, the Turks were being pushed back relentlessly; politically, the rich pickings of the Ottoman Empire were falling into British hands. Arab support for the British was extending dramatically, while, by the Balfour Dec-laration of November 8th declaring British support for a Jewish National Home in Palestine, it was hoped that Jewish support for the Allies—particularly in the United States—would be substantially gained. The fatal clash between reconciling Arab ambitions and creating a national home for the Jews in Palestine had not been appreciated. In the case of Salonika, Lloyd George was equally adamant. This vast Allied force—amounting to over a million men—had remained on the defensive since the end of 1915, but there were solid political reasons for retaining a large British presence in this area. Emotional considerations also played their part in Lloyd George's feelings towards this theatre.

The Italian front was even less appropriate for a substantial with-drawal of British forces in the aftermath of Caporetto, although one division was brought back. This meant that the reinforcements would have to come from England. Some 130,000 'A' men were sent to the Western Front between January 1st and March 21st and, on the advice of the General Staff, 120,000 troops were kept in England. Lloyd George subsequently made much of this in his War Memoirs, but there were sound military reasons for doing so, not the least of which was the fact that these men could be moved to France in the eighteen days for which Haig said his existing forces could hold an enemy attack.

Much harsh controversy subsequently raged over these actions and attitudes. The essential fact was that, as Lloyd George bluntly said, 'I don't trust Haig with men'. With good reason, given recent experience, he feared another futile offensive, whereas in fact Haig's principal interest was to maintain his existing positions. The result stemmed less from the situation itself than from the poisoned relations between the British commanders and the British Prime Minister. Both were grievously at fault, but Haig's case is marginally the better one. When the German attack began on March 21st, the British forces were well below the minimum level deemed by Haig to be essential.

Haig was beyond Lloyd George's reach, and the Prime Minister had to move cautiously. In November 1917, at his urging, a Supreme War Council, consisting of the Allied Prime Ministers and specially appointed military advisers, was set up at Versailles. It proved effective and valuable in all save military co-ordination. Robertson refused to work with the Council and when, at his promptings, the Liberal Opposition raised the matter in the House of Commons, Lloyd George hastily retreated. The Council, he explained, had only advisory powers, and he was 'utterly opposed' to the suggestion of an Allied Commander-in-Chief.

In February 1918 he tried again, and with more success. The Supreme Council decided to set up a general reserve of Allied forces, under the control of its own military advisers. Robertson refused to have anything to do with this, or even go to Versailles. The King and Asquith supported him, as did Derby, Lord Robert Cecil, Walter Long and Curzon. This time Lloyd George felt strong enough to deliver an ultimatum to his colleagues and to the King. Robertson's supporters swiftly vanished. Haig at once said that he would accept the view of the Cabinet, and gave practical demonstration of his willingness to assist the Supreme Council by accepting Marshal Foch as president of the Executive Committee. On February 18th the abandoned Robertson read in the newspapers that he had resigned, and had been replaced by Sir Henry Wilson. Wilson's slipperiness would have awed an eel, but he had a real understanding of the need for military and political agreement, particularly on his own terms. Robertson fell sheer. He did not even subsequently receive the comparable handsome financial rewards given to senior commanders after the war, although he was not wholly forgotten.

This was rough, but in Beaverbrook's memorable phrase, 'he had taken a pot-shot at Santa Claus—and missed'.

On March 21st the German attack fell upon the British Third and Fifth Armies, of which the greater part—some forty miles—was held by the Fifth Army under General Sir Hubert Gough. Haig was not convinced that it would fall on the Fifth Army, and he viewed the prospect of a major German attack with some confidence; indeed, on February 28th, he told the army commanders that he was 'only afraid that the enemy would find our front so very strong that he will hesitate to commit his army to the attack with the almost certainty of losing very heavily'. Perhaps this was partly to boost morale; he was still far short of the numbers of troops he had asked for in December.

The Fifth Army was swept aside, and by the afternoon of March 22nd Gough was ordering a general withdrawal. Within a few days the Germans advanced forty miles.

At the outset of the war the British were trained for open warfare, and had been totally unprepared for trench warfare; now they were professionals at trench warfare, and totally unprepared for the new conditions of open warfare. The Germans swept on.

Lloyd George now repeated what he had done in the previous April over the convoy crisis; he took over the direction of the War Office from Derby, discovered that nearly 90,000 troops were home on leave, and returned them and the reserve to Haig. It may be argued that it was Lloyd George's fault that Haig did not have enough troops in the first place, but he certainly acted energetically to meet the crisis. Like Julius Caesar, he was at his best when recovering from his own errors. On March 28th, without consulting Balfour, he asked President Wilson for the immediate use of all available American troops; Wilson agreed, and over-ruled the irascible and difficult General Pershing. This was leadership of a kind that would never have occurred to Asquith.

The Allies now faced a really grave crisis. Haig proposed to fall back on the Channel ports; Pétain had orders from the French Government to cover Paris at all costs. Furthermore, Pétain's defeatism was such that Haig was convinced that his replacement was essential; he asked on March 25th that Wilson and the Secretary of State for War should arrange that 'General Foch or some other determined general who would fight, should be given supreme control in France'. Lloyd George sent Milner, whom he appointed Secretary for War in Derby's place on April 19th.

It was quite evident that Pétain, whose nerve had been broken at Verdun, and who regarded the battle and the war as lost, could not remain in charge of the French effort, and there could be no question of Haig being subordinate to such a commander. Haig was now anxious that Foch should become supreme commander in order that he should keep Pétain in control. Foch accordingly was appointed to co-ordinate the British and French armies; on April 3rd—with Haig's full approval —he was given the 'strategic direction of military operations'. On April 14th Foch was named 'Commander-in-Chief of the Allied Armies'. This was somewhat grandiloquent; in his own phrase, he was merely a conductor who beat time well. It was, however, a very different beat to that which Pétain would have struck.

Before the German campaign eventually ran out of steam, it had serious effects on the course of British politics. The first affected Ireland. Protests in England against the calling-up of men had been accompanied with complaints that Ireland still enjoyed freedom from conscription, and Lloyd George thought he saw the solution— conscription would be extended to Ireland in return for Home Rule.

This maladroit manoeuvre, intended to placate the Conservatives and the Irish with one move, completed the work that General Sir John Maxwell had put in hand. The Irish M.P.s left the House of Commons in a body, and joined with Sinn Fein. Eamonn de Valera, a survivor of the Easter Rising, led the opposition, strongly supported by the Roman Catholic hierarchy, hitherto independent of the recent nationalist movements. On April 23rd there was a twenty-four-hour general strike. The Government reacted with a heavy hand. French was made Viceroy, his mandate to rule by force; the Sinn Fein leaders were arrested—many for the second time in two years—and imprisoned in England. Lloyd George dropped Home Rule. He also dropped conscription in Ireland, but the mortal damage had been done.

The German offensive also led to the most serious challenge yet to the Government. When Milner went to the War Office in succession to Derby he promptly removed Robertson's Director of Military Operations, General Sir Frederick Maurice. On May 7th Maurice, in a sensational public letter, brought out into the open charges that had been hitherto circulating privately in military and official circles. The allegation that Lloyd George had deliberately withheld troops from Haig to compel him to remain on the defensive had been denied by Lloyd George on April 9th in the Commons: 'Notwithstanding the heavy casualties in 1917', he said, 'the army in France was considerably stronger on January 1st 1918 than on January 1st 1917.' Now, Maurice in effect said that Lloyd George—abetted by Bonar Law— was a liar. There is now strong evidence to the effect that Maurice's charges were well founded, but the manner in which he made his revelations was intolerable. And the matter of whether Maurice's charges were justified is of less importance than the political consequences.[1] On May 7th, in answer to questions in the House from Asquith and others, Law foolishly agreed to set up a judicial enquiry into Maurice's charges; Asquith insisted on a debate first, which was fortunate for the Government, which hurriedly withdrew the offer of an enquiry.

On May 9th the famous Maurice Debate took place. Asquith spoke in a low key, and did not speak as though he were launching a Vote of Censure. But Lloyd George replied with a devastating counter-attack. He produced two defences; the first was that he made his statement of April 9th on the basis of figures supplied by Maurice himself; the second—rather less impressive—was that he had not included the non-combatant troops, and would have been justified in doing so.

But the real impact of Lloyd George's speech was personal. Here, he emphasised, was a Prime Minister, at a critical moment in the nation's fortunes, being forced to meet a fractious, disloyal, partisan attack. The self-portrait was irresistible. Perhaps Lloyd George really did believe—as he later stated in his memoirs—that this was all part of a plot to 'blow up the Government'; in any event, he emphatically pinned the badge of lack of judgement and patriotism upon Maurice and Asquith.

When the division was held, 100 Liberals—including two tellers— voted against the Government, supported by 6 Labour, 1 Unionist and 1 Irish Nationalist; 293 M.P.s supported the Government, of whom 71 were Liberals. This division marked the end of the Liberal Party as a unified force. The schism already created by the events

[1] See Jenkins, op. cit., 470–1, and A. J. P. Taylor: *English History 1914–1945*, 104–5.

of December 1916 was now substantially increased by the bitterness of the Maurice Debate.[1]

*

It was Lloyd George's last serious test. The German offensive congealed. The British and French forces held. The Americans were present in force. On July 15th the French withstood the last German offensive; on August 8th the British attacked north of Amiens, using 456 tanks in massed formation—the 'battering-ram' so long argued for by the tank experts. Haig checked the advance after two days, and attacked elsewhere. The Germans began to fall back. In September the new tactics were employed all along the line. There was no great break-through or triumph, and Allied casualties exceeded German when the attack was launched, particularly among the Americans.

But now, the Central Powers began to crumble. The last Turkish army was defeated by Allenby; the long immobile Salonika force at last advanced, and the Bulgarians hastily signed an Armistice. Ludendorff considered that the war was lost. And so it was. Apart from the British and the French, now pressing forward with renewed vigour and at last scenting victory, the impact of the fresh American divisions was psychologically overwhelming. On October 4th the German Government appealed to President Wilson for an immediate armistice and the opening of peace negotiations. Wilson eagerly accepted the opening to force the Fourteen Points upon both the Germans and the Allies. The principal Points were 'Open covenants of peace, openly arrived at'; absolute freedom of navigation on the seas in peace and war; the removal, so far as possible, of all economic barriers and equality of trade conditions; guarantees for arms reduction to the lowest point consistent with domestic safety; a free, open-minded, and absolutely impartial adjustment of all colonial claims, the interests of the population involved to have equal weight with the

---

[1] Not content with trouncing Maurice—whose military career was ended—Lloyd George returned to him with relish in his *War Memoirs*. The index references give a good indication of Lloyd George's ferocity:

'*Maurice, Sir Frederick:* comfortably placed as any politician . . . subservient and unbalanced . . . his astonishing arithmetical calculations . . . the instrument by which the Government was to be thrown out . . . intrigues against the Government, his mind being apparently unhinged . . . tool of astuter men . . . his double-dealing denounced by Lloyd George . . . his grave breach of discipline condoned by Asquith . . . dismissed.'

claims of the government making the claim; the evacuation of all Russian, French, and Belgian territory by the Germans; autonomous development for the peoples of Austria, Hungary and the Ottoman Empire; the creation of an independent Poland with a free and secure access to the sea; 'A general association of nations must be formed under specific covenants for the purpose of affording mutual guarantees of political independence and territorial integrity to great and small states alike.'

On October 23rd the Germans accepted the Points, and then, on November 4th, the Supreme War Council followed suit, with reservations by both the French and the British. On October 30th the Turks signed an armistice of surrender; on November 3rd the Austro-Hungarians concluded a similar armistice with the Italians. Morale in the German army was low, except in a few elite divisions; the fleet mutinied when ordered to sea; on November 9th the Kaiser fled to Holland and a Republic was proclaimed. At 5 a.m. on November 11th the Germans signed the armistice, which came into force at 11 a.m. For many, the delight at victory was tempered by other thoughts, not least of the joyous crusade that had ended in calamity for so many, and of the gay volunteer armies that were lost forever. In Siegfried Sassoon's words:

> And through some mooned Valhalla there will pass
> Battalions and battalions, scarred from Hell.
> The unreturning army that was youth;
> The legions that have suffered, and are dust.

*

Nations may weep or celebrate, but politics must continue. There had not been a General Election since 1910, and at the beginning of November Law and Lloyd George agreed to maintain the Coalition and to have an immediate election. Lloyd George had been planning for this eventuality for some time. After the events of December 1916 Asquith had taken much of the Liberal machine with him; Lloyd George had accordingly set up his own Liberal organisation and had started to create his personal political fund. Thomas Jones states[1] that 'During the summer of 1918, and indeed earlier, Lloyd George was planning an election which would give him a mandate from a

[1] T. J. Jones: *Lloyd George*, 158.

united nation not only to lead it to victory but to negotiate the peace'. At Manchester, in September, he made what was in effect the first election speech of the new campaign. Before the Armistice was signed the plans were ready. In the euphoria of victory, the doubts which Law had had about Lloyd George had now vanished. To Archibald Salvidge, boss of the Conservative organisation in Liverpool, he said emotionally: 'Salvidge, I tell you we must never let the little man go. His way and ours lie side by side in the future.'

Lloyd George, after an unconvincing attempt to bring Asquith—as Lord Chancellor—and Labour into the Coalition, fought the election as the head of the Government. His most violent diatribes were, however, directed against the Liberals who had tried 'to overthrow a Government that was in the midst of a crisis whilst wrestling for victory'; those who had repented were compared to Germans who cried 'Kamerad!' Such statements were not designed to heal the gaping wounds in the old Liberal Party. The position of the Asquithian Liberals in any event was a very difficult one. They were caught in the open between the Coalition and Labour. Only 159 Liberals were spared Coalition opposition and received the joint letter of commendation from Lloyd George and Bonar Law, derided by Asquith as 'the coupon'.

Contrary to Asquith's allegation—accepted by many subsequent historians—the Maurice Debate voting was not the decisive test for the bestowal of the 'coupon'. The choice of the favoured 159 was done on strange and arbitrary causes, but the effects were devastating. Only 18 Liberals survived opposition from a sponsored Coalition candidate. When the election dust cleared, the Coalition had 484 Members—338 Conservatives, 136 Lloyd George Liberals, and 10 other supporters; opposed to them were 59 Labour and 26 Asquithian Liberals. Asquith himself, although his opponent did not receive the 'coupon', was defeated; so were Henderson, MacDonald and Philip Snowden. MacDonald had not expected to be re-elected in Leicester, anticipating 'an . . . combination against everyone who has thought and acted independently upon the war'. He was swept away by 20,570 votes to 6,347, but in 1920 was adopted for Aberavon. In the meanwhile he was to keep the flame of the Labour nascence alive and vehement. He fell in good company. Only 229 members of the new Parliament had not received the 'coupon'. 541 'coupons' were issued; 478 'couponed' candidates were returned.

The 1918 General Election was remarkable for other reasons. It was a dirty fight. Lloyd George, in *The Truth About the Peace Treaties*, subsequently cited a speech at Bristol in which he had gone into the whole question of German reparations. This defence has been destroyed by Jones,[1] who comments that 'he was inclined to shout the popular demands and to whisper the qualifications'. On the matter of the treatment of the Kaiser, one commentator[2] claims that Lloyd George referred to 'hanging the Kaiser' on twenty separate occasions. One example of Lloyd George's style (December 6th) is sufficient:

> The Kaiser must be prosecuted. The war was a crime . . . a hideous, abominable crime, a crime which has sent millions of the best young men of Europe to death and mutilation, and which has plunged myriads of homes into desolation. Is no one responsible? Is no one to be called to account? Is there to be no punishment? Surely that is neither God's justice nor man's. The men responsible for this outrage on the human race must not be let off because their heads were crowned when they perpetrated the deed.

A statement to the Press on the eve of the election put prosecution of the Kaiser first, and reparations second, as the election issues; 'rehabilitation of those broken in the war' and 'domestic reform in all spheres' were bottom of the list of priorities. Apart from the speechifying about 'hanging the Kaiser' and 'squeezing Germany until the pips squeak', the real issue was whether the country wanted the victorious Lloyd George Coalition to continue. To this question the answer seemed to be overwhelming.

But there were some significant portents. The Labour national executive sponsored 363 candidates, and in fact a total of 447 Labour candidates (of whom 36 supported the Coalition) stood, and polled 2,374,385 votes. The Irish Nationalist Party had vanished, a remnant of seven returning to Westminster. Seventy-three Sinn Feiners had been elected—including the first woman M.P., the flamboyant Countess Markiewicz—but refused to take their seats in the English Parliament; 36, indeed, were in no position to do so, being in prison at the time. Most interesting of all, in the first General Election in British history

[1] Jones, op. cit., 161–3.
[2] S. Lauzanne: *Le Diable Aux Yeux Bleu*. Churchill, also, joined in the cry for punishing the Kaiser and harsh reparations.

that could truly claim to be such, with seventy-eight per cent of the adult population now entitled to the vote, only some fifty-six per cent actually voted. So far as could be seen, the women's vote had no impact whatever.

The election was, above all, a triumph for the Conservative Party and a catastrophe for the Liberals. Each had entered the war with approximately the same number of seats—260; now, the Conservatives had 338, and the Liberals were fatally split in twain. In 1914, the United Liberal Party had enjoyed Irish Nationalist and Labour support; by the end of 1918 the Irish Nationalists had disappeared, and Labour was an independent, hostile, party.

Thus, the Great War had not only changed the face of Europe; it had also transformed the features of British politics. For the time being, Lloyd George reigned supreme and unchallenged, hailed as 'the man who won the war'. But there were others who described him as 'a fire-brand scattering hate across England', and Augustine Birrell wrote to Asquith: 'You surely are better out of it for the time, than watching Ll.G. lead apes to Hell.' Lloyd George still remained in 10 Downing Street so long as the Conservatives were content to leave him there. He believed that they owed their victory to his leadership; for a time, many of them believed it as well.

*

The physical wounds of the Great War on Britain were not severe as they had been on other belligerents, although they seemed appalling at the time. The British economy had not been severely harmed, and in many fields—notably technological—her industries had advanced dramatically. The British people had withstood, and conquered, the perils and hardships of the war, and it had been for many a liberating experience. Thus, for those who had gone through the war and had emerged unscathed, there were high expectations for the future. But the desire to return to 'normalcy' now assumed the proportions of a cult. The war-time system of government direction and control was enthusiastically dismembered, as were many of the industries—notably the aircraft industry—that the war had in fact created. As Sir Llewellyn Woodward has written:

> The Brigade of Guards got back into Scarlet, and the Treasury set about restoring Treasury Control. After the march of armies, the

wrigglings of martinets. . . . Mr. Austen Chamberlain returned to
the Treasury to which he had first been appointed in 1903; Lord
Curzon presided over the Foreign Office, and Mr. Arthur Balfour,
fresh from the Congress of Berlin, exchanged reminiscences with
M. Clemenceau, whose memories stopped short at 1870. No
wonder that no one knew . . . whether we were going on or going
back.

And, in 1927, a group of young Conservatives that included Harold
Macmillan and Robert Boothby commented that:

The war period shattered preconceived economic notions, proved
possible theoretic impossibilities, removed irremovable barriers,
created new and undreamt-of solutions. Yet by far the greater part
of the legislation which today governs trade and industry dates from
before that period. We are surely entitled to ask whether it is now
adequate to meet the vastly changed conditions of the modern
economic era.

The question was well-based, and it was not to be answered. And
thus the victors returned to the problems of Ireland, of Empire, and
of how to administer a Free Trade economy. Men reared in Victorian
politics resumed their old, inconveniently interrupted, activities with
pleasure. They did not hesitate to dwell movingly on the mighty
sacrifices that had been made, insensitive to the surly anger of those
who had suffered. To quote Woodward again:

Laurence Binyon's noble words 'they shall not grow old as we who
are left grow old' took on an ironic meaning in the mouths of
speakers who were well content to grow old and fat, and who had
never asked the dead whether they had chosen to die young in
order to avoid old age. As time went on, I began to dislike more and
more the celebration of Armistice Day. I wished that all the formal
ceremonies might be abandoned, and that this commemoration
of the dead could be left to those for whom it had some personal
meaning. Darkness is not better than light, death is not better than
life; no praise from comfortable men can bring the dead back to
the sun they loved.

The war did not, in itself, make men disillusioned; it was the peace
that achieved this, which four bitter years of war had failed to do. In

the 1922 General Election Lord Winterton—a Conservative M.P. since 1904, who had served in the war at Gallipoli and in Mesopotamia—was 'shocked' to hear the following exchange at an election meeting:

The Chairman: Our candidate fought most gallantly in the war.
A Voice: More bloody fool he (Cheers and laughter).[1]

That exchange would have been unthinkable in 1918. But much occurred between then and 1922.

---

[1] Lord Winterton: *Orders of the Day*, 118.

CHAPTER THIRTEEN

POST-WAR, 1919–1922

The world's great age begins anew,
The golden years return,
The earth doth like a snake renew
Her winter weeds outworn;
Heaven smiles, and faiths and empires gleam,
Like wrecks of a dissolving dream.[1]

BRITAIN WAS STILL a very rich nation in 1914, and, had it not been for the substantial loans to her Allies, would have been even richer by 1918. The most significant feature of the British economy at the end of the nineteenth and beginning of the twentieth centuries was the change from an industrial to a trading nation; as R. C. K. Ensor has said, 'If she was no longer so much as formerly the world's workshop, she was more than ever its warehouseman, its banker, and its commission agent. And these were relatively the better-paid functions'.[2] These changes had not materially affected the nation's overall prosperity, but they were the essential background to the rise of the trade union movement in the 1890s and 1900s, and the serious industrial disputes of 1910–11. This industrial situation, coupled as it was with bad housing and urban conditions, did not lead directly to the emergence of the Labour Party, but it was the combination of industrial stagnation with doubts over the legal position of the Unions that had led to the movement to have working-class representation at Westminster. From the 'new Unionism' of the 1890s —given its greatest impetus by the success of the 1889 dock strike— the Labour Representation Committee of 1900 was an indirect growth; it was, in time, to be its most significant political consequence. The rise of the Labour Party up to the Great War was

[1] Shelley, *Hellas*, quoted by Curzon in the House of Lords, November 18th 1918, in moving an Address to the King.
[2] Ensor: *England 1870–1914*, 507.

something less than meteoric, but the groundwork had been laid for the subsequent edifice, and the first Labour leaders—Henderson, MacDonald, Clynes, and Snowden—had received their political apprenticeship. It is hypothetical to consider whether Labour would have grown into a separate party had it not been for the war and for the Liberal schisms, but the nature of the post-war Labour Party was largely shaped in the pre-war decade.

The emergence of Labour as a distinct—if not separate—political group was one of the most significant features of the pre-war period. It owed much in the first instance to the Liberal obsession with Irish Home Rule and schisms over Imperialism from 1886 to 1894, and to its consequent political impotence and divisions; its survival was ensured by the Taff Vale Judgement, the increased trade union financial support, and the MacDonald–Gladstone Pact of 1903. Nevertheless, up to 1914, it was essentially an appendage of the Liberal Party, without distinct leadership, policy, or philosophy. These only emerged in 1917–18.

Perhaps the most significant political fact of all in this period had been the dramatic extension of the electorate. In 1886 it had stood at just over one million; in 1883 it was 2·6 million; in 1886, after the 1885 Reform Act, it was some 4·4 million; by 1900 it had grown, by natural increase, to 6·7 million, or some 27 per cent of the total adult population; in 1910 it was just under 7·7 million, some 28 per cent of the total adult population; in 1918 it had swollen dramatically to 21,755,583, or 78 per cent of the adult population. This was not yet full adult suffrage, which was to come ten years later, but it was very nearly that. In these years Britain had come close to becoming a true democracy for the first time in her history.

This revolution—for such it was—had been much more considerable in local government before 1914. The Municipal Corporations Act of 1882 and the creation of the elective County and Borough Councils in 1888 had removed local government from a privileged minority and established a system which, with all its inadequacies, was a vast improvement on its predecessor.

But although Members of Parliament now received a small salary, national politics remained the privilege of a very small proportion of the nation until 1918. For those without private means or a substantial alternative income public service involved considerable sacrifices and careful husbandry of very limited resources. The early Labour M.P.s had to live frugally, and formed no part of the highly political and small world of London society. Politics remained remarkably centralised. The great and lesser men might sally forth into the country, but their base was London. The modern idea that a Member of Parliament should live in his constituency, or have some personal connection with it, was not widespread, in spite of the example given by those notable exceptions, the Chamberlains. The control exercised by Lord Derby over Lancashire Conservatism—which was to continue until his death—demonstrated that the days of the great territorial magnates had not wholly passed, but the influence and control of the Conservative Central Office were developing rapidly. The Liberal central dominance was less, but reflected the same tendency to draw political power and influence into a small central core of active London politicians. The powers of the central party machine, although perhaps exaggerated at the time, had substantially increased, and were moving political parties into nationally organised entities to a degree which had not been dreamed of in the early 1880s. The Primrose League proved to be a much clearer portent than the Birmingham Caucus, and Captain Middleton a more significant individual than Schnadhorst. Even in the Labour Party, the movement towards central direction was evident.

It was still not difficult for a rich man to buy his way into Parliament, but the Corrupt Practices Acts gave the advantage to central organisation rather than to the individual. Many constituency organisations in the Liberal and Conservative parties remained fiercely independent, but in the majority it was the voice of London which mattered. When Joseph Chamberlain first heard F. E. Smith speak he arranged for him to have a more hopeful constituency in Liverpool. It was not the Oldham Unionist Association which sought the candidature of Winston Churchill, but one of its M.P.s, an admirer of Lord Randolph Churchill. When Churchill made his political debut at Bath in 1897, it was arranged by Central Office. Politics remained a national pastime, but increasingly orchestrated from London.

Thus, it would be unwise to exaggerate the changes—considerable though they were—in the structure of British society and government between 1880 and 1914. Money and power were limited to a very small minority. The first steps towards a national education policy tended to emphasise further the vast gulf which separated the prosperous few and the many poor. The men and women who managed to bridge this gulf did so through intense application and self-education in very difficult circumstances. The much-hailed social reforms of the period 1880–1914 did not seriously affect the structure of a society in which the accident of birth remained the most crucial of all factors in one's prospects. The resilience and strength of the top element in this society lay in its willingness to accept new recruits and to instil in them the precepts of success and wealth, trinkets and honours. And these trinkets were highly attractive and very seductive.

London Society may have been vulgar in many respects between the 1890s and the outbreak of the war, but its outward appearances were glittering. The great country houses were run on a scale which had changed little over the years. King Edward VII, in his style, priorities, and standards, was not an unrepresentative monarch of this small but immensely powerful fragment of his realm.

The war did not wholly destroy this situation, but it aroused a new awareness—and not only among the deprived—of the perils and inequities of this society. The war itself had removed some of them, of which the greatly expanded franchise was the most portentous. The class structures remained, but the old assurances and acceptances had been altered. All classes had suffered in the war, and the rolls of honour of the public schools and universities testify to how heavy were the losses of the pre-1914 elite. There was a new militancy and expectation among those who had previously been poor but acquiescent to their fate. It was to be some time before these new attitudes became apparent in political terms, but the most perceptive commentators had the sensation of real, deep, social movement.

The façade remained largely unchanged, and the established institutions unaltered. The monarchy, certainly, emerged from the war more popular than ever.

The 'powers' of the monarchy had been recognised as limited to advice and influence by the middle of the reign of Queen Victoria; if King George V was a very different monarch to her, this owed more to the differences in character and experience than to a profound alteration in the position of the monarchy. King Edward VII and King George V lacked Queen Victoria's unique experience of politics, and their prejudices were less deep. But, after a difficult start, King George developed a style and technique of his own that gave him eventually a very considerable influence as well as much popularity. The 'powers' of the monarchy in reality were gone before the death of the Prince Consort, who had done more than any other individual to put it on the constitutional lines that have been followed ever since; the influence of the monarch still remained, could be important on occasions, and varied with the personality and experience of each sovereign. There were no indications before 1914 that the public respect for the monarchy had seriously waned, although, had King George accepted the advice urged on him by one of his advisers in the first crisis of his reign in 1911 and been seen to have been taking sides,[1] the situation might have been very different.

One really marked change had concerned the position of the House of Lords. Between 1868 and 1905 it was usual for the Foreign Secretary to be a peer; Lord Clarendon from 1868 to 1870; Granville from 1870 to 1874 and 1880 to 1885; Salisbury in 1885–6; Rosebery and Iddesleigh in 1886; Salisbury 1887–92; Rosebery 1892–4; Kimberley 1894–5; Salisbury, 1895–1900; Lansdowne 1900–5. Salisbury had been Prime Minister for over thirteen years between 1885 and 1902, and Rosebery for over a year in the same period. After 1886, the Lords became even more than in the past a Conservative stronghold. The Liberal campaigns against the peers in 1883–4 and 1892–5 did not have substantial immediate effect, but they were the first shots in the battle that developed fully between 1906 and 1909, and which reached its culmination in the constitutional crisis of 1910–11. The Liberal objections to Rosebery in 1894 were not principally the result of his being a peer, but after that disaster it was highly improbable that the Liberals would ever consider a member of the Lords as leader again. And in 1911 one of the arguments which had a strong influence with Asquith in appointing Churchill to the Admiralty over Haldane's claims was the belief that an office of that importance must be held by a member of the House of Commons. Thus, although the 1911 Parliament Act did not, in itself, grievously diminish the powers of the House of Lords, the accumulation of events leading up to it had shown that in the last analysis the Lords could no longer withstand a determined Government with a Commons majority and public support. The latter remained the key factor, as the examples of 1893 and 1906–9 had demonstrated.

But the blatant partisanship of the Lords had destroyed its influence. So long as the hereditary principle lasted, it could count upon a regular intake of young men interested in politics, but for

[1] See Volume I, 251.

those who were more fortunate the Commons was the centre of ambition. The Lords declined into the Valhalla of failed or ageing politicians, generals, and officials, addressed by fading titans of the past or undistinguished junior Ministers. The Salisbury–Rosebery debates had been the last occasion on which the party leaders had combated in the Lords, and after Salisbury's death the declined status of the Lords became increasingly evident. It still had its great days and great orators—Milner and Curzon, Birkenhead and Carson, Hailsham and Swinton. But the reality of power now lay elsewhere.

This had been the lesson of 1830–2, but it was not fully applied until 1911. Ministers still sat in the House of Lords, but the balance had now swung sharply towards the Commons. It subsequently became very uncommon for a peer even to be Foreign Secretary, the exceptions in the inter-war period being Curzon (1919–23), Reading (for three months in 1931) and Halifax (1938–40); in May 1923, when Law's succession was discussed, the fact that Curzon was a peer was held to be a significant objection. There *might* have been a peer as Prime Minister in May 1940 (Halifax), but this would have been seen as a major change in accepted practice, justified only by very exceptional circumstances. The Lords could still be a nuisance to a radical government, but little more.

Although the apparatus of the central Government affected the ordinary citizen very little in 1914, there had been a very considerable increase in the size and scope of government since the early 1880s. In 1880 there were over 50,000 civil servants of all categories, including those engaged in postal and telegraph services; by 1914 the figure had risen to 280,000. The creation of the Board of Agriculture (1889) and the Board of Education (1899) had been the first, rather timorous, steps in the direction of 'functional' Ministries. The operation of the National Insurance Act of 1911 required new organisation, which was created in the form of four linked commissions, represented by the Treasury in Parliament. This was an example—of which others were to come later—of government legislation leading directly to the creation of new organisation outside the existing government structure. The Labour Exchanges, on the other hand, were created within the structure of the Board of Trade. The non-contributory old age pensions scheme enacted in 1909 similarly did not merit a new department of State.

The volume of public expenditure was in itself an indication of what had happened. In 1901 the Civil Estimates were £23·6 million, and the Service Estimates were £60·9. By 1914 the Civil Estimates had risen to £57·6 million, and the Service Estimates to £80.39. The marked disparity between military and civil expenditure still remained, but the sharp increase in civil expenditure was a significant trend. This jump in public expenditure at home—principally on education and social remedial legislation—demonstrated a real movement away from the mid-Victorian philosophies of 'self-help'.

The dictum of Disraeli that 'the vicissitudes of politics are inexhaustible' had been demonstrated frequently in the years 1886–1918. The period opened with the thunderbolt of Gladstone's espousal of Home Rule, and the subsequent split in the Liberal Party that had taken Joseph Chamberlain and Hartington and ninety-one other Liberals into the Conservative lobby in June 1886, and that eventually resulted in the Unionist Alliance. Then, shortly after their victory in the 1886 General Election, the Conservatives had been shaken by the unexpected resignation of Lord Randolph Churchill: the policy of 'killing Home Rule by kindness', coupled with that of 'twenty years of resolute government' personified by Balfour, led to a revival of the Irish cause, a revival given enormous impetus by the Pigott forgeries, only to be temporarily crushed by the Parnell divorce case and the subsequent internecine feuds among the Irish Nationalists.

The Liberal victory of 1892 had been, accordingly, a barren one, and, particularly after the resignation of Gladstone, subsided feebly towards defeat. Between 1866 and 1886 the Liberals were in office for a total of eleven and a half years; in the twenty years following, they were in office, and only with the support of the Irish vote, for under three years.

The Liberal revival of 1903–5 was the result less of Liberal advances in thinking or activity than the collapse of the Unionist Alliance, and a startling swing of circumstances in their favour. But from December 1905 until May 1915 the Liberals were in office, and it was the Unionists who seemed to be doomed to perpetual opposition. It was this fact that imparted to the political crises of 1906–14 much of their bitterness.

This period also saw the decisive movement towards full Irish independence. After the setbacks of the 1890s, and the slow rebuilding of the Irish Nationalist Party by Redmond, Home Rule seemed very near in 1914, its proximity only shadowed—now that the absolute

veto of the House of Lords had been destroyed by the Parliament Act
—by the refusal of Ulster to be coerced into a Home Rule Parliament.
But the aftermath to the Easter Rising of April 1916 and the attempt
to impose conscription in 1918 had transformed the emphasis of the
movement away from limited Home Rule to full independence.
Between 1880 and 1916 the separatists had always been in a minority;
now they were, as the General Election of 1918 decisively demonstrated, the majority. The Irish Question was to torture the British
domestic political scene for another three years, and then to disappear,
but not permanently.

In the Empire, there had been a subtle but very significant development since 1880. By 1918 the Empire seemed more secure, united, and
confident than ever. Its members had rallied to the British cause, and
had shared the British sacrifice. The unhappy saga of British relations
with the Boer Republics had resulted in the fulfilment of Bartle
Frere's old dream of the South African Federation. Canada, Australia,
New Zealand and South Africa now enjoyed full self-government. In
India, a policy of 'gradualness' was slowly incorporating Indians into
the process of consultation—although not that of government. There
were, in 1918, few indications in London of the storm that was about
to break.

The years following the Boer War, and the Great War itself, far
from destroying the Empire, had apparently strengthened its cor-
porate sense and had certainly seen a substantial increase in its size.
The new possessions in the Middle East, and the acquisition of the
former German colonies, represented a very considerable accession of
British territorial possessions. These developments were of great
encouragement to what might be loosely described as the 'idealistic
imperialists' of the Milner school. They had, however, failed to learn
the real lessons of 1900–18. Every attempt to bring the Empire into
a closer federation—economic or military—had merely emphasised
the increasing sense of independence of its members. These attitudes
were to be formally enacted in the Statute of Westminster in 1931, and
their full implications were to be seen at the Imperial Conference of
1937 and in the Munich Crisis in 1938.

So far as the Colonies were concerned, British power and influence
remained strong. But the acceptance by Lloyd George of Woodrow
Wilson's concept of 'self-determination', and the fact that Britain had
gone to war ostensibly to preserve Belgian independence, provided

critics of British rule with formidable new weapons. And, by the Balfour Declaration of November 1917, the British had ensured that their occupancy of the Middle East was to be a difficult one. The dominant attitude of the British towards the Colonies remained that of Milner's conclusion on self-government in Egypt: 'The people neither comprehend it nor desire it. They would come to singular grief if they had it. And nobody, except a few silly theorists, thinks of giving it to them'.[1] But now, it was becoming less a question of giving than surrendering. It was to be many years before British politicians comprehended the vast aspirations to which their own rhetoric had contributed. Hobson had exaggerated—but not greatly—when he had written in 1902 that 'not five per cent of the population of our Empire are possessed of the political and civil liberties which are the basis of British civilisation'.[2] The blatant absence of these liberties was now beginning to arouse resistance and hostility which had little to do with theorists, silly or otherwise.

Thus, the war that had demonstrated so dramatically the cohesion of the Empire, was also to open large fissures in that cohesion. Ireland was to provide the first example.

*

But Britain emerged from the Great War militarily triumphant and seemingly more powerful than ever. The war had swept away all the other familiar landmarks in Europe. Germany and Russia, crushed by military defeat and internal collapse, had ceased to exist as great powers. The Austro-Hungarian and Ottoman Empires had literally vanished. France, although a nominal victor, was exhausted by her prodigious sacrifices—even more exhausted than was realised at the time. The German High Seas Fleet lay in sullen docility in Scapa Flow. The German colonies had been expropriated. Everywhere the British armies rested on their arms, with vast new areas of conquest to their name. The Empire revelled in the splendour of total victory. The Prime Minister of Britain, at the zenith of his fame, journeyed to Versailles to dictate terms to the defeated and to parley from a position of power to his allies. President Wilson journeyed across the Atlantic to build a new World Order, but in fact to meet and be vanquished by the implacable reactionary *realpolitik* of the Old.

[1] Milner: *England In Egypt.*
[2] Hobson: *Imperialism*, 123.

The economic effects of the war on Britain had been surprisingly small, and the war was followed by a boom—quickly to disappear. In many respects the war had had beneficial results, particularly on the chemical, scientific, and engineering industries. Before the war Britain had lagged badly behind her principal rivals in all three industries; by 1918 she could claim at least parity, and in many respects superiority. Britain had lost about a tenth of her overseas investments, which had amounted to some £4,000 million in 1914; she had also incurred a substantial external debt. This caused little concern, as the debt of £842 million to America was more than balanced by the £1,740 million owed to her by her allies. But £568 million of this was owed by Russia, and the other debtors were not in a condition to repay. It was some time before the British began to realise the full implications of this situation. In the immediate post-war euphoria it was assumed that Germany would substantially repay the Allies for their expenditure and that Britain's debtors would promptly meet their obligations. Neither assumption proved to be valid.

The psychological results of the war were to prove, in the long run, considerably more important than the physical, although the latter were serious enough. The British had lost some 744,000 men killed in the Army and Navy. This meant that one in ten men of the generation aged between twenty and forty-five during the war was dead. Most of them, it should be recalled, had been volunteers. In addition, 14,661 merchant seamen had been killed, and 1,117 civilians in German airship and aeroplane raids; the influenza epidemic of 1918–1919 killed 150,000 more, of whom more than 15,000 died in London alone. The British Empire mourned some 947,000 young men killed in action or dead of wounds; in addition, there were countless tens of thousands who had been physically or mentally scarred by the war. The available statistics can only afford us some idea of the physical results of the war. By 1921, in Britain, nearly 3,500,000 persons were receiving some kind of war pension or allowance;[1] some 160,000 wives had lost husbands in the war, and over 300,000 children had lost fathers.[2] The fact that struck commentators at the time, and

[1] *Report of the Departmental Committee of Inquiry into the Machinery of Administration of the Ministry of Pensions, p. 3.*

[2] The casualties of the other major belligerents were approximately as follows:
Russia: 1·7 million dead, 4·9 million wounded.
France: 1·3 million dead, 4·3 million wounded.
Germany: 1·8 million dead, 4·2 million wounded.

which has become one of the most potent phrases of modern history, was 'the missing generation', particularly among the traditional ruling classes. But it was not simply a phrase. No nation of Britain's size can afford to lose three-quarters of a million young men dead and another million and a half wounded without grievous consequences. The great majority had been volunteers, and included men in the highly skilled professions. It has been suggested that of those who returned, there was a marked distaste for public life and for politicians. As Woodward wrote:

> The men who came back from the war have counted for less, perhaps, in the political life of their country than any generation during the last two or three centuries.

This contention was not wholly merited. Among the survivors of the so-called 'lost generation' were Anthony Eden, Clement Attlee, Walter Elliot, Duff Cooper, Harold Macmillan, Oswald Mosley, Walter Monckton, and the future Lord Halifax. But the men who dominated British politics in the inter-war period were those who had been born and brought up in Victorian Britain. This was not altogether surprising since the pattern of British politics is such that it is unusual for men under forty to rise to Cabinet rank. But there seemed to be—and was—a gulf in experience and attitude between the men who had served in the war and those whose experience was essentially pre-war.

This was seen less in specific policies than in general attitudes. The dominant—and understandable—feeling among the leading personalities in public life after the war was to return to the comfortable 'normality' of the pre-1914 situation. As R. H. Tawney has commented: '"Back to 1914" became a common cry.' They had no wish to build on the structures that had been so painfully created by the exigencies of the war, and which they consequently regarded as exceptional measures for exceptional circumstances. Thus, the new functional Ministries spawned by the war were thankfully and

---

Austria-Hungary: 1·2 million dead, 3·6 million wounded.
Over 60 million men were mobilised by the European belligerents, of whom 57·6 per cent were casualties, with more than 8 million killed and over 21 million wounded. These figures are very approximate, but are certainly not an under-estimation, and it cannot be emphasised enough that they are almost entirely related to males between the ages of 18 and 45, and they give little hint of the psychological and physical effects upon the survivors.

swiftly obliterated. Free Trade was revived as the national lode-star, and those politicians who had fought for the Tariff Reform cause for so long resumed their wearying struggle. All parties worked towards a return to the Gold Standard. Nothing, it seemed, had changed. The trouble was that everything had changed. But those who saw this, and had no desire whatever to go back to 1914, did not occupy the commanding political heights.

The structure of politics itself had changed drastically. The condition of the Liberal Party was very comparable to that of the Whig Party in the 1840s, described by Disraeli as 'absolutely forlorn . . . spoken of as a corpse, it was treated as a phantom', its remnants divided between Lloyd George and the defeated Asquith. But Lloyd George and the Conservatives—in 1914 apparently doomed to indefinite Opposition, and now in 1919 so firmly in control—had not been the only causes of the Liberal débâcle.

The most significant event in the downfall of the Liberals had been the emergence of the Labour Party, with its own leaders, candidates and programme, and now a separate, distinct, and individual force in British politics. In 1910 Labour voters had amounted to less than eight per cent of the votes cast; in 1918 it was 22·2 per cent. The Labour Party was in no sense whatever a revolutionary element, but its emergence aroused intense apprehension in the older parties. From this point the obsession of keeping Labour out of office became their dominant, if often unspoken, motivation.

The Redmondite Irish Nationalists had vanished almost as completely as the Austrian-Hungarian Empire. Of the eighty-strong phalanx that had swayed British politics since the late 1870s, only seven returned. The seventy-three elected Sinn Fein candidates contemptuously refused to take their seats in the British Parliament, and established their own, the Dail, in Dublin. The profound significance of this action was only gradually perceived.

An observer of the House of Commons at the beginning of 1919 could accordingly see at a glance the political effects of the war. The Conservatives, in opposition for so long, sat triumphantly on the Government benches, enclosing in their midst their Lloyd George Liberal captives. The followers of Asquith sat in a pitiful group, in an apparent condition of shock. The Irish had gone. Labour, with fifty-nine Members, was the majority opposition party.

*

The dominant personality in British political life was Lloyd George. Many of his contemporaries, and a number of subsequent commentators, have endeavoured to recapture his extraordinary personality, but without success. He comes down to us in vague terms, Keynes' 'half-human visitor to our age from the hag-ridden magic and enchanted woods of Celtic antiquity', 'rooted in nothing', 'void and without content', 'a vampire and a medium in one'. To Beaverbrook he was the Archetypical Pragmatist:

> To keep the seat of power, the place of patronage, he was prepared to stand out as the leader of Empire-minded men—or appear as the Liberal Apostle of Free Trade: as the Man of Peace in Europe—or as the Man of War against Turkey and France: as the hammer of the Russian Bolshevists—or their noble conciliator: as the Tribune of the British Working Class—or the champion of the Tory landlords against Labour: stern enemy of the Irish—or their tender friend spreading his covering wings about another Celtic race ground under the heel of the oppressor. He took up each position in turn during those tragic years of 1921 and 1922.[1]

That Lloyd George was an opportunist and, in political terms, an adventurer, may be freely accepted. So had been Disraeli; so was Churchill. In 1918 this was not only accepted but positively admired; he was 'the man who won the war', and 'the man who got things done'.

But although Lloyd George had successfully stormed the citadel of power, he had triumphed at heavy cost. He had split the Liberal Party. He was wholly dependent upon Conservative votes and Conservative goodwill for his survival. He headed a Coalition in which the Conservatives were dominant. His own shifts of policy reflected the strains and difficulties of the Government that he headed. He was to become the convenient scapegoat when the electorate turned against the Coalition.

To those who appreciate natural justice in human affairs, this is agreeable. Lloyd George's personal standards of political probity were not high; his standards of loyalty to friends and colleagues were even less exalted; he was more than willing to pay the price of Tory support; in political matters great and small he had few scruples and few standards. But no portrait of this remarkable individual can discount

[1] Beaverbrook: *The Decline and Fall of Lloyd George*, 10-11.

his extraordinary charm. He was always bubbling with life and vigour, and could be an enchanting companion. One sensed in his presence a glow of energy and spirit which few could resist, and he had full comprehension of the value of flattery in human affairs. Bonar Law was one of many improbable politicians who found 'the little man' irresistible, however much he might disapprove of certain aspects of his public and private life. The fact that Lloyd George had a mistress, to whom he was not invariably faithful, was well known in political circles, but—like Asquith's drinking—was never mentioned publicly, and remained unknown to the public until long after his death. But, in the mood of 1919, it is perhaps doubtful that even this knowledge would have fatally affected his political eminence.

Political power and prestige of the kind that Lloyd George enjoyed immediately after the 1918 General Election is very heady wine. He became careless and greedy, in matters financial particularly, and the atmosphere in 10 Downing Street was not edifying. Everything revolved around the Prime Minister's whims and prejudices, and the only road to favour was subservience. Lloyd George became intoxicated by his power, relished its trappings to the point where they dominated his horizons, and made him forget how shallow were the foundations of his occupancy of Downing Street. From past experience he should have known that the Conservative Party would only follow him while his national popularity remained, and would abandon him without remorse or compunction when it was evident that his usefulness to them was at an end. It was said of Lloyd George in 1918 that he could be Prime Minister for the rest of his life; conceivably, he might have been, had he continued to produce political success for his nominal followers and effective masters. But *hubris* was to be for Lloyd George, as for so many others, his fatal characteristic.

The collective personality of the Government was essentially that of its leader. Lloyd George was the first—and, to the time of writing, the last—'Presidential' Prime Minister. He treated Parliament with contempt, and rarely went there. He filled 10 Downing Street with cronies and sycophants. He could be—and often was—brutal to those colleagues who crossed him or who aroused his jealousy, and merciless when his own position seemed in jeopardy. He created the Lloyd George Fund, whose purpose was simply 'to promote any political purpose approved by the Rt. Hon. David Lloyd George', and for which a major source of revenue was the sale of honours and other favours. Until 1922 the income was shared fifty-fifty with the Conservatives; afterwards it all went to Lloyd George, and only he controlled it. This must have seemed a brilliant stroke, giving him a power of the purse that would ensure his domination of the Liberal Party. But Lloyd George grossly exaggerated the value of money in the new circumstances created by the arrival of a mass electorate, and the revelation of its existence and how it had been built up was to be the final blow to his declining reputation in 1922.

But for most of the Coalition Lloyd George's style and manner dominated it, and were to be his undoing. Churchill became increasingly disenchanted with his old companion-in-arms; Bonar Law was to become totally disillusioned; and the revulsion that Lloyd George's imperious and cynical conduct of affairs aroused in the junior members of his Government was to prove fatal to him in 1922 and to pursue him relentlessly for the rest of his career.

The second man in the Government—indeed, almost on a level with Lloyd George—was Bonar Law, formerly highly sceptical of Lloyd George but now a warm admirer. His hold on the Conservative Party was a strong one, but was in the real sense a reactionary one; Law did not lead, he listened and followed what his supporters said. He was plainly, and manifestly, the lynch-pin of the Government. His natural caution and melancholy had been emphasised by the loss of two of his sons in the war. Pessimistic, matter-of-fact, cautious, modest to the point of appearing nondescript, Law was in marked contrast to the other Coalition leaders—in Beaverbrook's phrase the glittering birds of paradise.

The Coalition leaders could count upon nearly 500 supporters in the House of Commons. They basked in the glow of military victory, as the dominant personalities in the most powerful nation in the world. It was a dazzling, brilliant, all-powerful alliance. Yet, within four years it was to disintegrate, collapse, and to perish unmourned. The story of this downfall is among the most remarkable in modern British political history.

It is not simply hindsight to detect in the Coalition from the outset certain important weaknesses. 'The war fought for democracy', one perceptive observer has written, 'had produced at the centre an atmosphere more like an oriental court at which favourites struggle unceasingly for position.'[1] Its leading members, with the notable

[1] Francis Williams: *A Pattern of Rulers*, 19.

exception of Bonar Law, were remarkably detached from their rank and file. Lloyd George was to become, so far as the House of Commons was concerned, virtually an absentee Prime Minister. He also developed a marked taste for personal international diplomacy, an obsession that increasingly divorced him not only from the House of Commons but also from the Government.

Churchill had only recently emerged from a period of signal political misfortune. The prodigy of 1900–15 had stumbled badly, and although he was back in office, much—if not all—of the early glitter had been severely tarnished. The grim shadow of the Gallipoli disaster hung over his reputation. The Conservatives disliked and distrusted him; the Asquithian Liberals considered him a renegade; organised Labour regarded him as one of their most implacable foes. Churchill was totally dependent upon Lloyd George for his political survival. In 1908, when Churchill had first entered the Cabinet, A. G. Gardiner had pondered the question of whether the mercurial young man had staying power. 'How will forty find him?' Gardiner asked, '—that fatal forty when the youth of roselight and romance has faded into the light of common day. . . .' By 1919 Churchill was forty-five, yet he retained many of the more alarming features of the *enfant terrible* that prompted Lloyd George to compare him with a chauffeur who drove steadily for months and then drove one over a precipice. Churchill had no political or personal following. As an anonymous commentator wrote in *The Times* in November 1920: 'His first party will still have no good said of him, his second believes him to be hankering after his first love, and latterly he has been advertising for a new Centre Party which is to combine the charms of the other two. But even if this third match came off and then turned out ill, Mr. Churchill would not be greatly embarrassed, for wherever he is there is the party.'

In the event, however, Churchill was indeed 'greatly embarrassed' when the match was broken off by the other party and he was left, totally alone and grievously exposed, in a political No Man's Land.

In 1919 Churchill could point to many conspicuous achievements; among them, however, was not that of inspiring trust or notable affection—particularly in the Conservative Party, where Bonar Law eyed him with conspicuous reservations.

Churchill's closest friend in the Government was F. E. Smith, now transformed into Lord Birkenhead and Lord Chancellor at the age of forty-five—a step described by *The Times* as 'carrying a joke too far'. Birkenhead was probably the most brilliant individual in public life, 'the cleverest man in the kingdom', as Beaverbrook described him. Sardonic, sharp-witted, and irreverent, he was the best of company when in the mood, adored by his family and close friends, and a superb speaker. But his public virtues were not as apparent as his deficiencies. After a spectacular start he had failed to reach the heights that had seemed open to him. Like Lloyd George, he had no real roots. His cynical, cavalier attitudes made more enemies than admirers. If, in Cabinet, he was a silent and respected member, whose eventual opinion carried great weight, and if he was deeply loved by those who knew him best, in public he gave a rasping, intolerant, bullying and unprincipled impression. Even in an age of hard-living politicians, Birkenhead's drinking and extravagance stood out conspicuously.

Austen Chamberlain was in many ways the most attractive of the Conservatives; certainly, in most respects, he was the most attractive of all the Chamberlains. But although he faithfully emulated his father's appearance and revered his memory, there was a vast gulf between Joseph and Austen. Indeed, acutely conscious of the ill-feeling that remained over his father's political action, Austen Chamberlain sought a reputation for honourable conduct that rendered him peculiarly vulnerable and ineffective. Controversy exists about the author of the famous phrase 'Austen always played the game and always lost it'—Birkenhead is the most likely author, although it has also been credited to Churchill—but it had substantial justice. And, in spite of much *gravitas* and earnestness, there was always something faintly preposterous, if also rather touching, about the frock-coated, top-hatted, monocled, Austen.

Curzon was, on the face of things, even more preposterous, but he was in fact one of the most complex and deeply interesting figures of modern politics. Although born in rich circumstances, his upbringing had been a hard and loveless one. He suffered from a lifelong weakness of the spine, which required wearing an uncomfortable steel brace. He was rarely free from pain, a fact that no doubt contributed substantially to the stiffness, formality and on occasion downright pomposity of his public manner. But perhaps there were other, deeper, causes for this. For all his qualities and achievements, he lacked constancy of purpose and self-confidence to a surprising degree.

He was always threatening resignation, always complaining of the treatment of his colleagues, yet always irresolute. As Churchill has tartly commented: 'He was too much concerned with what might be said about things, and too little with the things themselves.' There was truth in this jibe, but it did not contain the whole truth.

Curzon's record was impressive by any standards. His careers at Eton and Oxford had been outstanding, and he had entered the House of Commons in 1886 almost as of right. He had travelled widely and thought much; he had, above all, written much (one book on Persia ran to some 1,300 pages). Nor did he lack shrewdness; he devoted one section of an enormous book on the Far East to an unknown hamlet in Indo-China called Dien Bien Phu which had, as he pointed out at length, substantial strategic importance. He was in every respect a formidably equipped man. Yet it all added up to surprisingly little. The House of Commons found him a bore. He never rose above junior office, until, in 1898, he was appointed Viceroy of India. That searing experience has been related.[1] But, like Milner, he had risen again. In 1915, at the age of fifty-six, he had held senior office for the first time. From October 1919 he was Foreign Secretary, and one of the best equipped of all modern holders of that office. But, again, it added up to not very much in terms of real influence. Throughout his strange career Curzon eagerly coveted and sought after eminence. Few men have worked harder to achieve it, nor have recovered more completely from severe misfortunes and disappointments. But the curious fact is that at no time was he ever taken seriously as a politician of the first order. There was something in his manner, his seriousness, his celebrated meanness, and self-important grandeur that made him an object of ribaldry rather than respect.

Balfour, the other leading Conservative in the Coalition, was perhaps even more remote than Chamberlain, Birkenhead and Curzon from the political rank and file. His detachment from the political hurly-burly, which had always been marked, had become greatly accentuated by the passing years. Still bland, affable, charming, remote, and cold-blooded, Balfour moved on a different plane from the new men who gave the Coalition their Parliamentary power.

*

This Parliament has become known to history as being composed of

[1] See Volume I, 215–16.

'hard-faced men who look as though they had done well out of the war'; the phrase was that of the then unknown Stanley Baldwin, but it was echoed by others. Austen Chamberlain described them as 'a selfish, swollen lot'. Some historians have demonstrated that, statistically, this Parliament did not differ greatly from its predecessors. As usual, such statistics are irrelevant. There was clearly something about that overwhelming Coalition majority that observers found loathsome;[1] yet it was this body that was to turn against the Coalition with revulsion, and permanently to affect the course of British politics in the inter-war years.

For most of 1919 Lloyd George was in Paris, and the main burden of his activity was directed towards the settlement of the peace treaty in particular and international affairs in general. A substantial part of the Foreign Office was moved to Paris, and the processes of Cabinet Government were rendered infinitely more complicated by the frequent absences not merely of the Prime Minister but the Foreign Secretary, and often the Chancellor of the Exchequer as well. This was perhaps inevitable in the circumstances, but the results were unfortunate. Almost at once, the Government was plunged into a series of domestic problems from which it extricated itself with some difficulty and without enhanced reputation.

The first shock—and it was a very real and serious one—came over demobilisation. The mood of the Army had been manifested quickly after the Armistice by the refusal of troops, in camps at Dover and Folkestone, to embark for France and by the burning of Luton Town Hall. It was a difficult situation for the Government as peace had not been signed, but the mood of the Army was ugly. The principal cause was the decision to grant priority releases not only to men with jobs awaiting them in certain trades but also to men on leave who could produce written offers of employment. In effect, this meant that priority discharges were being given to men who had been in the Army

---

[1] This was the adjective employed to the author by the late Sir Edward Fellowes, Clerk of the House of Commons, who entered the service of the House in 1919, and retired in 1962. These people—particularly on the Conservative side—did not disappear at the end of this Parliament, as Duff Cooper, elected in 1924, has related. 'I soon discovered that the Die-Hards were not the stern, unbending Tories of my imagination, the descendants of those who had supported Pitt against Fox, Wellington against Grey, and Disraeli against Gladstone. They were mostly business men who had recently made fortunes, often by methods that did not invite close inspection.' (Duff Cooper: *Old Men Forget*, 141.)

for a short time, and militated against those who had been under arms for a longer period. The Government's plans were justifiable in the national interest, but hardly skilfully designed to placate a citizen army aching for release. Lloyd George blamed Milner; Robertson wondered if he could rely on any troops to quell the disturbances. The impasse was resolved by Churchill, who took over the War Office in January and swiftly ordered that demobilisation was to be firmly based on length of service. The disturbances subsided, although there were further isolated episodes in the summer.

Matters were not improved by the lavish generosity with which Parliament rewarded the commanders of the war. Peerages, honours, and substantial financial rewards showered upon the deserving and undeserving alike. The widow of General Maude received £25,000, a particular grant which received the attention of Philip Snowden in *Forward*. The resentment which these generous rewards to the senior officer class caused in the Army was profound, and fully merited, when they are compared with the plight of disabled ex-soldiers, war widows, and orphans. In itself, it was a small episode, but it was symptomatic of an attitude which had been acceptable before 1914 but which was now not. The refusal of the Glasgow Federation of Discharged Soldiers to admit ex-officers was an extreme reaction, but understandable.[1] At the outset, the hope of many veterans that the comradeship of the trenches would be carried into peace was compromised. Back to 1914, again.

This anger in the Army coincided with widespread industrial unrest, and the Government—and particularly Lloyd George—took fright. The miners, the railwaymen, and the transport workers revived the 'Triple Industrial Alliance' in February. The engineers were also in a belligerent mood, and in Glasgow a series of stoppages culminated in a general strike in the area which had violent scenes, caused the dispatch of tanks and troops, and lasted from January 27th until February 11th. Among those arrested were James Maxton and Emanuel Shinwell, of whom much more was to be heard. By February 1919 the startled and apprehensive Government found itself coping with striking soldiers, a formidable nationwide federation of trade unions capable of inflicting virtually a national strike, and rioting in

[1] It was characteristic of the mood of the Government that, on June 6th, the Minister of Labour, Sir Robert Horne, declared that the Glasgow Federation was 'now in touch with the Russian bolsheviks', and likely to form a Soviet.

Glasgow, Edinburgh and Belfast. But, except in Glasgow—where the Red Flag was flown from the flagstaff of the Town Hall, and the leaders of the rising were arrested and imprisoned—the Government acted cautiously and sensibly. Nevertheless, they were already reacting to situations and problems at home on a piecemeal basis, while their Prime Minister and senior Ministers were occupied at Versailles with the future map of Europe.

The measures taken by the Government were essentially ad hoc. Milner told Henry Wilson on February 5th that 'we are in chaos in England as regards these strikes, which under Lloyd George's régime are being dealt with by every sort of man and every sort of department, each acting on a different principle from the others'. The minimum wage level was maintained until September 1920, although it had been originally designed to expire six months after the Armistice. An out-of-work donation to ex-servicemen and unemployed civilian workers was extended beyond the original plan to confine it to firms working for the Ministry of Munitions. A Coal Commission, presided over by Mr. Justice Sankey, was set up to examine the grievances of the coalminers. Lloyd George also called—at the end of February—a National Industrial Conference, a characteristic dramatic and futile step, but one that at least served to lower the temperature for the time being. The fact that the Government consistently ignored the Conference's recommendations resulted in the eventual withdrawal of the trade union members, and marked another stage in the growing disillusionment of organised labour with the Coalition.

The Sankey Commission's final Report—issued in June—disclosed the gulf between the views of the miners and the owners. The Government had already approved a compromise wage increase; it now firmly rejected any idea of nationalisation of the mines, and in this seemed to be going back on its acceptance of the interim report in March in which Sankey had recommended representation of the workers in the running of the mines, and either nationalisation or some other system of unification 'by national purchase and/or joint control'. This was now reduced to acceptance of a one-man minority report by a member of the Sankey Commission, Sir Arthur Duckham, for amalgamation of collieries into district companies, with a minority of workers' representatives and a limit on profits. The miners indignantly rejected this solution, and the possibility of a nationwide coal strike now grew nearer.

Meanwhile, the railwaymen had been active. In the dispute between the Government and the railwaymen the principal difficulty was caused by the fact that the latter were convinced that after decontrol the owners would not increase wages. The Government's offer was a fair one; the minimum wage was to rise to forty shillings a week but—given the sharp rise in the cost of living since 1914—this was not a substantial improvement on the pre-war level of eighteen shillings. The failure seems to have been essentially one of communication, for which the somewhat rasping manner of the President of the Board of Trade, Sir Auckland Geddes, must bear considerable responsibility. The railway strike began on September 26th, and on October 5th the Government agreed to maintain the existing system for one more year.

These compromises and devices for putting off serious examination of the problems may have been unheroic, but they were successful in damping down the somewhat revolutionary tone that had been evident earlier in the year. The continuance of the wartime boom kept up wages and kept down unemployment, and the apparent success of responsible labour leadership succeeded even more effectively in diminishing the influence of the extremists. A special Trades Union Congress was summoned in December to consider the particular case of the miners, and it was resolved to undertake a publicity campaign in favour of nationalisation rather than to strike. In March 1920 the T.U.C. voted overwhelmingly against a proposal by the Miners' Federation for a general strike; the Government reciprocated by granting a wage increase to offset increases in the cost of living.

Nothing had been solved by these essentially political measures, and the Government was concurrently eagerly dismembering the government machinery that was essential to a controlled economy. But the Government had at least bought time in which tempers could cool, and had divided the unions. It remained to be seen what use it could make of the opportunity thus created.

*

No international treaty of modern times has come under such widespread criticism and abuse as the Treaty of Versailles, which was concluded on June 28th, 1919.[1]

Lloyd George's position—although perhaps not as difficult as that

[1] Lloyd George was persuaded that it would be appropriate to write to the King informing him of the fact, which he did with some reluctance; the letter was conveyed by air to the King by J. C. C. Davidson, Bonar Law's private secretary. (Davidson: *Memoirs of a Conservative*, 92.)

of Clemenceau—was difficult enough. The bulk of the Coalition M.P.s looked to him for severe reparations on Germany, and reacted with alarm to any suggestions of leniency. Northcliffe, now in sad decline, and embittered with Lloyd George for not including him on the British delegation, kept up a running fire of criticism in *The Times* and the *Daily Mail*. The eventual Treaty was considerably more lenient towards Germany than the bulk of the Coalition supporters had expected or wanted; yet, within a relatively short time, they were echoing the vehement criticisms of J. M. Keynes against its severity.

The proceedings of the Conference were a triumph for Lloyd George and a disaster for President Wilson. In fact, Lloyd George's attitudes were very close to those of Wilson, and he was an infinitely more accomplished negotiator than the American. Wilson's lack of experience and understanding of the details were painfully exposed, and matters were not improved by the attitudes and actions of Herbert Hoover, who sabotaged a reasonable proposal put forward by the British to maintain shipping controls and establish an international administration to supersede the blockade. Hoover vetoed the proposal out of hand and ordered that nothing should be done about feeding Germany until he arrived in Europe. Three months elapsed before the Supreme Economic Council was set up, with him in the dominant role. The new organisation was no improvement on that originally suggested, and three vital months had been wasted. Hoover's disagreeable personality did not assist matters. An agitation began in Britain against what was called 'the hunger blockade'.

Here, Lloyd George was in a very real difficulty. The Germans had been sinking the world's transport shipping up to the Armistice, and there was a severe shortage of ships. The American farming and business interests were putting strong pressure for the resumption of exports to Europe; the Germans pointed out the difficulties of paying for the food and insisted that its supply should be definitely assured by British or American credits before handing over their mercantile marine to the Allies; the French were all for maintaining the blockade to bring pressure upon the Germans. There was another factor. The only tangible asset in the Reichsbank was the gold reserve of some £120 million, and the French Government had its eye firmly fixed upon this valuable asset; the prospect of it disappearing to America to pay for food was not relished.

The deadlock was broken by Lloyd George, in a masterly display of negotiating skill, at the Supreme War Council on 8th March. The French eventually withdrew their main objections and the Germans were more forthcoming over the ships. By April the food supplies were entering Germany. Difficulties remained, but the deadlock had been broken.

Over the League of Nations Covenant Lloyd George was less successful. The British saw the League essentially as an instrument for international conciliation, and their proposals—which had been carefully prepared—were practical and realistic. Wilson, who ignored a studied hint by Lloyd George that heads of delegations should not sit on the League of Nations Committee, became its chairman. His interest was less in organisation than in establishing a code of international ethics. Furthermore, his own isolationism and that of his advisers led to serious omissions in the Covenant. Any matter which by international law was solely within the jurisdiction of a party to a dispute was excluded; French plans for a permanent international General Staff and commission to watch over armaments were rejected by Wilson as an interference with national sovereignty; Hoover's opposition to international economic controls had been based on the same attitude. The result was a compromise document that, on the whole, leaned more to the British interpretation than to Wilson's, but which contained several important ambiguities. The most crucial point concerned the guarantee by the participants of 'political independence and territorial integrity to great and small alike'. The British opposed any automatic guarantee, and it was decided that in cases of aggression the Executive Council would advise upon the matter. The French text, however, used the word *aviser*, or 'look to', which left them with the conviction that the League was pledged to guarantee the security of its members.

To say this is not to dismiss Wilson's vision. The concept of the League owed much to the contributions of Norman Angell, Lord Robert Cecil, and Smuts, but it was Wilson who was the only major international leader to grasp it and espouse it with genuine enthusiasm. The League had immense potentialities. Tragically, the British and French, upon whose support the League's future rested, were unexcited. 'Nobody wished any ill to the League', Duff Cooper later recorded of his then colleagues in the Foreign Office, 'but few believed it could do any good.'[1] Hankey—who was seriously considered

[1] Duff Cooper, op. cit., 157.

as Secretary-General—also reflected official disdain for this idealistic experiment. Wilson returned to America to wage an exhausting and heroic national campaign to secure the ratification of the Treaty and American endorsement of the League, in the course of which he suffered a paralytic stroke. For the remainder of his Presidency he was a broken man. The Senate did not ratify Versailles, and the United States remained aloof from the League, from Europe, and from foreign entanglements generally. 'The people are tired', Walter Lippmann wrote in *The New Republic*, 'tired of noise, tired of politics, tired of inconvenience, tired of greatness, and longing for a place where the world is quiet and where all trouble seems dead leaves, and spent waves riot in doubtful dreams of dreams.'

America's refusal to join the League was a major misfortune, but not a disaster. The United States was potentially a major world power, but only potentially. American power and influence were insignificant, and in either economic or military terms she was not to be compared with Britain or France. The disaster to the League lay not in American aloofness, but in British and French stupidity. Back to 1914.

The new boundaries in Europe provoked further strains between the British, French and Americans. The Wilsonian concept of 'self-determination' became somewhat difficult to define in the highly confused situation that followed the collapse of the German, Austro-Hungarian and Ottoman Empires. The delineation of the new Polish State and that of Czechoslovakia proved particularly difficult, and the French proposal for a separate Rhineland state was vehemently opposed by the British and Americans. Eventually agreement was reached by authorising the extension of Allied occupation of the Rhineland for fifteen years and its permanent demilitarisation.

It was over reparations, however, that the most severe difficulties arose. The British representatives on the Reparations Committee—the Australian Prime Minister W. M. Hughes, Lord Cunliffe, and Lord Sumner—put forward extraordinarily unrealistic estimates of Germany's ability and liability to pay. Lloyd George could not accept their figures—which at one point suggested that Germany could and should pay some £24,000 million in a generation. The Treasury believed that £3,000 million was a more realistic sum; the estimate of the then obscure J. M. Keynes was £5,000 million. Lloyd George persuaded the Council that the Treaty should merely state the principle of Germany's liability to pay and that the sum should be fixed after a detailed examination of her resources.

But while Wilson deserves better of history than he has received, the view that an innocent, peace-loving, sincere American President was taken for a ride by a guileful, cynical, selfish, narrow-minded clique of wily European politicians cannot stand up to any serious examination. What had been painfully exposed was Wilson's ignorance of Europe and of the realities of international diplomacy, and the sheer impracticability of many of his proposals. But there was a deeper reason. The Americans—and not least their President—were intoxicated by their arrival on the world stage. The actual contribution of the United States to the Allied victory had been important, but the Americans developed a grotesquely exaggerated estimation of its significance, and assumed that Wilson was negotiating from a position of great strength and could dictate terms. The realities of the situation were quite different, and Wilson was in fact in a relatively weak negotiating position against the British and French. In his message to the Senate, Wilson emphasised that the League was not 'a counsel of perfection [but] . . . a plain counsel of necessity', but he added that 'America may be said to have just reached her majority as a world power', which was simply not the case. And there was also truth in the statement of Senator William E. Borah, a vehement opponent of the League, 'that we are a part of the European turmoils and conflicts from the time we enter this League'.

The Treaty was approved virtually unanimously in Parliament. It was not long before new attitudes manifested themselves. MacDonald —still out of Parliament—was one of the principal opponents of the Treaty in the Labour Party. Later in the year the former Treasury official, John Maynard Keynes, published *The Economic Consequences of the Peace*, a brilliant and mischievous philippic in which the American President was mercilessly held up to ridicule and the European members of the War Council accused of imposing a Carthaginian peace upon Germany, which was vital to the future of Europe. Keynes became a national figure overnight.[1] His book had an enormous sale and was excessively venerated on all sides; its long-

---

[1] 'About 1922 the world suddenly got very full of arrogant and languid young people of uncertain sex engaged in the new Bloomsbury sport of expressing their bored yet intolerant confidence that art and brains ended with them and Maynard Keynes' (Douglas Jerrold: *Georgian Adventure*, 240).

term effects on British attitudes towards the Versailles Treaty and the
League can hardly be exaggerated. His diatribe appeared *after*
disillusionment had set in; it followed an existing trend rather than
creating a new one. But it was a vitally important factor in the growth
of what Etienne Mantoux subsequently called *meaculpisme* over the
Treaty, which was to have baleful consequences in the 1930s. In
Germany, the new Weimar Republic was saddled with the double
stigma of having sued for peace and of having accepted an odious
Treaty. The Treaty of Versailles created enduring grievances in both
Germany and France, and fostered guilt and uncertainty in Britain.
In Britain it suddenly became fashionable to deride, and be ashamed
of, the Treaty of Versailles. France became the new menace to international peace and order, and Lloyd George her ally. Thus by a
remarkable shift of public attitude, Lloyd George's triumph swiftly
turned into reproach and even obloquy. And, from other quarters,
events were marching down relentlessly upon him and the Coalition
Government which were further to diminish its stature and authority.

*

Throughout 1919, while Lloyd George was negotiating peace in Paris
and his colleagues were coping with industrial unrest at home, the
British Government was involved in a complex and embarrassing
consequence of the war that brought it no credit and whose management provides us with an instructive illustration of the processes of the
Coalition.

When the Soviet Government ended the war with Germany in
December 1917, counter-revolutionary forces were raised by Generals
Kornilov and Denikin, which were supported by the Allies. In the
July of 1918 the British had landed forces at Archangel to protect
substantial supplies already landed there. These actions were perfectly
legitimate in the context of the war, but with its conclusion the position
of the British in Russia at once became more equivocal.

The situation in Russia was, in any event, somewhat confused by
November 1918. In the north, there was an Allied force of some 15,000
troops—of whom half were British—at Murmansk. In Siberia there
were over 100,000 Czech troops, and some British, French, American
and Japanese elements. In all, there were some 1,200 British troops
in Siberia. The various governments in the area had been concentrated
into a single Directorate at Omsk, whose War Minister was Admiral

A. V. Kolchak. In South Russia, General Denikin commanded a substantial army of over 30,000 men, which had received—and continued
to receive for some time—very heavy British assistance in material and
advisers.

Up to this stage there was no question of 'intervention' in Russia.
But in October 1918 some significant steps had been taken in this
direction. The British commander at Murmansk had been ordered to
take certain bases that clearly could only be of use against the Bolsheviks, and on October 18th the Cabinet in effect ignored Lloyd
George by deciding to retain the force at Murmansk, to recognise the
Omsk government, to maintain the force in Siberia, and also to
increase the scale of intervention by occupying the Baku-Batum
railway and stepping up supplies to Denikin. Three days later Kolchak
was declared head of the Omsk government. At this Cabinet Lloyd
George's opposition to any crusade against Bolshevism had been made
very plain; what had also become plain was that his views on this
matter were not shared by his colleagues. Smuts had been particularly
vigorous in his denunciation of Bolshevism, and the views of Milner
and Sir Henry Wilson were clear enough. Churchill was not at this
point a member of the Cabinet, but his views as Minister of Munitions
were of importance, and his alarm at 'the foul baboonery' of Bolshevism was very marked. Thus, although the Government had not
decided to intervene in Russia, it had decided not to reduce its
existing commitment of troops, and, by deciding to maintain Denikin,
had incurred a moral commitment of some importance.

On December 10th Lloyd George initiated another discussion in
the Cabinet on the issue of Russia, again making his personal views
very clear. The Foreign Office submitted a memorandum that stated
in effect that although there was substantial opposition in the country
to a major military intervention, any new governments set up under
British protection must be supported and maintained. Milner and
Wilson argued strongly against the withdrawal of the Murmansk
force, and Curzon said that the British were in honour bound to
remain until the anti-Bolshevik forces could properly organise themselves. Thus, the status quo was to be maintained. The troops stayed,
the blockade remained, and Denikin received his supplies of British
surplus war material. The Royal Navy policed the Baltic and the
Black Sea.

Early in January the division in the Cabinet became more marked.

On January 10th Churchill strongly opposed any suggestion of a withdrawal of men and support from the Omsk government. On the 16th, at a meeting of the Council of Ten in Paris, Lloyd George made a vigorous speech opposing Allied intervention in the Russian civil war, and suggesting the invitation of representatives of all sides to Paris. Wilson supported him, but the French and the Italians were not enthusiastic. On the 21st Wilson proposed that the representatives should meet after they had ended hostilities with representatives of the Great Powers on Princes' Island (Prinkipo) in the Sea of Marmara. The proposal was approved by the Council, and turned down by the White Governments of Siberia and North Russia, while the Red conditions for attendance were unacceptable. On February 12th, when the new Parliament met for the first time, the Prinkipo proposal came under strong criticism from the Conservative benches; in reply, Lloyd George put the case against intervention with vigour and skill.

In the Cabinet, however, his views were not prevailing. As soon as Churchill had gone to the War Office he had sent out a circular to station commanders enquiring if their men would accept service overseas, 'especially Russia'; the reply was to the effect that the men would muster for draft overseas except in Russia. It was accordingly necessary in future to have to raise volunteers for any forces in Russia. At Cabinet meetings on February 12th and 13th the gulf in attitudes between Churchill and Lloyd George became wider. Churchill wanted the Japanese to aid Kolchak, the British to declare war on the Bolsheviks and send volunteers to Russia, and accordingly 'crush' Bolshevism for ever. On February 14th he put his case personally to Wilson in Paris, who was hostile. On the following day Churchill put his plan to the Council of Ten, and Lloyd George—in London— hurriedly checked Churchill's activities.

Public debate on the situation was becoming more noticeable. The Labour leaders had never been enthusiastic about the Bolsheviks after the fall of Kerensky, but both they and the Asquithian Liberals now began to express concern about the British position. The Miners' Federation led the way; the Triple Alliance followed, and the T.U.C. followed this joint lead in opposition to the intervention. On March 3rd Churchill covered his flanks neatly by stating that 'in this theatre we have no special British interests of any sort to serve. . . . We are simply discharging a duty to the League of Nations . . . and endeavouring to prevent new areas of the world from degenerating into the welter of Bolshevik anarchy.' On the Conservative side, however, the Government was being urged not merely to maintain its position but actually to increase its assistance. This was in any event being done; volunteers and millions of pounds' worth of munitions were being sent to Denikin by Churchill. Already, the War Office was interpreting the decisions of the Cabinet in a vigorous spirit. On April 9th the Foreign Office joined in by issuing a horrifying list of alleged Red atrocities in a solemn Parliamentary Paper. Yet a week later, in the House of Commons, Lloyd George made one of his most powerful and effective speeches against intervention in the internal affairs of another country. On the previous day the General Staff had circulated its detailed plans for an offensive in North Russia!

It was now becoming clear even to observers outside the Cabinet that the Government was speaking with two voices. What was not sufficiently appreciated was the extent to which Churchill was operating not merely independently of the Cabinet but in some instances actually contrary to its decisions.[1] Nevertheless, enough was realised to make Churchill the particular object of the steadily mounting criticism in the Labour and Liberal parties of the enterprise. Nor was this unjustified. On June 14th Churchill and Henry Wilson secured Cabinet approval—both Lloyd George and Bonar Law being absent—for the offensive in the North on the grounds that it was essential for the preservation of the British force. Unfortunately for their plans, Kolchak at once suffered the first of a series of heavy defeats; the Cabinet reconsidered the offensive on June 27th, and assented to it when assured that it was vital for the preservation of the British force.

Up to this point the Government had been sustained by two hopes; the first was that a joint Allied policy would emerge from Paris, and the second was that the Russian situation would happily solve itself by the defeat of the Bolsheviks. By August 1919 it was evident that both these hopes had been dashed. Lloyd George, in May, urged the Supreme Council to aid Kolchak to make the Omsk regime the 'Government of all Russia'; any chances this overture had were

---

[1] Perhaps the best example of this occurred in May. On the 14th the Cabinet expressly rejected a proposal by Churchill to form additional units of the Slavo-British Legion. Churchill, after consulting Balfour, decided that it was a strictly War Office decision, and put the matter in hand. The Cabinet was informed of this *fait accompli* on June 11th.

dashed by Kolchak's military disasters.[1] Churchill put up a vigorous rearguard action, but the most that he could secure was the granting of a final batch of assistance to Denikin. By August 15th the Cabinet had decided to end all other intervention. But the War Office continued to assist Kolchak until October, and British troops were not withdrawn until the late autumn. The naval blockade continued until the winter, and on November 20th the Cabinet decided not to renew it in the spring. As late as September 25th, Churchill was still urging the Cabinet to approve 'war upon the Bolshevists with every means in our power . . . with a coherent plan on all fronts at once'. When, in the middle of October, it seemed that Denikin—whose forces were in the suburbs of Petrograd—might win, he issued a public letter that declared that 'There are now good reasons for believing that the tyranny of Bolshevism will be overthrown by the Russian nation'. It was, however, a false dawn. On November 8th Lloyd George, in a speech at the Guildhall, pronounced finally and definitely against intervention. On January 27th, 1920, the Cabinet was faced with a request for a new anti-Bolshevik combination: it decided that 'we have neither the men, the money, nor the credit, and public opinion is altogether opposed to such a course'.

Certainly the Labour opposition to the intervention had been vigorous. The party conference in June had passed condemnatory resolutions, and advocating 'the unreserved use of . . . political and industrial power' to change the policy of the Government. Those Labour leaders who opposed direct action were coldly received; the young Herbert Morrison described the intervention as 'a war against the organisation of the Trade Union movement itself, and as such should be resisted with the full political and industrial power of the whole Trade Union movement'. In September the T.U.C. had followed suit, and had set up the National 'Hands Off Russia' Committee. It has been argued[2] that this agitation had no effect on the Cabinet's decision, which had been taken before the activities of the Labour movement had developed. This is factually correct, but the nature of Labour opposition had been apparent long before the resolutions were carried, and it was an important element in strengthening the positions of Lloyd George and Austen Chamberlain in particular in the Cabinet. Bonar Law had acquiesced uneasily in

[1] Kolchak was captured and killed in January 1920.
[2] See S. R. Graubard: *British Labour and the Russian Revolution*, 82.

the intervention; his gradual shift against it was a decisive stage in the development of Cabinet re-assessment of the policy. Perhaps the clamour in the country had no bearing upon the decisions of the Cabinet, but it is difficult to accept this in its entirety, while rejecting the bold claims made at the time and subsequently by Labour leaders.

The entire episode did nothing to bring credit upon the Government. As Churchill had pointed out at the very beginning, it had a choice between full-scale intervention or withdrawal, and that any middle course would be the worst policy of all: '. . . he felt that if we did not decide upon a policy we should have a succession of disasters, followed by wholesale massacres and the extermination in one way or another of the whole of the people who had been supporting us. If we were unable to support the Russians effectively, it would be far better to take a decision now to quit and face the consequences.'[1] Nevertheless, given the prevailing political feeling at the time, the Government had some justification in continuing assistance so long as there was a fair chance of a White victory. If the gamble had come off, the policy would have had its own justification. It was not until the late summer of 1919 that majority opinion in the Cabinet definitely came round to Lloyd George's side and against Churchill.

By the policy of half-hearted intervention in Russia the Coalition had earned the hostility and contempt of Left and Right alike. Lloyd George was attacked by Labour for publicly opposing intervention and yet continuing with it, while he was under fire from the Conservatives for not seizing a chance of destroying Bolshevism once and for all. What the episode did reveal very clearly was that Lloyd George was no longer master in his own house, and that his personal influence, once so dominant, now stood for little when he was isolated in his own Cabinet. If the melancholy story of the British intervention in Russia brought no credit on the Government as a whole, it did even more harm to Lloyd George's already falling reputation, while Churchill became a particular target for Labour and Liberal vilification. The latter censure was rather more fair than the former, but it is not the least of the perils of personal government that all censure tends to concentrate upon its principal and self-styled exponent.

Thus, if 1919 was not a good year for the Coalition, it was an even

[1] War Cabinet Minutes, February 13th, 1919.

worse one for the Prime Minister, both in public esteem and in his control over his Cabinet.

*

As has already been noted, not the least of the crucial results of the 1918 election had been the virtual extinction of the old Irish Nationalist Party and the triumph of Sinn Fein. The victorious seventy-three members refused to go to Westminster, and met at the Mansion House in Dublin as the Irish Parliament, Dail Eireann. On January 21st they issued a declaration of independence and ratified the establishment of the Irish Republic that had been publicly proclaimed outside the General Post Office in Dublin on Easter Monday, 1916. They then made an appeal for recognition by the participants in the Peace Conference at Versailles. To the British, loudly adhering to the principle of 'self-determination' for small nations, this was an acute embarrassment. It was to become something substantially more than an embarrassment. The Paris attempt came to nothing, but the Irish Race Convention in Philadelphia sent a committee of three to Paris and Ireland to report back, and produced a bitter indictment of British rule that was written into the Congressional Record. De Valera visited America in 1919 to further the Irish cause, and raised some five million dollars for the Irish National Loan, although he did not escape some embroilment in the labyrinthine viciousness of Irish-American politics.

Meanwhile, the British were confronted by the uncomfortable fact that the self-styled Irish Government was usurping many of the functions of the administration, including a Ministry of Defence. Funds were raised by Michael Collins, the Minister of Finance, and arms and ammunition were smuggled into Ireland from England; the famed Volunteers became the Army of the Republic, the Irish Republican Army (I.R.A.). It was not long before it began to operate. On the day that the Dail had declared independence, two armed policemen were killed at Solohead, County Tipperary, while attempting to prevent the capture of a consignment of gelignite. They were the first victims of the events that were to be described with characteristic understatement as 'The Troubles'.

The first priority for the I.R.A. was to secure weapons, and all the initial attacks—principally directed against the Royal Irish Constabulary—were for this purpose. Small barracks were so consistently attacked that many had to be abandoned, and gradually the country-side fell into the control of the Nationalists, who became experts in the skilful use of the ambush. The I.R.A. technique was, in the words of Collins, 'an organized and bold guerrilla warfare', and set-piece battles on the lines of the Easter Rising, which Collins knew he could not win, were eschewed. It was not long before the R.I.C.'s morale began to drop sharply. Recruitment slumped, and resignations rose. This was the first victory for the new movement, and an important one. In 1919—which subsequently looked in retrospect a quiet year—there were eighteen murders and seventy-seven armed attacks, which included an attempt to ambush and assassinate the Viceroy, Lord French, on the outskirts of Dublin. The weapon of the boycott was revived, specifically against the R.I.C., and with considerable success.

The British Government decided to meet force with force. Sinn Fein was declared illegal in August 1919 and in September the Dail was also proclaimed. In March 1920 Sir Nevil Macready, Commissioner of the Metropolitan Police, was appointed Commander-in-Chief of the British forces in Ireland. As it was urgently necessary to increase the size of the R.I.C., recruits were sought in England, mainly among ex-soldiers. This was a creation of Churchill's, originally described as the 'Special Emergency Gendarmerie'. By the summer of 1920 they were arriving in Ireland, and were equipped with surplus khaki uniforms with the black belts and dark-green caps of the R.I.C. They were dubbed the 'Black and Tans', after a famous pack of hounds in County Limerick. In addition, another 1,000 men were recruited from among ex-officers in England, the Auxiliary Division of the R.I.C., the 'Auxis', who had a dark-blue uniform. The Black and Tans were paid ten shillings a day, and the Auxis a pound. Churchill subsequently claimed that they 'were selected from a great press of applicants on account of their intelligence, their characters, and their record in the war'. All other estimates have been considerably less favourable.

This decision to fight the I.R.A. was not surprising when the composition of the Coalition is considered. Bonar Law, Long and Birkenhead had been vigorous supporters of Ulster in the grim crisis of 1912–14; the Chief of the Imperial General Staff was Henry Wilson, who had always been a vehement supporter of Ulster and who had played an important part in the fatal decision to impose conscription in 1918; Churchill, who seriously misjudged the scale and nature of the situation, was certainly not a man to bow to rebellion; and Lloyd George himself was fully prepared to follow the course they charted.

The Irish rebellion developed slowly, and this fact reflected the divisions that still existed within the nationalist movement. Collins, who directed the I.R.A., was the only leading nationalist who was a member of the Irish Republican Brotherhood. His most open opponent in the movement was Cathal Brugha (hitherto known as Charles Burgess) who was a passionate fighter but lacked Collins' organising genius and subtlety—and, as events were to prove, his ability to compromise. De Valera endeavoured to mediate between them, without success. Arthur Griffith, the founder of Sinn Fein, to whom the example of Hungary's independence from Austria under the Dual Monarchy was always predominant sought freedom for Ireland through peaceful rather than violent means. He was Minister of Home Affairs in the Dail Government; De Valera was President (succeeding Brugha after his escape from Lincoln Jail in 1919), and Collins had become Minister of Defence.

Ireland raged throughout 1920 and most of 1921. The British forces in Ireland—military and police—numbered at least 40,000; the I.R.A. had about 15,000, but it has been claimed that there were never more than 5,000 men on active service at one time. Whatever their numbers, they sufficed. Losses have never been fully assessed, but one authority gives figures of 752 Irish killed and 866 wounded between January 1919 and July 1921, with the British losses put at 176 police and 54 soldiers killed, 251 police and 118 soldiers wounded. But the numbers were less relevant than the circumstances. On 'Bloody Sunday'—November 21st, 1920—fourteen British officers were hauled from their beds and shot by the I.R.A., in some cases in the presence of their families. That afternoon a party of Black and Tans opened fire into a football crowd in Dublin, killing twelve people and wounding sixty. Perhaps the burning of Cork by the Black and Tans in December 1920 was the most notorious single episode of all, while to Irishmen the death, after seventy-four days of hunger-fasting, of the Lord Mayor of Cork—Terence MacSwiney—in Brixton Jail was an example of English callousness. On October 9th, 1920, Lloyd George declared that 'we have murder by the throat'; other Ministers made frequent similar statements, Birkenhead promising that 'we shall use force and yet more force'; the situation only deteriorated further, and English opinion began to veer sharply against a Government that could neither make war nor achieve peace.

The fierce debates on the Irish situation brought into sudden and dramatic prominence a dashing, handsome, and highly articulate Coalitionist back-bencher. Oswald Mosley had been the youngest Member of the Commons when he had been elected for Harrow in 1918 at the age of twenty-two. His appearance was striking, he was clearly of a highly independent nature, he was rich, and he had swiftly developed into a most formidable debater. His genius at mob-oratory was as yet unknown. Shocked by the excesses of the Black and Tans, and contemptuous of the Government's blatant evasiveness on the issue of reprisals, he went for the Irish Secretary, Hamar Greenwood, Churchill, and the Prime Minister himself with a sharp-ness and skill that reminded older Members and observers of Lord Randolph in his prime, and others of the young Lloyd George. He crossed the Floor to assail Ministers to their faces, and was relentless in his probings and attacks. It was evident that the war generation had thrown up at least one politician of elemental fire and outstanding ability. It was also apparent to some shrewd observers that his per-sonality did not lack elements of arrogance and impatience. It was not long before the Conservatives of Harrow became embarrassed, and then enraged, by the insulting independence of their Member. But, at the age of twenty-five, 'Tom' Mosley had definitely arrived. Married to a daughter of Lord Curzon, untroubled by money matters, fascinating to women and with an air of complete self-control and manifest ambition, he was suddenly seen as the most exciting prospect in British politics. The laurels were to wither quickly, but in spite of subsequent follies and worse, at least the Irish never forgot that he had been their fiery and dedicated champion against the evil obscenity of the Black and Tans. Nor should it be forgotten by others.

What efforts that were made towards peace had an air of fantasy. The Government of Ireland Act of 1920 had something for everybody; there would be two Parliaments in Ireland, one for Ulster and another for the rest of the country, while the Irish representation at West-minster was to be retained on a reduced basis; a Council of Ireland, drawn from the two Irish Parliaments, would preserve or restore Irish unity. It was a good example of Lloyd George's skill at apparently reconciling all sides; apart from the Ulstermen, it placated nobody. In the South, the Government lost control of the legal process and of the taxation system. The local authorities took their orders from the Dail Ministry of Local Government. The clashes between the I.R.A. and the Black and Tans increased in their intensity.

This was an Irish struggle which, for the first time since 1800, had no counterpart at Westminster. Churchill commented that 'the two supreme services which Ireland has rendered Britain are her accession to the Allied cause on the outbreak of the Great War, and her withdrawal from the House of Commons at its close'. The Labour and Liberal parties could not be, in numbers or political vigour, a proper substitute. The Act of 1920, for all its high-sounding utterances and imposing façade, was a victory for Ulster and a further postponement of the real issue. With Ireland in turmoil, and with the British Press becoming progressively more appalled at the situation, the moment for decision could hardly be postponed longer.

*

And all this was taking place in a darkening economic situation.

In 1919, when the industrial situation had seemed so menacing, the one gleam of solace had been provided by the booming conditions of British industry and commerce. Then this gleam was suddenly extinguished. As Tawney has commented: 'In April 1920 all was right with the world. In April 1921 all was wrong.'

The causes are not difficult to detect. Encouraged by the dizzy prospects of vast world trade, British manufacturers had invested heavily. These prospects, after the immediate post-war demand, almost vanished. Producers of food and raw materials suddenly found no markets. Exports of coal and cotton were cruelly hit, bringing poverty to those cities whose total livelihood depended on the prosperity of those industries. Government spending had been cut by nearly two-thirds (£2,696 million in 1917–18 to just over £1,000 million in 1920–1) while taxation had gone up. Prices fell, and unemployment rose, until by June 1921 it passed two million, or over ten per cent.

The Government, which had contributed to this disaster by the wanton dismantling of all the laboriously created machinery for economic control, now further added to the chaos. The official monetary policy was severe. In April 1920 the Bank Rate was raised to seven per cent to check inflation. It also checked investment and confidence. The Government, pursuing its policy of decontrol, also decided to relinquish its paternal supervision over the railways and the mines. The miners and the owners at once clashed; the owners offered 'new' agreements by which wages were cut and the old hated system of district rates was to be resumed. On April 1st a lockout began. The Triple Alliance did not show up to advantage, as the railwaymen and transport workers would not strike in sympathy. By the beginning of July the miners were beaten, and forced to accept the harsh terms of the owners. The national depression, and the farsightedness of J. H. Thomas and Ernest Bevin, had averted what would have been virtually a national strike, but the divisions and bitterness in the coal-fields was an important contributory factor to the further decline of Labour sympathy for the Government in general and Lloyd George in particular.

More and more, the phrase 'a land fit for heroes to live in' came to be seen as a mocking, cruel joke. At the Ministry of Health, Christopher Addison had attempted to meet the housing shortage by lavish grants to local authorities; he had no control over the market in land and labour, and no machinery to control the work. By 1921 the Government was paying over £900 for each house, and a Parliamentary and Press uproar developed against this extravagance. In March Addison was abruptly dropped from the Ministry and, a few months later, from the Government altogether. Addison joined the lengthening list of men who had been ruthlessly abandoned by Lloyd George when their usefulness expired, and he joined the equally lengthening list of those men who had a real personal grudge against the Prime Minister. The irony of it was that although Addison went, and his grandiose schemes with him, the principle that the State had a responsibility for housing the people had been initiated and accepted; furthermore, the fact that the scheme operated through the local authorities was another revolution of a kind. These principles, utterly novel in 1919 and unthinkable in 1914, have never subsequently been challenged. But Addison's 213,000 new houses did not look well beside a figure of over two million unemployed.

By chance rather than design, the unemployed were catered for. The 1911 National Insurance Act had been limited to the building, engineering, and shipbuilding industries, and covered some three million workers; in the war it was extended to munitions workers. When the out-of-work donation ended in 1920, it was evident that something must replace it. The new scheme covered some twelve million workers; it was designed solely to provide insurance, to be contributed to by workers and employers, against casual short-term unemployment. It was not intended to meet the situation that now, in the winter of 1920–1, fell upon the nation. The scheme was arbitrarily extended by virtual subsidies from the Treasury to meet the exceptional circumstances; the circumstances went on being exceptional.

The author of the 1911 Act had, without meaning to, provided the working classes with an important buttress against total disaster. Between 1919 and 1924 over £525 million was provided for unemployment relief. But the fact won him no gratitude; by 1921 Lloyd George's personal position had fallen spectacularly from the glories of 1918. He sought to redeem that position by triumphs abroad. With mounting disaffection at home, Ireland in a state of civil war, Russia now abandoned, and the nation in the midst of what the *Economist* described as 'one of the worst years of depression since the industrial revolution', the reactionary Conservative phalanx on the Government benches eyed the Prime Minister with decreasing admiration. In March 1921 Bonar Law resigned on grounds of ill-health, and was succeeded by Austen Chamberlain as leader of the Conservative Party. In the subsequent reshuffle the obscure Stanley Baldwin entered the Cabinet, at the age of fifty-four, as President of the Board of Trade. The former change was a portent that was not detected at the time. The latter was to be a vital contributory factor in the downfall of the Coalition and its leader. The Coalition had lost its lynch-pin.

CHAPTER FOURTEEN

THE RETURN OF THE CONSERVATIVES, 1922–1923

BY THE END of 1921 the Coalition had lost almost all of its original authority and prestige. As early as 1919 Harold Laski had written of Lloyd George that 'he seems determined to sacrifice upon the altar of his private ambition the whole spirit of our public life'. Edward Grey subsequently wrote that the Coalition moved him to 'indignation and despair such as I have never felt about any other British Government'. Arnold Bennett noted after a weekend at Cherkley with Chamberlain, Lloyd George, and Birkenhead: 'I never heard principles or the welfare of the country mentioned.' A subsequent commentator has written of this period:

> What strikes one most as one looks back upon that period is the general disarray of public life, the absence of firm principle in most of the moves and counter moves hatched at the country house gatherings and private dinner parties round which political activity on its highest levels revolved.[1]

The remoteness and *insouciance* of the Coalition leaders from this mounting disillusionment were remarkable. The many warnings that they received were ignored or dismissed. 'Who is going to lead you to victory if you smash the Coalition?' Birkenhead imperiously and contemptuously demanded of a discontented Conservative: 'Someone like Bonar or Baldwin?'[2] Fortified by all the panoplies and appurtenances of power, they wholly failed to notice the remorseless slipping away of their authority and political position. The old Liberal Party was politically dead; the new Labour Party was only gradually emerging; it was in the Conservative Party that the real opposition to the Coalition was slowly generating.

[1] Francis Williams, op. cit., 19.   [2] Winterton, op. cit., 115.

Lloyd George's strength still lay in his alleged wizardry in international affairs, but it had already been compromised by the criticisms of the Treaty of Versailles, and it was difficult to judge the Russian Intervention or the handling of the situation in Ireland as outstanding triumphs. Between the end of the war and the fall of the Coalition Lloyd George attended twenty-four major international conferences. To his increasingly irritated contemporaries, the value of these exercises seemed limited. The last was at Genoa in April 1922, and was intended to settle everything. In the event it settled nothing. The Americans, who were cast in the amiable role of generously writing off the war debts of the Allies, refused to attend. The French only came to repeat their claims for full reparations. The Germans and the Russians—fearful (and with cause) that they were to be played off against the other—came to a previous arrangement at Rapallo. Lloyd George's 'personal diplomacy', which had briefly dazzled his countrymen, was now a rather poor political joke.

Elsewhere, success had been mixed. In the Middle East the British had been obliged, as a result of French and American pressures, to withdraw from Persia; they also withdrew from Afghanistan. Iraq and Palestine became British mandates, and the clash between Arab commitments and the obligation to provide the new national home for the Jews in Palestine was already becoming evident. The British stayed in Egypt, but the old authority and control had gone.

In India new forces were stirring. The British declaration of 1917 that India would have 'responsible government . . . as an integral part of the British Empire' was given legislative enactment in the Government of India Act of 1919. It had established 'dyarchy' and emphasised again that the process of 'gradualness' was to be slow. At Amritsar, in April 1919, troops under the command of General Dyer opened fire on a crowd and killed 379 persons, including many women and children. The ugliest aspect of this deplorable incident was the support that Dyer received in Britain, and not least on the Conservative benches. Dismissed by the Government, he received a public subscription and warm tributes. This in itself demonstrated the new nervousness with which the British regarded the situation in India. The emergence of Gandhi and the outbreak of serious communal violence, met with armed force and the proscription of Congress, were unpleasant portents.

The main crises were, however, nearer home. By the early summer of 1921 the British were becoming sickened of the Irish nightmare. 'There is something wayward, *diabolical* in them (the Irish)', Morley wrote at the time.[1]

There were several factors involved in the sudden *volte-face* of the British Government, but the dominant one was the increasing revulsion in Britain at the war and the manner in which it was being conducted. There were those Ministers who still believed that the war could be won, but their numbers and influence were declining. The King was personally deeply troubled and consulted Smuts, who was visiting London in the summer of 1921. Smuts was a strong advocate of conciliation, and drafted a statement which he urged upon Lloyd George. The Prime Minister, who was confronted by the possibility of even more intense fighting, a divided Cabinet and a restless public, assented readily enough. When the King spoke in Belfast in June and appealed for unity it had an immediate response from the Irish leaders, and a truce was signed on July 8th. The King's initiative, as Mr. Taylor has said, 'was perhaps the greatest service performed by a British monarch in modern times'.[2]

The Irish Treaty of December 1921 was in many respects Lloyd George's greatest diplomatic and political triumph, but at the time the feeling was more that he was belatedly bringing to an end a tragedy for which he bore a substantial personal responsibility. And it was, like all of Lloyd George's interventions in the affairs of Ireland, too clever by half. The Irish delegates were bullied and tricked into submission. The retention of Ireland in the Empire was nominally achieved, but at the expense of the reality. Ulster was preserved—thanks to Bonar Law threatening to lead a Unionist revolt if she was interfered with—and the twenty-six counties were given a greater degree of autonomy than Parnell or Redmond ever claimed. The Conservatives had to swallow the Treaty, but without pleasure, and Carson delivered a cruel attack on Birkenhead in the Lords for his apostasy. In Ireland, de Valera denounced the work of the Irish plenipotentiaries. Their offence was that they had reached an agreement under threat of renewed war, without consulting their colleagues in Dublin, and had abandoned the dream of United Ireland.[3] The Dail approved the Treaty by sixty-four to fifty-seven after a debate of great bitterness and drama. The nationalist movement split into two

[1] J. H. Morgan: *John, Viscount Morley*, 55.   [2] Taylor, op. cit., 157.
[3] The best account of the negotiations is F. Pakenham: *Peace by Ordeal* (1935).

powerful groups, and real civil war began to flare all over Ireland, in which many Irish leaders—including Collins and Erskine Childers[1] —were to meet their deaths. The new Irish Free State was formally agreed to by the British Parliament on December 5th, 1922. The last British troops left twelve days later. The civil war lasted until April 1923. The wounds that it inflicted on Ireland were to be even more lasting and debilitating than those of the fight against the British.

The Conservatives could only see that, once again, they had been led up the path by Lloyd George, and then betrayed. If Ireland had been conciliated, possibly all might have been well. But the fighting that raged throughout Ireland, and episodes, of which the assassination in London of Sir Henry Wilson was the most significant, destroyed what chances the Coalition had of securing the fading trust of the Conservative ranks.

When a Government runs out of fortune, nothing goes right at all. The record of the Coalition was far from one of total failure. The Treaty of Versailles had many imperfections, but was a masterpiece of compromise with the emphasis on the liberal and progressive side. The placating of Labour in 1919 and 1920 may have been ad hoc, unplanned, and opportunist, but at least Labour *had* been placated. The intervention in Russia may have been a folly, but at least the British had withdrawn in time. The decision to fight Irish nationalism with the Black and Tans may have been an outrage to civilised opinion, but there had been a settlement that was, in the difficult circumstances, magnanimous and workable. The depression of 1921 may have afflicted the prople grievously, but the effects were infinitely less cruel than they would have been without the acceptance of the principle of government support for the needy. Lloyd George may not have built a land fit for heroes to live in, but 200,000 new houses had been built, and the State had taken a responsibility for accommodating the people. Nothing of major importance that had been

[1] Childers, the author of *The Riddle of the Sands*, who had accompanied the Irish delegation in the Treaty negotiations as its secretary, had resigned from his Clerkship in the House of Commons before the war and had involved himself in the Nationalist cause. It was he who, in his yacht *Asgard*, had brought the rifles to Howth in July 1914 (see Volume I, p. 277), which had been used in the Easter Rising. In the war he served in the British Army with distinction, before returning to Irish politics. Churchill subsequently denounced him as a 'mischief-making, murderous renegade', a grotesquely harsh depiction of a very talented and brave man. He wrote shortly before his execution at the hands of an Irish firing-squad that 'I die loving England, and praying that she may change completely and finally towards Ireland'.

gained in the war had been lost. The Montagu-Chelmsford Reforms in India may have been too little and too late, but they existed, and the Government had disavowed Dyer and all he stood for.

In political terms, however, all this added up to very little. Labour steadily gained seats in by-elections; Asquith had returned to Parliament, and new hope existed among the Asquithian Liberals; the Conservatives chafed at their erratic leadership. On the Left there was disillusionment with the social reforms produced by the Government; on the Right there was resentment at a series of compromises which smacked of weakness and vacillation, and, in the High Tory school, an increasing suspicion of the adventurer image of Lloyd George, Churchill, and Birkenhead. The blatant trafficking in honours came into the open in the summer of 1922; no one had heard of Maundy Gregory, but his handiwork was there to behold.[1] The 'Garden Suburb' Secretariat came under increasing criticism. By the August of 1922, when the House of Commons adjourned for the summer recess, the Government supporters and junior Ministers were in a condition of simmering revolt. Yet, so long as the ruling circle held firm, how could the leadership of the Coalition be changed?

Whichever way men looked in the summer of 1922, there was misfortune and disillusion. Unemployment had become the burning issue of the day, and was to remain so for the next twenty years. By December 1921 36·1 per cent of insured workers in shipbuilding were unemployed; in the iron and steel industries the figure was 36·7 per cent, and for engineering 27·2 per cent. These grim facts were reflected in the areas most severely afflicted: Northern Ireland (25 per cent), Scotland (21 per cent), the Midlands and the North-East (18 per cent each). In August 1922 Barrow-in-Furness had an unemployment rate of 49 per cent, and Hartlepool had 60 per cent. Demonstrations took place in almost all the major industrial cities. Unemployment pay—the 'dole'—saved the people from starvation, but not from anger and disillusionment.

The Government had reacted by deliberately adopting deflationary measures. A committee mainly of business leaders, headed by Sir Eric Geddes, was appointed to review Government Estimates and recommend economies. The committee published three reports in February 1922 that recommended economies totalling over £86 millions. The biggest cuts were to be in the armed services, but Education was to

[1] See Davidson: *Memoirs of a Conservative*, 280.

lose £18 millions, Health £2½ millions, and War Pensions £3·3 millions. What really symbolised the 'Geddes Axe' was the emphasis on the social services; teachers' and police salaries were to be reduced, and contributions to the tuberculosis, maternity and child welfare services were to be cut. Scheduled for abolition were the Ministry of Transport, the Ministry of Labour, and even the Labour Exchanges. It was a typical rich man's economy drive. The Government eventually accepted cuts of £64 millions, and reduced income tax to five shillings in the pound. The economy campaign subsided, but the mood of Labour was justifiably bitter.

Nor were others much mollified by the Government's attempts to satisfy all parties. The old duel between Free Trade and Protection had never died, and now flared up again. Protection was still a word from which politicians shrank, and the Safeguarding of Industries Act of 1921, which provided for duties of thirty-three and a half per cent on certain imports, was too feeble to protect British industry adequately, yet significant enough to alarm the Free Traders in the Liberal and Conservative sections of the Coalition. Such storms passed, and the Coalition struggled on, yet with its position impaired still further.

Nevertheless, there was no desire on the part of any of the party chiefs to end the Coalition. Faced with the alternatives of Asquith or Labour, the leaders drew together. In February 1920 the prospects of a formal new party had been seriously discussed, but had been opposed by the respective rank and files, and the notion of 'fusion' had been allowed to fade away. Early in 1922 the idea of a General Election was seriously canvassed, and then thwarted by the adamant opposition of Sir George Younger, the head of the Conservative organisation. In February, Lloyd George offered to make way for Austen Chamberlain, and Chamberlain refused on the grounds that Lloyd George's departure would be a disaster for the country and the Conservative Party. His decision was accepted, but Law—returning to the Commons in February—at once noted a change of feeling in the party towards the Coalition. On April 5th a Conservative, Joynson-Hicks, moved a motion of censure on the Coalition, which was defeated by 193 votes.

In these circumstances it needed a major political convulsion to change the Coalition without also bringing down the Conservative Party as well. This was the essential problem, and one which the

Coalition's critics within the Conservative ranks found insoluble until September.

At first, the crisis that suddenly flared up in the Middle East seemed ideally suited for Lloyd George. In spite of the opposition and lack of enthusiasm of many of his colleagues, Lloyd George had pursued a consistent pro-Greek policy in Asia Minor. The emergence at Ankara of a new Turkish national movement led by Mustapha Kemal, the most significant of the Turkish commanders at Gallipoli, prompted the French and the Italians to abandon their grants under the Treaty of Sèvres of 1920; the Russians also treated with Kemal. The Greeks, encouraged by Lloyd George, hung on. In the summer of 1922 they began to fall back in disorder under a series of massive and brilliantly conducted attacks by the Kemalists. By August they were in full rout, and the exultant Kemalists, having swept the Greeks into the sea at Smyrna—or those that could not be evacuated by the Royal Navy—swung northwards to the Dardanelles, where they were confronted by a small British force at Chanak. Frances Stevenson, Lloyd George's mistress and future second wife, noted in her diary on July 20th:

> D. very interested in the Greek advance against the Turks. He has had a great fight in the Cabinet to back the Greeks (not in the field but morally) and he and Balfour are the only pro-Greeks there. All the others have done their best to obstruct and the W.O. have behaved abominably. However, D. has got his way, but he is much afraid lest the Greek attack should be a failure and he should be proved to have been wrong. He says his political reputation depends a great deal on what happens in Asia Minor, though I don't think people care a hang what happens there. . . . He is perfectly convinced he is right over this, and is willing to stake everything on it.

Churchill, Birkenhead, and Chamberlain, hitherto highly unenthusiastic over Lloyd George's pro-Hellenic adventure, now saw in the Kemalist threat a potential disaster to British honour and prestige in the Middle East. Beaverbrook has described a sharp discussion on October 4th:

> The debate became bitter in tone. The accusation made against the Peace party was a charge of 'scuttle'—a word thrown like a brick-

bat. Birkenhead referred to our duty to Christian minorities and showed a lively interest in the British Nonconformist Conscience. Churchill talked of the might and honour and prestige of Britain which he said I, as a foreigner or invader, did not understand, and of how it would be ruined for ever if we did not immediately push a bayonet into the stomach of anyone in arms who contested it. He was always ready to fight England's foes. He was not departing from his honest and sincere convictions. Birkenhead was in a different position. Hard-headed, clear-sighted, free from any profound political faith, he was a team man, dazzled by preferment, and influenced by the mistaken belief that Lloyd George could get the votes.[1]

The Cabinet—without Baldwin, holidaying in Aix, and often without Curzon—rushed towards a major confrontation. On September 15th the Dominions were appealed to for assistance. By a crass error in timing, most of the Dominion Premiers read of the appeal in the newspapers before they officially received it. Not surprisingly, their reactions were generally bleak. The British woke up with amazement to discover themselves almost at war. Law published a letter on October 7th that opposed the actions of the Government if they were to be unilateral. This action came after the real drama, which occurred on September 29th, when General Harington was ordered to issue an ultimatum to the Turks, and did not do so. The Chanak Crisis fizzled out, but to many people it was decisive. Baldwin read of the Government's action in the newspapers, and came hastening home to express his dismay, and to join with Curzon in opposing the dispatch of the ultimatum. Bonar Law's denunciation was curt and scathing.

The revolt against Lloyd George now gathered momentum. The junior Ministers had already been irked by a characteristic hectoring lecture from Birkenhead, and it was clear that the annual Conservative conference in November was going to be a difficult occasion. The decision was made to hold the election before then. The Conservative organisation men—Younger, Sir Malcolm Fraser, Leslie Wilson—strongly opposed the decision, and Baldwin was the sole dissentient voice among the Conservative Cabinet Ministers. Curzon's doubts and anxieties were also increasing. After a deliberately

[1] Beaverbrook: *The Decline and Fall of Lloyd George*, 116.

belligerent speech by Lloyd George at Birmingham on October 13th, Curzon ostentatiously stayed away from a dinner party given by Churchill on the 15th, at which it was decided to call a party meeting at the Carlton Club on the following Thursday, October 19th.

It must be emphasised that the decision was made by the Conservative leaders. The purpose was, as Chamberlain put it, 'to tell them bluntly that they must either follow our advice or do without us, in which case they must find their own Chief, and form a Government *at once*. They would be in a d——d fix.' Just to ram the point home, the meeting was timed to take place just after the result of a by-election at Newport was due to be announced, at which it was confidently expected that an independent Conservative candidate would be at the foot of the poll.

This left only three days for the rebels. As Leo Amery has written:

> Unionists felt that they no longer had any policy of their own, but were being dragged along in the wake of an erratic Prime Minister whom they once again profoundly distrusted, by a little group of their own leaders who had lost, not only their principles, but their heads.[1]

Everything depended on Bonar Law. Beaverbrook, Baldwin, Amery and a young confidant, J. C. C. Davidson, urged him to go to the Carlton Club and speak against the Coalition. Law was tortured by doubts and misgivings, and up to the morning of the 19th his decision seemed in doubt.

Meanwhile, although unaware of the vigour and the strength of the forces against them, the Coalition leaders were not inactive. As Beaverbrook has recorded:

> Between Sunday the 15th and Thursday the 19th the struggle became less like a battle than a series of single duels. Every man's political soul was required of him. Promises and promotions and honours were sprinkled from Downing Street on the green benches with a hose. The orthodox Tories appealed to the age-long traditions of a Party now caught fast in the house of semi-Liberal bondage.[2]

Every stratagem was employed to buttress the still wavering Law. A memorial signed by eighty influential—and carefully chosen—

---

[1] Amery: *My Political Life*, II, 232–3.   [2] Beaverbrook, op. cit., 190.

back-benchers against the Coalition was submitted to him; Baldwin, Beaverbrook and Davidson kept up their urgings, aided by Younger, Wilson, and Lord Derby; on the other side, Salvidge reminded him of his 1918 promise 'never to let the little man go'. Law wavered miserably throughout the 18th. At one point he had written a letter addressed to the chairman of his constituency declaring his intention to resign his seat and retire from public life. Beaverbrook persuaded him not to send it. The *Daily Express* on the morning of the 19th announced that Bonar Law would go to the Carlton Club. As Members entered it, the news of the Newport by-election came in. The independent Conservative had won; the Coalition candidate was a bad third.

The actual meeting itself was full of drama. Chamberlain made a somewhat condescending speech in support of the Coalition, supported by Balfour. But the real sensation was Baldwin's contribution, which revealed, as his biographer has written, 'a new eloquence; direct, conversational, monosyllabic; rising and falling without strain or effort between the homeliest humour and the most moving appeal'.

> I will not beat about the bush but will come right to the root of the whole difficulty, which is the position of the Prime Minister. The Prime Minister was described this morning, in the words of a distinguished aristocrat, as a live wire. He was described to me, and to others, in more stately language, by the Lord Chancellor, as a dynamic force, and I accept those words. He *is* a dynamic force and it is from that very fact that our troubles, in our opinion, arise. A dynamic force is a very terrible thing; it may crush you, but it is not necessarily right.
>
> It is owing to that dynamic force, and that remarkable personality, that the Liberal Party to which he formerly belonged, has been smashed to pieces; and it is my firm conviction that in time, the same thing will happen to our party . . . until the old Conservative Party is smashed to pieces and lost in ruins.

The decisive speech, however, was Bonar Law's. Following his advice, the party resolved to fight the next election as an independent party by 185 votes to eighty-eight. That afternoon Lloyd George resigned as Prime Minister. The Conservative ex-Ministers issued a pained statement, stating that the victors of the Carlton Club meeting would have to live with the consequences of their unpatriotic actions without any assistance from them. The Coalition, to the amazed glee of the rebels, had fallen. The task of replacing it now pressed urgently upon them.

*

Having toppled the Coalition, the dissident Conservatives were now faced with the very real problem of forming a Government to replace it that would be representative of the Party and that stood a chance of winning an election. Law insisted that his election as Leader of the Conservative Party should precede his acceptance of the Premiership, and this took place at the Carlton Club on October 23rd. For the first time, prospective candidates were invited to attend the 'election'. Curzon moved, and Baldwin seconded, the motion, which was unanimously adopted. It was no more an election than Law's first one, eleven years before, but it was an important endorsement of his position and a clear warning to the dissident Conservatives.

With Austen Chamberlain, Birkenhead, Balfour, and Sir Robert Horne standing studiously aloof, it was not surprising that Law's Cabinet had a somewhat makeshift appearance. Baldwin became Chancellor of the Exchequer, Curzon—who had left the sinking Coalition ship at the eleventh hour—stayed at the Foreign Office, Derby returned to the War Office. Bonar Law tried to bring Reginald McKenna back to active politics at the Treasury, but without success. The Bonar Law Cabinet was largely composed of unknown political figures, of whom six were Peers; derided by Churchill as 'a government of the second eleven', it uneasily took up the offices lately held by more glittering and arresting personalities. Parliament was dissolved immediately, and the General Election was held on November 15th.

There was much truth in the subsequent comment of Philip Guedalla:

Mr. Bonar Law . . . became Prime Minister of England for the simple and satisfying reason that he was not Mr. Lloyd George. At an open competition in the somewhat negative exercise of not being Mr. Lloyd George that was held in November 1922, Mr. Law was found to be more indubitably not Mr. Lloyd George than any of the other competitors; and, in consequence, by the mysterious operation of the British Constitution, he reigned in his stead.

The downfall of the Coalition had been principally a reaction against 'Lloyd George-ism', and in his election programme Bonar Law emphasised the differences; he promised 'the minimum of interference at home and of disturbance abroad', severe economies, and the reduction of the personal power of the Prime Minister. 'We are asked to choose', Asquith's daughter, Lady Violet Bonham-Carter, commented in what was, in the main, a dull campaign, 'between one man suffering from Sleeping Sickness and another from St. Vitus's Dance.'

In fact, Lloyd George's campaign was notably quiet. His isolation —and that of his Liberal supporters—was painful. Their only hope was to placate Conservative vengeance, and Lloyd George did not even issue a manifesto. Bonar Law could not prevent local Conservative Associations from putting up candidates against his former colleagues in the Coalition, but he did nothing to encourage them. This attitude was approved by the Conservative managers, who hoped to attract Coalition Liberal support for those of their candidates who were contesting Asquithian Liberals.

These genial arrangements were disrupted by several local Conservative Associations, who felt deeply about the Coalition, and by Beaverbrook, who put up, and in some cases, financed, independent Conservative candidates against the National Liberals. This sharply changed the tone of the campaign, which became notably more vigorous and outspoken. Birkenhead and Churchill—prostrate after an emergency appendix operation but still vehement—were particularly sharp in their criticisms of the Bonar Law Government.

It was, in any event, a highly confused election. The Conservatives fielded 442 official candidates, and in the course of the campaign Bonar Law—to Beaverbrook's dismay—gave an undertaking that another General Election would be held before there was any major change in fiscal policy. This virtual negative to Protection was necessary to preserve party unity—not least at the top—and it was not unpopular. Free Trade remained the fiscal orthodoxy of the majority in all parties. The National (Lloyd George) Liberals put up 138 candidates, of whom 56 found themselves opposed by Beaverbrook-inspired unofficial Conservatives; the Asquithian Liberals had 339 candidates, and Labour 408. Never before, and never since, have so many candidates appeared in a British election, and rarely have the differences between them been so difficult to discern.

The result, however, confirmed the decision made at the Carlton Club. The Conservatives won 345 seats; Labour 142; 60 Asquithian Liberals were elected, and 57 National Liberals. Of the 56 National Liberals opposed by independent Conservatives, all but two had been defeated. F. E. Guest, indeed, lost his seat in East Dorset to the son of Hall Caine, the novelist, in spite of flaunting the pictures of Lloyd George *and* Bonar Law in his Committee Rooms. Churchill was overwhelmingly crushed at Dundee in a peculiarly harsh and bitter contest.

In terms of the votes cast, the figures showed what the Conservatives owed to the disunity of the other parties. They had won 5,383,896 votes; Labour 4,236,753; Lloyd George Liberals 1,678,088; and Asquithian Liberals 2,507,204. The practical effects of the Liberal split could be clearly and explicitly seen.

Labour's triumph—in terms of votes won rather than seats—was perhaps the most remarkable feature of all. The pacifists who had lost their seats in 1918—MacDonald, Philip Snowden and George Lansbury—were returned. The composition of the new Parliamentary Labour Party was also significant; the trade union domination of 1918–22 was ended. From having formed virtually the whole of the Parliamentary Labour Party, they now constituted little more than half. From Glasgow there came 21 exultant I.L.P.'ers, including Maxton and Shinwell, fortified by the belief that the victory of Socialism had already been won. There was also an infusion of educated middle- and upper-class men, of whom one was Major Clement Attlee.

When Parliament met, the Parliamentary Labour Party elected a new leader. The voting figures are given as 61–56 for Ramsay MacDonald against Clynes in the accounts of MacNeill Weir and Shinwell; Dalton states that MacDonald's majority was four; Snowden says that it was two. There is, at least, no doubt that MacDonald won, nor that the Clydesiders voted solidly for him.

Looking back, it seems that MacDonald was virtually the only sensible choice the P.L.P. could have made. But he had been out of Parliament for four years, and Clynes was an established, well-liked, orthodox trade union M.P. Furthermore, MacDonald had—quite justifiably—criticised the Parliamentary Party for its generally listless and feeble performance since 1918. The proposal, made in April 1920 at the instigation of Thomas, that MacDonald should advise the party on day-to-day matters had been defeated by twenty-two votes to eleven. The decision was understandable, and MacDonald's position would have been highly anomalous; but the rejection stung him, and his criticisms of the lack-lustre performance of the P.L.P. did not diminish.

Others—notably the Clydesiders—were also critical of the P.L.P. but for different reasons. As MacDonald put the matter in an article in the *Socialist Review* in 1919:

> I am constantly meeting people who do not appear to be able to understand that there is anything possible but one of two positions: either a wild, reckless, disorganised fight, unprepared by scouting, surveying the ground, studying maps, and an examination of the enemy's strength and weakness, or an abject living from day to day with your ears on the ground listening to 'the man in the street', mistaking commonplaces for wisdom, and the shifting position of disorganised majorities for progress.

In the difficult years of 1918–22 in the Labour movement, MacDonald's was consistently the voice of sanity and realism. When he contemplated the sufferings of the miners and their families he inveighed against:

> those who think that we have only to lay down tools to build the City of God in our midst. . . . Direct action may be forced upon us, as it was upon the miners, but to choose it as an ordinary weapon for redressing grievances and bringing Governments to their knees betokens insanity.

On several issues—notably on the British involvement in Russian affairs—MacDonald was as fierce as any Labour man, describing Churchill as 'the man of most evil influence in the Government'. On another occasion he wrote that 'If Mr. Churchill had been an unlimited monarch, he could not have spent the money and lies of the nation with more unstinted generosity'. (*Forward*, July 10th, 1920.)[1] Nevertheless, even on the issue of the Russian civil war it was

[1] This, it might be noted, was mild comment compared with some others on Churchill in Labour journals at this time. In one article in *Forward*, by William Stewart in the July 17th 1920 issue, entitled 'The Marlborough Rat', he was described as 'a madman or a blackguard'.

significant that MacDonald only recommended limited direct action. 'When Governments have to be checked by industrial action', he wrote, 'do not let us deceive ourselves, it is an act of revolution.' In his attitude to the Bolsheviks—first welcoming, then cautiously approving, and then fiercely critical—the combination of idealism and realism that characterised MacDonald can be clearly seen. 'How often have we to say it', he wrote on one occasion: 'Wars and revolutions settle nothing; they only begin settlements under the most adverse conditions.' As the works of the Bolsheviks became plainer to see, his contempt for their methods increased, at a time when it would have been easy to win favour and cheers by identifying Bolshevism with Socialism and by talking away Bolshevik actions as natural and understandable. The seizure of the Georgian Republic aroused his particular fury. In 1921 he published his book, *Socialism: Critical and Constructive*, which revealed his moderate position very clearly. In all, he published four books in the years 1919–21, edited the I.L.P. *Socialist Review* and contributed to many journals.

When he returned to Parliament in November 1922—having failed to win a by-election at Woolwich—it was at once plain that he would be a formidable rival to Clynes. To the Clydesiders in particular Clynes was antipathetic. His reluctance to break with the Coalition in 1918—of which he had been Food Controller—had been unconcealed; he had contributed to Horatio Bottomley's scurrilous and super-patriotic *John Bull*; and, on a memorable occasion, he had been howled down at a Labour meeting in Glasgow. Thus, although MacDonald was a moderate in the eyes of the new men, when compared to Clynes he was a substantial improvement. Above all, his record of courageous and unvarying hostility to the war now stood him in excellent stead. By any standard he was the best qualified man in the party to lead it, and—looking back—the only surprise about his election was the narrowness of his majority.

Labour was not the only party that needed to make changes. But the Liberal schism remained as deep as ever. 'For the moment the thing that gives me the most satisfaction is to gloat over the corpses which have been left on the battlefield', Asquith wrote: '—Winston, Hamar Greenwood, Freddie Guest, Montagu, Kellaway—all of them renegades.' These emotions, although understandable, were hardly likely to lead to party reconciliation. In the rank and file there was some feeling towards re-unification, but the leaders remained aloof.

Throughout the spring of 1923 the two Liberal groups sat on the Opposition benches in uneasy proximity, a divided and largely ineffectual force.

The short-lived Bonar Law Government had some achievements to its credit. In December, Law had to move the Bill that gave legislative force to the Irish Treaty of 1921, a task that he undertook with reluctance and distaste but discharged with skill. The Irish Question thus faded out of the sphere of British domestic politics, and was to remain dormant for nearly fifty years.

The two major crises that the Government faced were economic in their origin. In December 1922 Baldwin went to the United States to discuss the American Loan. Bonar Law considered that Britain should pay only the equivalent of what she received from her debtors, thus following the policy implicit in the Balfour Note sent to the debtor nations stating that the British recognised their obligations to the United States but also that 'our undoubted rights as a creditor nation cannot be left wholly in obeyance. . . . In no circumstances does Great Britain propose to ask more from her debtors than is necessary to pay her creditors—not more, but not less.' The response had been not merely negligible, but actively hostile.

The debt itself, furthermore, had been incurred in the form of goods (some of which had been sold at inflated prices), but its discharge by these means was prevented by American tariffs and by the insistence of the Foreign Debt Commission set up by Congress which wanted the money, with interest.

Baldwin returned with a settlement that committed the British to paying 3 per cent interest for ten years and $3\frac{1}{2}$ for 52 years; in practical terms, this amounted to paying £34 millions per annum for ten years and £40 millions thereafter. Baldwin considered that these terms, although stern, were reasonable. On his arrival at Southampton he held a highly injudicious press conference in which he announced the terms of the settlement and gave his opinion on them. Bonar Law was violently opposed to the settlement and carried his objections to the point of threatening resignation at a Cabinet meeting on January 30th. Derby's account informs us that:

With the exception of Lloyd-Graeme we were absolutely unanimous in saying that we ought to accept the terms, and it looked at the moment as if there would be a break-up of the Government there and then, but luckily somebody—I cannot remember who—suggested that we might adjourn and meet again the next day.[1]

The Times carried a letter, signed 'Colonial', which repeated the arguments put forward by Bonar Law in the Cabinet; some Ministers, noting the many similarities, suspected that Law may have inspired it. In fact, he had actually written it, an extraordinary action for a Prime Minister to take. But on the following day, faced by the unanimous opinion of the Cabinet, the Treasury, and the City of London, Law reluctantly withdrew his objections, and this storm passed.

With the French, however, no progress whatever was made. Poincaré's insistence upon immediate payment by Germany of her reparation commitments resulted in two unsuccessful meetings in December 1922 and January 1923 in London and Paris respectively. Law urged Poincaré 'to allow Germany a breathing space to restore her shattered credits before pressing her for payments she cannot at the moment make', but to no avail. After an unhappy and unfruitful meeting in January, the Prime Ministers parted with the cold regret 'that there should be irreconcilable differences on a subject so serious'. On January 11th the French started to occupy the Ruhr. The British, although hostile to the French policy, acquiesced in it. The Germans boycotted the French; the supplies of coal stopped, and German industry with it. By the end of the year there were ten millions unemployed in Germany, and the value of the mark had collapsed from 2,000 to the pound in January to 100,000 in May and to 5,000,000 in September. The banking system of Central Europe was in chaos. In September, after receiving assurances from a new German Government, the French withdrew. This was an ominous milestone on the downward march of Europe.

Meanwhile, the Government had achieved a major diplomatic success at Lausanne, where Curzon had been grappling single-handed with the aftermath of the Kemalist uprising. The Turks gained much, but Curzon secured the neutralisation of the Straits and the retention of the oil wells of Mosul. It was one of those rare conferences from which all the parties emerged reasonably satisfied.

Thus, by April 1923, the Government had weathered its immediate

[1] R. S. Churchill: *Derby*, 495. Philip Lloyd-Graeme, later Cunliffe-Lister, later Lord Swinton, was President of the Board of Trade.

storms, and the confidence of Ministers and back-benchers alike had risen. And it was at this point, when some stability seemed to have arrived at last, that the political situation was once again hurled into turmoil.

*

For some months Bonar Law had experienced difficulty in speaking, and his voice had actually failed during the 1922 election. This caused no great concern, and it was expected that a relaxing holiday would quickly restore him. He accordingly sailed to Genoa with his son Richard in the liner *Princess Juliana* on May 1st. They were met at Genoa on the 8th by Davidson, who was taken aback to see that Law's condition had not improved at all, and that he looked decidely worse. Law decided not to stay in Genoa, and to travel to Aix to spend some days with the Baldwins. Baldwin's cousin, Rudyard Kipling, was staying at Aix, and was shocked by Law's appearance. Beaverbrook was telegraphed to come out at once. Law went on to Paris, where Beaverbrook had arranged for Sir Thomas Horder to examine the Prime Minister. Even at this stage, although there was considerable concern, there was no serious anxiety.

Horder examined Law on the morning of April 17th at the Hotel Crillon, and diagnosed terminal cancer of the throat. Law was now under heavy sedation, and could hardly speak. For some weeks he had spoken yearningly of retirement, and Beaverbrook had argued strongly against entertaining such thoughts. Now Beaverbrook had to change course abruptly; but Law's condition was such that he was overwhelmed with relief at the prospect of his deliverance.

Law returned to London on Saturday, May 19th. Confronted by the precedent of March 1894,[1] Law let the King know that he would prefer not to be consulted about his successor, and on the morning of May 20th he laboriously wrote out his letter of resignation to the King.[2]

While he was writing it, Davidson was dictating a memorandum in another room. This document he had promised to Stamfordham 'as

[1] See Volume I, 142–3. The precedent was not, of course, exact, but it impressed Law.

[2] It was on this day that he told Thomas Jones that if his advice had been required, 'he would put Baldwin first'. (R. K. Middlemas (ed.): *Whitehall Diaries*, Volume I, p. 236.)

representing back-bench opinion'. It went to Aldershot together with Law's letter, and was conveyed by Law's son-in-law Sir Frederick Sykes and his secretary, Sir Ronald Waterhouse.

Both Davidson and Waterhouse were very keen that the succession should go to Baldwin, and Davidson's memorandum—which was unsigned—while carefully prepared to give an apparently balanced portrait, was in fact a cogent argument for Baldwin as against Curzon. According to Stamfordham, Waterhouse said that 'it practically expressed the views of Mr. Bonar Law'. Davidson has firmly denied that Waterhouse had any knowledge of its contents, and doubted that it had any real effect on the course of events. A lively dispute later developed as to whom Law did in fact prefer, and whether his views were deliberately misrepresented. Davidson and Waterhouse, supported by Amery and Jones, believed that on balance Law favoured Baldwin. Beaverbrook has argued vigorously in the other direction. None of these witnesses are, however, wholly reliable.[1] But the fact that Law, who was well enough to have conveyed advice, did not, was a powerful implicit voice against Curzon.

The King sought formal advice from Lord Salisbury and Balfour. Salisbury favoured Curzon, and Stamfordham records of his conversation with him:

> Lord Salisbury then told me that he had seen Bonar Law this morning and in discussing the question of his successor he gave Salisbury the impression that in this very grave and complex situation he would on the whole be disinclined to pass over Curzon: but he added that he would rather not take the responsibility of any decision.

This was something less than a ringing endorsement of Curzon, and Balfour's advice was strongly against Curzon, basing his case firmly on the impossibility of the Prime Minister being in the Lords. No doubt Balfour found his task highly congenial. On his return he was asked 'And will dear George be chosen?', to which he retorted with evident satisfaction, 'No, dear George will not'. Although Balfour's argument against Curzon was constitutionally fallacious, it was persuasive. The King concurred in this opinion. On the afternoon of Tuesday, May 22nd, Baldwin was summoned to the Palace and invited to form an Administration. Meanwhile Curzon, out of telephone communication

[1] See Davidson, op. cit., 150–5, and Blake, op. cit., 520–5.

with London at Montacute, was summoned to London by Stamfordham. To Curzon, this summons could only have one meaning, and he travelled to London discoursing to his wife on his plans for the Premiership. He was greeted at the station by a large crowd of photographers. On his arrival at Carlton House Terrace an emissary from Austen Chamberlain—Oliver Locker-Lampson—arrived with a message that 'he and his friends earnestly hope for my appointment and that some of them, including Chamberlain himself, would willingly consent to serve under me, but could not do so under Baldwin'. Curzon replied that one of his first acts 'would be to end the breach in the Tory Party and ask him [Chamberlain] to rejoin the Government'.[1]

Then, Stamfordham called. He came, not with the expected invitation, but with the information that Baldwin was already at the Palace. Poor Curzon's dreams were shattered in an instant. And not only his. According to Davidson, the former Conservative Coalitionists were awaiting the news of Curzon's accession at Sir Philip Sassoon's Park Lane house. Beaverbrook was present, and eventually telephoned Downing Street. Davidson, already there, recorded the conversation:

I went into the Private Secretary's room, picked up the receiver, and heard the familiar voice of Beaverbrook. He said, 'David, you know that Curzon has been sent for', and I replied 'Yes, I know he has been'. He then said 'I am at Philip's house and the old gang have sent a message to Curzon to tell him that they will serve under him as Prime Minister', to which I replied, 'I am sorry Max, but it's too late: Baldwin has just come back from the Palace and is busy in the Cabinet Room making the new Government'. There was a roar like a lion and it sounded as though the telephone had been thrown across the room and crashed against the wall.[2]

Thus did the news come to Park Lane. Elsewhere, there was equal astonishment and, in many quarters, equal dismay. Beaverbrook claims that Bonar Law was astonished at Baldwin's selection, Davidson that 'Law was very pleased that the Prime Minister was to be in the House of Commons'.

The King's action was endorsed by a special meeting of Conservative M.P.s and Peers—candidates were not invited—on May 28th, in which Curzon proposed Baldwin's election as leader of the

[1] Mosley: *Curzon*, 271–2.   [2] Davidson, op. cit., 161.

party in a speech of superb malice. 'In a sense', he remarked, 'it may be said that the choice of Mr. Stanley Baldwin as Leader of the whole Conservative Party has been determined by the action of the King. But we all felt, and I am sure you will agree, that it was right that the choice of the Sovereign should be ratified and confirmed by the vote of the entire Party.' After a somewhat unenthusiastic recital of Baldwin's virtues, Curzon concluded that 'lastly (I breathe this almost *sotto voce*), Mr. Baldwin possesses the supreme and indispensable qualification of not being a peer'. Baldwin was duly 'elected'.

Curzon died in 1925, still to the majority a preposterous personality, but to some, for all his failings and foibles, a man of exceptional quality beset by exceptional misfortune. Curzon deserved the memorable tribute paid to him by Winston Churchill: 'The morning was golden, the noon-time silver, the afternoon bronze, and the evening lead. But each was polished until it shone after its own fashion.'

Curzon had only two years of life left to him, Law had even less. On October 20th his sufferings ended, and his ashes were buried in Westminster Abbey. 'It is not inappropriate', Asquith is alleged to have remarked caustically, 'that we have buried the Unknown Prime Minister beside the Unknown Soldier.'

Beaverbrook has given a moving account of the last meeting between Law and Lloyd George, at Beaverbrook's little house in Fulham, in September:

> Here were two men who had served in the highest office of state and each had come to an end. Bonar Law had come to the end of his life and the shadows of death were already gathering round him. Lloyd George had many years to live, but the shadows of decline were gathering round him. There were to be flashes of revived activity, moments of brilliance and an occasional false hope of further greatness still to be achieved. But these manifestations meant nothing. The path led inexorably downwards. The heights were behind and the valley was ever deepening before. Lloyd George was never again to hold any public office.[1]

*

By the time that Stanley Baldwin made his unexpected advance to the Premiership, the condition of European affairs already dem-

[1] Beaverbrook, op. cit., 233–5.

onstrated a sharp descent from the high hopes of November 1918. The first Assembly of the League of Nations at Geneva in November 1920 emphasised the divisions rather than the strengths of the new European and world order. It was a victors' assembly. None of the former enemy states were present—Austria and Bulgaria were admitted at the end of 1920, Hungary in 1922, Germany in 1926, and Turkey in 1932—and the United States of America and Russia were even more conspicuously noticeable absentees.

The effects of American withdrawal were immediate, and substantial. In the lengthy discussions at Versailles in which Wilson had persuaded Clemenceau to abandon the French demand for cession of the Rhineland, the Americans and the British had promised, in return for French withdrawal on this point, to give a guarantee to France against any future German attack. The action of the Senate in denying ratification of the Treaty until the Presidential elections of 1920 repudiated Wilson's pledge. The British Government decided that the new situation rendered their pledge inoperative. The French, to their dismay and chagrin, found that they had lost the joint guarantee that had been the prime advantage that they had secured from Versailles.

This episode blighted Anglo-French relations, never really to be restored. For the British, although less dramatically and obviously than the Americans, had demonstrated that their inclination was equally isolationist. The 'lessons' of the First World War were already being absorbed, and the pre-Entente policy of freedom from European entanglements was again in the ascendant. Such an attitude was strongly supported by the Dominions, whose influence on British policy was infinitely stronger than it had been before the war. As the events of September 1922 had served to emphasise, the Dominions were ill-disposed to become implicated in another European conflict unless Britain was specifically and manifestly imperilled.

The gulf in attitudes between Britain and France became steadily more evident. The French, deprived of their Versailles pledge, now attempted to secure protection from the League of Nations. The British saw the League as a conciliation body and an international forum, rather than as an organisation with executive functions and responsibilities. In short, the French wanted to give the League binding commitment upon its members to resist aggression; the British did not. In 1923 the French brought forward the Draft Treaty of

Mutual Assistance, which proposed that once the Council had declared that a member state was the object of aggression, all other members were obliged to come to its assistance. In 1924 they proposed the Geneva Protocol, which provided for the submission of disputes to the International Court of Justice or to the Council of the League; any refusal to do so would constitute an act of aggression. Both these proposals were defeated, principally as a result of British official and Dominion opposition.

The French were pursuing other lines in their search for the security that the war and the Peace Treaties had failed to provide. An elaborate series of defensive alliances was intended to avert a repetition of the 1914 situation, when British intervention had hinged on the neutrality of Belgium. Such treaties were negotiated and agreed with Belgium in 1920, Poland in 1921, and Czechoslovakia in 1924. These involvements led to others. Poland had an alliance with Romania, and Czechoslovakia had joined with Rumania and Yugoslavia in 'the Little Entente'; France joined, and, in 1927, forged additional military ties to cement the diplomatic alliances.

There were many flaws in the French strategy. The pursuance of security clashed with France's membership of the League, a fact that was emphasised in 1923 when she supported Poland in an attack on Lithuania and blocked League intervention. The new alliance, furthermore, increased the mistrust with which the British regarded French policies and their apprehension of European entanglements.

These divisions in the Anglo-French entente were aggravated and accentuated by the German question.

The central point of division was that of Reparations. By 1920 the British had come to the conclusion that to continue a policy of heavy reparations was probably impracticable and even undesirable. To a Cabinet in which Lloyd George and Churchill were members the spectre of Bolshevism was a very substantial one. The Rapallo Treaty, that had destroyed Genoa, alarmed the British in this direction, whereas it made the French even more determined to insist upon their rights under Versailles. This was the background to the elaborately staged action of January 1923, when the French occupied the Ruhr, which must be adjudged the most important single event of the 1920s to damage democratic forces in Germany and give encouragement to those of reaction.

A year earlier—indeed less than two weeks after Lloyd George had fallen at the Carlton Club Meeting—Mussolini had come to power in Italy.

Of all the 'victorious' nations, Italy had been a most conspicuous loser. The territorial gains at the head of the Adriatic were hardly adequate to compensate for the losses in the war; the war itself had not succeeded in endowing the Italians with a reputation for military competence; and it had plunged the national economy into appalling debts. Disillusion and bitterness stalked the land on the morrow of victory. The political parties were divided, venal, and incapable of providing stable government or competent administration. A series of coalition governments presided helplessly and feebly over a country increasingly riven with faction and disorder.

Three important elements viewed this situation with dismay and contempt. The wealthy landowners and industrialists wanted stability and security; the nationalists who had backed intervention in 1915 and who still believed in Italian greatness were bitterly hostile towards the pusillanimous Socialists and Liberals, a hostility that was based on the recognition of Yugoslav rights on the Dalmatian coast in 1920 and the evacuation of Albania in the same year; then, there were the ex-servicemen, abandoned and derided. These groups found their man in Benito Mussolini.

Mussolini had formed his first *Fascio di combattimento* in Milan in March 1919. For a time the movement seemed powerless, divided, and faintly absurd. Mussolini's authority was far from being accepted, and at times his position seemed precarious. But he was indispensable to the movement. For all his deficiencies as a leader, as a writer and an orator he towered over all his contemporaries. His subsequent career, and its dismal conclusion, must not blind the historian to Mussolini's very real abilities and popular appeal.

In 1920 and 1921 Italy was ravaged by industrial and agrarian disorder, which the Government was unable to meet. The Fascists posed as the champions of law and order, and the true patriots of Italy. In the elections of May 1921 the Fascists became bolder, and their tactics more open. They won only thirty-five seats, but the Fascist movement was now on the offensive; the declaration of a general strike in August 1922 gave the movement its great opportunity. The nation was yearning for stability, and when the Fascists embarked upon a policy of fighting socialism there was general approval. Emboldened, the Fascist leaders took command of the major cities of northern Italy. Negotiations with royalist, religious, and industrial representatives convinced Mussolini that the moment was ripe for a national *coup d'état*. With some trepidation, Mussolini ordered the Black Shirts to mobilise and march on Rome. The King —Victor Emmanuel III—refused to sign the declaration of martial law put forward by the government, and, urged by a Fascist mission led by Count Grandi, appointed Mussolini Prime Minister. The hero arrived in Rome by sleeping car from Milan on the morning of October 30th.

Other nations were quickly made aware of what the change meant. In August 1923 an Italian general and his staff were killed on the Greco-Albanian border. Mussolini issued an ultimatum to the Greek Government, and then bombarded and occupied the island of Corfu. Greece appealed to the League of Nations. The Western Powers referred the matter to arbitration; Corfu was returned to Greece in return for the payment of substantial damages to Italy. Mussolini had gained a cheap triumph. What was more significant was the refusal of the European Powers to apply the principles of the League. The Corfu Incident, small in itself, was of profound significance for those who wished to emulate Mussolini's achievement.

The Weimar Republic in Germany was buffeted most brutally from its birth. It was born in the shadow of defeat, humiliation, and internal anarchy. For the first four years of its existence it was involved in constant crisis, internal and external.

The first attempt to overturn the Republic came in March 1920, in the so-called Kapp *Putsch*. This episode exposed the equivocal position of the Army, as the Defence Minister—Noske—could not persuade the commanders to envisage troops firing on troops. The Kapp 'government' was brought down by the Socialists and the trade unions, and the Republic was saved. But the ugly demonstration of where power really lay in Germany poisoned the air; the army, allegedly aloof from the political foray, bided its time and awaited the leader who would restore their former supremacy. On the Left, opposition to the army was increased after a rising in the Ruhr, in March 1920, was put down with severity. This episode, coming so swiftly after the Kapp *putsch*, also demonstrated the fact that the Republic needed the army.

But the problem of reparations, in an economy severely hit by the war, was the dominant and perpetual crisis. In strict logic, the case for reparations—particularly to France and Belgium—was justified. But the brutality of the French attitude occasioned the crisis. The occupation of the Ruhr in January 1923 sent inflation, which had been serious since 1919, spiralling catastrophically. The life savings of respectable, thrifty people became of absolutely no value. The reserves of the trade unions were obliterated. Violence swept across Germany. Walter Rathenau, the foreign minister and author of Germany's economic war planning, was assassinated in June. Other leaders of the Republic were in mortal danger. On November 9th Adolf Hitler and General Ludendorff led the Munich *putsch* which, easily crushed, destroyed the until then potentially serious situation in Bavaria. 'Hitler was arrested and imprisoned', the British Ambassador wrote in his memoirs—published in 1932—'and thereafter disappeared into oblivion'.

But the ailments of the Republic were on the mend. In August 1923 Gustav Stresemann became Chancellor of a coalition. His first action was to end the policy of passive resistance to the French occupation of the Ruhr, which ended in September. Draconian measures, worked out by Schacht and Luther, were introduced to restore the economic situation. Britain and the United States responded to appeals for assistance, and, with reluctant French agreement, the Dawes Plan revalued the rate of reparations. Foreign loans—principally from the United States—were arranged to invigorate the German economy and German industry. It was an essential step, and one that restored Germany with dramatic suddenness in the 1920s. The protests of the extreme Right were impassioned, but as Germany recovered her economic position and her diplomatic respectability, these shrill accusations of betrayal faded into apparent insignificance. But the bitterness against Versailles could not be obliterated, and awaited darker days to be exploited again.

*

It was at this hour that Stanley Baldwin came to the Premiership.

A more complex personality has seldom held the supreme political position in the State. It is still difficult to focus accurately on him. He comes down to us in many vignettes, sniffing at books, muttering restlessly to no-one in particular in the House, parading as the simple country gentleman, the romantic Celt, the modest scholar, or the Man

of Reliability, the personification of Trust. That he was also at root
an honest and sincere man is also incontestable. What is not clear is
when he was being devious and when he was honest. It was also a
matter of bafflement to his contemporaries, and in this lay perhaps
his greatest strength. He portrayed himself as a practical, commonsense Englishman; as a commentator in *The Times* remarked in 1930,
he 'cultivates the character of an amateur in politics to a point which
is maddening to ardent politicians'. He had been selected as Bonar
Law's Parliamentary Private Secretary because, in the words of Lord
Edmund Talbot, he was 'discreet enough to be safe and stupid enough
not to intrigue'. If his Ministerial career had not been outstandingly
successful, he had cultivated the House of Commons assiduously, and
with quiet skill. As has been written of him, 'the House of Commons
was his village. He had an ear like an old man sitting in the sun outside a village inn.' Harold Macmillan has written of him that he:

> had a unique hold on all sections of his party and the House as a
> whole. He was rarely attacked with any vigour, and if the House
> was excited or unruly he would usually and without difficulty
> reduce the temperature. His fairness in debate, the width and
> generosity of his approach to life, the charm of his manner, and even
> the skilful way in which he could avoid a difficult argument or
> awkward situation by a few minutes of reminiscence or philoso-
> phising; all these qualities made him a supreme Parliamentarian.[1]

The decline of the Coalition had brought to the surface emotions
and attitudes hitherto unappreciated. As Thomas Jones wrote of
Baldwin, 'he felt things deeply, and his conscience was more active
than his intellect'. His reaction to the Coalition had been perhaps the
most decisive element in its downfall. 'Beaverbrook and I fought for
the soul of Bonar Law', Baldwin once commented on that episode.
'Beaverbrook wanted to make him a great man after his fashion. I
showed him there were better things to be'. The Coalition Conservatives had been astounded at his apostasy, and much of their subsequent bitterness was directed against him personally. They found
it impossible to take him seriously as a major political figure, and had
yet to learn that he was, like Gladstone, 'terrible on the rebound'—
or, as *The Times* commentator of 1930 put it, 'his spiritual home is
always the last ditch'.

[1] Harold Macmillan: *Winds of Change*, 313.

Not the least of his most valuable political attributes was the fact that he was a most likeable man. As Leo Amery has written of him, 'Baldwin was a personality, with a breadth of outlook, a tolerance and a warm humanity which commanded the admiration, as well as the affection, of those who chafed under the weaknesses of his leadership'.[1]

The contrast between this agreeable, tolerant, broad-minded man of business and the personalities of the Coalition was marked indeed, and did him no harm at all. The real exhaustion of the war was now becoming apparent. Like a victim grievously wounded yet alive and exhilarated by his survival who subsequently plunges into deep shock and depression, Britain by 1922 was at last feeling the full psychological and physical consequences of the war. The indications were apparent on all sides, and had been manifested by the general approval of the fall of Lloyd George and by the almost alarming conservatism of the Labour Party. The revulsion against suppressing Ireland was, as Austen Chamberlain (among others) noted, deeply significant. The reaction to Chanak was no less revealing. The British had had enough of fighting, of adventurous living, of sacrifice. Unemployment hung like a pall over the land, particularly in the north. The spectre of grievous industrial disputes haunted all men of sensitivity, glancing nervously at the situation on the Continent. As Europe struggled and seethed in the grim aftermath of the war, the British drew in upon themselves.

Baldwin enjoyed particular support on the Left and in the more liberal sections of the Conservative Party. Attlee has written of him that 'he always seemed more at home with our people, particularly the older trade union people, than with his own lot'. Macmillan has written:

The young and progressive wing of his party had a special regard for him. His speeches, particularly on industrial problems, struck just the note which we thought appropriate and illuminating. The fact that the Right Wing and especially the so-called 'industrials' had little love for him, confirmed our feelings.

Baldwin had already given a demonstration of that quality, in a speech in February 1923:

Four words of one syllable each are words which contain salvation

[1] Amery, op. cit., 398.

for this country and for the whole world. They are 'Faith', 'Hope', 'Love', and 'Work'. No Government in this country today which has not faith in the people, hope in the future, love for its fellow men, and which will not work and work and work, will ever bring this country through into better days and better times. . . .

The historian must often ponder on why it is that, so often, a single speech or a single phrase in a speech, establishes or destroys a political character. It is something that is inexplicable for those who were not there. It is a matter of the combination, the magical combination, of orator, theme, words, audience, and occasion. That phrase struck the House of Commons like a bullet. It was widely reported, a fact which in itself demonstrates how wide and deep was the appeal of Baldwin's message.

But his real strength lay in the fact best expressed by John Buchan in his biography of Montrose:

There is a moderation which is in itself a fire, where enthusiasm burns as fiercely for the whole truth as it commonly does for half-truths, where moderation becomes not a policy but an act of religion. . . . The moderate man can never become a barren dogmatist.

Baldwin was a deeply sensitive man. Lloyd George once remarked of him that 'Baldwin is one of us, he is a Celt at heart and that is why many of you find him difficult to understand'. And his son has written that 'Before an important speech the colour would leave his face, the sweat would sometimes roll off his brow, and he has confessed time and time again that he felt he might be sick'.

Baldwin's successes over the next ten years so astonished men who regarded themselves as superior to him in capacity and experience that they tended to endow him with qualities that he did not in fact possess. Lloyd George described him as 'the most formidable antagonist whom I ever encountered'. Churchill has described him as 'the greatest party manager the Conservatives ever had'. Beaverbrook, so often worsted by Baldwin, left a posthumous portrait of a man of almost diabolical cunning.

All this came later. At the time, it seemed impossible that this amiable nonentity would be anything more than a *locum tenens*. But Baldwin had many shocks in store for his critics, his party, and his country.

He made no really serious overture to the Coalition Conservatives to return to the fold. One historian[1] has written that he 'badly muffed the opportunity to bring about a reconciliation', but Baldwin's timing was much better than this implies. It was Baldwin's view that the time had not yet come for a reconciliation, an impression increased after a bleak interview with Austen Chamberlain. Of greater importance was the fact that in the party as a whole, and particularly in the Cabinet, there was no great urge towards reconciliation. The actions of Birkenhead and Horne in particular since the fall of the Coalition were resented, and those who had been subjected to the collective and individual arrogance of the Coalition Conservatives had no desire to repeat the experience. Furthermore, if they returned they would have to be given senior offices, a factor which was no doubt on the minds of those who held those offices. There was not only no real desire for reconciliation, but no real need. The only change of real note that Baldwin made was to appoint Austen's half-brother, Neville, to the Treasury, after yet another attempt to woo McKenna back to politics had failed. Neville Chamberlain had entered Parliament in 1918 after a successful period as Mayor of Birmingham and a very unsuccessful one as Director of National Service in the Lloyd George Government, which left an enduring impression on both men. He was nearly fifty when he entered national politics.

It was in fact Neville Chamberlain who was responsible for the only measure of note produced by the first Baldwin Government, the Housing Act of 1923, which gave a subsidy of £6 a year for twenty years for each house built within certain dimensions by local authorities or private enterprise. These were houses built only for sale, and the Act benefited the lower middle classes. This fact, when combined with the wretchedly small size of the houses to be subsidised, the restriction to houses for sale, and the emphasis on private enterprise, caused bitter hostility from Labour. Neville Chamberlain's somewhat grim version of State paternalism, well laced with characteristic superciliousness at the stupidity of his critics and a certain moral sanctimoniousness, enraged the Opposition, and made him a special target even from this early stage of his official career.

Nevertheless, the significance of what Neville Chamberlain had done was considerable. A Conservative Government had perpetuated rent restriction; it had accepted the principle of the Addison scheme

[1] C. L. Mowat: *Britain Between the Wars*, 164.

that the State had a responsibility for housing; and it had accepted the importance of the local authorities in any housing programme. At the time these facts were obscured by the outcry that the limitations of the scheme aroused.

The economic situation showed no sign of improving. By October the national average of unemployment was 11·7 per cent. Talk of protective tariffs was heard again, and was a dominant topic at the Imperial Economic Conference held in London in October. Nevertheless, the nation was wholly unprepared for the statement of Baldwin on October 25th at the annual party conference at Plymouth, to the effect that Protection was essential. The actual words are worth recording:

> Mr. Bonar Law's pledge given a year ago, was that there should be no fundamental change in the fiscal arrangements of the country. That pledge binds me, and in this Parliament there will be no fundamental change, and I take those words strictly. I am not a man to play with a pledge. . . . This unemployment problem. is the most crucial problem of our country . . . I can fight it. I am willing to fight it. I cannot fight it without weapons. . . . I have come to the conclusion myself that the only way of fighting this subject is by protecting the home market (*loud and continued cheering*). I am not a clever man. I know nothing of political tactics, but I will say this: Having come to that conclusion myself, I felt that the only honest and right thing as the leader of a democratic party was to tell them, at the first opportunity I had, what I thought, and submit it to their judgement.

Baldwin had decided to raise the Protection issue while on holiday in Aix in August after, in the words of G. M. Young, 'meditating deeply on his own discomforts as Prime Minister and the precarious condition of his party'. But there is no evidence that he envisaged an election on the issue, nor that he proposed to fulfil Bonar Law's pledge, at this stage. This only matured in September, after consultations with his colleagues, but Baldwin's Plymouth speech envisaged a full autumn session and made no reference to an election. But the fact of the speech—and the manner in which it had been received—aroused apprehensions that Lloyd George might seize the issue and the initiative. The Protectionists were eager for an election, and were confident that with Liberal divisions and the fear of Labour the party

A FORLORN APPEAL.

Mr. Asquith. "COALITION, ERE WE PART, GIVE, O GIVE ME BACK MY—ER—PARTY!"

18   Asquith by Ravenhill in *Punch*, 1918

19   A Young Man in a Hurry. Winston Churchill by Bert Thomas
in the *World*, 1919

THE NEW CONDUCTOR.

OPENING OF THE 1917 OVERTURE.

20   Lloyd George by Ravenhill in *Punch*, 1916

Lord Oxford.

Low

21 Asquith by Low in *The New Statesman*, February 1926

22   Ramsay Macdonald addressing the House of Commons, 1923.
By Sir John Lavery, R.A., R.S.A.

THE SOFT-WORD PUZZLE.

Mr. Baldwin. "CAN ANYBODY THINK OF ANOTHER WORD FOR 'SUBSIDY'?"

23   *Left to Right:* Austen Chamberlain, Baldwin, Birkenhead, Churchill, Neville Chamberlain, Joynson-Hicks

24 Baldwin by Low in *The New Statesman and Nation*, November 1933

Sir Austen

25   Austen Chamberlain by Low in *The New Statesman*, March 1926

26   Philip Snowden by Low in the *Graphic*, 1927

27   Lloyd George by Low in *The New Statesman*, March 1926

28 'The Recruiting Parade' by Low, 1924. Lords Rothermere (*left*) and Beaverbrook (*right*) hold the banner of Anti-Socialism over Mr Churchill's motley army, which includes Birkenhead (in busby) and Baldwin

29 Strube in the *Daily Express*

Max, Lord Beaverbrook.

30 Beaverbrook by Low in *The New Statesman*, March 1926

The Right Honourable J. H. Thomas, P.C., M.P.

31   J. H. Thomas by Low in *The New Statesman*, July 1926

32   Sir John Simon by Low in *The New Statesman and Nation*,
December 1933

STILL HOPE

33   Illingworth in *Punch*, 21st September 1938

34   In Low's bitter commentary on Munich, Neville Chamberlain and
Halifax play with the innocent little lambs (led by Sir John Simon)
while Beaverbrook rejoices on the right

35   Winston Churchill by Low in *The New Statesman*, May 1926

would win easily. Baldwin had forced the issue, but he did not, as was subsequently charged, stampede his colleagues into an election. The decision was reached on November 12th.[1]

At the time, and for many years afterwards, it was commonly said that Baldwin had been guilty of an act of political lunacy. The Conservatives had a comfortable majority. Protection could be brought in, if need be, by the back door by the process of 'safeguarding' more industries on an ad hoc basis. It was only some time later that the shrewdness of Baldwin's move was seen. Perhaps he has been credited with more skill and subtlety than he deserved, and his precise motivation remains somewhat obscure. Nonetheless, the effect of his action was to bring Austen Chamberlain, Birkenhead and their supporters scuttling back from any tentative alliance with Lloyd George. It removed any possibility of Lloyd George himself raising the banner of Protection. By securing the agreement of the Cabinet to the election he took the issue away from the party to the country.

The gamble did not come off electorally when the election was held in December. Free Trade still had powerful allies. The total Conservative vote dropped only slightly, and that of the Labour Party rose only fractionally. The Liberals, hurled into an uncomfortable embrace by the old unifying cry of Free Trade, improved their position slightly. But the Conservatives lost badly in terms of seats. Although they were still the largest party in the Commons, with 258 seats (as opposed to 346 in 1922), they were in a minority in the Commons and the country to a Liberal-Labour coalition. Labour had won 191 seats, and the Liberals 158. As 1923 came to a close, the nation suddenly realised that it was confronted by the real possibility of a Labour Government taking office with Liberal support. There was a wave of violent criticism against Baldwin for having exposed the nation so wantonly to this peril, and wild schemes were devised for a Conservative-Liberal Coalition against Labour with, possibly, Balfour as Prime Minister—the 'impossibility' of a Peer being Prime Minister evidently now forgotten.

The sudden emergence of the hideous spectre of a Labour Government convulsed London. The City trembled. The ample proportions of the Carlton Club could scarce contain the prophets of doom and sulphurous mutineers. Brutal intrigue flourished at every groaning table, and savage mutiny was discussed nakedly over the port wine.

[1] See Keith Middlemas and John Barnes: *Baldwin*, 239.

Defeated Conservative candidates hastened back to London, aflame with resentment that their services had been so incontinently denied to the State at this critical juncture. Heads were seen to wag mournfully in the most influential circles. Visions of the Red Flag floating insolently over the Palace of Westminster loomed before the outraged eyes of The Elect (but, alas, unelected). The Empire was doomed! Trade would fall! Britain was finished! And Baldwin must go!

There are, indeed, few spectacles more heart-rending than the Conservative Party on the morrow of defeat, seeing the country going to the dogs, and helpless to avert the catastrophe. But seldom has this assumed such tragical proportions as it did in December 1923. The fate of civilisation fluttered in the balance, and it was infinitely galling for the Conservatives to behold the calm indifference with which the British people proceeded upon their daily tasks. If only they knew what was in store for them! Bolshevism! Misery! Devastation! The mockery of the world! And the fools don't give a damn! In such moods of sedition, fury, and contempt did the Conservatives angrily adjourn to celebrate a gloomy, but not frugal, Christmas. There are occasions when the historian's emotions of pity and distress overwhelm him, and thus he must avert the gaze of his reader from this melancholy episode in the annals of this historic political confederation.

After a good Christmas, the mood of the party was more benign. After all, things were not as bad as all that. If Mr. MacDonald and his Muscovite collaborators assumed office, they would do so under the lowering gaze and majority votes of the Conservatives and Liberals. The latter, after all, were not all *that* bad, and could be relied upon to demonstrate some lingering traces of patriotism. There would be a brief interlude, which would prove once and for all that Labour was unfit to govern, and then The People would recover their senses.

Baldwin was under heavy pressure to resign, but stood calmly apart from this absurd clamour. On January 21st the Liberals marched to their doom. The Government was defeated in the House of Commons on a motion of no confidence moved by Clynes and supported by Asquith. On the following day Baldwin resigned and Ramsay MacDonald kissed hands as the first Labour Prime Minister, inspiring the King to sombre reflections on what 'dear Grandmama' would have thought.

CHAPTER FIFTEEN

THE TRIALS OF LABOUR AND THE
DIFFICULTIES OF BALDWIN, 1924–1929

IF THE GENERAL ELECTION of December 1923 was, both in its
origins and its result, one of the more perplexing episodes of modern
British politics, its consequences were to be of weighty significance.
The principal casualty was the Liberal Party, so hurriedly flung
together in such embarrassing circumstances, and so dismally unsatisfied by the sensation and the results of its loveless consummation.
This melancholy reunion has been well described by Asquith:

> At 7 o'clock Sat. evening the rites of Liberal Reunion were cele-
> brated at an enthusiastic meeting in the Town Hall [at Paisley].
> Ll. G. arrived with his Megan, and I was accompanied by Margot
> and Violet. I have rarely felt less exhilaration than when we got to
> the platform amid wild plaudits and a flash-light film was taken,
> 'featuring' me and Ll. G. separated only by the chairman—an
> excellent local Doctor. I spoke for about quarter of an hour, and
> Ll. G. then plunged into a characteristic speech—ragged and
> boisterous, but with quite a good assortment of telling points. He
> was more than friendly and forthcoming, and the meeting was full
> of demonstrative fraternity. When it was over, Ll. G. and Megan,
> and their bodyguard of secretaries and detectives, were swept off
> by their host, Lord Maclay, to some baronial retreat, and we
> supped here in peace.[1]

The old flame of Free Trade had prompted this reconciliation. For
Asquith the issue was so fundamental that the prospect of a Protectionist Conservative Government was anathema. His attitude was
supported by Lloyd George at a party meeting on December 18th.

[1] Jenkins, op. cit., 499.

From that moment it was certain that the Baldwin Government
would fall.

But there were many Liberals—including Churchill, who had lost
again, this time at Leicester as a Liberal Free Trader—to whom
Asquith's decision was the moment of final rupture from the Liberal
Party, and who regarded the prospect of a Labour Government with
horror. Asquith commented sardonically:

> You would be amused if you saw the contents of my daily post-bag;
> appeals, threats, prayers from all parts, and from all sorts and
> conditions of men, women, and lunatics, to step in and save the
> country from the horrors of Socialism and Confiscation . . . The
> City is suffering from an acute attack of nerves at the prospect of a
> Labour Government.

By putting in the Labour Government, Asquith had done the
Liberal Party irreparable damage. No doubt, the Liberals' false
position would have been exposed sooner or later, and the necessity
for choice could not have been postponed indefinitely. But, as Asquith
and Lloyd George had each repeatedly emphasised, a wide chasm
separated Liberalism from Socialism. Certainly, a wide gulf separated
most Liberals from the Labour Party. Churchill was not the only
Liberal who viewed Asquith's decisions with dismay, and who
concluded that British politics were moving towards a choice of two
parties and two philosophies, in which the ancient Liberal creeds were
increasingly irrelevant. There was to be no real co-operation between
Labour and Liberals throughout 1924. The Labour M.P.s tended to
regard the Liberals with scorn; the feeling was reciprocated, Asquith
describing the new Government (in private) as 'a beggarly array'.

It is also arguable that the election had been unfortunate for the
Labour Party. The Red Dawn had broken unexpectedly soon. The
National Executive boldly declared on December 12th that 'should
the necessity for forming a Labour Government arise, the Parliamentary party should at once accept full responsibility for the government of the country without compromising itself with any form of
coalition'. But behind these brave words there was much unease and
uncertainty. At a meeting of the Labour leaders on December 11th
at the Webbs' house it was accepted that Labour could not refuse
office, but MacDonald's reluctance was manifest and understandable.
They agreed that their approach should be a moderate one. This

reflected MacDonald's ambition to 'gain the confidence of the country'; it also recognised the reality of the minority position of a Labour Government; but, most important of all, it demonstrated that Labour had little positive to offer in legislation or policies. Labour came into office with a multitude of attitudes and beliefs but with few positive proposals and little agreement on the few that there were.

Apart from its psychological unpreparedness, Labour had a marked shortage of men who could claim to have any apparent qualifications for public office. MacDonald appreciated this very clearly, and the barrenness of the field was apparent when the new Government was announced. Lord Parmoor—a former Liberal M.P. and brother-in-law of Beatrice Webb—became Lord President of the Council; Haldane became Lord Chancellor, for the second time in his interesting career; Lord Chelmsford became First Lord of the Admiralty, a surprising elevation for a former Viceroy of India with allegedly Conservative inclinations. The Labour Left was almost totally ignored, the most conspicuous absentees being E. D. Morel and George Lansbury. The only Clydesider in the Government was John Wheatley, who turned out to be its only major success. The principal posts went to Snowden (Treasury), Arthur Henderson (Home Office), and J. H. Thomas (Colonial Office). This Ministry could not be described as revolutionary in personality or in policy. The spectacle of Ramsay MacDonald in Court Dress with silver-buckled shoes and sword, and Jimmy Thomas in full fig brought solace to those apprehensive of the coming Bolshevik Revolution and aroused unease in those who had anticipated more radical attitudes. The new Ministers seemed enchanted at their positions, and quickly brought to their tasks that solemnity of mien and pomposity of manner that are deemed appropriate for those who nobly bear on their shoulders the destinies of a great nation and a mighty Empire. As Clynes (Lord Privy Seal) subsequently wrote:

> As we stood waiting for His Majesty, amid the gold and crimson of the Palace, I could not help marvelling at the strange turn of Fortune's wheel, which had brought MacDonald the starveling clerk, Thomas the engine-driver, Henderson the foundry labourer, and Clynes the mill-hand, to this pinnacle.

But the Conservative Right Wing was still aghast at the prospects. 'The enthronement in office of a Socialist Government', Churchill thundered wildly from his wilderness, 'will be a serious national misfortune such as has usually befallen great states only on the morrow of defeat in war. It will delay the return of prosperity, it will open a period of increasing political confusion and disturbance, it will place both the Liberal and Labour parties in a thoroughly false position. . . . Strife and tumults, deepening and darkening, will be the only consequence of minority Socialist rule'.

*

In these difficult circumstances, Labour did surprisingly well and laid the foundations for its own future. There were two really substantial achievements in social reform. John Wheatley—whose early death was to be a tragedy for the Labour Party—took Chamberlain's housing policy and entirely re-cast it. He increase the subsidy from £6 a year for twenty years to £9 a year for forty years, with the option open to local authorities to add a further £4 10s. for forty years if the controlled rent was insufficient to meet the cost; he put the main burden and responsibility firmly on the local authorities, and insisted that the houses must be built to rent. He secured an expansion of the building industry by promising that the scheme would operate for at least fifteen years. The Wheatley Act was a real revolution, and it was noticeable that its main principles were unchallenged. Its principal deficiency lay in the fact that it did not tackle the problem of slum-clearance; the building of new houses was, of course, vital, but did not meet the problems of overcrowding and wretched conditions in the worst areas. And, once again, the unemployed and the really poor did not immediately benefit.

Only in the field of education did Labour have a policy, largely the work of the historian R. H. Tawney. The Minister, Charles Trevelyan, restored much of the work of H. A. L. Fisher between 1918 and 1921 that had been scrapped or shelved by the Geddes economies, particularly in secondary education; but he initiated studies that resulted in the system whereby the compulsory minimum school-leaving age was to be raised to fifteen[1] and a separation was created by examination between primary and secondary education at the age of eleven, thus creating two categories of talent. Subsequently, this latter arrangement came under heavy and justified criticism in the 1960s and was

[1] The Fisher Act of 1918 had established it at fourteen and had abolished all previous exemptions.

abandoned. At the time it was regarded as a remarkable step forward, and as completing the transformation of British state education that had had its first tentative advances in the Forster Act of 1870 and in the Balfour Act of 1902.

In foreign affairs, to which MacDonald devoted almost all his attention and energies, some real progress was made. Labour in this respect at least was lucky. The Franco-German dispute had passed its peak, and the Dawes Plan was the first realistic assessment of reparations that had a chance. It was to MacDonald's credit that the British Government seized upon it, and urged France and Germany to accept it. The British reaped some tangible benefit from their role of honest broker; the share of reparations from Germany, together with some payments from France, enabled the British to meet the obligations to the United States incurred by Baldwin.

MacDonald also set the tone for the improvement in international relations which Austen Chamberlain was to develop subsequently. He personally attended the League of Nations, and actively supported the Geneva Protocol: the Government fell before it was ratified, and the Conservatives were hostile to it. But the role of international conciliator was one to which MacDonald took naturally, and one which he accomplished well. He was never, as some of his admirers (and many of his critics) have averred, a devout believer in the League of Nations as an effective replacement for the international bilateral system. But he did believe that in a forum such as the League the rules of international politics could be reorganised to avert a repetition of the disastrous pre-1914 system. In this, as in so many other matters, the difference between MacDonald's outlook and that of the Conservative leaders was one of degree; but that degree was important. The Geneva Protocol would not have stopped Hitler or Mussolini or Japan; it imposed no obligations not already inherent in the Covenant. But the principle of the reference of all disputes to arbitration was an important one, and might possibly have borne fruit if it had been wholeheartedly pursued and backed by successive Governments.

All this was viewed with suspicion by the Liberals and alarm by the Conservatives, who viewed another aspect of the Labour foreign policy with open hostility. Anglo-Russian relations since the end of the war had veered between the bad and the critical. Continued anti-British propaganda from Russia, studied insults, and hectoring communications, had not disposed any British Government to view the

Soviet Government with anything but reluctant acceptance of the unpleasantness of its existence. There was some substance in Churchill's concluding words in *The Aftermath* that 'Russia, self-outcast, sharpens her bayonets in her Arctic night, and mechanically proclaims through half-starved lips her philosophy of hatred and death'.

Suspicion of international Bolshevism ran very deep in British political circles, and touched even level-headed men like Baldwin. The Conservative-dominated Press never omitted to emphasise the barbarous intentions of the Soviets, and the blood-curdling utterances of Zinoviev—the bellicose president of the Communist International —did not help to warm Anglo-Russian relations.

In this unpromising situation the Labour Government acted with what could be regarded as courage or foolhardiness. On February 1st the Soviet Government was officially recognised, and was invited to a conference in London to settle outstanding differences. This gesture was bleakly rewarded. The conference began in mid-April, and dragged on inconclusively throughout the summer. It was resumed in August, and broke down on the evening of August 5th; under heavy Labour back-bench pressure the Government reconvened the conference, and agreement was reached on the following evening. Two treaties—covering commercial relations and pre-Revolution obligations—were signed on the 8th; the British Government also agreed to recommend to Parliament the granting of a loan to the Soviet Union. The treaties and the loan were immediately vehemently attacked both by the Conservatives and the Liberals, Lloyd George being among the most vigorous of the critics. Largely as a result of Russian intransigence, the position of the Government had been fatally compromised by the embarrassing *volte-face* of August 5th–6th.

If these Bolshevik flirtations aroused the wrath of the Opposition, Labour supporters had been profoundly disappointed by the failure of Labour to effect a miraculous cure in the economic situation. The claim that 'only Labour can speak to Labour' had had an unexpectedly early repudiation.

Snowden's views on national economic policy showed little advancement, if any, on those of Mr. Gladstone. In his 1924 Budget expenditure was cut and taxes reduced; even the McKenna Duties were abolished. This was, of course, the reason why the Liberals had backed Labour—to preserve Free Trade. But in Snowden they had discovered an advocate more ardent and bigoted even than themselves. The McKenna Duties had, after all, been introduced when Asquith was Prime Minister and maintained by Lloyd George. Now, even that fig-leaf of Protection was removed.

This did nothing to alleviate the condition of the unemployed or the part-employed. Eventually, and with manifest reluctance, Snowden announced a scheme of public works costing £28 millions, a modest enough nod in the direction of Keynes, the only foremost economist now advocating such policies. Labour did not merely accept the *status quo*; in many respects it demonstrated an alarming conservatism on economic matters, combined with a reluctant acquiescence in the system among the rank and file.

In industrial disputes the Government did not fare much better. Faced with strikes of dockers and London tramwaymen, the Government threatened to use the Emergency Powers Act. The unions were astounded, and their leader—Ernest Bevin—called the strikes off. An angry division opened between the T.U.C. and the Government.

By the late summer of 1924 the Liberals were becoming increasingly impatient with their leaders for continuing their support of the Government. Lloyd George's opposition to the Anglo-Russian Treaties forced Asquith's hand, and it was evident that the Government would be defeated on this issue when Parliament reassembled in the autumn. But before then, the Government sealed its own doom. A prosecution was initiated against the Communist J. R. Campbell for publishing a 'Don't Shoot' appeal to soldiers in *The Workers' Weekly*. Urged by back-benchers, and with MacDonald's approval, the case was dropped by the politically inexperienced Attorney-General, Sir Patrick Hastings. At once the Conservatives alleged improper interference in the course of justice, and received substantial Liberal support. A Vote of Censure was tabled at the end of September. Asquith proposed a characteristic compromise, whereby the matter would be considered by a Select Committee. This was rejected by the Government, which was defeated by 364 to 191. Parliament was dissolved.

Behind the Campbell case there lay the same prejudices and apprehensions that had greeted the Russian Treaties. Were there, in fact, mysterious and sinister forces at work behind the apparently moderate façade of the Labour Government? Such fears were sedulously fostered by the Conservatives, and appeared to have had some justification when, shortly before polling day, a letter from Zinoviev giving instructions to the British Communists was made public by the Foreign Office. The matter was handled clumsily by MacDonald, with the result that the Conservatives were able to allege that the Prime Minister was incompetent as well as being implicated in the great Bolshevist Conspiracy.

In fact, as we now know, and many suspected at the time, the Zinoviev Letter was a forgery. The Conservative Central Office had been partly responsible for its publication. Although it is doubtful if it had much effect on the eventual result, it did give a very neat clincher to the Conservative allegations concerning the Peace Treaties and the Campbell Case. It seemed to give strong emphasis to the dire and alarming warnings of Churchill that Labour was indeed 'driven forward by obscure, sinister, and in part extraneous forces'. It was a squalid episode.

But the Zinoviev Letter was a misfortune for Labour for another reason, as it provided it with a magnificent excuse for failure and defeat. The inadequacies that had been exposed in the Government in its brief existence could be ignored and forgotten by the movement. All could be blamed on misrepresentation by the Opposition, the hostility of the capitalist Press, and the unscrupulous use made of the 'Red Scare'. Thus, when Labour returned to office in 1929, it proceeded to repeat its more grievous errors of 1924 with fervent exactitude.

But the election was far from being a disaster for Labour. It lost sixty-four seats and gained twenty-four, and was still ten seats better off (151) than in 1922; largely as a result of running more candidates, it put up its national vote by a million. The real losers were, again, the Liberals. They lost a hundred seats, and among the fallen was Asquith, whose long career thus came to a sad close. He went to the Lords as Earl of Oxford and Asquith; he did not find the new atmosphere congenial: 'It is an impossible audience; as Lowe said fifty years ago, it is like "speaking by torchlight to corpses in a charnel-house",' he glumly recorded. In his last years he wrote a certain amount, without much distinction, and presided benignly over his brilliant and loud-speaking family, a genial and much-loved patriarchal figure. His last years were clouded by persistent financial difficulties, which were only partly alleviated by the commercial success of the irrepressible Margot's memoirs and articles. He died in 1928 and, in spite of several studies and two full-length biographies, remains an enigma.

But Asquith did not relinquish the Liberal leadership until 1926, and in the meanwhile the forty surviving Liberals in the Commons had only Lloyd George to lead and guide them there, a prospect that not all found heartening.

The Conservatives returned triumphantly with 419 Members. There was now no criticism to be heard of Baldwin. The nation settled down to five placid years of solid Conservative rule. Her first little Labour fling was over.

*

Understandably, Protection had been notably absent from the Conservative programme in the 1924 General Election. It would have to wait for 'clear evidence that on this matter public opinion is disposed to reconsider its judgement'. This, although it did not satisfy the more ardent Protectionists, went far to close the divisions in the Conservative ranks, removed the only common ground of unity in the Liberal leadership, and focused the issue on whether or not Labour was 'fit to govern'. To emphasise the remarkable contrast with 1923, Baldwin, in an unhappy hour for his Administration, offered the Chancellorship of the Exchequer to Churchill, now returned as 'Constitutionalist' Member for Epping, and ardent exponent of antisocialism.[1]

The other rebels returned to the Conservative fold. Horne was offered, but refused, the Ministry of Labour, and never held public office again. But Birkenhead became Secretary of State for India; Austen Chamberlain went to the Foreign Office; Balfour, in 1925, succeeded Curzon as Lord President on the latter's death. One by one the great pre-war and wartime political figures were disappearing. Bonar Law and Curzon were dead; Asquith was in retirement, Carson was a spent force, McKenna was out of politics, and, although it was not certain at the time, Lloyd George's star was definitely in the descendant. Milner died in 1925, Asquith in 1928, Rosebery—long

[1] Churchill had contested the Abbey Division of Westminster as an 'Independent and Anti-Socialist' candidate in March with strong but unofficial Conservative support, and had lost to the official Conservative candidate by only forty-three votes. In May he had spoken at a meeting organised by Sir Archibald Salvidge—now the dominating figure in Liverpool—and addressed a gathering of Scottish Unionists in Edinburgh presided over by Arthur Balfour. Although nominally a 'Constitutionalist' at Epping, his candidature was warmly supported by the local Conservative Association, and a year later he renewed his membership of the Carlton Club.

forgotten—in 1929, Balfour in 1930, and Birkenhead in 1931. Each had been out of office and responsibility for some time before their deaths, although Balfour had been by far the most durable.

Curzon has received more biographies and biographical studies than his colleagues and contemporaries could have expected. There is always something irresistibly attractive about early success and eventual near-triumph, but this cannot wholly explain Curzon's great subsequent fascination for biographers and historians. Behind his excessively deliberately impressive façade, Curzon was a passionate and sensitive man. He had a real scholar's approach, and was genuinely learned and a man of taste and discernment. He bore disappointment with public fortitude, and although he was mocked for his idiosyncrasies and airs, his capacities as a negotiator were formidable. As Churchill and others who had cause to resent him have emphasised, he was a difficult man to dislike for very long. His financial meanness was proverbial—and is well-attested—and he was inordinately vain. But he was also very generous with time, kindness, and attention to young people whom he wished to help, and many of the best stories about him either originated with him or were told by him cheerfully against himself. He had wit, style, intelligence, and a profound devotion to public duty. The more one examines his life and career, the less is one surprised by the interest and admiration which he subsequently aroused.

Curzon's decline and death made Baldwin's task much easier. The Conservative Party was at last formally reunited. And British politics could, after nearly a decade of violent fluctuations of fortunes, alliances, and allegiances, resume a coherent pattern. The Liberal Party had been the most spectacular casualty of this decade. In July 1914 it stood, 260-strong in the House of Commons, fortified in the country by a substantial and effective organisation. Now, it had forty Members of the House of Commons, and its once-formidable organisation was reduced to isolated and embittered fragments. Driven out of the cities by Labour, and out of the counties by the Conservatives, it found succour only in the Celtic fringes. The Labour Party, despite its first somewhat hapless experience of office, viewed the future with a new confidence and spirit.

We may conclude this account of the events of October 1922–November 1924 with some comments made by Churchill in a newspaper article on October 5th, 1924:

When the Coalition Government was destroyed at the Carlton Club only two years ago, it was perfectly clear to many of us that a period of political chaos would ensue. To the best of my ability, I warned the public of what was in store. But nobody would listen. Everyone was delighted to get back to party politics. Dear to the hearts of all the small politicians were the party flags, the party platforms, the party catchwords. How gleefully they clapped their hands and sang aloud for joy that the good old pre-war days of faction had returned!

They have had their wish. We have had two years of insensate faction.

*

The Baldwin Government of 1924–9 operated in the context of continuing decline and hardship in the old industries—particularly in the North of England—and mounting prosperity elsewhere. The historian viewing the 1920s is struck by the sharpness of the contrasts —the misery in the mining towns, for example, and the glittering revival of London Society, the utterly different worlds of Aneurin Bevan and Michael Arlen, of James Maxton and Lady Cunard, George Orwell and Dornford Yates. Unemployment never fell below one million, yet by 1927 there were nearly two million motor vehicles, and the era of the private car, mass-produced and relatively cheap, had arrived. Income tax was low, and was to be made even lower by the Baldwin Government; virtually all the wartime restrictions had gone; Europe at long last reposed in apparent tranquillity and peace. With the United States of America locked in its isolation, and passing through a period of confusion, introspection, wealth and hedonism under the distant supervision of a succession of nondescript and often corrupt leaders, and Stalin's Soviet Union occupied with its ferocious internal difficulties, the position of Britain and her Empire appeared stronger than ever. The Labour Government's controversial Russian Treaties were curtly abrogated; the Geneva Protocol dropped. The phenomena of Gandhi in India and Adolf Hitler in Germany seemed to have passed. The British viewed the policies of Mussolini in Italy with benignity. Europe, demonstrating its extraordinary resilience and strength, was recovering rapidly physically, politically, and economically. There was a freshness in the atmosphere, a resurgence of hope and of confidence, symbolised by the Treaty of Locarno, signed in London on December 1st, 1925, and regarded as Austen Chamberlain's greatest achievement.

Locarno was a non-aggression pact between France, Germany, and Belgium, guaranteed by Britain and Italy. It also ended military staff talks between Britain and France. It was a perfect example of politicians successfully stopping the last war, but at the time it was widely applauded, and not least because it seemed to remove Britain definitely from any close commitments in Europe, and particularly in Eastern Europe. To all outward signs, 'normalcy' had indeed been achieved. It was 'back to 1914' accomplished, and a 1914 with distinct improvements. There was no sense of the shortage of time, and certainly none that this was a transient gleam of sunlight in the darkness of the twentieth century.

But it was not sunlight for all. One per cent of the population of Britain still owned some two-thirds of the national wealth. Three-quarters of the people earned less than £100 a year. Rural and urban poverty remained stark and grim. Imports were higher than before the war, and exports never recovered their previous position. British agriculture endured another prolonged slump, until by 1931 only 5·67 per cent of the employed population worked on the land and land values had plummeted. The European economic recovery was not matched by the British. And, over all, hung the concentration of depression and unemployment among the pre-war industrial giants, coal and cotton, shipping and steel.

For many years it was fashionable to depict the General Strike of May 1926 as a catalytic event. Before it, it was asserted, Labour and employers were set on a collision course. The strike, this version runs, 'purged the poison' in industrial relations, which from then onwards were harmonious, reasonable, and sympathetic. 'Our old country can well be proud of itself', King George wrote when it was all over, 'as during the last nine days there has been a strike in which 4 million men have been affected; not a shot has been fired and no one killed; it shows what a wonderful people we are.' Foreign observers were astonished and impressed by what had *not* happened. And the strike entered a familiar realm—that of historical mythology. But in fact it was a clear reflection of a very serious social and economic situation.

The dominant feature of that situation was the persistent unemployment level of over one million. This experience was unique and unprecedented. There had been cyclical unemployment before the war, but nothing in memory comparable to what the Cambridge economist Pigou called 'the intractable million'. This unemployment tended to be explained by the dislocation of the international trading monetary systems caused by the war. By this reasoning, the only hope lay in the restoration of this system which involved currency stabilisation (by means of return to the Gold Standard) and the reduction of wartime tariffs. Free Trade remained the economic doctrine in firm possession of the field, and, as the General Election of December 1923 seemed to demonstrate, the belief of the people. Of the main political parties, only a minority of the Conservative Party was wedded to Protection. Labour, the Liberals, and a substantial element in the Conservative Party, were vehement advocates of Free Trade. Philip Snowden was a dedicated Free Trader; so was Churchill. These two men were at the Treasury from January 1925 until November 1931.

The politics of 1925–31 were to be the politics of unemployment, which dominated all other issues, but which defied the endeavours of the politicians, and notably those of the pre-1914 era. Early in his career, in 1902, Winston Churchill and his friends had entertained Joseph Chamberlain, then at the zenith of his fame, to dinner. As the young men present had just combined to embarrass the Government of which they were supporters and Chamberlain one of its principal members, the evening had begun uneasily. But the mood warmed, and at the end Chamberlain had repaid his hospitality by telling his hosts that 'Tariffs are the politics of the future'.[1] But in 1924 no politician of the first rank had grasped that unemployment was now the politics of the future, and that the kind of unemployment that now afflicted millions of people and darkened the lives of millions more was not susceptible to the machinery and attitudes of the past. A few younger men grasped this fact, but they were outcast and ignored voices. There was, accordingly, an air of marked and real irrelevancy about the speeches and actions of Government and Opposition alike during these vital years. They took the wealth of the nation for granted; they understood that there would be ebbs and flows in the process of economic expansion; they endeavoured to mitigate the unfortunate consequences of recessions; but their eyes were usually on more traditional and exciting concerns. It was not wholly without significance that the fiercest schism in the Conservative Party in the period was over Churchill's attempt to reduce the cruiser-building programme, nor that the finest debates in the House of Commons were

[1] Churchill: *My Early Life*, 385.

over the revised Book of Common Prayer. The political centre was drifting away from the true concerns of the people.

Normal unemployment, based on pre-war experience, was about four per cent. It was considered that the problem centred on the remaining six per cent—the 600,000 persons who formed the 'new unemployed'. Concentration of unemployment was in the north and in the Celtic fringe, where the ailing industrial giants of pre-war years were situated. Coal and cotton together accounted for about sixty per cent of the 'abnormal' unemployment. Together they employed 1,500,000 workers, and were the largest industries in the country. The textile and coal industries had formed fifty-five per cent of the total value of British exports in 1913; in 1913, cotton alone provided a quarter of this total value of exports, but exports fell by nearly half between 1912 and 1929. In 1913 Britain had exported 73 million tons of coal; by 1921 this had shrunk to 25 million, and although there was a recovery, the average figure in the 1920s was 50 millions. Accordingly, coal production fell by some 30 million tons a year comparing 1913 with 1929. The principal causes were the increase of coal exports by Germany in the 1920s, the loss of the Baltic markets to Poland, and the elimination of the valuable trade with Russia. The movement to oil, gas, and electricity at home was an additional, but not a crucial factor.

Cotton had been killed by competition. Britain's best market had been India; here, domestic production trebled between 1913 and 1929. By 1929 Japan—not a competitor at all in 1913—had captured nearly twenty per cent of the world market. Thus, in both coal and cotton the British were severely undercut in prices and at least equalled in quality.

The iron and steel industries were heavily dependent on the shipbuilding industry. Shipbuilding contracted sharply after the war. There was an immediate post-war shipping boom that had abruptly stopped before the end of 1921. The decline in exports aggravated what would have been in any case a serious situation. The war had resulted in a dramatic boom in iron and steel, the installation of new equipment, and the building of new factories. Much of this now stood idle. The production capacity of British steel was some 12 million tons; only twice in the 1920s did actual production exceed 9 million tons.

The solutions to these chronic problems were sought along two separate but not unconnected lines.

Free Trade was an integral and essential part of the gold standard system. But a return to the gold standard was regarded as essential for other reasons. The pre-war rate was seen as a crucial token of London's financial leadership, and it was believed that its restoration would re-establish its former primacy. In this attitude there was some realism. In the disordered condition of Europe in the early 1920s *some* estab-lished economic leadership was required, and Britain was considerably better equipped to undertake this than any other single nation. Prestige and confidence are crucial to success in international banking. There was accordingly much to be said for the arguments that were brought forward by the City and the Treasury and that were accepted by all Governments.

Furthermore, the messianic quality of Free Trade must never be under-estimated. The belief that Free Trade encouraged international co-operation and good feeling was deeply imbedded. The return to general Free Trade had much political content in it. A series of international conferences agreed that the elimination of trade barriers was highly desirable, if not actually essential, for international har-mony. But, of all the international trading nations, Britain was the only one that kept it in effect. Throughout the 1920s, as a result of the assistance given to the few safeguarded industries, there was a tariff level of some five per cent for foreign imports, which was negligible. At the same time, the tariff barriers abroad to British exports were steadily, if stealthily, rising. But at the same time as the restoration of the pre-war trading and monetary system was thus being eagerly sought, there was a general refusal to accept the permanence of the decline of the staple export industries. The cause of their decline, it was argued, was the high cost of their products. But the solution was sought not in better equipment and marketing but in the reduction of wages, and what was, after 1927, described as 'rationalisation' to re-duce production costs. The former became an article of faith, shared even by Baldwin, who said (July 30th, 1925) that 'All the workers of this country have got to take reductions in wages in order to help put industry on its feet'. The effects of this attitude were to precipitate the confrontation between the coal-owners and the miners that reached its culmination in May 1926.

It is to over-simplify the matter to state that Free Trade as practised in Britain in the 1920s implied *no* government control of the economy. What was important was *how* it attempted to do so.

The function of the Treasury was principally to regulate government expenditure. Monetary policy was the field of the Bank of England. Industrial policy was the responsibility of the Board of Trade and the Ministry of Labour, which were subordinate to the Treasury. 'Balancing the Budget' was a hallowed principle. In this, as in other fields, the Government was expected to give the nation a lead. Every Chancellor was expected to provide for a surplus and to achieve it by taxation and reductions in government expenditure. As it was generally agreed that taxation—particularly direct taxation—was too high at even five shillings in the pound—and which Churchill reduced to four shillings—this meant that the real 'balancing' was to be achieved by the latter. It was also regarded as essential that the Budget contained interest payments on the national debt, for moral rather than for practical purposes. Thus, every Budget in the 1920s contained a provision for about £60 millions which went on the 'debit' side automatically, and had to be met from the static 'credit' side.

With these attitudes and this machinery, and having turned its back upon Protection, and with a dramatic but thinly informed Free Trade Chancellor of the Exchequer, the Baldwin Government had little to offer towards the restoration of the old exporting industries. It is fair to add that Labour had little to offer, either. If Churchill was an hereditary Free Trader, Snowden was a fanatical one.

Baldwin's personal obsession was with industrial peace, haunted by the potentialities of employer–employee antagonism. 'There is only one thing which I feel is worth giving one's strength to', he said on January 1st, 1925, 'and that is the binding together of all classes of our people in an effort to make life in this country better in every sense of the word. That is the main end and object of my life in politics.' In a party in which there were strong elements on the front and back benches burning for a confrontation with the unions, Baldwin's voice was one of sanity and compassion. On March 6th, 1925 he destroyed a back-bench Bill to abolish the political levy, the Labour Party's principal source of income, with a speech in his own distinctive style, rambling, sincere, modest, and yet compelling. He ended with the words 'Give peace in our time, O Lord', and the Bill was dead. But it was only a temporary victory.

Neville Chamberlain proved a progressive and reasonably imaginative social reformer at the Ministry of Health. The implications of Birkenhead's reactionary views on India were not yet fully evident.

Only Joynson-Hicks, at the Home Office, was an obviously unfortunate appointment. It was, in Churchill's words, 'a sedate, capable, government'. It gave financial incentives to exporters; it relieved industry of three-quarters of local rating assessments; it financed public works on a modest scale; it restored the McKenna Duties ; it provided unemployment relief for an indefinite period by abandoning the insurance principle; it introduced contributory old-age pensions; it put into practice—on Churchill's urgings—the principle that the Defence estimates should be based on the assumption that no war with a major power would break out within ten years; it established, in the British Broadcasting Corporation and in the Central Electricity Board, the machinery for national corporations that was later to be used as precedents by their opponents; it lowered the voting age for women from thirty to twenty-one, and gave them the same residence qualification as for men. But it could not, and did not, resolve the fundamental problems.

The first serious blunders occurred in Churchill's first Budget in 1925, when he imposed new taxes on artificial silk at a time when the textile industry was seriously turning to the development and production of man-made fibres, and when he announced the return of Britain to the Gold Standard at the pre-war parity of $4.86. It was the last decision that was the major error. Churchill had not taken it lightly, but he was seriously out of his depth in this field. 'We are often told,' he said in introducing the Gold Standard Bill, 'that the gold standard will shackle us to the United States . . . I will tell you what it will shackle us to. It will shackle us to reality. For good or ill, it will shackle us to reality.' At the time, the decision was enthusiastically applauded, particularly as a further indication that 'normalcy' was returning. But Keynes spelt out in a series of articles in the *Evening Standard*—subsequently published as *The Economic Consequences of Mr. Churchill*—some of the implications:

> The whole object is to link *rigidly* the City and Wall Street . . . The movement of gold or of short credits either way between London and New York, which is only a ripple for them, will be an Atlantic roller for us.

The principal consequences may be swiftly categorised:
The primacy of the Bank of England over monetary policy was restored. The Bank saw its relationship with the Government as that

of 'the ordinary duties of banker to client', and the supremacy of the Treasury over the Bank, which had seemed to be established in 1917 when Bonar Law had secured the resignation of Lord Cunliffe, was lost. This might not have been so serious were it not for the fact that the Bank of England was inadequately equipped to meet its responsibilities.

The fact that the pound was over-valued in relation to other currencies reduced the value of British exports.

The consequent necessity to build up reserves to support the new value of the pound removed sums that could—and should—have been used to assist industry.

The British economy was henceforth linked to a world-system which the British did not dominate. The conditions of 1925 had no relevance to those of 1914. A large proportion of British assets had been sold to pay for the war, and exports could no longer produce the surplus necessary to finance and buttress her position.

Above all, the decision was symbolic of the fact that neither the Government nor its principal advisers had grasped the enormity of the new problems facing the British economy and British industry. It was a step backwards into a dream-world in which Britannia ruled the waves and the pound sterling commanded awe and respect throughout the world. The reasons *why* the pound sterling had commanded this respect were inadequately appreciated.

It is relevant to look at what was written in warning and in retrospect by Hubert Henderson, perhaps the wisest of contemporary economists, and certainly among the most percipient. On April 4th he wrote warningly:

> We make bold to say that a return to gold this year cannot be achieved without terrible risk of renewed trade depression and serious aggravation of unemployment.

And, on May 9th:

> In short, it was Mr. Churchill's duty, if he decided to take the plunge back to gold, to insist that expensive social measures must be ruled out meantime. Nor is that all. Relief to the income-tax payer should no less have been ruled out. The sacrifices of the return to gold fall entirely upon business and do not touch the salaried man. Mr. Churchill should accordingly have used his

Budget surplus . . . exclusively to help industry through the transition . . .

We are driven to the conclusion that Mr. Churchill's great but peculiar abilities are not well suited to the realms of finance. . . . It is with regret that we are disposed to write him down as one of the worst Chancellors of the Exchequer of modern times.

Perhaps most important of all was the point made by Keynes:

He [Churchill] was just asking for trouble. For he was committing himself to force down money-wages and all money values, without any idea how it was done . . . [the result] must be war, until those who are economically weakest are beaten to the ground.

*

The resultant confrontation, long developing, was immediate.

Churchill's Budget had not only been massively irrelevant to the general economic problem, it had actually been harmful to industry, and particularly to the textile and coal industries. For the latter, 1925 was the worst year on record and the return to $4.86 substantially increased the cost of British exported coal. With the recovery of the Ruhr coalfields, this additional burden—estimated by some as an increase in cost of two and a half per cent, by others as high as ten per cent—was catastrophic. The owners proposed to meet it by the classic methods of revoking the existing wage and working condition agreements, reducing wages, and increasing the working day. But the miners had had enough, and were backed strongly by the General Council of the T.U.C. in their 'resistance to the degradation of the standard of life of their members'. There was strong workers' solidarity with the miners, and by July the situation had become critical. Baldwin's proposal for a subsidy to the industry was strongly opposed by the bulk of his colleagues, but, confronted by the real possibility of a General Strike, the Government agreed to an interim subsidy for a period during which a Royal Commission would examine the industry. This had Churchill's support, albeit with reluctance at any surrender to the Unions—a reluctance not diminished by the statement of the miners' leader, A. J. Cook, that 'we have already beaten not only the employers but the strongest government in modern times'. Herbert Samuel was made chairman, and nine months' peace had been purchased. The satisfaction of the unions at the Government's apparent climb-down stirred angry mutterings on the Conservative benches and in the Cabinet, which were not appeased by the prosecution in October of twelve members of the Communist Party.[1] Certainly in the Cabinet the view was beginning to prevail that a confrontation with the T.U.C. was inevitable, and that it should come soon, on ground of the Government's own choosing. On the unions' side, the approach was less clear. The Government perfected its plans for a national emergency; the unions did nothing in particular.

It was clear to observers—and also to Baldwin—that there was a considerable gulf in attitudes between the Prime Minister and a substantial element in the Conservative Party towards the crisis. Duff Cooper and Harold Macmillan were not the only progressive younger Conservatives who sat for industrial constituencies—Oldham and Stockton-on-Tees respectively—and who were shocked not only by the condition of their constituents but by the indifference of a considerable number of their colleagues towards these conditions. Baldwin's 'hard-faced men' and what the progressives called 'the industrials' were active, influential, and vocal in the party, and constituted one of Baldwin's principal difficulties. They despised his moderation, and were fearful of the menace of Socialism which Baldwin rightly regarded with relaxed indifference. Thus, as Baldwin greatly increased his reputation with the Opposition, his authority within his own party was constantly imperilled. It was to this audience that Joynson-Hicks, Churchill, Birkenhead, and even Neville Chamberlain, with his rasping contempt for the Labour Party, constantly played. Baldwin believed strongly that vital constitutional principles were involved in the threat of a General Strike, but his own instincts for conciliation were affected by the need to retain his party's support. The clash between these instincts and the political reality explain his actions in 1926 and 1927.

The Samuel Commission reported on March 11th, 1926. Parts of its proposals were positive, but the key recommendation was for the immediate reduction of wages. The owners were unimpressed by the positive proposals, the miners were incensed at the endorsement of the owners' principal demand. Cook urged 'not a penny off the pay, not

---

[1] All were convicted under the Incitement to Mutiny Act, 1797, and given moderate prison sentences, a fortunately very rare example in modern times of a purely political trial in Britain.

a minute on the day', and was obdurate to all proposals that did not meet this central criterion. Birkenhead's celebrated remark that he thought the miners' leaders the most stupid men he had ever met until he met the owners seems ill-merited. Negotiations continued throughout April, with little movement on either side. The agreement expired at the end of the month, and on May 1st the owners resorted to another classic tactic, the lock-out.

On the same day a special union conference placed authority in the general council of the T.U.C. and approved the proposal for a General Strike on May 3rd. The Government and the T.U.C. stumbled into confrontation. There were two days of confused negotiations and discussions, eventually broken off by the Government late on May 2nd when the Cabinet learned that the machine-men of the *Daily Mail* —acting entirely independently—had refused to print the Monday edition unless a fiery leading article by the editor, Thomas Marlowe, was amended. There is still considerable doubt whether this provocation was or was not deliberate. Certainly Marlowe hastened to inform the Cabinet. There is no doubt that it was welcomed by a majority of the Cabinet as a *casus belli*. Their plans—carefully matured by the permanent under-secretary of the Home Office, Sir John Anderson, and J. C. C. Davidson—were ready, and a State of Emergency had already been proclaimed. Baldwin, although deeply depressed, really had no choice but to break off negotiations. In the previous August, in defending the interim subsidy, he had given a strong warning to any who intended to have 'a deliberate and avowed policy to force a stoppage of this kind on the country', and his authority could hardly have survived another apparent climb-down. He was, like the T.U.C., caught irrevocably by events. The T.U.C., also trapped in a false position and unsure of its course, had to press on. The General Strike began at midnight on May 3rd.

Both sides surprised themselves and each other. The strike was virtually total, an unpleasant shock for the Government; the Government's emergency plans, and the flood of eager volunteers to work them, were a considerable surprise to the unions. Baldwin was calm and moderate, as were most of the union leaders. Churchill was given the relatively harmless job of editing a government newspaper, the *British Gazette*, which he did with characteristic élan. It was an inflammatory, one-sided, and provocative propaganda broadsheet, which aroused a considerable degree of resentment, and not least in its insistent demands for 'unconditional surrender'. The counter-attack took the form of the *British Worker*, which never attained the *Gazette*'s circulation nor could match its frenzied style.

More serious was Churchill's attempt to commandeer the B.B.C., which its managing director, John Reith, successfully repelled with the support of Davidson and Baldwin. But a price had to be paid. The B.B.C., behind an impressive façade of impartiality, was in fact strongly supportive of the Government, and its influence was far greater than that of the *British Gazette*. Its most notorious action was to refuse permission to the Archbishop of Canterbury to broadcast an appeal for a settlement drawn up by leaders of the Church and the Nonconformists on May 7th; it was eventually broadcast, in amended form, on May 11th. But it was also, like Baldwin and unlike Churchill, in favour of a negotiated settlement. On May 12th the T.U.C. gladly accepted a compromise formula proposed by Samuel and called off the strike. By this stage the mood had grown ugly, and there was general agreement by contemporary observers that it was as well that the strike ended when it did. Certainly, Churchill did not emerge with an enhanced reputation. 'Throughout the 1930s', as George Isaacs has written, 'suspicion of Churchill was one factor in preventing any attempt by the trade unions to make a closer alliance with him in opposition to the foreign policy of the Baldwin and Chamberlain governments.' A reading of the issues of the *British Gazette* gives part of the answer.

The announcement of the end of the strike had shocked the majority of the strikers, exhilarated by their solidarity, and they determined to fight on. When some employers tried to capitalise on the Government's victory, the strike was in effect resumed voluntarily until Baldwin categorically denounced the owners' tactics. But the memories of this attempt by some employers to cut wages and impose humiliating conditions for accepting men back were to prove very enduring.

The abandoned miners maintained their stand, and the owners were relentless. Baldwin and Churchill—who followed his characteristic principle of 'in victory, magnanimity'—could not persuade the latter otherwise, and eventually the miners had to capitulate unconditionally. As Amery has written, they 'struggled back to the pits on the owners' terms, including longer hours, a beaten and resentful army'. But they had not fought entirely in vain. The crude tactic of the general strike was never to be repeated, and its failure gave strength to those union leaders, notably Ernest Bevin and Walter Citrine, who had always believed in compromise, and it seriously damaged the wilder union leaders. But the solidarity of the workers had made a deep impression upon many sensible employers. With Government support, Sir Alfred Mond, the head of Imperial Chemicals, initiated employer–union discussions which achieved little of immediate practical value, but which were highly significant of the new mood.

Unhappily, this did not include the politicians. The die-hard Conservatives were determined to capitalise on their success, and carried Baldwin reluctantly with them. The Trade Disputes and Trade Union Act of 1927 deliberately set the clock back twenty years, although not quite to the Taff Vale Judgement.[1] Sympathetic strikes, or any strike designed to coerce the Government, were made illegal, and union members who wished to pay the political levy now had to 'contract in' rather than 'contract out', thereby jeopardising a substantial part of the income of the Labour Party. It was a mean and useless act of vengeance that only temporarily affected the Labour Party income and created a lasting and justifiable resentment. Given the overwhelming feeling in his party and in the Cabinet, Baldwin had little choice but to acquiesce. It won him no further friends in the Conservative ranks, but it was a remarkable tribute to the estimate that his opponents had formed of him that the respect and trust he had created in the Labour Party were not seriously affected.

It was a persistent criticism of Baldwin at the time—and subsequently—that he did not 'lead' his Government, that he waited upon events, was vacillating, and was usually unsure of his course. These strictures had justice in them, but in retrospect they enhance, rather than diminish, his character and intelligence. His principal mistakes had been to bring back Birkenhead, Churchill, and Joynson-Hicks, and particularly to the posts he offered them, but he had had little choice if he was to re-unite the Conservative Party after the schism of 1922–3. He held together his Cabinet effectively for five years, and during that period did much to reduce the venom in industrial relations that had built up so ominously since the war. Baldwin did not have the answer to unemployment, but at least he understood what it meant. Although not a political innocent, and quite capable of swift, severe, and effective action in the lower levels

[1] See Volume I, pp. 212 and 231.

of public life, he had a humanity and basic moral standards that were far higher than those of Lloyd George or many men then active in politics. He was a refreshing personality, and it is probably more to Baldwin than to any other British politician that the nation owed the fact that it faced the terrible crisis of 1939–40 united. But for this imperishable achievement he was to receive little gratitude, particularly in the Conservative Party.

*

Regarded in retrospect, the years 1924–9 represented a lull in the international anarchy that had been rampant since 1914 and which was to be resumed in the 1930s, and through which we have been living ever since. The Treaty of Locarno was described by Austen Chamberlain as 'the real dividing line between the years of war and the years of peace', and such it appeared to be. In 1926 Germany joined the League, and in the same year the Preparatory Commission of the League on Disarmament was established. The international renunciation of war by the signatories of the Kellogg Pact in 1928 seemed another important step forward. The problem of reparations seemed to have been definitely settled by the Young Plan in May 1930. The Allied troops left the Rhineland. In Russia Zinoviev and his associates were removed in 1927–8, and the strident propagandist interference of the Third International was replaced by belated attention to the lamentable circumstances of the internal affairs of the Soviet Union; the presence of a Soviet representative on the Disarmament Commission from 1927 was seen as a hopeful portent.

In reality, nothing much had changed, despite a greatly improved atmosphere. But, after the inter-European relations of 1906–25, anything would have seemed an improvement. Europe remained the dominant centre of the world, on which all attention was fixed and whose actions directly affected virtually every part of the world. International affairs were still conducted wholly on a national or at best a regional basis. The pre-1914 system of local alliances had not disappeared. The smaller new nations were still subservient to the big ones. The tendency towards autocratic government throughout the world was sharply apparent, and was seen particularly in Russia, Italy, Spain, Portugal and Greece. The triumph of democracy, so freely forecast at the end of the war, had failed to materialise.

This was not how the British saw the situation at the time. The condition of Europe was enormously better in 1929 than it had been even five years before. An incident here and there might rattle the tiles, but such breezes quickly faded away. The calm warmth of peace, prosperity, and optimism glowed throughout Europe. The scars of the war had healed. The nightmare was over.

Yet, for those who wished to see them, there were some ominous signs. Mussolini, addressing a large audience at Florence, on May 17th, 1930, struck what was to become the dominant theme of the 1930s:

> Words are a very fine thing; but rifles, machine-guns, warships, aeroplanes and cannon are still finer things. They are finer, Blackshirts, because right unaccompanied by might is an empty word. . . . Fascist Italy, powerfully armed, will offer two simple alternatives: a precious friendship or an adamantine hostility.

And, in an article in the *Saturday Evening Post* in February 1930, Churchill pointed to the necessity to form a 'United States of Europe', and wrote:

> The Treaty of Versailles represents the apotheosis of nationalism. . . . The empire of the Habsburgs has vanished. That immense, unwieldy, uneasy but nevertheless coherent entity has been Balkanized. Poland has escaped from her eighteenth century dungeon, bristling with her wrongs and dazzled by the light. The whole zone of Middle Europe, from the Baltic to the Aegean, is split into small states vaunting their independence, glorying in their new-found liberty, acutely self-conscious and exalting their particularisms. They must wall themselves in. They must have armies. They must have foundries and factories to equip them. They must have national industries to make themselves self-contained and self-supporting. They must revive old half-forgotten national languages just to show how different they are from the fellows across the frontier. No more discipline of great empires: each for himself and a curse for the rest. What a time of jubilee!

It was perhaps not without significance that 1929 saw the publication in Britain of several outstanding anti-war books, of which the most popular were Robert Graves's *Good-Bye To All That*, Edmund Blunden's *Undertones of War*, and Siegfried Sassoon's *Memoirs*. R. C. Sherriff's play *Journey's End* was also firmly in the spirit of revulsion against the Great War that was now so apparent.

One other development of the 1920s must be recorded. At the Imperial Conference of 1926 a report of a committee presided over by Balfour was accepted. For the first time an attempt was made to define the relationship of the members of the Empire. Britain and the Dominions, the vital sentences ran, were 'autonomous Communities within the British Empire, equal in status . . . united by a common allegiance to the Crown, and freely associated as members of the British Commonwealth of Nations'. This definition was formally ratified in the Statute of Westminster in 1931. The formula was in reality merely a statement of the existing situation and the relationship between the 'old' Dominions. Virtually no consideration was given to the implications for the future; significantly, the Report stated (paragraph III) that:

> It will be noted that in the previous paragraphs we have made no mention of India. Our reason for limiting their scope to Great Britain and the Dominions is that the position of India in the Empire is already defined by the Government of India Act, 1919 . . .

This bland assumption was to be swiftly challenged.

*

By 1928 it was apparent that the Baldwin Government was losing ground. It had had its achievements, but it seemed dull, uninspired, and was clearly unable to solve the intractable problem of unemployment. As John Boyd Orr wrote in 1927:

> A ruling class living on dividends, masses of the people on the dole, and a Government trying to maintain an uneasy status quo, is a picture which fills thinking people with despair.

It was particularly in economic and industrial matters that the Government's performance was regarded, with good cause, as pedestrian and incomprehending. Churchill's last three Budgets were characterised by ingenious but unsatisfying expedients to provide a technical surplus; it was only too clear that there was a complete absence of strategic and serious economic thinking at the level that the Liberals were now advocating, which John Strachey and Sir Oswald Mosley were proselytising, and which some Conservative back-benchers—notably Robert Boothby, Harold Macmillan and Oliver Stanley—were urging. Churchill robustly dismissed Keynes's proposals as 'camouflaged inflation', entranced the Commons with his brilliant speeches, and proceeded on his temporising way.

Keynes declared that his principal objective was 'the transition from economic anarchy to a regime which deliberately aims at controlling and directing economic forces in the interests of social justice and social stability', and the adamant rejection of such attitudes disturbed many Conservatives. As Amery subsequently wrote:

> The combination of deflation and free imports which he [Churchill] stubbornly maintained bore its immediate fruit in wage reductions, long-drawn industrial conflict and continuous heavy unemployment; its long-term results in the conviction of the working classes that Socialism alone could provide a remedy for unemployment.

But could Labour provide this remedy? This was certainly the impression that it confidently gave. But closer inspection revealed that Labour thinking on the subject had not advanced at all since 1924, and that the differences between Labour and Conservative attitudes and policies were minimal.

For years Labour speakers had convinced themselves, and their audiences, that sufficient national wealth was available for assisting the unemployed, but by the middle of the 1920s they concluded that it was not. Snowden had a horror of inflation, and wrote in 1920 that 'Government borrowing in this country has reached a point which threatens national bankruptcy'. In 1924 he had pursued a rigid Treasury policy. In 1925 Labour abandoned the proposal of raising funds for unemployment assistance from direct taxation. In 1927 Snowden was warning that 'the microbe of inflation is always in the atmosphere', and he was undoubtedly, and unhappily, correct when he wrote in 1929 that 'there is a good deal more orthodoxy in Labour's financial policy than its critics appear to appreciate'. Echoing Snowden was William Graham, who in many respects was even more 'orthodox' than Snowden, and who was declaring in 1929 that 'Labour has no desire to increase expenditure, but to decrease it'. These were not merely election-year soothing noises. As events were to demonstrate, Snowden and Graham meant what they said.

The one really constructive Labour programme was put forward by Oswald Mosley, John Strachey, and Allen Young in 1925 in *Revolution By Reason*, which emphasised that:

At present Socialist thought appears to concentrate almost exclusively upon this transfer of present purchasing power by taxation, and neglects the necessity for creating additional demand to evoke our unused capacity which is at present not commanded either by the rich or the poor.

They recommended the nationalisation of the banks, planning by an Economic Council, subsidies to industry, and bulk purchasing of raw materials. Mosley also was prepared to abandon the Gold Standard and let the pound sterling fall to its true value. Such proposals were regarded with distaste and incomprehension by the party hierarchy, and Labour took office in 1929 still firmly committed to the vaguely defined attitudes of 1924.

The only other serious thinking on the subject came from the Liberals.

In 1925 the Liberal Industrial Enquiry had been initiated, in which politicians and economists collaborated at length and in detail, and in which the prominent intellects were those of Keynes, Hubert Henderson, Philip Kerr and Seebohm Rowntree. The first fruit was the first 'Yellow Book', published in February 1928, entitled *Britain's Industrial Future*, which advocated government planning and substantial investment in industry. It was the parent of the 'Orange Book' *We Can Conquer Unemployment*, issued in March 1929. Its central features were an emergency programme of public works—principally in roads and housing—and long-term planning. It caused a sensation, and may be regarded as the most brilliant and far-seeing programme put forward by any political party in Britain in this century.

It was at once subjected to vehement counter-attack and distortion by both main parties. On this at least they were united. The Government issued a reply which described the Liberal proposals as irresponsible and impracticable, and which would require a dictatorship to operate. Keynes retorted with justification that 'Mr. Baldwin had invented the formidable argument . . . that you must not do anything because it will mean that you will not be able to do anything else'.

The Conservatives, after deriding the Liberal programme as being unsound and impracticable, then dwelt heavily upon their own record since 1924. The De-Rating of Industry Act had relieved industry of some £27 million, which could be used for investment. There had been a record of steady development in the public services which would be continued, though a Conservative Government would not follow 'hasty and ill-considered schemes which could only lead to wasteful and unfruitful expenditure'. The 1925 Pensions Act had been of substantial benefit; 930,000 houses had been built since 1925; infant mortality had been reduced from 75 to 65 per 1,000 births, and much more besides. It was a familiar Conservative refrain—'Safety First', 'You never had it so good', 'Don't let Labour ruin it'.

Labour produced a reply of sorts to the Liberal programme, written by G. D. H. Cole, which was singularly unimpressive, and contained not a single original thought or proposal. The Liberals' scheme was assailed for its 'irresponsibility', and vague references were made to Labour's 'more diversified plans'. What were they? In MacDonald's account at the Albert Hall on April 29th, 1929, they consisted of the following:

> Roads will be built as a system, bridges broken and reconstructed, railways reconditioned, drainage carried on, afforestation advanced, coasts protected, houses built, emigration dealt with, colonial economic expansion planned and carried out.

Thus the Conservatives went to the country in May 1929 with considerable confidence on the cry of 'Safety First'. The strategy misfired for several reasons, of which the principal one was that the fears of Labour, which had been whipped up so successfully in 1924, had virtually disappeared. The Liberals were much more formidable than they had been five years before. And the Conservatives, running on their record, had little positive to offer. The aftermath of the General Strike—particularly the Trade Disputes Act and the breaking-off of diplomatic relations with the Soviet Union on the flimsiest of pretexts in 1927—had hurt it in the traditional Tory working-class electorate, and undid much of the good done by Baldwin's common sense and reason. A party political broadcast by Churchill set the tone:

> We have to march forward steadily and steadfastly, along the highway. It may be dusty, it may be stony, it may be dull; it is certainly uphill all the way, but to leave it is only to flounder in the quagmires of delusion and have the coat torn off your back by the brambles of waste.

The election contained two innovations—broadcasts by the party leaders, of which Baldwin was the most impressive and Lloyd George the least—and the use by the Conservatives of mobile cinemas, which were particularly effective in remote rural areas.

The results were inconclusive for Labour and Conservatives, but a bitter disappointment to the Liberals. In this, the distrust of Lloyd George may have been the major factor; the strength of the Labour and Conservative organisations was certainly another; but perhaps the most important element was the fact that the Liberal programme was too revolutionary in the context of 1929. Nevertheless, the Liberal performance was not unimpressive. They put up 512 candidates and secured 5·31 million votes. It was in terms of seats won that the acute disappointment lay. Labour, with 8·4 million votes, won 287 seats; the Conservatives, with 8·6 million, won 261; the Liberals, with their 5·31 million, won only 59. The election had at least been a decisive vote of no confidence in the Baldwin Government. 13·7 million votes cannot be lightly disregarded. But it had been wholly indecisive about the alternative.

Another remarkable—and historic—statistic about this election should be emphasised. The total registered electorate was now nearly 29 million, an increase of 7½ million since 1918—and those figures had then included Southern Ireland. Even more remarkable was the fact that the number of women electors (15,196,000) exceeded that of male voters by some 1½ million. It may be recalled that the total electorate, including Southern Ireland, had been 7,267,000 in the 1906 General Election. This comprised some 27 per cent of adults over 21, and only 58 per cent of male adults. The 1918 electorate had been 78 per cent of all adults. By 1929 virtually the entire adult population was entitled to the vote. What Churchill lamented as 'the age of mass effects' had arrived.

Baldwin did not meet Parliament as he had in 1924, and promptly resigned. MacDonald formed his second Administration.

MacDonald's leadership had come under serious criticism after the 1924 defeat, and there had been talk of replacing him by Henderson, which Henderson himself had effectively quenched. But the uneasiness remained, and was not assuaged by the revelation that MacDonald had accepted the gift of a Daimler car from a Scottish biscuit manufacturer (who had received a baronetcy) while he had been Prime Minister, nor by his fierce counter-attacks to criticisms levelled against him by the I.L.P. Those who viewed him closely increasingly doubted his commitment to socialism, and were alarmed by his enjoyment of

London society. 'Ramsay MacDonald,' Beatrice Webb sharply noted, 'is a magnificent substitute for a leader. He has the ideal appearance. . . . But he is shoddy in character and intellect.' But there was no serious move to challenge his leadership in the Parliamentary Labour Party, and although many of his colleagues—notably Snowden—had their views on his capabilities, they judged that any attempt to change the leadership would be doomed to failure. But this did not mean that they accepted the high estimates of his leadership that were widely held in the Labour movement.

The *Annual Register* for 1929 comments:

> The fall of the Baldwin Ministry, while hailed with exultation by the progressive parties, was not deeply regretted by the bulk of its own supporters, who found much to criticise in its leading personages. Mr. Baldwin had been more amiable than forcible, and had shown himself too much inclined to wait on events instead of trying to direct them. Mr. Churchill had proved himself the most able debater in the party, if not in the House, but as a financier his success had been questionable; he had not fulfilled his promises of reducing expenditure, and he left to his successor a formidable task in the financing of the de-rating scheme.

Thus, not greatly mourned, Mr. Baldwin's Ministers gathered their political belongings and reluctantly moved from the balmy warmth of office into the cool shades of Opposition. 'We all parted very happily' Amery wrote in his diary, 'voting ourselves the best government there has ever been, and full of genuine affection for S.B.'

CHAPTER SIXTEEN

THE TURNING-POINT, 1929–1931

THE MORROW OF defeat in 1929 found the Conservative Party in an ugly and fractious mood. As in 1923, the bulk of the criticism fell upon Baldwin and his closest associates, particularly J. C. C. Davidson, the party chairman, and the author of 'Safety First'. The party was, as Austen Chamberlain noted, 'divided, disgruntled, and confused', and in an article in the *Saturday Review* in November, Harold Macmillan wrote:

> The Conservative Party has no clear policy on immediate problems; it has no clear goal towards which it feels itself to be striving. It has too many 'open questions' and too many closed minds.

Beaverbrook had been politically quiescent for some time. He had been absorbed by his rapidly expanding and highly successful newspaper empire, and had been downcast by variations in his own health and by the deaths of his mother and wife. Now he made a dramatic return with the 'crusade' of Empire Free Trade, which was in fact Tariff Reform and Imperial Preference jumbled up and clothed in a new guise. It was not a coherent programme, and perhaps it was simply because of this that it had such success. It became fashionable in the top Conservative circles to depict Beaverbrook as an evil, unscrupulous, calculating megalomaniac of limitless ambition. He certainly had many faults, but these were hardly to be numbered among them. Beaverbrook had beliefs, and he loved crusades. Above all, his greatest joy lay in stirring things up, a characteristic that deeply shocked respectable public men—particularly when they were on the receiving end of Beaverbrook's disfavour or mockery. He was a marvellous raconteur and mimic; he was also a superb journalist and public speaker and, when in the mood, wonderful fun. His political judgement veered from the wrong to the execrable, and his devotion to his friends and relentless hostility to his foes belied the label of 'calculating'. He was warm, opinionated, often intolerable, always brash, yet to the end possessed of a magnetism and vitality that made all others seem bleak and dreary. Empire Free Trade was much more of an imposture than Tory Democracy had been, but when Beaverbrook hurled himself into a crusade things were likely to happen.

In July 1929 the first happening occurred. At a by-election at Twickenham, the Conservative candidate announced his conversion to the new creed; he was disowned by the Central Office, but several Conservative M.P.s announced their intention of speaking for him and did so. The Conservatives lost the seat; each faction ascribed the loss to the action, or inaction, of the other. This was an interesting beginning.

At least two ex-Ministers, Amery and Neville Chamberlain, were dedicated Protectionists, and several back-benchers—particularly the right-wingers who had grumbled against Baldwin since 1923—were sympathetic to Beaverbrook's crusade. Baldwin, who could scent trouble more quickly than most politicians, sought a *modus vivendi*, but by the end of the year no real progress had been made. The Rothermere and Beaverbrook newspapers were in full cry, and their cause gave a good excuse for critics of Baldwin to group themselves behind it. The 'crusade' became a party—the United Empire Party. At a public dinner early in 1930 Rothermere proposed Beaverbrook as the new leader of the party, to which Beaverbrook replied by describing Rothermere as 'the greatest trustee of public opinion that we have ever seen in the history of journalism', and declaring that he would serve loyally under Baldwin 'subject of course to his adoption of the policy in which I so earnestly believe'. He went on to announce that Empire Free Trade candidates would be put up wherever necessary.

This challenge could not be lightly dismissed. Serious attempts were made to provide a formula that would placate Beaverbrook and not alarm the Free Traders in the party hierarchy. At one stage, at the beginning of March 1930, it seemed as though an arrangement had been reached. Beaverbrook seemed to be soothed, and Rothermere was angered by Beaverbrook's apparent betrayal. To the dismay of the Conservative leaders this rift proved to be brief. Early in April Beaverbrook charged that the Conservative leaders had broken their side of the bargain by nominating a candidate at a by-election at Nottingham who was opposed to Empire Free Trade. Beaverbrook virtually demanded that the candidate be disowned; Davidson refused. A few days later, basing his case on a Conservative party policy circular, Beaverbrook declared open war again against the leadership. He refused to appear on the same platform as Baldwin. At another by-election, at East Fulham, a Conservative with Beaverbrook–Rothermere support won a Labour seat, which was hailed by the *Mail* and *Express* as evidence of the strength of the cause of Empire Free Trade. By now, the United Empire Party had a membership of 170,000.

The Conservative Party was becoming extremely nervous at these uncomfortable developments. An immediate scapegoat was Davidson, who resigned in June under fire, and was replaced by Neville Chamberlain.[1] But the assaults on Baldwin, far from abating, drew new encouragement. As one commentator noted:

> The Conservative revolt against Mr. Baldwin's leadership is gaining strength, and preparations are being considered for definite open actions. The resignation of Mr. Davidson from the Chairmanship of the party organization has stimulated the movement . . . it is hailed by the anti-Baldwin faction as a success in the campaign against Mr. Baldwin himself.

Baldwin was twice compelled in the summer and autumn to summon party meetings to pass motions of confidence in himself (in October he won by 462 to 116)—a sure sign of declining authority. By the end of the year it seemed certain that his tenure of the leadership could not be prolonged much further.

But the disruptive activities of the Press barons, and the considerable success of Empire Free Trade, did not constitute the only strains within the Conservative Party.

As has been related, the steps towards Indian self-determination had been cautious. The Morley–Minto and Montagu–Chelmsford Reforms had improved Indian representation without affecting the reality of British supremacy. The fact that Britain was in India, and would remain there indefinitely, was subject to little active dispute in British politics, and particularly in the Conservative Party. Seeley's statement of 1883 that withdrawal 'would be the most inexcusable of

---

[1] Davidson's achievements had been many, but perhaps the most durable was the establishment of the Conservative Research Department, subsequently often— and wrongly—credited to Neville Chamberlain.

all conceivable crimes and might possibly cause the most stupendous of all conceivable calamities' represented the established view. Radical criticism of Empire had been assuaged by the gradual—and very gradual—movement towards self-government. Reform and the widening of Indian responsibilities was one thing; abandonment was quite another. As Morley had declared:

> There is a school of thought who say that we might wisely walk out of India and that the Indians could manage their own affairs better than we can. Anybody who pictures to himself the anarchy, the bloody chaos that would follow from any such deplorable step might shrink from that sinister decision.

The first step in the revival of Indian nationalism had been taken in reaction to Curzon's partition of Bengal in 1905. Nevertheless, India had been relatively quiescent until the end of the Great War. The Amritsar massacre in 1919, the anti-Turkish policies of the Lloyd George Government, and the general ferment of ideas aroused by the war all played their part. But there had been cause enough for dis-affection in the past. The factor that added a crucial new dimension to the situation was the personality of Mohandas Gandhi. In this frail, determined, saintly but politically highly acute man all the streams of Indian protest merged and met. 'An Englishman', he wrote, 'never respects you till you stand up to him. Then he begins to like you. He is afraid of nothing physical; but he is very mortally afraid of his own conscience if ever you appeal to it, and show him to be in the wrong.'

Gandhi's first campaign of non-violence had begun in August 1920, and developed into civil disobedience a year later. Ugly flames began to glow. Communal and race riots had totalled sixteen between 1900 and 1922; between 1923 and 1926 they rose to seventy-two.

On the British side, the key figure in the 1920s was Birkenhead. He accepted the principle of 'gradualness' only in the sense that 'rendered the final attainment so remote as to be incalculable'.[1] In a speech made in 1925 he said that 'I am not able, in any foreseeable future, to discern a moment when we may safely, either to ourselves or to India, abandon our trust'. In private he was even more explicit: 'To me it is frankly inconceivable', he wrote to the then Viceroy, Reading, in December 1924, 'that India will ever be fit for Dominion self-govern-ment.' Birkenhead knew nothing about India. His faculties were now

[1] Gopal: *The Viceroyalty of Lord Irwin*, 3.

in decline, and the defects of his personality were now becoming distressingly apparent.[1] He had not long to live, but in his relentless quest for money he was to sadly compromise his once glittering reputation, signing his name to books he had never read, and dictating bored and inaccurate reminiscences to a secretary after dinner. When he had his first serious haemorrhage he said to his brother, 'I'm done for, Fred'. In reality, he had been 'done for' many years before. After 1922, all was melancholy anticlimax. He died just before the vulture descended. He was bankrupt, and with nothing to leave save gleaming memories and the haunting sense of undefinable and irrevocable loss.

Birkenhead's two most important actions as Secretary for India were the establishment of the Simon Commission in 1926, required by the 1919 Act to review its workings and appointed by Birkenhead to forestall a possible Labour-nominated body and which was boycotted by the Indian political leaders, and the appointment of the Hon. Edward Wood (who was created Lord Irwin) as Viceroy. The majority of the Simon Commissioners—who included Clement Attlee—were as adamantly opposed to the idea of Dominion Status for India as was Birkenhead; for, as he wrote to Irwin, it meant 'the right to decide their own destinies'. This was, of course, the point.

To Birkenhead's surprise and dismay, Irwin proved to be a shrewd, sympathetic, and sensitive Viceroy. He pursued a humane, enlightened and realistic policy. The Independence for India League was founded in 1928, and plans were prepared for further campaigns of civil disobedience. Gandhi's dramatic Salt March to Dandi (March 1930) focused Indian and world attention on the movement. The demand for Dominion Status was being rapidly overtaken by the campaign for complete independence.

It was Irwin's outstanding quality that although he realised that law and order must be preserved, he recognised the eventual need to negotiate. When the Conservatives fell in June 1929 he had no difficulty in persuading Wedgwood Benn, the new Secretary of State, to call a conference attended by representatives from Britain, the Indian States, and British India. A public correspondence was carefully prepared, in which Simon would propose a conference and MacDonald would state the view of the Government that the granting of Dominion Status was inherent in the 1917 Declaration of the Montagu–Chelms-

---

[1] One episode was the provision to him of £10,000 out of Party funds as compensation for loss of earnings (Davidson, op. cit., 276–7).

ford proposals. But the Simon Commission objected to being involved in a correspondence about Dominion Status, and the two announcements—the conference and the interpretation of the 1917 Declaration —were published in the *Gazette of India* on October 31st. The so-called 'Irwin Declaration' came as a thunderbolt to the Conservative Party.

Birkenhead and Reading assailed the Declaration at once, vehemently supported by Churchill. Baldwin first approved it, and then, when he realised that the Simon Commission had not been involved and that the bulk of his party was opposed to it, back-pedalled. This was hardly impressive, but as the months passed it became increasingly clear that Baldwin's sympathies lay more with Irwin and the Labour Government than with their opponents in the Conservative Party. The Conservative reactions to the Irwin Declaration confirmed many in India in their suspicions of British good faith, and the good effects of the Declaration were quickly lost. The Congress Party turned once again to civil disobedience.

The lead was quickly taken by the fading Birkenhead, and by Churchill. After Birkenhead's final decline and death in 1931, Churchill was the dominant figure in the Tory rebellion. Churchill vigorously denounced the granting of Dominion Status, and urged that 'it is necessary without delay to marshal the sober and resolute forces of the British Empire and thus preserve the life and welfare of all the people of Hindustan'. This had been an ominous warning shot, but worse was to follow. The Government, with Baldwin's support, called the first Round Table Conference in 1930, which was boycotted by Congress. By the end of 1930 Churchill was the leading spokesman of the newly formed India Defence League, and his speeches were becoming increasingly frenetic. Gandhi-ism', he declared (December 12th, 1930), 'and all it stands for will, sooner or later, have to be grappled with and finally crushed.' He demanded that Congress be broken up and its leaders deported. On February 12th he alleged that 'every service that has been handed over to Indian administration has been a failure'. On February 23rd:

It is alarming and also nauseating to see Mr. Gandhi, a seditious Middle Temple lawyer, now posing as a fakir of a type well known in the East, striding half-naked up the steps of the Viceregal Palace, while he is still organizing and conducting a defiant campaign of civil disobedience, to parley on equal terms with the representative of the King-Emperor.

When, in January 1931, MacDonald called for further consultations with the Indian leaders, and the Congress leaders were released unconditionally from jail, Churchill came into open division with Baldwin on January 26th in the Commons. He violently attacked the Round Table Conference; in one of his best speeches, Baldwin made it plain that he supported the Government. Churchill resigned from the 'Parliamentary Business Committee' and left the front benches. He was not to return to them for eight years. On March 12th he and Baldwin clashed again, and again Baldwin more than held his ground in the debate, quoting from Churchill's celebrated speech on General Dyer a decade before, with devastating effect. Wedgwood Benn, the Secretary of State for India, followed Baldwin with the words 'After the historic speech to which we have just listened there is really, from the point of view of the Indian situation, nothing to add to this debate'. This was not Churchill's opinion.

India was the issue, but it was not the only factor in Churchill's departure. He himself has described his position:

> My idea was that the Conservative Opposition should strongly confront the Labour Government on all great Imperial and national issues, should identify itself with the majesty of Britain as under Lord Beaconsfield and Lord Salisbury, and should not hesitate to face controversy, even though that might not immediately evoke a response from the nation.[1]

He had made his dissatisfaction with Baldwin's unheroic attitudes evident immediately after the 1929 election, and following the Irwin Declaration in October he had written an article in the *Daily Mail* in which he described the granting of Dominion Status as 'a crime'. He became the leading spirit of the India Defence League, and drew a black picture of an India dominated by 'Brahmins who mouth and patter the principles of Western Liberalism and pose as philosophic and democratic politicians', in which 'the British will be no more to them than any other European nation, when the white people will be in India only upon sufferance, when debts and obligations of all kinds will be repudiated, and when an army of white janissaries,

---

[1] Churchill: *The Gathering Storm*, 32–3.

officered if necessary from Germany, will be hired to secure the armed ascendancy of the Hindu'. The dismissal by the Labour Government of the High Commissioner in Egypt, Lord Lloyd, had also incensed Churchill. 'The British lion', he informed a large audience in Liverpool, 'so fierce and valiant in bygone days, so dauntless and unconquerable through all the agony of Armageddon, can now be chased by rabbits from the fields and forests of his former glory. It is not that our strength is seriously impaired. We are suffering from a disease of the will. We are the victims of a nervous collapse'.

Not the least of the consequences of the Churchill–Baldwin dispute over India—which Duff Cooper described as 'the most unfortunate event that occurred between the two wars'—was that it alienated Churchill from the younger and liberal-minded Conservatives. For his principal supporters he was thrown back upon those elements in the Party whose knowledge of the subject was as limited as his, and who were impelled forward not only by reactionary ignorance about India but by their loathing of what they regarded as Baldwin's 'neo-Socialism'. It was bad company to keep, and most of it swiftly deserted Churchill after the India dispute was eventually resolved. But an even greater tragedy was that, by the extreme violence of his speeches, Churchill debased the coin of alarmism, with the result that when, from 1933 onwards, he was warning his fellow-countrymen of the real perils from Germany, they remembered his dire prognostications of doom if India received even a mild version of Dominion Status. They also remembered much else about this flamboyant, melodramatic, disturbing politician. Thus it was that he became, in Beaverbrook's words, 'a busted flush', a haunted, and sometimes desperate, impotent observer of the events of the next eight years.

But his campaign seriously embarrassed successive Governments in their attempts to find an agreed settlement. This campaign lasted from 1931 until 1935. In 1933 there was a well-planned attempt to destroy the Government's policy at three levels in the Conservative Party machinery. In February, an attempt to get the National Union to disavow the policy was only defeated by 189 to 316. In October, at the Annual Conference, the Government won by 737 to 344. In October 1934 it survived by only 17. Churchill led the attack with unmatched brilliance; it was melancholy that such oratory should have been so devoted. In February 1935, in a national broadcast, he declared that 'two million bread-winners in this country would be tramping the streets and queuing up at the Labour Exchanges', and warned that one-third of the population of Britain 'would have to go down, out, or under, if we ceased to be a great Empire'.

Thus, from 1929 to 1935, the Conservative leadership was exposed to constant harassment from the Right in its attempts to achieve a settlement in India. Indian nationalist opinion was outraged by descriptions of Gandhi as 'a half-naked fakir', and by the repeated statement that Indians were not in a condition even to have Dominion Status. And the Government itself, by being forced to make some concession to its critics, provided a form of Dominion Status that was infinitely less generous than that accorded to the 'white' Empire. All this gave an immense impetus to the total Indian Independence movement.

This lay in the future at the beginning of 1931. The language of the disputes within the party had got notably sharper throughout 1930. At the party meeting on June 24th, Baldwin had described the Press Lords as 'an insolent plutocracy', and read out a letter from Rothermere demanding consultation as to offices in a future Conservative Government. Beaverbrook retorted with spirit by calling on Conservatives to send their party subscriptions to the Empire Crusade, and wrote that 'Baldwin's successive attempts to find a policy remind me of the chorus of a third-rate review. His evasions reappear in different scenes and in new dresses, and every time they dance with renewed and despairing vigour. But it is the same old jig'. The manner in which his newspapers handled the news was well demonstrated when a banner headline declared an 'Australian Resolution for Empire Free Trade'. It transpired to be a resolution passed by the Kyabram Urban District Council in favour of E.F.T., 'provided there was no interference with the tariffs set up to protect Australian industries'. A not insignificant qualification!

Neville Chamberlain was writing as early as July 1930 that 'I have come to the conclusion that if S.B. would go the whole party would heave a sigh of relief. Everywhere I hear that there is no confidence in his leadership or belief in his determination to carry any policy through.'

These movements against Baldwin were unhappily more symptomatic of internal confusions exacerbated by frustration at loss of office than evidence of serious re-thinking in the Conservative Party about the philosophies and future of Conservatism. In any event, Baldwin's critics did not combine. The cause of the Protectionists was not helped by the fact that Beaverbrook's crusade was so obsessed with the Imperial aspect, and was linked to Rothermere's avowed aim to supplant Baldwin as leader. Churchill did not warm greatly to Empire Free Trade, which he regarded as a somewhat unreal cause; the raising of the banner of Britain's Imperial greatness by Churchill did not, however, greatly attract Beaverbrook. Nonetheless, although the forces against him were divided, it was evident that Baldwin's position was precarious at the beginning of 1931.

*

The short-lived Labour Government of 1929–31 was not, as its detractors claimed, standing evidence of Churchill's often repeated charge that Labour was unfit to govern. Its principal failure lay in only one field, that of unemployment, but it was the deep misfortune of that Government and of the party that it was the one field in which Labour had claimed special qualifications—with flimsy evidence. It was also the one that really mattered.

A perverse political godparent seems to have attended the birth of the Labour movement. She gave to it a fine cause for which to fight; she tended it carefully in its fledgling years, enabling it to grow and prosper under the benevolent and condescending guardianship of the Liberal Party; she permitted it to have sufficient independence in which to gain experience, yet without the opportunity to court disaster; she so arranged matters that, when the child was gaining in strength and confidence, those of its Liberal guardian faltered and failed, enabling it to seize its inheritance. But this political godparent failed to bestow the one priceless gift on the child when it emerged from youth; she denied it fortune when in office. There are indeed times when one feels warm sympathy with the bitter complaints of the Labour movement that on no occasion has it ever come into office in calm, or even reasonably calm, times. The political godparent of the Conservative Party denied that federation much, but she ensured that it had generous amounts of good luck in the matter of the taking and leaving of office. In 1929, as in 1945 and even 1964, the Conservatives were removed from the scene a fraction before the political tempests began to rage, leaving Labour to turn haggard and dismayed into the unexpected storm.

Ramsay MacDonald was sixty-two in 1929, and was in reality older

than his years. He had been in at the birth of the party, and had borne
almost alone the righteous opposition to the Great War. His origins
had been humble, yet there had always been about him, in manner,
speech and talents, a certain aristocratic aloofness which many found
attractive, and many others impressive. He was absolutely convinced
of the constitutional road to social reform, contemptuous and even
fearful of any suggestions for direct action or outside interference in the
proper processes. Yet he was never a House of Commons man; as he
once remarked on the Treasury Bench to Herbert Morrison, 'I hate
this place'. He was the nominee of the I.L.P. members in 1922, and
yet a vast gulf of attitude separated him from them. In 1923 he
declared that 'public doles, Poplarism,[1] strikes for increased wages,
limitation of output, not only are not Socialism, but may mislead the
spirit and policy of the Socialist movement'. What, then, was
MacDonald's road to Socialism? Indeed, what *was* his Socialism?

Whenever one approaches this central problem, the man and his
message seem to take on a vague, empty, mystical, entity. MacNeill
Weir wrote that it was

> that far-off Never-Never-Land born of vague aspirations and de-
> scribed by him in picturesque generalities. It is a Turner landscape
> of beautiful colours and glorious indefiniteness. He saw it, not with
> a telescope, but with a kaleidoscope.

This was perhaps a true, although hardly kind, estimate. Mac-
Donald was certainly a romantic. He was also a shy and remote man.
After the death of his wife in 1911 he wrote:

> I feel the mind of the solitary stag growing upon me. My fireside
> is desolate. I have no close friends in the world to share either the
> satisfaction of success or the disturbance of defeat. So I get driven
> in upon myself more and more, and I certainly do not improve.

It is at once apparent on reading MacDonald's articles and letters
that here is a man of exceptional intelligence and sensitivity. The
shadow of his illegitimacy[2] certainly assisted this latter aspect, and his
enjoyment of the company of the great and the rich was probably

---

[1] In 1921 the Poplar Borough Council refused to pay its share of the expenses
of the London County Council in protest against inequities of local rates in rich and
poor boroughs, and the word 'Poplarism' was used to describe local authorities'
defiance of the Government.

[2] Something that he shared with Ernest Bevin.

more the result of very human gratification at acceptance and security rather than of simple vanity or snobbery. But such traits in a Labour leader were bound to be misinterpreted—and were. Furthermore, his intellectual intolerance of others—and particularly his colleagues— may have been often justified, but was not calculated to make relation- ships any easier. He was jealous of possible political rivals, and as he aged he at times seemed obsessively concerned to demonstrate his own omniscience. A magnificent public speaker—Beatrice Webb probably did not exaggerate when she called him 'the greatest artist of British politics'—his diffuseness, impatience with detail, and vague but sincere Utopianism served better on a public platform than in dry debate in the Commons or technical discussions in Cabinet. And, even by 1929, his intellect was fading. This was at least partly the consequence of sheer exhaustion and strain. In 1924 he had doubled the offices of Prime Minister and Foreign Secretary, and the pressures of this double burden had played an important part in the maladroit handling of the Campbell Case and the Zinoviev Letter. He was bad at delegating responsibility, was not an efficient administrator, forever conscious of the precariousness of his position and both suspicious and contemptu- ous of most of his colleagues. And he did not lack vanity.

But in 1929 MacDonald was not able to be his own Foreign Secretary. Arthur Henderson had insisted upon this office, and Mac- Donald had conceded his claim with reluctance and ill grace. Hender- son was sixty-five, and since 1903 he and MacDonald had worked closely together, although often in disagreement. Henderson was warm-hearted, approachable, and gregarious. The Labour Party was the sum total of his life, and his Socialism was confined to what has been appropriately described as 'a vague gradualism'. As the same commentator has written:

> . . . his speech-making was mediocre, he wrote nothing. He was dull, practical, teetotal and deeply religious, with all the sterling qualities and limitations of his type. Above all, he was utterly devoted to the Labour movement, which he came to regard as an end in itself. He was, as his biographer has written, 'the incarnation of the Party as a Party'.[1]

Henderson was at least likeable, and was liked. MacDonald was respected. But Philip Snowden was perhaps even more remote than

[1] R. Skidelsky: *Politicians and the Slump*, 68.

his leader. He was working-class self-help Yorkshire, crippled, proud, independent, and bitter. He regarded MacDonald and Henderson with almost equal contempt and dislike. His wife, Ethel, was not an endearing personality, and was deeply disliked in the Labour movement. By this stage, Snowden had no time for the I.L.P. and perhaps even less for the trade union leaders. His political phraseology fully merited the adjective 'vitriolic'. It is possible to say harsh words and yet still be liked, but Snowden's virulent invective had an unforgivable quality about it. He meant every word. But there was no question that Snowden should not be Chancellor of the Exchequer again. Like Mac-Donald and Henderson, he was one of the party's veterans, in a confederation already excessively awed by the principle of seniority. Like them, he believed in gradualism. Unlike almost anyone else in the party, he actually wanted to be Chancellor. His vigour in debate, and authority of manner when discussing financial and economic matters, made the place his for the asking. As Boothby has written:

> To every outworn shibboleth of nineteenth century economics he clung with fanatic tenacity. Economy, Free Trade, Gold—these were the keynotes of his political philosophy; and deflation the path he trod with almost ghoulish enthusiasm.

This was a bad appointment, if inevitable, but another was much more disastrous. With justifiable unease, MacDonald appointed the garrulous, and indolent J. H. Thomas to be Lord Privy Seal with special responsibilities for unemployment, assisted by a three-man committee consisting of George Lansbury (Ministry of Works), Thomas Johnston (Under-Secretary for Scotland) and Sir Oswald Mosley (Chancellor of the Duchy of Lancaster).

Mosley's imperious march from Coalitionist gadfly to Socialist intellectual had been viewed with scepticism and distaste by many in the Labour movement. When one appreciates Mosley's wealth, glamour, manner, and the publicity his every action almost effortlessly acquired, these emotions are understandable. But the combination with John Strachey, which had produced *Revolution By Reason*, brought to the Government the only serious intellectual force that it possessed. He was also its only serious revolutionary. In the words of Harold Nicolson: 'The exuberant dynamism of the Chancellor of the Duchy was ill-attuned to the cheerful lethargy of the Lord Privy Seal.' But there was a good deal more to the situation than that. Mosley was still in a tearing hurry. Fame, and the discovery that he was by far the best public orator in the country, reminding many of the not-forgotten brief glories of Victor Grayson, had encouraged neither the slender elements of modesty in his character nor his patience for slower minds. Humourless and implacably self-confident, he firmly believed that he had the answers to all the ills that plagued the nation. Furthermore, he entertained few apprehensions of his capacities to lead it. Here were the ingredients of a famous disaster, and a major national misfortune.

It would be difficult to conceive a more ill-assorted quartet, but the appointment of Thomas ensured that nothing very revolutionary was likely to emerge. As Mr. Skidelsky comments with justice of him:

> Totally devoid of constructive ideas, intimate with the City and big business, the boon companion of half the House of Commons, the jingoistic upholder of imperial and national unity, his appointment gladdened the conservatives and dismayed the radicals.[1]

These were the diverse and fallible human instruments with which the new Government would endeavour to cure the chronic disease of mass unemployment. It was highly improbable that any positive agreed proposals would emanate from the Thomas group, but the presence of Snowden at the Treasury ensured that any which did slip through would be met with freezing hostility and the certainty of rejection.

*

Although Henderson was Foreign Secretary in title, foreign affairs remained the obsession of the Prime Minister. He warmly supported Irwin's policies in India, pressed forward eagerly with international disarmament, and had his reward in the London Naval Conference of March 1930, in which Britain, America and Japan agreed to ratios which were certainly not to the advantage of the British. Henderson, for his part, worked successively for the resumption of full diplomatic relations with the Soviet Union; the final withdrawal of Allied troops from the Rhineland; the acceptance of the principle of compulsory arbitration in international disputes; and a sharp reversal of policy in Egypt, starting with the removal of Lord Lloyd as High Commissioner and culminating in negotiations towards an Anglo-Egyptian Treaty.

[1] Skidelsky, op. cit., 70.

These initiatives, in the context of 1929–30, can be fairly regarded as enlightened, progressive, and sensible. In this field at least, Labour had gone far to prove that it was responsible and fully fitted for government.

But in October 1929, with the sudden and dramatic collapse of the American stock market, there came the first of a series of events that was to shatter the illusory tranquillity of the second half of the 1920s. The impact upon Britain, it requires emphasis, was not so grievous as it was elsewhere in Europe, but it was bad enough. British exports fell in value from £839 million in 1929 to £666 million in 1930, and then to £461 million in 1931. By July 1930 unemployment had gone over two million, and by December had risen to over 2½ million.

In this darkening situation, Ministers looked helplessly about them In February 1930 Mosley produced a dramatic programme of increased pensions and allowances, protection of home industries by tariffs, import restrictions, bulk purchase agreements; a far more extensive use of public money to finance development; and the rationalisation of industry under central control. These were in fact the same proposals as he had enunciated in 1925, with a certain watering-down of some of the more extreme proposals.

The 'Mosley Memorandum' was submitted to the Cabinet in February; it was definitely rejected in May. Mosley resigned—to be succeeded by the more docile Clement Attlee—and took his case to the Parliamentary Party, where he was defeated by 202 votes to twenty-nine. He then put it before the annual party conference in October, and was only narrowly defeated. In December he published his manifesto, and was supported by seventeen M.P.s, who included Strachey and Aneurin Bevan, a young miner who had recently been elected for Ebbw Vale. In February 1931 Mosley announced the formation of the New Party to put his policies into effect. He was expelled from the Labour Party, supported only by Strachey. Thus did the Government lose perhaps the most able man in its ranks, and turned away from the only policies that had any real hope of success in the deteriorating situation. Thereafter, Mosley's career took him into channels that were to lose him the support of Strachey and of most of his other adherents, and to lead him to the bathos of the British Union of Fascists, and to the immortal denunciation of A. P. Herbert —'A curse on both your blouses!'

All the Government could do, and all that it did do, was to increase the unemployment benefits to the unemployed and abandon the principle of contributory relief. For this they were assailed by the Opposition for their extravagance and from the Labour back benches for their niggardliness. The Government retreated into a cloud of impressive-sounding Commissions and Committees. A Committee of Enquiry into Finance and Industry under Lord Macmillan was appointed in November 1929; in 1930 an Economic Advisory Council under MacDonald's chairmanship was set up. Later in 1930 a Liberal-Labour committee was established, followed by a Royal Commission. Most serious of all, Snowden virtually abdicated the Government's responsibility when he agreed to the appointment of a Committee on National Expenditure chaired by Sir George May in February 1931. Until the Committee reported the Government could only mark time. Meanwhile, what Churchill called 'the economic blizzard' grew even more fierce. The collapse of the Credit Anstalt in May caused further drainage of gold from London. Unemployment approached the figure of three million.

*

One solace for Labour throughout this turbulent period had been the acute divisions within the Conservative ranks, culminating in Churchill's resignation from the front bench over India at the end of January 1931 and a crucial by-election at St. George's Westminster in March. This was, as the *Annual Register* remarked, 'a campaign of unusual scurrility, instigated not by Communists or Socialists, but by titled Conservatives'. Hostility to Baldwin's leadership had become so acute that Baldwin had seriously considered resignation, but had been persuaded to stand and fight. Baldwin in a corner was a very formidable quantity. At St. George's the Beaverbrook–Rothermere factions propelled forward a candidate of little capacity but imposing support. At one point Baldwin brooded over the possibility of fighting the by-election himself, but thought better of it. Duff Cooper, who had lost his Oldham seat in the 1929 election, was nominated as the official Conservative candidate.

Baldwin now exercised again his genius for a diversionary attack. The 'Press Lords' were an easy target, of whom Baldwin had made good use in the past, but now came the opportunity for a knock-down blow. On March 18th he spoke on behalf of Duff Cooper, and turned on the 'Press Lords':

They are engines of propaganda for the constantly changing policies, desires, personal wishes, personal likes and dislikes, of two men. What are their methods? Their methods are direct falsehood, misrepresentation, half-truths, the alteration of the speaker's meaning by publishing a sentence apart from the context, such as you see in these leaflets handed out inside the doors of this hall; suppression and editorial criticism of speeches which are not reported in the paper. These are methods hated alike by the public and by the whole of the rest of the Press. . . . What the proprietorship of these papers is aiming at is power, and power without responsibility—*the prerogative of the harlot throughout the ages.*

It was this final phrase—proposed by Baldwin's cousin, Rudyard Kipling—which electrified the audiences and a wider public. 'I saw the blasé reporters, scribbling self-consciously, jump out of their skins to a man', Duff Cooper's wife later recorded, with vividness rather than total factual accuracy. Duff Cooper rode to an easy victory, Beaverbrook swiftly came to terms with Baldwin, and the latter's critics in the Conservative Party relapsed either into sullen silence or hastened to proclaim their fealty. Neville Chamberlain, whose hand had been reaching eagerly for the succession, had to maintain his patience. Never again, except in the difficult summer of 1936, was Baldwin's leadership in any serious jeopardy.

*

The Conservatives resolved their internal difficulties only just in time. By the early summer of 1931 the Labour Government was in serious trouble. Unemployment continued to rise with inexorable force, the value of British exports fell, Ministers became distraught and helpless, awaiting the solemn judgement of the May Committee. The party was confused and demoralised. By the time the May Committee reported at the end of July, withdrawals from London were running at nearly £2·5 million a day, and unemployment was over three million.

The Report of the May Committee was released after Parliament had risen for the summer recess. Its salient conclusions were that there would be a deficit of £120 millions by April 1932; that new taxation, to raise £24 millions, was required; and that immediate economies, totalling £96 millions, were needed, of which £66½ millions were to be achieved by the reduction of unemployment relief, including a twenty per cent reduction in benefit payments. By this time the situation was almost out of control; a run on sterling had already begun, and the May Report caused a panic among foreigners with short-term British investments.

The Bank of England obtained credits at the beginning of August, but by the 11th the drain was resumed; MacDonald returned hurriedly from Lossiemouth to be told by the bankers that the crisis was one of confidence in the Government, which the Government alone could restore. A balanced Budget and a determined drive for economies—in unemployment benefit in particular—was required. They also proposed meetings between the Government and Opposition leaders, to which MacDonald agreed. The first meeting took place on August 13th, when MacDonald and Snowden met Baldwin and Chamberlain, with Samuel and Donald Maclean representing the Liberals in the absence of Lloyd George, who was recuperating from an operation.

A Cabinet Economy Committee drew up a tentative list of economies totalling £78½ millions; after long sessions, the Cabinet agreed to £56¼ millions on August 19th. But at a meeting with the Opposition leaders on the next day (August 20th) the impression was given that the £78 millions had been agreed. On the same afternoon there was a confused meeting with the General Council and the National Executive, at which it had become clear that the T.U.C. would not accept any reductions in unemployment benefit.

On the afternoon of the 21st, after a day of Cabinets, Snowden and MacDonald reported to the Opposition leaders the true figure of £56 millions; they retorted that these were wholly inadequate. The Opposition was now dominating the Government. On the following morning the Cabinet was summoned again to be told by MacDonald and Snowden that further economies were required. A major split among Ministers now appeared, but there was agreement to submit to the Opposition a new set of proposed economies of £68½ millions, including £12¼ million saved by a ten per cent cut in unemployment allowances.

The Government was now tottering towards collapse, without leadership, hopelessly confused, sorely divided, and subjected to the fierce blasts of conflicting pressures. MacDonald, Snowden, and J. H. Thomas now clutched towards other possibilities of rescue. A cool head and a refusal to be stampeded might have saved the situation, but these were not provided. The waves of the prevailing panic in London swept into the Cabinet Room, and Ministers swayed helplessly in its harsh billows.

It is not possible to decide exactly when the idea had been implanted in MacDonald's mind of extricating himself simultaneously from his acute dilemma and his quarrelling colleagues by seizing the possibility of heading a National Administration. Perhaps the basic psychological need had been there throughout, and he had been sending signals to the Conservatives since 1929. The circumstances of August 1931 were sufficient to tempt him profoundly.

Others were thinking on similar lines, if from different perspectives.

The momentum towards coalition was greatly assisted by the fact that Lloyd George was convalescent, and, although consulted by Samuel and Maclean, was effectively removed from the real negotiations. The Press—and notably *The Times*—was by now pushing the Government hard. But of far greater significance was the mounting concern of the King, who returned from Balmoral and saw MacDonald on the morning of August 23rd. MacDonald told him of the gravity of the position in the Cabinet, and the King decided to consult Samuel and Baldwin. In the normal course of events Baldwin, who was strongly opposed to the idea of coalition, would have been the first to be summoned, but he could not be found immediately (he was discussing the crisis with the editor of *The Times* at the latter's house, and later lunched with Sir Samuel Hoare at the Travellers' Club). Accordingly, as a result of Baldwin not having told the Davidsons— with whom he was staying—of his plans, Samuel, who did favour coalition, was the first to see the King.

Possibly this did not make much difference. The King was now firmly in favour of the principle of coalition, and his dominant and overriding concern was—properly—with national unity at an hour of crisis. Samuel strongly fortified these attitudes. His advice was that if the Government could not agree on the necessary economies, it should be replaced by a National Government, preferably led by MacDonald himself. This suggestion fell upon very receptive ears. Thus, when the King saw Baldwin in the afternoon, the main question put to him was *not* his general advice on the crisis but whether he and his colleagues would serve in such a Government. Put in such terms—virtually an appeal to Baldwin's patriotism—there could only be one answer. The King 'was greatly pleased with Mr. Baldwin's readiness to meet the crisis which had arisen, and to sink Party interest for the sake of the Country'. Baldwin was not, however, enthusiastic or optimistic about the prospects. It remained very much the King's solution, which —for different reasons—also attracted Samuel and Neville Chamberlain.

That evening the crisis reached its culmination when the Cabinet received the reply to its enquiry to the American bankers J. P. Morgan and Company, about the prospects of a loan; it was to the effect that this could only be considered if the bankers were convinced that the Government was sufficiently in earnest. The Government was now firmly in the hands of its opponents. MacDonald appealed to the Cabinet to agree to the larger sum of £78 millions; eleven Ministers were prepared to do so, but ten were not. Accordingly, MacDonald asked all Ministers to place their resignations in his hands, to which they consented. The distracted and perplexed Cabinet adjourned in circumstances of considerable confusion, under the impression that it would be replaced on the following day by a Conservative–Liberal Coalition. But the King urged MacDonald to reconsider the matter, and told him that 'he was the only man to lead the country through this crisis'. The King also agreed to MacDonald's request for a meeting of the party leaders on the next morning. Later that evening Baldwin, Samuel, and Chamberlain entered 10 Downing Street by a back entrance; in the discussion Chamberlain and Samuel urged MacDonald to remain Prime Minister, as head of a Coalition Government. Baldwin said nothing.

Thus was the situation on the night of August 23rd–24th. The Government had in effect resigned, but MacDonald, at the personal appeal of the King, had agreed to reconsider his own position. Samuel was enthusiastic for coalition, but Baldwin was not. His judgement was that the best, as well as the most obvious, course was for the Government to resign, for him to form a Conservative Government with suitable guarantees for immediate legislation, and then to dissolve.

But the meeting at Buckingham Palace on the morning of the 24th was dominated by the King, who opened by saying that he trusted that there was 'no question of the Prime Minister's resignation: the leaders of the three Parties must get together and come to some arrangement. His Majesty hoped that the Prime Minister, with the colleagues who remained faithful to him, would help in the formation of a National Government, which the King was sure would be supported by the Conservatives and the Liberals. The King assured the Prime Minister that, remaining at his post, his position and reputation would be much more enhanced than if he surrendered the Government of the country at such a crisis.'[1] After this, there was very little to say, and this momentous meeting took little over thirty minutes. The agreement was that the new Government 'will not be a Coalition in the ordinary sense of the term, but co-operation of individuals' and that its task would be purely to resolve the economic crisis. Thus was born the National Government.

Baldwin and Samuel left to inform their colleagues, and MacDonald to break the astounding news to the Cabinet. Ministers were too stunned to protest. Perhaps most did not grasp the enormity of what had happened. 'We uttered polite things, but accepted silently the accomplished fact', Sidney Webb recorded. 'Lord Sankey proposed a vote of thanks to MacDonald which was passed unanimously and, without further leave-taking, his colleagues left the room.'[2]

In a very literal sense, this was the King's Government. If he had not pressed the idea on MacDonald and had not asked him to reconsider his resignation, and had not conducted his meetings on the 23rd and 24th with the determination to have a National Government, it is very unlikely that it would have been created. If Lloyd George had not been prostrated, it is doubtful whether the King would have been as enthusiastic, and Baldwin would have shied violently from the prospect. If MacDonald's vanity had not been so vulnerable to the urgings of the King, Chamberlain and Samuel . . . But these speculations must remain of academic amusement. For good or ill, the Second Labour Government had gone, and much else besides. Baldwin's instinctive suspicion of coalitions was to be fully justified, and MacDonald's proven inability and weakness in stress were to become even more marked. But in the apprehension and drama of the hour the unhappy long-term consequences of the King's leadership were impossible to discern.

[1] Harold Nicolson: *King George V*, 465–6.   [2] Skidelsky, op. cit., 383.

CHAPTER SEVENTEEN

NEW DANGERS AND TRIBULATIONS, 1931–1935

T HE 'ECONOMIC BLIZZARD' of 1929–31 was the turning-point not only for Britain. It marked the doom of the Weimar Republic, and gave Hitler the chance that had seemed so forlorn when his Munich *putsch* had been so ignominiously scattered. It plunged the United States into a terrible depression, from which it was slow to emerge. It rocked, and sometimes fatally disturbed, governments and financial institutions across Europe. The growing confidence of the 1920s was dispersed and destroyed. Anarchy, confusion, and dismay renewed their briefly interrupted dominance.

It was not surprising that in the vital years 1931–5 the majority of British politicians were obsessed by primarily domestic problems, of which the economic situation was the most central. The principal exception was India, and the passage of the Government of India Act, eventually achieved in June 1935, evoked prodigious debate in Parliament—covering some four thousand pages of *Hansard*—and very considerable and heated controversy outside it. For all its imperfections, in its recognition of Indian rights it did indeed constitute 'a monument to the sincerity of declared British intentions'.[1] The adoption of a general ten per cent tariff in 1932 and the Ottawa Conference of the same year marked a significant change from the temporising economic policies of the 1920s without representing a shift of sufficient substance to meet the remaining problem of concentrated industrial unemployment. Neville Chamberlain's Unemployment Act of 1934 abolished the hated 'means test' that had been introduced in 1931, and established an Unemployment Assistance Board intended to provide a more fair and consistent system. But it was still based on the

[1] *Oxford History of Modern India*, 370.

insurance principle, and did not receive the warm approval from Labour that it merited.

The British were oppressed by their own concerns. There was an increasingly evident isolationist mood. 'Right or Left, everybody was for a quiet life', as the Permanent Under-Secretary at the Foreign Office, Sir Robert Vansittart, subsequently wrote. To arouse apprehension and a sense of awareness of what was happening in Europe was, as Boothby has written, 'like boxing a stone wall'. Nor was this particularly surprising. The British were engaged in the process, which was not fully achieved by 1939, of pulling themselves out of another major economic crisis. Although they experienced no hardship on the scale of the American Depression, it was a grim period for many. The intractable million of unemployed remained intractable, and there was consequently little interest in foreign affairs. To most, what happened in Germany was of insignificant interest, no more relevant to the lives of the multitude than upheavals in Egypt or difficulties in India—indeed, probably less relevant. It was only very slowly that the realisation dawned that the emergence of Hitler did indeed have a direct and personal relevance, and by then it was too late.

Throughout the 1930s—and, indeed, until 1945—Britain was ruled by essentially Conservative Governments. The National Government formed on August 24th, 1931, consisted of MacDonald, Baldwin, Neville Chamberlain, Sir Samuel Hoare, Cunliffe-Lister, Samuel, Snowden, Lord Sankey, Thomas and Lord Reading. By his actions over India, Churchill had excluded himself; Austen Chamberlain—who was chagrined by the offer of the Admiralty—was evidently ageing; a more surprising omission was that of Amery who, after a lifetime of battling for the cause of Protection, was left out of the Government that at last accepted it. The Liberals did not fight hard for their former faith; under the formula of 'agreement to differ' initiated by Lord Hailsham, they opposed Chamberlain's Import Duties Bill, with little effect or even enthusiasm, and in 1932 resigned (with Snowden) when they considered the results of Ottawa—which were largely nugatory, and admirably described as 'a repudiation of Free Trade principles in theory, though not in practice'[1]—the final apostasy. Lloyd George denounced Ottawa vigorously: 'the mutilated statues of Peel, Cobden, and Bright have been finally relegated to the scrap-heap to be melted down to provide material for the bronze

---

[1] Taylor, op. cit., 334.

figures of Chamberlain (père et fils) on a pedestal showing in bas-relief the great anti-food taxers MacDonald, Snowden, Runciman, and Samuel as pouting supporters; at the base Baldwin gazing triumphantly at a prostrate Beaverbrook with his Empire Free Trade banner in the dust'. This did not aid the cause of Liberal reunion. In reality, the Liberals were broken, even more so than Labour.

The economic crisis that had created the National Government was not miraculously averted; indeed, after Snowden[1] brought in an emergency Budget on September 10th that substantially carried out the recommendations of the May Committee and cut unemployment benefits and the salaries of Government-paid persons by an average of ten per cent, the crisis actually got worse. The main cause was a disturbance in the Fleet at Invergordon which was described as a mutiny and involved ten thousand men; this necessitated a hasty re-vision of the Government's plans, but not before Britain had been un-ceremoniously forced off the gold standard. The heavens did not fall.

Snowden's Budget had been vehemently opposed by the embittered Labour Party, and the Conservatives now pressed for an election. Neville Chamberlain is generally credited for evolving the formula in which the National Government appealed to the country for 'a doctor's mandate' whereby the three parties would fight independently but together under this ingenious banner, and not oppose each other. It was, in practical terms, a ganging up on Labour. Thus, the Con-servatives campaigned for a modest Protectionist policy, the National Liberals heroically stood by Free Trade, and National Labour pledged that the tariff issue would be impartially examined after the election. Baldwin, with even greater vagueness, said that the Government 'must be free to consider any and every expedient which may help to estab-lish the balance of trade'.

The election was, of course, a direct vote of no confidence in Labour and left the Lloyd George Liberals in limbo. It was, as Mowat has commented, 'the coupon election all over again, though, let it be granted, without the coupons'.[2] It was not the most elegant of cam-paigns, and the Labour Party was justified in feeling sore about the alarmist character of the National programme, and not least by Snowden's charge that their modest proposals were 'Bolshevism run

---

[1] Snowden went to the House of Lords in November as Lord Privy Seal, and was replaced as Chancellor of the Exchequer by Neville Chamberlain.

[2] Mowat, op. cit., 409.

mad'. But the tide was running harshly against them. In a mood of uncharacteristic panic, impregnable Labour citadels collapsed, and a considerable number of young Conservatives fighting forlorn ventures found themselves in the House of Commons. In the Northumberland mining constituency of Morpeth a Labour majority of more than 16,000 in 1929 produced in 1931 a comfortable Conservative majority; in Gateshead, Ernest Bevin, fighting his first election, experienced a Labour majority of 16,700 becoming a Conservative one of 12,938. Many former Liberals clearly voted Conservative; evidently a considerable number of Labour voters did not bother to vote at all; probably many who did switched their allegiance. The results were devastating—not only for Labour but for Lloyd George, and for Mosley, whose New Party fought twenty-four seats without success, Mosley himself losing his seat. The New Party did even worse in total votes (36,377 in 24 constituencies as opposed to 70,844 in 26) than the Communists.[1]

Labour, deserted and reviled by its former leaders, had gone down to catastrophic defeat, only a stunned fragment of fifty-two crawling back to the House of Commons. Of the former front bench, only Lansbury—who became leader—Attlee and Stafford Cripps survived. Lloyd George's party was reduced to a family quartet. Suddenly, there was no Parliamentary Opposition, and, although Labour was to win back a hundred seats in 1935 and make a modest revival, it was to remain a minority party with no real prospect of office until the events of 1940 brought its leaders into a very different Coalition than that which reigned in 1931.

*

Throughout the 1930s, Britain made a considerable economic recovery. In 1932 Chamberlain introduced his modest tariff of ten per cent, and cut Bank Rate to two per cent. Although there was still a tendency for governments to shy violently away from anything that savoured of 'planning', Government interventions were far more substantial—if unsystematic—than they had been in the 1920s. Keynes was still regarded as heretical, and unemployment was only slightly reduced. (It was 1·2 million in 1929, 2·7 million in 1931, 2·5 million in 1933, and 1·4 million by 1937.) The general level of British exports remained depressingly low. But the overall picture was one of substantial improvement, particularly in the consumer and service

[1] R. Skidelsky: *Oswald Mosley*, 279.

industries, and in the south there was a really remarkable transformation in the 'white collar' professions and industries. The 1930s were, in fact, the golden years of the British middle class.

But although this Parliament was not initially dominated by issues of foreign affairs or rearmament, these gradually consumed its increasing attention, acting as a darkening back-drop to the concerns of Members of Parliament with the economic depression, unemployment, and the apparently interminable India debates, in which Hoare conducted the Government of India Bill through its complex and extended stages with considerable skill and moderation, thus marking him out for future promotion. His young Under-Secretary, R. A. Butler, was clearly a rising man, as were Duff Cooper, W. S. Morrison, Walter Elliot, and a notably flamboyant and publicity-conscious Minister, Leslie Hore-Belisha, Minister of Transport from 1934 to 1937, and immortalised by the flashing 'Belisha Beacons' for pedestrian crossings introduced under his regime. Each was spoken of as a future Prime Minister. But the star of Anthony Eden was rising much faster —perhaps too fast for his own good. Little notice was taken of Harold Macmillan, who, rebellious and intense, aroused irritation in the party hierarchy and made little immediate impact.

Of the senior Ministers, only Neville Chamberlain enhanced his reputation, his massive competence and self-assurance evoking respect but little affection, particularly in the Labour Party. Simon's arrogant legalisms were equally resented. MacDonald, contemptuously dismissed by Churchill as 'The Boneless Wonder', was in marked and pathetic decline. Cunliffe-Lister, although outstandingly able, was too acerbic for most tastes. Jimmy Thomas blundered along harmlessly enough at the Colonial Office, delighting the King with his racy conversation and enjoying his celebrity as a favourite of the House of Commons.

But what of Baldwin? Although only a year younger than MacDonald, and sixty-four in 1931, he was clearly still highly alert and physically very fit. But, as has been emphasised, he was a very sensitive man, and the events of 1929–31 had hurt him deeply. He had been much closer to quitting in January 1931 than most contemporaries —and several historians—have realised. He was still estranged from a substantial element in the Conservative Party, which, with Churchill's vigorous encouragement, was incessantly barking at his heels over India throughout the Parliament. He was held in politics partly through sheer habit, partly because he had not abandoned his vision of the Conservatives as a truly national party, partly because he felt that the task of national reconciliation which he had begun had not been completed, and, perhaps principally, through a profound sense of national duty at a time of serious crisis. But these were not the only factors. His reluctance to see Neville Chamberlain take his place, which was entirely natural after recent events, and his strong desire to defeat Churchill and the die-hards over India, also played their part.

But although Baldwin was, as Bonar Law in the Lloyd George Coalition, its lynch-pin, he was not the Prime Minister, and he was excessively meticulous in recognising and emphasising this fact. It would have been far better if MacDonald had been quietly shunted into retirement in 1932 or 1933 and Baldwin had taken his place, but Baldwin's loyalty stood against such a desirable action. Such attitudes might have been appropriate in quiet times, but by 1933 it was evident that the international situation was deteriorating rapidly, and that the brief Age of Locarno had ended. These were not circumstances in which MacDonald would have shone at any time of his career, and were certainly ill-fitted for its melancholy twilight.

Since the war, successive British Governments had followed policies of non-commitment—particularly in Europe—wary association with the League, and the pursuit of the goal of disarmament. What was lacking was any realistic assessment of the perils facing the European system and any sense of the shortage of time available. These failings were apparent in politicians of all parties. But in their defence it must be emphasised that nothing comparable to the advent of Hitler had been seen in Europe before, and, even now, it is a phenomenon that still astonishes and awes. The old concept of the Balance of Power in Europe had been tacitly abandoned, and had been replaced by what Lord Strang has called 'an almost Cobdenite non-interventionism'. It is difficult to improve upon Strang's estimate:

In the inter-war years . . . no clear policy was framed. The new problems of a changed and changing world tended to be interpreted in terms of old conceptions. Our position in the world had altered for the worse and we did not seem to recognise this in our actions. We continued too long to believe the horrors of the war of 1914–18 would have convinced all civilised powers that they must not have another war. We behaved as though we could play an effective part in international affairs as a kind of mediator or umpire without providing ourselves with the necessary arms and without entering into firm commitments, whereas the truth was that, for lack of international solidarity in face of the common menace, we were in mortal peril.[1]

Hitler came to power early in 1933 at a time when France was weakening and her political structure was crumbling, and the British were preoccupied with other concerns. Their reactions to Hitler were confused. In October 1932, when the pattern of future events was becoming more clear, Baldwin warned the annual Conservative conference of the deteriorating situation in Europe and that 'we are coming to the parting of the ways in Europe'. Two months after Hitler's assumption of power Sir Horace Rumbold, the British Ambassador in Berlin, reported that his regime had brought to the surface 'the worst traits in German character, i.e. a mean spirit of revenge, a tendency to brutality, and a noisy and irresponsible jingoism'. Anthony Eden reported to Baldwin after a meeting with Hitler in February 1934 that 'he has simplicity of manner and a sense of humour', and gave it as his opinion that 'I find it very hard to believe that the man himself wants war. My impression is much more that this country has plenty to do internally and to be thus preoccupied for five years to come.' The only British politicians who took Hitler seriously from the outset were Baldwin, Churchill, and Austen Chamberlain, the last saying in the Commons on April 13th, 1933:

What is this new spirit of German nationalism? The worst of all-Prussian Imperialism, with an added savagery, a racial pride, an exclusiveness which cannot allow to any fellow-subject not of 'pure Nordic birth' equality of rights and citizenship within the nation to which he belongs. Are you going to discuss revision with a nation like that?

But this was exactly what most people were very willing to do. The alleged iniquities of Versailles had been sedulously cultivated by German propagandists since the setting up of the 'War Guilt Section' in the German Foreign Ministry in the 1920s. The success of these methods may be seen from a statement of Lord Lothian in 1939:

I do not think it possible to understand British policy without

---

[1] Lord Strang: *Home and Abroad*, 154.

realising the fact that a great many people felt that the internal
persecution in Germany was in great part the result of the denial
to Germany of the rights which every other sovereign nation
claims.

Arthur Henderson, in *War and Peace* (1934), wrote that the injustices
of Versailles must be redressed, and that Labour would not fight to
defend them; he added that sanctions would be sufficient to curb
Hitler, and that there was no need to rearm.

The gradual revelation of what Nazism really was did not invariably carry with it the assumption that it denoted aggressiveness
outside Germany. *The Times* claimed (July 10th, 1934) that the violent
and aggressive speeches of the German leaders were only for home
consumption. Indeed, there was a respectable body of opinion that
constantly reiterated that internal revolutions were always ugly
affairs, and that responsibility came with power. We find even
Churchill writing in October 1937:

> Although no subsequent political action can condone deeds or
> remove the guilt of blood, history is replete with examples of men
> who have risen to power by employing stern, grim, wicked and even
> frightful methods, but who, nevertheless, when their life is revealed
> as a whole, have been regarded as great figures whose lives have
> enriched the story of mankind. So it may be with Hitler.

And, again, in September 1937:

> One may dislike Hitler's system and yet admire his patriotic
> achievement. If our country were defeated, I hope we should find
> a champion as indomitable to restore our courage and lead us back
> to our place among the nations.

The argument that a strong Germany was a powerful 'bulwark
against Communism' was one that was emphasised repeatedly by the
Nazis, and it was one that gained particular approval in the British
business and conservative communities. The reports of pogroms
against the Jews tended to be discounted by people cynical of propaganda; there were some who actually applauded the Nazi attitudes.
Lord Londonderry—admittedly a notable example—wrote to Ribben-
trop in 1936:

As I told you, I have no great affection for the Jews. It is possible to trace their participation in most of those International disturbances which have created so much havoc in different countries.

The Anglo-German Fellowship contained many leading people from these backgrounds who firmly believed in the truth of this argument. As Michael Astor has commented:

> In the nineteen-thirties the majority of Conservatives thought that Fascism was, in some ill-defined way, more or less all right. And the majority of Socialists thought that Communism was more than more or less all right. And in these judgements they were both all wrong.[1]

Thus, even those who accepted the essential evil of Nazi Germany and distrusted its presence in Europe, did not accept that conflict was in any sense unavoidable. Indeed, it was this group—substantially in the majority in the Cabinet—that was particularly susceptible to the argument that a policy of controlled and judicious concessions would damp the fires of German chauvinism and make it a tolerable neighbour. Lothian was not unrepresentative when he said in 1933:

> Like most Liberals, I loathe the Nazi regime, but I am sure that the first condition to reform it is that we should be willing to do justice to Germany. The second is that Liberal nations should be willing to stand together to resist any unjust pretension which she herself may later put forward.

The tragedy of Europe was that the latter condition became increasingly obscured. The development of Lothian's argument may well be seen in a leading article in *The Times* written by Geoffrey Dawson in 1936:

> The truth is that British public opinion is probably far ahead of the Government in its conviction that a clear understanding with Germany will have consequences more profound and more conducive to a stable peace than any other single object of our foreign policy. There is little sympathy here with the view, which has sometimes seemed to prevail on the Continent, that the proper way

[1] Michael Astor: *Tribal Feeling*, 143

to treat Germany is to ring her about with vigilant allied states, sometimes masquerading as the League of Nations, like trained elephants round a tiger in the jungle, to prevent her expansion in any direction beyond the limits imposed twenty years ago.

Behind all British attitudes there lay the haunting terror of another war. The argument of Sir Edward Grey that the 1906–14 arms race had somehow 'caused' the Great War was particularly emphasised in radical circles; it accordingly became logical to argue that a refusal to rearm oneself would in itself reduce the chance of war. The prevalent attitudes were well described by Churchill in a newspaper article in 1932, before Hitler came to power:

> There is such a horror of war in the great nations who passed through Armageddon that any declaration or public speech against armaments, although it consisted only of platitudes and unrealities, has always been applauded; and any speech or assertion that set forth the blunt truth has been incontinently relegated to the category of 'war-monger'. . . . The cause of disarmament will not be obtained by Mush, Slush, and Gush. It will be advanced steadily by the harassing expense of fleets and armies, and by the growth of confidence in a long peace.

All commentators agreed that the next war would be unspeakably worse than the last. 'Who in Europe', Baldwin asked, 'does not know that one more war in the West and the civilisation of the ages will fall with as great a shock as that of Rome?' Churchill also painted the picture in colours so appalling that the effect, far from stimulating his audiences to a comprehension of the perils of evasion of the issue, confirmed them in their fears.

If diagnosis of the new threat to Europe was confused, cure was even more controversial. MacDonald was fading rapidly. 'The thought that this vain old man, whose mind was only just turning over, was Prime Minister of a still great country, was rather depressing', as one sardonic observer has written.[1] Simon had little of value to contribute, and was markedly hostile to the idea of rearmament. He presided, furthermore, over a very divided Foreign Office. The retirement of Rumbold from Berlin and the appointment of Sir Eric Drummond, the former Secretary-General of the League of Nations,

[1] Kenneth Clark: *Another Part of the Wood*, 185.

to Rome were to prove major errors. Of Rumbold's successor, Sir Eric Phipps, Baldwin complained that his reports 'had too much wit and not enough warning; they did not alarm the Cabinet enough'. Drummond's association with the League was not the swiftest road to Mussolini's confidence. With a pacific, aloof, and limited Foreign Secretary, a vehemently divided Foreign Office, and confusing reports from the principal capitals, the Cabinet was not well served.

In the Labour Party the dominant phrase was 'collective security', a perfectly respectable and sensible theoretical philosophy but one that tended to wither into generalities when closely approached. Until 1935 at any rate, the one thing on which Labour agreed was the futility of rearmament. Richard Crossman has commented on the attitude of the *New Statesman*:

> Week by week throughout the 1930s we predicted the imminent collapse of Western capitalism and denounced in despairing terms successive betrayals of Western democracy . . . At home we attacked appeasement as a base surrender to Hitler and simultaneously opposed rearmament and predicted the total destruction of London by Hitler's air force if war broke out. I doubt whether any other periodical in modern history has preached such a despairing, self-immolating gospel with such gusto as we did in the 1930s.[1]

The essential conflict in Labour attitudes can be best seen in a resolution passed at the annual conference in October 1936, which was strongly condemnatory of the dictatorships, urged that 'the armed strength of the countries loyal to the League of Nations need be conditioned by the armed strength of the potential aggressor', but 'declines to accept responsibility for a purely competitive armament policy'.

If 'collective security' meant anything, it meant rearmament and the League of Nations. Yet here British politicians were in a quandary. The concept of the League as a centre of conciliation was a practicable one in the atmosphere and conditions of the 1920s, yet, as had been demonstrated in the Corfu Incident and was shown again by Japan in Manchuria in 1931, the League could be flouted at will. If, on the other hand, one interpreted 'collective security' in the sense of a series of national treaties, one was brought back to the sombre 'lesson' of 1914 that such entanglements deprived Britain of freedom

[1] *New Statesman*, May 3rd, 1968.

of manoeuvre, encouraged German chauvinism, heightened tensions, and led to war.

Britain's natural ally was France, even if few British Ministers recognised this fact. As a result of Locarno, there was no military co-operation. And France was herself entering a period of severe domestic difficulties that made a consistent policy almost impossible and sapped the initiative of French politicians, to whom it became an accepted fact that no war could be launched on Germany without British assistance. French foreign policy—particularly towards Germany—was increasingly dominated by concern about what the British felt. In the meanwhile, unperceived in London, the French military superiority over Germany was being remorselessly eroded.

There were few enough other potential allies. Fear of Russia had faded, but deep suspicions remained. On a practical basis, what could Russia do in the event of a western European war? Her army was to be grievously weakened by the purges of 1936–8. Her fleet and air force were derisory. The Left in Britain always favoured rapprochement with Russia on ideological grounds, but few suggested Russia's incorporation into any kind of western European military alliance beyond her current obligations. There was no movement in British foreign policy in the 1930s to make any serious overtures to Russia, and it is difficult to see how any practicable arrangements could have been made. The prevalent view was that put forward by H. A. L. Fisher in his *History of Europe*, published in 1936: 'The Hitler revolution is a sufficient guarantee that Russian Communism will not spread westward. The solid German bourgeois hold the central fortress of Europe'. 'A Communist Germany', Lloyd George said (September 27th, 1933) 'would be infinitely more formidable than a Communist Russia'.

The United States of America hardly counted at all in these considerations. Preoccupied by her own severe domestic problems, still aloof from the League, concerned by the rise of Japan, her remoteness from the grim drama that was unfolding in Europe was complete. The occasional international forays by President Franklin D. Roosevelt were regarded with impatience by the British, and it must be conceded that a considerable emptiness of purpose lay behind the European activities of the United States. In retrospect, the unwillingness of the British to try to draw the United States out of isolation is almost as strange as their apprehensions of American naval strength in the

1920s had been. But all the evidence demonstrates that any such attempts would have been futile.

Thus, everything depended upon the British.

As this menacing situation slowly unfolded, a critical difference of attitude became evident in Britain among the ranks of those who increasingly chafed against policies of inaction.

In this respect, it is instructive to return to Churchill, whose voice was the most challenging and insistent throughout this period. Churchill was not particularly concerned about Fascism *per se*. It would be tolerable only, he wrote, 'if the sole alternative was Bolshevism'. He expressed warm admiration for Mussolini, of whom he was writing in October 1937:

> It would be a dangerous folly for the British people to underrate the enduring position in world-history which Mussolini will hold; or the amazing qualities of courage, comprehension, self-control and perseverence which he exemplifies.

On every issue of flagrant aggression in the 1930s apart from those inflicted by Germany, Churchill's reactions were muted. He said in February 1933 of Japan's invasion of China:

> I do not think the League of Nations would be well advised to have a quarrel with Japan . . . I hope we shall try in England to understand a little the position of Japan, an ancient state, with the highest sense of national honour and patriotism and with a teeming population and a remarkable energy. On the one side they see the dark menace of Soviet Russia. On the other, the chaos of China, four or five provinces of which are now being tortured under Communist rule.

In the Abyssinia crisis of 1935 his position was highly equivocal. He said that 'no one can keep up the pretence that Abyssinia is a fit, worthy and equal member of a League of civilised nations', and warned that Britain must not become 'a sort of bell-wether or fugleman to lead opinion in Europe against Italy's Abyssinian designs . . . We are not strong enough to be the lawgiver and the spokesman of the world'. On the issues raised by the Spanish Civil War he was more emphatic —at least until the spring of 1938. A strong supporter of non-intervention, he also made it quite clear that he preferred a Fascist Spain to a Communist one.

Throughout, from the end of 1933 onwards, Churchill had his eye fixed upon the revived menace of German militarism. He considered that, compared to this threat, all other dangers were minor. But although this determination of priorities was to prove absolutely correct, it contained a very serious political and moral deficiency. For, if Italian aggression in Abyssinia or Japanese aggression in Manchuria were somehow morally and politically defensible as acts of national policy in which the League of Nations had no *locus standi*, what about the remilitarisation of the Rhineland? And if Fascist governments in Italy, Japan and Spain were perfectly tolerable, why not tolerate that of Germany? By taking these stands, Churchill cut himself off from a very real element in Britain that was increasingly nauseated by Fascist excesses everywhere; his lack of sympathy and understanding for the young men who went to fight in Spain was significant of the gulf of attitudes between himself and them. Abyssinia brought the Labour movement out of its feckless slumber; Spain aroused the young. Churchill's limitation to *German* ambitions failed to take advantage of a very sizeable group of British opinion. Thus, when he belatedly attempted to stir the still substantial League of Nations Union constituency in Britain in the 'Arms and the Covenant' crusade, his own position was severely compromised.

'Appeasement' has become one of the most dangerous and misleading of all modern political phrases. Briand had used the word to differentiate his policies from those of Poincaré; everybody subscribed to Anthony Eden's statement in 1936 that 'the appeasement of Europe' was the prime objective of British policy. This was, of course, the classic policy of England if, by appeasement, one meant the preservation of peace. But there was a substantial difference of emphasis between the foreign policy, and the circumstances, of 1933–7 and those of 1937–9. Indeed, it can be well argued that there was no foreign policy in 1937–9 apart from the avoidance of war at virtually any price.

British foreign policy between 1933 and 1937 was unquestionably lacking in distinction or purpose. Simon's tenure of the Foreign Office (1933–5) was hapless, and Hoare's brief occupancy in 1935 was a fiasco. 'Everyone seemed to be over-excited', he subsequently complained. 'There appeared to be no generally accepted body of opinion on the main issues. Diametrically opposed views were pressed upon me, and sometimes with the intolerance of an *odium theologicum*.'[1] Eden

[1] Templewood: *Nine Troubled Years*, 137.

(1935–8) was far from being the vigilant foe of the dictators that he has been subsequently portrayed as. The central features of British policy in these years were to reach accommodations with Germany on specific issues—as demonstrated in the Anglo-German Treaty of 1935—to avoid conflicts arising in Europe—as in the Rhineland crisis of March 1936—and to attempt to retain the co-operation of Italy— as in the so-called British, French, and Italian 'Stresa Front' of 1935. The latter policy collapsed over Abyssinia in the storm that followed the revelation of the Hoare–Laval Pact,[1] and the Stresa Front was accordingly a dead letter almost from the outset. Nevertheless, the thinking behind the Hoare–Laval Pact was very enduring, and lasted until May 1940. There were many serious fallacies in this approach, but a case could be made out to the effect that here was a valid policy of cynical realism. But it was not conducted in that spirit on the British side up to 1937, and after that it became part of Chamberlain's approach of all-round conciliation. By then, as the Italians rightly estimated, the British had little to offer as a potential ally, and little to be fearful of as an opponent.

The fundamental fallacy that ran through British policy and attitudes—and not only Governmental—was the assumption that Britain's unilateral efforts would be sufficient. Any attempt to 'encircle' Germany would have met strong opposition from all sides, and yet if this was regarded as unacceptable and unrealistic, what was the alternative?

As the reactions to the German reoccupation of the Rhineland in March 1936 were to emphasise, the concept of a preventive war was even less acceptable. The comment of the *Spectator* (March 27th) was representative: 'The reoccupation of German territory by German troops is no cause for war.' The coup was denounced by the *New Statesman* and the *Manchester Guardian*, consistent opponents of re-armament, and vehemently opposed to all war. But all the latter could suggest was that Britain and France should insist on the withdrawal of the troops under the threat of 'international ostracism'. If war was unthinkable between civilised nations, and was the most stupendous of all conceivable evils, what remained except a series of bilateral deals? And, in the context of relative British and German military strength, how could this result in anything save a series of capitulations? By March 1938, when the first major act of German

---

[1] See pp. 286–9.

aggression occurred, the British had moved into a situation in which the options had been reduced to one between concessions and war.

So far as an effective British foreign policy was concerned, the issue of armaments was much more crucial *before* 1938 than it was then. 'The practical choice', Simon wrote in January 1935, 'is between a Germany which continues to rearm without any regulation or agreement, and a Germany which, through getting a recognition of its rights and some modification of the peace treaties, enters into the comity of nations, and contributes, in this and other ways, to the European stability.' It was significant that in the summer of 1935 the Cabinet authorised the Service Ministries to make their defence preparations 'with a view to achieving a reasonable state of preparedness by 1939'. Preparedness for what? It was all too reminiscent of the War Council's resolution on the Dardanelles in January 1915. But at least it recognised the significance of time. The 1934 assessment had envisaged 1942 as the likely period of crisis, now the odds were dimly seen to be shortening. But the major crisis was to occur a year earlier. In 1938 the military imbalance between Britain and Germany was still considerable, but was closing. But by then the conviction of British inferiority was dominant in Chamberlain's mind. Thus, the paramount object in 1938 was to maintain peace, even if Czechoslovakia had to be sacrificed for this purpose. It was in the period 1934-7 that British weakness was so fatal for the peace of Europe.

*

In the writing of recent history it is very necessary for the participants to get in first. First impressions tend to be dominant; if they are formidably deployed no amount of subsequent revisionism can match the effect created by the original version. Churchill's opening volume of his Second World War memoirs, *The Gathering Storm*, has perhaps had a greater impression on post-war attitudes—and not least in the United States—than any other single work. Although its impact upon historians is diminishing, it is still considered a reliable primary source for examining the 1930s.

Churchill's thesis is a very simple one. The Second World War was 'the Unnecessary War'. As he writes:

It was a simple policy to keep Germany disarmed and the victors adequately armed for thirty years. But this modest requirement the might, civilisation, learning, knowledge, science, of the victors were unable to supply.

But, in reality, it was not nearly as simple as that. This policy required several crucial elements—not the least of which was to deny to Germany one of the rights of a sovereign state while at the same time building her up as one. The policy also required a situation whereby, in order to enforce German inequality, the European Powers would be prepared to revert to military action. By 1933 this situation did not exist. In one of his earliest speeches on the subject, in August 1933, Churchill warned that 'there is grave reason to believe that Germany is arming herself, or seeking to arm herself contrary to the solemn treaties *extracted from her in her hour of defeat*' (my italics). It was the latter comment that contained the difficulty.

It was with very profound reluctance that the British turned away from the chimera of total disarmament. None of the former Great Powers had given so much practical demonstration of their good faith. By 1933 the R.A.F. was numerically sixth in the world; the Navy had a smaller complement of men than at any time for forty years, and the Fleet was substantially ageing; the condition of the Army was the worst of all. Nine cavalry regiments, sixty-one batteries and twenty-one infantry battalions had been scrapped in the Regular Army; the Territorials were 40,000 below strength; mechanisation had virtually stopped; equipment was obsolete and in small supply; the Ordnance Factories were virtually phased out. Total Defence expenditure in 1926–7 had been £116 millions; in 1932–3 it was down to just over £100 million. The Disarmament Conference limped along until 1934. At the celebrated by-election in East Fulham in 1933 an anti-war Labour candidate rode to triumphant victory. No election is ever won or lost on a single issue, and there were other factors involved in East Fulham. But it was the successful candidate's principal theme, and the impact it made upon other politicians was understandable. In 1934 the Peace Pledge Union was created, followed by a Peace Ballot organised by the League of Nations Union— whose most interesting (but rather unnoticed) feature was the statement by some 6¾ million people that they favoured military sanctions by the League in the face of aggression. But sanctions by the League of Nations was not the same as unilateral rearmament. In the 1935 election, accordingly, Baldwin had to maintain a precarious balance; in the context of 1932–4 this balance was even more delicate.

There was, of course, a genuine and highly vocal pacifist anti-war element in the rearmament debate after 1933. In the Labour Party George Lansbury and Stafford Cripps were its most vehement exponents, Cripps actually declaring in November 1936 that he 'did not believe it would be a bad thing for the British working class if Germany defeated us. It would be a disaster to the profit-makers and capitalists, but not necessarily for the working class.' If these were extreme views, they were very close in content to those of moderate men like Attlee and the Liberal leader Sir Archibald Sinclair. In the debate on the 1935 Air Estimates the Labour spokesman attacked 'the squandering of so much money on the enlargement of the Air Service. . . . We are sick to death of all this mad talk about rearming.' In the 1935 General Election Herbert Morrison described Neville Chamberlain and Churchill as 'fire-eaters and militarists. . . . Chamberlain would spend money on the means of death, but not on the means of life.' In the 1935 election one Labour pamphlet declared that:

> The Unionist Party wants war. Your husbands and sons will be cannon-fodder. More poison gas will mean dearer food. Register your distrust of the war-mongers by voting Labour.

In the debate on the Defence White Paper in 1935, Attlee said that 'We reject the use of force as an instrument of policy. We stand for the reduction of armaments and pooled security . . . Our policy is not one of seeking security through rearmament but through disarmament.' The impossibility of reconciling the desire to 'fight' Fascism without rearming made all Labour Party contributions to the debate in the 1930s singularly unhelpful. There were, however, some voices of realism, and the most brutal was that of Ernest Bevin who, at the party conference on October 8th, 1935, destroyed Lansbury's leadership.[1]

In the Government, the reluctant acceptance in 1933–4 of the necessity to begin a modest rearmament to repair the ravages of years of neglect and low expenditure clashed with the optimism of a European settlement. As Lord Halifax (the former Lord Irwin) commented in December 1935:

[1] See p. 278.

Are we in fact to judge the question so serious that everything has to give way to the military reconditioning of our Defence Forces? Such a conclusion, in fact, appears to me to rest on premises not only of the inevitability but of a certain degree of certainty as to the early imminence of war, which I am not prepared to accept.

In this, Halifax represented a very substantial view—and not only in the Conservative Party. War remained the supreme, the total, horror. As Churchill himself said, 'Another Great War would cost us our wealth, our freedom, and our culture, and cast what we have so slowly gathered of human enlightenment, tolerance, and dignity to different packs of ravening wolves . . . It would be like the last—only worse.'

Thus, the British rearmed in a spirit of depression, believing almost to the end that the weapons would never be used.

The governmental organisation for rearmament was itself cumbersome and complicated. Sir Maurice Hankey had established himself into a position of immense influence in Whitehall, greater than that of any other single official and more substantial than that of most Ministers. He was hostile to all proposals for reorganisation, and his negative attitudes almost invariably carried the day. Hoare's portrait of the situation is confirmed by subsequent knowledge:

The complicated machinery that Hankey had most efficiently developed had become so intricate that it was often difficult to obtain a quick or clear decision upon specific questions. Rearmament had ceased to be the sole concern of the Service Departments and almost every Minister, Service and Civil, had come to take an interest in it. The result was the creation of innumerable committees for dealing with every kind of defence question, and an inevitable tendency to defer decisions until most of them had been consulted.[1]

This might not have been serious were it not for the fact that the Prime Minister was incompetent and vacillating, the Foreign Secretary was blandly untroubled by the European situation and instinctively hostile to rearmament, the Chancellor of the Exchequer was obsessed by the economic problems and profoundly reluctant to allocate expenditure for rearmament, and the Service Ministers—two of whom, Hailsham and Londonderry, were in the Lords—were

[1] Templewood, op. cit., 330.

politically weak and technically limited. Of the entire Cabinet, only two men grasped the realities and the new necessities—Baldwin and Cunliffe-Lister. But Cunliffe-Lister was Colonial Secretary, and Baldwin, checked by his unfortunate loyalty to MacDonald, could not at that stage move too far ahead of his colleagues and his party—at least not too obviously. But he at least sent up some public warning signals, and made evident the reality of his concern. In private his alarm was much greater, and it was principally because of his efforts that the rearmament programme was begun, and the Ten Year Rule abandoned.

It is not the case that MacDonald was the determined believer in disarmament, with Baldwin a reluctant follower. Up to 1933 Baldwin believed strongly in it, and particularly in the elimination of what he regarded as the barbarism of aerial bombing—a factor that made the Air Minister, Londonderry, and his chief bombing zealot, Trenchard, highly uncongenial to him. On this matter he tried very hard in 1932 to get an agreement at Geneva, and in his celebrated speech of November 10th he meant every word:

> I think it is well also for the man in the street to realise that there is no power on earth that can protect him from being bombed. Whatever people may tell him, the bomber will always get through. The only defence is in offence, which means that you have to kill more women and children more quickly than the enemy if you want to save yourselves.

This often-derided statement was, in the context of 1932, absolutely true. But by 1933 Baldwin realised that the moment for genuine all-round disarmament had probably passed; by the beginning of 1934 he was absolutely convinced that it had. But his preoccupation was always to be on aerial defence. For this he was prepared to cut official corners and give to those engaged in this task virtually everything they wanted that he could supply. 'A country which shows itself unwilling to make what necessary preparations are recognisable for its own defence will never have force—moral or material—in this world', he said in 1935. Again, emphasis must be placed on the word *defence*. It was the key to Baldwin's thinking and activity on rearmament questions, a key that almost all observers and historians have missed. By 1933, and even more by 1934, Baldwin had developed what can be best described as 'the Armada complex'. The Defence of the Realm—particularly from the air—was his personal, and almost total, obsession.

Baldwin was not—and nor did he pretend to be—an expert on foreign affairs. As Prime Minister in the twenties he had worked on the old principle of letting each Minister run his own shop without interference unless a particular crisis or problem arose, much as Asquith had done, and Lloyd George had not. If the Ministers were well chosen and able, this arrangement had much to be said for it. But as number two to MacDonald, and with Simon at the Foreign Office for purely domestic political reasons, it had very little to be said for it. But Baldwin, although no expert, saw the reality of the danger looming in Europe and the need to take some action to counteract it. But he concentrated on one particular aspect, the negative one of air defence, and could not and did not see the matter in the wider perspective that it desperately needed. And, by 1935, he was tired, and assailed by other problems.

Baldwin's other great concern was to carry public opinion with him. The many speeches, some elliptical and confusing ('the bomber will always get through', 'When you think of defence of England you no longer think of the chalk cliffs of Dover; you think of the Rhine'), that he gave on the subject did not provide the clarion call that Churchill and some others sought, but they went far further than any others made by Ministers. He was convinced that the British could not be, and would not be, stampeded into increased expenditure on armaments unless the necessity was very evident. Perhaps he read too much in the East Fulham by-election, but all the evidence we possess emphasises that Baldwin's general diagnosis of the public mood was correct. He therefore concentrated upon building the foundations not only of rearmament itself but of a cautious change in public awareness of the seriousness of the European situation. In this, Hitler was his best ally, but in this period Hitler was demonstrating that the portrait of him as a mere ranting paranoid gutter politician of considerable brutality left out a great deal. At home, ruthlessness and rearmament, the consolidation of his own position, the support of the Services, and the dramatic revival of nationalism, brilliantly stage-managed by Goebbels; abroad, the combination of menacing threats to the weak, and bland overtures to the strong. He played on fears and hopes, weaknesses and optimism, with intuitive genius. Hitler and Baldwin were the two best politicians in Europe, and every violent action or gesture by Hitler enabled Baldwin to carry his own policies further forward; but at this stage Hitler, too, had to act warily.

Furthermore, despite Baldwin's real affection and regard for the Labour Party—a regard greatly increased by the gallant manner in which the diminutive Parliamentary Party kept going in the 1931–5 Parliament, and to which he paid a noble and merited tribute in 1935 —he was convinced that it was in no condition to take office again in the immediate future. He was particularly alarmed about its attitude towards rearmament. With Lansbury and Cripps—with Attlee not far behind them—denouncing all armaments, even defensive, and deriding warnings about present or future dangers, this apprehension was not surprising. Baldwin also had considerable respect for the recuperative powers of the Labour Party. He understood, as did no other Conservative politician of the inter-war period, the strength of the foundations of the party, and he noted its ever increasing membership and voting power. He regarded the 1931 election, rightly, as a freak, and it was not only East Fulham that impressed him; all indications were of the revived spirits and increased public support for the Labour Party.

These apprehensions were fully confirmed by the by-election results, which were devastating for the Government from the autumn of 1933 until the summer of 1934. East Fulham was the first shattering blow in October 1933, when the Labour candidate John Wilmot campaigned on a shrill pacifist platform and was warmly supported by Lansbury, who pledged that he would disband the Army and disarm the Royal Air Force, close every recruiting station, and 'abolish the whole dreadful equipment of war'. The swing to Labour was 26·5 per cent. In November the pattern was repeated at Kilmarnock (24·8 per cent), Shipton (25·2 per cent), Rusholme and Rutland (18·6 per cent in each case) and Market Harborough (23·6 per cent). In February 1934 Cambridge was held, but with a large anti-Government swing, and in April the Government held Basingstoke with a greatly reduced majority, and lost Hammersmith North and West Ham. In March, Labour gained control of the London County Council for the first time ever, and in the autumn of 1934 the movement against the Government was even greater than at East Fulham. The disarmament issue was obviously not the only factor, but the disturbing element for Baldwin was that these by-elections, held in very different constituencies in very different regions, demonstrated the same ominous pattern of Labour recovery. The fact that when Admiral Sir Roger Keyes hung on to Portsmouth against an 8·8 per cent swing this was regarded as a signal triumph gives some indication of the seriousness of the situation. A Labour Government, with Lansbury as Prime Minister, was, on the basis of these indications, a very real possibility.

Baldwin's operations were, therefore, on several levels. Within the Government he pushed his very reluctant colleagues, and supported by only a relatively few senior officials, of whom Vansittart was the most notable and outspoken, in the direction of rearmament, particularly in the air. In public, without being alarmist he gave his warnings—on occasions in terms more dire than his experts believed were merited by the facts. But he also heavily stressed the specifically defensive nature of rearmament. It was a calculatedly gradual and cautious exercise, intended to get the results without inflaming the Labour Party or opening irreparable divisions in his own Government. And, in the main, he succeeded.

It was generally accepted—and in this Baldwin and Churchill were in full agreement—that the threat to Britain came from the air. This was the dominant obsession of the 1930s. In October 1933 the Cabinet had set up a Defence Requirements Committee under Hankey, to examine 'the worst deficiencies' in the Armed Services; it reported in February 1934, and stated that Germany was 'the ultimate potential enemy'. The fact that Germany was rearming—and rearming fast—was well known; indeed, there was little attempt made to conceal it. But it was the rebuilding of the Luftwaffe that caused the British the greatest alarm. This was partly the result of recognition of the fact that the German Army was not a direct menace to the British, but it was principally based upon a very widespread fear of an aerial pre-emptive strike of devastating proportions. At that stage the German Navy seemed to pose no serious threat to the British, and exponents of naval expansion usually spoke in terms of the dangers presented by the Japanese and Italian navies. Once again, the submarine danger was discounted.

Thus, the debate on rearmament was from the beginning essentially about *air* rearmament, with the result that both the older Services—and particularly the Army—fared badly in the distribution of what funds were made available. The lamentable condition of the Army, and particularly in its equipment, when war did break out was commentary enough on this order of priorities. But it also reflected the general refusal to consider the possibility of it being involved once again in a major land war. The British remained convinced that they were, in Churchill's phrase, 'sea-animals rather than land-animals', and of all the Services the Navy had suffered least from the rigorous economies of the 1920s. But the Great War had demonstrated the superlative quality of the British soldier, however ill-commanded, and very serious deficiencies in the Navy. The latter were not adequately met; the former was forgotten. Duff Cooper, one of a string of undistinguished Secretaries of State for War, subsequently complained that he had spent most of his time at the War Office—during which he wrote a lengthy and flattering biography of Haig—writing papers about the role of the Army, and that it was a relief to move to the Admiralty where no doubts about the role of the Navy existed.[1] His even less distinguished successor, Hore-Belisha, wrote to Neville Chamberlain in 1937 that 'My view after the fullest survey, including a visit to France, is that our Army should be organised to defend this country and the Empire, [and] that to organise it with a military pre-possession in favour of a Continental commitment is wrong'. When he introduced the Army Estimates for 1936–7 Duff Cooper apologised to those cavalry units that were to be mechanised, remarking sympathetically that 'It is like asking a great musical performer to throw away his violin and devote himself in future to a gramophone'. The 1920s and early 1930s had been a miserable period for the Army; now, when rearmament at last began, it remained at the bottom of the list in terms of material, finance, and political leadership. No serious thought was given to what its role in a future conflict was to be. Again, the essentially defensive nature of the Government's military thinking, and the blind reliance on the French—a view in which Churchill, crying 'Thank God for the French Army', fully concurred —dominated. And so, the Army continued to languish. Its subsequent feelings about politicians were understandable and merited.

In taking these views, Ministers demonstrated the basic insularity of British attitudes, and their complete failure to comprehend the wider picture, which was a threat to the whole of Europe and to that balance of power to which they dutifully gave lip-service. It was France, and Central Europe, that were in mortal peril, not Britain. And it was the Wehrmacht, with its air arm and massive mechanisation, that held the reality of political-military power in Europe. But

[1] Duff Cooper, op. cit., 207.

while the British Government was not particularly concerned about the Wehrmacht or the German Navy, although it should have been, it became progressively excessively frightened by the emergence of the Luftwaffe. No one—including Churchill—appreciated the basic fact that the Luftwaffe was essentially the air arm of the German Army, and that it was this combination that posed such a threat to Europe. In 1937 the Cabinet was informed that it must expect an immediate German air attack of sixty days in the event of a war, with probable casualties of 600,000 dead and 1,200,000 injured (the actual civilian casualties in the whole of the Second World War were 295,000, of whom 60,000 were killed). Churchill, in 1934, described London as 'the greatest target in the world, a kind of tremendous fat cow', and dwelt upon the hideous effects of air attack. In March 1934 he warned that Germany would be strong enough in the air within a year or eighteen months to threaten 'the heart of the Empire'. Baldwin gave an assurance that such an eventuality would not be permitted to arise. A year later, again in response to Churchill, he acknowledged that Germany had indeed achieved 'parity' in the air—as will be seen, incorrectly—and that a greatly enhanced programme would have to be introduced. It is very difficult indeed to escape the conclusion that Churchill's campaign was extremely helpful to Baldwin, so far as *air* rearmament was concerned.[1]

It is important on these matters to separate the true facts from those that people believed at the time. In July 1934 the Luftwaffe possessed

[1] Although Churchill urged rearmament for all Services, he devoted himself principally to the Air Force. Indeed, some of his evaluations of future military and naval conflicts read very curiously indeed in the light of later—and even current—experience. He himself later admitted that he had not fully appreciated the revolution in mechanised warfare which had been propagated by Captain Basil Liddell Hart, to whom the Germans had listened with great respect and profit. He was sceptical of the value of the tank. He discounted the effectiveness of aerial attacks on modern warships and greatly exaggerated the advances in anti-submarine techniques. He was convinced that a future land war would be essentially static, and that 'One thing is certain about the next war, namely, that the armies will use their spades more often than they use their bayonets' (April 24th, 1938). 'The idea that enormous masses of mechanical vehicles and tanks will be able to overrun [modern] fortifications will probably turn out to be a disappointment.' But Churchill assumed that the major land powers in Europe likely to be opposed to Germany—France, Czechoslovakia, and Poland—would act together and were reasonably well equipped. He assumed also the paramount need for such an alliance, with the British playing their part on the sea and in the air. For all his errors, Churchill had a vision of the kind of alliance that was essential to meet the German threat. In this he was virtually alone.

some 400 military aircraft, and some 250 that were readily convertible to military uses; it had, in addition, some 1,450 civil and training aircraft of various types. The threatening factor was that Germany had an aircraft industry that was capable of producing at least 100 aircraft a month; by December 1934 the Luftwaffe consisted of 1,888 aircraft, of which 584 were operational military aircraft. These figures were bound to cause concern, but gave no reason for panic.

The issue was bedevilled by the fact that the Foreign Office—and Churchill—possessed much more alarming figures of German expansion. Vansittart was by now absolutely obsessed by the German threat, and particularly by the fear of 'a knock-down blow from the air' at the outset of a war, and his alarming memoranda descended upon Ministers like a cataract. The Air Ministry indignantly defended its estimates of German air strength, and the struggle gradually took the strange form of the Air Ministry producing arguments *against* the dramatic expansion of the Air Force for which Vansittart and Churchill were clamouring.

In point of fact, the Air Ministry figures were accurate, and the Foreign Office estimates of German aerial rearmament between 1933 and 1938 were greatly exaggerated. In 1934 Baldwin took a figure roughly between the two extremes, and was right. But when, in March 1935, Hitler made a false claim to Simon and Eden of air 'parity', it seemed that he had been wrong.

It has become almost an article of faith in Britain—and elsewhere —that, had it not been for Churchill's loud and insistent voice in the wilderness, the National Government would not have rearmed at all, and that the Battle of Britain would have been lost. As Churchill himself once wrote in a very different context, these broad effects are capable of refinement. In particular, the obloquy he and others heaped on Baldwin is now clearly seen to be grossly unfair.

It is impossible, of course, to gauge the effect on Ministers of Churchill's speeches on this issue. Probably Baldwin welcomed them. His celebrated 'confession' of May 22nd, 1935, that he had been 'completely wrong' the previous November in his estimate of future German air expansion was certainly not unhelpful to his own cause. But Churchill was a solitary and discredited figure with no following worth taking seriously. When he forced Baldwin into making apparently very damaging admissions of government inadequacy in aerial rearmament, he aroused many Conservatives who might despise

Churchill personally but who were alarmed by his message. Baldwin arranged for Churchill to receive confidential information through his friend Desmond Morton; he also, as will be recorded, brought him in as a member of the Air Defence Research Committee. The Statement on Defence published in March 1935 was by far the clearest statement of the Government's concern and marked the vital step away from deficiency programmes to real rearmament. But these were not in response to Churchill's speeches; they were the result of Baldwin's own activities. When Baldwin became Prime Minister in June 1935 and was master of his own house again, he at once removed Londonderry and appointed Cunliffe-Lister—who went to the Lords as Lord Swinton—as Secretary of State for Air, with his full support and encouragement to undertake a revolutionary programme of expansion and innovation. 'It could not have been achieved without Baldwin's support', Swinton has recorded: 'we knew it and were grateful.' 'It is by no means clear', Churchill's latest biographer has conceded, 'that Churchill was able to assist significantly in the technical development of air defence.'[1] Other estimates are even less enthusiastic.

It is necessary to emphasise that the really vital decisions were taken between 1933 and 1935 within the Government circle. It may also be noted that Churchill's 'ten-year rule' had been abandoned in 1932, and that the run-down of the armament industries in the 1920s meant that the process of rearmament was likely to take a long time. In these circumstances Baldwin's initiation of a study of British industrial potentiality by Lord Weir, Sir James Lithgow, and Sir Arthur Balfour, which produced the scheme for 'shadow' factories, which could be swiftly moved to the production of military equipment, was to be of central importance. Under the chairmanship of Sir Henry Tizard, a committee for the scientific survey of air defence was set up at the end of 1934, and swiftly produced a most remarkable discovery, developed by Robert Watson-Watt—Radio Direction Finding. It then moved towards the next vital step, that of incorporating this new technique into the operational tactics of the R.A.F. By itself, radar was a valuable technical assistance; incorporated operationally, it could give the R.A.F. an outstanding defensive capability.

[1] H. Pelling: *Winston Churchill*, 371. See also R. Rhodes James: *Churchill: A Study in Failure 1900–1939*, Chapter Six.

Meanwhile, the Air Defence Research Committee—the policy overlord of the Tizard Committee—was moving towards the courageous decisions to order the Spitfire and Hurricane off the drawing-board and to set up the 'shadow' factories to produce them. These decisions owed everything to Cunliffe-Lister and Baldwin.

Exactly what *was* achieved requires emphasis. In 1934 the R.A.F. had based in Britain 564 aircraft, which were wooden biplanes with fixed undercarriages. By 1939 this had increased to 1,476 aircraft, of the most modern type. The personnel was increased from 30,000 regulars and 11,000 reservists in 1934 to 118,000 regulars and 68,000 reservists in 1939. In 1934 there were 52 airfields in the United Kingdom available for war needs; by 1939 there were 138, and in that year the expenditure on 'works' was more than three times the cost of the entire R.A.F. in 1934. Indeed, if Kingsley Wood in 1938 had not abandoned one of the 'shadow' factories at West Bromwich, the total of Spitfires available would have risen by some 1,000 by 1940. Swinton's 'Scheme F', approved by the Cabinet in February 1936, provided for the construction of eight thousand aircraft in three years; in April 1938 'Scheme L' provided for twelve thousand in two years. The creation of the R.A.F. Volunteer Reserve was in many respects equally significant. The British had started late, but their quality in aircraft and pilots was exceptional. The former owed little to successive Governments, and everything to private enterprise, funding, and initiative, as did the invention of the jet propulsion engine by Frank Whittle. Swinton deserves all praise for his actions, but the true heroes were the British air pioneers, and particularly the designers and engineers.

In immediate political terms, the price paid for this quality was substantial. In terms of numbers, the R.A.F. was not impressive in 1938. Calculations were based on the necessity for providing for 1939; thus, in the crucial year of 1938, the R.A.F. had only 93 of the new fighters in operation, all of which were Hurricanes, and which experienced difficulties in firing their guns above 15,000 feet. Certain aircraft—notably the turret-firing Boulton Paul Defiant, which Churchill greatly favoured—turned out to be quite useless, and the twin-engined bombers Wellington and Blenheim were highly vulnerable, although excellent aircraft in many respects. The Hampden was a more prescient design for the needs of war. The Hurricane and Spitfire, moreover, were under-gunned, and the latter never achieved its full performance until equipped with three-bladed propellers in 1940—a development urged for some time by the de Havilland Company. By 1938—and even by 1939—the R.A.F. was not an impressive deterrent force. The Germans did not know of its unique R.D.F. defensive operational capacity. Bomber Command had less than 100 obsolete long-range bombers. Meanwhile the Luftwaffe had a fully efficient first-line strength of 3,609 aircraft, supplemented by 552 modern transports; personnel numbers had risen from 20,000 in 1935 to over half a million by 1939. If the Government—on Vansittart's urgings—had expanded the R.A.F. dramatically, it would have been a quantitative expansion, with obsolete aircraft.

The public debate on the situation was becoming very confused. The MacDonald–Baldwin Government had taken a definite decision to rearm in 1934, and the White Paper of March 1935 seemed to mark a very decisive moment. But the unhappiness of the Government was manifest, and in discussion of the ratio of strength in the air the term 'parity' introduced a highly complicated element into the controversy. Was parity meant in numerical or qualitative terms? What, indeed, *was* 'front-line strength'?

Matters were not made easier by Baldwin's decision to appoint Churchill to the Air Defence Research Committee in the summer of 1935. Churchill insisted on maintaining his freedom of action in Parliament and on the admission of his friend Professor Lindemann to the Tizard Committee.

Lindemann had been Professor of Experimental Philosophy at Oxford since 1919. He had had a brilliant beginning as a physicist, and the Clarendon Laboratory stands as his monument—a poor joke in 1919, and under his aegis developed into the most advanced low temperature physics laboratory in the world. He fought for the status of science with absolute and concentrated ardour. But by the 1930s Lindemann no longer moved among the foremost figures of his profession, by whom he was generally regarded with aversion. Lindemann was not an attractive man. He was a snob; he could be savagely vindictive; he had a very high estimate of his own intellectual calibre and a low one of other people's. Sir Roy Harrod has written of him:

His experience of men was very limited. One might gain the impression, and he himself perhaps believed, that he knew everyone who was everyone. But his acquaintance really only extended to a thin top crust—prominent people in politics, diplomacy and London Society. . . . He was quite out of touch with the course of contemporary thought, and this considerably cramped his style.

He had sedulously cultivated Churchill since the 1920s. Each man was fascinated by the other. As Lindemann was a total abstainer, a non-smoker, a philistine in art and literature and a fastidious vegetarian the connection of interest between himself and Churchill may seem difficult to diagnose. Churchill has written that 'Lindemann could decipher the signals of the experts on the far horizons and explain to me in lucid homely terms what the issues were'. One commentator has surmised that:

> Through Churchill, Lindemann could vicariously enjoy the pleasures of life; through Lindemann, Churchill could vicariously engage in mathematical calculations and scientific investigations.

There is no need to examine the controversial question of whether Lindemann was or was not Churchill's evil genius. What is undeniable is the fact that he was a divisive and almost disastrous influence on the Tizard Committee. He and Tizard had been colleagues and close friends in the past; swiftly there developed a deep and bitter enmity between them that poisoned relations and hindered the work of the Air Defence Research Committee to the point that Swinton—in order to keep the Committee together—had to disband it in 1936 and recreate it without Lindemann. But Lindemann had his revenge later.

Regarded now, many of Lindemann's arguments and theories verge on the farcical. The most ludicrous of all was a proposal for research on aerial mines, which has been rightly described as 'a completely blind alley for research on which valuable time and money were wasted'. Another proposal for a 'cloud of substance in the path of an aeroplane to produce detonation' seems to belong more appropriately to bad scientific fiction than to a serious understanding of scientific and technological matters. Lindemann put forward his ideas with intense vigour, and reacted harshly to criticism; Churchill urged them on the A.D.R.C. with comparable energy. Much time was lost in the pursuit of these fantasies. Swinton became exasperated. 'The differences of opinion on the Tizard Committee', it has been written, 'could have had a serious effect on the rapid growth of radar.'

There was another disadvantage to these arrangements. Churchill, as a member of the A.D.R.C. was privy to what was going on; he was also to some extent an associate in the decisions taken. This did not prevent him from attacking the Government incessantly in public for its dilatoriness. On this matter Swinton has written:

> Winston certainly believed in my expansion plans. . . . At the same time he was determined to use anything he could find to attack the Government. So he used every evidence, good or bad, relevant or irrelevant, he could find about German air strength to attack the Government. The meaningless phrase of Baldwin's about 'parity' played into his hands. And the last thing he bothered about was consistency. He knew I should go on with the plans we both believed in; and at the same time he could go for the Government.
>
> He was, I am sure, genuinely horrified when the result of attacks on the Government, to which he had contributed so much, resulted in Neville sacking me.

In this debate, it is very easy to make out a good case for each side. The Baldwin Government was in effect introducing rearmament by stealth, and making long-term plans for air defence that were far-seeing, courageous, and absolutely right. Churchill did not believe in rearmament by stealth, particularly in the air. He wanted a bold, well-publicised, defiant programme that would provide Britain with her defence needs and warn Germany of the perils of incurring Britain's enmity. Ministers could point to the progressive expansion of expenditure on armaments after 1934; £102·7 millions in 1932–3 to £198 millions in 1937–8. Churchill could point to the fact that this was not nearly enough *relative* to Germany, and this was the vital point.

But what was rearmament *for*? Hardly anyone—perhaps not even Churchill—accepted the inevitability of war. Was it to strengthen British diplomacy in a new appalling jungle world? Was it merely for national defence? Was it to check German and Italian ambitions? Baldwin's view—which he never set out clearly in public—was that the defence programme should have as its main objective that of deterrence. When Churchill made the same point in a meeting with Baldwin in November 1936 Baldwin interrupted him to say 'I am with you on that' . . . 'I am with you there wholeheartedly'.[1] Although the development of Bomber Command was a notable exception, the

[1] See R. Rhodes James, op. cit., 294.

priority of Ministers was, and remained, strictly defensive. Chamberlain reluctantly supported the need for a rearmament programme, but watched jealously over its cost. As he wrote in February 1936, 'If we were to follow Winston's advice and sacrifice our commerce to the manufacture of arms, we should inflict a certain injury on our trade from which it would take generations to recover, we should destroy the confidence which now happily exists, and we should cripple the revenue'. Principally as a result of his insistence, the 1936 White Paper on Defence pledged to rearm 'without impeding the course of normal trade'. For the MacDonald–Baldwin Governments, rearmament was a grim necessity, undertaken without zest and, with the exception of the Air Ministry, carried on without urgency.

We are accordingly presented with a very curious situation. By 1936, it is evident Ministers were at last deeply disturbed at the imbalance—which they exaggerated—between the British and German air forces. They were quite unconcerned at the other military imbalances. They were oppressed by the horrors of a future war. They accepted the fact that Germany was already approaching the capability of waging a substantial war. Yet they did not see rearmament as the answer. Nor was it the answer; but, having accepted that it was necessary, they did not see its place in the determination of policy towards the Dictators. There was a crucial absence of interest and urgency in the Cabinet on the subject—with the exceptions of Baldwin and Swinton, whose attention was concentrated on the R.A.F. Accepting military weakness as a fact, their colleagues gradually moved to accepting the solution to the European problem by other means. From this there came the conviction, almost the obsession, that Hitler could and must be negotiated with, and that the problems of Europe were fully capable of a peaceful solution. The 'deterrent' argument faded, even before Baldwin's retirement. By 1937 there was a tacit assumption in the Cabinet that Germany possessed overwhelming military superiority. We find Chamberlain writing in January 1938:

> Until our armaments are completed, we must adjust our foreign policy to our circumstances, and even bear with patience and good humour actions which we should like to treat in very different fashion.

None of this is to deny the existence of an imbalance by 1937. But what is so striking is the failure to enter into military conversations with the French, to examine the true nature of the German military threat—which was on the land—or to take the kind of measures that a Government which feels its national existence imperilled would be expected to take. Ministers became paralysed by the spectacle of German military renaissance, and accepted its preponderance. Thus by the time that Chamberlain succeeded Baldwin in May 1937, there was a general acceptance of the argument that diplomatic settlement provided the only hope of escape from disaster. Their general attitude was enshrined in the words of Castlereagh:

> This country cannot and will not act upon abstract and speculative principles of precaution.

By the end of 1937 even Churchill was hesitant. In an article written in October he declared that:

> Three or four years ago I was myself a loud alarmist . . . In spite of the risks which wait on prophecy, I declare my belief that a major war is not imminent, and I still believe that there is a good chance of no major war taking place in our time. . . . Well was it written: 'Agree with thine adversary quickly whilst thou art in the way with him.'

This was indeed the policy of the new Prime Minister. But much was to occur between the summer of 1935 and Neville Chamberlain's accession to the Premiership in May 1937.

CHAPTER EIGHTEEN

THE LAST BALDWIN GOVERNMENT, 1935–1937

B Y THE early summer of 1935 the fluctuating fortunes of the National Government began to show clear signs of marked improvement. Although the chronic problems of the most afflicted industrial areas remained, the Government could claim that it had taken some positive action to alleviate their most severe difficulties. It was true that here the realities of unemployment, part-employment, and wretched conditions of work for those who could obtain employment were still overwhelming features of the daily lives of the people, but elsewhere in the country prosperity was rising. After the trauma and fears of 1930–2, national confidence had returned. In Parliament, the divisive and protracted India dispute was approaching its conclusion. The Labour and Liberal leadership was feeble and tentative. Both parties were weighed down by public memories of the 1929–31 débâcle, particularly in the middle classes. The Roehm purge, and Hitler's claims, had led to the general acceptance of the principle of cautious rearmament. The Anglo-German Naval Treaty of June 1935, which limited the German Navy to thirty-five per cent of the British, and submarines to forty-five per cent, was criticised, and not vehemently, only by a small group of Conservatives. To the majority, it appeared to be a notable coup for the Government; the fact that it was a unilateral revision of Versailles, undertaken without any consultation with France, and accordingly a severe blow to the concept of the 'Stresa Front', was not widely appreciated. Thus, after the strains of the previous two years, the Government seemed to be moving into a calmer and more hopeful period. In by-elections, the Labour resurgence fell away. It was Jubilee year. Conservative morale began to mount.

In June came the long expected reshuffle when MacDonald at last stepped down as Prime Minister and was replaced by Baldwin. MacDonald's career had dwindled into a pathetic twilight, in which his always somewhat diffuse speaking style had drifted into meaningless vapidity. To the younger politicians it was difficult to recognise in this often rambling and vain old man the architect of the Labour Party, the courageous and reviled opponent of the war, and the first national leader that the Labour movement had produced. He deserves much better of history than the derisive mockery which has followed him beyond his death in 1937. But it had been a profound national misfortune that he had held the Premiership so long after it was clearly evident that he was no longer capable of holding any serious public office.

Baldwin's belated resumption of power gave him the opportunity of making several overdue changes. The pompous and legalistic Simon was moved from the Foreign to the Home Office, and was replaced by Hoare. This was only a marginal improvement. Hoare was a prim and not wholly lovable personality, witheringly immortalised by Birkenhead as 'the last of a long line of maiden aunts', but he was very ambitious and undoubtedly able, and had a heightened reputation as a result of his patient handling of the Government of India Act. No one realised the price that had been paid in mental and physical exhaustion during this struggle. Anthony Eden became Minister Without Portfolio for League of Nations Affairs, also in the Cabinet. Eden, high-strung and eager to advance, was unhappy about this dual arrangement, and with good cause, but Baldwin persuaded him to accept. Although Eden seemed too young and inexperienced to take the Foreign Secretaryship, Baldwin had developed a high estimate of him. He was certainly by far the most exciting, attractive, and impressive of the new generation of Conservatives that had emerged from the war, with a good intellect, an excellent record, and considerable personal charm, and who was dedicated to his work. It was difficult to discern at that stage of his meteoric career that behind this most impressive façade there was a brave, sensitive, honourable, but nervous and irresolute personality.

Halifax, whom Baldwin had long admired and liked greatly, became Secretary of State for War, and two young Conservatives of high promise, Oliver Stanley (Education) and Walter Elliot (Agriculture), entered the Cabinet. The National Labour presence was rather disproportionately represented by Ramsay and Malcolm

MacDonald and the perennial Jimmy Thomas, with Lord de la Warr as a senior Minister. The most significant appointment was that of Cunliffe-Lister to the Air Ministry. His energy and ability as chairman of the Air Defence Research Committee had impressed Baldwin, who was also resolved to get rid of the imperious Lord Londonderry. The latter took his removal to the leadership of the Lords badly, and took his dismissal from the Government in November even more ill. Londonderry has received rather more praise for his tenure of the Air Ministry—notably from Churchill—than he really merited, but there were other factors in his downfall. He and his wife ran what was virtually the last *grande tenue* establishment in London, and the fact that their great wealth was based substantially upon coal revenues did not heighten his stature in Baldwin's eyes. The Londonderrys' sedulous courting of MacDonald also distressed Baldwin, who had a genuine affection and respect for his colleague and disliked seeing him basking foolishly amidst the glories of Londonderry House. But there were considerations of policy as well. Londonderry was a 'bomber', and in October 1934 had made a boastful speech on the subject which had been a source of considerable public embarrassment to the Government and of great personal annoyance to Baldwin. Londonderry was furthermore, a member of London Society that was markedly friendly to the German government and notoriously hostile to Jews.

Cunliffe-Lister was by far the best of Baldwin's new appointments, but it was a deep misfortune—as he himself subsequently realised—that in November he accepted a peerage and went to the House of Lords as the Earl of Swinton. This removed from the Commons not only one of the most able Ministers in the Cabinet but the architect of the renaissance of the Royal Air Force and the most emphatic exponent of effective rearmament. Cunliffe-Lister's abrasiveness and lack of respect for exalted reputations had prevented him from developing a real following in the party, but the respect he had gathered might have made him a strong challenger to Neville Chamberlain for the succession. As he remarked in his old age, 'I still kick myself. I was a damned fool.'

Londonderry's removal in November enabled Baldwin to transfer Halifax to the office of Lord Privy Seal and to bring in another promising young Conservative, Duff Cooper. Again, this promise was not to be fulfilled. In the Government, but outside the Cabinet, were other coming young men favoured by Baldwin—W. S. Morrison,

Thomas Dugdale, James Stuart, R. A. Butler, and Leslie Hore-Belisha. For some time Baldwin had been deeply concerned at the lack of young men of ability and sense of public service in the Conservative ranks that he was looking for in the party, and he was understandably worried about the advanced average age of the Cabinet. But his promotions look odd in the light of later experience. Of his personal favourites only Eden and Butler proved to be of top calibre, and he overlooked equally promising men, most notably the rebellious Harold Macmillan and the rapidly developing Victor Cazalet. Nonetheless, it was a bold infusion of new blood, and emphasised the fact that the Labour Party had nothing comparable in talent, in Parliament or out of it, in this generation at this level.

Baldwin himself was ageing, if not as noticeably as MacDonald, and the virtually twenty years of high office and thirteen of the party leadership had taken their toll. He commanded unequalled respect and affection, and he was, like the old Gladstone, still capable of rising from time to time to great events and important occasions. But the capacity to cover all aspects of Government without becoming too immersed, of surveying the operations of an Administration with a keen eye for the most critical, had been eroded. He cared deeply about rearmament—'a country which shows itself unwilling to make what necessary preparations are recognisable for its own defence will never have force—moral or material—in this world'—and had done more than any other senior Minister to put the Government on this unpopular but necessary course. But he did not see the whole picture. He was tired, under strain, and he recognised the fact. Chamberlain was to be the dominating influence in his last Government. But he felt that he should remain to take the Government through a General Election that could not be long postponed; he was concerned about Neville Chamberlain's likely approach to rearmament as Prime Minister; and he had deep forebodings about the monarchy. King George had never fully recovered from a major illness in 1929, and the Jubilee in the summer of 1935, although a personal triumph, had been a further strain on a weakened physique. The personality of his heir, and his fitness for the tasks before him, were matters of concern. Baldwin, accordingly, stayed on. His final Premiership was to be dismally undistinguished, and, indeed, marked by only one major public achievement and a series of public humiliations. But at least

Swinton was given his head at the Air Ministry, and that was to prove a major element in the salvation of the nation in 1940.

No places were found for Amery, Churchill, or Lloyd George. The former was becoming regarded, cruelly, but not wholly without cause, as an over-serious long-winded bore, and he had no following. But he had also proved himself an able and courageous Minister, and his continuing exclusion—in which Neville Chamberlain played some part—was a major misfortune. Churchill was deeply chagrined by his ostracism, but it would have been a most remarkable act of charity to have given office to a man whose dominant occupation over the previous four years had been to denounce the Government on almost all possible occasions, and often in the most violent terms. In these circumstances the fact that Baldwin was 'very hostile' to the idea of Churchill's return was wholly understandable.[1] Chamberlain was also strongly opposed to the reinstatement of what he called 'this brilliant, erratic, creature', and the opinions of the evident heir-apparent had to be taken into serious account. The only really surprising aspect was that Churchill, both before and after the 1935 election, thought that he had a serious chance of inclusion.[2] Subsequently he was more philosophical. 'There was much mocking in the Press about my exclusion. But now one can see how lucky I was. Over me beat the invisible wings. And I had agreeable consolations. I set out with my paintbox for more genial climes without waiting for the meeting of Parliament.'[3] The possibility of a Lloyd George–Baldwin coalition—although discussed—was never realistic.

The new Government was swiftly presented with an ominous challenge to the assumptions of the 'Stresa Front', when Italian designs upon Abyssinia moved from threats to active preparations for invasion.

The Cabinet received very conflicting advice. The Minister in Addis Ababa, Sir Sidney Barton, cabled that 'I can think of only one course likely to prevent perpetration of what may be widely regarded as an

[1] Thomas Jones: *A Diary with Letters*, 145.
[2] In January he had spoken on behalf of his son, Randolph, who had put himself forward as Independent Conservative candidate in a by-election at Wavertree (Liverpool). This was not inspired by the older Churchill, as was generally believed at the time, but Randolph Churchill got over ten thousand votes and Labour captured the seat. This episode, coming so soon before the change of Government, was in itself sufficient cause for Churchill to be passed over by Baldwin. But it was only one element.   [3] Churchill, op. cit., 141.

international crime, and that would be for England and France to tell Italy that she cannot have Ethiopia'. But the counsel of Sir Eric Drummond, formerly the first Secretary-General of the League, and now Ambassador in Rome, was dismissive of the League and of any conciliation procedures and favoured pressure on the Emperor Haile Selassie to make concessions to the Italians. His attitude reflected the firm views of Simon and Vansittart to exploit Mussolini as a counter-weight to Hitler, and the urgings of Barton were ignored. There was little enthusiasm among Ministers for making this a major issue, let alone a *casus belli*, and certainly none at all among the Chiefs of Staff. Their annual review of the condition of Imperial Defence was a very sombre document. 'By the signing of the Treaty of Locarno', they observed, 'the United Kingdom undertook definite commitments and to that extent made our participation in a European war more likely without in any way reducing our responsibilities in the Far East.' Confronted with a rearming Germany and a powerful and menacing Japan, the prospect of making an additional enemy was not alluring.

The bulk of the Conservative Party shared Churchill's view that it was 'a very small matter' and that 'no one can keep up the pretence that Abyssinia is a fit, worthy, and equal member of a League of civilised nations'. But the possibility of an Italian invasion aroused surprising passions outside Westminster, and was a major element in the downfall of George Lansbury, who was savaged and humiliated by Ernest Bevin at the annual Labour conference in October. The full extent of public feeling was not fully evident until December, but even in June and July Ministers realised—particularly with an election looming within twelve months—that they had to walk warily. While they sought in private a formula that would extricate themselves from this unpleasant embarrassment, in public Hoare was dispatched to Geneva to pledge on September 12th the full commitment of the British Government to the Covenant of the League, and, in particular, to 'steady and collective resistance to all acts of unprovoked aggression'. Eden was not the only Cabinet Minister to be startled by the vigour of a speech that, in the words of Lester Pearson of Canada, 'moved us to cheers and almost to tears'. Hoare had trapped the Government in its own self-made snare. Its policy was now reduced to big words, the League, and the private resolution not to put these grave matters to the test.

The Labour Party was passing through deeply emotional heart-searchings about its attitude towards national and collective security, which was now sharply exacerbated by the mounting crisis over Abyssinia. Lansbury, an avowed and dedicated pacifist, was greatly loved, and his offer to resign if his extreme views were an embarrassment to the party had been rejected at the 1934 party conference. By October 1935 this embarrassment had become very real with the majority of the party and the T.U.C. strongly supporting the League. The key issue was sanctions, which Lansbury passionately opposed, but there were other factors which had made his leadership a source of irritation to many in the party. With an election looming, Lansbury's age and lengthy emotional speeches jarred on many of his colleagues, but none dared challenge his overwhelming popularity. His speech to the 1935 conference opposed sanctions and won a tremendous ovation. But in a speech of notable brutality Ernest Bevin stamped upon the possibility, which Lansbury had clearly hinted at, that he might remain as leader despite the division of view between himself and the bulk of the party, in one passage: 'You are placing the Executive and the Movement in an absolutely wrong position to be taking your conscience round from body to body asking to be told what you ought to do with it.' Some who were present claim that Bevin used the words 'trailing your conscience', others 'hawking your conscience', but the exact words were not the point. The resolution against which Lansbury had spoken so vehemently was passed by more than two million votes, and his speech in reply to Bevin was listened to with impatience and had no effect. Lansbury resigned, and the Parliamentary Party, after asking him to reconsider his decision, elected Attlee for the remainder of the session. It was assumed that this would be a very temporary measure. This assumption was to prove wrong.

Thus, the trade union and Labour movements had committed themselves to the principle of firm action through the League against Italy. Their reasoning may have been confused, but the meaning was clear. A surge of emotion seemed to be sweeping the country, and to this Ministers could not be indifferent.

In June Hoare had warned the Cabinet that there was every prospect of it being placed in 'a most inconvenient dilemma' over Abyssinia, and had informed his colleagues that 'Either we should have to make a futile protest, which would irritate Mussolini and perhaps drive him out of the League into the arms of Germany, or we should make no protest at all and give the appearance of pusillanimity'. The same basic point was made more bluntly by the head of the Civil Service, Sir Warren Fisher: 'If Italy persists in her present policy', he wrote to Baldwin, 'is England really prepared not merely to threaten, but also to use force, and is she in a position to do so?' The answer to both questions was clearly negative. Thus, by September, the British were exactly in the dilemma that Hoare had warned about in June, and he was very substantially responsible for making the situation even worse by his dramatic Geneva speech. Electoral factors undoubtedly played a considerable part in this chaos. As Ministers read it, the Peace Ballot—published in June—demonstrated strong support not only for non-military League action against an aggressor but also for military. It was certainly Hoare's judgement that 'there would be a wave of public opinion against the Government if it repudiated its obligations under Article 16 [of the Covenant]. . . . It was abundantly clear that the only safe line for His Majesty's Government was to try out the regular League of Nations procedure'.[1] By this stage the Chiefs of Staff had laid out to the Cabinet the full military and diplomatic implications of years of neglect of the armed forces. The French, still embittered by the Anglo-German Naval Treaty, remained only very guardedly co-operative. When the French Foreign Minister, Laval, put the question of full British adherence to the Covenant to Eden with characteristic bluntness on September 2nd, he got a lame answer.[2] On September 9th and 10th Hoare met with Laval, and reached agreement that they would take no action at Geneva that would lead to war.

Why, then, did Hoare proceed to Geneva and deliver his dramatic call to arms? Chamberlain's account of a dinner with Hoare and Baldwin on September 5th relates that it was he who urged a firm line which 'might force Italy to a halt, which in turn might make Hitler waver',[3] and that Hoare and Baldwin agreed. But Hoare went further than this in public. He later wrote that he was personally determined to make 'a revivalist appeal to the Assembly. At best it might start a new chapter of League recovery, at worst it might deter Mussolini by a display of League fervour. If there was any element of bluff in it, it

[1] Quoted in Correlli Barnett: *The Collapse of British Power*, 361.
[2] Lord Avon: *Facing the Dictators*, 258.
[3] Keith Feiling: *Neville Chamberlain*, 268.

was a moment when bluff was not only legitimate, but inescapable.'[1] A cynic might observe that it was the only option left. But there was another consideration, to which Hoare referred in his speech: 'The recent response of public opinion [in Britain] shows how completely the nation supports the Government in the full acceptance of the obligations of League membership.'

Hoare had gone considerably further than the discussions in the Cabinet had warranted, and it is not clear whether Baldwin saw the final text of his speech. But although Hoare returned to a hero's welcome the reactions of other Ministers were understandably less glowing. At a long Cabinet on September 24th these mounting apprehensions surfaced, but Ministers had to conclude that 'the serious consequences of receding from the previous attitude [of support for the League] were emphasised from the point of view of domestic policy no less than from that of foreign policy. It was pointed out that any weakness or vacillation would bring serious consequences'. Baldwin was not the only Minister who remarked upon the equal perils of maintaining the present course. But now they had no choice.

Throughout this dismal proceeding Baldwin had not given any serious lead to his colleagues, and the error of having two Cabinet Ministers from the Foreign Office was being revealed. Baldwin's position and attitudes are extremely difficult to describe, let alone analyse, during these critical weeks. The evidence is confused and fragmentary, but the very absence of clear evidence in his own papers or in the Cabinet archives leads to the conclusion that Baldwin was himself very confused, baffled, and profoundly concerned. He did not let the crisis slip turbulently past him while he observed it serenely from a sage shore, as many have implied. He watched the terrible maelstrom with bewilderment and fear, but with his mind concentrated upon other matters. He left far too much to his subordinates, whom he had just appointed, and he had committed himself too deeply to the League in the appointment of the ardent Eden and the newly converted and unstable Hoare. And, then, there was the startlingly belligerent Neville Chamberlain, whose influence as the heir-apparent was rising sharply, and who had informed the Cabinet on May 27th that 'the Italians had behaved so badly that it would be impossible morally, and indeed, almost indecent to come to terms with them'. Hoare had taken his lead from Chamberlain.

[1] Templewood, op. cit., 166.

Thus, with a Cabinet whose senior members were so confident, yet himself knowing of the dismal inadequacies of the force behind these fine challenges, his attention concentrated on other priorities, Baldwin struggled along and hoped for the best. His Government had drifted into a position from which only a dramatic and humiliating climb-down by the Italians could possibly save them. And the possibility of this deliverance was rapidly disappearing.

Meanwhile, Baldwin was receiving conflicting advice about the best time for the General Election that must come before the autumn of 1936. The view of the Conservative Central Office was that the main issue of the election would be unemployment, and particularly the conditions in the depressed areas; it was also obvious that Labour would continue to exploit the armaments issue. Neville Chamberlain, somewhat surprisingly in view of his fiscal opposition to rearmament, urged that the Government should fight on rearmament and foreign policy, but his arguments were based less on national than on party political calculations. Baldwin disagreed strongly with these calculations. He wanted his mandate for rearmament, and was equally prepared to exploit the public feeling over Abyssinia, but he did not want another single-issue election on the 1923 pattern, and in any event he was convinced that rearmament was not an issue on which an election could be won. He therefore proposed to fight it over the broad front of the Government's achievements and the deficiencies of Labour. He held his counsel about the timing until the European situation seemed clearer. At the party conference at the beginning of October he had, in the account of Thomas Jones, 'a great ovation. Denounced the isolationists, reconciled the Party to the League by supporting rearmament, and reconciled the pacifists to rearmament by supporting the Covenant. Spoke strongly in favour of Trade Unions. All with an eye to the election, on the date of which he was inscrutable.'[1]

But on October 3rd the Italians actually invaded Abyssinia. The League branded Italy as an aggressor, and the question of economic sanctions was urgently considered. The dominant factors in the British approach were their refusal to act alone—and certainly not without full French support—their apprehensions of the situation in the Mediterranean if war broke out with Italy, and, above all, the desire of Ministers and the Foreign Office not to antagonise Mussolini

[1] Jones, op. cit., 155.

fatally. Sanctions were accordingly imposed, but with the notable exception of oil. It was something more than a slap on the wrist, and something less than a harsh blow. Ministers groped towards a convenient escape from their predicament, while making strong pronouncements about support for the League. Greater attention should have been given to Baldwin's warning in his October 3rd speech that 'His Majesty's Government have not, and have never had, any intention of taking isolated action in this dispute'. On this point Baldwin was emphatic, but he left the actual details to Hoare and Eden. It is a serious charge against Baldwin—and a just one—that he did not devote as much attention to what was going on in the Foreign Office at this time as he should have. As Vansittart, the chief author of the looming disaster, subsequently wrote:

> It is wrong to suppose that he [Baldwin] had no care for foreign affairs; he had some, but not enough: he could not find time to masticate the mass of Foreign Office papers. Seeing the limitations of time and himself he preferred to leave details to experts without authority.[1]

This is a severe judgement, and one not merited as a general one on Baldwin's involvement in foreign affairs throughout his career; but it was certainly justified in the context of the Abyssinian crisis.

It is not clear what were the decisive factors that prompted Baldwin to decide on an autumn election. He wanted his 'mandate' for rearmament, and his concern at the deficiencies revealed by the latest report of the Defence Requirements Committee was genuine. With the international situation so ominous, the prospect of taking the Government into the last months of a dying Parliament was not an alluring one. There was also the incalculable factor of Baldwin's sensitivity to public opinion. He sensed, rather than knew, that the Labour resurgence was receding, and that the Liberals offered no real threat. In the period when polling on the Gallup pattern was unknown (its first tentative appearance in Britain was in 1938) politicians had to rely upon visits to their constituencies, by-election results, the advice of the party officials, the economic indicators of confidence or recession, and the newspapers. When they had done all this, the judging of this vast new electorate was basically one of guesswork. In 1923 and 1929 Baldwin had guessed wrong; this time he was right. Parliament

---

[1] Vansittart: *The Mist Procession*, 352.

was dissolved, and the election held on November 14th. Meanwhile, the labyrinthine discussions in Geneva and Paris continued on their uneasy course.

Mr. Taylor has summarised the subsequent campaign:

> It was a confused election. Essentially both Labour and the National parties, apart from a few extremists on either side, were saying the same thing: all sanctions short of war. Labour implied that the government were not operating sanctions seriously: Conservatives alleged that Labour, if in power, would topple over into war. Both sides were in a muddle themselves and therefore muddled their charges against each other.[1]

But this was not the whole story. The election was not fought over Abyssinia or rearmament in isolation from other issues, of which economic ones were the most significant, but they figured so prominently in the debates between the major politicians that it is unwise to accept that, as Mr. Taylor claims, 'the electors showed little interest in these questions'. The Labour accusations of Conservative 'warmongering' did not diminish after the removal of Lansbury, and were intense throughout the campaign. The Labour Manifesto declared that 'This Government is a danger to the peace of the world, to the security of this country. . . . Whilst paying lip service to the League, it is planning a vast and expensive rearmament programme which will only stimulate similar programmes elsewhere . . . the best defence is not huge competitive national armaments, but the organisation of collective security against any aggressor and the agreed reduction of national armaments elsewhere.' One particularly vitriolic accuser was Herbert Morrison, a bitter and ambitious former Minister of Transport who had built up a formidable and ruthless organisation in the London County Council (and also a very formidable enemy in Bevin) and who was consumed by the conviction that if he had not lost his seat in 1931 it would have been he, and not Attlee, reigning in Lansbury's place. Perhaps he was right, but it was a lucky escape for the Labour Party and for the nation.[2] But in the 1935 election Morrison's was the dominant Labour voice, and he was relentless on

[1] Taylor, op. cit., 383.

[2] After the election, when he was in Parliament again, he and Arthur Greenwood stood against Attlee. In the first ballot the votes were: Attlee 58, Morrison 44, Greenwood 32. Greenwood withdrew, and on the second ballot Attlee defeated Morrison by 88 votes to 44.

the charge of armaments, with Attlee, a trenchant speaker on occasion, but no demagogue, limping behind.

Baldwin's responses subsequently earned Churchill's withering contempt—and not only his. At the time Churchill confined himself to Epping, equivocated on Abyssinia, was strong on rearmament, and pledged his warm support for his leader. 'Things are in such a state that it is a blessing to have at the head of affairs a man whom people will rally round', he wrote enthusiastically to Baldwin on October 7th. '. . . I will abide with you in this election, and do what little I can to help in the most serviceable way.'

Baldwin in fact handled the matter of rearmament not only with considerable political skill but also with rather more honesty than later evaluations—principally Churchill's—afford him credit. He reiterated the point that rearmament was necessary for defence, but defence alone. He pledged that 'there will be no great armaments', and in further response to the drum-beat of Labour attacks—'What they really want is big armaments in order to play the old game of power politics', Attlee was charging—issued a statement just before voting that made this point again:

> The Government will undertake a programme planned only, so far as all the defensive services are concerned, to provide adequately for our country's safety. The sole desire of Ministers is to secure that the country and the Empire are again placed in a position to safeguard their interests in case of any eventuality. Beyond that point it is not intended to go.

The allegation has persisted that Baldwin tricked the electorate over rearmament in 1935, and, in Churchill's devastating accusation, that 'having gained all that there was in sight upon a programme of sanctions and rearmament, he became very anxious to comfort the professional peace-loving elements in the nation, and allay any fears in their breasts which his talk about naval requirements might have caused. . . . Thus the votes both of those who sought to see the nation prepare itself against the dangers of the future, and of those who believed that peace could be preserved by praising its virtues, were gained.'[1] This was harsh, and not justified. Churchill's case would be strengthened if the evidence supported his own claim that

---

[1] Churchill, op. cit., 180.

'I fought my contest in the Epping Division upon the need for re-armament and upon a severe and *bona fide* policy of sanctions'. In fact, he ran it on classic anti-Socialist lines, warmly supporting the economic and social programmes of the Government, warning about the German peril but praising Baldwin, whom he described as 'a statesman who has gathered to himself a greater fund of confidence and goodwill than any man I recollect in my long public career'. Believing, as he did, that it would be 'a terrible deed to smash up Italy', references to sanctions—*bona fide* or otherwise—were not at all prominent in his campaign. It is in no sense to denigrate Churchill's prolonged and courageous campaign for rearmament in the 1930s to emphasise that all aspects of his subsequent version, and particularly the violent assault on Baldwin, should not be accepted. Churchill himself was a tough, and not always wholly scrupulous, professional politician. In his memoirs, although Baldwin receives more than his deserved share of criticism, there is one passage of genuine admiration: 'He had a genius for waiting upon events and an imperturbability under adverse criticism. He was singularly adroit in letting events work for him, and capable of seizing the right moment when it came . . . I should have found it easier to work with Baldwin, as I knew him, than with Chamberlain.'[1]

Baldwin received what he later described as his mandate for the continuation of his policies. It was, in a very real sense, a personal triumph. Baldwin had the capacity to inspire trust and respect that no British politician of the century has possessed. Normally a hum-drum commonsense speaker, with an instinctive understanding of his audiences, he had the capacity to move unexpectedly into heights of oratory that constantly astounded his colleagues and critics. As a radio speaker he was particularly impressive. In contrast, Attlee was waspish and sounded mean, like an embittered tax inspector; Morri-son was cockney and vicious; Cripps was learned and politically wild; Churchill seemed to belong to another age, almost as absurd as MacDonald; Lloyd George was a gone goose, courted only by those with flickering memories and vague expectations.

The real and valid charge against Baldwin in 1935 is not that he deceived the nation on rearmament, but that his Abyssinian policy was a fraud. The Opposition was deeply split on the issue, and in these circumstances the apparently balanced and judicious approach of the

[1] Churchill, op. cit., 221-2.

Government had an appearance of statesmanship and responsibility. It was this façade that was probably decisive in the Conservative victory, and laid the foundations for the subsequent tumult within and outside the party.

But it had not been a landslide. The Conservative vote was 11·8 million, that of Labour 8·3 million—a margin that emphasises how justified had been Baldwin's apprehensions of the Labour revival in 1933 and 1934. But in terms of seats the majority was much greater —432 to 154. The Liberals dropped again, and both MacDonalds were defeated, the elder by Emanuel Shinwell at Seaham in a particularly unpleasant contest. Both quickly returned to the Commons for other constituencies. Churchill departed with his family and paint-box to Spain. Ministers turned again to the embarrassments of Abyssinia.

*

By this stage, these had become acute. The strategy of the Government —if such a patched-up inchoate process can be adorned with such a description—was to create sufficient European moral, political, and economic pressure to make Mussolini draw back from his adventure and then offer him the hand of warm friendship and closer alliance in the Stresa Front. This overlooked the fact of French disillusionment over the Anglo-German Naval Treaty. Also, unknown to Ministers, there was a serious security leak in the British Embassy in Rome, and Mussolini had other sources in London that gave him the true picture of the flickering British resolve. He pressed forward to 'avenge Adowa', and the wretched poverty-stricken people of Abyssinia found themselves facing modern weapons and an exultant, cruel, and inept invader. Partly through their courage, but principally through Italian incompetence, logistical difficulties, and the sheer size of the country, the Italian onslaught was something less than a *blitzkrieg*. But in Britain, disgust at the Italian excesses rose sharply.

Hoare and Vansittart—principally the latter—devised an escape-route. With French aid, Mussolini would be offered most of Abyssinia, but not all of it; Selassie would retain his title and a fragment of land. This tactic had a considerable element of practical sense in it, but it took no account whatever of the passions building up in Britain. It also conveniently ignored the warm approval given to Hoare's September speech, and the fact that an election had just been fought and won on strong support of the League. It therefore included all factors save that of public opinion and practical politics, and presents us with a perfect example of political insensitivity by a leading official born and brought up in an age when everything was settled in the Westminster Square Mile. But the weak Hoare eagerly went along with it, and so did a not totally comprehending Baldwin.

The proposal that Hoare and Vansittart took to Paris on December 7th to present to Laval, was that Abyssinia would be partitioned, with Italy receiving the principal—and most valuable—areas, while the Emperor Selassie would retain his former limited kingdom with a corridor to the sea. The war would end, the Stresa Front would be triumphantly re-created, sanctions dropped, and the regrettable inter-lude successfully terminated. Laval enthusiastically endorsed it, and made proposals (which were accepted) even more favourable to Italy. The plan ignored the fact that Mussolini was under no serious pressure to end his campaign—and on this the British and French greatly exaggerated reports of discontent and difficulty in Italy—and that political and public opinions in Britain and France, and particu-larly the former, were wholly unprepared for such an abrupt *volte-face*.

The Hoare–Laval Pact was deliberately leaked in Paris—it is still not clear by whom—and in London Ministers and Members of Parliament were subjected to a storm of protest which Duff Cooper subsequently described as the most violent and intense he experienced in his political career. *The Times* blasted the proposals with a leader headed 'A Corridor For Camels', and Conservative back-benchers reported an unparalleled outburst from their constituents.

But the real revolt came from the new Conservative M.P.s, who had taken the election pledge that 'the League of Nations will remain the keystone of British foreign policy' seriously, and were outraged by the rapidity with which their election speeches had been made to look, at the very best, absurd. The Foreign Affairs Committee, chaired by Austen Chamberlain, was the centre of the revolt, and when fifty-nine Government supporters signed a motion critical of the Pact Ministers belatedly realised the full dimensions of the storm. The League of Nations Union, then at the height of its membership and influence, was in itself a force not lightly to be mocked, and made its fury known. As the events of June 1936 over the ending of sanctions were to demonstrate, the League by itself could not have changed the policy. The revolt was within the Conservative Party, and particularly by the new M.P.s. This was what brought Hoare down.[1] When the Chief Whip told Baldwin that 'our men won't stand for it' Hoare's doom was sealed.

Austen Chamberlain became the spokesman of this angry dissident group, and with the Conservative Party, the Press, and the Opposition in uproar, it became evident that Hoare, contentfully resting in Switzerland and believing that he had pulled off a major diplomatic coup, must be sacrificed. In such situations Baldwin could act swiftly. Hoare, his nose encased in plaster after a heavy fall while skating, was summoned back to be given his quietus. Forlorn, undignified, incredulous, and overwhelmed, he tearfully pleaded his case, but unavailingly. Hoare had cause for his unhappiness at the brutality of his treatment, although his colleagues also had merited grounds for complaint of his conduct of affairs. They considered that he had over-committed them on September 12th, and they had certainly not expected him to come to firm undertakings with Laval at this stage, nor to issue a communiqué after his talks with Laval that announced the creation of a formula 'which might serve as a basis for a friendly settlement of the Italo-Ethiopian dispute', which had precipitated the initial intense international speculation before the full details were leaked in Paris. Hoare noted that the Cabinet had agreed on December 10th that the terms were 'the best, from the Abyssinian point of view, that could be obtained from Italy' and 'the lowest terms which the French Government and the Secretary of State for Foreign Affairs thought that Italy might agree to'. On grounds of collective responsibility, all Ministers were implicated. But then the unexpected storm hit them, the party went into open rebellion, and the mob had to have a victim.

Baldwin, in one of the worst speeches of his career, tried to explain matters away in the House of Commons without success. A party revolt of real magnitude was only narrowly averted. Hoare was replaced by Eden, and the Hoare–Laval Pact was emphatically dead. So, too, was the League of Nations. All that remained was the inevitable Italian victory, the exile of Selassie who had become, improbably, an inter-

---

[1] For a recent study of the crisis see D. Waley: *British Public Opinion and the Abyssinian War, 1935–6.* The crisis also occasioned one of the King's more memorable utterances when he remarked (in private), 'No more coals to Newcastle, no more Hoares to Paris'.

national hero, and, in June 1936, the abandonment of sanctions, mocked into their grave by Neville Chamberlain as 'the height of midsummer madness'.

For the Government, this had been a very ugly shock. At no time in the life of the National Government, not even at the height of the storms over India, had there been a party revolt of such intensity and gravity. No one could recall an occasion when a newly elected Government had been plunged so swiftly into a crisis of survival. Luckily, Churchill had been studiously absent and had made no comment whatever, and Austen Chamberlain was hardly an intimidating leader of a *putsch*. But Ministers went on their Christmas holidays profoundly shaken and very perplexed, and none more than Baldwin. The overwhelming majority of a month earlier suddenly looked much less secure.

As has been emphasised before in this narrative, every Parliament has its particular and peculiar characteristics. This one was to prove exceptionally volatile and unpredictable throughout the ten years of its life, and was to provide Ministers with frequent and salutary surprises. It was to humiliate, and then to revere, and finally to excoriate, Baldwin; it was to give Neville Chamberlain the very rare tribute of a standing ovation and then to destroy him; it was to howl Churchill down, then to ignore him, and later to give him support of a kind that neither Gladstone nor Lloyd George had ever experienced —but on its own terms. It was to prove itself a restless, disturbed, emotional, apprehensive, and bloody-minded Parliament, at no time to be taken for granted. It was, both in its leading personalities and in its collective character, the most brilliant and passionate Parliament of the century. A strong and glorious lustre shines upon all who served in it.

As Ministers dispersed for Christmas, some vague inklings of these remarkable and disturbing characteristics had been forcibly borne upon them.   *

When Parliament returned, it was to mourn the passing of the Sovereign. King George V had succeeded to the throne in 1910 in the midst of a major constitutional crisis, for which he was ill-equipped by experience or temperament, and from which he had emerged with a healthy and abiding suspicion of most politicians. Throughout the war his influence had been on the side of the soldiers, and his relationship with Lloyd George had never been close. The King was a sensible, formidable, man, not an intellectual but possessed of considerable intelligence; deeply conservative, yet he never permitted his personal prejudices—which were very strong—to interfere with his conception of his public duty. His crucial intervention in the Irish war in 1921 has already been noted, as has his selection of Baldwin over Curzon in 1923. His treatment of the Labour Ministers was always scrupulously correct, and his personal friendship with Jimmy Thomas was warm and genuine. His part in the creation of the National Government in 1931 was based upon deep concern for the national interest.

The inevitable remoteness of the monarchy had been remarkably diminished by his annual Christmas radio broadcasts. Together with Franklin Roosevelt and Baldwin he had instinctively understood the fundamental technique of this new medium, and mastered it effortlessly. His calm, gentle, conversational, guttural, friendly and sincere homilies had a considerable impact, and the intense enthusiasm with which he had been greeted at his Jubilee in the summer of 1935 had startled most observers and had astonished the King himself. He regarded himself as the Father of his people, and to a remarkable degree was thus regarded by them.

He spent the Christmas of 1935, as always, at Sandringham, but it was evident to those close to him that he was seriously unwell. His condition deteriorated suddenly. On the evening of January 20th it was announced by his doctors that 'the King's life is moving peacefully to its close', and he died during the night. In the January bleakness his body was borne to Sandringham station after lying in state in the small Sandringham church guarded by his tenants and estate workers, and thence to an ice-cold Westminster Hall. 'The coffin remains there', Harold Nicolson, just elected as National Labour M.P. for West Leicester, wrote, 'just a wreath of flowers and the crown, its diamonds winking in the candle-light.' For several days a huge silent procession filed past the catafalque, soldiers with bowed heads standing at the corners. It was an unforgettable, awesome, intensely moving, spectacle. On one occasion the place of the soldiers was taken by the King's four sons.[1] Then the King was taken to Windsor. The public grief and gloom were genuine, and widespread.

[1] King Edward VIII, the Duke of York, the Duke of Gloucester, and the Duke of Kent.

In that same bleak January King Edward VIII was proclaimed with due ceremony. Remote from his parents, he was in public a charming and accomplished performer, but also known to those who had observed him closely to be moody, shallow, and self-indulgent. Although far from being a misogynist, he had not married, and had a marked prediction for what was derided as 'Café Society'. But it was his association with a married American woman, Mrs. Ernest Simpson, which gave those in the know the principal source of alarm, and not least because the relationship was deliberately flaunted. The people knew nothing of this, it was a London story. The new King inherited the vast respect for the monarchy that his father had increased in his reign, and the admiration that he had established in his own right as a fresh, vital, and glamorous personality. His admirers believed that he would provide excitement, and would inject new life into the monarchy. But others, including the Prime Minister, looked on with apprehension, hoped that their fears were groundless, but were still assailed with many forebodings. They could not have calculated how the brief reign of King Edward was to have such a major effect upon the course of British politics in 1936.

*

Ministers had little respite after the Hoare–Laval catastrophe. The pressure for a Minister of Defence from Conservative back benchers became so insistent that some response had to be made to it, in itself an indication of the Government's new nervousness about its supporters. With the notable exception of Swinton, few Ministers were enthusiastic, most were strongly opposed, and the strong influence of Hankey was cast in the balance against the proposal. The fact that Churchill, now returned but studiously restrained, was known to be thirsting for the position did not improve its chances, particularly as far as Neville Chamberlain was concerned. The result was a classic and lamentable Whitehall compromise, whereby a 'Minister for the Co-ordination of Defence' was created, with no powers and little staff. Furthermore, the new Minister was the Attorney-General, Sir Thomas Inskip, whose surprise at the appointment was widely shared. But the choice had been deliberate, and Neville Chamberlain had been the key voice in Inskip's selection; as he approvingly noted, Inskip 'would excite no enthusiasm but he would involve us in no fresh perplexities'. It was one of Baldwin's worst appointments. Inskip was to prove a

thoroughly bad Minister, secretive, nervous, difficult to work with or
for, and with none of the drive and energy that the post required. If
he had possessed these qualities, of course, he would not have been
selected. It was not without significance that Churchill's speeches
subsequently began to strike a nastier note after this final (as it
appeared) blow to his career. 'He thought, no doubt,' he later wrote
of Baldwin, 'that he had dealt me a politically fatal stroke, and I felt
he might well be right.' In reality, the stroke had been delivered by
Chamberlain.

The announcement was made on March 12th, five days after Hitler
had marched German troops into the demilitarised Rhineland in
flagrant violation of Versailles and Locarno, swiftly following this
coup by proposals for settling outstanding issues, the first example of a
technique of swift actions followed by soothing words that was to
become grimly familiar. But this was the first time, and everyone was
caught off balance. The French looked frantically towards London,
but the Government willingly accepted the advice of Eden that the
French should be strongly discouraged from taking any military
action—not that they intended any—and that renewed attempts
should be made to reach 'as far-reaching and enduring a settlement
as possible while Herr Hitler is still in the mood to do so'. Harold
Nicolson noted that 'The feeling in the House is terribly "pro-German", which means afraid of war'.[1] The *Spectator*'s dismissal of the
event as 'a small thing in itself' was excessive, but there was remarkably
little disposition to criticise the Germans for, in Lothian's memorable
phrase, walking into their own back-garden, and considerable impatience at alleged French belligerence. Even Churchill, who knew
that the proposed appointment of the Minister of Defence (as he
thought it would be) was at hand, was cautious. There was widespread
agreement with the statement of Eden that Hitler's offer of negotiations was evidence of Germany's 'unchangeable longing for a real
pacification of Europe', and that 'it is the appeasement of Europe as a
whole that we have constantly before us'. There was no wave of public
opinion faintly comparable to the revulsion against the Hoare–Laval
Pact; indeed, all the evidence was that the British were largely
indifferent to the event, and certainly strongly opposed to any steps
that contained the possibility of war. As the French leaders well
knew, the same attitudes prevailed in their country. The Russians

[1] Nicolson: *Diaries and Letters, 1930–1939*, 254.

proposed League sanctions against Germany, which killed what little
hope there might have been of any serious reaction from the League.
Hitler's soothing assurances turned out to have no real content, and
no serious negotiations took place. He had won his first major victory
at no cost. But the stirrings of unease in Europe that had begun in
1933 were now given substantial impetus. Austen Chamberlain's
fame was now far eclipsed, and he had become a forlorn and even
faintly comical figure, but when he warned the House of Commons
that Austria would be next, and that 'if Austria perishes, Czechoslovakia becomes indefensible', Members were now beginning to
listen.

The Government endured a wretched summer. The collapse of
Abyssinian resistance, the flight of Haile Selassie, his hopeless and
moving appeal to the League, the ignominious abandonment of sanctions, and his exile in England, were eloquent commentaries enough
on the policy pursued by the Government. But when Neville Chamberlain denounced sanctions in June, and the League of Nations Union
rose in its wrath, this time the Conservatives did not rise with it. The
incident was instructive in another sense. It was the first serious public
intervention in foreign affairs made by Chamberlain, was made without reference to his colleagues, and could be read as a humiliation for
the young Foreign Secretary. As Swinton subsequently wrote, 'a man
beaten once in politics at this level can be beaten again. Chamberlain
knew from that moment that he had the measure of Eden.'[1] The
Government's supporters accepted the inevitability of the facts, but
the episode made them restless. In the House of Commons Arthur
Greenwood denounced 'this trembling, vacillating, cowardly government, which is leading people backward instead of forward', and
Lloyd George depicted Ministers as being in full retreat, 'running
away, brandishing their swords—still leading!' The speeches and
articles of Churchill had now real bite in them again. He accused
MacDonald and Baldwin of excelling 'in the art of minimising political
issues, of frustrating large schemes of change, of depressing the
national temperature, and reducing Parliament to a humdrum level.
. . . If the supreme need of John Bull after the war and its aftermath
was a rest-cure, no two nurses were better fitted to keep silence
around a darkened room and protect the patient from anything in the
nature of mental stress or strong emotion.'

[1] Swinton: *Sixty Years of Power*, 166.

Then, the Spanish Civil War erupted. At first it seemed a simple military coup by the Spanish Army, but the supporters of the left-wing Government resisted fiercely. Italy and Germany sent military aid to General Franco's rebels, and the Soviet Union assisted the Government. The 'simple military coup' had flared into a terrible civil war, conducted with great brutality on both sides, and now expanded as a major international issue. But it was something more than this. The ideological struggle of Socialism against Fascism excited a considerable number of British people, notably the young, and with a strong element of the intellectuals. Others, who were uninterested in the ideology, saw the war as another part of the collective Fascist menace to Europe. On the other side were those who strongly supported Franco, were fearful of the possibility of the 'Reds' winning, and saw in the war the dread form of international Communism penetrating Western Europe. It became a deeply divisive issue, on which each group held to its opinions with fierce passions.

But it did not seriously divide the Conservative Party. The Government—with the strong support of Churchill, for some time a devout Franco supporter—decided to keep out; so did the French. A Non-Intervention Committee was established in London, and found its endeavours literally thankless. Labour, which originally supported non-intervention, switched into strong opposition when it was obvious that the Germans and Italians were intervening massively and in contemptuous indifference to the wails of the farcical and impotent Non-Intervention Committee. The League did absolutely nothing. Its new Secretary-General, the malevolent and obsessed Frenchman, Avenol, was a dedicated anti-Communist, and the atmosphere in Geneva itself was poisonously pro-Fascist. Interest in the League had dropped sharply in Britain after the Abyssinian débâcle, and although it continued its normal proceedings in its monstrous new edifice rising beside Lake Leman, it did so in an atmosphere of disillusionment and declining morale. It neither sought, nor was it offered, any role in the Spanish crisis.

But although the war was much more divisive on the Left than on the Right in Britain, the Government's compromises did not appear heroic even at the beginning, and increasingly looked distinctly like intervention on the Franco side when the scale of German and Italian intervention became evident. As Labour concern, anger, and contempt grew, Ministers found it increasingly difficult and embarrassing to hold to their chosen line. They did so, but were evidently highly uncomfortable as they battled the rising tumult of scorn.

There were several indications that Baldwin himself was becoming severely rattled by the storms through which his Government was passing. He over-reacted to Press rumours of a Churchill-led plot against his leadership and startled the House by the observation that it was 'the time of year when midges come out of dirty ditches', a comment both crude and absurd. But he had good cause for his alarm and confusion. The Government seemed incapable of getting anything right. First Hoare–Laval, then the Rhineland, then the Inskip appointment, then in May it was discovered that Jimmy Thomas had leaked to friends in the City the fact that income tax was going to rise by 3d and had to leave public life in a hurry, then the sanctions storm, and now Spain. Meanwhile, Churchill was maintaining his hostile salvoes from the back benches and in the columns of the *Evening Standard*, Austen Chamberlain was becoming a regular spokesman of doom,[1] and there were several other areas of turbulence behind the Prime Minister. It was not surprising that Baldwin was very close to a nervous breakdown. But his mounting army of critics did not fully appreciate the true cause of his weariness, strain, and preoccupation. Throughout this crucial summer the Prime Minister's principal concerns and attentions were concentrated upon what became known as 'the King's Matter'.

*

The relationship between the King (then still the Prince of Wales) and Mrs. Ernest Simpson had been well known in London Society for over a year. Mrs. Simpson was an American lady of much grace, intelligence, and charm, who had been married once before, and was whispered to have 'a past'. The Prince of Wales was clearly infatuated with her, and several of his friends considered her influence upon him a good one, but none had any idea that he contemplated marriage. When he became King his reliance upon her became, if anything, even greater. While the British Press maintained a discreet silence over the affair, those of Europe and the United States blazoned it. The

[1] He died in March the following year, and was the subject of a memorable tribute in the Commons by Lloyd George. 'The younger members felt that they had been carried back through Lloyd George to Gladstone away to the battles of the Reform Bill and the administration of the Duke of Wellington' (Nicolson, op. cit., 296).

King himself did little to conceal his feelings, and a cruise in the Mediterranean on the yacht *Nahlin* in the summer with Mrs. Simpson in prominent attendance further alarmed Ministers. On October 27th Mrs. Simpson obtained a *decree nisi* from her husband, and the loyal Press merely reported the fact without comment. This action was the direct result of an appeal by the King to Beaverbrook, who persuaded his colleagues in the newspaper industry to handle the divorce with the minimum of publicity. Beaverbrook had no knowledge that the King intended to marry Mrs. Simpson, and in fact received assurances from her solicitor, Mr. Theodore Goddard, to that effect. 'Even if I had known that he did propose marriage', Beaverbrook later wrote, 'I would still have done what I did. But the fact remains that I did not know, although I was having conversations with the King almost every day.'[1] The nation as a whole had no inkling of the situation, but in London it was the main topic of gossip and speculation. 'King and Mrs. Simpson only source of conversation', Victor Cazalet, M.P. for Chippenham, noted at the beginning of November. 'Everyone has ideas, nearly everyone is miserable about it . . . Some think he will have to abdicate, others think he will marry her, still again some think he may do it morganatically.' On November 19th Cazalet was present at a dinner given for the King and sat next to Mrs. Simpson:

> Every minute he [the King] gazes at her and a happiness and radiance fills his countenance such as makes you have a lump in your throat. She believes that if she left he would deteriorate and drink. I think she's right; she is the one real friend he has ever had. She does have a wonderful influence over him, but she knows how stubborn he is, and how difficult to influence.[2]

Not all estimates were as favourable, particularly in the Royal Family itself. Baldwin approached the problem with embarrassment and caution. There is no evidence at all to support the view held by some that he was intent on removing the King from his throne. Indeed, it is clear that he was groping for a solution which would avert what he and many others genuinely regarded as a disaster. For all his faults and weaknesses, King Edward was a highly attractive man, and it was believed that he had great potentialities. But Baldwin believed—and probably rightly—that the possibility of Mrs. Simpson

[1] Beaverbrook: *The Abdication of King Edward VIII*, 33.
[2] R. Rhodes James: *Victor Cazalet*, 186.

as Queen of England was wholly unacceptable to the British people. It can be argued with some merit that Baldwin and the Cabinet were assuming an attitude which they never tested, and that the King was being judged by a wholly unrepresentative segment of the nation on standards which belonged more suitably to Victorian times than those of 1936. But it is significant that Labour supported Baldwin completely, and there are other indications that the British belief in the Royal Family as a standard-bearer of moral rectitude was very strong.[1]

Baldwin's caution and embarrassment were in part responsible for the misunderstandings which arose between himself and the King, but the latter was less than frank with the Prime Minister about his intentions. He also concealed his determination to marry Mrs. Simpson from his solicitor, Beaverbrook, and close adviser Walter Monckton. As Monckton recorded:

> I thought throughout, long before as well as after there was talk of marriage, that if and when the stark choice faced them between their love and his obligations as King-Emperor, they would in the end each make the sacrifice, devastating though it would be.[2]

Indeed, it was not until November 17th that the King informed Baldwin of this fact. Up to this point Baldwin had fought against the fact, but with waning optimism, that the King was serious, but it was now evident that he was utterly resolved. Baldwin, and many others, were torn by conflicting emotions. It was obvious that the King was deeply in love, and his determination to marry his mistress was honourable. But monarchs had had lovers before and had not married them, a point which Baldwin—who was not a puritan—gently put to the King. But the King was adamant.

The position was impossible. The Royal Family, the Cabinet, the Liberal and Labour leaders and Dominion leaders would not have Mrs. Simpson, either as a 'real' Queen or a morganatic one. On November 25th Baldwin told Attlee and Sinclair of the situation, and asked their attitude if the King persisted in rejecting the advice of his Ministers and they resigned. Attlee and Sinclair said that in that event they would refuse any invitation to form an alternative Administration. Churchill was also present at this crucial meeting, and

---

[1] See, for example, Hugh Dalton: *Call Back Yesterday*, 114.
[2] F. Donaldson, *Edward VIII*, 207.

Baldwin's biographers state that he said that 'though his attitude was a little different, he would certainly support the Government'. The attitude of other Ministers—notably Neville Chamberlain—was much less sympathetic than that of Baldwin to the King, and there was a strong feeling that Baldwin was not pressing the matter urgently enough. It was to Baldwin's credit that he refused to issue the virtual ultimatum which had been originally drafted by Sir Warren Fisher and Sir Horace Wilson, and toughened up further by Chamberlain. Baldwin's caution and care were more appropriate to the situation, both in human and in political terms. For these qualities he was to be harshly treated by the ex-King in his embittered exile, but historians have endorsed Baldwin rather than his accusers.

But the crisis could not be averted indefinitely, and the Press was becoming justifiably restive and unhappy at remaining silent on one of the most sensational and important stories in modern journalistic history while the American and European newspapers devoted great resources of time and space to the story.

Until December 3rd, the British public was wholly unaware of the crisis. The catalytic event was the statement by the Bishop of Bradford, Bishop Blunt, on December 1st that he wished the King were more aware of his duties as head of the Anglican Church. The innocent Bishop was referring to the King's lax attendance at church, but when the *Yorkshire Post* seized the statement, the London Press decided to break its long and wholly voluntary silence. To the dismay and surprise of the King and Mrs. Simpson, the general tone was one of hostility and censure. The King was not used to public criticism, and had clearly reckoned—even if subconsciously—on the power of his enormous popularity.

A swift turmoil followed. A proposal for a morganatic marriage—originally aired in discussion with the King by Esmond Harmsworth—briefly flared into prominence in the discussions, and then was curtly and definitively quenched by the Cabinet and by the uniformly hostile reaction of the Dominion leaders. Attlee wholly concurred that the suggestion was unacceptable. By the time that Baldwin informed the King of the unanimous rejection of this alternative, the matter had at last become public knowledge. Mrs. Simpson left London for the South of France, and was persuaded to urge the King publicly to abandon her and thereby to retain his throne. He refused. Beaverbrook and Churchill became strong advocates for delay, but it was apparent to Beaverbrook that the King had made up his mind. As he put it bluntly to Churchill, 'our cock won't fight'. Churchill, however, plunged on vehemently to the dismay of his friends. On December 5th he issued an emotional appeal for 'time and patience', and by implication accused the Government of acting unconstitutionally. 'They have no right whatever to put pressure upon [the King] to accept their advice by soliciting beforehand assurances from the Leader of the Opposition that he will not form an alternative administration in the event of their resignation, and thus confronting the King with an ultimatum . . . if an abdication were to be hastily extorted, the outrage so committed would cast its shadow forward across many chapters of the History of the British Empire.'

Churchill's actions were motivated principally by his reverence for the monarchy and personal friendship for the King. He was shocked by the King's evident fatigue and the effects of the prolonged emotional pressures to which he had been subjected. But his bitterness against the Government came through in his statement, and aroused intense resentment, and not less in the Labour and Liberal leaders who knew that Churchill had been present at the November 25th meeting. His intervention was not only clumsy, but it was based on wrong information—his statement said that it was quite possible that the King's marriage 'may conceivably, for various reasons, never be accomplished at all'—and it was also much too late. Churchill later realised that Baldwin 'undoubtedly perceived and expressed the profound will of the nation'. This may have been going too far, as the nation was never consulted, but it certainly was the profound will of Parliament. 'I do not find people angry with Mrs. Simpson', Harold Nicolson recorded on December 3rd, 'but I do find a deep and enraged fury against the King himself. In eight months he has destroyed the great structure of popularity which he had raised.'[1] This popularity was undeniable. When in the mood—and, as he had grown older, this was an increasingly important qualification—he had a magnetism and persona which a wide variety of individuals found irresistible. He was genuinely kind and interested in individuals, and his evident melancholy was very attractive. David Kirkwood, who regarded himself as a fervent republican, was among many who succumbed completely to his interest in and sympathy for the problems of his constituents. But, quite unconsciously, he had built up expectations far beyond his

[1] Nicolson, op. cit., 282.

capacity—or, indeed, any man's—to fulfil. Thus the revelations of early December had a far greater effect upon his millions of admirers than they would have in the case of most monarchs. He had, in short, become excessively idealised. It was not his fault, but when it was evident that he fell far below these high estimations the reaction was disproportionately severe.

In any event, the die was cast on December 5th. The King, through Walter Monckton, informed Baldwin of his intention to abdicate. Mrs. Simpson's offer to withdraw was made on December 7th, but it was superfluous, although sincere.

London was torn between 'the King's Friends', known as 'the Cavaliers', and 'the Roundheads'. This was rather overdramatic. There could only be one outcome, given the incompatibility of the position of the King and that of his constitutional advisers. When Churchill rose on December 11th in the House of Commons to renew his plea for patience and delay he was shouted down, and angrily stalked out of the Chamber. Winterton has described this episode as 'one of the angriest manifestations I have ever heard directed against any man in the House of Commons',[1] and Amery recorded that Churchill 'was completely staggered by the unanimous hostility of the House'. His last duty to the King was to assist him in preparing his farewell wireless message to the nation. On December 10th he abdicated, and was succeeded by his shy and retiring brother, the Duke of York, who became King George VI, and whose first act was to create his brother the Duke of Windsor. After his farewell broadcast, the Duke drove down to Portsmouth and embarked in H.M.S. *Fury* for France. King Edward VIII's brief reign was over.

The Abdication Crisis, although dramatic and intense, left few visible scars. The monarchy was strengthened rather than weakened by Edward's departure. His successor was a tense and nervous man, with none of the bonhomie of his father or brother, inexperienced and unprepared. But he was clearly a good and sincere man, devotedly and happily married to a woman of exceptional charm and intelligence. His nervousness manifested itself in a stutter which was a source of intense worry to himself but which became as distinctive and as familiar as Churchill's lisp. His sense of duty was profound, and he gradually established a position of trust with the British people equal to—and perhaps even greater than—that of his father.

[1] Op. cit., 223.

But the Abdication Crisis had had other serious long-term consequences, which historians have tended to underrate. For one thing, 'the King's Matter' had occupied a wholly disproportionate amount of the time and energies of the Prime Minister and his colleagues for many crucial months. It was almost certainly a major contributory factor in Baldwin's near-breakdown in the summer, and it dominated everything else in his mind. His plea to Anthony Eden 'not to trouble me too much with foreign affairs just now' was the result of this central preoccupation. The crisis had probably delayed Baldwin's retirement for perhaps a year, and had dramatically restored his position. Churchill's, on the other hand, had been well-nigh destroyed.

Baldwin's speech to the House of Commons on December 10th was a Parliamentary masterpiece, and it completely restored the position he had appeared to have lost through the year. The speech itself appears somewhat confused, and it was certainly not a carefully prepared oration, but at the time these characteristics deeply impressed that most critical of public audiences. 'It was Sophoclean and almost unbearable', Harold Nicolson wrote, '. . . We file out broken in body and soul, conscious that we have heard the best speech that we shall ever hear in our lives. There was no question of applause. It was the silence of Gettysburg. . . . No man has ever dominated the House as he dominated it tonight, and he knows it.'[1]

To his enemies this was yet another example of Baldwin's superb Parliamentary guile, his unique capacity to enter into an informal blundering conversation with the House of Commons which could almost hypnotise the assembly and win it over completely to his cause. But it is very doubtful whether, on this occasion, Baldwin had deliberately calculated the effect. He was a very tired man, under a very heavy strain. But, whether deliberately conceived or not, this speech and his conduct during the crisis destroyed the last rebellion against him which he had faced since he had unexpectedly become Prime Minister in 1923. Fate was to deal with him harshly in his last years, which he bore with uncomplaining fortitude. He was to be subjected to virulent abuse from his embittered and frightened countrymen, not discouraged by those whom he had politically worsted. He remains a strange, not precisely delineated, personality. But, at the close of the disastrous year of 1936, his control of the House of Commons was, once again, total.

[1] Nicolson, op. cit., 286.

These events had profound implications on the wider political situation. Churchill had been endeavouring to create a national movement that would give his personal campaign for rearmament and an aggressive approach towards the Dictators a much greater constituency than he had previously achieved. One attempt had been the 'Focus' group, which held its first meeting in June 1935, and which included Violet Bonham-Carter, Gilbert Murray, Kingsley Martin— the editor of the *New Statesman*—but which achieved very little. Nonetheless, it formed the basis for the 'Arms and the Covenant' movement which made real progress in 1936, and whose first meeting was due to be held at the Albert Hall on December 3rd.

On November 12th Churchill had had one of his greatest personal triumphs in the House of Commons. The House had reconvened after the summer recess in an ugly mood. The Opposition was deeply stirred by developments in Spain and the Conservatives were still distraught by almost a year of Ministerial ineptitude and vacillation. On the debate on the Address Churchill delivered perhaps the most brilliant of his philippics on the condition of British air deficiencies, which included this unforgettable passage:

> The Government simply cannot make up their minds, or they cannot get the Prime Minister to make up his mind. So they go on in strange paradox, decided only to be undecided, resolved to be irresolute, adamant for drift, solid for fluidity, all-powerful to be impotent. So we go on preparing more months and years—precious, perhaps vital, to the greatness of Britain—for the locusts to eat.

Baldwin's reply was one of the most disastrous in his career, and has shadowed it ever since. He took the House into his confidence, and said that he would speak with 'appalling frankness'. He spoke of the situation that he confronted in 1933:

> Supposing I had gone to the country, and said that Germany was rearming and that we must rearm, does anybody think that this pacifist democracy would have rallied to that cry at that moment? I cannot think of anything that would have made the loss of the election from my point of view more certain.

As a statement of historical fact it was incontrovertible, but the House of Commons was genuinely shocked. Churchill's subsequent distortion of this passage, and his deliberate claim that it referred to the 1935 election,[1] should not delude the historian to underestimate the impact of that speech on the House of Commons. 'His voice and thought limp as if he were a tired walker on a long road', Harold Nicolson noted. 'The House realises that the dear old man has come to the end of his vitality.'[2]

But from these depths the Abdication Crisis had rescued Baldwin; it had also hurled Churchill down. As Harold Macmillan has written: 'It was not possible to restore the situation.' The Arms and the Covenant movement struggled on with little effect, and Churchill's already waning public prestige had received so devastating a blow that, as he himself subsequently wrote, 'it was the almost universal view that my political life was at last ended'.

[1] The literature on this speech is somewhat disproportionate, but the glee with which Churchill and G. M. Young jumped on it and misquoted it has resulted in a powerful counter-attack, notably by R. Bassett in *The Cambridge Journal*, November 1948, and by Barnes and Middlemas, op. cit., 970–3.

[2] Nicolson, op. cit., p. 178.

CHAPTER NINETEEN

TOWARDS THE ABYSS, 1937–1939

STANLEY BALDWIN RETIRED in a warm glow of popular esteem immediately after the Coronation of King George VI in May 1937, and became Earl Baldwin of Bewdley. 'No man', Nicolson wrote, 'has ever left in such a blaze of affection.' There was no challenge or question as to who his successor should be. Neville Chamberlain, the most successful Minister in the 1924–9 Government, had been second to Baldwin since 1929, and, as has been related, had nearly succeeded him early in 1931. Since 1931 he had been the architect of Britain's modest economic recovery, and as Chancellor had dominated both the National and the last Baldwin Governments—albeit at a discreet public distance. He worked hard, was a dedicated public servant, and was a first-rate Departmental Minister with a mind of his own and an incisive manner that although it did not attract over-much affection aroused considerable respect. His succession to Baldwin was a formality. Churchill proposed his election as leader of the Conservative Party and it was unanimously approved.

Neville Chamberlain is one of the most difficult of modern British politicians to portray with accuracy and justice. Only Baldwin was subsequently more denigrated and reviled, but with the distance of time a more objective portrait must be attempted.

Chamberlain had been brought up in the heavy shadow of his father, and his early life had been one of relative failure. After a disastrous attempt to make Joseph Chamberlain another fortune by growing sisal in the Bahamas, he had immersed himself in Birmingham business and politics with only modest success. In 1917 he had been briefly Minister for National Service, and had been summarily dismissed for alleged incompetence by Lloyd George, thus establishing a mutual and unrelenting antipathy. When he entered Parliament in 1918 he was in his fiftieth year, having achieved little of note in his

584

life. Even the fact that he had been Mayor of Birmingham was regarded more as the result of his name than of his capacities.

But from this point his rise had been swift. He worked hard, and his experience had made him a practical social reformer. But although in private charming, sensitive, kind, and warm, his public façade was bleak. 'Neville's manner freezes people', as Austen Chamberlain wrote. '. . . Everybody respects him, but he makes no friends.' 'In manner he is glacial rather than genial', Arthur Salter wrote in 1939. 'He has neither the spontaneous ease of intercourse of some of his colleagues, nor the *fausse bonhomie* of others. It is unfortunate, and of some importance, that his expression often tends to something like a sneer, and his manner to something like a snub, even when there is nothing in either his intentions or his feelings to correspond . . . His instinctive attitude to a critic, even one who intends to be helpful and constructive, is to bear down, not to consolidate or to compromise. An opponent must be opposed; and a supporter who shows signs of independence must be disciplined.'[1]

It must be admitted that Chamberlain's disdain for the bulk of his political contemporaries was not wholly unmerited, nor his contempt for the vapid temporisings which are the stock-in-trade of most politicians, and which were particularly evident in the inter-war Parliaments. But it was his most conspicuous political defect that he could not and did not conceal these emotions. Furthermore, he appeared to have a sadistic pleasure in exposing ignorance, laziness, and shallow thinking. Although a limited man, he towered over most of his colleagues, and not least in his application. His shyness was a major element in his failure to make those casual friendships which are so essential to popularity in the House of Commons. It was his place of business, never his home. His only recorded visit to the Smoking Room was artificial, embarrassing, and not successful. Like Stafford Cripps, he was contemptuous of what he perceived to be the idleness and lack of dedication to the public service of the great majority of his fellow politicians. Admittedly, he was too quick to pass hostile judgement. But, if he was intolerant—as he was—it can be argued that he had much to be intolerant about.

Chamberlain was, as Lord Strang has written, 'a man of cool, calm mind, strong will and decisive purpose, wholly devoted to the public cause and with a firm confidence in his own judgement'. The last was

[1] Arthur Salter: *Security, Can We Retrieve It?*, 284–5.

both the key to his success and to his eventual failure. 'Unhappily', he once wrote, 'it is part of my nature that I cannot contemplate any problem without trying to find a solution to it.' But his solutions were created from a narrow base of knowledge of human nature.

Initially, Chamberlain did not entertain any illusions about Nazi Germany, as a long letter he wrote to the Secretary of the United States Treasury, Henry Morgenthau, in March 1937 demonstrates.[1] But the passage by the United States Congress of the Neutrality Act and the pacifist tone of the Commonwealth Prime Ministers' Conference in the summer of 1937 were important—indeed, crucial—influences. Equally influential were the attitudes and despatches of the British Ambassador in Berlin, Sir Nevile Henderson, a persistent, skilful, and lamentable advocate of settlement with Germany. Gradually, Chamberlain moved in the direction of a rapprochement with Germany, and from there it was but a short step to an almost obsessional search for peace, which characterised the policy of 1938 and culminated in Munich.

As the months passed, Chamberlain's personal control grew. At the beginning of 1938 Vansittart was shunted into honorific impotence at the Foreign Office; Eden was in effect dismissed shortly afterwards, and Swinton was removed. Halifax, although nominally Foreign Secretary, played a minor role in 1938, but his attitudes were close to those of the Prime Minister. Even closer were those of Sir Horace Wilson, his former Chief Industrial Adviser.

This was entirely deliberate. Chamberlain's first objective was to get the Cabinet that he wanted and the advisers whose judgements coincided with his own assessments. Chamberlain did not share Baldwin's relaxed and somewhat old-fashioned view of the role of the Prime Minister. Certainly, he did not welcome strong personalities or divergent views in his immediate or official circle. This feature of his personality could be put down to extreme self-confidence, to authoritarianism, or to a fundamental insecurity. Whatever the real motivation—which was probably a combination of these three factors—the result was that men of independence and high calibre were either ignored or got rid of. Churchill made hopeful overtures, which were rejected out of hand. Amery was left to languish in his political wilderness. Eden, Vansittart, Swinton and Ormsby-Gore were fired, and replaced by docile nonentities. 'To a somewhat exceptional extent',

[1] See James: *Churchill*, 359.

Salter wrote of Chamberlain, 'he regards unquestioning loyalty, obedience, pliability, as giving better claims to his favours than signs of personal initiative or judgement. . . . He prefers the even running of his craft to the vigour of the individual oar.' By March 1938 Chamberlain had established a congenial, subservient, and mediocre Government which he personally dominated, usually ignored, and, as some thought, bullied. If he had none of Austen's public charm, he had certainly inherited that element in his father's personality that frightened men. The Labour Party hated him; he had succeeded in building up a small group of dissident young Conservatives who were shocked at Eden's removal; but his mastery of the House of Commons and the Cabinet was complete. His weapons were immense application, mastery of his subject, and a freezing belligerence which his opponents found profoundly intimidating.

Some of his contemporaries, seeking for the clue to his character, have noted his intellectual vanity and implacable self-assurance. Others have remarked upon his conviction that no problems were beyond resolution by analysis and consequent clear policy, with the result that, once his mind had clamped down upon a matter and the policy determined, there could be and would be no turning back. These critics felt that life, and particularly political life, is a much more complex business than this, and also that Chamberlain consistently omitted the personal elements in his calculations. In short, he jumped to conclusions too quickly, was secretive and solitary, was unsparing in his dedication to his chosen solution and contemptuous of its critics, had little understanding of human nature, and pursued policies that were both superficial and dangerously rigid.

There was certainly much truth in these criticisms. The most merited of all was Chamberlain's distaste for criticism and his solitariness. Very few people had any clear understanding at the time of what his policies were. The Cabinet was usually bypassed and then told what had been done. Only a very limited group of officials had his ear. It was only many years later, with the availability of his papers and those of his colleagues, that it was possible to discern the movement of his thought. At the time, the majority were perplexed onlookers of events of massive importance to them yet in whose outcome they were denied any role. Subsequently, we have a clear picture in 1937 of a man puzzled and alarmed by the foreign situation, by the slow pace of British rearmament, by the timorous attitudes of the Commonwealth

Prime Ministers at their conference in the summer of 1937,[1] by the evident realities of German strength and French pusillanimity, and, above all, by the deep fear of Britain being sucked into another European war virtually by mistake or for reasons not central to British interests. 'I do not see', he wrote in November 1937, 'why we shouldn't say to Germany "give us satisfactory assurances that you won't use force to deal with the Austrians and Czechoslovakians, and we will give you similar assurances that we won't use force to prevent the changes you want, if you can get them by peaceful means".'

By the beginning of 1938, however, one is presented with a man who has reached his conclusions. This was not, as has so often been alleged, a policy of surrender, nor was it simply a desperate search for peace at any price. It was at root a matter of priorities. The integrity of France and the Low Countries was one; German ambitions to the East were not. This, at any rate, was how it began. Increasingly, however, the policy of 'appeasement' acquired in 1938 a self-righteous and even sanctimonious character which repelled its few critics at the time and subsequent commentators. But it was a gradual development. There was no public declaration of doctrine or policy; it was only as events unfolded, and government reactions seen, that the development of Chamberlain's attitudes could be discerned. Thus, throughout 1938, the House of Commons, the Cabinet, and the British people, all anxious for peace yet bewildered and dismayed, jogged nervously along the mysterious course that the imperious Prime Minister had vaguely charted in 1937 but to which he became irrevocably committed.

With the exception of Spain, 1937 had been a relatively quiescent year in European affairs, and even Churchill's independent trumpet was giving a more uncertain note. British rearmament, particularly in the air, proceeded, but hardly with coherence or fervour. What was more serious was the general Ministerial acceptance of German superiority, and their grossly exaggerated fear of the German air potential. They were also puzzled and concerned by the fact that the very large increases in the Air Estimates since 1934 did not appear to be giving them the large air force that they had expected. The real price for their neglect of the aircraft industry was now having to be

[1] See D. C. Watt: 'The Commonwealth and the Munich Crisis' in *Personalities and Policies*, 159–74.

met. The decision to go for the next generation of fighters and bombers had been courageous and right, but the facilities simply had not existed for this leap forward and had to be created. This inevitably caused delays that seemed inexplicable to Ministers, and was one of the factors in Swinton's unmerited downfall. The fact remained that although by the beginning of 1938 the British were not in a good position *vis-à-vis* the Germans they were in nothing like as bad a position as Ministers and their advisers believed. To remedy the situation there would have had to be a complete reversal of the distant attitude towards France, the acceptance of French guarantees to Czechoslovakia, a sharp and dramatic increase in rearmament, the introduction of military conscription, the purchase of war material from abroad—particularly the United States—and the concentration of British and Dominion forces closer to the area of crisis. None of these were done, or even seriously contemplated, by the Prime Minister. He freely negotiated from a position of weakness that could, even at this late hour, have been strengthened.

The British Government was, accordingly, severely and excessively frightened of Germany. Eden had written after the reoccupation of the Rhineland that 'The myth is now exploded that Herr Hitler only repudiates treaties imposed on Germany by force. We must be prepared for him to repudiate any treaty even if freely negotiated (a) when it becomes inconvenient, and (b) when Germany is sufficiently strong and the circumstances are otherwise favourable for doing so.' Baldwin warned the Dominion Prime Ministers in 1937 that 'the only argument which appeals to the dictators is that of force'. But the Government continued to view the situation as Britain *versus* Germany, and at no point seriously considered the strategical potentialities of an effective European alliance. Indeed, under Chamberlain, such a combination was anathema. Thus, the chimera of maintaining freedom of action and of playing a major European role without entering into any European commitments danced enticingly before the new Prime Minister.

Accordingly, Chamberlain was dominated by conflicting illusions. The first was his Victorian assumption that Britain, as the dominant world power, could deal directly and independently with the German leaders on a realistic and indeed *realpolitik* level. The second was that Germany was militarily so powerful and Britain so relatively weak that everything possible must be done to avert a war crisis. The third, which became increasingly central in his mind, was that reasonable men could always find reasonable solutions to problems, once the latter were identified. Alliances against Germany would be provocative; Halifax was able to inform the Cabinet, without protest, after the German occupation of Austria in March 1938 that 'nothing was more likely to aggravate the difficulties of the present situation than any suggestions that our ultimate objective was to unite France, Italy and ourselves against Germany'. Thus Ministers, while privately sharing Churchill's celebrated sentiment of 'Thank God for the French Army', kept the French carefully at a distance, and flirted vaguely with the Italians. 'If only we could get on terms with the Germans, I would not care a rap for Musso', Chamberlain wrote in his diary. The dream of an all-encompassing deal with the Germans increasingly obsessed the Prime Minister.

Viewing this situation in calm retrospect, with all the facts at his disposal, the historian can easily be contemptuous and condemnatory of the Chamberlain Government. But the situation that confronted them at the time must be clearly appreciated.

All of its members had passed, either personally or very closely, through the agony of the Great War. Those who had not fought in it had experienced the bitter loss of close relatives and friends. They had seen the subsequent turmoil in Europe, and the advent of a vast and malignant Communist state in Russia. Their own nation was barely recovering from the consequences of that war. They had hoped for, and had worked for unavailingly, a comprehensive disarmament programme. They had been compelled to rearm in the face of the German military renaissance. But they could not believe that another and more terrible catastrophe could not be averted. They could not believe that reason could not prevail. Few had any illusions about the character of Nazi Germany, but they could not accept that a deal could not be made with its leaders. But it was to be a *British* deal. No more fatal *ententes*!

This was certainly the progression of Chamberlain's logic, coupled as it was with his lack of serious interest in any Eastward ambitions that Germany might have. He shared the opinion of Eden, set out to the Imperial Conference in 1937, that any declaration of British willingness to regard an attack on Austria or Czechoslovakia as a *casus belli* with Germany 'would be going far beyond our obligations under the Covenant and far beyond where the people of this country were prepared to go'.[1] The same point was made by Halifax in his discussions with Hitler in November 1937 when he told the German leader that on matters such as Danzig, Austria, and Czechoslovakia 'we were not necessarily concerned to stand up for the *status quo* as today, but we were concerned to avoid such treatment of them as would be likely to cause trouble'. While this was not precisely an open invitation, it was perilously near one. Chamberlain made the same point in his discussions with the new French Foreign Minister, Delbos, at the end of November 1937. This looked like cold-blooded *realpolitik*. What British interests were involved in the independence of Austria or Czechoslovakia? Was either worth a war? Why should not they be sacrificed, and used as British bargaining offers in the achievement of an Anglo-German settlement? It was certainly a cold-blooded approach, but it was certainly not *realpolitik*.

With this narrowing of British concerns there went an earnest search for concrete British proposals—which included the possibility of the return of the annexed German colonies—to put before the Germans as part of the overall settlement which was developing into an obsession with the Prime Minister and his senior colleagues— among whom Eden must be included. Eden's abrupt removal from office early in 1938 owed less to fundamental differences on foreign policy than personal factors. There was at least one element of principle in their rift, their very differing judgements of how to handle Mussolini. But Chamberlain had been eyeing Eden very carefully and closely since 1935, and had been unimpressed. Perhaps he had detected the irresolution beneath the confident façade, and the intense emotionalism and ambition of this glittering but unsure young man. His confidence in his judgement could not have been reduced by Eden's feeble and deferential resignation speech. Chamberlain felt that he had little to fear from that quarter, and events were to prove him right.

Eden's successor, Halifax, was a man of several complexities. Brought up in a strange home, heir to his title only through the deaths of his brothers, deformed at birth with a withered arm, a Fellow of All Souls and a highly successful Viceroy of India, he skilfully erected an impassable wall between himself, his contemporaries, and historians. He was shrewd, yet also naïve. He was calculating, yet also sensitive and emotional. His shyness and apparent aloofness perplexed and

[1] Cabinet Papers. Quoted in Barnett, op. cit., 465.

antagonised many, but his kindness and sincerity won him a multitude of friends and admirers. He was at times sentimental and innocent, at others cold and realistic. He had common sense, yet also a capacity for wishful thinking. His strong dedication to the Church often tore at his innate Yorkshire pragmatism and sense of cynical reality. A devout man of principle, yet he was one whom one would compare in some respects to Balfour, of whom Churchill wrote that, had he been alive at the time of the Renaissance, he would not have needed to read the works of Machiavelli. Thus he was, through 1938, an eager and docile follower of Chamberlain's strategy and yet was the first to wake up to its implications and consequences. The more one examines this perplexing man the less is one surprised that he was to be, in May 1940, the first choice of the King and the Conservative Party to be Prime Minister, nor that the Labour Party was willing to serve under him. There were depths in that austere personality that historians have consistently failed to recognise, yet which contemporaries understood.

Unhappily, Halifax was barely given a walking-on part in the events of 1938. His meeting with Hitler and his colleagues in November 1937 had persuaded him that a deal could indeed be made with the German leaders, loathsome though they were. But while Halifax was impressed by Hitler's expressed contempt for the British 'fairy-land of strange, respectable, illusions' Chamberlain was more struck by the fact that Halifax's visit had created 'an atmosphere in which it is possible to discuss with Germany the practical questions involved in a European settlement'. This decision now developed into his dominant preoccupation. Throughout 1938 Halifax—and the Foreign Office— were little more than observers of the drama. This role was also given to the Cabinet, the House of Commons, and the British public. Chamberlain took in 1938 an even more arbitrary and personalised 'Presidential' role than even Lloyd George had established at the height of his power, and his awed and undistinguished colleagues followed dutifully and in ignorance.

Halifax's own attitude in 1938 was substantially based upon his profound personal admiration and affection for Neville Chamberlain. In Chamberlain there was a most marked, and remarkable, contrast between the public and private persona that was without parallel in modern British politics before the advent of Edward Heath. Chamberlain, who in public was so sharp, sneering, and unappealing, was in private beloved and revered by his family and close friends. As Halifax has himself written:

> It was not universally known with how many sides of life Chamberlain moved on terms of close and intimate relationship. Few men had a more real enjoyment of all things of beauty and art, whether in the world of nature or of men, which make life colourful and rich, and few had his knowledge and deep appreciation of all that is greatest in music. No one was a truer lover of the countryside.

These words have sometimes been quoted mockingly, but they partly open the door to why Chamberlain received the love and veneration that he did. His gentleness and kindness moved people who had had experience of other types of politicians. He was, in private, shy and modest, and he was a devoted husband and father. Those who penetrated the public façade—including Churchill[1]—were surprised and impressed by the real man. His total control over his Government was not merely that of being Prime Minister. He had surrounded himself with some men who loved him and others who feared him. Those who did neither had been cut down. Neville Chamberlain was a decent, kind, sensitive, vain, authoritarian and ruthless man. By March 1938 he was in complete command, and marched forward without fear or doubt into the eager arms of his enemies. They, too, believed that a deal could be made. But it was to be on their terms.

*

The first shock to Conservative confidence in Chamberlain was the forced resignation of Eden and his Parliamentary Under-Secretary, Lord Cranborne, on February 20th; twenty-five Government back-benchers abstained in protest in the subsequent debate. Eden's speech of explanation left most Members wondering what the dispute had really been about, and Eden himself was scrupulously—some felt excessively—loyal to the Government. But it was a nasty jolt. In reality, the causes of his departure had been personal rather than on policy. Chamberlain's increasing absorption with foreign affairs, his growing self-assurance, and his impatience with Eden and the Foreign Office were the main causes. Chamberlain's discouraging reply in January to a vague suggestion by Roosevelt for a world conference

[1] Churchill, op. cit., 494–5.

was made without consultation with the Foreign Secretary, and had been another episode in a lengthening list of incidents in which Eden had been virtually ignored. The final dispute was over the precise wording of a formula to give Mussolini *de jure* recognition of his Abyssinian empire in return for the withdrawal of Italian intervention in Spain. But the event not only provoked the first Conservative revolt against Chamberlain, but began the movement that was to deflect his course in 1939 and bring him down in 1940.

Then, on March 13th, Hitler annexed Austria. 'Europe', Churchill told the House of Commons, 'is confronted with a programme of aggression, nicely calculated and timed, unfolding stage by stage, and there is only one choice open, not only to us, but to other countries who are unfortunately concerned—either to submit, like Austria, or else to take effective measures while time remains to ward off the danger and, if it cannot be warded off, to cope with it.' Hitler's strategy was in fact not as carefully planned as Churchill and others assumed, and the *Anschluss* was a hurriedly launched affair, but apprehension began to mount sharply.

Chamberlain did not see matters thus gloomily, nor did Halifax. Both had become convinced by the 'encirclement' theory, whereby alliances would drive the Germans into some mad-dog act to escape. 'The more closely we associate ourselves with France', Halifax informed his colleagues, 'the more we produce on German minds the impression that we are plotting to encircle Germany and the more difficult will it be to make any real settlement with Germany.' Chamberlain said that 'the seizure of the whole of Czechoslovakia would not be in accordance with Herr Hitler's policy, which was to include all Germans in the Reich but not to include other nationalities'. Halifax 'distinguished in his own mind between Germany's racial efforts, which no one could question, and a lust for conquest on a Napoleonic scale which he himself did not credit'.[1] The Cabinet Foreign Policy Committee, to which these words were addressed, accepted their argument. Any resolution that there might have been was effectively dampened by a grim assessment of the British military situation by the Chiefs of Staff. But, again, it was an assessment only of the *British* position, and took no account whatever of the Czechoslovakian forces, the French Army, nor the German deficiencies which had become evident in the invasion of Austria. British military weak-

[1] Barnett, op. cit., 474.

ness was not the major factor—if, indeed, a factor at all—in Chamberlain's mind, although later it was to be used as an excuse for the policies of 1938. But it did have its impact upon other Ministers.[1]

As Austen Chamberlain, Churchill, and others had warned, this *coup de main* placed Czechoslovakia, with its three million Germans, immediately in a highly vulnerable position. Hitler's strident denunciations of the treatment of the German minority made the point clear. 'The overriding consideration with Chamberlain and his colleagues', Hoare, now back in office at the Admiralty, has recorded, 'was that the very complicated problem of Czechoslovakia ought not to lead to a world war and must at almost any price be settled by peaceful means.'[2] Chamberlain's strategy was to take the initiative and to place the maximum pressure upon the Czechs to come to terms with their German problem on German terms and thereby to deny Hitler the excuse to attack their country on that issue and draw in their French allies. Meanwhile, some bold words were used publicly about honouring obligations which perplexed the House of Commons, made the position of Chamberlain's small band of Conservative critics difficult, but did not deceive Hitler. As Strang later wrote: 'The ambivalence of our policy of trying to deter the Germans from armed action by pointing out the probability of British intervention, and to discourage the Czechs from fighting by hinting at its improbability, was not long concealed.' British politicians and the Press did not expect an immediate crisis, and tended to take at face value the resolution of the Government. The French, although they suspected that Hitler's menacing threats against Czechoslovakia were militarily unrealistic, went along—if uneasily—with the British strategy. The Sudeten German Nazi leader, Konrad Henlein, made a highly successful visit to Britain, even impressing Churchill. The discussions about the situation became increasingly confused. Hitler divined that the moment was approaching for another opportunistic coup.

The crisis came in September. In a daring stroke, looking to London and Paris, President Benes appeared to concede all the Sudeten German demands, knowing that even this would be inadequate for Henlein and Hitler. He also discovered that it was

---

[1] Even Duff Cooper, the most Francophile and anti-German member of the Cabinet, told Harold Nicolson in May that 'the Germans are so beastly powerful'. (Nicolson, op. cit., 344.)

[2] Templewood, op. cit., 344.

inadequate for London and Paris. On September 13th there were manufactured disturbances in German regions against the Government which were easily controlled, but on the 15th an alarmed but determined Chamberlain flew to Berchtesgaden with Sir Horace Wilson and Strang to see Hitler and to try to achieve his all-European settlement. There was no question in Chamberlain's mind of consultation with the Cabinet, of a concentrated policy with the French, and none whatever of any consultation with the Czechoslovak leaders. This was to be a straightforward Anglo-German negotiation—and one, furthermore, in which neither the British Cabinet nor the Foreign Office were involved. The two men discussed the matter alone. Chamberlain's proposal was that, in return for the preservation of the rest of the country, the Sudeten German areas would be separated from the rest of Czechoslovakia if they so desired. Lord Runciman, who had been dispatched on a special mission in August to 'mediate' between Henlein and Benes, had initially concluded that the claims of the Germans could be met within the framework of the Czechoslovak state; in his final report he switched hurriedly to the cause of 'self-determination'.

But Chamberlain returned to find his colleagues troubled and to learn of ominous rumblings in the Conservative Party. *The Times* had published an infamous leading article which remarked that 'the general character of the terms submitted to the Czechoslovak Government could not, in the nature of things, be expected to make a strong *prima facie* appeal to them'. At last, the true nature of Chamberlain's purpose was becoming more clear. But Eden, who had the most substantial influence on the Conservative back-benchers—much greater than Churchill's—would not express publicly his private consternation. Nonetheless, the alarm spread that a spectacular betrayal was at hand. A sense of impending humiliation reached out through the scattered Conservative Party. The French, also, were alarmed, and sought—and received—a British military guarantee for the 'new' emasculated Czechoslovakia. Although the Berchtesgaden talks had achieved nothing, they had persuaded Chamberlain that Hitler must be given a higher offer. Runciman had recommended the immediate transfer of all frontier districts where the Germans were a substantial majority; Chamberlain now proposed the transfer of all areas where the Germans constituted more than half of the population. The French agreed, and the Czechs were handed a plain ultimatum by their ally. Bitterly, they had no choice but to agree. Thus, Chamberlain seemed to have won over his critics, and on September 22nd flew to Godesberg to tie up the details, only to be confronted with larger demands. Hitler wanted immediate occupation by German troops of the disputed territories. After an angry discussion, he agreed not to act before October 1st.

By now the mood in London had turned hostile to any more concessions. The Cabinet was shocked, and it was evident that opinion in the House of Commons—Labour as well as Conservative—had swung violently again and would not tolerate the Godesberg proposals. The French Government reacted similarly. Suddenly everyone was highly belligerent, even—although mutedly—*The Times*. The Fleet was mobilised by Duff Cooper—with Chamberlain's acquiescence—on September 27th. There were startling evidences of air-raid precautions in London parks, in the distribution of gas-masks, and in plans for evacuating children to the country. The silver balloon-barrages rose into the clear autumn skies. But the crisis had come so suddenly, without any governmental warning or explanation, and seemed not only alarming but unreal. To even the most ardent, the spectacle of puny slit-trenches and the hasty distribution of gas-masks seemed inadequate preparations for the aerial onslaught that all expected. 'When war comes', Nicolson mused on the 21st, 'it will be a terrible shock to the country. The bombing of London by itself will provoke panic and perhaps riots. All those of us who said "We must make a stand" will be branded as murderers.'[1] Thus, the exaggerated fears of devastation from the air, so sedulously argued both by anti- and pro-rearmers for years, now had their effect. This apprehension was certainly not diminished by Chamberlain's broadcast on the 27th, which was markedly egotistical, and which included the lugubrious words, uttered in a tone of numbed melancholy that was unforgettable:

How horrible, fantastic, incredible it is that we should be digging trenches and trying on gas-masks here because of a quarrel in a far-away country between people of whom we know nothing.

Was Czechoslovakia worth a war? This was not, of course, the real question. But it was the question posed to himself by Chamberlain, as it had been for months, and now to the public, and his answer was clear. Through Nevile Henderson he suggested renewed negotiations

[1] Nicolson, op. cit., 368.

with Hitler. Godesberg had distressed his usually supine colleagues, and the popular mood was highly uncertain. But Chamberlain had certainly never given up, and in Paris the Daladier Government was now wavering again. Both directly to Hitler, and to Mussolini, Chamberlain proposed a meeting of the leaders of the four powers.

On September 28th the House of Commons, called back from its recess, reassembled in a confused mood of perplexity and tension, looking for some kind of lead. There was no war-fever, nor defeatism, in its temper. The majority of Members, clearly representing the principal view of their constituents, were baffled by the ugly turn of events. What did it all mean? What was the Government going to do? Most Ministers were in the same quandary. This was the atmosphere when Chamberlain rose in a packed and uneasy House of Commons. He described the events of the past two weeks precisely and calmly, and with considerable skill; as he approached his culmination, which was unclear to Members, but which seemed to be an admission of the failure of negotiation and British solidarity with France and her Czechoslovak ally, there was a famous dramatic moment, described by Harold Nicolson that evening in a radio broadcast:

> 'Yesterday morning', began the Prime Minister, and we were all conscious that some revelation was approaching. He began to tell us of his final appeal to Herr Hitler and Signor Mussolini. I glanced at the clock. It was twelve minutes after four. The Prime Minister had been speaking for exactly an hour. I noticed that a sheet of Foreign Office paper was being rapidly passed along the Government bench. Sir John Simon interrupted the Prime Minister and there was a momentary hush. He adjusted his pince-nez and read the document that had been handed to him. His whole face, his whole body, seemed to change. He raised his face so that the light from the ceiling fell full upon it. All the lines of anxiety and weariness seemed suddenly to have been smoothed out; he appeared ten years younger and triumphant. 'Herr Hitler', he said, 'has just agreed to postpone his mobilisation for twenty-four hours and to meet me in conference with Signor Mussolini and Signor Daladier at Munich.'

> That, I think, was one of the most dramatic moments which I have ever witnessed. For a second, the House was hushed in absolute silence. And then the whole House burst into a roar of

cheering, since they knew that this might mean peace. That was the end of the Prime Minister's speech, and when he sat down the whole House rose as a man to pay tribute to his achievement.[1]

Chamberlain departed on his mission to Munich in a blur of excitement and undisguised self-satisfaction. He was seen off at the airport by his beaming Cabinet colleagues, present to a man, and leaving only a very small minority of deeply troubled men. At Munich he virtually ignored Daladier, and the miserable business of the destruction of Czechoslovakia did not take very long. The German occupation of the Sudeten territories would be spread over ten days, and the 'new' Czechoslovakia would be guaranteed by the Powers. Thus was the peace of Europe secured. On the following morning Chamberlain offered Hitler a statement that this agreement was 'symbolic of the desire of our two peoples never to go to war with one another again', which Hitler gladly signed. Chamberlain returned to London with this paper to frenzied applause. Daladier, who had expected, understandably, to be lynched, also rode into Paris in triumph, rather more bemused. Addressing the crowd in Downing Street from an upper window, Chamberlain, invoking Disraeli's return from the Congress of Berlin in 1878, declared that 'This is the second time that there has come back from Germany to Downing Street peace with honour. I believe it is peace for our time'. He stood with the King and Queen on the balcony of Buckingham Palace, amid tumultuous cheers. His friends and supporters have subsequently argued that he was very tired, that the Downing Street crowd had to be told something, and that Chamberlain almost immediately regretted his rash words. Other observers were more struck by his personal elation and by his conviction that he had achieved a major and enduring triumph. He reacted negatively to Halifax's proposal to bring Churchill and Eden into the Government. He told his colleagues and friends that he was confident that 'Hitler is a man of his word'.[2]

[1] Nicolson, op. cit., 370-1. Nicolson did not add in his broadcast that he had refused to join the ovation; nor did Churchill, Eden, Amery, and the Communist M.P., William Gallacher. But accounts of the scene vary considerably, and Nicolson's immediate version is the most vivid. It is still not clear whether the drama was deliberately contrived, and no hard evidence that it was, in Mowat's words, 'all but a put-up job'. (Mowat, op. cit., 616.)

[2] Staying at Chevening, the exquisite Kent home of Lord Stanhope, early in 1939 he gave this opinion to Lord Rosebery at breakfast. Rosebery found that he had entirely lost his appetite.

His vanity was certainly not unaffected by the extraordinary wave of emotion that the Munich Agreement aroused in Britain and France. Chamberlain had become the Peacemaker of Europe.

It is as well to remember that Chamberlain had never experienced popularity in the House of Commons or in the country. Nor, to be fair to him, had he ever courted it. In Birmingham he was respected both as a Chamberlain and as a devout son of the city, but he had never aroused anything comparable to the enthusiasm and adulation that his father and Austen had evoked. Now, he had eclipsed them both, and the gratitude and admiration was both intense and widespread. This was his hour. It was to be very brief.

The enthusiasm and relief which greeted Chamberlain on his return were genuine enough, but the Munich terms shocked, embittered, and humiliated a small but very vocal minority. The passions which the previous German demands had aroused had abated somewhat in the circle of Chamberlain's critics, but were still present. Duff Cooper was the only Minister who resigned—'the pioneer along the nation's way back from hysteria to reason', in Vyvyan Adams' words. Duff Cooper was a man who was beloved and excessively admired by his friends, but in the House of Commons—after one of the best maiden speeches in the post-war period—he had become generally regarded as a lightweight, and his antipathy towards Germany and love of France made many discount him as unbalanced in his attitudes. He had been successively Financial Secretary to the Treasury, Secretary of State for War, the First Lord of the Admiralty, and his tenure of these offices had not been very distinguished. His friends considered him brilliant, sensitive, and perceptive; his critics regarded him as opinionated, hot-tempered, emotional, and rather lazy. His resignation over Munich was the making of his career, and his resignation speech completely restored his faltering position. But he quickly found, as did the other Conservative opponents of Munich, that to oppose Chamberlain at that time was not a popular move.[1] The Labour attacks on Munich provoked some Conservatives to talk eagerly of a General Election.

In these circumstances, the size and the calibre of the Conservative rebellion against Munich was remarkable. Churchill, in one of his greatest speeches, described the agreement as 'a total and unmitigated defeat', to the fury of the bulk of the Conservative Party, and thirty

[1] Duff Cooper, op. cit., 253.

Conservatives abstained in the post-Munich vote. These included Churchill, Eden, Amery, Cranborne, Duff Cooper, Sir Roger Keyes, Boothby, Macmillan, and J. P. L. Thomas. Several others voted for the Government only with heavy hearts, and their emotions were very similar to those of A. P. Herbert, who later wrote 'I voted sadly for Munich; and the whole thing made me ill',[1] and Victor Cazalet, who could only bring himself to accept it as 'a regrettable decision'.

The tests of public feeling about Munich were not conclusive. In November there was a vehement by-election at Oxford, where the Master of Balliol, A. D. Lindsay, stood against the official Conservative candidate Quintin Hogg (the son of Lord Hailsham) with Labour and anti-Government Conservative backing. Harold Macmillan campaigned for Lindsay, as did the young Edward Heath. It was a passionate affair, but when the result came in it was seen that although the Conservative majority had been reduced by 3,000 votes, the hopes of the opponents of the Government had been severely disappointed. At Bridgwater, however, Vernon Bartlett stood as an anti-Government Independent and won, but the excitement this caused was checked when the Duchess of Atholl resigned her seat in protest against the Government's foreign policy and stood in the resulting by-election as an Independent and lost.

But the indications of popular attitudes, although confused, are that Munich was accepted, even though the immediate euphoria was replaced by a more sober realisation of what had happened. 'At our almost daily conferences with our friends', Macmillan has written, 'we had the gloomiest forebodings. The tide was, at present, too strong and it was flowing against us.'[2] Churchill only narrowly won a motion of confidence in Epping, and other Government critics in the Conservative Party had a difficult winter. But it should be noted that these difficulties were principally with the party faithful, who are liable to be outraged by any serious opposition against party conformity.

But Chamberlain's personal popularity was unquestionable, and surprised even those close to him. Unlike Baldwin, this was never seriously harmed. His enemies put this down, then and later, to the fact that he had duped the people with a spurious peace. This does not explain, however, the continued respect and gratitude which he

[1] A. P. Herbert: *Independent Member*, 113.
[2] Harold Macmillan: op. cit., 567.

evoked. Some of his critics actively wanted war, and saw as its alternative an endless series of abject political defeats which would give Germany control of Europe and make her invincible. 'Better now' was their belief. The majority of the Government's critics regarded war as an inevitable necessity. But there is little evidence that the British public accepted either alternative at that time. Some observers noted a new grim fatalism abroad in the land in the winter of 1938–9, but others a genuine belief that Chamberlain had indeed brought peace in their time, and were overwhelmed with gratitude. It is not surprising that the politicians, trying to read the signs of the popular temper, came up with sharply contradictory impressions. The Government's position in the House of Commons had, however, been shaken by the Conservative defections and the unexpectedly critical attitude of the Opposition. The Labour Party's attitude to the European situation remained full of contradictions and contrasts, but the majority sentiment—particularly on the Front Bench—was becoming one of repugnance against the long catalogue of Government capitulations to the Dictators, and there was genuine outrage—well expressed by Attlee in one of the best speeches in the Munich debates —at the treatment of the Czechs. The universal Labour dislike for Chamberlain personally did not make them disposed to accept his claims.

Ministers comforted themselves with the fact that their Conservative critics were themselves divided. Churchill could count on only three supporters—the mysterious Brendan Bracken, Boothby, and his son-in-law Duncan Sandys—but although the bulk of the dissidents (derided by the Whips as 'the glamour boys') grouped around Eden, he gave little leadership and seemed highly reluctant to criticise Ministers strongly in public. Furthermore, as Munich receded, and Ministers struck highly optimistic notes about the heartening prospects in Europe, it seemed possible that Chamberlain really had been able to come to a deal with Hitler. But this remarkable House of Commons seemed impossible to placate, and sensitive on matters such as the abandonment of the 1936 proposal to partition Palestine and lack of assistance to European refugees. Not only the dissident Conservatives but the loyal ones passed an uneasy winter.

The turning-point came on March 15th, when the Germans annexed the rest of Czechoslovakia. Five days before, Chamberlain had declared that Europe was settling down to a period of tranquillity, and that the Government was contemplating the possibility of a general limitation of armaments. The Nazi occupation of Czechoslovakia left his policies in ruin, and a surge of anger rippled through the Conservative ranks. Urgently advised by the party managers, and for once his own composure shaken, Chamberlain made a hurried *volte-face*.

*

By no extension of charity can the conduct of British foreign and defence policies between 1933 and 1939 be described as distinguished, but most accounts have been seriously distorted by the emotional and often political commitment of successive historians and politicians, given their lead by Churchill, Lewis Namier, Wheeler-Bennett and G. M. Young. A. J. P. Taylor's *Origins of the Second World War*, published in 1961, may be open to challenge and criticism on several points, but it marked the moment at which historians started thinking of the 1930s in more detached and historical terms. As Mr. Taylor has written:

> Hitler, it seems to me, had no precise plans of aggression, only an intention, which he held in common with most Germans, to make Germany again the most powerful state in Europe and a readiness to take advantage of events. I am confident that the truth of this interpretation will be recognised once the problem is discussed in terms of detached historical curiosity, and not of political commitment.[1]

This judgement has been borne out by subsequent scholarship, but it does not give sufficient importance to the very peculiar and frightening aspects of Hitler's appetite, greed, and cruelty. He was not the insensate madman that he is often depicted; but nor was he the calculating yet opportunistic politician of some portraits. He was inconstant, emotionally unstable, mentally twisted, yet with a natural understanding of harsh power politics. He read Chamberlain very clearly, and became convinced that the British would not interrupt his Eastward ambitions. He had reckoned without the House of Commons. But, so had Chamberlain.

The central dilemma is whether Hitler was ever 'stoppable' short of war. It is the argument of many—and of which Churchill was the

[1] *English History 1914–45*, 424, footnote 1.

most vigorous—that he was, and that a policy of British firmness backed by strong European alliances and effective rearmament would have contained him, and would in all probability have led to his downfall at home. In this particular argument, the attitudes of senior German Army officers are cited as evidence of dislike and distrust of Hitler and of fear about the direction in which he was moving.

This commentator is doubtful of this argument. With some exceptions, the hostility to Hitler in the German Army seems to have been based partly on personal distaste but principally on the belief that he was moving too rapidly, rather than in the wrong direction. The claim that the Army could have toppled Hitler is doubtful after the S.S. was fully organised and the senior commanders had been quietly purged or persuaded of Hitler's strength; all the evidence suggests that any attempt at a coup was very improbable after 1934, and must have resulted not merely in civil war but in deep divisions within the German Army itself.

The British had no conception—and still have no conception—of what life under a modern, centralised, ruthless dictatorship is like. They do not recognise the devastating simplicity of the power of an all-pervasive police state, which rules less on terror than on the elementary principles of the sense of self-preservation and political apathy of the individual. Nor do they realise how easy it is to manipulate information, distort history, and remove from individuals the basic facts on which they can exercise their judgements. Today, we have a much clearer understanding of how easy it all is, and how complete can be its effects. In the 1930s, these things were only dimly realised, if they were realised at all, by the British. And the Nazis were geniuses at this new art, compared with which the Tsars and Stalin were incompetent butchers. They were masters of propaganda and staged show-pieces. Hitler's oratory may have sounded in turns turgid and comically hysterical to British ears, but it aroused some deep emotions in the German personality. The Nazis may have been a bunch of gangsters, but they raised gangsterism to a new level. Thus the British dream of a coup, both then and later, was based upon a complete misunderstanding of how a modern dictatorship operates at every level of a society, how total is its power, how intimidating its warnings, and how pernicious its influence on intelligent people.

Grotesque though many of the Nazi attitudes were, their appeal to German instincts was in many cases profound. In the character of the

German people—and in this they are not unique—there lies a belief that Germany's proper role is in the front rank. There also lay the conviction that Germany's position was always under threat, and had been under threat since 1870. They envied the British their island protection, their vast possessions, and their assumption of security. They could also point out that the virility of other European nations —principally Britain, France, Holland and Portugal—had been manifested in gigantic territorial expansion outside Europe. For reasons of history and geography, this opportunity had been denied to Germany, and for the whole of the life of the nation she had been surrounded with hostile alliances. On these emotions the Nazi leaders played with very great skill.

It should also be remembered that, of all the nations engaged in the Great War, Germany had proportionately suffered physically the least. She had been defeated—a fact which most Germans denied— but it had taken a vast Coalition to achieve this. As Churchill wrote at the end of *The World Crisis*:

> For four years Germany fought and defied the five continents of the world by land and sea and air. The German armies upheld her tottering confederates, intervened in every theatre with success, stood everywhere on conquered territory, and inflicted on their enemies more than twice the bloodshed they suffered themselves. To break their strength and science and curb their fury, it was necessary to bring all the greatest nations of mankind into the field against them. Overwhelming populations, unlimited resources, measureless sacrifice, the Sea Blockade, could not prevail for fifty months. Small states were trampled down in the struggle; a mighty Empire was battered into unrecognisable fragments; and nearly twenty million men perished or shed their blood before the sword was wrested from that terrible hand. Surely, Germans, for history it is enough!

Europe's tragedy was that it was not enough. Throughout the 1920s, while the Weimar Republic was struggling to achieve European stature, the plans were being laid for Germany's military renaissance. This does not mean that the intentions were aggressive at the time; armaments were a symbol of national regeneration, the mark of sovereignty, and escape from the shameful ignominy of Versailles. It was Hitler who gave the Wehrmacht its political direction.

The British failure to support the League actively, and to make it a central part of its European strategy, was the result of a deeper repugnance for foreign entanglements. Surges of emotion over Spain and Abyssinia were brief, and—particularly in the former case— confined to an articulate minority. The emphatic rejection of the Lloyd George Coalition's sabre-rattling over Chanak had been a significant episode. The British had had enough of this nonsense, and the cause of the failure of Churchill's career in the inter-war period was this revulsion from bellicosity and threatening rhetoric. And thus Britain withdrew herself physically and mentally from European affairs. 'We behaved as though we could play an effective part in international affairs as a kind of mediator or umpire without providing ourselves with the necessary arms and without entering into firm commitments', as Strang had commented. Churchill, in 1933, put the same point when he said that 'if we wish to detach ourselves and lead a life of independence from European entanglements, we have to be strong enough to defend our neutrality'. But the desire, in Churchill's words again, 'to live our life in our island without being again drawn into the perils of the continent of Europe' was a fatal chimera. The most important single factor in the collapse of Europe in the 1930s was British isolationism. But the question persists—even if Britain had been armed to the teeth for purely defensive purposes, how would this have checked Hitler's expansionism in *Europe*? Britain was not Hitler's main target.

As has been emphasised, the acceptance by many in Britain of the essential evilness of the Nazi regime did not carry with it the inevitable corollary that its policies meant a European war. It was against this particular scepticism that Churchill argued so long, and unavailingly. Indeed, as its internal outrages increased, there were those who urged with even greater insistence that a true nobility lay in accommodation with such men—as though a truly Christian stance was to shake hands with the dictators while holding one's nose. Margot Asquith wrote in March 1939:

There is only one way of preserving Peace in the world, and getting rid of the enemy, and that is to come to some sort of agreement with him—and the *viler* he is, the more you must fight him with the opposite weapons than his . . . The greatest enemy of mankind today is *Hate*.

Chamberlain wrote to his sister on July 30th, 1939:

My critics think that it would be a frightful thing to come to any agreement with Germany without giving her a thorough thrashing 'to larn her to be a toad'. But I don't share that view; let us convince her that the chances of winning a war without getting thoroughly exhausted in the process are too remote to make it worthwhile. But the corollary of that must be that she has a chance of getting fair and reasonable consideration and treatment from us and others if she will give up the idea that she can force it from us, and convince us that she has given it up.

It was the dogged retention of these attitudes even after March 1939 that precluded any chance of bringing Churchill into the Government. As Chamberlain wrote, 'Churchill's chances improve as war becomes more possible, and *vice versa*. If there is any possibility of easing the tension and getting back to normal relations with the dictators, I wouldn't risk it by what would certainly be regarded by them as a challenge.'

Mr. Michael Astor has written:

It is astonishing to think that people who were almost professionally high minded, who abhorred violence, and who were prepared to act with the courage of their convictions, could seriously believe that it was possible to come to any honourable arrangements with Hitler.

Yet, surely, it was not astonishing at all. The moral fervour and faith that lay behind a policy of accommodation was in some respects its most impressive feature. How, may it be asked, can you accommodate with gangsters? How can you make deals with a man like Hitler? But, it would be retorted, what is the alternative? The alternative was the polarisation of Europe, the acceleration of the arms race, and war, when their sons would suffer the fate of Wilfred Owen's 'Doomed Youth', for whom:

> *The pallor of the girls' brows shall be their pall;*
> *Their flowers the tenderness of silent minds,*
> *And each slow dusk a drawing-down of blinds.*

*

But, after the cynical occupation of Czechoslovakia on March 15th, 1939, Chamberlain was temporarily jolted out of his policies. Two days later, in Birmingham, he was drawn by the evident mood of the audience into an unprepared denunciation of the German action, which was wildly applauded. There were suddenly fears for Romania and Poland. At once, Churchill's depiction of a German grand strategy of calculated aggression and acquisition seemed only too real. It was clear to the party managers that the House of Commons, and particularly the Conservatives, were not prepared to accept any more Munichs. The Franco-British guarantee to Poland of March 31st was a hastily-considered absurdity, and only makes sense in the context of a sudden desperation and desire to appear resolute. Harold Nicolson's account of this event should not be omitted:

> Chamberlain comes into the House looking gaunt and ill. The skin above his high cheekbones is parchment yellow. He drops wearily into his place. David Margesson proposes the Adjournment and the P.M. rises. He begins by saying that we believe in negotiation and do not trust in rumours. He then gets to the centre of his statement, namely that if Poland is attacked we shall declare war. That is greeted with cheers from every side. He reads his statement very slowly with a bent grey head. It is most impressive.[1]

The concomitant steps towards an Anglo-Russian agreement were dismally half-hearted. The once-confident Government was being stampeded into new alliances for which it had no enthusiasm and which were in their view impracticable and unnecessary. 'I must confess to the most profound distrust of Russia', Chamberlain wrote at the end of March. Outside the Labour Party it was widely shared. But this was one of those occasions when Governments are not masters of their own destinies. The Polish Guarantee was a case in point.

Halifax had been one of the first to realise that the Munich mood could not last, and after Prague there was a sharp reaction away from any further conciliation, a fact that was signified by the startling public restoration of Churchill's position. Few people could remember any of his individual speeches, but his persistent reiteration of the German menace had got through. The realisation, however vague, that he had been 'right' when virtually everyone else had been 'wrong' oversimplified the matter, but was certainly not unjustified. Personal abuse directed against him by the German leaders did him no harm at all. His stock rose rapidly in the House of Commons. A letter urging his

[1] Nicolson, op. cit., 393.

recall to the Government signed by a number of prominent people was published in the *Daily Telegraph* (after being rejected by *The Times*). He was being hailed by the *Daily Mirror* as 'Britain's most trusted statesman', and there were many other indications of his suddenly changed status.

Thus, in the early summer of 1939 Chamberlain was being forced by the evident feeling in the House of Commons into a reluctant belligerent posture while still believing that peace could be maintained. The introduction of military conscription—strongly opposed by Labour—was not a true indication of British resolve. The Government also announced in April the appointment of a Minister of Supply; the Minister himself was not appointed until July. The conscription was not immediate, and was limited to six months' preparatory training. The new Minister turned out to be Leslie Burgin, another Inskip. In May came the announcement of the 'Pact of Steel' alliance between Italy and Germany. The Anglo-Russian discussions were the touchstone of the British resolve towards Poland. Seldom has a matter of such importance been handled with such lethargy. The dispersal of the House of Commons on August 2nd was the occasion for angry scenes, in which pro-Chamberlain Conservatives shouted angrily at those who urged that Parliament should not adjourn.

Chamberlain stated that he would regard a vote on the matter as one of confidence, and the temperature rose rapidly. Forty Conservatives abstained, nonetheless, and Parliament adjourned in a sulphurous atmosphere. On August 22nd the thunderclap of the Nazi-Soviet Pact was announced, and Parliament was hastily summoned. 'The P.M. was dignified and calm', Nicolson wrote on the 24th, 'but without one word which could inspire anybody. He was exactly like a coroner summing up a case of murder. I see mighty little chance of peace.'

Some Ministers, however, still clutched at the hope that war might be averted. On September 1st Germany invaded Poland, but no British declaration of war followed. The House of Commons met in agitation, and received no clear indication of the Government's policy. Desperate efforts to avert the inevitable continued, but the mood of the House of Commons was no longer amenable to these endeavours. On the evening of September 2nd, Chamberlain's statement to the House was so equivocal that when Arthur Greenwood (deputising for Attlee, who was unwell) rose from the Front Opposition bench he was greeted with a bitter cry from Leo Amery, 'Speak for England!' In that instant the accumulated tensions of months exploded memorably. 'It was an astonishing demonstration', as Nicolson recorded. 'Greenwood almost staggered with surprise. When it subsided he had to speak and did so better than I expected. He began to say what an embarrassing task had been imposed on him. He had wanted to support, and was obliged to criticise. Why this delay? We had promised to help Poland "at once". She was being bombed and attacked. We had vacillated for 34 hours. What did this mean? He was resoundingly cheered. Then tension became more acute, since here were the P.M.'s most ardent supporters cheering his opponent with all their lungs. The front bench looked as if they had been struck in the face . . .'.[1] Chamberlain intervened lamely, and the House adjourned in 'great confusion and indignation', in Nicolson's words.

Immediately after the House rose, there was an even more unexpected revolt, this time from within the Government. Ministers decided upon immediate and direct action. The Minister of Agriculture—Sir Reginald Dorman-Smith—has related that:

> reports are quite wrong about stormy scenes. This was a plain *diktat* from the Cabinet . . . I remember that the P.M. was calm, even icy cold, all the time . . . The climax came most dramatically. The P.M. said quietly: 'Right, gentlemen, this means war.' Hardly had he said it when there was the most enormous clap of thunder, and the whole Cabinet Room was lit up by a blinding flash of lightning.

The most vehement single group against the impending war was Mosley's Fascists, declaring that 'The War on Want is The War We Want', and endeavouring to create a Peace Front. It was a motley collection of the good, the bad, the enlightened and the idiotic, bound together with the inextricable links of irrelevance. Dean Inge and Lord Alfred Douglas gave their full support. A vast rally—attended by some 20,000 people—had taken place at Earls Court on July 16th, at which Mosley excoriated the major parties and the Jews. 'We fight for Britain, yes, but a million Britons shall never die in your Jews' quarrel.' Mosley's arguments were in fact more subtle and realistic than his oratory would imply, but he had once again fatally misunderstood the mood of the times. It was to be his last misunderstanding. The political career that had opened so brilliantly and excitingly,

[1] Nicolson, op. cit., 419.

and which had shown such genuine promise, collapsed in derision and contempt.

There was no possible escape for Chamberlain short of resignation, and the British ultimatum to Germany was dispatched. It expired at 11 o'clock on the morning of September 3rd. At 11.15 Chamberlain spoke to the nation, in terms of melancholy acceptance which were strangely moving. The House of Commons was due to meet at noon, but was delayed by a false air-raid warning. The evening and night of September 2nd had been wild and stormy, but September 3rd was a perfect late-summer day. The House of Commons met in a strange atmosphere of calm, as if a prolonged and agonised nightmare had been concluded. Churchill had been invited to join the Government on September 1st, but had heard nothing since then, and was still on the back benches, from which he rose to make his last speech from the political wilderness. Later he recorded:

> As I sat in my place, listening to the speeches, a very strong sense of calm came over me, after the intense passions and excitements of the past few days. I felt a security of mind, and was conscious of a kind of uplifted detachment from human and personal affairs. The glory of Old England, peace-loving and ill-prepared as she was, but instant and fearless at the call of honour, thrilled my being and seemed to lift our fate to those spheres far removed from earthly facts and physical sensation.[1]

Not all enjoyed this sense of comfort and relief. Chamberlain spoke in terms of anguish. 'Everything I have worked for, everything that I have hoped for, everything that I have believed in during my public life, has crashed in ruins.' The mood was not one of exaltation, but of grim resignation. The euphoria and exhilaration of 1914 were gone, yet there was a remarkable lack of realisation of the scale and extent of the task which lay before the British people, and certainly little comprehension of the dangers which confronted them. But the British, like the Chamberlain Government, went reluctantly to war. 'At 1.50', Nicolson wrote in his diary for September 3rd, 'I motor down with Victor Cazalet to Sissinghurst. There are many army lorries passing along the road and a few pathetic trucks evacuating East End refugees. In one of those there is an elderly woman who shakes her fist at us and shouts that it is all the fault of the rich.'[2]

[1] Churchill, op. cit., 320.   [2] Nicolson, op. cit., 422.

RETROSPECT

PRESIDENT WILSON DECLARED in December 1918 that 'I believe that . . . men are beginning to see, not perhaps the golden age, but an age which at any rate is brightening from decade to decade, and will lead us some time to an elevation from which we can see the things for which the heart of mankind is longing'. The story of the inter-war years is how that vision quickly faded, then returned, only to be destroyed for ever.

It is easy for the historian, many years later, to point morals and deliver judgements. It is always important to remember that, to the contemporary, matters are always confused, and that it is always difficult to distinguish the meaningful from the irrelevant, the great issues from the small, the significant portent from the passing transient phenomenon. Consistency may be the hobgoblin of little minds; it is also a perilous attitude in an always changing situation.

It may also be a pleasant pastime for the historian to select his politicians and his parties and to impose upon them the policies and attitudes which he, with his subsequent wisdom, may deem to have been the most appropriate. The post-war Lloyd George Coalition should have striven to create and maintain the Weimar Republic in Germany and create a viable European order in the League. It should have entered into immediate negotiations for a settlement of the Irish Question. It should have addressed itself most seriously to industrial relations at home. It should have made use of the experience of the Great War in managing and developing a national economy. It should have pursued a mildly inflationary policy, invested heavily in the new industries while enabling the older ones to rehabilitate themselves. It should have eschewed romantic dreams of Free Trade, laissez-faire, and the return to gold. It should have recognised the fact of Soviet Russia, and the enormous potentialities of the United States. It should not have disarmed so quickly and completely.

But the Coalition was a liaison of individuals and parties that had had its origins in the darker period of the War. It was subject to the strong tides of electoral opinion. It was composed of men whose political lives and experiences had been well advanced before that war began. The policies that that Government followed were compounded of the respective attitudes, experiences, and prejudices of its members, and necessarily reflected their political background in the pre-war years. Victorians all, the experience of the war had confirmed them in their conviction that the foundations of that victory had been laid in the previous decades. The desire to return to 'normalcy' was accordingly a reactionary attitude in the best—if also the most disastrous—sense of the word. But, as we have seen, this essential conservatism did not apply to the Coalition leaders alone. The leaders of the nascent Labour and dying Liberal parties were also children of the Victorian era.

It was the misfortune of the Coalition leaders that they were the first to discover, the hard way, that so much had changed. The privileged and unchallenged dominance of the old political classes was itself fading. In 1918 Britain had taken a giant step towards becoming a full democracy, a process that was completed ten years later. It was significant that Churchill, in *My Early Life* (1930), looked back with such nostalgia to the good old days when 'we had a real political democracy, led by the hierachy of statesmen, and not a fluid mass distracted by newspapers. There was a structure in which statesmen, electors and the Press all played their part . . . All this was before the liquefaction of the British political system had set in.' By 1934 he was denouncing the British political system as 'a timid Caesarism refreshing itself by occasional plebiscites', and was declaring that 'all experience goes to show that once the vote has been given to everyone, and what is called full democracy has been achieved, the whole [political] system is very speedily broken up and swept away'.

In fact, the structure of British politics had been affected in more subtle manners than this gloomy diagnosis would suggest. The glittering personages of the Lloyd George Coalition—their manner, their style, their assumptions, their arrogant acceptance of authority —parade before us as characteristic figures of a political era that had gone. It is doubtful if any of them fully realised the true cause of their downfall, which was simply that they were out of date. At this distance of time it is possible to form a less severe judgement upon the Coalition and to appreciate more fully the magnitude of the burdens that it endured, than many contemporaries had been prepared to concede. But, if people expected too much, it may be remarked that they had been led to expect too much. Justice, in politics, usually is somewhat rough, but it is difficult to deny that the Coalition did receive justice.

It was unfortunate that power fell from the hands of one type of pre-war politician to another. Baldwin emerges as the most sensitive and sensible of the major inter-war political figures, to whom belated justice must be given for much wisdom and perceptiveness, yet his vision of a Britain in which Master and Worker lived in harmony and mutual respect was in many ways as unreal, as romantic, and as historically false as were the Imperial dreams of Churchill and Amery, and MacDonald's respectable, Utopian, socialism. Snowden's tenacious seizure of the Holy Grail of Free Trade ensured that the advent of Labour, far from heralding revolution and change, marked a decisive step backwards into nineteenth-century Radicalism. The claims of Mosley, Keynes, and Hubert Henderson to have found the cures for Britain's industrial and economic ailments may be viewed with some scepticism, but their remedies offered infinitely more hope than the essentially reactionary and unimaginative attitudes of Ministers, officials, and orthodox advisers in the 1920s and even in the 1930s.

One may notice the continuance of many of the problems and dilemmas in other fields from the pre-1914 era, often in a more acute form. Home Rule was at last conceded to Southern Ireland, but only after the British had been compelled to seek negotiations—and not the least of the significant features of this episode was the fact that it was British public opinion, for so long hostile to Irish ambitions, that was the decisive factor. The long struggle over Ireland ended with a virtual war in which the British resorted to methods that appalled decent opinion everywhere, and was followed by a Civil War that cost Ireland the lives of many of the men who could have made the new nation operate successfully in its formative years.

In Imperial matters we can see the development of the relationship of the self-governing Dominions carried to its logical conclusion in the definition of Dominion Status and the Statute of Westminster. The attempts of successive British Ministers and believers in Empire to bind the Empire into a more formal relationship failed, and the

continued failure to achieve co-operation in Defence matters emphasised the fundamental separatist tendencies of the new nations. The
existence of this separatism was covered up by phrases and formulae,
and by the genuine mutual affection and regard that existed between
the Dominions and Britain. But, as the Chanak Crisis of 1922 and the
Imperial Conference of 1937 demonstrated once again—if further
evidence had been required—British policy was becoming more
dominated by Dominion attitudes than the other way around. In her
continued faith in Empire, Britain had become imprisoned by it, and
had become grossly over-extended in military and economic terms.

British Governments had not lost their interest in Imperial affairs.
But, at the top, the emphasis was now on maintaining what existed
rather than engaging in any serious attempt to change the *status quo*,
and far less to extend British Imperial commitments. The revised
terms of association with Egypt may be seen to be particularly
significant. The dismissal of Lord Lloyd and the abandonment of the
Cromer–Milner approach marked a new attitude and, some might
say, a new realisation, however dimly perceived, that national interests
could be preserved without the apparatus and authority of virtual
complete rule.

Elsewhere—and India is the most conspicuous example—we can
see the further development of ideas of association that were the
logical conclusion of previous measures and attitudes. But here we can
also see a failure to realise that the pace, particularly in the East, had
sharply accelerated, and that what was offered was too little and,
above all, too late. In the debates on the Government of India Act
we can clearly see three distinct attitudes emerging—that represented
by Churchill and his associates; that espoused by men like Amery,
who believed in the future of the Empire as a world confederation of
vast significance in which nationalism and supra-nationalism could
dwell together; and that put forward by a minority in Parliament, but
by a not derisory minority, to the effect that the movement must be
towards complete independence and, if necessary, separatism. This
may be said to represent a return to the Radical attitudes towards
Empire of the first half of the nineteenth century. Had not the Second
World War vastly increased the pace of the desire for independence,
this development might have taken longer to achieve. It is difficult,
however, to believe that it could have been averted. The pattern had
been established in the case of the 'white' Dominions, and the illogicality

of denying it to other peoples was clearly exposed in the lengthy debates on the 1935 Act. And the minority that argued thus in the early 1930s was to find itself in a majority after 1945. The Indians, as had the Irish, learned that their battle was to be won in England and that Disraeli had been right when he declared that 'the keys of India are in London'.

Nevertheless, we shall note that a sharp differentiation still existed between the African and non-African states. The unscrambling of Africa was to be essentially a post-Second World War phenomenon.

In British domestic politics the outstanding feature of this period, and most particularly of the inter-war years, was the dominance of the Conservative Party. This unique federation, constantly changing yet with its essential characteristics unchanged, survived all others in the years 1886 to 1939. Only in the years 1906–14 was it seriously out of office. For the rest, the history of these years is that of almost complete Conservative rule, with occasional and very fleeting interludes of Opposition. The fundamental reason for this remarkable durability lies in the development into unspoken doctrine of the Disraelian philosophy that change must come, but that it must be change conducted on the terms of the propertied classes. The Reform Acts had widened the franchise, but had still concentrated it upon a minority—and a minority with a profound stake in cautious, ordered, change. When Labour emerged in 1917–18, it, too, was dominated by this approach, and could not compete on level terms with the Conservative experience and ruthlessness in this particular limited political market.

Between the two, the Liberals were crushed into extinction. They could not command the mass of cautious conservatism which exists in all classes in Britain and which serves as the bed-rock of the Conservative Party. They were detached from the new masses which progressed from active trade unionism into dedicated support for the Labour Party. The Liberals accordingly drifted into a middle ground between two powerful combinations, each of which had a substantial unwavering constituency and the capacity to appeal to the uncommitted. It could be argued that Liberalism as a general philosophy had not died, and that its tenets had been accepted and appropriated by the other parties. But the schism of 1916 and the Asquith–Lloyd George feud had been more significant than issues of ideology. Its bold programme of 1928–9 was the last burst of energy from a party whose intellectual and practical contribution had transformed the political and social character of the nation. But it had become divided and irrelevant, and it perished.

The Conservatives certainly moved to the Left between 1919 and 1939. In essentials, this tendency was not more marked than that between the 1860s and the beginning of the Great War, but in most respects—and particularly in domestic reform—it was more coherent and better based. The eager social-reform Conservatives who came into politics from the trenches were disillusioned and disappointed by what was achieved, but their contribution had been significant. In particular, the nascent battle with trade unions had been averted in the 1920s, and the general approach of the Conservatives in the 1930s had been one of tolerance and reform. The overwhelming rejection of extreme policies, both in Dominion and home affairs, was of real historical significance in heralding the final decline of the 'two nations'. It was here that Baldwin's personal contribution was of such importance, and his defeats of his right-wing critics so fundamental to the continued relevance of his party. This was Baldwin's supreme achievement; like Disraeli, he 'educated' his party, and it was his misfortune that power came to him again in 1935 in circumstances in which neither he nor the nation had sufficient time for gradual change.

Labour had not presented an impressive picture in office. It lacked experience, leadership, and a real philosophy. Suddenly projected into prominence and office, it never enjoyed power. The roots of the Parliamentary Party lay deep in Victorian Liberalism, and the passionate craving for respectability and acceptability dominated its fevered and distracted counsels. Both in 1924 and in 1929–31 it demonstrated these characteristics with sad clarity. In some spheres— and not least in foreign affairs—Labour often had the right attitudes, but these were not accompanied with either practical experience or profound thinking. Labour's real chance came in 1940; war was to provide it with the experience and the stature and the freedom to operate which had always been denied to it before. But the lessons of the 1920s and the 1930s were to be of even greater importance in the establishment of the Labour Party as the natural and unchallengeable successor to the Liberal Party. Out of the tumults, the errors, the agonies and the heart-searchings of this formative period the modern Labour Party was born.

*

This narrative opened in 1880. The flaring gas-jets above the great glass ceiling of the House of Commons—that ceiling which had been built over the bitter objections of Sir Charles Barry—had, in 1880, flickered and illuminated Gladstone, Joseph Chamberlain, Parnell, Lord Randolph Churchill, Arthur Balfour, Harcourt and Hartington. In the same Chamber, on September 3rd, 1939, the sons of Joseph Chamberlain and Lord Randolph Churchill were prominent, the one white, tense, and temporarily crushed, the other pink-faced, determined, and grimly elated. On the Conservative benches there sat Leo Amery, who had fought his first election in 1906; opposite, there was Lloyd George, his hair now a shock of white mane, but his eyes still clear and crisp, first elected in 1890. Baldwin was in retirement, MacDonald, Balfour, Asquith and Campbell-Bannerman were dead. Yet in that tawny chamber, soon to be destroyed for ever, where Disraeli and Gladstone had debated, where Lord Randolph Churchill had risen and fallen, where the young Lloyd George had denounced the South African War and the even younger Winston Churchill had seen his party walk out contemptuously as he addressed the House in 1904, where Campbell-Bannerman had swept Balfour aside and Asquith had been howled down in the tempests of the 1911 Constitutional Crisis, a mysterious sense of continuity still existed. And it was this indefinable element, this incalculable sentiment of history and of fundamental justice, which was to bring the British Parliament and people through an ordeal unparalleled in the long annals of their turbulent history. The Britain of 1939 was very different from that of 1880. A vast, almost silent, revolution had been accomplished. Much more remained to be done, and many more injustices to be resolved. But the Britain of 1939 was in almost every respect a better nation, a more equitable nation, and a more united nation, than it had been when the gas-lights flared upon the House of Commons seventy years before.

Of course, the history of a people is not a stable, fixed, thing. The achievements of one generation may easily be lost by the next. There is little pattern in the past, few hints of what tomorrow may bring. But if the British can point to their survival as their principal achievement in the twentieth century, this is, in itself, no idle or unworthy claim. And it is in this spirit and resilience that we may find the answer to the quandary of how the British were to survive two World Wars, the loss of much of their wealth, the disappearance of their Empire, a reduction to minor status among the world powers, the continued follies of their leaders, and their manifest inadequacies in material possessions and economic systems when compared with other nations. How this was achieved must be the theme of a subsequent volume. But even in 1939, after these seventy years of triumph, tragedy, change and revolution, the British people could console themselves with Aeschylus' dictum:

Why repine at Fortune's frowns? The gain hath the advantage, and the loss does not bear down the scale.

And thus, on September 3rd, 1939, with none of the excitement of August 1914, and with grim forebodings, this remarkable, perplexing, and defiant people entered another stage of their curious, many-faceted, and unfinished odyssey.

SELECTED
BIBLIOGRAPHY

The quantity of books, monographs and articles concerned with the period 1880–1939 is very substantial indeed, and this bibliography is intended for the guidance and assistance of the reader who wishes to study the period further rather than as a comprehensive list of all the works consulted.

1. 1880–1914

POLITICAL PAPERS

The principal collections that I have used during the preparation of this volume are, in alphabetical order, the papers of Sir Henry Campbell-Bannerman (British Library), Victor Cazalet (in private possession), Lord Randolph Churchill (Chartwell and Blenheim Palace), Sir Charles Dilke (British Library), Herbert and W. E. Gladstone (British Library), Sir Edward Hamilton (British Library), W. V. Harcourt (then in the possession of the present Lord Harcourt, and now in the Bodleian Library, Oxford), Lord Kitchener (Public Record Office), Sir Stafford Northcote (then in private possession, now in the British Library), Lord Rosebery (now in the National Library of Scotland), Lord Salisbury (Christ Church, Oxford, and Hatfield House), Lord Ripon (British Library), and W. H. Smith (British Library). I have also made use of the complete correspondence between Prime Ministers and the Sovereign (Public Record Office) and the Cabinet papers.

PUBLIC WORKS

On general histories of the period, R. C. K. Ensor: *England 1870–1914* (1936), in spite of much subsequent research and discoveries, still holds the field, and is a work of abiding quality. Halévy's *The Rise of Democracy* (1943) is certainly in the same class. Of more recent books, particular note must be taken of H. Pelling: *Popular Politics and Society in Late Victorian Britain* (1968), R. Shannon: *The Crisis of Imperialism 1865–1915* (1974), and S. Maccoby: *English Radicalism 1886–1914* (1953). R. T. Mackenzie's *British Political Parties* (1955; revised editions 1964 and 1970) covers a considerable part of this period, while on economic matters the best single work is W. Ashworth: *An Economic History of England 1870–1939* (1960). On the parties, R. Blake's *The Conservative Party from Peel to Churchill* (1970), although exhilirating, is not the substitute for the detailed history of this remarkable confederation that is urgently needed. P. Smith: *Disraelian Conservatism and Social Reform* (1967) is a step in the right direction. Lord Chilston's *Chief Whip* (1961) throws some further light, and E. J. Feuchtwanger: *Disraeli, Democracy and the Tory Party* (1968) is good on the 1870s and 1880s. H. Pelling's work on the Labour Party—particularly *The Origins of the Labour Party* (1965) and *A Short History of the Labour Party* (1965) is excellent, as are A. M. McBriar: *Fabian Socialism and English Politics 1884–1918* (1962) and R. McKibbin: *The Evolution of the Labour Party 1910–1924* (1975); R. Harrison: *Before the Socialists—Studies in Labour and Politics, 1861–1881* (1965) is an indispensable work. The Liberals have also been better served by historians than the Conservatives, notably in D. Southgate: *The Passing of the Whigs* (1962), J. R. Vincent: *The Formation of the Liberal Party 1857–1868* (1966), D. A. Hamer: *Liberal Politics in the Age of Gladstone and Rosebery* (1972), P. Stansky: *Ambitions and Strategies—The Struggle for the Leadership of the Liberal Party in the 1890s* (1964) and R. B. MacCullum: *The Liberal Party from Earl Grey to Asquith* (1963). H. J. Hanham: *Elections and Party Management—Politics in the Time of Disraeli and Gladstone* (1959) was a pioneering work of high quality, as were M. Cowling's *Disraeli, Gladstone and Revolution: The Passing of the Second Reform Bill* (1967), C. O'Leary's *The Elimination of Corrupt Practices in British Elections 1868–1911* (1962), R. T. Shannon's *Gladstone and the Bulgarian Agitation, 1876* (1963), and N. Blewett: *The Peers, The Parties and The People,* (1972).

On specific episodes, attention should be given to several excellent studies, notably F. B. Smith: *The Making of the Second Reform Bill* (1966), T. Lloyd: *The General Election of 1880* (1968), A. Jones: *The Politics of Reform, 1884* (1972), A. B. Cooke and J. R. Vincent: *The Governing Passion, Cabinet Government and Party Politics in Britain 1885–86* (1974), R. Jenkins: *Mr. Balfour's Poodle* (1954), A. K. Russell: *Liberal Landslide—The General Election of 1906* (1973) and W. L. Arnstein: *The Bradlaugh Case* (1965).

For the House of Commons, the best accounts are those of H. W. Lucy, whose 'diaries' of the Parliaments from 1874 to 1906—in fact the compilation of his weekly columns as a lobby correspondent—provide the best contemporary portrait available to us.

It is when the historian comes to biographies that he begins to fell overwhelmed by the sheer mass of published material. On Disraeli, the volumes of F. W. Monypenny and G. E. Buckle, published between 1910 and 1920, still have a powerful attraction and much interest. R. Blake's long, but in comparison brief, biography published in 1966 is by far the best biography yet published. On Gladstone, the publication of his Diaries has proved a most lengthy process, and they have not yet begun to approach the period covered by this volume. Morley's classic three volume biography (1903) maintains its position, but is now greatly supplemented by J. L. Hammond and M. R. D. Foot: *Gladstone and Liberalism* (1952) and Sir Philip Magnus's *Gladstone* (1954). An admirable brief study was published by E. J. Feuchtwanger in 1975. One of the best sources is *The Political Correspondence of Mr. Gladstone and Lord Granville*, edited by Agatha Ramm, which covers the years 1868–76 (published in 1952) and 1876–86 (1962).

J. L. Garvin's huge and idiosyncratic biography of Joseph Chamberlain first began to appear in 1932, and was greeted with warm praise. Later evaluations, however, have been less admiring. Now that the work has been completed by J. Amery, it is evident that a new single volume biography is very much needed. P. Fraser: *Joseph Chamberlain, Radicalism and Empire, 1868–1914* (1966), although of interest, does not really meet this requirement. M. Hurst's *Joseph Chamberlain and Liberal Reunion: The Round Table Conference of 1887* (1967) deals with one episode in Chamberlain's career (at great length). Chamberlain's *A Political Memoir 1880–1892* (1953), edited by C. H. D. Howard, is a valuable source, but should be approached with considerable caution.

Lord Randolph Churchill was (at least initially) more fortunate. Winston Churchill's biography (1906) and Lord Rosebery's memoir, published the same year, are classics of British political literature. Rosebery's vignette tells us much more about the man. R. Rhodes James's biography, published in 1959, added new material from sources not available to the earlier biographers. Lord Randolph's fascination, for not only his contemporaries but later generations, is evident in each of these biographies. Lord Randolph not only 'forgot Goschen', but so have historians, apart from A. D. Elliot's sombre biography (1911) and P. Colson's *Lord Goschen and His Friends* (1946).

Lady Gwendolen Cecil's uncompleted biography of Salisbury (published in four volumes between 1921 and 1931) is a superlative work of political biography, but a single-volume new biography is very much needed. A. L. Kennedy: *Salisbury* (1953) does not adequately supply this. R. Taylor's brief biography (1974) is an excellent short study but necessarily limited in scope. Campbell-Bannerman received massive treatment by J. A. Spender in 1923, and an admirable—if perhaps rather too admiring—biography by J. Wilson in 'C-B' (1973). Milner—like Curzon—has been heavily assailed by biographers. *The Milner Papers*, edited by C. Headlam (1931, 1933) were, we can now see, rather too well edited. J. E. Wrench: *Milner* (1958), V. Halperin: *Lord Milner and the Empire* (1952), E. Crankshaw: *The Forsaken Idea: A Study of Lord Milner* (1952) and A. M. Gollin: *Proconsul in Politics* (1964) view this intriguing man from varying angles and with sympathetic skill.

A really satisfying biography of Lloyd George has yet to be written but J. Grigg: *The Young Lloyd George* (1973) is a first-rate study of his early career. H. du Parcq's *Life of David Lloyd George* (1911–13), although written before the most dramatic part of his career and with all the disadvantages of contemporary biography, remains an indispensable source. F. Owen's *Tempestuous Journey* (1954) has been consistently underrated; its style is certainly an acquired taste. W. George: *My Brother and I* (1958) and K. Morgan: *Lloyd George, Family Letters 1885–1936* are of considerable value and interest. The biography by T. Jones (1951) is more illuminating on Lloyd George's later career than the earlier; M. Thompson's *David Lloyd George: The Official Biography* (1948) is not very illuminating on any period. K. O. Morgan: *Wales in British Politics 1868–1922* (1963) is essential reading in its own right, but is invaluable in the context of Lloyd George's rise.

A. J. Balfour similarly lacks a biography that does full justice to his complex character and career. Mrs. Blanche Dugdale's biography (1939) provided some excellent family glimpses, but was too admiring and deficient on certain vital episodes to be an acceptable political biography. K. Young's new biography (1963) was a bold attempt to remedy the situation, but was not wholly successful. A. M. Gollin's *Balfour's Burden* (1965) deals with the 1903–5 crisis in the style of Lord Beaverbrook—a somewhat startling metamorphosis, and not convincing. D. Judd: *Balfour and the British Empire* (1968) has good material and interesting insights, but Balfour remains as inscrutable as ever.

Asquith published his own *Memories and Reflections* in 1928, which have occasional flashes of real interest. Margot Asquith's *Autobiography* (1920–2) also has the same characteristic, but is much more fun. The official biography by J. A. Spender and C. Asquith (1932) is a solemn work of veneration; R. Jenkins's biography (1964) is the best study yet provided, although not devoid of flaws, and rather more sympathetic than is required in a revising biography.

The list of biographies of Curzon, started by Lord Ronaldshay (1928), seems endless. Of the recent attempts the best are D. Dilks: *Curzon in India* (1969–70), M. Edwardes: *High Noon of Empire—India Under Curzon* (1965) and K. Rose: *Superior Person* (1969). None, however, is really a biography; L. Mosley: *Curozn—The End of an Epoch* (1960) is a caustic and somewhat dramatised study, but with many virtues.

On Sir Edward Grey, the only complete biography is that by K. Robbins, published in 1971, but his own *Twenty-Five Years* (1925) should not be neglected. The biography of C. F. G. Masterman by his wife Lucy (1939) and Masterman's own *The Condition of England* (1910) emphasise the significance of this now virtually unknown man, whose career ended so prematurely. John Morley's *Recollections* (1921) are highly haphazard and not easy to follow, but of great value. D. A. Hamer's biography (1968) is a major attempt to portray Morley, but hampered—as in the case of Grey—by the disappearance and scattering of his papers. J. Pope-Hennessy: *Lord Crewe—The Likeness of A Liberal* (1958) gives belated justice to a minor but far from unimportant public personality, as does C. Cross: *Philip Snowden* (1966). The biography of Beatrice Webb by K. Muggeridge and R. Adam (1967) only tends to emphasise the need for more full treatment. Lord Zetland's biography of Cromer (1932) has been supplemented most interestingly by Afaf Lutfi Al-Sayyid's *Egypt and Cromer* (1968). Sir Philip Magnus's biography of Kitchener (1958) is a vast improvement on the previous attempt by Sir George Arthur, but leaves the reader vaguely unsatisfied. The same can be said of the biography of Northcliffe by R. Pound and G. Harmsworth (1959). In contrast, A. M. Gollin's *The Observer and J. L. Garvin* (1960) and A. J. P. Taylor: *Beaverbrook* (1972) are excellent studies of two other major journalistic and political figures. C. Mallet: *Herbert Gladstone—A Memoir* (1932) is an important book, but subsequent research on his papers demonstrates that a new biography would be of value. Lord Newton's biography of Lord Lansdowne (1929), falls into the same category. Haldane's *Autobiography* (1929) has been supplemented by Sir Frederick Maurice's official biography (1937), and by D. Sommer's rather disappointing *Haldane of Cloan* (1960). S. E. Koss: *Lord Haldane— Scapegoat for Liberalism* (1969) is excellent in its early chapters, but thereafter must be treated with reservations. Austen Chamberlain wrote his own memoirs (*Politics From The Inside* (1936)) and his biography was written by Sir Charles Petrie in 1939. Now that his papers are available it is to be hoped that a new study may be attempted. R. Blake's biography of Bonar Law (1955) is difficult to fault on any count.

Lord Birkenhead's biography of his father, first published in 1933, and revised in 1960 under the title 'F.E.', has many of the virtues, but also many of the deficiencies, of filial biography. Randolph Churchill's biography of his father Winston (Vol. I 1966, Vol. II 1967) was a project flawed both in conception and execution, excessively documented and excessively admiring. Volume One made a good beginning, but the second was a sad disappointment. Churchill's own autobiography: *My Early Life* (1930) and his *Great Contemporaries* (1937), and Lady Violet Bonham Carter's *Winston Churchill As I Knew Him* (1965) should be read in conjunction with the Randolph Churchill volumes. H. Pelling's single volume biography (*Winston Churchill* (1974)) is surprisingly uncritical and rather bland. R. Hyam: *Elgin and Churchill At the Colonial Office 1905–08* (1968) is essential reading both in the context of the South African policies and in Churchill's development and characteristics as a young Minister. The essays in *Churchill—Four Faces and the Man* (1969) provide a more critical appraisal than was then fashionable, as did R. Rhodes James: *Churchill, A Study In Failure 1900–1939* (1970), whose ironically intended sub-title deluded those who read no further into the belief that this was a denigratory biography. But it may be stated with confidence that, even after M. Gilbert has completed the gargantuan task which he assumed on the death of Randolph Churchill, this extraordinary career will continue to fascinate historians and biographers.

Other biographies that merit attention are E. Marjoribanks and H. M. Hyde on Carson (1932 and 1953 respectively), Lord Askwith's *Lord James of Hereford* (1930), Viscount Chilston: *W. H. Smith* (1965), K. Morgan: *Keir Hardie* (1975), and R. Rhodes James: *Rosebery* (1963).

On Ireland, the list of books and studies is so substantial—and of such high quality—that only a very limited selection can be given. N. Mansergh: *The Irish Question 1840–1921* (1965) is perhaps the best single study of the period. On Parnell, the best studies by far are R. Barry O'Brien's magnificent biography, published in 1898, Conor Cruise O'Brien's *Parnell and His Party* (1957), and F. S. L. Lyons: *The Fall of Parnell* (1960). There have been many other biographies and studies of Parnell, but none of this quality. D. Thornely: *Isaac Butt and Home Rule* (1964) L.P. Curtis: *Coercion and Conciliation In Ireland 1880–1892* (1963), F. S. L. Lyons: *The Irish Parliamentary Party 1890–1910* (1951) and *John Dillon* (1968) are fully up to the high standard of modern Irish histories. J. L. Hammond: *Gladstone and the Irish Nation* (1938) still holds its eminence as a work of outstanding scholarship and literature. M. Davitt's *The Fall of Feudalism In Ireland* (1904) should be read in conjunction with F. Sheehy-Skeffington's biography of Davitt, published in 1908 and deservedly republished in 1967. J. C. Beckett: *The Making of Modern Ireland 1603–1923* (1966) covers a large canvass with skill and objectivity.

The same dilemma confronts the historian of the Empire. The *Cambridge History of the British Empire, Volume III, 1870–1919* (1959) in a basic work. On African matters the indispensable works are E. A. Walker: *A History of Southern Africa* (3rd edition, 1957), the Cambridge History of the British Empire, Volume VIII—South Africa (1963), R. Robinson, J. Gallagher, and A. Denny: *Africa and the Victorians* (1963), D. M. Schreuder: *Gladstone and Kruger* (1969), J. S. Marais: *The Fall of Kruger's Republic* (1961), G. H. Le May: *British Supremacy in South Africa 1899–1907* (1965). Also of value are E. Pakenham (Lady Longford): *Jameson's Raid* (1960), P. Mansfield: *The British in Egypt* (1971), J. L. Lockhart and C. M. Woodhouse: *Cecil Rhodes* (1962), J. E. Flint: *Sir George Goldie and the Making of Nigeria* (1960) and M. Perham: *Lugard* (1956, 1960). On the South African War, L. S. Amery's history for *The Times* (1905–9) is detailed, but heavy going. D. Reitz: *Commando* (1929) is a classic of military autobiography: W. B. Pemberton: *Battles of the Boer War* (1964) is clear and well written, as are J. Symonds: *Buller's Campaign* (1963) and the appropriate chapters of W. K. Hancock's excellent biography of Smuts (1962). R. Kruger's *Good-bye, Dolly Grey* (1959) gives a lively account of the war, as does E. Holt: *The Boer War* (1958). An interesting study of domestic reactions is given in R. Price: *An Imperialist War and the British Working Class* (1972). The best account of the Sudan Campaign of 1897–8 is to be found in Winston Churchill's superb *The River War* (1899, 1900), and no student of this area should ignore R. Slatin's: *Fire and Sword in the Sudan* (1896) nor G. Brook-Shepherd's biography of Slatin, *Between Two Flags* (1973), and R. Wingate: *Wingate of the Sudan* (1955). A new account of the Sudan campaign is given in P. Ziegler: *Omdurman* (1974). Although a good history, it is written in a colourful style that reads oddly from the sombre biographer of King William IV and Addington.

On the wider subject of Imperialism, J. R. Seely: *The Expansion of England* (1883, and in print until 1956) and the counter-attack in J. A. Hobson: *Imperialism: A Study* (1902) are essential, as is C. A. Bodelsen: *Studies in Mid-Victorian Imperialism* (1924). Also strongly recommended are M. Beloff: *Imperial Sunset, Vol. I 1897–1921* (1969), I. M. Cumpston: *The Growth of the British Commonwealth 1880–1932* (1973), A. P. Thornton: *The Imperial Idea and Its Enemies* (1959), R. Koebner and H. D. Schmidt:

Imperialism (1964), C. J. Lowe: *The Reluctant Imperialists* (1967), and C. C. Eldridge: *England's Mission. The Imperial Idea in the Age of Gladstone and Disraeli* (1974).

The period has produced a very considerable number of published memoirs, diaries and letters. The most important single collection is G. E. Buckle (ed.): *Letters and Journals of Queen Victoria* (Second and Third Series, 1928–30). On Queen Victoria herself, the best studies of her during this period are F. Hardie: *The Political Influence of Queen Victoria* (1938) and E. Longford: *Victoria R.I.* (1964), but this historian feels that much more work could and should be done on the Queen in the latter part of her reign. The publication of Sir Almeric Fitzroy's *Memoirs* (1925) caused Royal displeasure; of value also are Sir Frederick Ponsonby's delightful *Recollections of Six Reigns* (1951). The almost total destruction of the papers of King Edward VII by Lord Knollys and others has probably hurt rather than improved his subsequent treatment by historians. Sir Philip Magnus's biography (1964), although of characteristic quality and insight, certainly suffered from this lamentable incendiarism. Lord Ponsonby's *Henry Ponsonby; His Life From His Letters* (1942) and H. G. Hutchinson: *The Private Diaries of Sir Algernon West* (1922) are of considerable value and interest. Sir Harold Nicolson's *King George V—His Life and Reign* (1952) is by far the best modern Royal biography.

On political memoirs, in addition to those already mentioned, particular note should be taken of M. V. Brett: *Journals and Letters of Viscount Esher* (1934), G. P. Gooch: *Under Six Reigns* (1958), Lady St. Helier: *Memoirs of Fifty Years* (1909), Lord Kilbracken: *Reminiscences* (1931), F. E. Hamer (ed.): *The Personal Papers of Lord Rendel* (1931), J. A. Spender: *Life, Journalism, and Politics* (1927), Lord Winterton: *Orders of the Day* (1953), and A. Clark: *A Good Innings, The Private Papers of Viscount Lee of Fareham* (1974). Parts of the copious diaries of Sir Edward Hamilton have now been published, edited by D. W. Bahlman (1972), and Lord Carlingford's Journal for 1885, edited by A. B. Cooke and J. R. Vincent (1971).

On military matters, there is nothing to compare with A. J. Marder: *From the Dreadnought to Scapa Flow*, in five volumes (1961–70), although D. E. Morris's *The Washing of the Spears* (1966), a brilliant and sensitive history of the Zulu Wars, Churchill's *The River War*, and Reitz's *Commando* describe individual episodes with exceptional skill.

On foreign affairs, which do not occupy a substantial part of this volume, in addition to the biographies of Gladstone, Disraeli, Salisbury, Rosebery, Balfour, Grey, Campbell-Bannerman, Churchill and Asquith to which reference has been made, two works by A. J. P. Taylor, *The Troublemakers* (1957), and *The Struggle for Mastery in Europe 1848–1918* (1954) should be particularly mentioned, as should G. Monger: *The End of Isolation* (1963) and W. Langer: *The Diplomacy of Imperialism* (1951).

2. 1914–1939

GENERAL

The best brief book on the period is A. F. Havighurst: *Twentieth Century Britain* (1962), although H. Pelling: *Modern Britain, 1885–1955* (1960) runs it close. The best general studies are C. L. Mowat: *Britain Between The Wars, 1918–1940* (1955) and W. N. Medlicott: *Contemporary England, 1914–1964* (1967), but as both were written before the official archives were available some of their judgements require revision. The same applies to A. J. P. Taylor: *English History 1914–1945* (1965), which may fairly be described as brilliant but erratic. C. Barnett: *The Collapse of British Power* (1972) is a bitter denunciation of many villains, some of which seem to this author to have been harshly treated. S. Beer: *Modern British Politics* (1965) is excellent, as is

D. Thomson's brief *England In The Twentieth Century* (1965). E. H. Carr: *The Twenty Years Crisis* (1939) is of considerable value, despite the correctives necessarily needed in the light of later knowledge; the same caution applies to W. McElwee: *Britain's Locust Years, 1918–1940* (1962), although it has tended to be underestimated by historians. G. H. Le May: *British Government 1914–1953; Select Documents* (1955) is invaluable, as is P. and G. Ford: *A Breviate of Parliamentary Papers 1917–1939* (1951). There is, alas, no Parliamentary commentator in the period comparable to H. W. Lucy or the younger A. G. Gardiner, but Lord Winterton: *Orders Of the Day* (1953), Harold Nicolson's diaries, volume one (1961), and those of Sir Henry Channon (1967) provide interesting sidelights on the House of Commons. On the general scene, to be recommended are M. Muggeridge: *The Thirties* (1940), R. Graves and A. Hodge: *The Long Week-End* (1940), and P. Quennell: *Life In Britain Between The Wars* (1970). The appropriate chapters of G. D. H. Cole and Raymond Postgate: *The Common People, 1746–1946* (1955), E. Shinwell: *Conflict Without Malice* (1955), W. Citrine: *Men and Work* (1964), A. Bullock: *Ernest Bevin*, Vol. I (1960), *Herbert Morrison: An Autobiography* (1960), and the diaries of Hugh Dalton *Call Back Yesterday* (1953) and *The Fateful Years* (1957) give a darker aspect to life in the period.

On economic matters, particularly recommended are A. J. Youngson: *The British Economy 1920–1957* (1960), H. Henderson: *The Inter-War Years and Other Papers* (1955), R. S. Sayers: *A History of Economic Change in England, 1880–1939* (1967), U. K. Hicks: *British Public Finances, 1880–1952* (1954), R. F. Harrod: *John Maynard Keynes* (1951) and R. Skidelsky: *Politicians and the Slump* (1967), which rightly goes farther and deeper than its account of the collapse of the 1929–31 Labour Government. W. Ashworth: *An Economic History of England, 1870–1939* (1960) is perhaps the best single book of all.

On foreign affairs the massive *Documents on British Foreign Policy* provides vital basic material for much of the period. F. S. Northedge: *The Troubled Giant* (1966), W. N. Medlicott: *British Foreign Policy Since Versailles* (second edition, 1968), and P. A. Reynolds: *British Foreign Policy In The Inter-War Years* (1954) are good, but would benefit from revision to take account of new information from the Cabinet and Foreign Office archives. Winston Churchill's *The Gathering Storm* (1948) is an overwhelmingly convincing personal view of the inter-war years, and should, accordingly, be treated with great caution. Lord Avon: *Facing the Dictators* (1962), Lord Templewood: *Nine Troubled Years* (1954), Lord Vansittart: *The Mist Procession* (1958), I. Colvin: *Vansittart In Office* (1965), Lord Simon: *Retrospect* (1952), Duff Cooper: *Old Men Forget* (1953) also give points of view that are highly personal. Lloyd George's *War Memoirs* (6 volumes, 1933–6) are heavy going, and unreliable. Churchill's *The World Crisis* (5 volumes, 1923–9) is a classic of literature and also of personal vindication that does not totally convince all historians. A. J. P. Taylor: *The Origins of the Second World War* (revised edition, 1963) caused a highly satisfying sensation when it first appeared in 1961; it can now be seen as a most valuable and stimulating corrective to the then general thesis of Hitler's saturnine and calculated policies of aggression, and is now almost respectable. M. Howard: *The Continental Commitment* (1970) and R. K. Middlemas: *Diplomacy of Illusion* (1972) are two excellent recent additions to the literature, and D. C. Watt: *Personalities and Policies* (1965) remains fresh, invigorating, and shrewd. A. Bullock: *Hitler, A Study in Tyranny* (revised edition, 1964) still stands up remarkably well in spite of the torrent of books on Hitler since then. Dennis Mack Smith's biography of Mussolini (1976) is a comparably remarkable achievement. M. Gilbert: *The Roots of Appeasement* (1966) argues a thesis ably but not, in this author's view, convincingly. Hugh Thomas: *The

Spanish Civil War (1961) is an outstanding history. L. S. Amery: *My Political Life*, Volumes II and III (1953, 1955) is particularly useful on Commonwealth and Colonial matters in the 1920s, when he was in office, and Harold Nicolson: *Curzon, The Last Phase* (1934) is a dramatic and very sympathetic account of the negotiations leading to the Treaty of Lausanne. K. Young's biography of Balfour (1963) is not very strong on the final part of Balfour's remarkable career; R. K. Middlemas and J. Barnes put up a valiant defence of Baldwin (1969) which is marred by excessive length and detail, and perhaps protests too much. It is, however, a much-needed corrective to Churchill, G. M. Young, and Beaverbrook.

Mention should also be made to C. Thorne: *The Approach of War, 1938–9* (1967). K. Feiling: *Neville Chamberlain* (1946) remains the best biography of this controversial man; Iain Macleod's biography (1961) was a deep disappointment, and not least to the author. For all the mass of studies of foreign policy in the 1930s, no single volume as yet masters the complexities nor fully escapes the charge of emotional involvement.

BIOGRAPHIES AND MEMOIRS

In addition to those already mentioned, particular attention must be paid to M. Gilbert's continuing marathon biography of Winston Churchill, of which volume V (1976) takes the story up to 1939. It is such a remarkable personal achievement that it seems unkind to comment that it is in fact so long and so massively documented that the immense complexities and fascination of Churchill's extraordinary personality have become somewhat submerged. H. Pelling's single-volume biography (1974) is rather uncritical. R. Rhodes James: *Churchill, A Study In Failure 1900–1939* (1970) endeavoured to treat Churchill as a fallible, erratic, human being of immense ability but uneven judgement. Later discoveries have tended to confirm the validity of this then revolutionary approach to a post-1939 national idol.

R. Jenkins' admiring biography of Asquith (1964) has now been supplemented by a cooler perspective from S. Koss (1976). Lloyd George's later career still lacks its historian, and there is nothing to compare with J. Grigg's study of the early period. R. Blake: *The Unknown Prime Minister* (1955) is superb on Bonar Law, and H. Nicolson and Lady Donaldson have written admirable biographies of King George V (1952) and King Edward VIII (1974) respectively, although the latter cannot be called an official or authorised biography—perhaps the better for that. In R. Rhodes James: *Memoirs of a Conservative* (1968) the obscure but important J. C. C. Davidson gives his account of the 1920s, with some important insights and documents. Also of value are B. H. Liddell Hart: *Memoirs* (1965 and 1966), S. Roskill: *Hankey, Man of Secrets* (three volumes, 1970, 1972, and 1975), R. J. Minney: *The Private Papers of Hore-Belisha* (1960), H. Macmillan: *Winds of Change* (1966), R. Boothby: *I Fight To Live* (1947), P. J. Grigg: *Prejudice and Judgement* (1948), C. Addison: *Politics From Within* (1924), Mary Hamilton: *Remembering My Good Friends* (1944), T. Jones: *Diary With Letters* (1954) and his *Whitehall Diary*, edited by R. K. Middlemas in three volumes (1969–71). These are all, of course, personal views of men and events, but each is of use. Lord E. Percy: *Some Memories* (1958), Lord Swinton: *I Remember* (1948) and *Sixty Years of Power* (1966), and Lord Butler: *The Art of the Possible* (1971) are far above the average standard of politicians' memoirs, although none quite reaches the standard of Duff Cooper's.

It cannot be pretended that the period has yet produced biographies of the exceptional quality of the previous one. There is certainly none to compare with Morley on Gladstone, Monypenny and Buckle, and R. Blake, on Disraeli, Churchill and Rosebery on Lord Randolph Churchill, R. Barry O'Brien and Conor Cruise O'Brien on Parnell, or Lady Gwendolen Cecil on Salisbury. This does not mean that the standard is low. Of particular merit are A. J. P. Taylor: *Beaverbrook* (1972), H. Thomas: *John Strachey* (1973), Bullock on Ernest Bevin, M. Foot on Aneurin Bevan (Volume I, 1966), R. Skidelsky on Mosley (1975), and R. W. Clark: *Tizard* (1965). Also of value are Lord Birkenhead's biographies of Halifax (1964), his own father, F. E. Smith (1959), Walter Monckton (1969), and Lindemann (*The Prof in Two Worlds* (1964)). R. F. Harrod also wrote an interesting personal memoir of this strange man (1959). Randolph Churchill's *Lord Derby, King of Lancashire* (1959) contains some important raw material. Also recommended are C. Cross: *Philip Snowden* (1966), L. Mosley: *Curzon, The End of an Epoch* (1960), J. R. M. Butler: *Lord Lothian* (1960), M. Hamilton: *Arthur Henderson* (1938), Sir Charles Petrie's second volume of his biography of Austen Chamberlain (1940), and R. Rhodes James: *Victor Cazalet* (1976).

MISCELLANEOUS

The literature on the Great War is primarily military; the best brief study is that by C. Falls (1960), but the general standard is very high. On the political side, in addition to the titles already mentioned, Hankey's *The Supreme Command* (1961) has now been superseded by Roskill's biography, but remains of value. Beaverbrook's entrancing volumes (*Politicians and the War* (1928), *Men And Power* (1956), and *The Decline And Fall of Lloyd George* (1963)) should be read and enjoyed, but with Taylor's biography close to hand to pour cold water on some of the better stories. R. Blake: *The Private Papers of Douglas Haig* (1953), Sir William Robertson's *Soldiers and Statesmen* (1926), and V. Bonham-Carter's biography of Robertson, *Soldier True* (1963) are essentially political rather than military sources. C. Hazlehurst: *Politicians At War, 1914–15* is a belligerent book, at times unnecessarily so, but based on solid research. T. Wilson: *The Downfall of the Liberal Party 1914–1935* is valuable on the war-time schisms, and there are useful contributions to the history of war-time politics in A. J. P. Taylor: *Politics in Wartime* (1964). There is, as yet, no single satisfying study of war-time politics, but the material is rapidly building up in biographies and special studies.

GENERAL POLITICAL

Finally, particular mention should be made of certain books that deal with specific aspects or periods. M. Cowling: *The Impact of Labour* (1971) hammers an important and valuable thesis almost into the ground, but is essential—if difficult—reading. His *The Impact of Hitler* (1974) also contains a mass of new material, but is also rather hard going. R. Blake: *The Conservative Party From Peel to Churchill* (1970) is fluent and perceptive, but is not the history of the Party that is so needed. Roy Douglas's *History of the Liberal Party 1895–1970* is not particularly informative. One of the best books on inter-war Labour politics is R. K. Middlemas: *The Clydesiders*, but its scope is necessarily limited. H. Pelling: *A Short History of the Labour Party* (1961) is excellent, but does not probe deeply. Of considerable use are C. A. Cline: *Recruits To Labour, 1914–1931*, R. W. Lyman: *The First Labour Government, 1924* (1957), R. Bassett: *1931— Political Crisis* (1958), and S. R. Graubard: *British Labour and the Russian Revolution* (1956). C. Cross: *The Fascists in Britain* (1961) and H. Pelling: *The Communist Party* (1958) deal rather unsatisfactorily with these fringe, but not insignificant, elements in inter-war politics.

Index

Law, Andrew Bonar—*contd.*
316, 343, 362, 363, 379, 387, 410, 424,
439, 441, 464, 484; American Loan
settlement and, 449–50; Asquith, loyalty to, 347–8, 350; Asquith, in movement against, 350–3; Bevin's humiliation of, 536, 557, 558; Coalition's fall
and, 442–4, 460; forms Government
(1922), 444–5; illness, resignation, and
death, 451–4; independent War Committee and, 348–50, 353; invited to form
Government, 354, 355; Irish Home
Rule and, 265, 268, 269, 273–4; Keynes
on, 263; Lloyd George, admiration for,
390, 408, 409; Lloyd George, last meeting with, 454; Lloyd George mistrusted
by, 321, 323, 344, 347–9; Lloyd George
on, 264, 265; Nigeria and, 346, 347;
1915 Ministerial Crisis and, 318–19;
1918 election and, 389–90; personal
characteristics of, 262–5; Russia, intervention in, 425–6; Ulster and, 428, 436;
as Unionist (Conservative) leader,
261–2, 409, 433, 444; on War Committee, 327

League of Nations, 458, 471, 490, 524,
532, 535, 574; British failure to support,
418–19, 559, 561–2, 573, 606; 'collective
security' and, 529; creation of, 418–19;
French-British differences over, 455–6;
Geneva Protocol, 456, 471, 477; Italian
invasion of Abyssinia and, 557–62,
568–9, 573; United States refusal to
join, 419, 420, 455

League of Nations Union, 532, 535, 567,
573

Lee, Arthur (later Viscount Lee of Fareham), 8–9, 11, 253, 272, 347

Leveson-Gower, Granville George, *see*
Granville, 2nd Earl

Leyds, W. J., 173–4, 180, 186

Liberal Coalition, 4, 18, 19

Liberal Imperialists, 106, 147, 204, 224

Liberal League, 204, 219, 226

Liberal Party, 102, 174, 209, 210, 214, 283
and *n.*, 289, 293, 310, 311, 397, 399, 401;
Anglo-Russian Convention and, 238;
Asquith-Lloyd George split in, 379,
389–90, 406, 448–9; Balfour and, 114;
Birmingham as stronghold of, 8, 38, 92;
Boer War and, 195, 200, 204–6, 224;

Bradlaugh Case and, 51; coalition
party, proposals for, 93, 98, 99, 249–50;
conscription and, 237, 329, 331, 332;
decline and extinction as unified force,
387, 392, 406, 407, 434, 616; disunity in
(1886–7), 17–18, 95–7, 99–102, 104,
107–9, 113; economic programme of,
494–6; Egypt, occupation of, 67; in
1860s, 4–5; 1874 election and, 26–7;
1880 Cabinet, 47–8; 1880 election and,
45–8; 1885 defeat, 79–81; 1885 election
and, 92–3; 1892–5 Governments,
135–6, 138–9, 141–2; 1895 election and,
155; 1900 election and, 201–2; 1903–14
superiority of, 218–21; 1906 election
and, 228–30; 1916 Ministerial Crisis
and, 345–55; 1918 election and, 390,
392, 406; 1922–3 elections and, 445,
446, 465, 467; 1924 collapse of, 466–8,
474, 476; 1929 election and, 496; 1931
election and, 521, 522; 1935 election
and, 546; Hardie and, 133; Hartington
as leader of, 19, 37, 45, 93, 99, 105;
Imperialism and, 31, 36, 67, 68, 106,
142, 224; Irish policy of, 40–1, 53 (*see
also* Liberals and Irish Home Rule);
Labour Representation Committee
and, 212; leadership of (1870s), 37–8;
leadership problems of (1880s), 48,
81–2, 105; Maurice Debate and, 387;
in National Government, 517, 518,
520–1; National Liberal Federation
and, 38–9; 'nation in arms' concept
and, 306, 323; Parnell-O'Shea scandal
and, 118, 120–5, 135; Radicals, *see*
Radicals; reform and, 26, 27, 48, 132,
244–6; Rosebery Government resigns
(1895), 154; 'Round Table' Conference
(1887), 108, 113; *Times* charges against
Parnell and, 115–18; Victoria's bias
against, 28, 137; Welfare State and,
245–6; women's suffrage and, 238–9;
working class and, 126, 129, 131–4,
161–2; *see also* Asquithian Liberals;
Lloyd George Liberals; *and specific Liberal leaders*

Liberals and Irish Home Rule, 31, 44–5,
104–7, 138–42, 147, 149, 273–7; Con-
servative-Irish relationship and, 84–6;
1885–6 crisis, 84–6, 95, 97–8, 100–2;
1886 election, 100–1; 1892–5 Govern-

Robert Rhodes James is the author of several works on modern British politics, of which *Lord Randolph Churchill* (1959), *Rosebery* (1963), *Gallipoli* (1965), *Chips: The Diaries of Sir Henry Channon* (1967), *Memoirs of a Conservative* (1968) and *Churchill— A Study in Failure 1900–1939* (1970) are the best known. He has also edited the complete speeches of Sir Winston Churchill (1974). His work has received the Llewellyn Rhys Memorial Prize and the Heinemann Award of the Royal Society of Literature. He was a Clerk of the House of Commons from 1955 to 1964, and subsequently a Fellow of All Souls College, Oxford (1964–8), Director of the Institute for the Study of International Organisation at the University of Sussex (1968–73), and Principal Officer of the Executive Office of the Secretary-General of the United Nations (1973–6). He was, in 1968, Kratter Visiting Professor at Stanford University, California, and is a Fellow of the Royal Historical Society. He is now Conservative Member of Parliament for Cambridge.